# Sybex's Quick Tour of Windows 95

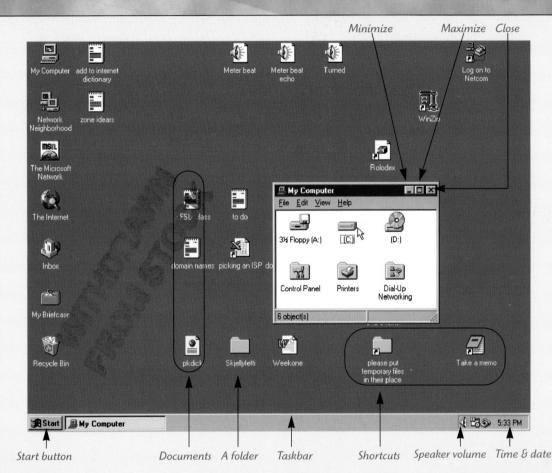

Minimize    Maximize    Close

Start button    Documents    A folder    Taskbar    Shortcuts    Speaker volume    Time & date

**The Desktop** *is where your programs, files, and shortcuts reside.*

**My Computer** *allows you to browse the contents of your computer, open folders, open documents, and run programs.*

**Network Neighborhood** *gives you direct access to other computers (and shared resources, such as printers).*

**The Microsoft Network** *dials up your connection to Microsoft's online service.*

**The Internet** *starts up the Internet Explorer, a World Wide Web browser (available only with Plus!).*

**Inbox** *starts Microsoft Exchange and opens your inbox, so you can see if you have any new mail.*

**My Briefcase** *is a new feature for keeping documents consistent as you move them between computers.*

**Recycle Bin** *makes it easy to delete and undelete files.*

**The Start button** *pops up the Start menu, from which you can run just about every program.*

**The Taskbar** *displays a button for every running program.*

*Create* **shortcuts** *on your Desktop for frequently used programs and documents.*

*Every window has a* **Minimize, Maximize** *(alternating with Restore), and* **Close** *button. The Close button is new; the others just look different.*

# FORMATTING A FLOPPY DISK

To format a floppy disk, first double-click the My Computer icon. Put the floppy in the disk drive. Then right-click the 3½ Floppy icon in the My Computer window and choose Format. The Format dialog box appears.

If you want some density other than the standard 1.44MB, click the Capacity drop-down list box and choose another option. To give the disk a label, click in the Label box and type one. Then click Start.

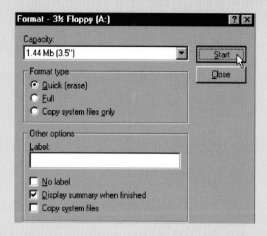

# USEFUL KEYBOARD SHORTCUTS

| TASK | KEYSTROKE |
| --- | --- |
| Get help | F1 |
| Quit a program | Alt+F4 |
| Pop up shortcut menu for selected item | Shift+F10 |
| Pop up the Start menu | Ctrl+Esc |
| Cut a selection | Ctrl+X |
| Copy a selection | Ctrl+C |
| Paste a selection | Ctrl+V |
| Delete a selection | Delete |
| Undo the last action | Ctrl+Z |
| Select all items in window | Ctrl+A |
| Refresh a window | F5 |
| Open folder one level up from current one | Backspace |
| Close a folder and all its parents | Shift and click Close button |
| Rename a selection | F2 |
| Find a file starting with current folder | F3 |
| Delete a selection without putting it in Recycle Bin (be careful!) | Shift+Delete |
| View a selection's properties | Alt+Enter or Alt+double-click |
| Copy an icon | Ctrl+click and drag |
| Create a shortcut from an icon | Ctrl+Shift+click and drag |

**Sybex Inc.**
2021 Challenger Drive
Alameda, CA 94501
Tel: 510-523-8233 · 800-227-2346
Fax: 510-523-2373

SYBEX®

# CHANGING THE WAY WINDOWS 95 LOOKS

You have all kinds of control over the appearance of Windows. You can get to the Display Properties dialog box to change the look via the Control Panel, but the easiest shortcut is to right-click in any empty area of the Desktop and select Properties. The Display Properties dialog box comes up with the Background tab selected.

- *Choose a desktop pattern or wallpaper design.*

- *Choose **Screen Saver** to select a screen saver or stop using one.*

- *Choose **Appearance** to change the look of the windows and dialog boxes.*

- *Choose **Settings** to change the color palette or screen resolution.*

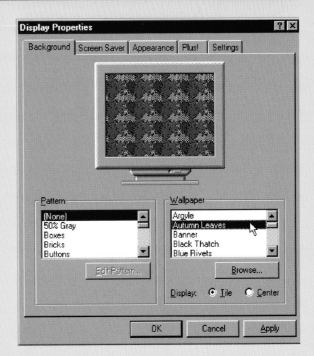

# SETTING UP YOUR PRINTER

No one likes having to set up a printer, but Windows has made it fairly unthreatening. Choose Start ➢ Settings ➢ Printer (or open My Computer and double-click Printers). Your Printers window will open.

- *To modify an existing Printer, right-click it and choose Properties.*

- *To create a new Printer, double-click the Add Printer icon and follow the instructions in the Add Printer Wizard.*

- *To change the default printer, right-click a printer and choose Set as Default.*

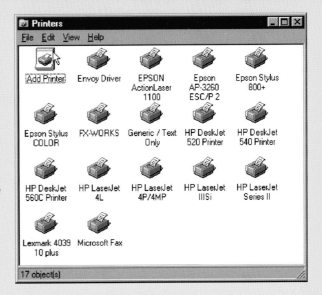

Sybex's Quick Tour of Windows 95

Just press the Start button to do almost anything.

## Running a Program

To start a program, click Start ➢ Programs, choose a program folder (if necessary), and then point to a program.

- *Choose a program or program group from a submenu.*
- *Reopen one of the last 15 documents you've worked on.*
- *Change the way Windows is set up or add a printer.*
- *Search for a missing document, folder, or program.*
- *Get online help.*
- *Run a program directly, the old-fashioned (DOS) way.*
- *Turn off or restart your computer.*

## Putting a Program, Folder, or Document on the Start Menu

First, open the folder that contains the program you want to put on the Start menu. Then click the program icon and drag it onto the Start button. (If you want to get a look at the hierarchy of the programs on the Start submenus—so that you can move things around—right-click on the Start button and choose Open.)

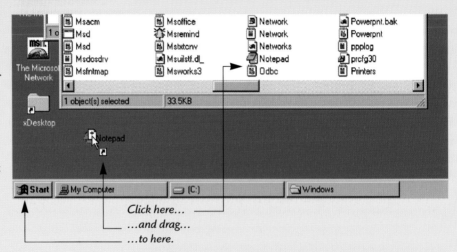

*Click here…*
*…and drag…*
*…to here.*

## Finding Files and Folders Quickly

Unlike Windows 3.1's cumbersome Search command in the File Manager, Windows 95 has a simple-to-use Find command. To try it, select Start ➢ Find ➢ Files or Folders.

*Type the name of the file you're looking for (or just part of it), then click Find Now.*

*A window will open, showing the files as Windows finds them.*

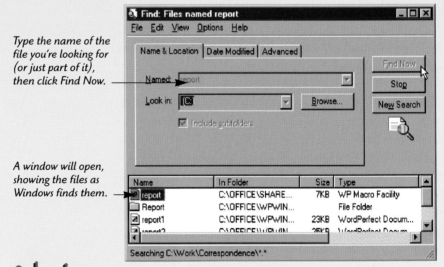

One of the best new features of Windows 95 is shortcuts. Each shortcut you create takes up only a small amount of disk space, but can save you time and energy by opening a program or document that you'd otherwise have to hunt around for. You can recognize a shortcut by the little doubling-back arrow in the bottom-left corner of its icon.

## Putting a Shortcut on the Desktop

There are many ways to do this. If you have a document or program already visible on the screen and want to create a shortcut to it on the desktop, right-click on the icon, drag it onto the Desktop, and then choose Create Shortcut(s) Here. You can also start from the Desktop when the "target" of your shortcut-to-be is not readily available.

Right-click on the Desktop, select New, and then Shortcut.

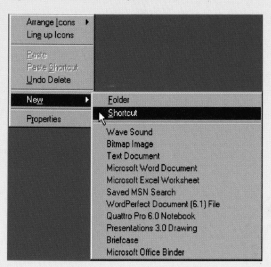

This brings up the Create Shortcut wizard. If you don't know the command line for the program you want, click the Browse button. This brings up an Open-style dialog box; work your way through various folders until you find the program you want to make a shortcut to. Then click the Open button, click Next (or type a different name for the shortcut and click Next), and click Finish when you're done. Voila! Your shortcut appears on the Desktop.

## Making a Keyboard Shortcut

Once you've created a shortcut icon, you can also set up a keyboard shortcut to launch the program (or open the document) automatically.

Right-click the shortcut icon and choose Properties. Click the Shortcut tab in the Properties dialog box, click inside the Shortcut Key box, and then press the keyboard shortcut you want. It will appear in the box as you press it.

*Shows the default folder for the program*

*Controls how the program's window appears when you first run it (other choices are Minimized and Maximized)*

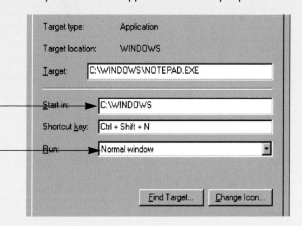

The basic routine for poking around your computer is to double-click on folder icons and select programs or documents from folder windows.

## Starting with My Computer

Usually, you'll start by double-clicking My Computer, which gives you a view of all the drives and devices attached to your computer. Double-click the C: icon to look at the contents of your hard disk.

Then double-click one of the folders in the C: window to open another window, and so on, and so on.

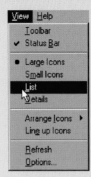

Besides the Large Icons view, you can also choose List view (shown below). Or you can choose Details view to see more information about a folder or file, such as size, type of file it is, and date it was last changed.

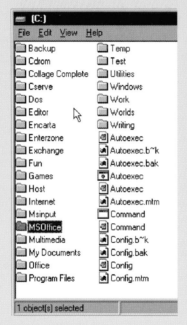

If you'd prefer that each new folder opens up in the same window, instead of creating a new window (which can get very irritating when you end up with numerous open windows on your screen), select View ➤ Options ➤ Browse folders by using a single window.

## Renaming, Copying, or Moving an Icon

In Windows 95, an icon can represent a document, folder, program, or short-cut. The rules for manipulating an icon are the same no matter what the icon corresponds to.

To rename an icon, select it and click in the label below it (wait a few seconds for the text in the label to become highlighted). Then type a new name (up to 255 characters, including spaces if you like) and press Enter.

To copy an icon, the easiest way is to right-click on it and select Copy. Then move to the destination, right-click again, and select Paste. To move an icon, right-click on it and select Cut. Then move to the destination, right-click, and select Paste.

This is a big change from Windows 3.1! Before, the convenience of cutting, copying, and pasting was limited to the text and other contents of application windows. Now just about every item on the screen can be dragged, dropped, cut, copied, and pasted.

Or, you can just hold down Ctrl and drag a copy of an icon to a new location. (A safer way to copy an icon is to right-click on it, drag to a new location, and then choose Copy from the menu that pops up.)

Every running program, open folder, and drive gets a button on the Taskbar. Dialog boxes do not.

You can switch to any task by clicking its button. When you get a lot of things going at once, the Taskbar can get crowded, as you can see in example 1 below.

## Making the Taskbar Bigger

To make more room on the Taskbar, click it along its top edge and drag it up. You'll get something more like example 2.

## Moving the Taskbar

If you'd prefer to have the Taskbar at the top of the screen, so the Start menu will pull down like a menu on the menu bar, just click the Taskbar (not one of the buttons on it) and drag it to the top of the screen. It will look similar to example 3.

You can also put the Taskbar at the left or right edge of the screen to get something that looks like the taskbars shown to the right. In either position, the Taskbar can be stretched up to half the width of the screen.

## Changing the Way the Taskbar Works

You can customize the Taskbar by right-clicking on an empty portion of it and choosing Properties. This brings up the Properties dialog box.

Check or uncheck the options (the preview area shows you the effects of your choices). Uncheck **Always on top** if you want the Taskbar to be covered by other windows. Check **Auto hide** if you want the Taskbar to stay hidden until you move your mouse toward it.

## Task-Switching with Alt+Tab

Another easy way to switch from task to task is to hold down the Alt key and press Tab repeatedly. This worked in Windows 3.1 too. But now when you do this, a plaque will appear showing all the running programs as

icons, with the currently selected one labeled in a box at the bottom of the plaque. Press Tab until the program you want is highlighted and then release both the Tab and the Alt keys.

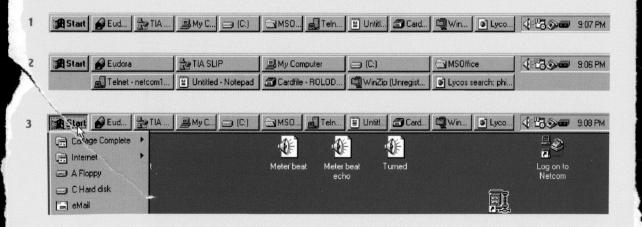

Sure, Windows 3.1 enabled you to use the mouse to scroll, click menus, and interact with dialog boxes, but now just about every feature of Windows can be clicked on (with either button), double-clicked, and/or dragged.

## Selecting Things

Click most things to select them. Shift-click to add all intervening items to a selection. Ctrl-click to add an individual item to a selection. Click and drag to lasso and select several items (click in an empty space before starting to drag—otherwise, you'll drag the item itself).

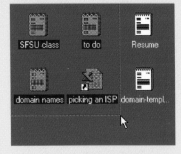

## Right-Click Dragging

If you click with the left button and drag, Windows 95 will either copy the icon (for example, when dragging from or to a floppy) or move the icon (for example, when dragging from one folder to another).

For more control, right-click on an icon and drag it. When you release the mouse button, a menu pops up.

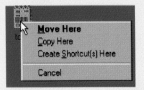

## Things You Can Right-Click On

Right-click on an item to pop up a shortcut menu. Every icon's shortcut menu has Properties as its last choice —each object on your computer has a set of properties associated with it, which you can view or change.

■ **My Computer**

**Explore** displays a File Manager-like view of folders and files.

■ **Any folder, document, or program icon**

**Send To** sends documents directly to a floppy, printer, or fax machine.

■ **The Start button**

**Open** lets you make changes to the Start menu.

■ **The Recycle Bin**

■ **The Desktop**

**Arrange Icons** sorts them by name, type, size, or date.

**New** creates a new folder, document, or shortcut on the Desktop.

■ **The Taskbar**

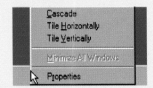

■ **A Taskbar button**

■ **Undo** After you move, copy, create a shortcut from, or delete an icon, the next time you right-click anywhere you can undo your last action. The menu will have a choice like Undo Move or Undo Delete.

# Mastering Lotus® SmartSuite® 97
## for Windows® 95

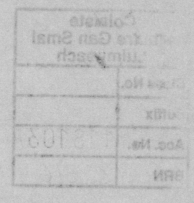

Sandra E. Eddy

San Francisco ▲ Paris ▼ Düsseldorf ▲ Soest   SYBEX®

ASSOCIATE PUBLISHER: Amy Romanoff
ACQUISITIONS MANAGER: Kristine Plachy
ACQUISITIONS & DEVELOPMENTAL EDITOR: Sherry Schmitt
EDITOR: Pat Coleman
PROJECT EDITOR: Linda Good
TECHNICAL EDITOR: Darralyn McCall
BOOK DESIGNER: Suzanne Albertson
ELECTRONIC PUBLISHING SPECIALIST: Stephanie Hollier
PRODUCTION COORDINATOR: Nathan Johanson
INDEXER: Matthew Spence
COVER DESIGNER: Design Site
COVER PHOTOGRAPHER: David Bishop

Screen reproductions produced with Collage Plus.

Collage Plus is a trademark of Inner Media Inc.

SYBEX is a registered trademark of SYBEX Inc.
Mastering is a trademark of SYBEX Inc.

SmartSuite is a registered trademark of Lotus Development Corporation.

TRADEMARKS: SYBEX has attempted throughout this book to distinguish proprietary trademarks from descriptive terms by following the capitalization style used by the manufacturer.

The author and publisher have made their best efforts to prepare this book, and the content is based upon final release software whenever possible. Portions of the manuscript may be based upon prerelease versions supplied by software manufacturer(s). The author and the publisher make no representation or warranties of any kind with regard to the completeness or accuracy of the contents herein and accept no liability of any kind including but not limited to performance, merchantability, fitness for any particular purpose, or any losses or damages of any kind caused or alleged to be caused directly or indirectly from this book.

An earlier version of this book was published under the title *The Compact Guide to Lotus SmartSuite* copyright ©1994 SYBEX Inc.

Library of Congress Card Number: 96-68126
ISBN: 0-7821-1780-5

Manufactured in the United States of America
10 9 8

For Elizabeth Eddy

*It were not best that we should all think alike; it is difference of opinion that makes horse-races.*

MARK TWAIN

# ▶▶ Acknowledgments

Writing a computer book is not a lonely pursuit. Although the author may be working in an ivory tower in some remote spot, there is friendly support from the editors and the production team from the first chapter to the last appendix and beyond. In this section, I'd like to thank all the people whose efforts have been so important.

I especially thank the people at Sybex for all their help and encouragement. Special thanks go to Developmental Editor Sherry Schmitt, Project Editor Linda Good, and Production Coordinator Nathan Johanson. Thanks also to Stephanie Hollier who typeset the book, and Dan Schiff who debabelized the graphics.

A warm thank you to my editor Pat Coleman, who is a great partner.

For accuracy and attention in reviewing every page and figure, a special thank you to the Technical Editor, Darralyn McCall.

Thanks to John E. Schnyder, who helped with advanced spreadsheet techniques.

To Michael Oltedal, Nancy Oltedal, Barbara Keyes, and Eric Lindhardt at Southern Vermont Computer Services: Thanks for your support.

For their continued encouragement, my family and friends—you know who you are.

For their special and continuing contributions—Toni and Bart. In loving memory of Indy.

> *The one absolutely unselfish friend that man can have in this selfish world, the one that never deserts him, the one that never proves ungrateful or treacherous, is his dog.*

> GEORGE GRAHAM VEST

Sandra E. Eddy
73510.3154@compuserve.com
eddygrp@sover.net

# Contents at a Glance

# Table of Contents

# ▶▶ *Introduction*

Welcome to *Mastering Lotus SmartSuite* 97 *for Windows 95*, a comprehensive guide to the powerful Lotus SmartSuite package and its individual components: 1-2-3, Word Pro, Approach, Freelance Graphics, and Organizer. Whether you are using one, two, or all five SmartSuite applications, this book will help to answer most of your questions—from how to start and familiarize yourself with the five award-winning SmartSuite applications to how to use their most advanced features.

One of the primary advantages of SmartSuite is that the diverse applications work together so well. For example, you can create an Organizer address book and import some or all its data into a form letter designed in Approach or Word Pro to create a mailing to go out to all your clients or friends. You can create an Approach database using data you've compiled with 1-2-3. When you prepare a Freelance Graphics presentation, you can write its outline in Word Pro, import 1-2-3 ranges or charts or Approach data to build your case, and then top it all off with a logo you created in Word Pro. You can then import parts of your presentation into a Word Pro report.

1-2-3, Word Pro, Approach, and Freelance Graphics all provide you with *SmartMasters*, templates that help you get started with any project. For example, in 1-2-3 you can find SmartMasters for standard financial workbooks, and using a Word Pro SmartMaster, you can create a fax cover sheet, a letter, and a memo. The Freelance Graphics Smart-Masters include many professionally designed backgrounds and graphics for presentations, topic contents produced by experts, and 11 page designs you can use as a basis for your own projects. You never have to stare at a blank computer screen again!

All five SmartSuite applications also have *SmartIcons*, toolbar buttons that allow you to perform common tasks. As you jump from application to application, you'll find many SmartIcons that look and behave the same throughout SmartSuite. For example, to open any file—regardless of the SmartSuite application—click on the Open an Existing File or Open a Document SmartIcon. The name varies from application to application, but the appearance is identical. To print, click on the Print SmartIcon.

The *SmartCenter* feature allows you to start any SmartSuite application (or any application that you want to add to the SmartCenter) by clicking on an icon palette that's always on your computer screen. In the

SmartCenter, you can also find a drop-down appointment calendar and a drop-down address book, both of which you can use to update your Organizer Calendar and Address Book.

You've never gotten as much help support as you'll get in SmartSuite. Each SmartSuite application provides its own full-featured help facility. You can run tours in all the applications. When viewing any dialog box, you can click on the question-mark icon or press F1 to get help about that dialog box. In any SmartSuite application, simply place the mouse pointer on a SmartIcon, and you'll see a "bubble" with a description of what that icon does. Opening the Suite Help drawer in the SmartCenter tells you how to use one SmartSuite application with another. You can even view movies that show you how to use common SmartSuite functions.

# ►► Who Should Read This Book

This book is designed for people who are familiar with Windows but may be new to one or more of the SmartSuite applications. If you are a SmartSuite or Windows novice, be sure to review Chapters 1, 2, and 3, in which you'll learn the basics.

# ►► How to Use This Book

This book is both a reference and a tutorial. Throughout the book, you'll find useful tables, illustrations, and sets of procedures to guide you through SmartSuite applications. You'll also find these special features:

 ►►**N O T E S**

**emphasize important information about a topic.**

▶▶ **T I P S**

provide shortcuts and easy-to-use methods for
performing functions.

▶▶ **W A R N I N G S**

inform you about potential problems and pitfalls.

You can use this book along with your SmartSuite manuals and help facilities to get a comprehensive picture of SmartSuite features and functions. The book is arranged in the following six parts.

**Part One: Organizing Your Business with Lotus SmartSuite** Part One introduces you to each SmartSuite application, provides information about the elements of application windows, and teaches you the basics of working with the applications.

**Part Two: Mastering Finances with 1-2-3** Part Two introduces spreadsheets and teaches you how to plan and create them. It also provides information about editing and formatting spreadsheets—from an individual cell to the entire spreadsheet. Also covered are 1-2-3 charting and data analysis tools.

**Part Three: Processing Words with Word Pro** Part Three teaches you to work with the Word Pro word processor, create a document, and use the thesaurus and the grammar checker. You'll learn to format text, select print options, create and modify pictures, work with long documents, create and edit tables, and use power fields.

**Part Four: Organizing Information with Approach** Part Four introduces databases and teaches you how to plan and create them. You'll learn how to design a form, define fields and field types, and create a report. You'll also find out how to join databases, import and export, and use Approach macros.

**Part Five: Presenting Information with Freelance Graphics** Part Five teaches you to plan, create, and edit a presentation with Freelance Graphics. You'll learn how to import and add tables and charts, insert symbols and pictures on a presentation page, run and edit screen shows, and add special effects to a screen show.

**Part Six: Managing Time with Organizer** Part Six covers using the Organizer Calendar, To Do, Address, Notepad, Planner, Anniversary, and Calls sections and shows you how to select print options.

**Appendices** Four appendices provide detailed information about installing SmartSuite, customizing your environment in all five Smart-Suite applications, using SmartSuite's Internet features, and using SmartSuite workgroup commands.

# ►► *Conventions Used in This Book*

This book provides the following keyboard and text conventions.

## ► *Keyboard Conventions*

Windows applications such as 1-2-3, Word Pro, Approach, Freelance Graphics, and Organizer support both the mouse and the keyboard.

Press a *key combination* (pressing two or three keys simultaneously) as a shortcut to execute commands or perform actions. In this book, key combinations are shown as two or three keys, each separated by a plus sign (for example, Ctrl+P). Many, but not all, commands have key combinations. To execute a key combination, press and hold down the first key, and then press the next key or keys.

Press a *key succession* (pressing two or three keys in succession) as another keyboard shortcut. In this book, key successions are shown as two or three keys, each separated by a comma (for example, End,End). To execute a key succession, press the first key and release it, press the second key and release it, and so on.

## ▶ *Text Conventions*

In this book, *italicized* text represents both variables (for example, a file-name or value to be typed) and new terms.

This font

```
=123 Main Street
123 Main Street
```

indicates statements that you type or emulate when creating your own statements.

**Boldfaced** text generally indicates text that you should key in.

## ▶ *Command Syntax Conventions*

In this book, command lines follow this syntax:

( )   Parentheses enclose variables and must be entered in the command line.

[ ]   Brackets indicate optional parts of a command line. When you enter the option in the command line, you do not enter the brackets.

,   Commas separate options and must be entered in the command line.

|   Vertical lines separate choices. Select one and enter it in the command line. When you enter the option in the command line, do not enter the vertical line.

*Italicized text*   Indicates variables that you name and enter in the command line.

Underlined text   Indicates default options.

Organizing Your Business
with Lotus SmartSuite

# PART ONE

▶ ▶ CHAPTER 1

# What Is SmartSuite?

►► **L**otus SmartSuite provides all the applications that you need to run your business or department efficiently. The SmartSuite applications are the 1-2-3 spreadsheet program, Word Pro word processor, Approach relational database, Freelance Graphics presentation software, and Organizer personal information manager (PIM). SmartSuite applications are designed to work together, and the elements and options in each look and function almost identically. Thus, once you learn one application, you are well on your way to being familiar with the others. Each SmartSuite application has a similar set of menu commands and dialog boxes and a complete help facility.

## ►► *What Can I Do with SmartSuite?*

SmartSuite applications are designed so that you can transfer information from one application to another quickly and easily. And because SmartSuite runs under Windows, you can also import to and export from other Windows applications. If you are part of a network or mail group and if you have either cc:Mail or Lotus Notes installed on your computer system, you can send and receive mail from within any SmartSuite application.

SmartSuite applications are sophisticated and extensive, yet easy to use. Each application is based on the Windows *graphical user interface* (GUI, pronounced "gooey"), a display format that allows you to select commands, choose functions, and even start other Windows applications by double-clicking on the application's icon with your mouse. If, however, you do not want to use a mouse or if you like to use shortcut keys for functions that you use often, you can still access every command and function by pressing keys on your keyboard.

All the SmartSuite applications fit together so well that if you are more comfortable working with one of them, you can often launch any of the

other applications and crea...
cation. For example, if you crea...
or part of it into a Word Pro docume... **SmartSuite?**
you can copy a report from Approach or ...
Freelance Graphics presentation.

within that appli-
...u can copy all
...-2-3. Or
...to a

## ► *SmartSuite Features*

These are some of the SmartSuite features:

- True WYSIWYG ("what you see is what you get"). The printed page looks just like the contents of your screen.

- A spelling checker with a main dictionary and user-defined dictionaries.

- *SmartIcons*—customizable toolbar buttons that reduce the steps necessary to perform a task.

- *SmartMasters*— professionally designed, predefined documents and templates that allow you to bypass design and creation.

- *View Tabs*—labels on which you can click to move to another section of a document, to another document in a set of documents, or to another form.

- An active Status bar with which you can see your current settings and even the current date and time.

- Automatic save, in which the current file is automatically saved every few minutes.

- The context-sensitive InfoBox with which you can change attributes and formats for the selected object. With the Info box open, click on another object, and then modify it.

- In many dialog boxes, a yellow section that includes brief descriptions of the purpose of the dialog box.

- Context-sensitive menus whose names change depending on the object that you select.

- Shortcut menus associated with the active object. Simply click your right mouse button to display a menu from which you can select commonly used commands.

recognition of other spreadsheet, word processor, database, presentation, and graphic file formats for easy export and import.

- Team-computing features: TeamMail, TeamSecurity, TeamReview, and TeamConsolidate.

- Internet access, opening files from the Internet, saving to the Internet, and other options.

# ►► *The SmartSuite Components*

Let's look a little more closely at the SmartSuite applications and the major features that each offers.

## ► *1-2-3*

Lotus 1-2-3 is a spreadsheet program with which you can organize and graph information on your computer Desktop. Some 1-2-3 features are:

- Almost 300 built-in math, engineering, financial, and statistical functions.

- In-cell editing, alignment, and formatting.

- Three-dimensional worksheets with which you can organize an entire category of spreadsheets (for example, this year's actual expenses and next year's budgeted expenses).

- Tabbed worksheet pages, which you can name and color-code and which help you quickly move from one spreadsheet in a file to another.

- Palettes of 256 colors and 64 fill patterns to help you custom-format your spreadsheets.

- Twelve types of easy-to-edit charts and many variations.

- The Version Manager, which allows several users to set up what-if scenarios related to alternate values and formulas. View the Version Manager index to see a master list of scenarios.

- Database queries, which can evaluate data from within 1-2-3, from Approach, or from other popular database programs.

For information about 1-2-3, see *Part Two: Mastering Finances with 1-2-3.*

## ▶ *Word Pro*

Word Pro is a full-featured word processor with which you can create any type of document—from a one-page memo or letter to a large manual with headers, footers, footnotes, a table of contents, and index.

Some Word Pro features are:

- A thesaurus and an optional grammar checker with rules that you can set for several levels of checking
- An easy-to-use mail merge
- Character, paragraph, and document formatting
- Multiple column formatting
- Styles
- Large document features, including tables of contents and indexes
- Frames in which you can insert graphics or text

For information about Word Pro, see *Part Three: Processing Words with Word Pro.*

## ▶ *Approach*

Approach is a relational database with which you can plan, design, create, and manage your information. Approach allows you to work with data using forms, reports, form letters, and mailing labels.

Some Approach features are:

- Predesigned databases and templates for business and home for conference room scheduling, checkbook management, loan amortization, contact management, Internet resource tracking, customer service, employee management, inventory management, invoicing, and personal time management
- Free-form and easily edited reports, forms, form letters, and mailing labels
- Report Assistant, with which you can automate report creation
- Built-in forms

- Self-contained mail merge facility
- Avery label support
- Joined database files so that you can use information from several databases
- Comprehensive sort and retrieve capabilities
- Point-and-click data entry

For information about Approach, see *Part Four: Organizing Information with Approach.*

## ▶ *Freelance Graphics*

With Freelance Graphics you can create business presentations complete with slides, overheads, handouts, and speaker notes. You can enhance your presentation by using graphics, charts, and text from other applications or by generating them from within Freelance Graphics. You can create portable presentations and take them on the road. Some Freelance Graphics features are:

- Many SmartMaster design sets—most designed by experts—that guide you through the creation process. Select the look and page layout, and then start filling in each page.
- Galleries of charts, tables, organization charts, maps, movies, sound files, clip art, and diagrams.
- Smart Charts, which are predesigned charts in some SmartMasters.
- Outliner view, which lays out a presentation as an outline and converts the outline to a series of presentation pages.
- Page Sorter view, with which you can see all presentation pages on your desktop, quickly move from page to page, and change the order of the pages.
- Current Page view, with which you can work on all the elements of a single page and see the changes instantly.
- Screen shows with transitional effects and onscreen drawing, to which you can add sound and animation.

For information about Freelance Graphics, see *Part Five: Presenting Information with Freelance Graphics.*

## ► *Organizer*

Organizer, your own personal information manager (PIM), tracks your work and personal calendars, automates your address book, keeps notes, reminds you of anniversaries and birthdays, and displays your to-do list.

Organizer's pages are divided into tabbed sections, each representing a different information category. Click on a tab, and the application displays the opening "page" of that section.

With Organizer you can do the following:

- Schedule appointments and set alarms that remind you of the time.
- Type to-do lists that appear on your calendar until you remove them.
- Keep an up-to-date address book and anniversary list. You can import names and addresses from Approach or other database programs.
- Print any section on pages that are compatible with almost any label or personal organizer binder.
- Add or customize sections within the Organizer notebook.
- Import text and graphics into the Notepad section.
- Keep a chart of your activities or projects.

For information about Organizer, see *Part Six: Managing Time with Organizer.*

## ► *Team Features*

Using SmartSuite team features, you can exchange messages and files with people whose computers are networked with or attached to yours. Team features include TeamMail, TeamReview, TeamConsolidate, TeamShow, and TeamSecurity.

## TeamMail

With TeamMail, you can send messages, files, and selected data to individuals defined to your e-mail system. You can send to your entire team or to a distribution list simultaneously or sequentially and receive an automatic acknowledgment whenever a message or a file is received. Using TeamReview, members of your team can review and comment on the information that you distribute. TeamMail is a feature in 1-2-3, Word Pro, Approach, Freelance Graphics, and Organizer.

## TeamReview

After you send information using TeamMail, members of your team can examine the file and use TeamReview to add comments. Reviewers can add freehand drawings and typed notes to the information but cannot edit or delete the file itself. Reviewers then send the files back to you so that you can incorporate comments. TeamReview is a feature in 1-2-3, Word Pro, and Freelance Graphics.

## TeamConsolidate

With TeamConsolidate, you can split parts of a 1-2-3 workbook or Word Pro document, save them as individual versions or documents, and distribute them to members of your team on disks, over your network, or in a Lotus Notes database. After members of your team work on their assigned documents, you can gather the documents and merge them into a single workbook or document.

## TeamShow

Use the Freelance Graphics TeamShow feature to play screen shows on computers that are connected in one of three ways: by cable, by network, or by dial-up connection.

## TeamSecurity

With TeamSecurity, you can password-protect the current Word Pro document or Approach (APR) file to restrict the files to the original author and selected editors and to specify levels of access. In addition, you can name the individuals who are allowed to define TeamSecurity passwords and define the ways in which they verify themselves.

## ▶ *LotusScript*

LotusScript, which is a version of the BASIC programming language, enables you to create and run applications within 1-2-3, Word Pro, Approach, and Freelance Graphics. You can use LotusScript to extend the features of SmartSuite applications, to automate procedures, or to get the most out of your computer resources.

# ▶▶ *Working Together with SmartSuite Applications*

One of the major advantages of working with Windows applications such as SmartSuite is that it's easy to exchange data among open applications, as shown in Figure 1.1. You can transfer data in three ways:

- By copying, moving, and pasting it using the Windows Clipboard
- By using Dynamic Data Exchange (DDE)
- By using Object Linking and Embedding (OLE)

## ▶ *Copying, Moving, and Pasting Data*

You can transfer data and objects from one Windows application to another. You can select data or an object in the source application and either place a copy or move the selection to the target application. Then, if you want to edit a copied or moved selection, you have two choices: Edit the selection in all its locations, or edit in one place and copy or move it again. You'll learn about copying and moving selections in Chapter 3, *Editing SmartSuite Applications.*

## ▶ *Linking and Embedding with OLE*

You can use Windows' Object Linking and Embedding (OLE) feature to exchange data between two or more active Windows applications and to edit in only one work area. If you have linked applications by choosing the Link or the Paste Link command from the Edit menu, when you change an object or information in one application, it automatically changes in all linked applications.

**FIGURE 1.1** ►

*Exchanging data among applications*

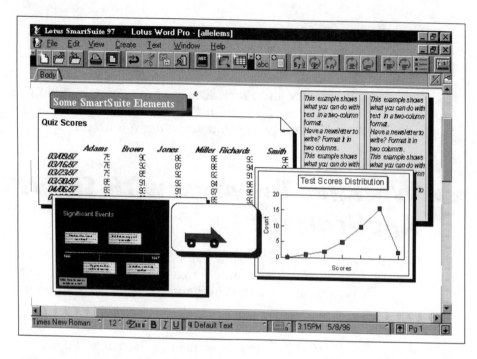

When you want to edit an object, you don't have to leave the *client application*, in which it is embedded and in which you are currently working; you can call up the *server application*, the application in which the object was created, from within the client.

# ►► *Using SmartMasters*

You can use SmartMaster applications and templates to skip the planning and design stages and jump right to using a 1-2-3 workbook, a Word Pro document, an Approach database, or a Freelance Graphics presentation. You can adapt and change SmartMasters so that they better fit your working environment.

## ► *1-2-3 SmartMasters*

1-2-3 provides ready-to-use SmartMasters for a variety of uses, including business expenses, analysis, sales, personal budgets, and loan amortization. For more information about 1-2-3 SmartMasters, see Chapter 4, *Planning and Creating Your First Spreadsheet.*

### ▶ *Word Pro SmartMasters*

Word Pro SmartMasters include templates for calendars, fax cover sheets, invoices, letters, memoranda, newsletters, and tables of contents and indexes for long documents.

### ▶ *Approach SmartMasters*

Approach SmartMasters come in two flavors: applications and templates. Applications are finished databases with professionally designed forms. These SmartMasters include menus with which you can move from form to form. Templates are databases with appropriate fields defined for you. To get the best use from templates, you should edit and format the default forms and/or create custom forms.

### ▶ *Freelance Graphics SmartMasters*

Freelance Graphics provides SmartMaster sets with professionally designed pages and page backgrounds. In addition, you can choose templates created by experts and associated with particular page designs. Templates include business plans, competitor analysis, market research, meetings, sales, training, and so on.

## ▶▶ *Accessing the Internet*

When you are using Lotus 1-2-3, Word Pro, or Approach, you can access the Internet to open files and save files on FTP servers. Using the Internet Options dialog box, you can set up automatic connections and edit connection information. In Freelance Graphics, you can publish a presentation on the World Wide Web. You can choose to include links, speaker notes, and a table of contents with links to each presentation page. For more information about accessing the Internet from within SmartSuite applications, see the *SmartSuite and the Internet* appendix.

► ► **CHAPTER 2**

# Getting Acquainted with SmartSuite

▶ ▶  *T**he** best way to learn how an application works is not by reading a manual and applying the information that you have read
at a later date, but by starting to use the application right away.

One of the biggest advantages of working with Windows applications is
that after learning how to use one application, you know many features
common to all. In this chapter, you'll learn about starting and exiting
applications; opening, editing, saving, and printing files; and more. As
you read this chapter, try using each feature. Before you start, however,
turn on your computer and wait for Windows to start. If you are new to
Windows, learn about some of its features in *Sybex's Quick Tour of Windows 95* insert.

# ▶ ▶ *Using the Lotus SmartCenter*

Lotus
SmartCenter
97

If you installed SmartSuite with the Default Install, the SmartCenter bar
(see Figure 2.1) appears when you start Windows. If the SmartCenter bar
is hidden, you can reveal it by *double-clicking* (quickly pressing the left
mouse button twice) on the Lotus SmartCenter icon (if it is on your
Desktop) or by *clicking* (pressing the left mouse button once) on the Start
button, moving the mouse pointer to Programs, moving the mouse
pointer to Lotus SmartSuite, and clicking on Lotus SmartCenter. (If you
need help in using the mouse, see the "Using the Mouse" section,
which appears later in this chapter.)

The SmartCenter is to SmartSuite as the Taskbar at the bottom of the
Desktop is to Windows. From the SmartCenter, you can start a program,
open a document, or create a document using a SmartMaster; display or
schedule an event in a calendar—text or Organizer-based; display or edit
an address entry in an address book—text or Organizer-based; or get
help (from the help system, movies, guided tours, and so on) about
SmartSuite and its applications.

**FIGURE 2.1** ▶

*The Lotus Smart-Center bar with its Control menu displayed*

## ▶ *Managing SmartCenter Drawers*

By default, the SmartCenter is a "cabinet" with four "drawers" and the Control-menu icon in its usual top-left position. You can add, modify, and delete drawers. In fact, you can use the SmartCenter to operate any Windows applications or Notes databases.

From left to right, these are the default SmartCenter elements:

**SmartCenter Control-Menu**    Click on this icon to display a menu from which you can change cabinet properties, add a drawer, access help, or close the SmartCenter.

**SmartSuite**    Open this drawer to display icons for all the SmartSuite applications, for SmartMaster templates, and for recently opened documents. Table 2.1 shows the icons for each of the SmartSuite applications; Table 2.2 illustrates the icons for SmartMaster templates.

**Internet**    Open this drawer to access Internet resources arranged under these categories: News, Stock Quotes, Weather, Web Reference, and Bookmarks. You must be connected to the Internet to link to these resources.

**Calendar**    Open this drawer to reveal a text calendar file with the current time marked. You can choose to use your Organizer calendar instead of the text file.

**Addresses**    Open this drawer to reveal a text address book file. From the Addresses drawer, you can add names and addresses, dial your telephone, send mail, write a letter, or show names and addresses. You can choose to use your Organizer address book instead of the text file.

Getting Acquainted

▶ ▶

*Ch.*
**2**

► **TABLE 2.1:** *Icons for SmartSuite Applications*

| Icon | Application |
| --- | --- |
| Lotus 1-2-3 97 | Lotus 1-2-3 |
| Lotus Approach 97 | Lotus Approach |
| Lotus Freelance Graphics 97 | Lotus Freelance Graphics |
| Lotus Organizer 97 | Lotus Organizer |
| Lotus ScreenCam 97 | Lotus ScreenCam |
| Lotus Word Pro 97 | Lotus Word Pro |

► **TABLE 2.2:** *Icons for SmartMaster Templates*

| Icon | Template |
| --- | --- |
| | Lotus 1-2-3 SmartMaster |
| | Lotus Approach |
| | Lotus Freelance Graphics |
| | Lotus Word Pro |

**Reminders**　　Open this drawer to type a home or business reminder. When you have completed a task, check it off or delete it.

**Reference**　　Open this drawer to check the spelling of a word or to find a synonym in the thesaurus.

**Business Productivity**　　Open this drawer to access Smart-Masters to be used as templates for business documents.

**Suite Help**　　Open this drawer to access SmartSuite Help for SmartCenter, view online documentation using Adobe's Acrobat Reader, view a ScreenCam movie about SmartCenter or about how two SmartSuite applications work together, take a guided tour of a SmartSuite application, or go to a Lotus or an IBM site on the Internet—if you have an Internet browser application.

## Opening and Closing Drawers

When you open a SmartCenter drawer (see Figure 2.2), it looks and sounds—if you have a sound card—like a file cabinet drawer being opened and closed. You can open a drawer in two ways:

- Click on its drawer front.

- Right-click on its drawer front and choose the Open Drawer command from the shortcut menu.

**FIGURE 2.2** ▶

*The SmartSuite drawer—open and ready to use*

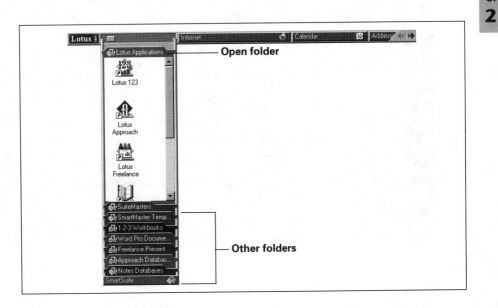

# ▶ USING LOTUS SCREENCAM

You can record both sounds (if you have a sound card, micro-phone, and sound software installed) and activities on the computer screen using Lotus ScreenCam. You can then distribute those files to train users, demonstrate applications, or respond to colleagues. For example, you can illustrate how to edit a Word Pro document, open a 1-2-3 file, embed a ScreenCam demo in a Free-lance Graphics presentation, or show the changes that you would like in another Windows application document.

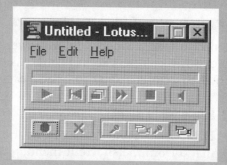

The Lotus ScreenCam window contains controls arranged as follows:

| | |
|---|---|
| Play | Plays the current movie or sound file |
| Rew | Rewinds the current movie or sound file |
| FF | Fast-forwards the current movie or sound file |
| Exit | Closes Lotus ScreenCam |
| Vol | Controls the volume of sound |
| Rec | Records a movie or sound file |

| Clear | Clears the current movie so that you can record a new one. (To delete a movie, open Windows Explorer, click on the movie filename, press Delete, and respond to any prompts. Another way to delete a movie is to find it using the Windows File utility, click on the movie filename, press Delete, and respond to prompts. To learn more about Windows, see the *Overview of the Windows Environment* appendix.) |
|---|---|
| Mic | Records a sound file |
| Both | Records a movie with sound |
| Cam | Records a movie without sound |

Before creating a movie, plan it carefully. Keep in mind that a long movie takes a great deal of computer or disk space. Before recording, turn off your Windows wallpaper to save computer memory. Because a Lotus ScreenCam movie shows every movement of the mouse, know ahead of time the directions in which you'll move the mouse; don't record extraneous movements, plan to move the mouse in a straight line, and move it more slowly than you usually do.

To create a movie, follow these steps:

1. Start Lotus ScreenCam.

2. Click on the Mic, Both, or Cam button to indicate whether you will record sound, a movie with sound, or a movie without sound.

3. Click on the Record button or press F12. Lotus Screen-Cam places a Stop box in the lower right corner of the current window. Before moving the mouse pointer or recording a sound, wait for the stopwatch cursor to change to an arrow (which may occur so fast that you won't see it). You may have to close a dialog box before the Stop box appears.

**4.** Record mouse movement and/or sound. When you have completed recording, click on the Stop button.

To show a movie or hear a sound file, click on the Play button or press the spacebar.

To save a movie or a sound file, choose one of these options:

○ Choose File ➤ Save or press Ctrl+S to save a new Screen-Cam movie (SCM).

○ Choose File ➤ Save As to save a movie as a ScreenCam movie (SCM) in a different directory or drive or under a new name.

To embed a Lotus ScreenCam movie in a Windows application with the Create ➤ Object command, follow these steps:

**1.** Open the application in which you want to embed the movie.

**2.** Choose Create ➤ Object. The application opens the Create Object dialog box.

**3.** Double-click on Lotus ScreenCam 97 Movie. The Lotus ScreenCam window appears.

**4.** To open an existing movie file, choose File ➤ Read in the ScreenCam window or press Ctrl+O.

**5.** In the Read dialog box, select a movie, and click on the Load button or double-click on the filename of the movie.

**6.** In the ScreenCam window, choose File ➤ Update *Application* to embed the Lotus ScreenCam logo in the application at the insertion point.

7. Choose File ➤ Exit & Return to *Application* to close Lotus ScreenCam and return to the application.

8. To play the movie, double-click on the ScreenCam icon in the application.

You can also embed a movie in a Windows application by choosing Edit ➤ Paste Special. For instructions, see *Embedding Screen Movies* in the Lotus ScreenCam Help facility.

To continue the file cabinet analogy, some drawers contain folders in which the icons reside. To open a folder, click on its title. To browse through the contents of a folder, use the vertical scroll bar.

You can close a drawer in three ways:

- Click on its drawer front, which is at the bottom of the open drawer.
- Click on the SmartCenter bar above the open drawer.
- Point to the SmartCenter bar above the open drawer, right-click, and choose the Close Drawer command.

## Adding a Drawer

If you want to run other applications from the SmartCenter, you can add a drawer.

 ▶▶ **N O T E**

> If you add drawers to the SmartCenter bar, be aware that space is limited; extra drawers may be out of sight. When the SmartCenter bar contains more drawers than can be seen at one time, Smart-Center adds arrow buttons on which you can click to display left or right drawers on the bar.

To add a drawer, follow these steps:

1. Click on the Control-menu icon or point to an area of the SmartCenter bar that doesn't have a drawer front and click the right mouse button (that is, right-click). A small menu opens.

2. Click on the New Drawer command. The New Drawer dialog box (see Figure 2.3) appears.

3. In the Drawer Label text box, type the drawer front name (see Figure 2.4).

4. From the Drawer Handle drop-down list box, select a handle. Use the scroll bar to view the entire list of handles. Click on Done. The new drawer is added to the SmartCenter bar.

5. To move a drawer to another location on the SmartCenter bar, simply point to the drawer front, hold down the left mouse button, and drag the drawer front to its new location.

6. To change the width of a drawer, click on the drawer front to open the drawer, move the mouse pointer to the right side of the drawer, hold down the left mouse button, and drag the side of the drawer to the right (see Figure 2.5).

**FIGURE 2.3** ▶

*The New Drawer dialog box*

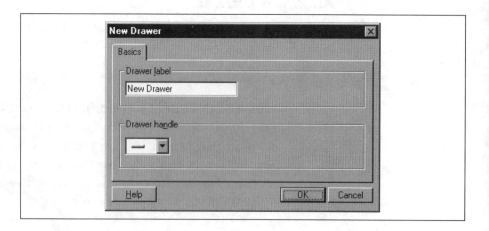

**FIGURE 2.4** ▶

*The filled-in New Drawer dialog box*

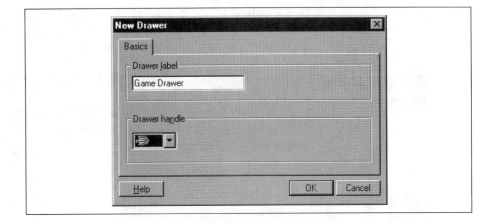

**FIGURE 2.5** ▶

*A SmartCenter drawer as it is made wider*

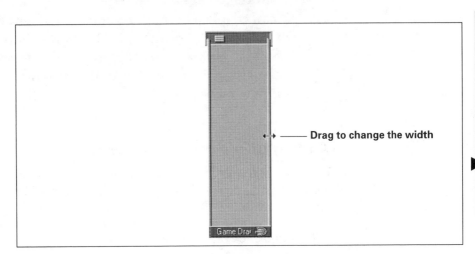

Drag to change the width

## Adding an Application Icon to a File Drawer

You can add an application icon to a file drawer using the same techniques that you use to create a Windows shortcut. (See the insert *Sybex's Quick Tour of Windows 95* for more information about Windows.) You can add an application icon to a file drawer in three ways:

- Drag a shortcut from the Desktop into an open drawer.

- Drag an application icon from a window (such as Windows Explorer or My Computer) into an open drawer.

● In a window, create a shortcut by clicking on an application icon, choosing File ➤ Create Shortcut, and dragging the Shortcut to *Application* icon into an open drawer.

**▶▶NOTE**

**After you create a shortcut, you can rename its label by clicking on it twice, typing its new name, and clicking outside the label.**

**▶▶TIP**

**You can create a file drawer and copy an application icon to it in one step. Simply drag an application icon to the SmartCenter bar. When you release the mouse button, a new drawer appears and a new folder is created. (For more information about folders, see the following pages.)**

## Adding a Folder to a File Drawer

If you want to put icons in categories (for example, solitaire games, war games, and so on), you can create folders inside the file drawer. To create a folder, follow these steps:

1. Right-click on the drawer in which you want to create the folder.
2. Choose the New Folder command. The New Folder dialog box appears.

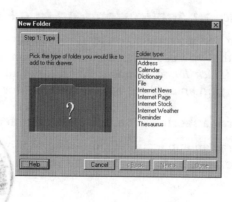

▶▶**N O T E**

If you misspell a word while creating or editing a Word
Pro document, the Spell Check button changes color
and becomes more visible. When this happens, click on
the button to open a menu with four commands (Add
to Dictionary, Skip, Skip All, and Replace) and
suggested replacement words. Use the commands
exactly as you would while using the Word Pro Spell
Check bar.

## Moving Folders in a File Drawer

The folder immediately on top of an open drawer is active. To make active
another folder, click on its title. To make active the space between the top
of the drawer and the first folder, click on the gray bar above the first
folder's title. Figure 2.6 shows a new drawer with two folders and an icon.

**FIGURE 2.6** ▶

*A new drawer with
two folders and
an icon*

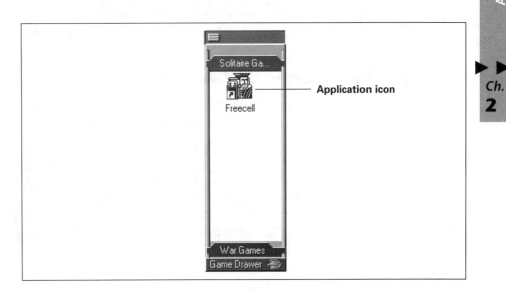

Application icon

### Moving Icons to a New Folder

To move an icon from one section of a drawer to another, drag it on top of its destination folder's title. When the title moves to the top of the drawer, release the left mouse button.

### Deleting a Drawer

To delete a drawer, follow these steps:

1. Right-click on the front of the drawer to be deleted.

2. From the shortcut menu, choose Delete Drawer. A confirmation message box appears.

3. Click on Yes. If you have a sound card, you'll hear a loud tearing noise.

## ► The SmartSuite Drawer

The SmartSuite drawer (see Figure 2.7) is loaded with icons representing applications, templates, and documents.

The Lotus Programs folder contains icons for 1-2-3, Approach, Freelance Graphics, Organizer, ScreenCam, and Word Pro. The Smart-Master Templates folder contains icons representing professionally designed SmartMasters for 1-2-3, Approach, Freelance Graphics, and Word Pro. The remaining folders in the file drawer include icons representing files that you have created either from SmartMasters or from a blank document.

**FIGURE 2.7** ▶

*The open SmartSuite drawer showing the contents of the Lotus Programs folder*

## ▶ *The Calendar Drawer*

The open Calendar drawer (see Figure 2.8) reveals a text file (by default, C:\LOTUS\SMARTCTR\CALENDAR.TXT) containing activities that you have entered for the day. Instead of the text file, you can define another text file or use your Organizer calendar.

**FIGURE 2.8** ▶

*The open Calendar drawer shows part of today's schedule and a small dot indicating the current time.*

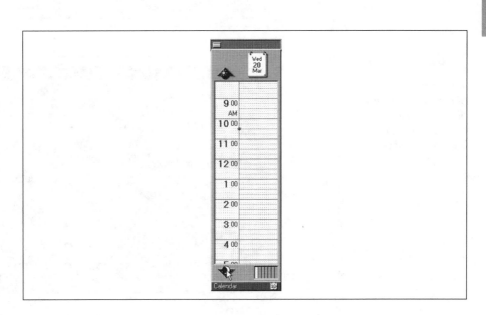

**Getting Acquainted**

▶ ▶

**Ch.**

**2**

### Defining a Calendar File

To define a calendar file for the Calendar drawer, follow these steps:

1. Right-click on the folder name, and choose Folder Properties. The Basics section of the Folder Properties dialog box (see Figure 2.9) appears.

2. Click on the Calendar tab. The Calendar section of the Folder Properties dialog box (see Figure 2.10) opens.

**FIGURE 2.9** ▶

*The Basics section of the Folder Properties dialog box for a Calendar drawer*

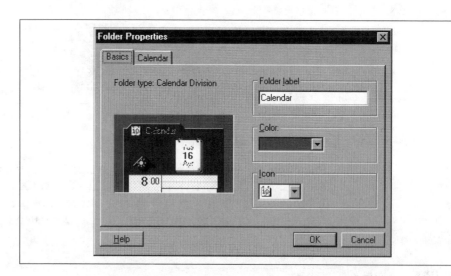

**FIGURE 2.10** ▶

*The Calendar section of the Folder Properties dialog box with an open Calendar Data drop-down list box*

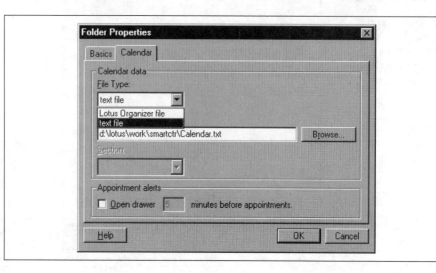

3. Choose Lotus Organizer File or Text File from the Calendar Data drop-down list box.

4. To search for a Lotus Organizer or text file, click on the Browse button. (If you know the name and location of the file, type it in the Name of Lotus Organizer File or Name of Text File text box.) The Browse for Lotus Organizer File or Browse for Text File dialog box opens.

5. Select a file. (By default, Lotus Organizer files are located in C:\LOTUS\WORK\ORGANIZE\, if Organizer has been installed on your C: drive.)

6. Click on OK. The new calendar file is associated with the Calendar drawer.

## Moving around the Daily Calendar

The default calendar display is today from 8 AM to 5 PM. To move up the calendar toward the first minutes of today, point to the upward-pointing arrow and press and hold down the left mouse button. To move down the calendar toward the last minutes of today, point to the downward-pointing arrow and press and hold down the left mouse button.

## Adding an Appointment

To add an appointment to the calendar, follow these steps:

1. Point to the time of the appointment and click. The Create Appointment dialog box (see Figure 2.11) appears.

**FIGURE 2.11** ▶

*The Create Appointment dialog box with the description of an appointment filled in*

2. Click on OK. The appointment is inserted into the calendar. If the calendar is linked to an Organizer file, the appointment is added to the Organizer Calendar section.

Getting Acquainted

▶▶

Ch.
2

3. To move the appointment, move the mouse pointer to the appointment. When the mouse pointer looks like a hand, drag the appointment box to its new location.

4. To show the duration of the appointment, drag its bottom border to the appropriate ending time.

## Moving around the Calendar Day by Day

 To display the previous day's calendar, move the mouse pointer to the bottom left side of the calendar page at the top of the drawer. When a left-pointing arrow appears next to the mouse pointer, click the left mouse button.

 To display the next day's calendar, move the mouse pointer to the bottom right side of the calendar page at the top of the drawer. When a right-pointing arrow appears next to the mouse pointer, click the left mouse button.

## Displaying Additional Days

 To display up to seven days at a time, click on the Days to Display icon at the bottom of the calendar drawer. If you click on the second bar, two days display; if you click on the fifth bar, five days display, and so on. To return to the default of one day displayed, click on the first bar. Notice that when you select a number of days, the drawer becomes wider and pushes the drawers to the right of the Calendar drawer toward the right side of the Desktop. If the SmartCenter bar extends beyond the right side of the Desktop, two arrows appear at the top right of the Desktop. To view the leftmost drawers on the bar, click on the left-pointing arrow. To view the rightmost drawers, click on the right-pointing arrow.

## Moving around Days and Months Using a Monthly Calendar

To jump from month to month, click on the center or top of the date at the top of the drawer. (If you click on the lower left or lower right side, you'll change the date display.) A monthly calendar appears:

Today's date is marked in red or highlighted, if the drawer displays today's date.

- To change the calendar drawer display to a day in the current monthly calendar, click on it.

- To move to the prior month, click on the left-pointing arrow at the top left corner of the monthly calendar.

- To move to the next month, click on the right-pointing arrow at the top right corner of the monthly calendar.

### Launching Lotus Organizer from within the Calendar Drawer

If you are using an Organizer file for the Calendar drawer, you can start Organizer so that you can define repeating appointments or access another Organizer section. To start Organizer, click on the Organizer icon at the top of the drawer. To learn more about Organizer, see the *Scheduling with Organizer* and *Managing Data with Organizer* chapters.

## ▶ The Addresses Drawer

The open Addresses drawer (see Figure 2.12) reveals a text file (by default, C:\LOTUS\SMARTCTR\ADDRESS.TXT) containing names and addresses. Instead of the text file, you can define another text file or use an Organizer address section.

**FIGURE 2.12** ▶

*The open Addresses drawer shows the names of six people whose last names start with the letter C.*

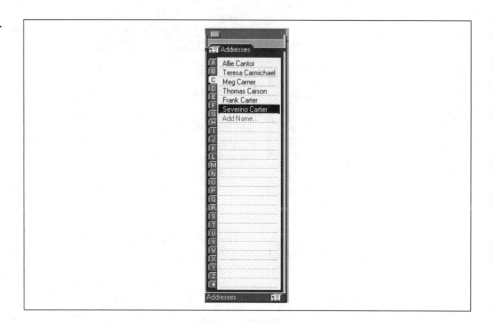

 ▶▶ **N O T E**

**Using an Organizer file for your Calendar drawer does not mean that you have automatically defined it for your Addresses drawer. This means that you can use different Organizer files for each drawer—including any new Calendar and Addresses drawers that you define.**

## Defining an Address File

To define an address file for the Addresses drawer, follow these steps:

1. Right-click on the folder name, and choose Folder Properties. The Basics section of the Folder Properties dialog box (see Figure 2.13) appears.

2. Click on the Name & Address tab. The Name & Address section of the Folder Properties dialog box (see Figure 2.14) opens.

3. Choose Lotus Organizer File or Text File from the Name & Address Book drop-down list box.

**FIGURE 2.13** ▶

*The Basics section of the Folder Properties dialog box for an Addresses drawer*

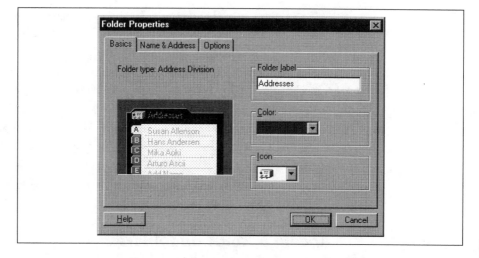

**FIGURE 2.14** ▶

*The Name & Address section of the Folder Properties dialog box with an Organizer file defined*

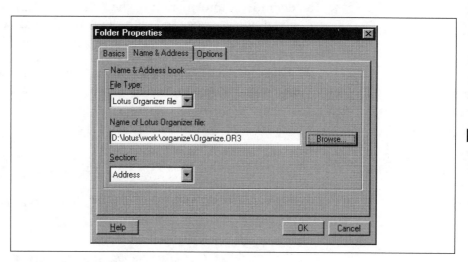

**Getting Acquainted**

▶ ▶

*Ch.*
**2**

**4.** To search for a Lotus Organizer or text file, click on the Browse button. (If you know the name and location of the file, type it in the Name of Lotus Organizer File or Name of Text File text box.) The Browse for Lotus Organizer File or Browse for Text File dialog box opens.

5. Select a file. (By default, Lotus Organizer files are located in C:\LOTUS\WORK\ORGANIZE\, if Organizer has been installed on your C: drive.)

6. Click on the Options tab and click on one of the Display Names option buttons. By default, names are displayed in a first name—last name order.

7. If you want to access a particular Word Pro SmartMaster for letter writing from the Addresses drawer, either type the path and name or click on the Browse button to find a SmartMaster.

8. Click on OK. The new address file is associated with the Addresses drawer.

### Adding a Name and Address

To add address information to the Addresses drawer (and to the Organizer file, if one is associated with the Addresses drawer), follow these steps:

1. Click on Add Name in the drawer. A dialog box (see Figure 2.15) appears.

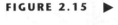

**FIGURE 2.15** ►

*An Add Name and Address dialog box*

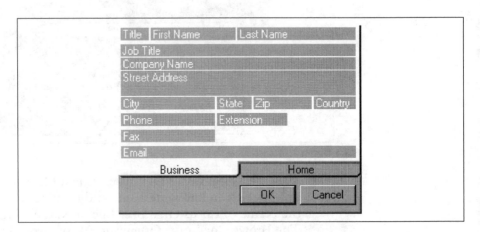

2. Fill in the text boxes in the dialog box:

   • Click in a text area.

   • To move from the current text area to the next, either press Tab or click in the next text area.

- To move from the current text area to the prior text area, either press Shift+Tab or click in the prior text area.

3. Click on OK to close the dialog box and add the name and address information to the Addresses drawer. If the Addresses drawer is associated with an Organizer file, the name and address information is added to the Organizer file. Click on Cancel to close the dialog box without adding the name and address information.

### Making a Telephone Call

To make a telephone call from the Addresses drawer using a telephone attached to your modem, follow these steps:

1. Click on the letter tab representing the first character in the last name of the person that you intend to call.

2. Click on a name listed under the selected tab. The name and address information for that person appears next to the number you want to dial.

3. Click on the Call button. The Dialing dialog box (see Figure 2.16) appears, quickly followed by the Call Status message box (see Figure 2.17).

4. To talk after successfully dialing, lift your telephone receiver and click on the Talk button.

5. To indicate completion of the call, click on the Hang Up button.

*Getting Acquainted*

▶ ▶

*Ch.*
**2**

**FIGURE 2.16** ▶

*The Dialing dialog box shows the dialed number.*

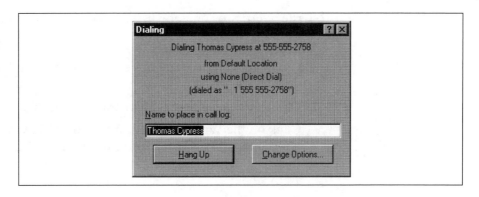

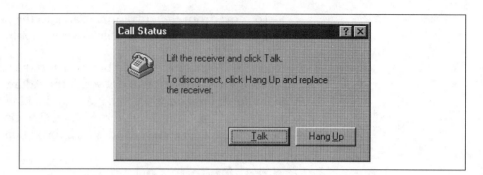

## Sending Mail

To use SmartSuite's TeamMail feature to send mail to a selected individual listed in the Address drawer, click on the Send Mail button.

## Writing a Letter

When you write a letter to an individual listed in the Addresses drawer, you automatically use a Word Pro SmartMaster template as the basis for the letter (or memo, fax cover sheet, invoice, and so on). If you have chosen a default template in the Options section of the Folder Properties dialog box, that template is always used for the letter. However, if you have not chosen a default template, you are asked for the name of a SmartMaster after selecting a recipient. So, if all your correspondence requires one SmartMaster template, select it as the default. Otherwise, select the SmartMaster at the time you are creating the letter.

To write a letter to someone listed in your Addresses drawer, follow these steps:

1. Click on the letter tab representing the first character in the last name of the person to whom you want to write a letter.

2. Click on a name listed under the selected tab.

3. Click on the Write a Letter button. If you have not defined a default SmartMaster, the Word Pro SmartMaster dialog box (see Figure 2.18) appears. If you have defined a default SmartMaster, go to step 5.

**FIGURE 2.18** ▶

*The Word Pro Smart-
Master dialog box
with a fax Smart-
Master template
selected*

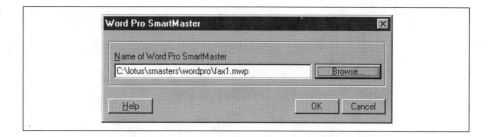

4. Type the path and name of a SmartMaster template, or click on
   the Browse button and double-click on a SmartMaster template.
   Click on OK. Click on the Business or Hometab in the address
   box (see Figure 2.19). After a few seconds of processing, Word
   Pro starts with the filled in template onscreen.

**FIGURE 2.19** ▶

*The Word Pro Address
dialog box*

5. Complete the document by typing the body text and editing as
   needed.
6. Save the document using a unique name.

### Editing a Name and Address

To edit a name and address entry in the Addresses drawer, follow these
steps:

1. Click on the letter tab representing the first character in the last
   name of the person whose name and/or address you want to change.
2. Click on a name listed under the selected tab.

3. Click on the button in the upper right corner.
4. Edit the Business section, the Home section, or both.
   Click on OK.

## ▶ *The Business Productivity Drawer*

It provides SmartMaster templates arranged under business topics.

## ▶ *The Suite Help Drawer*

The open Suite Help drawer (see Figure 2.20) reveals several folders: Help, DocOnline, Tours, and Helpful Web Sites. Each of these folders contains a different type of help resource. To learn about each part of the Suite Help drawer, see a following section, "Getting Help."

**FIGURE 2.20** ▶

*The open Suite Help drawer with the Smart-Suite Help icon displayed*

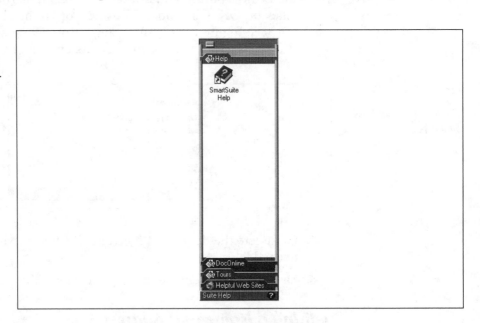

# ▶▶ *Starting a SmartSuite Application*

You can start a SmartSuite application in several ways: by selecting it from a SmartCenter drawer, by clicking on a SuiteStart icon, by selecting it from the Start menu, or by double-clicking on a shortcut on the Desktop.

## ► *Starting an Application from the SmartCenter*

It's easy to start any SmartSuite or Windows application by using the Lotus SmartCenter. Open a drawer in the SmartCenter and double-click on an icon to launch an application. By default, icons representing SmartSuite applications are located in the SmartSuite drawer. If the SmartCenter is hidden, open it by clicking on the Start button, pointing to Programs, pointing to Lotus SmartSuite, and clicking on Lotus SmartCenter.

## ► *Starting an Application Using SuiteStart*

In the Windows Taskbar, SuiteStart is composed of six small icons (see Figure 2.21) representing SmartSuite applications: 1-2-3, Word Pro, Freelance Graphics, Approach, Organizer, and ScreenCam. Click on an icon to start the application.

**FIGURE 2.21** ►

*The default SuiteStart icons*

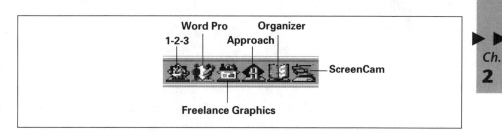

To remove all the SuiteStart icons from the Taskbar, point to SuiteStart, right-click, and choose Exit.

►► **W A R N I N G**

**Although the shortcut keys for Exit are Alt+F4, it is best not to press Alt+F4 because you might inadvertently start to shut down Windows. If this happens, click on No when the Shut Down Windows dialog box opens.**

Getting Acquainted

►►

Ch.

2

To remove one SuiteStart icon, right-click on the icon and choose Remove Shortcut to *Application* Icon.

If you have inadvertently removed an icon from SuiteStart, you can add it by following these steps:

1. Create a shortcut icon using the instructions in this chapter's prior section, "Adding an Application Icon to a File Drawer."

2. Drag the shortcut icon to the \LOTUS\SMARTCTR\ SUITSTRT folder.

3. Right-click on the SuiteStart bar.

4. Choose the Refresh command to display the new version of the SuiteStart bar.

 ▶▶ **N O T E**

> The SuiteStart bar is not limited to SmartSuite applications; you can add a shortcut for any application.

 ▶▶ **N O T E**

> By default, the SuiteStart icons appear on the Taskbar when you start Windows. During installation, the install program places the SuiteStart shortcut icon in the Startup window. If you want to be able to hide or reveal the SuiteStart bar, create a Desktop shortcut using the instructions in this chapter's prior section, "Adding an Application Icon to a File Drawer."

# ▶ *Starting an Application from the Start Menu*

If you don't use an application often (for example, every year you create or edit one Freelance Graphics presentation for an annual conference), there is no need to add a shortcut to your Desktop. Instead, when you want to start the application, use the Start menu.

To start an application using the Start menu, follow these steps:

1. Click on the Start button. Windows opens the Start menu.

2. Move the mouse pointer to Programs. Windows opens another menu to the right of the Start menu.

3. Move the mouse pointer to Lotus SmartSuite. Windows opens another menu to the right of the Programs menu. Figure 2.22 shows three open menus—Start, Programs, and Lotus SmartSuite—on a Desktop and shows Lotus 1-2-3 selected.

4. Point to an application and click. The application starts.

**FIGURE 2.22** ▶

*The open Start, Programs, and Lotus SmartSuite menus and 1-2-3 selected*

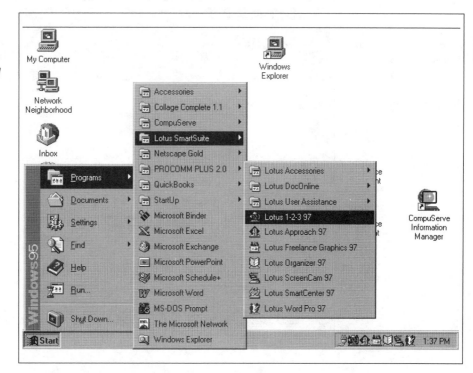

Getting Acquainted

▶▶

Ch. 2

## ▶ *Starting an Application from the Desktop*

To start a program for which you have created a shortcut, start one of the SmartSuite applications—preferably the one with which you'll be working most often—by moving the mouse pointer to the icon representing the application and double-clicking. To learn how to create a shortcut, see a prior section, "Adding an Application Icon to a File Drawer."

> **Shortcuts are analogous to program icons in the Windows 3.1 environment.**

Once you start an application, you'll see an application window such as the 1-2-3 window shown in Figure 2.23 or the Word Pro window shown in Figure 2.24.

**FIGURE 2.23** ▶

*An opening 1-2-3 application window with typical Windows elements: title bar, menu bar, toolbar, work area, and Status bar*

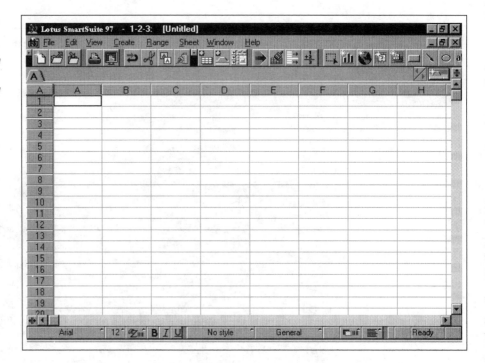

FIGURE 2.24 ▶

*A Word Pro application window with typical Windows elements and a document in the work area*

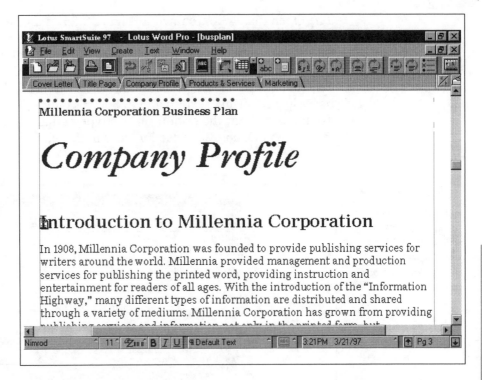

Before you learn about the elements of a typical application window, let's open BUSPLAN, a sample document from the \LOTUS\SAMPLES\WORDPRO subfolder, which is installed during a default Word Pro installation. With an open file in the application window, you'll be able to see how all the pieces of the window work.

# ▶▶ *Opening a File*

Opening a Word Pro file is very similar to opening a file in any other SmartSuite or Windows application. The process involves opening a *dialog box*, a small window in which you select or change application settings or specify how you want to perform an action.

▶▶
Ch.
2

Getting
Acquainted

The Open dialog box, shown in Figure 2.25, is an example of a common Windows dialog box. You'll find similar dialog boxes in the other SmartSuite applications. In fact, as you read through this chapter, you'll notice that the Save As dialog box is almost identical to the Open dialog box. You'll learn more about the elements of Windows dialog boxes in a following section and in Sybex's Quick Tour of Windows 95. To find out about the options in this type of dialog box, see the "About the Save As Dialog Box" section later in this chapter.

**FIGURE 2.25** ▶

*In Word Pro's Open dialog box, you can open a Word Pro document located on a specific drive in a particular folder.*

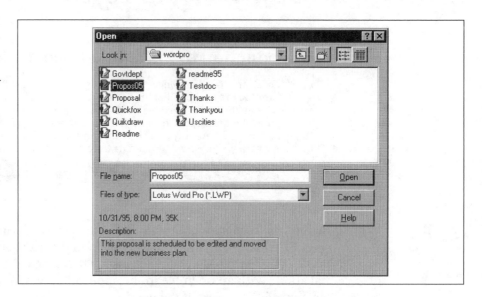

The document to be opened, BUSPLAN, is in the \LOTUS\SAMPLES\WORDPRO subfolder. Figure 2.26 shows most of the \Lotus folder and its subfolders, including \SAMPLES\WORDPRO, the subfolder in which BUSPLAN is located.

To open a Word Pro file, follow the steps below. (Before opening the file, if the Welcome to Lotus Word Pro dialog box is displayed, click on Cancel to close it.)

**1.** Click on the Open a Document SmartIcon, choose File ▶ Open, or press the shortcut key combination Ctrl+O on the keyboard. Word Pro displays the Open dialog box, shown in Figure 2.25, earlier in this chapter.

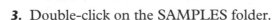

**2.** Click on the Up One Level button twice. The \LOTUS folder should be displayed in the Look In drop-down list box.

samples  **3.** Double-click on the SAMPLES folder.

wordpro  **4.** Double-click on the WORDPRO folder.

busplan  **5.** Double-click on the Word Pro icon preceding BUSPLAN. The BUS-PLAN document (see Figure 2.24 earlier in this chapter) opens.

**FIGURE 2.26** ▶

*The Windows Explorer window showing the \LOTUS folder and many of its subfolders, including \SAMPLES\ WORDPRO, which is the active folder*

The open folder

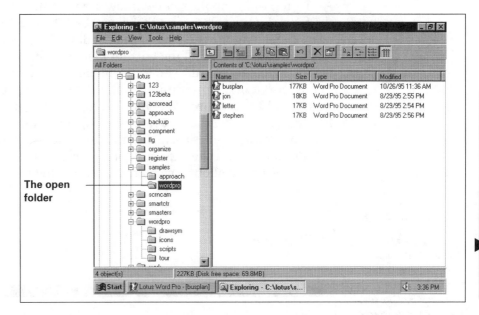

**TIP**

**If the file that you want to open is one of the last few on which you have worked (the number of files listed depends on the SmartSuite application you are using), you can select it from the bottom of the open File menu. Either click on the filename or type the underlined number preceding the filename.**

# ▶▶ The Elements of the Application Window

Much of the application window is similar to most Windows applications windows, but a few elements are unique to each SmartSuite application. Let's look more closely at the Word Pro window.

At the top of the application window are the title bar, the menu bar, the SmartIcons toolbar, and the view tabs. The *title bar* (see Figure 2.27), along the very top of the window, displays the name of the application, the name of the current file, or both. Before you open a file, the title bar typically shows the name of the Windows application—in this case, Lotus SmartSuite 97, the suite of which this application is a part, and Lotus Word Pro. Once you open a file, its name (that is, BUSPLAN) is added to the title bar. For some applications, the title bar sometimes provides useful information; whenever you open a menu, the title bar shows a short description of the menu or command. For more information about how menus work, see the following section.

**FIGURE 2.27** ▶

*The Lotus Word Pro title bar. Notice the name of Lotus Smart-Suite 97, the name of the application, and the name of the current file. Other SmartSuite title bars look just the same.*

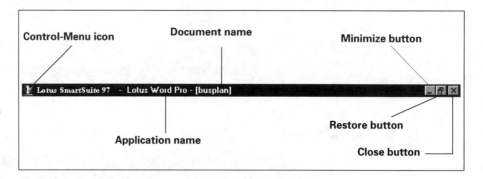

The title bar also contains the Control-Menu icon and three small buttons: the Minimize button, and either the Maximize button or the Restore button, and the Close button.

## ▶ Using the Menu Bar

Immediately below the title bar is the *menu bar* (see Figure 2.28), which displays the menus from which you can select commands. Menu commands begin an action, open a dialog box, or open a *cascading menu* or a *submenu*, branching off to the right.

**FIGURE 2.28** ▶

*The Word Pro menu bar contains seven menus from which you can select commands.*

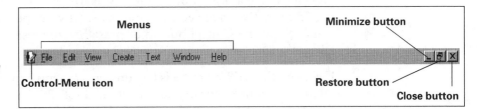

The standard Word Pro menus are File (from which you opened BUS-PLAN), Edit, View, Create, Window, and Help. Some menus—File, Edit, View, Window, and Help—are common to most Windows applications; Create appears with other SmartSuite applications. The Text menu appears on this particular menu bar, but is replaced by other menus in other sections of Word Pro. Text is a context-sensitive menu. If the mouse pointer points to text, the menu name is Text, and if the mouse pointer points to a frame in which a graphic is located, the menu name is Frame. All SmartSuite applications but Organizer have context-sensitive menus.

## ▶ Using SmartIcons

Under the menu bar are the *SmartIcons*, a series of toolbar buttons. When you click on a SmartIcon, you tell the application to do something (such as open, save, or print a file) that would otherwise take a couple of steps using menus, commands, and dialog boxes. The display of SmartIcons varies depending on the current SmartSuite application and your situation within that application.

The way buttons are positioned indicates their relationship. For example, the leftmost three buttons (Create a New Document, Open a Document, and Save the Current Document) in the Word Pro application window are closely related because they help in file management, but the fourth button (Print) is not related to the third.

►►**TIP**

**Move the mouse pointer over any SmartIcon in any SmartSuite application to view bubble help, a short description in a yellow cartoonlike balloon.**

Now let's take a brief look at a few SmartIcons. As you read, try clicking on SmartIcons to see what happens. (If you open a dialog box, you can click on the Cancel button or press Esc to close it without taking any action.)

For every SmartIcon, there is a counterpart menu command and quite often a shortcut key or key combination. Table 2.3 illustrates and describes some of the most common SmartSuite SmartIcons. (You won't see all of them on your starting Word Pro application window.) For information about SmartIcons used for specific applications, see the tables at the beginning of each part in this book. To learn how to customize Smart-Icons, see the *Customizing Your SmartSuite Environment* appendix.

► **TABLE 2.3:** *Common SmartSuite SmartIcons*

| Smart-Icon | Description | Equivalent Command | Shortcut Keys |
|---|---|---|---|
| | Starts a new document | File ➤ New Document | N/A |
| | Opens an existing document | File ➤ Open | Ctrl+O |
| | Saves the current document | File ➤ Save | Ctrl+S |
| | Prints the current file using the options in the Print dialog box | File ➤ Print | Ctrl+P |
| | Closes this window | File ➤ Close | N/A |
| | Exits this application | File ➤ Exit | Alt+F4 |
| | Undoes the last action, if allowed | Edit ➤ Undo | Ctrl+Z |

▶ **TABLE 2.3:** *Common SmartSuite SmartIcons (continued)*

| Smart-Icon | Description | Equivalent Command | Shortcut Keys |
|---|---|---|---|
| | Cuts the selection and places it in the Clipboard | Edit ➤ Cut | Ctrl+X or Shift+Del |
| | Copies the selection to the Clipboard | Edit ➤ Copy | Ctrl+C or Ctrl+Ins |
| | Pastes the contents of the Clipboard into the file at the current cursor location. (Other buttons with the glue bottle graphic also perform pasting actions.) | Edit ➤ Paste | Ctrl+V or Shift+Ins |
| | Opens or closes the InfoBox with which you can change the attributes of the selected object or text. (Other buttons with the yellow diamond open specific types of InfoBoxes.) | *Object* ➤ *Object* Properties | Alt+Enter or Ctrl+E (in Approach only) |
| **B** | Applies or removes boldface from the selection | Text ➤ Text Properties; click on the Text tab; click on Bold | Ctrl+B |
| *I* | Applies or removes italics from the selection | Text ➤ Text Properties; click on the Text tab; click on Italic | Ctrl+I |
| U | Applies or removes a single underline from the selection | Text ➤ Text Properties; click on the Text tab; click on Underline | Ctrl+U |
| ABC | Runs the spelling checker | Edit ➤ Check Spelling | Ctrl+F2 |
| | Goes to another section of the document | Edit ➤ Go To | Ctrl+G |
| | Finds and optionally replaces text and/or special characters | Edit ➤ Find & Replace Text | Ctrl+F |

## ► *View Tabs*

In Word Pro, Approach, and Freelance Graphics, view tabs are navigation tools. For example, in Word Pro, you can click on view tabs (see Figure 2.29) to move from one section of a large document to another; in Approach, you can move from one input form to another; and in Freelance Graphics, you can change from one way of viewing presentation pages to another. In 1-2-3, these tabs are known as sheet tabs. Figure 2.30 shows sheet tabs in the REVQRTLY sample workbook.

**FIGURE 2.29** ►

*View tabs for a five-part Word Pro document*

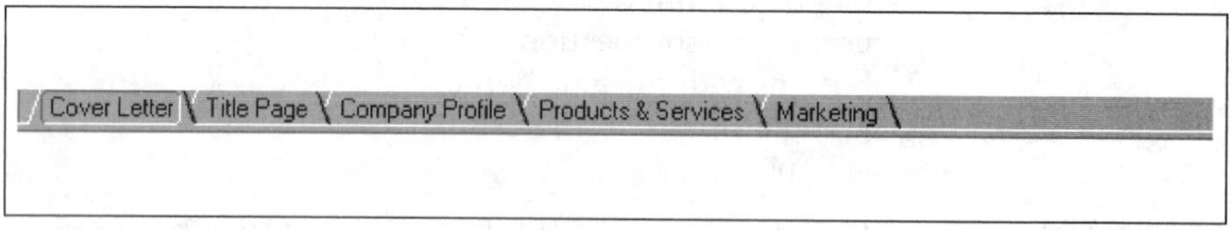

**FIGURE 2.30** ►

*Sheet tabs in a four-part 1-2-3 workbook; three tabs have been named.*

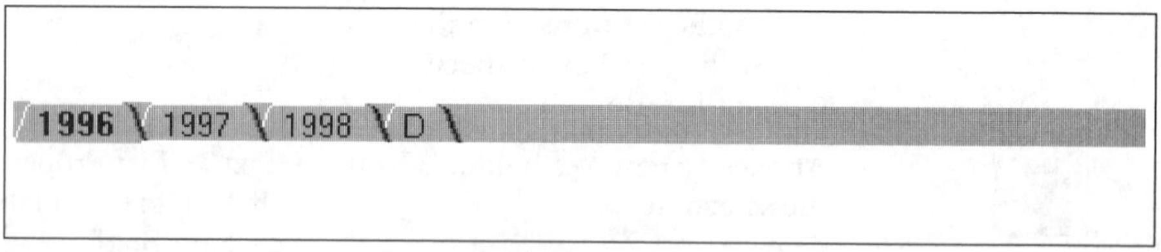

## ► *The Work Area*

The largest part of the window is the work area, in which you work on your files. If you have been testing features and functions as you read this chapter, you have already seen dialog boxes, menus, and changes to the contents of the work area.

## ▶ *The Status Bar*

At the bottom of the window, the Status bar (see Figures 2.31, 2.32, and 2.33) shows you a variety of information and allows you to perform certain actions. For example, in Word Pro, if you click on the Default Text button, you display a list of *styles* (that is, formats) that you can apply to paragraphs:

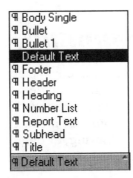

As you learn about each SmartSuite application, you'll find out about its unique Status bar.

*Getting Acquainted*

**FIGURE 2.31** ▶

*The Word Pro Status bar provides information about the application and allows you to take some actions.*

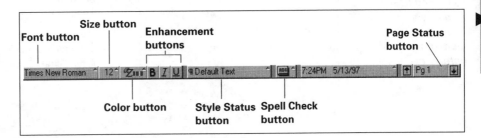

▶▶

Ch.

**2**

**FIGURE 2.32** ▶

*You can use the Approach Status bar to change attributes, change your view of the contents of the work area, or change modes or forms.*

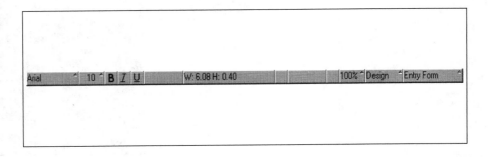

**FIGURE 2.33** ▶

*The Freelance Graphics Status bar is similar to yet different from Word Pro's Status bar.*

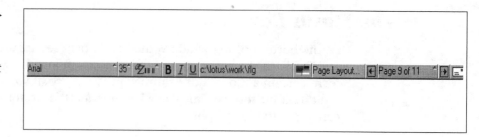

## ▶▶ *Selecting a Command*

Now that you have learned some application window basics, the next step is to find out some of the details. Let's open a menu from the menu bar and select a command. The 1-2-3 Create menu (see Figure 2.34) and its submenus provide tools with which you can create a sheet, chart, map, drawing, or database; add a button or text; insert an object from another application; and so on.

**FIGURE 2.34** ▶

*From the Create menu and its submenus, you can create a sheet, chart, map, drawing, or database, and more.*

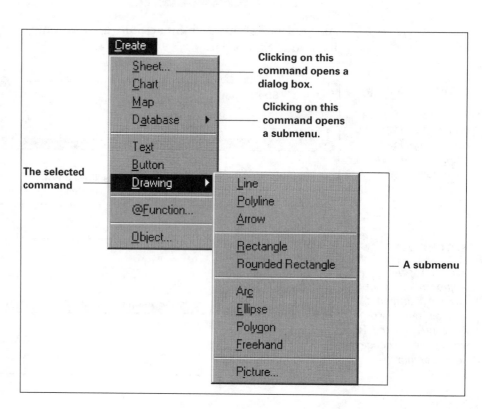

Choose Create ➤ Object to display the Create Object dialog box (see Figure 2.35), with which you can create an object to insert into a sheet. (The Create Object command is also available in Word Pro, Approach, and Freelance Graphics.) If you're using a mouse, click on Create, and when the menu opens, click on Object. To open a menu using the keyboard, press Alt, the underlined selection letter on the menu (**C** for Create), and the selection letter on the command (**O** for Object). For information about Windows menu and command syntax, see the insert *Sybex's Quick Tour of Windows 95* at the beginning of this book.

**FIGURE 2.35** ▶

*The Create Object dialog box, from which you can create objects to add to a document*

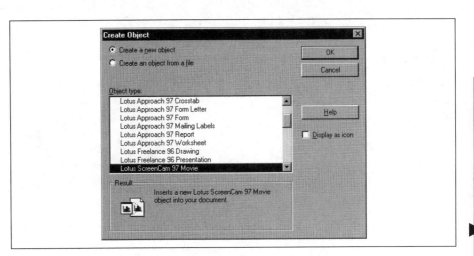

## ▶ *Selecting Options in Dialog Boxes*

Most dialog boxes, such as the Create Object dialog box, contain a variety of boxes and buttons with which you instruct the active application. For example, you can click in the Create an Object from a File box to display a version of the Create Object dialog box that you can use to create an object from a file that already exists. Or to select a particular object type, you can click on an item listed in the Object Type scroll box. You can even get help on using the dialog box by clicking on the Help button. When you finish selecting options and typing values, click on the OK command button or press Enter. To close a dialog box, click on the Cancel command button or press Esc. To close a menu, press Esc or click outside the menu. Without taking any action, click on the Cancel command button or press Esc.

## ▶ *Selecting Commands from Shortcut Menus*

As you learn more about SmartSuite applications, you'll find that there are often many ways to do a job. For example, you can copy a selection to the Clipboard by clicking on the Copy SmartIcon, by choosing Edit ▶ Copy, or by pressing either Ctrl+C or Ctrl+Ins. If you are working on an item, the quickest way to copy it is by clicking on the right mouse button (that is, right-click) to reveal a shortcut menu (see Figure 2.36), which contains the most common commands—in this case, text properties in Freelance Graphics. Then select Copy (by pressing either the left or right mouse button).

**FIGURE 2.36** ▶

*A Freelance Graphics text properties short-cut menu*

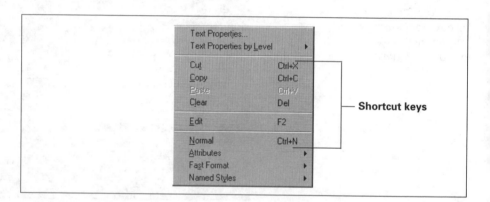

In the following sections, you'll learn some of the details of using the mouse and the keyboard to open menus, select commands, and specify options.

# ▶▶ *Using the Mouse*

Although you can move around the current window and the active application using either the mouse or the keyboard, it's easier for a novice to use the mouse (after learning how to move the mouse around the mouse pad and click the mouse buttons). In contrast, using the keyboard requires knowledge of the application; selection letters on menus and commands provide clues for getting around, but you have to know the application to know its shortcut keys. In addition, the only way to use some objects, such as SmartIcons, is to click a mouse button. As you find out about each SmartSuite application, however, you'll discover that using shortcut keys is the fastest way to perform an action.

So you'll probably issue commands—especially those that you use often—using both the mouse and the keyboard.

The mouse pointer changes shape depending on its location in the window and the action that you are taking. Table 2.4 shows many types of mouse pointers and provides a description of each.

▶ **TABLE 2.4:** *Common SmartSuite Mouse Pointers*

| Mouse Pointer | Description |
|---|---|
| | Points to objects (menus, buttons, boxes, windows, icons, and so on) on the screen so that you can select them. This is the default mouse pointer. |
| | Indicates that the computer is busy and that you must wait before performing another action. |
| | Indicates that the application is working and that you must wait before performing another action. |
| | Adjusts the width of a column. |
| | Adjusts the height of a row. |
| | Adjusts the height of a window. |
| | Adjusts the width of a window. |
| | Adjusts both the height and the width of a window. |
| | Moves or sizes a window using the Control menu. |
| | Marks the insertion point for text or data entry. |
| | Indicates that the area to which you are pointing is unavailable. |
| | Shows that you are ready to drag a selection. |
| | Shows that you have started to drag a selection. |

► **TABLE 2.4:** *Common SmartSuite Mouse Pointers (continued)*

| Mouse Pointer | Description |
|---|---|
| | Shows that you have started to drag a copy of a selection. |
| | Marks the starting position of a new chart, drawing, or frame. |
| | Points to text in a chart. |
| | Points to a series in a chart. |
| | Points to lines and borders in a chart. |
| | Points to Y-axes in a chart. |
| | Adds cells to the selection. |
| | Marks help text that when clicked on either displays terminology or a description or jumps to a related help topic. |
| | Magnifies or reduces the size of the clicked-on window. |
| | Cycles through the sizes of the clicked-on window. |
| | Opens a help window for the object on which you click. |

You can use the mouse in five basic ways:

**Point** Move the mouse around the mouse pad or table top until the mouse pointer is located at the desired position on the screen.

**Click** Press and release a mouse button once. In this book, the term *click* indicates clicking the left mouse button. When you see the term *right-click*, click the right mouse button.

**Double-Click**   Rapidly press and release the left mouse button twice.

**Drag**   Press and hold down the left mouse button, and move the mouse around the mouse pad or table top. Finally, release the left mouse button to end dragging.

**Drag-and-Drop**   Press and hold down the left mouse button while pointing to an object, and move the mouse around the mouse pad or table top until the mouse pointer is pointing at a particular location. Finally, release the left mouse button to end dragging and to drop the object in the new location.

# ▶▶ *Using the Keyboard*

If you have more experience with the keyboard than with the mouse, you can execute commands by using just the keyboard. As you learn about an application, however, you'll probably find that you'll use a combination of the mouse and the keyboard.

You can activate commands by pressing shortcut keys, which are single keys or *key combinations* (pressing two or three keys simultaneously). In this book, key combinations are shown as a series of keys, each separated by a plus sign (+). For example, the key combination used to print a file in any SmartSuite application is Ctrl+P. Table 2.5 lists some common SmartSuite shortcut keys and key combinations used to execute commands and perform other actions.

▶ **TABLE 2.5:**   *SmartSuite Shortcut Keys and Key Combinations—Commands and Actions*

| Shortcut Key or Key Combination | Description |
| --- | --- |
| Alt | Activates the Menu bar or inactivates an active Menu bar |
| Alt+↑ | Opens and closes a drop-down list box in a dialog box |
| Alt+↓ | Opens and closes a drop-down list box in a dialog box |

Getting Acquainted

▶▶

Ch.
2

▶ **TABLE 2.5:** *SmartSuite Shortcut Keys and Key Combinations—Commands and Actions (continued)*

| Shortcut Key or Key Combination | Description |
| --- | --- |
| Alt+- | Opens the Control menu for the current window |
| Alt+spacebar | Opens the Control menu |
| Alt+Esc | Cycles through all active Windows applications |
| Alt+F4 | Closes a window or application |
| Alt+F4 | Closes a dialog box without taking any actions |
| Ctrl+Esc | Opens the Windows Start menu from which you can perform a variety of Windows operations |
| Ctrl+F4 | Closes the current window |
| Ctrl+O | Opens the Open dialog box |
| Ctrl+P | Opens the Print dialog box from which you can print all or part of the current file |
| Ctrl+S | Saves the current file |
| Enter | Signals the completion of filling in the dialog box, then closes the dialog box |
| Esc | Closes the dialog box or some windows without taking any actions |
| F1 | Displays a help window—either the last Help Topics window you viewed or a window related to the active object |
| F10 | Activates the menu bar and inactivates an active menu bar in 1-2-3, Word Pro, Freelance Graphics, and Organizer |

# ▶▶ *Moving around a File*

You can use the mouse or the keyboard to move around any Smart-Suite file. Some SmartSuite applications offer other means of navigation; you'll learn about those methods in later chapters.

## ▶ *Scrolling around the Work Area Using the Mouse*

You can move around a file using the mouse in two ways:

- Move the mouse pointer around the work area currently displayed in the active window.

- Press and hold or drag the mouse pointer in the horizontal scroll bar (see Figure 2.37) and vertical scroll bar to display other parts of the file.

**FIGURE 2.37** ▶

*Use the arrows, the scroll box, and the area within the horizontal scroll bar to move around a file.*

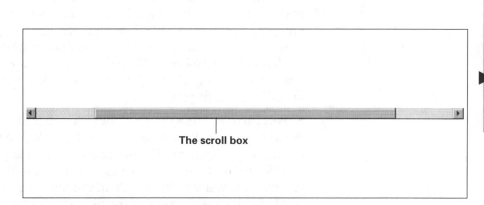

The scroll box

▶▶ **N O T E**

> If your file is small enough to fit within the work area, the scroll bars will either be dimmed (which indicates that they are unavailable) or will not appear in the work area.

Getting Acquainted

▶ ▶
Ch.
**2**

Except for the position in which they are displayed, vertical and horizontal scroll bars look exactly the same. Use the vertical scroll bar to move through a file from top to bottom, and use the horizontal scroll bar to move from side to side.

A scroll bar consists of arrows, the area within the scroll bar and between the arrows, and the *scroll box* (the box within the scroll bar). You can use any part of a scroll bar to scroll through a file.

**Scroll bar arrows**      Move horizontally or vertically through a file by moving the mouse pointer to the arrows at either end of a horizontal or vertical scroll bar and pressing and holding down the left mouse button on the scroll bar arrows. As your file scrolls side to side or up and down the Desktop, the scroll box also moves to indicate the part of the file currently in the work area. If you click once on a scroll bar arrow, the file moves a small amount (for example, one row or column in 1-2-3).

**Within the scroll bar**      The area within the scroll bar represents the entire length or width of your file. If you click on any part of this area other than the scroll box, you'll see the next or previous screen of the file. For example, in 1-2-3, if you are currently viewing columns J–Q, you'll see columns A–I if you click to the left of the scroll box. Then if you click to the right of the scroll box, once again you'll see J–Q. Again, click to the right and columns R–Y are displayed.

**Scroll box**      Drag the scroll box (which is also called the *thumb*) to a new position on the scroll bar. When you release the left mouse button, you'll move to a comparable position in the file. For example, if you move the scroll box to the middle of the scroll bar, you'll see the middle of the file. The size of the scroll box indicates the amount of the file that you are viewing. So, a long scroll box demonstrates that you are viewing a great deal, and a short scroll box indicates that you are viewing only a small part of the file.

## ▶ *Scrolling around the Work Area Using the Keyboard*

When you are typing, you'll find that you can move around a file more quickly with the keyboard than with the mouse. After you learn the basics of an application, you'll find that you memorize and use certain command keystrokes. Table 2.6 lists the keys and key combinations with which you can scroll around SmartSuite files.

▶ **TABLE 2.6:** *SmartSuite Shortcut Keys and Key Combinations—Navigation*

| Shortcut Key or Key Combination | Description |
| --- | --- |
| ↑ | Moves up to the previous item in a group or to the previous line |
| ↓ | Moves down to the next item in a group or to the next line |
| ← | Moves up to the previous item in a group or to the previous character on the current line |
| → | Moves down to the next item in a group or to the next character on the current line |
| Ctrl+← | Moves the cursor to the left of the previous word (label); moves to the beginning of the value (values) |
| Ctrl+→ | Moves the cursor to the left of the next word (label); moves to the end of the value (values) |
| Ctrl+End | Moves the cursor to the bottom of the last page in a Word Pro document, to the last record in an Approach database |
| Ctrl+Home | Moves the cursor to the first cell in the current file (the first cell in the first sheet in the workbook), to the first record in an Approach database, or to the top of the first page in a Word Pro document |
| Ctrl+PgDn | Moves the cursor to the first cell in the prior sheet in the workbook, to the prior form in an Approach database, to the next page in a Freelance Graphics presentation, or to the top of the next page in a Word Pro document |

▶ **TABLE 2.6:** *SmartSuite Shortcut Keys and Key Combinations—Navigation (continued)*

| Shortcut Key or Key Combination | Description |
|---|---|
| Ctrl+PgUp | Moves the cursor to the first cell in the next sheet in the workbook, to the next form in an Approach database, to the prior page in a Freelance Graphics presentation, or to the top of the previous page in a Word Pro document |
| End | Moves the cursor to the end of the entry or line |
| End,Ctrl+Home | Moves the cursor to the bottom right corner of the last sheet in the workbook |
| End,Ctrl+PgDn | Moves the cursor to the same cell address in the next sheet |
| End,Ctrl+PgUp | Moves the cursor to the same cell address in the prior sheet |
| Home | Moves the cursor to the beginning of the entry or line |
| Shift+Tab | Moves to the previous option, from right to left and from bottom to top order |
| Tab | Moves to the next option, from left to right and from top to bottom order |

# ▶▶ *Checking Spelling*

After you have created a 1-2-3, Word Pro, Approach, or Freelance Graphics file and have spent some time editing it, you should check its spelling and the occurrence of duplicate words. These SmartSuite applications have two dictionaries—the language (main) dictionary and the user dictionary into which you add your own words, such as unique technical terms, product and company names, and so on. You can check only one part of a file by selecting it; otherwise, the spelling checker evaluates the entire file.

To set spelling checker options and run the spelling checker, click on the Check Spelling SmartIcon, choose Edit ➤ Check Spelling, or press Ctrl+F2. The Check Spelling dialog box appears (see Figure 2.38). (In Word Pro, a Spell Check bar is inserted above the work area.)

**FIGURE 2.38** ▶

*In the opening Check Spelling dialog box for 1-2-3, you can set spelling checker options.*

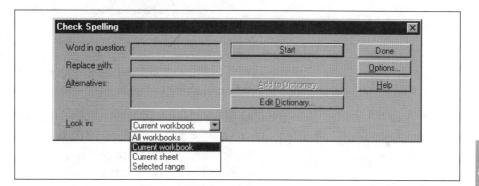

▶▶ **N O T E**

**If you misspell a word while creating or editing a Word Pro document, the spell check button in the Status bar changes color and becomes more visible. When this happens, click on the button to open a menu with four commands ( Add to Dictionary, Skip, Skip All, and Replace) and suggested replacement words. Use the commands exactly as you would while using the Word Pro Spell Check bar.**

The starting Check Spelling dialog boxes for 1-2-3, Word Pro, Approach, and Freelance Graphics contain some of these options:

**Language Options**  Click on this button to display the Language Options dialog box (see Figure 2.39), in which you can change the language that the spelling checker uses to check text.

**FIGURE 2.39** ▶

*In the Approach Language Options dialog box, you can select the language that the spelling checker uses.*

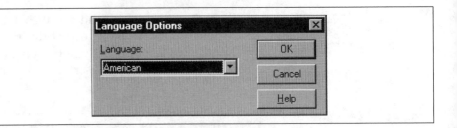

**Speller Options**   Click on this button to display the Speller Options dialog box (see Figures 2.40 and 2.41) with which you can specify checking options:

- Check for Repeated Words determines whether the spelling checker checks for repeated words.
- Check Words with Numbers determines whether the spelling checker checks for words including numbers (for example, Address1).

**FIGURE 2.40** ▶

*In Approach's Speller Options dialog box, you can specify four options.*

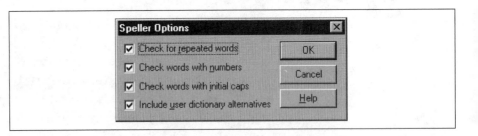

**FIGURE 2.41** ▶

*In Word Pro's Spell Check Options dialog box, you can specify four options as well as set the color for unrecognized words and choose custom dictionaries.*

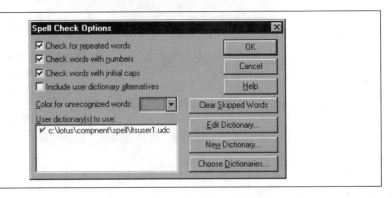

- Check Words with Initial Caps determines whether the spelling checker checks for words starting with uppercase characters (that is, proper nouns such as surnames and company names).

- Include Macro/@Function Keywords, Punctuation (only in 1-2-3) determines whether the spelling checker uses a dictionary of keywords and functions when checking words.

**Edit Dictionary**     Click on this button to display the Spell Check User's Dictionary dialog box (see Figure 2.42), which allows you to add, view, or delete words, such as new terms and proper words, from the user's dictionary. You can also add words as you run the spelling checker, as you will see shortly.

**FIGURE 2.42** ▶

*In the Freelance Graphics Spell Check User's Dictionary dialog box, you can add, view, or delete words from the list in your user's dictionary.*

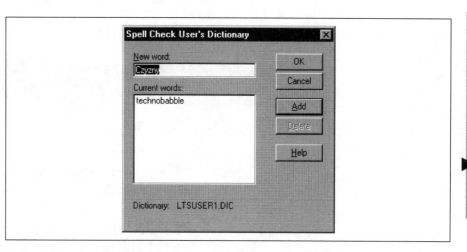

When you have set spelling checker options, click on OK to start the spelling checker. When it encounters its first unknown word, another Spell Check dialog box (see Figure 2.43) appears. In Word Pro, the Spell Check bar (see Figure 2.44) is already in place.

Common options in the Spell Check dialog box and the Word Pro Spell Check bar are as follows:

| | |
|---|---|
| **Word in Question** | Displays a word that is not in the language or user dictionary |
| **Replace With** | Contains the first alternative word |

*Getting Acquainted*

Ch.
**2**

**FIGURE 2.43** ▶

*In the main Freelance Graphics Spell Check dialog box, you can control the spelling checker as it reviews your file.*

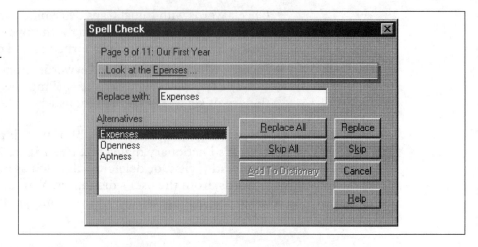

**FIGURE 2.44** ▶

*The Word Pro Spell Check bar with a misspelled word and the suggested alternative*

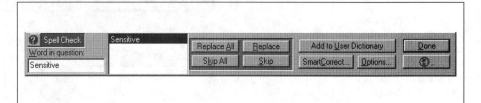

| | |
|---|---|
| **Replace All** | Replaces all occurrences of the unknown word with the word in the Replace With text box |
| **Replace** | Replaces this occurrence of the unknown word with the word in the Replace With text box |
| **Skip All** | Skips all occurrences of the unknown word in the rest of this file |
| **Skip** | Skips this occurrence of the unknown word |
| **Add To Dictionary** | Adds the unknown word to the user dictionary |

When the spelling checker has completed its work, it displays an information box:

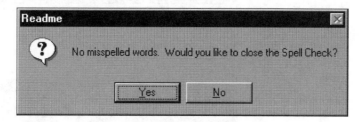

or

Click on OK, Yes, or Done to return to your file.

# ▶▶ *Saving a File*

Once you have put a certain amount of work into a file, you'll want to save it so that you don't have to reconstruct it later. You can save a file any time—even before you type your first character—using the commands listed below:

File ▶ Save (or click on the Save SmartIcon or press Ctrl+S)

If you are saving the file for the first time, your SmartSuite application displays the Save As dialog box (see Figure 2.45). If you are saving the file after that, this command simply saves the file using its original name. Note that in Approach, the command is File ▶ Save Approach File.

**FIGURE 2.45 ▶**

*In the Word Pro Save As dialog box, you name a file and provide other information about it.*

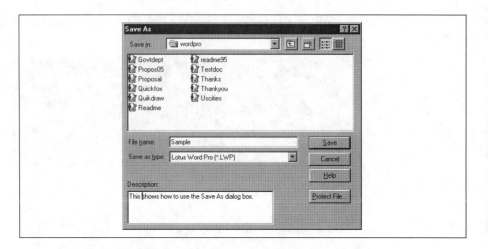

| File ➤ Save As | Displays the Save As dialog box so that you can save a file using a different name, location, or save option. Use this command to create a backup file. |
| File ➤ User Setup ➤ *Application* Preferences | Displays the *Application* Preferences dialog box (see Figure 2.46) in which you can define options for automatically saving your files every few minutes as you are working on them. |

You'll learn how to use each of these Save commands in the sections below.

## ▶ About the Save As Dialog Box

You save a file in several ways:

- Choose File ➤ Save.
- Press Ctrl+S.
- Click on the Save SmartIcon.
- Choose File ➤ Save As.
- Turn on the automatic save feature.

FIGURE 2.46 ▶

*In the Word Pro Prefer-ences dialog box, you can specify file-saving options and other customization options.*

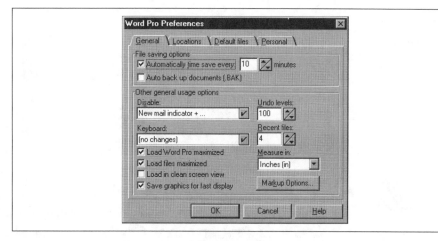

If you save a file by choosing File ➤ Save, pressing Ctrl+S, or clicking on the Save SmartIcon, and if you have saved this file before, your application will save the file using its current name and location. If the file you are saving has never been saved before, the Save As dialog box appears. Regardless of whether this file has been saved before, if you choose File ➤ Save As, the application displays the Save As dialog box. This dialog box may look complex when you first see it, but it is in fact easy to use.

▶▶**NOTE**

**The Save As dialog box is a typical Windows dialog box. It's almost identical to the Open dialog box (used when you opened the current file).**

These are the parts that the SmartSuite Save As dialog boxes have in common:

**Save In**     A drop-down list box (see Figure 2.47) from which you choose the folder in which you will save the file. In the large text box below the drop-down list box is a list of all the files in the current folder. You can check this list to ensure that the name you give a file is unique. To learn about valid filenames, see the next section of this chapter.

**FIGURE 2.47** ▶

*Sample contents of the
Save In drop-down list box*

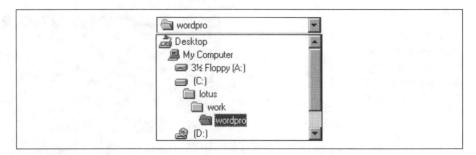

▶▶ N O T E

A computer's folder structure is like an upside-down tree. The *root* folder, at the top, is the trunk from which all the branches, or subfolders, come. (To see a better picture of your computer system's folder structure, open Windows Explorer and look at the Folder pane, on the left side of the Windows Explorer window.) Alignment in the Save In drop-down list box shows how far a subfolder is from the root folder, which is aligned against the left border of the box. If you open the drop-down list box, you'll see the C: ROOT folder icon (or the name of the drive in which you are currently working). Immediately underneath and to the right of the ROOT folder icon is the LOTUS folder icon, under that (and farther to the right) is the WORK folder icon, and under that is the WORDPRO folder icon. Notice that these four icons illustrate the path. LOTUS is a subfolder of the C: ROOT folder, WORK is a subfolder of the LOTUS subfolder, and WORDPRO is a subfolder of the WORK subfolder.

**Up One Level**   Click on this button to move to the parent folder of the current subfolder.

 **Create New Folder**   Click on this button to create a new folder.

 **List/Details**   Click on one of these buttons to display the file-names in this box in rows (the default) or display each filename, its size, its type, and the last modification date in a row.

**File Name**   In this text box, type a filename (it can be a maximum of 255 characters). You need not type a file extension; the application automatically assigns one.

**Save As Type**   When you open this drop-down list box, you can see the file types to which you can save this file. For example, in Word Pro, you have several choices of saving files: in six Microsoft Word formats alone.

**Description**   In this text box, type a description of the file that you are saving. Then when you want to find it to open it, the description will appear at the bottom of the Open dialog box.

The Save As dialog box also provides other options that are related to the specific type of application:

- In Freelance Graphics, you can save a presentation and prepare it for a mobile screen show at the same time.

- In Word Pro, 1-2-3, and Organizer, you can protect the file with a password and optionally assign access rights to those reading or editing the file.

- In 1-2-3, you can save a range of cells.

- In Approach, you can save a database or just an Approach file.

- In Organizer, you can grant single user access, and you can map (that is, assign) a drive on the network to which your computer is attached.

**Getting Acquainted**

*Ch.*
**2**

One of the most important reasons to save a file is to create a backup copy of it. The best way to back up a file is to save it to disk and store the disk in a location away from your computer—in another room or even in another building. To back up a file, insert a disk in the appropriate disk drive and choose File ➤ Save As. In the Save As dialog box, type or select the filename in the File Name text box and select a disk drive. Then either click on OK or press Enter. After saving, be sure that before you save or open your next file, you change the disk identifier back to the hard drive, if necessary.

The quickest way to move files to a disk is to use drag-and-drop. For example, in the Contents pane of the Windows Explorer, select the files to be backed up. Scroll to the top of the Folders pane until the 3 1/2 Floppy or 5 1/4 Floppy icon appears, depending on the drive in which the disk has been inserted. Then, drag the selected files toward the floppy icon. When the floppy icon is highlighted, release the left mouse button.

## ▶ Naming a File

When you save a file that is unnamed, the Save As dialog box highlights the File Name text box and sometimes suggests a name (for example, in 1-2-3 the suggested name is Untitled but in Word Pro the File Name text box is empty).

If you want to assign a filename other than the one suggested, follow these naming rules: Select a filename (it can be a maximum of 255 characters), and select valid characters (except for | ? : * " < >). When a SmartSuite application saves a file, it automatically adds a period (.) and the appropriate extension to the filename. Table 2.7 lists SmartSuite extensions and the applications to which they are related. You can use long filenames as built-in descriptions (for example, *Voting Pattern Report - 3/6/98* or *May 31 cover letters*), which are excellent memory joggers.

▶ **TABLE 2.7:** *SmartSuite File Extensions*

| Extension | Application |
| --- | --- |
| 123 | 1-2-3 |
| LWP | Word Pro |
| APR | Approach |
| PRZ | Freelance Graphics |
| OR3 | Organizer |

**TIP**

**If you will be using a combination of Windows 95 and Windows 3.1 computers, it is best for you to restrict yourself to eight-character filenames to conform to Windows 3.1 standards.**

## ▶ *Setting Up the Automatic Save Feature*

Anyone with any amount of computer experience can tell you at least one horror story about losing a file when the power went out. To prevent losing too much of your valuable time, take advantage of the automatic save features in Word Pro and Freelance Graphics.

• In Word Pro, choose File ➤ User Setup ➤ Word Pro Preferences. In the Word Pro Preferences dialog box (see Figure 2.46, earlier in this chapter), check the Automatically Time Save Every checkbox, select or type a value from 1 to 99 minutes (the default is 10 minutes) between saves, and click on OK or press Enter.

- In Freelance Graphics, choose File ➤ User Setup ➤ Freelance Preferences. In the Freelance Graphics Preferences dialog box (see Figure 2.48), check the Auto Timed Save checkbox and type or select a value from 1 to 99 (the default is 10 minutes, and click on OK or press Enter.

**FIGURE 2.48** ▶

*In the Freelance Graphics Preferences dialog box, you can change or specify many options, including the Auto Timed Save feature.*

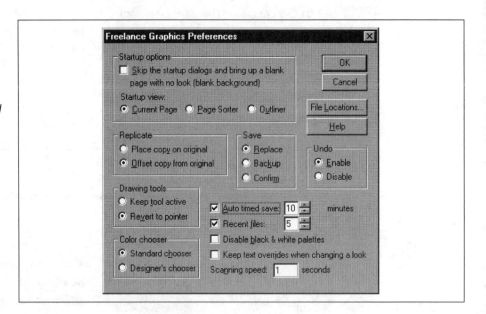

When the automatic save feature is turned on, the current application counts the minutes since the last save, either automatic or manual. Since this count goes on in the background, you can continue your work. When the count equals the specified number of minutes, the application is ready to save your file. The next time you pause (perhaps to look up a number or to think of the next word), the application quickly saves the file. The count then begins again.

# ►► *Printing a File*

Once you have previewed your file and have edited it, as needed, you can print it. SmartSuite applications provide three ways to print a file:

- Click on the Print SmartIcon in either the Print Preview window or the application window.
- Choose File ➤ Print.
- Press Ctrl+P.

Whichever method you use, the Print dialog box (see an example in Figure 2.49) appears. Each SmartSuite Print dialog box provides a combination of common options and application-specific options. Application-specific printing options are covered in these chapters: *Editing and Formatting a Spreadsheet, Formatting and Editing a Document, Editing a Presentation*, and *Managing Data with Organizer*.

**FIGURE 2.49** ►

*Word Pro's Print dialog box has several options that are common to any Windows application Print dialog box and several that are application specific.*

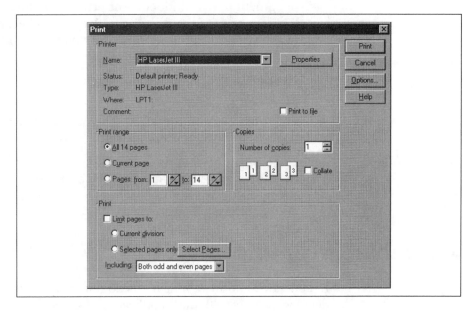

Ch.
2

These are some of the common options in the Print dialog boxes for SmartSuite applications:

**Number of Copies** or **Copies (Organizer)**    In this text/list box, select the number of copies of the file to be printed.

**From**    In this text/list box, select the starting page number.

**To**    In this text/list box, select the number of the last page to be printed.

**Current Sheet, Current Record,** or **Current Page**    Click on this option button to print only the page in which the insertion point is located.

**All Worksheets, All, All Pages, All *n* Pages, Entire Workbook,** or **All Records**    Click on this option button to print the entire file.

**Print to File**    Check this checkbox to print the selected document and its formats to a file for printing at a later time.

**Collate**    Check this checkbox to print all the pages in one document in a multidocument print job before starting to print the next copy of the document. A cleared checkbox tells the printer to print multiple copies of one page, multiple copies of the next page, and so on.

**Properties**    A button on which you click to specify attributes for the default printer.

**Options**    A button on which you click to specify application-dependent print and update options for this print job.

**Page Setup, Preview & Page Setup,** or **Setup**    To change the default page settings, click on this button. When the Page Setup dialog box appears, select from its options and either click on OK or press Enter.

# ▶▶ *Deleting Files*

In general, Windows applications do not provide explicit commands for deleting files. Instead, most applications take advantage of the file maintenance capabilities of the Windows Explorer feature or other windows (such as the Find utility's window or the Printer window). You can also delete files from certain dialog boxes that you can open from the File menu: Open, Open File, Save As, or Import Picture.

**N O T E**

> When you delete a file, Windows moves it to the Recycle Bin; the file is not removed from your computer. To permanently remove the file, double-click on the Recycle Bin icon on your Desktop. To delete one file, select it and choose File ➤ Delete. To delete all the files from the Recycle Bin, either choose File ➤ Empty Recycle Bin or choose Edit ➤ Select All (or press Ctrl+A) and then choose File ➤ Delete. If you have installed File Manager under Windows 95, remember that File Manager is a Windows 3.1 feature. Deleting files using File Manager results in permanent removal with no Recycle Bin to allow for second thoughts and "undeletion."

If you are running Windows with its default settings, you will open Windows Explorer from the Start menu. Once the Windows Explorer window is on your Desktop, delete a file by clicking on it and pressing the Delete key.

To delete a file, follow these steps:

**1.** Click on the Start button, point to Programs, and click on Windows Explorer. The Windows Explorer window (see Figure 2.50) opens.

**2.** In the All Folders pane on the left side of the Windows Explorer window, click on the icon that represents the folder in which the file to be deleted is located. You may have to click on several icons until you find the subfolder in which the file is located. (Most of your work is in a subfolder under the WORK subfolder.)

**3.** On the right side of the window in the Contents Of pane, find the name of the file to be deleted and select it.

**4.** Delete the file by choosing File ➤ Delete or by pressing the Delete key. A message box (see Figure 2.51) prompts you to confirm the deletion.

**5.** Close Windows Explorer by clicking on the Close button or choosing File ➤ Close.

Getting Acquainted

▶▶

*Ch.*
**2**

**FIGURE 2.50** ►

*The Windows Explorer window has two panes: the All Folders pane on the left side and the Contents Of pane on the right.*

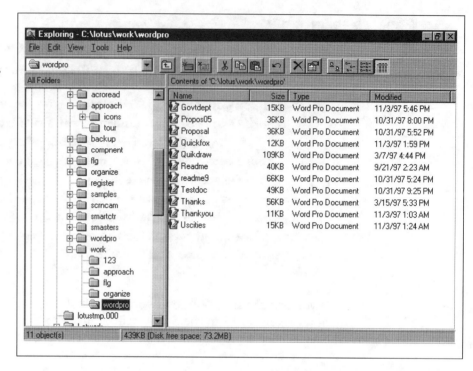

**FIGURE 2.51** ►

*Click on Yes to confirm the deletion.*

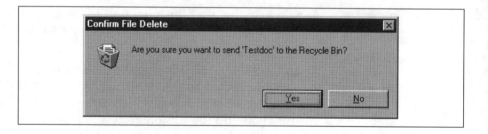

# ▶▶ *Getting Help*

Once you have found out how to get help in one Windows application, you will know how most Windows Help facilities work. If you have a question about a SmartSuite feature, element, or procedure, you can get help in several ways:

- To get general help about an application, from an application window click on Help on the menu bar; a menu (see Figure 2.52) opens from which you can choose.

**FIGURE 2.52** ▶

*The open Approach Help menu*

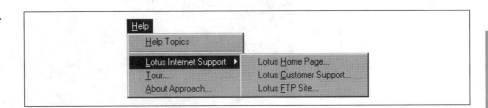

- To open a Help Topics window (see Figure 2.53), press F1 or choose Help ➤ Help Topics.

**FIGURE 2.53** ▶

*The Contents section of the Approach Help Topics window*

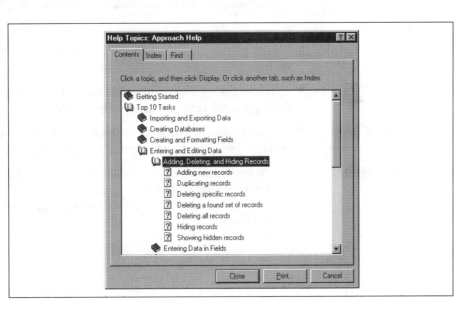

Getting
Acquainted

▶▶

Ch.
2

- To take an automated tour of an application, either choose Help ➤ Help Topics or open the Suite Help drawer in the SmartCenter and double-click on an icon in the Tours folder. Tours are available for Lotus 1-2-3, Lotus Approach, Lotus Freelance Graphics, and Lotus Word Pro.

- To view copyright and registration information (see Figure 2.54) about an application, choose Help ➤ About *Application*.

**FIGURE 2.54** ▶

*The About Approach message box*

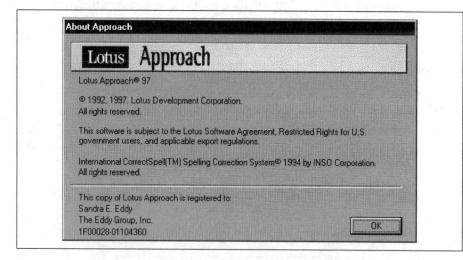

- To get Windows help, press F1 from an active Help window. To return to the application, click on Back.

- In some dialog boxes, click on the ? button and click on an object to open a context-sensitive help window.

- In some dialog boxes, right-click on an object and click on the What's This? button to open a context-sensitive help window.

- From the SmartCenter, click on the Suite Help drawer to get help from the SmartSuite help system, the DocOnline online Smart-Suite manuals, movies, guided tours, and access to Lotus and IBM Internet sites.

## ▶ *The Help Topics Window*

The Help Topics window has three sections: Contents (see Figure 2.53, earlier in this chapter), Index (see Figure 2.57, later in this chapter), and Find (see Figure 2.59). The first time you use a SmartSuite application, the default window is Contents. After you have used the help system, the default is the last window that you used.

### *Using the Contents Section of the Help Topics Window*

In the Contents section of the Help topics window, you can reveal or hide help windows.

- To reveal a list of topics, double-click on the closed book icon preceding the title of a main topic. When a topic is preceded by a question mark icon, you can display the help window discussing that topic.

- To reveal another list of topics, click on the open book icon preceding the title of a topic. To close a list of topics, double-click on the open book icon.

- To reveal a help topic window, click on the question mark icon preceding the title of a topic.

At the top of a help topic window are three buttons: Help Topics, Print, and Go Back.

- To return to the Help Topics window, click on Help Topics.
- To print the topic, click on the Print button.
- To return to the previous help window, click on the Go Back button.

Help windows have distinct features: jump text (see Figure 2.55) and buttons (see Figure 2.56).

- To reveal a short description related to a term underlined with dashes, click on the term.

> **Browse**
> The environment in Approach for entering, editing, and viewing data in a database.
> To go to Browse, do one of the following:
> • Click the Browse button in the action bar.
> • Click the Environment button in the status bar and select Browse.
> • Choose View - Browse & Data Entry.

*details*

● To jump to a help window related to a term with a solid underline, click on the term.

**FIGURE 2.55** ►

*An Approach help window with two types of jump text*

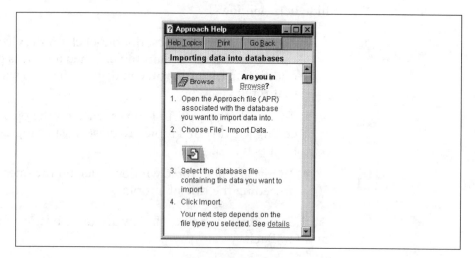

**FIGURE 2.56** ►

*An Approach help window with buttons on which you click to open a list of topics or another help window*

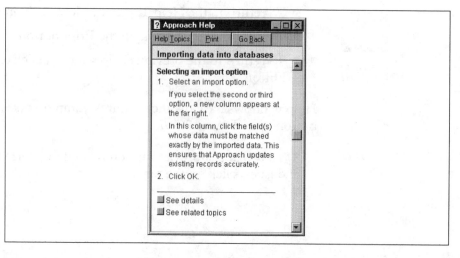

- To open a help window related to the current help window, click on a button. You can view both windows by dragging them by their title bars until both are completely revealed.

## Using the Index Section of the Help Topics Window

The Index section (see Figure 2.57) of the help topics window enables you to search for a term or a phrase. You can find a topic and open a help window for the chosen topic in two ways:

- Type the first characters in a topic name and click on the Display button.

- Scroll down the list of topics until you find a topic. Then either click on the topic and click on the Display button or double-click on the topic.

▶▶

Ch.

2

**FIGURE 2.57** ▶

*The Index section of the Approach Help Topics window*

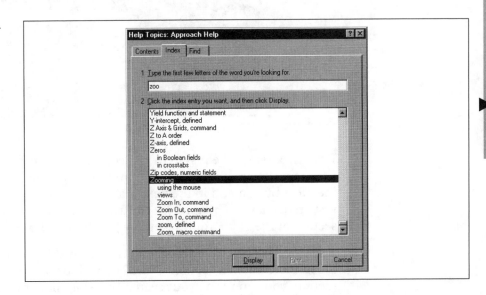

Then view and use the help topic window as you learned in the previous section, "Using the Contents Section of the Help Topics Window."

## Using the Find Section of the Help Topics Window

In the Find section of the Help Topics window, you can search for a particular word or phrase in the entire help system for an application. The first time you click on the Find tab in the Help Topics window, the help system displays the Find Setup Wizard dialog box (see Figure 2.58) so that the help system can set up the master list of words and phrases.

**FIGURE 2.58** ►

*The opening dialog box of the Find Setup Wizard*

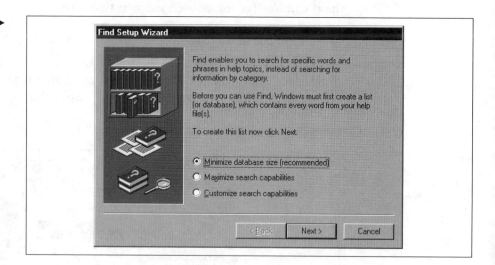

Because a typical help system can contain thousands of words, it is best to accept the recommendation to minimize database size. So, click on the Next button and in the next dialog box, click on Finish. The help system displays a Creating Word List message box and fills the Find section of the Help Topics window (see Figure 2.59).

Searching for a word or phrase from the word list is similar to searching in the Contents section of the Help window. However, in the Find section, you can refine your search by using these buttons:

**Clear**    Click on this button to delete the current text from the Type the Word(s) You Want to Find text box/drop-down list box.

**FIGURE 2.59** ▶

*The filled-in Find section of the Approach Help Topics window*

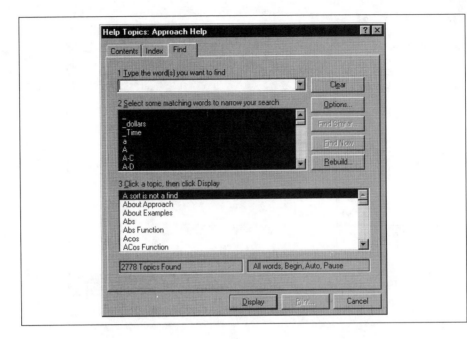

**Options**    Click on this button to open the Find Options dialog box in which you can customize searches. If you click on the Files button in this dialog box, you can choose the Lotus help files in which to search.

**Find Similar**    Click on this button to search for topics that are similar to the current search topic.

**Find Now**    Click on this button to start the search.

**Rebuild**    Click on this button to set up the word list again.

## ▶ *Getting Help from the SmartCenter*

You can get a variety of SmartSuite help from the SmartCenter bar—if it is on your Desktop. To learn about the SmartCenter, refer to the earlier section, "Using the Lotus SmartCenter." To get help from the SmartCenter bar, click on the Suite Help drawer. When the drawer is open (see Figure 2.60), click on a folder to get help.

Getting Acquainted

▶ ▶
Ch.
**2**

**FIGURE 2.60** ▶

*The open Suite Help drawer with the DocOnline folder available*

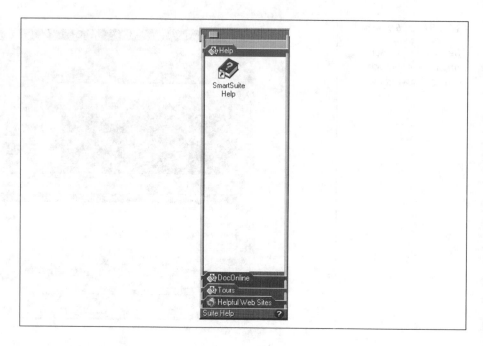

## The Help Folder

Click on the Help folder to access SmartSuite Help, which offers help topics about the SmartCenter and SuiteStart as well as using the SmartSuite applications together. Double-click on the SmartSuite Help icon to open a standard Help window with three sections: Contents, Index, and Find. To learn about using a standard Help window, see a prior section, "The Help Topics Window."

## The DocOnline Folder

Click on the DocOnline folder to access online documents for all the SmartSuite applications, including user's guides, exploring manuals, and information for upgraders. All documents are presented in Adobe Acrobat (PDF) format. To open a document for viewing, double-click on its icon.

**▶▶NOTE**

> The DocOnline files are not automatically installed when you install SmartSuite. If you have installed SmartSuite from CD-ROM, the files are in the \ACROREAD folder. Because of the size of these files, it is best to read them from the CD-ROM disk and not copy them onto your hard drive.

### The Tours Folder

Click on the Tours folder to access guided tours of SmartSuite applications. Double-click on a tour icon, sit back, and learn about selected features of 1-2-3, Word Pro, Approach, and Freelance Graphics.

### The Helpful Web Sites Folder

Click on the Internet folder to be able to go sites on the Internet. To fully use this, you must have an Internet browser that can access the World Wide Web and FTP sites. In addition, you must have Internet access and dial-in ability. To access a page on the Internet, double-click on an icon. This starts your browser, opens a Connect To dialog box, dials in to your Internet provider, and goes to the desired site. If you are already using your Internet browser, go to a site by double-clicking on one of the icons in the Internet folder.

For more infomation about accessing the Internet from within Smart-Suite, see the *SmartSuite and the Internet* appendix.

**▶▶TIP**

> If you have problems logging onto the Internet and going to one of these sites simultaneously, start your browser, dial in, and then double-click on an icon.

Getting Acquainted

▶▶

Ch.
**2**

# ▸▸ *Exiting an Application*

Exiting an application is the same whether it is the only active application or one of several; Windows is intelligent enough to realize that other open applications should continue running.

You can exit an active SmartSuite application in several ways:

- Click on the Close button in the upper right corner of the application window.

- Click on the End the Application Session SmartIcon.
- Choose File ➤ Exit.
- Type the key combination Alt+F4.
- Double-click on the Application Control-Menu icon.

After issuing the Exit command, the application will prompt you to save any unsaved work before you actually end the work session.

# ▸▸ *Exiting Windows*

To exit Windows, follow these steps:

1. Click on the Start button.
2. Click on the Shut Down command. Windows opens the Shut Down Windows dialog box and dims the Desktop.
3. Click on the Shut Down the Computer? option button (the default) and click on Yes. After a few seconds, the Desktop goes dark.
4. When the "It's now safe to turn off your computer" message appears, turn off the power to your computer.

# CHAPTER 3

# Editing in SmartSuite
# Applications

———

►► **O**nce you have created a file, whether it's a 1-2-3 sheet, a Word Pro document, an Approach database, a Freelance Graphics presentation, or even an Organizer calendar entry, you can edit it to change its content or look or enhance it to improve its appearance.

In this chapter, you'll learn some of the basic editing and enhancement capabilities of SmartSuite applications. Then as you read about and learn to use each application in future chapters, you'll find out the particulars of editing and enhancing a file in a specific application.

## ►► Magnifying and Reducing Your File in the Application Window

*Zooming* the information displayed on the computer screen helps you to see things in two ways: magnified (see Figure 3.1) or reduced (see Figure 3.2). If you zoom in to magnify the information, you can see the details of a file (for example, a piece of clip art in a document or presentation or a particular number in a sheet). If you zoom out to reduce the information, you'll see how the information looks on your desktop (for example, how the text fits using the margins that you have specified, how the headers compare with the body text, and how graphics look on the page).

The way in which you zoom varies by the SmartSuite application you are using, but in 1-2-3, Word Pro, Approach, and Freelance Graphics you can choose a command from the View menu to magnify, reduce, or change the view in another way. In addition, any SmartIcon that looks like a magnifying glass changes the view in some way. Each of these

**FIGURE 3.1** ▶

*Part of a Word Pro document magnified to 150% to show details of a graphic*

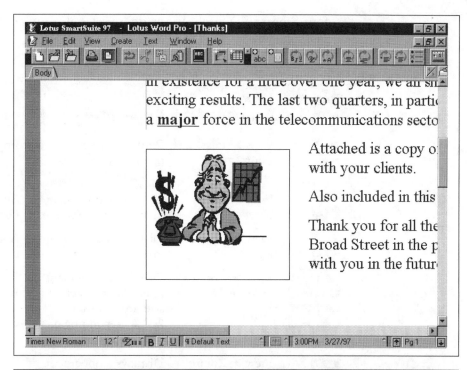

**FIGURE 3.2** ▶

*A Word Pro document reduced to 75% to show the page layout*

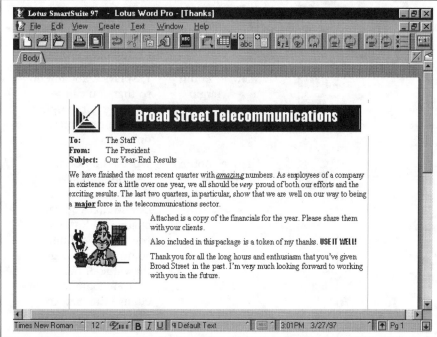

Editing
SmartSuite

▶ ▶

Ch.

**3**

four SmartSuite applications offers several zoom commands, as listed in Table 3.1.

▶ **TABLE 3.1:** *SmartSuite Zoom Commands*

| Smart-Icon | Menu Command | Description | Application(s) |
|---|---|---|---|
| | View ➤ Last Zoom | Returns to the previously selected zoom level | Freelance Graphics |
| | View ➤ Zoom In | Displays a document in an increased size | Approach, Freelance Graphics |
| | View ➤ Zoom Out | Displays a document in a reduced size | Approach, Freelance Graphics |
| | View ➤ Zoom to ➤ *nnn*% | Displays a document at *nnn*% of its actual size, from 25% to 200%, depending on the application | 1-2-3, Approach, Word Pro |
| | View ➤ Zoom to ➤ Custom Level (*nn*%) | Displays a document in a size that you select (from 1% to 999%) from the View Preferences dialog box | Word Pro |
| | View ➤ Zoom to ➤ Margin Width | Displays a document so that you can see both the left margin and the right margin onscreen | Word Pro |
| | View ➤ Zoom to ➤ Other | Opens the Zoom section of the View Preferences dialog box so that you can change to draft mode, specify the default zoom level, change the value of the custom zoom level, or change the view to show multiple pages | Word Pro |

► **TABLE 3.1:** *SmartSuite Zoom Commands (continued)*

| Smart-Icon | Menu Command | Description | Application(s) |
|---|---|---|---|
| | View ➤ Zoom to ➤ Page Width | Displays a page so that you can see both the left edge and the right edge onscreen | Word Pro |
| | View ➤ Zoom to Actual Size | Displays a page at its actual size—usually larger than the full page | Freelance Graphics |
| | View ➤ Zoom to Custom Level (xx%) | Displays this and future workbooks in a size that you select (from 25% to 400%) in the View section of the Workbook Properties dialog box (choose View ➤ Set View Preferences) | 1-2-3 |
| | View ➤ Zoom to Full Page | Displays a complete page on the desktop—showing all edges of the page—on the desktop | Freelance Graphics |
| | View ➤ Zoom to Full Page | Displays a complete page | Word Pro |

# ►► *An Introduction to Editing*

In most cases, you can expect a newly created file to be around for a long time—in one form or another. You'll probably have to modify its look and contents throughout its lifetime. For example, you might create a 1-2-3 sheet or an Approach database to use as the basis for your inventory or payroll systems and their weekly, yearly, and annual reports. You could put your business plan in Word Pro, 1-2-3, and even

Freelance Graphics and let it evolve as your business and business conditions change. In fact, every time you use Organizer, you might add, delete, or change items on your To-Do or anniversary lists and modify entries in your address book.

# ▶ Making a Selection

Before you edit a file, you'll have to identify the area of the file on which the editing command will act. As you work, you can select blocks of varying size—from a single character all the way to the entire file—so that you can copy, move, delete, or change the look of the selection.

## Using the Mouse to Select

As you have already learned, using the mouse when you first learn an application is easier than using the keyboard. When you use a mouse, you can set the boundaries of a selection without having to learn keystrokes for each type of selection.

To select with the mouse, move the mouse pointer to a starting position (that is, a corner, character, line, row, or column). Then press and hold down the left mouse button and drag the mouse pointer toward the other end of your selection. As you move the mouse, your selection is highlighted. If you are working in monochrome, the highlight is in inverse video. If you are working in color, the highlight is either the complementary color of the original (for example, blue becomes red and yellow becomes green) or black. When you reach the end of the selection, release the mouse button.

Below is a list of mouse shortcuts for selecting particular items in a file.

| To select this: | Move the mouse pointer here: |
| --- | --- |
| One or more characters in a 1-2-3 edit line, an Approach database, a Word Pro document, a Freelance Graphics Click Here box, or many Organizer text editing dialog boxes | To the first character and drag to the last character. |
| A word in a Word Pro document, an Approach field, a Freelance Graphics Click Here box, or many Organizer text dialog boxes | To the word and double-click the left mouse button. |

| **To select this:** | **Move the mouse pointer here:** |
|---|---|
| An object | To the object and click. |
| Several objects | To the first object and click, press the Shift key, and click on the other objects. |
| An element of a chart | To the element and click. |
| An entire chart | To an empty area in the chart and click. |
| Several words in a Word Pro document, an Approach field, a Freelance Graphics Click Here box, or many Organizer text-editing dialog boxes | To the first word, double-click the left mouse button, and drag to the end of the last word in the range. |
| A row in a 1-2-3 sheet | The left side of the row and click the left mouse button. |
| Several contiguous rows in a 1-2-3 sheet | The left side of the row and click the left mouse button. Then either: |

- continue to hold the left mouse button down and drag the mouse up or down from the point at which you first clicked, or
- press the Shift key and either click on rows to be added to the selection or click at the row on the other end of the selection.

| **To select this:** | **Move the mouse pointer here:** |
|---|---|
| Several noncontiguous rows in a 1-2-3 sheet | The left side of the row and click the left mouse button. Then press the Ctrl key and click on rows to be added to the selection. |
| A column in a 1-2-3 sheet | The top of the column and click the left mouse button. |
| Several contiguous columns in a 1-2-3 sheet | The top of the column and click the left mouse button. Then either: |

- continue to hold the left mouse button down and drag the mouse to the left or to the right from the point at which you first clicked, or

- press the Shift key and either click on columns to be added to the selection or click on the column on the other end of the selection.

| To select this: | Move the mouse pointer here: |
| --- | --- |
| Several noncontiguous columns in a 1-2-3 sheet | The top of the column and click the left mouse button. Then press the Ctrl key and click on columns to be added to the selection. |
| A sentence in a Word Pro document or an Approach memo field | To the sentence, press and hold down the Ctrl key, and click the left mouse button. |
| Several sentences in a Word Pro document or an Approach memo field | To the first sentence, press the Ctrl key, click the left mouse button, and drag to the end of the last sentence. |
| A paragraph in a Word Pro document or an Approach memo field | To the paragraph, press Ctrl, and double-click the left mouse button. |
| Several paragraphs in a Word Pro document or an Approach memo field | To the first paragraph, double-click the left mouse button, and drag to the end of the last paragraph. |
| A page in a Freelance Graphics presentation | To the page and click the left mouse button. |
| Several pages in a Freelance Graphics presentation in Page Sorter view | To the next page in the selection, press the Shift key, and click on the page. Then repeat to add more pages to the selection. |
| An entire 1-2-3 sheet | The selection button (above row 1, to the left of column A, and labeled with the default letter on its tab) and click the left mouse button. |

To remove the highlight from the current selection, simply move the mouse pointer off the selection and click the left mouse button. To remove the highlight from parts of the selection, continue to hold down the left mouse button and move the mouse back toward the start of the selection.

## *Using the Keyboard to Select*

For every mouse selection action, there is a keyboard method. Table 3.2 lists the keys and key combinations that you can use to select characters for later editing.

**TABLE 3.2:** *SmartSuite Keyboard Selection Shortcuts*

| Shortcut Key or Key Combination | Description |
| --- | --- |
| ← | Selects or reduces the selection of the prior character or a cell in 1-2-3 |
| → | Selects or reduces the selection of the next character or a cell in 1-2-3 |
| ↑ | Selects or reduces the selection of the character or the cell above the current cursor location in 1-2-3 |
| ↓ | Selects or reduces the selection of the character or the cell below the current cursor location in 1-2-3 |
| Ctrl+Shift+← | Selects one word to the left or reduces the selection one word to the left in Approach |
| Ctrl+Shift+→ | Selects one word to the right or reduces the selection one word to the right in Approach |
| F4 | Selects all the objects on a page in Freelance Graphics |
| Shift+← | Extends or reduces the selection one character or space to the left of the current cursor location |
| Shift+→ | Extends or reduces the selection one character or space to the right of the current cursor location |
| Shift+↓ | Extends or reduces the selection one line below the current cursor location |

Editing SmartSuite

**Ch. 3**

► **TABLE 3.2:** *SmartSuite Keyboard Selection Shortcuts (continued)*

| Shortcut Key or Key Combination | Description |
| --- | --- |
| Shift+↑ | Extends or reduces the selection one line above the current cursor location |
| Shift+Home | Extends or reduces the selection from the current cursor location to the top of the file in 1-2-3 |
| Shift+Home | Selects characters to the beginning of a line or to the beginning of a cell in 1-2-3 |
| Shift+Ctrl+Home | Extends or reduces the selection from the current cursor location to the top of the file in Word Pro |
| Shift+End | Extends or reduces the selection from the current cursor location to the bottom of the file in 1-2-3 |
| Shift+End | Selects characters to the end of a line or to the end of a cell in 1-2-3 |
| Shift+Ctrl+End | Extends or reduces the selection from the current cursor location to the bottom of the file in Word Pro |

You can always change the dimensions of the selection by pressing selection keys. For example, to remove the last line or row from a selection in 1-2-3, press the up arrow, or to remove the last character from a word selection, press the left arrow. You can also remove larger blocks from a selection by pressing the reverse of the last key or key combination you used. For example, if you pressed Shift+PgDn to select a screenful of characters, reverse the selection by pressing Shift+PgUp.

Making a selection usually means that you're going to do something with it. You can copy or move the selection to another part of the current file or even to a file in another Windows application. Or you can keep the selection in its location and change the way it looks: You can apply boldface to it or increase its size. Let's find out more about your choices in handling a selection.

## ▶ *About the Windows Clipboard*

The *Clipboard*, an application that runs under Windows, is a temporary storage facility that almost any Windows application can use to copy or move (cut) selected characters or graphics. You can use the Clipboard to copy or cut a selection within one Windows application or among several Windows applications.

The Clipboard holds only one selection at a time. Every time you copy or cut a selection, the last contents of the Clipboard are replaced with the new selection. If you exit an application but keep Windows running, the contents of the Clipboard remain. Once you exit Windows, however, the Clipboard is emptied (unless you have saved the contents to a file). Because of the differences in formatting options from one Windows application to another, a pasted item may not look exactly the same as it did in the source application.

Through the *Clipboard Viewer* (see Figure 3.3), a Windows accessory, you can see the contents of the Clipboard, and you can manipulate its contents. For example, you can choose File ➤ Save As to save its contents to a file, or you can open a Clipboard file (which has the extension CLP) to insert its contents back into the Clipboard.

**FIGURE 3.3**

*The Clipboard Viewer with an open File menu and a stored selection behind it*

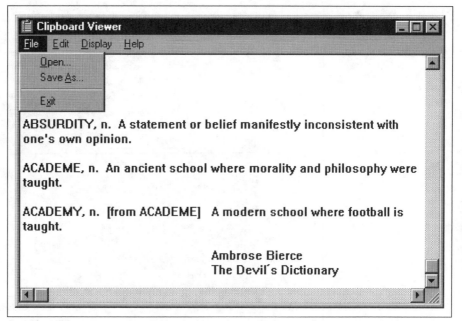

▶ ▶

*Ch.*

**3**

▶▶ **NOTE**

> **If the Clipboard Viewer (its path is C:\WINDOWS\ CLIPBRD.EXE) is not installed on your computer, you can do so by clicking on the Start button, pointing to Settings, and clicking on Control Panel. Double-click on the Add/Remove Programs icon, click on the Windows Setup tab, click on the word Accessories, and click on the Details button. If Clipboard Viewer is preceded by a checked checkbox, Clipboard Viewer is installed. If the checkbox does not contain a check, click on it, and click on OK. Click on OK again. Then follow the instructions: You may have to insert disks, clicking on OK after each.**

You can open the Clipboard Viewer in two ways:

- Click on the Start button, point to Programs, point to Accessories, and click on Clipboard Viewer (see Figure 3.4).

- Create a shortcut icon on your desktop and double-click on the icon.

**FIGURE 3.4** ▶

*The open Start, Programs, and Accessories menus with Clipboard Viewer selected*

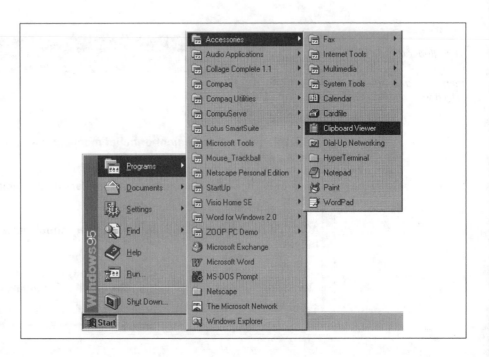

Table 3.3 presents shortcut keys and key combinations related to using the Windows Clipboard.

▶ **TABLE 3.3:** *Windows Clipboard Keys and Key Combinations*

| Shortcut Key or Key Combination | Description |
|---|---|
| Alt+Print Screen | Copies the active window into the Clipboard |
| Ctrl+C | Copies a selection from a Windows application into the Clipboard |
| Ctrl+Ins | Copies a selection from a Windows application into the Clipboard |
| Ctrl+V | Pastes the contents of the Clipboard into a Windows application |
| Ctrl+X | Removes a selection from a Windows application into the Clipboard |
| Del | Clears the contents of the Clipboard once you confirm the deletion |
| Print Screen (PrtSc) | Copies the current screen into the Clipboard |
| Shift+Del | Removes a selection from a Windows application into the Clipboard |
| Shift+Ins | Pastes the contents of the Clipboard into a Windows application |

## ▶ *Copying and Pasting a Selection*

Once you have made a selection, you can copy or move it to another location in the current document or to another document altogether. To leave a copy of the selection in its current location and to place a copy in another location, follow these steps:

**1.** Click on the Copy to the Clipboard SmartIcon, choose Edit ➤ Copy, right-click and choose Copy, or press Ctrl+C or Ctrl+Ins to copy the selection to the Clipboard.

Editing SmartSuite

▶▶

Ch.

**3**

**2.** Move the cursor to the location where you want to insert the selection. You can move the cursor within the current document or to a document in this or another Windows application.

**3.** Click on the Paste the Clipboard Contents SmartIcon, choose Edit ➤ Paste, right-click and choose Paste, or press Ctrl+V or Shift+Ins to insert the selection from the Clipboard in its new location. Remember that the selection also remains in its original location.

Once a selection is in the Clipboard, you can paste it as often as you desire in any location in a Windows application file. (Remember that when you copy or cut a new selection, it overwrites the previous contents of the Clipboard.) Simply move the cursor to the place at which you want to insert the selection and click on the Paste the Clipboard Contents SmartIcon, choose Edit ➤ Paste, right-click and choose Paste, or press Ctrl+V or Shift+Ins.

## ▶ Cutting and Pasting a Selection

With one important difference, cutting and pasting a selection is the same as copying and pasting. *Copying* leaves the selection in its original location; *cutting* removes the selection from its original location. To cut and paste a selection, follow these steps:

**1.** Click on the Cut to the Clipboard SmartIcon, choose Edit ➤ Cut, right-click and choose Cut, or press Ctrl+X or Shift+Del to cut (move) the selection to the Clipboard.

**2.** Move the cursor to the location where you want to insert the selection. You can move the cursor within the current file or to a file in this or another Windows application.

**3.** Click on the Paste the Clipboard Contents SmartIcon, choose Edit ➤ Paste, right-click and choose Paste, or press Ctrl+V or Shift+Ins to insert the selection from the Clipboard to its new location. Remember that the selection is no longer in its original location.

## ▶ *Moving a Selection Using Drag-and-Drop*

In many Windows applications, including those in SmartSuite, you can use a shortcut cut-and-paste method, *drag-and-drop,* to move a selection. As you might guess, drag-and-drop involves dragging a selection and then dropping it in its new location either within the active window or from one window to another. To drag-and-drop a selection in 1-2-3, follow these steps:

*1.* Move the mouse pointer to the edge of your selection. When the mouse pointer changes from an arrow to a miniature hand, you are ready to drag.

*2.* Press and hold down the left mouse button. The hand closes to indicate that it is holding the selection, and the application adds a dashed border to show the current location in which the selection would be dropped.

*3.* Drag the selection to its new location.

*4.* When you reach the new location, release the left mouse button. The mouse pointer changes back to an arrow.

 ▶▶ **T I P**

> **To cut a selection without replacing the contents of the Clipboard, press the Delete key. To move a selection without replacing the contents of the Clipboard, drag-and-drop the selection.**

## ▶ *Undoing an Action*

As you edit a file, you'll take some actions that you might think are irreversible. Fortunately, you can correct many mistakes immediately after you make them by choosing Edit ➤ Undo—*action,* pressing Ctrl+Z, or clicking on the Undo the Last Command or Action SmartIcon.

Editing
SmartSuite

▶▶

*Ch.*

**3**

You can't undo all actions. For example, you can't undo printing, saving to disk, or recalculating, and you can't undo an undo. If the Undo—*action* command can't undo an action, it will be dimmed and, therefore, unavailable on the Edit menu. (The Undo the Last Command or Action SmartIcon is also dimmed.)

# ▶▶ *Using SmartIcons*

SmartIcons are an important part of any SmartSuite application. As you work in an application, you can click on SmartIcons to open dialog boxes or perform certain actions without selecting a series of menus and commands. For example, click on the Open a File SmartIcon to display the Open dialog box, click on the Print Preview SmartIcon to view the current file as it will print, or click on the Cut to the Clipboard SmartIcon to remove a selection and place it in the Windows Clipboard. All three of these SmartIcons are part of the Universal SmartIcon bar (in 1-2-3, Word Pro, and Freelance Graphics) and the Default bar (in Approach and Organizer), which contains SmartIcons used for the many common actions in a particular application. Figures 3.5, 3.6, 3.7, 3.8, and 3.9 show the Universal or Default SmartIcon bars for 1-2-3, Word Pro, Approach, Freelance Graphics, and Organizer, respectively.

**FIGURE 3.5** ▶

*1-2-3's Universal SmartIcon bar*

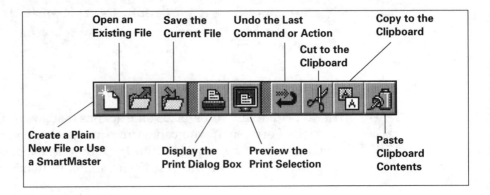

**FIGURE 3.6** ▶

*Word Pro's Universal SmartIcon bar*

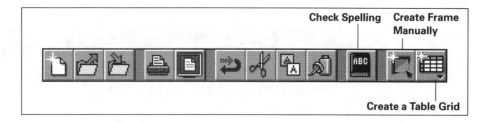

**FIGURE 3.7** ▶

*Approach's Default SmartIcon bar*

**FIGURE 3.8** ▶

*Freelance Graphics' Universal SmartIcon bar*

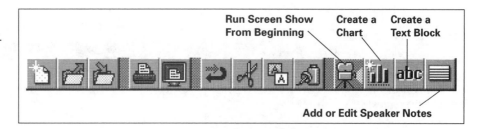

**FIGURE 3.9** ▶

*Organizer's Default SmartIcon bar*

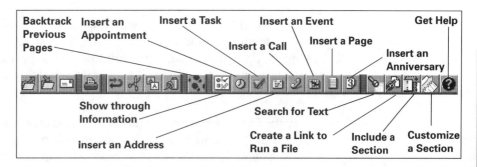

Other bars, typically on the right side, are context-sensitive: Click on an object, and a new set of SmartIcons appears. For example, in 1-2-3, click on a chart and the Chart bar replaces the current set on the right side of the SmartIcons bar.

Editing
SmartSuite

▶▶
*Ch.*
**3**

Or click in a header in Word Pro, and the Header bar is inserted on the light side of the SmartIcons bar.

A SmartIcons bar (see Figure 3.10) is composed of the Universal (or Default) bar for the application and a context-sensitive bar, whose appearance depends on the current selected object. For example, if you click on text, a Text bar is displayed; and if you click on a chart, a set of chart-related SmartIcons appears.

**FIGURE 3.10** ▶

*A Freelance Graphics SmartIcons bar made up of the Universal bar and the context-sensitive Page bar, as well a shortcut menu*

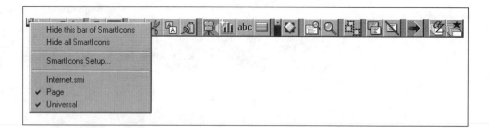

In 1-2-3, Word Pro, Approach, and Freelance Graphics, you can display or hide all or some SmartIcons bars or customize SmartIcons by clicking on the small downward-pointing arrow between the sets. In the shortcut menu that drops down, simply click on the appropriate command:

**Hide This Bar of SmartIcons**    Hides the SmartIcons bar to the right of the menu and the downward-pointing arrow with which it is associated. To display this bar again, click on a downward-pointing arrow in the remaining SmartIcons, and click on the bar name.

**Hide All SmartIcons**    Hides all the SmartIcons bars previously onscreen. To display the SmartIcons again, choose View ➤ Show/Hide ➤ SmartIcons or press Ctrl+O.

**SmartIcons Setup**     Opens the SmartIcons Setup dialog box with which you can customize SmartIcons and add or delete Smart-Icons from particular bars. To learn how to customize SmartIcons bars, see the *Customizing Your SmartSuite Environment* appendix.

**Bars**     Click on the name of a bar to hide or display it. An arrow preceding the command indicates that the SmartIcons bar is onscreen.

# ▶▶ *Changing the Look of the Contents of a Selection*

You can change the appearance of the characters in a selection. In SmartSuite applications, you can change the design or size of the characters, and you can enhance a selection with boldface, italics, underlines, and so on. In 1-2-3, Word Pro, Approach, and Freelance Graphics, you use an InfoBox to make these changes and much more. In the following sections, you'll learn about InfoBoxes and how to use them to change certain common enhancements and formats. In other parts of this book, you'll find out how to use InfoBoxes to change objects such as bitmaps, charts, tables, and so on. Table 3.4 shows all the SmartSuite InfoBox SmartIcons and lists the applications in which they can be found. Simply click on one of these SmartIcons to open an InfoBox.

## ▶ *Using an InfoBox*

InfoBoxes are special types of dialog boxes created for SmartSuite applications. An InfoBox is similar to a typical dialog box in that you can use an InfoBox to change attributes and select options, grouped into several sections, for a particular object. Unlike typical dialog boxes, InfoBoxes are context-sensitive. With an InfoBox onscreen, click on a different object, and the InfoBox either changes to another type of InfoBox or allows you to display a new InfoBox by selecting from a drop-down list. When you change an attribute in an InfoBox, you immediately see the result in your selection. For example, if you change the font for selected text in a Word Pro document, you can see the effect on your document and its layout. Because an InfoBox is a dialog box, you can drag it into a corner of the application window so that you can get a clear view.

▶ **TABLE 3.4:** *SmartSuite InfoBox SmartIcons*

| InfoBox SmartIcon | Object/Properties Affected | Application(s) |
|---|---|---|
| | Universal | 1-2-3, Word Pro, Approach, Freelance Graphics |
| | Font, font size, and text color | 1-2-3, Word Pro, Freelance Graphics |
| | Lines and borders | 1-2-3, Word Pro, Freelance Graphics |
| | Text and text blocks | 1-2-3, Word Pro, Freelance Graphics |
| | Text image | Freelance Graphics |
| | A drawing | 1-2-3, Word Pro, Freelance Graphics |
| | Bullets and numbers | Freelance Graphics |
| | Bullets and numbers | Word Pro |
| | Click Here Block | Freelance Graphics |
| | Table | Freelance Graphics |
| | Table | Word Pro |
| | Range of cells | 1-2-3 |
| | Table cell | Freelance Graphics |

▶ **TABLE 3.4:** *SmartSuite InfoBox SmartIcons (continued)*

| InfoBox SmartIcon | Object/Properties Affected | Application(s) |
|---|---|---|
| | Table cell | Word Pro |
| | Column | Word Pro |
| | Column and row | Freelance Graphics |
| | Column and row | Word Pro |
| | Table Layout | Freelance Graphics |
| | Page | Freelance Graphics |
| | Page | Word Pro |
| | Chart | 1-2-3, Freelance Graphics |
| | SmartChart | Freelance Graphics |
| | Sheet | 1-2-3 |
| | OLE object | 1-2-3, Freelance Graphics |
| | Map | 1-2-3 |
| | Query | 1-2-3 |
| | Print preview and page setup | 1-2-3 |
| | Connector | Freelance Graphics |
| | Bitmap | Freelance Graphics |

▶ **TABLE 3.4:** *SmartSuite InfoBox SmartIcons (continued)*

| InfoBox SmartIcon | Object/Properties Affected | Application(s) |
|---|---|---|
| | Collection | Freelance Graphics |
| | Group | Freelance Graphics |
| | Metafile | Freelance Graphics |
| | Image | Freelance Graphics |
| | Frame | Word Pro |
| | Movie | 1-2-3, Word Pro, Approach, Freelance Graphics |
| | Screen show | 1-2-3, Word Pro, Approach, Freelance Graphics |
| | Named styles | 1-2-3, Word Pro, Approach, Freelance Graphics |
| | Header | Word Pro |
| | Footer | Word Pro |
| | Organization chart | Freelance Graphics |
| | Organization chart box | Freelance Graphics |
| | Organization chart frame | Freelance Graphics |
| | Organization chart connecting lines | Freelance Graphics |

To open an InfoBox, either click on a SmartIcon (see Table 3.4 earlier in this chapter), press Alt+Enter, choose a Properties command from the top of certain menus, or right-click and choose a Properties command from a shortcut menu. For example, in 1-2-3, you can choose Range ➤ Range Properties, Sheet ➤ Sheet Properties, Chart ➤ Chart Properties, and so on. In Freelance Graphics, you can choose Page ➤ Page Properties, Text ➤ Text Properties or Text ➤ Text Properties by Level, or Table ➤ Cell Properties or Table ➤ Table Properties, and so on. Both Approach and Word Pro provide many Properties commands as well. Or you can right-click on an object or part of a document and choose a related Properties command.

An InfoBox (see Figure 3.11) is a compact dialog box loaded with options. You can display related InfoBoxes by selecting from the Properties For drop-down list box, and you can show other sections of the InfoBox by clicking on a tab.

**FIGURE 3.11** ➤

*The Text section of the Word Pro Text Properties InfoBox*

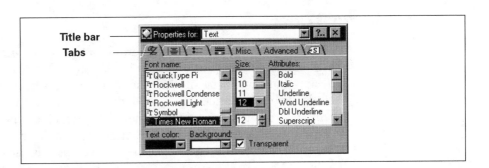

You can open an entirely different InfoBox (see Figure 3.12) either by clicking on another part of the document or by clicking on another part of the document and selecting from the Properties For drop-down list box:

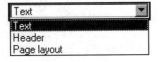

Editing SmartSuite

▶▶

*Ch.*
**3**

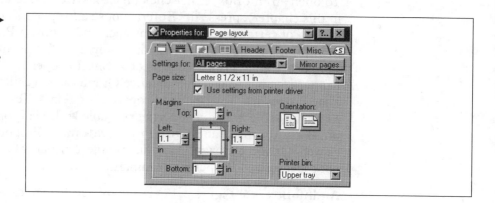

 To close an InfoBox, either click on the SmartIcon for that InfoBox or click on the Close button.

## ▶ About Fonts

One way of emphasizing a selection (such as sheet and document headings or specific rows or columns in a database) is to change its *font*, the design that applies to an entire set of characters. For example, as you read this book, notice that the heading text and body text differ, not only in size but also in design. Headings, which are generally short pieces of text that draw your attention, are unembellished and simple. Body text, which can go on for page after page, is meant to be readable. It's easy to differentiate between headings and body text because of their different fonts and sizes.

An important font factor is whether it is proportional or monospace (or nonproportional). Letters in *proportional* fonts are of different widths; letters in *monospace* fonts are of the same width. For example, in a proportional font the letter *I* needs less space than the letter *M*. In a monospace font, however, the letter *I* takes the same amount of space as the letter *M*. For this reason, monospace fonts are very useful in tables where you want to align characters from one row to the next. In general, body text is proportional because it is much easier to read.

A SmartSuite file starts out with a default font. For example, when you open a blank 1-2-3 sheet, the default font is Arial, a plain font that can be reduced in size and still be readable. In Word Pro, the default font is Times New Roman, which is an easy-to-read font for lines and lines of text.

## ▶ About Point Size

As you compare headings and body text in this book, notice that headings and body text differ in size as well as font. In general, the larger a character is, the more you notice it. The height of a character (from the top of a letter such as *h* to the bottom of a letter such as *q*) is measured in *points*, with one point being $\frac{1}{72}$ of an inch. The available point size for SmartSuite applications starts at 6 or 8, which is about $\frac{1}{9}$ or $\frac{1}{12}$ of an inch tall, and increases to 72, which is about one inch tall.

## ▶ About Text Enhancements

Enhancing text draws attention to it and separates it from the rest of the text in a document. SmartSuite text enhancements include bold-face, italics, color of the text and/or the background, three types of underlines, subscript (subscripted characters are somewhat below the rest of the characters on a line), superscript (superscripted characters are above the other characters on a line), strikethrough, change of case, and so on.

## ▶ Changing Text Attributes Using the InfoBox

To open an InfoBox in which you can change text attributes, do one of the following:

- Click on the InfoBox SmartIcon and then select Text from the Properties For drop-down list box at the top of the InfoBox.

- Choose Text ➤ Text Properties. In Word Pro, you can choose Text ➤ Font & Color to open the Text section of the InfoBox, or you can choose Text ➤ Bullets & Numbers to open the Bullets & Numbers section of the InfoBox.

- Point to some text, right-click, and select the Text Properties command.

- Press Alt+Enter and optionally select Text from the Properties For drop-down list box at the top of the InfoBox.

- Select some text and click on the Text SmartIcon.

- Select some text, open an InfoBox, and, if needed, select Text from the Properties For drop-down list box. Then click on the Text tab.

Standard options in the Text section of an InfoBox are:

**Font Name**    From this scroll box, select one of the fonts installed on your computer and under Windows.

**Size**    From this scroll box, select a point size for the selected text. You also can type or select a point size from the option box/text box at the bottom of the scroll box. Point sizes vary by the application and by the text that you have selected.

**Attributes**    In this scroll box, click on effects with which you can enhance the selection. In Word Pro, attributes include Bold, Italic, Underline, Word Underline, Dbl (Double) Underline, Superscript, Subscript, Strikethrough, Small Caps, Upper Case, Lower Case, Hidden, Protected, and No Hyphenation. In most Windows applications, you can also press shortcut keys and key combinations to apply or remove character emphasis. Table 3.5 lists SmartSuite shortcut keys and key combinations for character emphasis.

▶ **TABLE 3.5:** *Character Emphasis Shortcut Key Combinations*

| Key Combination | Action |
| --- | --- |
| Ctrl+B | Applies or removes boldface |
| Ctrl+I | Applies or removes italics |
| Ctrl+N | Removes boldface, italics, and underlines and returns to normal text, the default |
| Ctrl+U | Applies or removes single underlines |

**Text Color**   Click on any part of this drop-down box to reveal a palette of colors from which you can choose for the selected text—either for display onscreen or for printing on a color printer installed on your computer system.

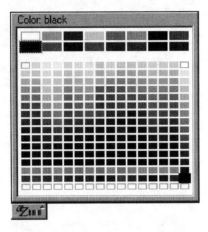

**Background**   Click on any part of this drop-down box to reveal a palette of colors from which you can choose for the background of the selected text.

**Transparent**   Place a checkmark in this checkbox to make the background transparent (that is, to remove any background color).

## ▶ Changing Text Attributes with a SmartIcon

To emphasize selected characters, you can click on one of the text enhancement SmartIcons. This means that you don't have to open an InfoBox; if the SmartIcon is onscreen, simply click on it to change the selected characters. Table 3.6 shows text enhancement SmartIcons and lists the applications in which they can be found.

 ▶▶**N O T E**

Some of the SmartIcons shown in this section are not on the Default SmartIcons bars. To learn how to add SmartIcons to a bar, see the *Customizing Your SmartSuite Environment* appendix.

Editing SmartSuite

▶▶
Ch.
**3**

►► **TABLE 3.6:** *SmartSuite Text Enhancement SmartIcons*

| SmartIcon | Description | Application(s) |
| --- | --- | --- |
| B | Applies or removes boldface | 1-2-3, Word Pro, Approach, Freelance Graphics |
| I | Applies or removes italics | 1-2-3, Word Pro, Approach, Freelance Graphics |
| U | Applies or removes a single underline | 1-2-3, Word Pro, Approach, Freelance Graphics |
| U | Applies or removes a single underline to words, but not to spaces | Word Pro |
| U | Applies or removes a double underline | 1-2-3, Word Pro |
| aA | Applies or removes uppercase letters | Word Pro |
| S$^s$ | Raises characters above the baseline or returns characters to the baseline | Word Pro |
| S$_s$ | Lowers characters below the baseline or returns characters to the baseline | Word Pro |
| 🖌 | Applies the formats of the previously selected characters to the newly selected characters | Word Pro, Approach |
| N | Removes the formats from the selected characters | 1-2-3, Freelance Graphics |
| A⸱A | Increases the size of the selected characters | Freelance Graphics |
| A⸱A | Decreases the size of the selected characters | Freelance Graphics |

In Word Pro, you can *cycle* through and choose from a list of related enhancements using Cycle SmartIcons and associated CycleKeys, shortcut keys. You can customize the settings for Cycle SmartIcons and CycleKeys.

## ► Changing Text Attributes Using the Status Bar

To change the font, to change the point size, or to emphasize text, you can select from the Status bar (see Figure 3.13) of any application but Organizer.

**FIGURE 3.13** ►

*The Word Pro Status bar with the point list displayed. Every Smart-Suite application except Organizer provides the same point list.*

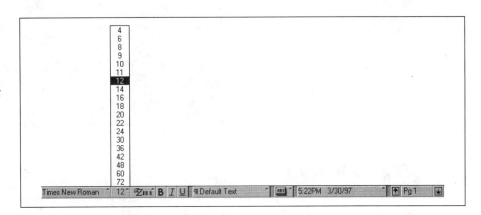

## ► About Lines and Color

The Lines and Color section of an InfoBox varies by application and by the object that you select. For example, if you select a field in Approach's Design environment, you can use the Lines and Color section (see Figure 3.14) to change the box style, the border, and colors.

The Lines and Color section of 1-2-3's Sheet Properties InfoBox (see Figure 3.15) is designed so that you can change the pattern and color of a selected cell and its background and text colors and make negative values red.

Editing SmartSuite

► ►

*Ch.*

**3**

**FIGURE 3.14** ▶

*The Lines and Color
section of the Field
Properties InfoBox in
Approach*

**FIGURE 3.15** ▶

*The Lines and Color
section of the Sheet
Properties InfoBox in
1-2-3*

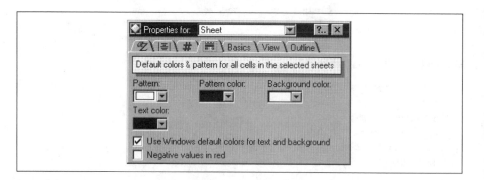

▶▶ **N O T E**

**The Lines and Color section of Freelance Graphics' All
Text Levels Properties InfoBox is very similar to the
Lines and Color section of 1-2-3's Sheet Properties
InfoBox.**

By contrast, in the Lines and Color section of Word Pro's Text Properties InfoBox (see Figure 3.16), you can define almost everything about
a line drawn around a paragraph.

**FIGURE 3.16** ▶

*The Lines and Color section of the Text Properties InfoBox in Word Pro*

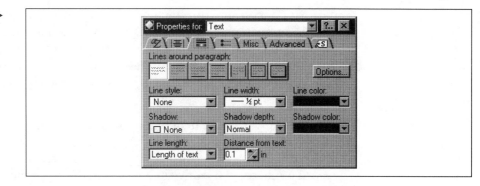

To open an InfoBox in which you can change attributes of lines and specify colors and patterns, do one of the following:

- Click on the InfoBox SmartIcon and then select the object to be changed from the Properties For drop-down list box at the top of the InfoBox.

- Choose Text ➤ Text Properties or another Properties command from a context-sensitive menu between the Create and Window menus.

- Point to the object to be changed, right-click, and select a Properties command.

- Press Alt+Enter and optionally select the object to be changed from the Properties For drop-down list box at the top of the InfoBox.

- Select some text, open an InfoBox, and, if needed, select the desired object from the Properties For drop-down list box. Then click on the Lines and Color tab.

# ▶▶ *An Introduction to Macros*

When you perform the same task over and over again, it's time to think about whether you can have the current application repeat the steps for you. A *macro* is a series of steps that have been recorded or written into a script. When you run a macro, the steps are automatically performed without your having to actually open the menus, select commands, or change settings. Using macros, you can save and print a document, change the spelling or format of a particular word throughout a document, change the font and point size of a certain level of headings, or find records that meet certain criteria and do something with them.

The easiest way to create a macro is to record the steps. You can record macros in 1-2-3 and Word Pro. To start recording, choose Edit ➤ Script & Macros ➤ Record Script. In Approach, although you cannot record a macro, you can write one using the Approach macro language or Lotus Script. In Freelance Graphics, you can write one using Lotus Script. For more information about macros in 1-2-3, see *Advanced 1-2-3 Techniques;* for more information about macros in Word Pro, see *Advanced Word Pro Techniques.*

# ▶▶ *An Overview of Finding and Replacing*

When you edit a file, automating your actions whenever possible is the way to go. For example, if you need to change the same name or value throughout a file, why manually change the text page by page when you can issue a single command?

Simply choose a find or search command in 1-2-3, Word Pro, Approach, or Organizer to open a dialog box (see Figures 3.17, 3.18, and 3.19). Then type the *search string*, the text you want to locate. If you want to replace the search string, also type a replace string. Then

**FIGURE 3.17** ▶

*Use the 1-2-3 Find and Replace dialog box to search for search strings in labels, formulas, and/or numbers and optionally replace them.*

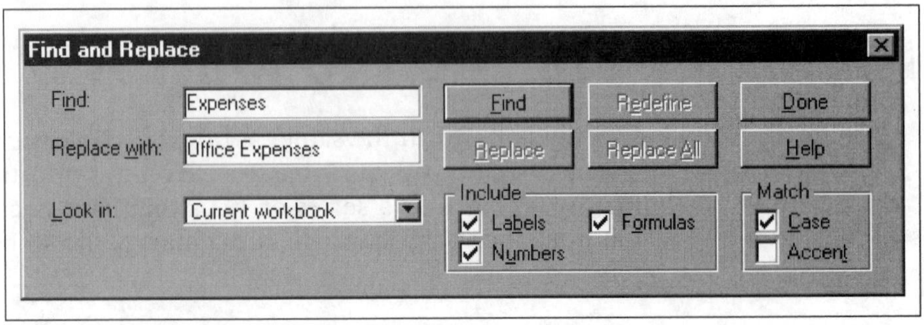

click on a command key to start the search and optional replace process. You'll find out more about find and replace commands as you learn about each SmartSuite application. Table 3.7 summarizes SmartSuite search and replace commands.

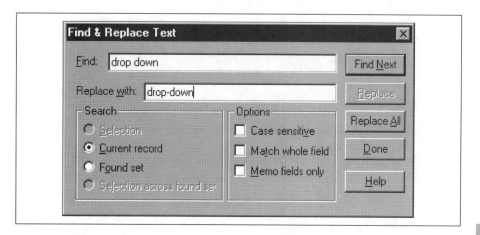

▶ **TABLE 3.7:** *SmartSuite Search and Replace Shortcut Keys and Menu Commands*

| Application | Shortcut Keys | Command |
|---|---|---|
| 1-2-3 | Ctrl+F | Edit ➤ Find & Replace |
| Word Pro | Ctrl+F | Edit ➤ Find & Replace Text |
| Approach | N/A | Edit ➤ Find & Replace Text |
| Organizer | Ctrl+F | Edit ➤ Find |

Editing SmartSuite

▶▶ Ch. 3

# PART TWO

# CHAPTER 4

# Planning and Creating Your First Spreadsheet

*I*n this chapter, you'll create a spreadsheet from scratch. As you work, you'll learn about spreadsheets, or *sheets*, in general. You'll find out about the elements of the 1-2-3 application window and a 1-2-3 sheet, the type of data that you can put in a sheet, how to use formulas, and some of the most common 1-2-3 @functions. Remember that you can find the basics of opening and saving files in the *Getting Acquainted with SmartSuite* chapter.

# ▶▶ *Introducing 1-2-3*

To control your company's finances, a spreadsheet program is invaluable. Using a 1-2-3 sheet, you can do all the following:

- Perform statistical analyses on your sales and expenses by region, division, office location, product, cost center, or individual employee.

- Calculate and graph how much you spent on office supplies or computers last year and budget for this year.

- Analyze demographic information for your region to determine the location of your next plant or decide how to target your advertising budget.

- Track your inventory, accounts receivable, accounts payable, and wages paid.

- Manage projects from beginning to end and perform date calculations to see if you are on time throughout your schedule.

# ▶▶ *What Is a Sheet?*

Before computers, accountants, and bookkeepers kept track of income, expenses, and other financial information on worksheet paper, which is made up of grids of rows and columns. The *rows* run horizontally, and the *columns* run vertically. The point at which a row and column meet is a *cell*, which holds one piece of information.

Rows, columns, and cells form the body of an electronic spreadsheet or worksheet—known in 1-2-3 as a sheet. To help you find your way around when the cells contain numbers and other characters, 1-2-3 labels columns and rows. At the top border of a sheet are column labels: A–Z, then AA, AB, and so on (all the way to IV, for a total of 256 columns). On the left border of a sheet are row labels: 1–8192. You can have as many as 256 sheets in one 1-2-3 file, or *workbook*, which means that you can hold a great deal of information in a single file.

# ▶▶ *Planning a Sheet*

To be fully effective, a sheet requires careful planning. You should be sure that you provide only the appropriate data—superfluous information clutters the sheet. In the beginning, it's a good idea to sketch out your sheet on paper before you create it. As you become more familiar with 1-2-3, you'll be able to design sheets right in the program, adjusting labels and formats "on the fly." Here are some useful guidelines to help you plan your sheet:

- Make your first sheet small enough so that all its rows and columns appear on your desktop at one time. In this way, you can learn about moving around and see the effect of formulas and formats.

- Provide label names that are as short as possible, yet understandable. When planning your sheet, think of the other people who will use or view it.

- When naming a sheet, use a name that helps you identify it in its folder, particularly if you plan to use it only occasionally.

Once you have a plan on paper, you can simply start entering the title and labels. But before that, start 1-2-3 so that you can learn about the 1-2-3 application window.

# ▸▸ *Viewing the 1-2-3 Window*

The 1-2-3 application window (see Figure 4.1) contains many of the elements that you found out about in the *Getting Acquainted with Smart-Suite* chapter. Because you are now working with a spreadsheet application, its window includes unique elements to help make your job easier. In this section, you'll find out about the edit line, special 1-2-3 Smart-Icons, the document window and its tabs and buttons, and the 1-2-3 Status bar.

**FIGURE 4.1 ▸**

*The 1-2-3 application window provides many helpful elements to help you create and edit sheets.*

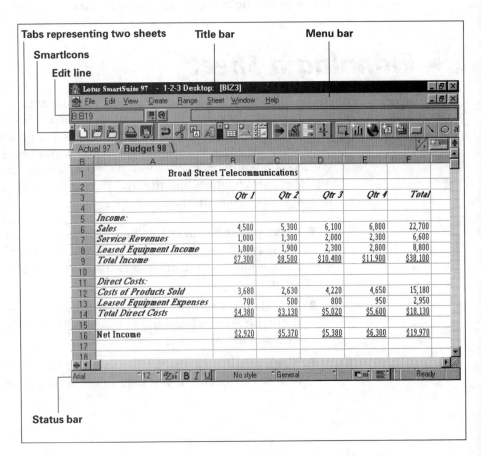

## ▶ *The Edit Line*

The *edit line* (see Figure 4.2) shows information about the current selection and provides tools with which you can edit it. If there is a blank sheet on your desktop, A1 appears on the left side of the edit line. This tells you that the *cell pointer* highlights column A, row 1. When you start typing labels, data, and formulas into the sheet, the edit line shows the contents of the current cell, which contains the cell pointer.

**FIGURE 4.2** ▶

*The 1-2-3 edit line*

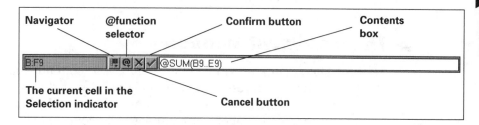

The edit line contains these components:

> **Selection indicator**     Displays the sheet letter (if there are multiple sheets in this file), the cell or range address, or the name of the object.
>
> **Navigator**     Goes to and/or selects any named range. You can select a named range to insert in a formula, @function (explained later in this chapter), or text box.
>
> **@function selector**     Displays a menu with common @functions and allows you to see a complete list of all @functions. If you select List All, 1-2-3 displays the @Function List dialog box, in which you can insert an @function or customize the @function menu.
>
> **Cancel button**     Cancels the entry on the edit line. The Cancel button is hidden unless you have clicked in the Contents box.
>
> **Confirm button**     Completes the entry on the edit line. The Confirm button is hidden unless you have clicked in the Contents box.
>
> **Contents box**     Contains the information, formulas, or @functions that you type for this cell.

## ▶ *1-2-3 SmartIcons*

The pages starting Part Two (the beginning of the 1-2-3 section) show many of the SmartIcons for 1-2-3. To get an introduction to Smart-Icons, see the *Getting Acquainted with SmartSuite* chapter. To learn how SmartIcons and SmartIcons bars work, see the *Editing in SmartSuite Applications* chapter. When you start 1-2-3 for the first time, the Universal and Range SmartIcons appear. As you work on various parts of 1-2-3 sheets, context-sensitive SmartIcons are displayed to the right of the Universal SmartIcons.

## ▶ *The Document Window*

The document window (see Figure 4.3) contains the sheet itself—with the letters representing column labels across the top and the numbers representing row labels going down the left side. Each set of numbers or characters, labels, or formulas will occupy a cell.

**FIGURE 4.3** ▶

*The 1-2-3 document window, in which you enter names, titles, values, and formulas, and do other work*

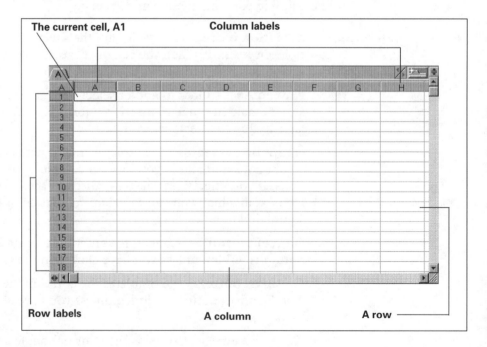

Each cell in a sheet has a unique *cell address*, the combination of row and column labels. For example, the cell in the top left corner of the work area, in column A and row 1, is known as A1. Notice on your desktop that A1 is surrounded by a dark border and both A and 1 appear to be pressed. As you move the cell pointer, notice that the highlight moves, other labels are pressed, and the contents of the edit line change.

The top of the sheet contains the items shown below, which aid you in using multiple sheets within a single file.

Click on a tab (from A to IV) to reveal the desired sheet:

Click on an arrow to move to the previous or next sheet in a set:

Click on this button to create a new sheet within the same file:

Drag this object down to split the window horizontally so that you can work in two areas of the sheet.

Drag this object toward the right edge of the document window to split the window vertically.

## ▶ The 1-2-3 Status Bar

You use the 1-2-3 Status bar (see Figure 4.4) to change formats, specify the number of decimal places for certain number formats, name a

**FIGURE 4.4** ▶

*The 1-2-3 Status bar, consisting of various buttons with which you can change formats and enhancements and check your current status*

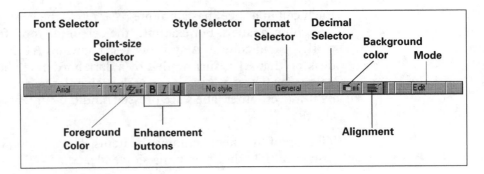

user-defined style, select a font, specify a point size, check the date and time or the row height and column width of the selected cell, check for possible circular references, and find out the current mode.

**Font Selector**    Click on this button to reveal a list of the installed fonts (see Figure 4.5).

**FIGURE 4.5** ▶

*A list of some of the fonts installed on one computer system*

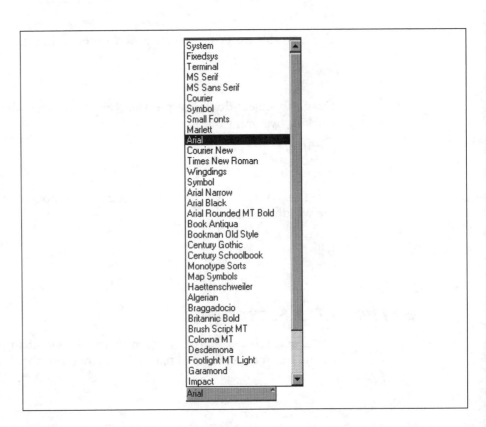

**Point-size Selector**    Click on this button to display a list of point sizes (6, 8, 10, 12, 14, 16, 18, 24, 32, 48, and 72) for the selected cell.

**Foreground Color**    Click on this button to display a palette (see Figure 4.6) from which you can choose a color for the characters in the selected cell.

**FIGURE 4.6**  ▶

*The Foreground Color
palette*

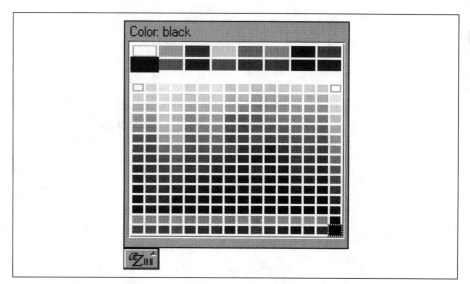

**Enhancement buttons**    Click on any or all of these buttons to apply or remove boldface, italics, or an underline to the characters in the selected cell.

**Style Selector**    If you have defined any custom styles in the Style section of the Range Properties InfoBox  click on this button to show a list of choices.

**Format Selector**    Click on this button to reveal a list of formats (see Figure 4.7) for number and text values.

**FIGURE 4.7** ▶

*The list of 1-2-3 for-
mats for number and
text values*

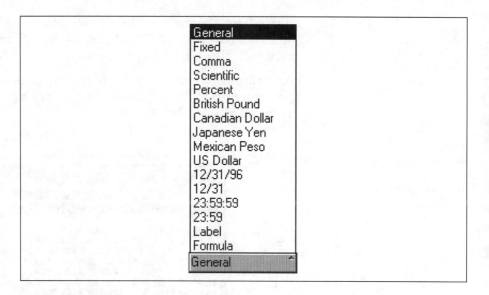

**Decimal Selector**    If the current cell contains a number, click
on this button to provide a list of decimal places, from 0 to 15.

**Background Color**    Click on this button to display a palette
(see Figure 4.6 earlier in this chapter) from which you can choose
a color for the background of the selected cell.

**Alignment**    Click on this button to display the buttons from
which you can choose to align the contents of the selected cell.

**Mode**    This area shows the current mode as listed in Table 4.1.

▶ **TABLE 4.1:** *1-2-3 Modes*

| Mode | Description |
|------|-------------|
| Edit | You are editing the contents of a cell, you are typing or editing text in a text box, or 1-2-3 senses that your last entry is in error. |
| Error | You are reading a 1-2-3 error message. |
| Files | 1-2-3 Classic is displaying a list of files. |
| Label | You are typing a label. |
| Menu | You have opened a menu or a dialog box. |
| Point | You are specifying a range. |
| Ready | 1-2-3 is ready for you to perform an action. This is the default mode. |
| Value | You are typing a value. |
| Wait | You are waiting for 1-2-3 to complete an action. |

# ▶ ▶ *Creating Your First Sheet*

After planning a sheet, the next step is to start entering information—titles, labels, data, and formulas. In this section, you'll enter a title, row labels, and column labels.

## ▶ *Entering Titles and Labels*

All you have to do to enter any type of information in a sheet is to start typing. You can either type in the cell itself, or double-click in the Contents box of the edit line and start typing there. Whether you start typing in a cell or activate the Contents box, 1-2-3 changes the edit line by adding the Cancel and Confirm buttons. If you type in a cell, 1-2-3 places the *insertion point*, the vertical bar that shows you the location of the next character to be typed, in the cell itself. As you type, 1-2-3 also adds the characters in the Contents box. If you type in the edit line, 1-2-3 places the insertion point in the Contents box and changes the background color of the Contents box.

When you type the first character for a cell, 1-2-3 recognizes whether you are entering a title or a label, a formula, or a value. If the first character in a cell is alphabetic, 1-2-3 understands that you are typing a title or a label. A mathematical symbol, such as a plus or minus sign, indicates that you have started to enter a formula. If you type a number, 1-2-3 automatically recognizes that you are typing a value.

When you finish typing the last character, press Enter or click on the Confirm button. This signals that your entry is complete and that you are ready to perform your next action.

When you type a series of alphabetic or numeric characters that extend beyond the borders of the current cell, 1-2-3 treats labels and values differently, sometimes depending on the contents of adjacent cells:

- When you press Enter or click on the Confirm button after typing a label that extends over several empty cells, 1-2-3 displays the entire label in its original cell, in adjacent cells, and in the edit line.

- When you press Enter or click on the Confirm button after typing a label that extends over several cells, some of which are filled, 1-2-3 displays as much of the label as it can until a filled cell is encountered.

- When you press Enter or click on the Confirm button after typing a number that extends over several cells, 1-2-3 automatically converts the value so that it fits within the cell. However, the value in the edit line remains as originally typed. For example, if you type 123212321232123, that value remains in the edit line, but the contents of the cell change to $1.2E+14$.

If you type values or labels for a series of adjacent cells, you can use shortcut keys to avoid typing extra keystrokes. For example, if you are filling in several cells in a column, you can press Enter and the down arrow to move to the next cell. However, if you press the down arrow, 1-2-3 realizes that you have finished working in the current cell and implicitly presses Enter for you. Other keys that perform the same action are right arrow, left arrow, up arrow, Home, and End.

1-2-3 enables you to automatically enter certain labels, such as months, years, and quarters. Just type the first label, select the *range* of cells to be filled in, and click on the Complete a Sequence in a Selected Range SmartIcon. Table 4.2 lists the values that 1-2-3 automatically fills in.

 ▶▶ **N O T E**

**You can fill in the first two cells in a range and have 1-2-3 fill in the remaining cells using its Fill by Example feature, if it can find the relationship between the two values.**

▶ **TABLE 4.2:** *1-2-3 Sequence Item Names*

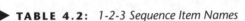

| Sequential Item | Examples |
| --- | --- |
| Integers | 1, 2, 3, 4, 5,... |
| | 1994, 1995, 1996,... |
| Letters | A, B, C, D, E,... |
| | x, y, z, a, b,... |
| Letters and Integers | A1, A2, A3, A4, A5,... |
| | Part 1, Part 2, Part 3, Part 4, Part 5,... |
| Months | Jan, Feb, Mar, Apr, May,... |
| | January, February, March, April,... |
| Days | Mon, Tue, Wed, Thu, Fri,... |
| | mon, tue, wed, thu, fri,... |
| | Monday, Tuesday, Wednesday,... |
| Quarters | Q1, Q2, Q3, Q4, Q1,... |
| | Quarter 1, Quarter 2, Quarter 3, Quarter 4, Quarter 5,... |

To create your first sheet, follow these steps:

1. Highlight cell B1. (If the cell pointer is not close to the upper left corner of the sheet, press Home and then press the right arrow.)

2. Type the title **Broad Street Telecommunications**. You also could have typed the title in the edit line.

3. Press Enter. If you click in cell B1, you'll notice that 1-2-3 adds a single quote before the title in the edit line. Figure 4.8 shows the title in cell B1 and in the edit line.

**FIGURE 4.8** ▶

*The top of a new sheet with the company name appearing in the edit line as well as in the sheet*

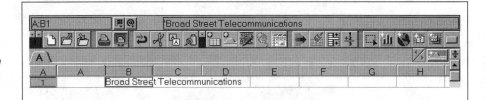

4. Move the cell pointer to A5 and start typing row labels:

| Cell | Label |
|------|-------|
| A5 | **Income:** |
| A6 | **Sales** |
| A7 | **Service Revenues** |
| A8 | **Leased Equipment Income** |
| A9 | **Total Income** |
| A11 | **Direct Costs:** |
| A12 | **Costs of Products Sold** |
| A13 | **Leased Equipment Expenses** |
| A14 | **Total Direct Costs** |
| A16 | **Net Income** |

5. Move the cell pointer to cell B3, type **Qtr 1** (that is, the first quarter), and press Enter.

**6.** Enter the remaining column labels by selecting B3–E3 and click-
ing on the Fill by Example SmartIcon (if it is on your desktop).
Otherwise, choose Range ➤ Fill, select Fill by Example from the
Fill Type box, and click on OK. 1-2-3 fills in Qtr 2, Qtr 3, and
Qtr 4.

**7.** In cell F3, type **Total** and press Enter. Figure 4.9 shows your
sheet with titles and labels.

**FIGURE 4.9** ▶

*The sample sheet with
titles and labels. Al-
though you typed the
title in cell B1, it ap-
pears to be located in
B1, C1, and D1, but
remains in B1.*

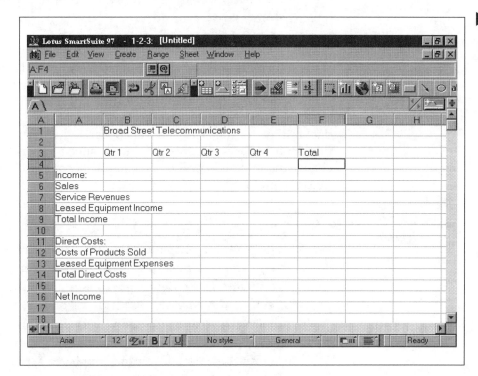

## ▶ *Adjusting Column Width*

When the contents of cells in one column appear to run into the contents of cells in the next column (such as columns A and B as they now
appear in the sample sheet), you can adjust column widths so that the
contents of each row are separated from adjacent rows. You can drag a
column border using the mouse, select the column and click on the
Size Columns to Fit Widest Entry SmartIcon, or choose Range ➤
Range Properties to change the width of selected columns. You can

also permanently change the default width of all columns in new sheets. (Existing sheets are not affected by this change in the column width default.)

▶▶ **N O T E**

As a default, a 1-2-3 column is eight valid characters followed by one space. Valid characters are alphabetic characters, numbers, spaces, decimal points, commas, dollar signs, and percent signs.

If the information typed or calculated for a cell is longer than can be shown given the cell's dimensions, 1-2-3 displays a series of asterisks in the cell, depending on the cell's format type. If the value takes up almost the entire width of the cell and is currency, +/-, percent, or any date or time format, asterisks will appear. Other formats, especially those that don't use as much space, do not change to asterisks. Asterisks do not change the underlying value; they simply act as placeholders for values that are too long to display onscreen.

▶▶ **T I P**

1-2-3 allows you move around a large sheet and always keep the row and column labels onscreen. This enables you to fill in or view a particular cell without scrolling back to the row or column label to make sure that you are in the proper location. First position the insertion point: To freeze row labels, click in a cell immediately below the row containing labels; to freeze column labels, click in a cell immediately to the right of the column containing labels; and to freeze both row and column labels, click in a cell below row labels and to the right of column labels. Then, choose View ➤ Titles. In the Titles dialog box, place a check mark in one or both check boxes. Finally, click on OK. To "unfreeze" labels, clear the check boxes in the Titles dialog box, and click on OK.

### *Using the Mouse to Adjust Column Width*

To widen a selected column to the width of the cell containing the most characters, move the mouse pointer to the line that separates that column from the next column and double-click. For example, if you want to adjust column A to its longest value, place the mouse pointer between A and B above the top row (that is, 1) in the worksheet. When the pointer changes to a double-pointed arrow, double-click.

You can also use the mouse to drag the column to a new width. Notice that as you drag the border between two columns, 1-2-3 displays its current width in the sheet below the column labels.

### *Using a SmartIcon to Adjust Column Width*

To adjust column width using a SmartIcon, select one or more columns and click on the Size Columns to Fit Widest Entry SmartIcon.

### *Using the Range InfoBox to Adjust Column Width*

To use the InfoBox to adjust a column's width to fit its longest value, select the column that you want to adjust and either click on the Range Properties SmartIcon, choose Range ➤ Range Properties, or press Alt+Enter. When 1-2-3 opens the Range Properties InfoBox (see Figure 4.10), click on the Size Columns to Widest Entry button in the center of the InfoBox. To adjust the width of another column, click in it and then click on the Size Columns to Widest Entry button. When you have finished, click on the Close button to close the InfoBox.

**FIGURE 4.10** ▶

*In the Range Properties InfoBox, you can change the width of the selected column.*

You can also set a column value for the selected column. Once again, click on the Range Properties SmartIcon, choose Range ➤ Range Properties, or press Alt+Enter. In the Range Properties InfoBox, select or type a value from 1 to 240 in the Width list/text box.

Figure 4.11 shows the sample sheet, now named and saved, with column A adjusted to fit the widest label.

**FIGURE 4.11** ▶

*Our sample sheet with column A adjusted to fit the longest label*

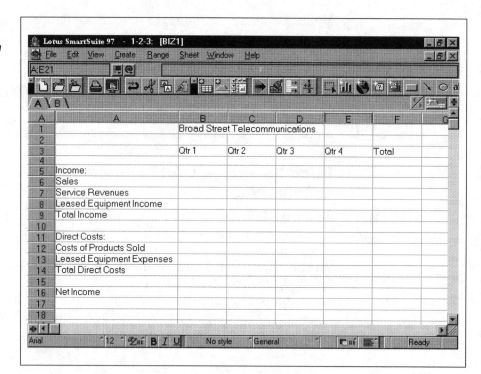

## Setting a New Default Column Width

To permanently change the column width for all new sheets only (until you change this option again), either click on the Sheet Properties SmartIcon, choose Sheet ➤ Sheet Properties, or press Alt+Enter. In the Sheet Properties InfoBox (see Figure 4.12), either type or select a value in the Default Column Width list/text box.

**FIGURE 4.12** ▶

*The Sheet Properties InfoBox, in which you can change sheet defaults such as column and row dimensions, font, point size, alignment within cells, colors, and number*

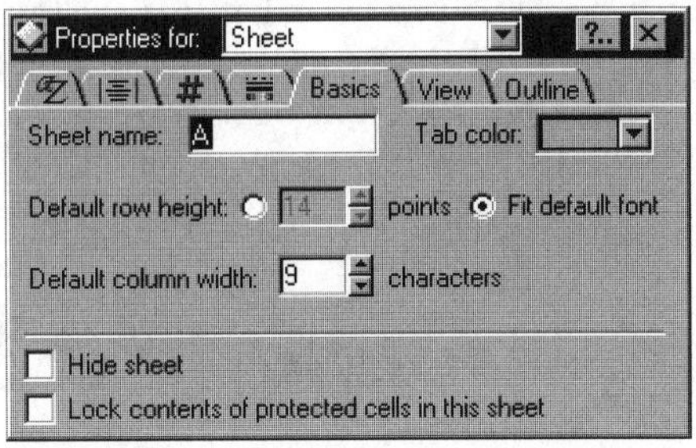

[Properties for: Sheet]

Sheet name: A    Tab color:

Default row height: ○ 14 points ● Fit default font

Default column width: 9 characters

☐ Hide sheet
☐ Lock contents of protected cells in this sheet

## ▶ Adjusting Row Height

Changing row height works almost the same as changing column width. You can use either a mouse shortcut or a menu command (but not a SmartIcon, as you can when adjusting column width).

### Using the Mouse to Adjust Row Height

To adjust the height of a row, you can drag the row boundary. Notice that as you drag the border between two rows, 1-2-3 displays the current row height in the sheet near the row labels. The default row height is 14 points.

### Using the Range Properties InfoBox to Adjust Row Height

To adjust row height using an InfoBox, select a row and either click on the Range Properties SmartIcon, choose Range ➤ Range Properties, or press Alt+Enter. When 1-2-3 opens the Range Properties InfoBox (see Figure 4.10 earlier in this chapter), you can have 1-2-3 find the largest font in the row or you can select a point value for the row height. Either click on the Fit Largest Font option button or select or type a value from 1 to 240 in the Height list/text box. To adjust the height of another row, click in it and then click on the Fit Widest Font option button or type or select a value in the Height list/text box. When you have finished, click on the Close button to close the InfoBox.

### Setting a New Default Row Height

To permanently change the row height for all new sheets only (until you change this option again), either click on the Sheet Properties SmartIcon, choose Sheet ➤ Sheet Properties, or press Alt+Enter. In the Sheet Properties InfoBox (see Figure 4.12 earlier in this chapter), click on the Default Row Height option button and then either type or select a value in the list/text box.

# ►► Moving Around in a Sheet

You learned all about general SmartSuite navigation keys in Table 2.6. 1-2-3 has additional navigation keys, key combinations, and key successions, shown in Table 4.3.

► **TABLE 4.3:** *1-2-3 Navigation Keys, Key Combinations, and Key Successions*

| Key/Key Combination/ Key Succession | Does This: |
|---|---|
| End, Ctrl+PgDn | Moves the cursor to the next sheet with a cell that contains data and is next to an empty cell in the same cell position as the current one |
| End,Ctrl+PgUp | Moves the cursor to the prior sheet with a cell that contains data and is next to an empty cell in the same cell position as the current one |
| Home | Moves to cell A1 |
| PgUp | Moves up one screen |
| PgDn | Moves down one screen |
| Ctrl+← | Moves left one screen |
| Ctrl+→ | Moves right one screen |
| End, ↑ | Moves up to the next cell adjacent to an empty cell or to the top of the spreadsheet, staying in the same column |
| End, ↓ | Moves down to the next cell adjacent to an empty cell or to the bottom of the spreadsheet, staying in the same column |

▶ **TABLE 4.3:** *1-2-3 Navigation Keys, Key Combinations, and Key Successions (continued)*

| Key/Key Combination/ Key Succession | Does This: |
|---|---|
| End, ← | Moves left to the prior cell adjacent to an empty cell or to the first column (that is, A), staying in the same row |
| End, → | Moves right to the next cell adjacent to an empty cell or to the last column (that is, IV), staying in the same row |
| End, Home | Moves to the lower-right corner of the spreadsheet in the last row or column that contains data |

# CHAPTER 5

# Entering Formulas
# and Data

►► **I**n this chapter, you'll build on your knowledge from the previous chapter. In the last chapter, you built the "skeleton" of a sheet. You added a title and column and row labels. In this chapter, you'll find out how to add the actual data—either by typing it in or by computing it. You'll learn about 1-2-3 data formats before you start creating your first formulas. Finally, you'll discover how to put a formula together, including how to use @*functions*, 1-2-3's built-in formulas.

## ►► Entering Data

The main purpose for a sheet's existence is to store data. Then once you have information to work with, you can perform mathematical and statistical calculations and edit, graph, and analyze it.

### ► Manually Entering Data

You'll enter most information manually, one cell at a time. As you learned when you entered labels for quarters of the year, however, there are ways to enter values automatically. Enter data just as you enter labels and titles, pressing Enter, right arrow, left arrow, down arrow, or right arrow to move from cell to cell or clicking in cells in which you want to enter data. For example, for our sample sheet, enter the following data, making sure to skip the cells that will store the results of calculations:

| Row Label | B | C | D | E |
|---|---|---|---|---|
| Sales | 4300 | 3100 | 4906 | 5400 |
| Service Revenues | 775 | 620 | 1708 | 2110 |
| Leased Equipment Income | 900 | 640 | 1023 | 1263 |

| Row Label | B | C | D | E |
|---|---|---|---|---|
| Costs of Products Sold | 3680 | 2630 | 4220 | 4650 |
| Leased Equipment Expenses | 700 | 500 | 800 | 950 |

If you type a value in the wrong cell, the easiest way to move it to its proper cell location is to use drag-and-drop. Click on the cell that currently holds the value, and move the mouse pointer to one of the cell borders. When the mouse pointer changes to an open hand, press and hold down the left mouse button. When the mouse pointer changes to a closed hand holding a small box, drag the cell contents to the desired location.

Figure 5.1 shows the sample sheet with income and expense data entered.

**FIGURE 5.1** ▶

*Our sample sheet with several rows of data entered*

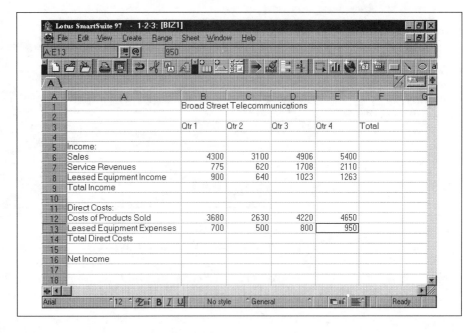

## ► *Automatically Entering Data in Ranges of Cells*

In the previous chapter, you learned how to fill in certain values with the Fill by Example SmartIcon or the Range ➤ Fill command. An alternate way of filling cells is to choose Range ➤ Fill and choose another option. When 1-2-3 opens the Fill dialog box (see Figure 5.2), you have several ways to manipulate the fill values. For example, you can't use the Fill By Example command to fill in a series of payroll dates (for example, every Friday); 1-2-3 places sequential dates in the cell (for example, 28-Nov-97, 29-Nov-97, 30-Nov-97, and so on). However, if you choose Range ➤ Fill, fill in the date for the starting Friday in the Start At text box, click on the Week option button, accept the default Increment of 1, and either click on OK or press Enter, 1-2-3 fills in the appropriate dates (for example, 28-Nov-97, 05-Dec-97, 12-Dec-97, and so on).

**FIGURE 5.2** ►

*The Fill dialog box, with a starting date, interval, and increment selected to fill a selected range of cells*

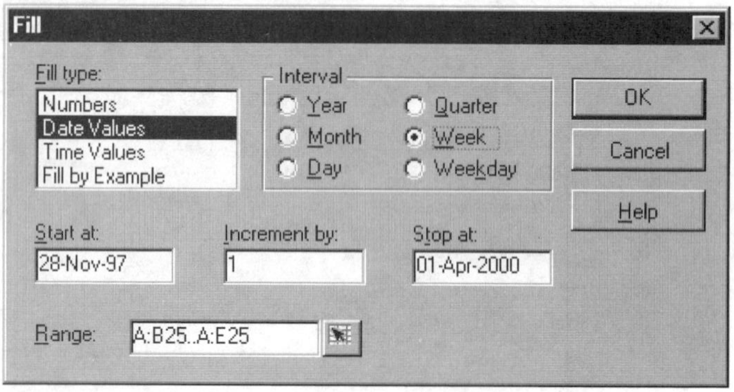

The fill types in the Fill dialog box are:

**Numbers**   Select this fill type to automatically enter numbers in a sheet. You can enter positive or negative values.

**Date Values**   Select this fill type to automatically enter dates in a sheet. 1-2-3 automatically inserts a starting date of the current month and year formatted *mon-nn* (where *mon* represents a three-letter month abbreviation and *nn* represents the last two digits of the year). Click on an Interval option button to specify the date value by which 1-2-3 increments the values.

**Time Values**   Select this fill type to automatically enter times in a sheet. 1-2-3 automatically inserts a starting time of 00:00 (representing a two-digit hour and a two-digit minute). Click on an Interval option button to specify the time value by which 1-2-3 increments the values.

**Fill by Example**     Select this fill type to have 1-2-3 find the relationship between the two entered values and fill in the remaining selected cells. Table 4.3 lists valid values for Fill by Example.

▶▶ **N O T E**

In selected 1-2-3 dialog boxes, you'll find text boxes with range selector arrows on the right side. To select a range, click on the range selector. 1-2-3 returns you to the sheet in which you select a range and then redisplays the dialog box.

Range:   A:B25..A:E25

▶▶ **T I P**

Fill in the same numeric value in selected cells by choosing Range ➤ Fill. In the Fill dialog box, type the value to be placed in all cells in the Start text box. In the Increment box, type 0, and either click on OK or press Enter. 1-2-3 closes the dialog box and fills all the selected cells with the same value.

▶▶ *Types of Data*

1-2-3 recognizes several types of data formats: General, Fixed, Comma, Scientific, Percent, five currency formats, two date formats, two time formats, Label, and Formula. In this section, you'll learn how each works.

## ▶ *Applying Data Formats*

For selected cells, you can apply data formats from the Status bar or from the menu bar:

- Click on the Format selector (see Figure 5.3) in the middle of the Status bar and select a format. You can revert to the original cell format by selecting that format from the list.

- Click on the Range Properties SmartIcon or choose Range ▶ Range Properties to open the Range Properties InfoBox. Then click on the Format tab to display the Format section of the Range Properties InfoBox (see Figure 5.4).

**FIGURE 5.3** ▶

*The Format selector, from which you can choose the appropriate format for the contents of the current cell*

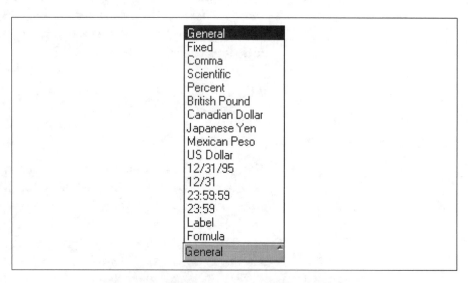

**FIGURE 5.4** ▶

*The Format section of the Range Properties InfoBox, showing its default settings*

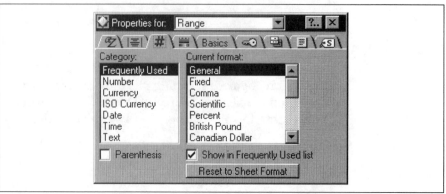

In the Format section of the Range Properties InfoBox, you can select from these options:

| | |
|---|---|
| Category | Select a format category from this list. |
| Current Format | Select a number or text format from this scroll list. |
| Parenthesis | Check or clear this checkbox to indicate whether negative numbers are displayed within parentheses for certain number formats. |
| Decimals | In this text/list box, either type or select the number of decimal places (from 1 to 15) for particular types of number formats: Fixed, Comma, Scientific, Percent, and currency formats. |
| Reset to Sheet Format | Click on this button to revert to the default format and category for this sheet. |
| Shown in Frequently Used List | Check this checkbox to add a Format to the Format Selector list in the status bar. |

You can change number and text format defaults for the current sheet by selecting Sheet ➤ Sheet Properties. (If the InfoBox is open, select Sheet from the Properties For drop-down list.) In the Sheet Properties InfoBox, click on the Format tab, select a Category and Current Format, and then click on the Close button.

## ▶ General Format

General format is the default 1-2-3 format. After you type data into a cell having General format, 1-2-3 analyzes the characters in order to change the data format to one of the other data formats.

| If 1-2-3 finds: | The new data format is: |
| --- | --- |
| A comma embedded in a number | Comma |
| The default currency symbol preceding a number | A currency format related to that currency symbol |
| A percent sign following a number | Percent |
| *dd-Mon-yy, dd-Mon,* or *mm/dd/yy* (see the Date format for the syntax) | The closest date format: 12/31/95 or 12/31 |
| *hh-mm, hh-mm-ss, hh-mm* AM, or *hh-mm* PM (see the Time format for the syntax) | The closest time format: 23:59:59 or 23:59 |
| *n*E+*n* (where *n* represents a number with one or more digits) | Scientific |

General format displays numbers as entered, but without thousands separators, leading zeros, and trailing zeros. Negative numbers are preceded by a minus sign. For example,

| If you type: | 1-2-3 converts to: |
| --- | --- |
| 99,999.9 | 99999.9 |
| .10 | 0.1 |
| −4.3 | −4.3 |

## ▶ Fixed Format

Fixed format displays numbers with a maximum of 15 decimal places and no thousands separators. This format displays negative numbers preceded by a minus sign and displays both leading and trailing zeros. For example, when using two decimal places:

| If you type: | 1-2-3 converts to: |
| --- | --- |
| 99,999.90 | 99999.90 |
| 0.1 | 0.10 |
| −4.3 | −4.30 |

# ▶ *Comma Format*

Comma format displays numbers with embedded thousands separators and with a maximum of 15 decimal points. Negative numbers are surrounded by parentheses. Simply type a number and apply Comma format. The only difference between this format and Currency format is the lack of a currency symbol. For example, when formatting with five decimal places:

| If you type: | 1-2-3 converts to: |
| --- | --- |
| 0.10003 | 0.10003 |
| 99999.9009 | 99,999.90090 |
| −49786.3023 | (49,786.30230) |

If the current cell is formatted as General, you can type a number including a comma, and 1-2-3 converts the format to Comma.

# ▶ *Scientific Format*

Scientific format displays positive or negative numbers as exponential numbers, with a maximum of 15 decimal points. Simply type a number and apply Scientific format. For example, when formatting with two decimal places:

| If you type: | 1-2-3 converts to: |
| --- | --- |
| 0.1 | 1.00E−001 |
| 99999.90 | 1.00E+005 |
| −4.3 | −4.30E+000 |

If the current cell is formatted as General, you can type an exponent (that is, $n$E+$n$, where $n$ represents a number with one or more digits), and 1-2-3 automatically converts the format to Scientific.

## ▶ *Percent Format*

Percent format displays a number as a percent, with a percent sign suffix, without thousands separators, and with a maximum of 15 decimal places. Negative numbers are preceded by a minus sign. Simply type a number and apply Percent format. For example, when using four decimal places:

| If you type: | 1-2-3 converts to: |
| --- | --- |
| 0.1 | 10.0000%. |
| 9999990.0000 | 9999990%. |
| −49786.3023 | −4978630.2300%. |

If the current cell is formatted as General, you can type a number with a percent sign suffix, and 1-2-3 converts the format to Percent.

## ▶ *Currency Formats*

Currency formats (that is, the default British Pound, Canadian Dollar, Japanese Yen, Mexican Peso, and US Dollar on the Format Selector list and several more that you can add to the list) display numbers preceded by a currency symbol, with embedded thousands separators, and with a maximum of 15 decimal points. Negative numbers are surrounded by parentheses. Simply type a number and apply a currency format. For example, when formatting the US Dollar with two decimal places:

| If you type: | 1-2-3 converts to: |
| --- | --- |
| 0.1 | $0.10 |
| 99999.9 | $99,999.90 |
| −4.3 | ($4.30) |

If the current cell is formatted as General, you can type a dollar sign (or your selected currency symbol) and a series of numbers, and 1-2-3 converts the format to Currency.

If you plan to use a currency other than the five on the Format Selector list, you can click on the Range Properties SmartIcon or choose Range ➤ Range Properties. In the Range Properties InfoBox, click on the Format tab, click on Currency or ISO Currency in the Category box, and select a currency from the Current Format scroll box. Then check the Show in Frequently Used List to add it to the Format Selector list in the Status bar.

## ▶ Date Formats

1-2-3 provides two default date formats—12/31/96 and 12/31—on the Format Selector list. Enter any number, select a date format, and 1-2-3 converts the number to that format.

If the current cell is formatted as General, you can enter a date in any of these formats: *dd-Mon-yy*, *dd-Mon*, or *mm/dd/yy*, where:

- *dd* is a two-digit day
- *Mon* is a three-character month
- *yy* is the two-digit year
- *mm* is a two-digit month

and 1-2-3 automatically applies the appropriate date format. If you enter a date using the *mm/dd* format, 1-2-3 interprets the value as a formula that divides *mm* by *dd*.

If you plan to use a date format other than the two listed on the Format Selector list, you can click on the Range Properties SmartIcon or choose Range ➤ Range Properties. In the Range Properties InfoBox, click on the Format tab, click on Date in the Category box, and select one of 13 date formats from the Current Format scroll box. Then check the Show in Frequently Used List to add it to the Format Selector list in the Status bar.

## ▶ Time Formats

1-2-3 provides two default time formats—10:59:59 and 10:59—on the Format Selector list. Enter any number, select a date format, and 1-2-3 converts the number to that format. In the Range Properties InfoBox, you can find seven other time formats, including 12-hour (AM|PM) and 24-hour military, where:

- *hh* or *h* represents the hour.
- *mm* represents minutes.
- *ss* represents seconds.
- AM is the period from one minute after midnight until noon.
- PM is the period from one minute after noon until midnight.

Enter any number, select a time format, and 1-2-3 converts the number to that format.

If the current cell is formatted as General, you can enter a time in any of these formats: *hh-mm*, *hh-mm-ss*, *hh-mm* AM, or *hh-mm* PM; 1-2-3 automatically applies the appropriate time format. If you type an hour between 13 and 24, 1-2-3 formats the time based on the 24-hour clock. If you type a number greater than 24, 1-2-3 interprets it as a label rather than as a time.

## ► Label Format

Label format displays text as a label and numbers using the General format.

## ► Formula Format

Formula format displays numbers and formulas as they are entered. Use this format to display a formula rather than the result of the formula.

# ►► Entering Formulas

Up to this point, you have used 1-2-3 just to store numbers and text. Remember that one of the most important reasons for using a sheet program is to manipulate numbers. There are three types of 1-2-3 formulas: numeric, logical, and text. A *numeric formula* computes numbers using the arithmetic operators +, −, *, /, and ^. Table 5.1 describes each arithmetic operator.

▶ **TABLE 5.1:** *1-2-3 Arithmetic Operators*

| Operator | Mathematical Operation Performed |
|---|---|
| + | Addition |
| – | Subtraction |
| ⋆ | Multiplication |
| / | Division |
| ^ | Exponentiation |

A *logical formula* determines whether a condition is true or false using these logical operators: =, <, >, <=, >=, <>, #AND#, #NOT#, and #OR#. Logical operators are described below:

| Operator | Logical Operation Performed |
|---|---|
| = | Tests value A against value B and returns True (1) if they are equal or False (0) if they are not equal |
| <> | Tests value A against value B and returns True (1) if they are not equal or False (0) if they are equal |
| < | Tests value A against value B and returns True (1) if A is less than B; otherwise, 1-2-3 returns False (0) |
| <= | Tests value A against value B and returns True (1) if A is less than or equal to B; otherwise, 1-2-3 returns False (0) |
| > | Tests value A against value B and returns True (1) if A is greater than B; otherwise, 1-2-3 returns False (0) |
| >= | Tests value A against value B and returns True (1) if A is greater than or equal to B; otherwise, 1-2-3 returns False (0) |

Entering
Formulas & Data

▶ ▶

*Ch.*
**5**

| Operator | Logical Operation Performed |
|----------|------------------------------|
| #AND# | Tests two combined values with these results: |

- if value A is False *and* value B is False, 1-2-3 returns False (0)
- if value A is False *and* value B is True, 1-2-3 returns False (0)
- if value A is True *and* value B is False, 1-2-3 returns False (0)
- if value A is True *and* value B is True, 1-2-3 returns True (1)

| Operator | Logical Operation Performed |
|----------|------------------------------|
| #NOT# | Reverses a value so that if value A is False (0), 1-2-3 returns True (1), and if value A is True (1), 1-2-3 returns False (0) |
| #OR# | Tests two separate values with these results: |

- if value A is False *or* value B is False, 1-2-3 returns False (0)
- if value A is False *or* value B is True, 1-2-3 returns True (1)
- if value A is True *or* value B is False, 1-2-3 returns True (1)
- if value A is True *or* value B is True, 1-2-3 returns True (1)

A *text formula* uses text and the text operator & to display combined text strings. For example, you can combine the strings "John "&"Doe" in a cell.

Operators determine the order in which a formula is processed. Table 5.2 lists the order of precedence for 1-2-3.

The simplest way to enter a formula is to build it one step at a time using combinations of names of cells, mathematical and logical operators, strings, or numbers. For example, suppose you have the value 22.5 stored in cell F16. To add 22.5 to a formula, you could type **22.5** or **F16**. Referring to a cell name makes changing values in your sheets and keeping track of those values easier. So in most cases, using the cell name within formulas is preferable.

To write a very simple formula using just cells and operators, highlight the cell in which the results will appear. Type a mathematical operator (typically, the plus sign), which tells 1-2-3 that you are about to enter a formula. Then click on a cell to add it to the formula. Type another mathematical operator, click on another cell to add it to the formula, and so on. When you have completed the formula, press Enter or click on the Confirm button in the edit line.

▶ **TABLE 5.2:** *1-2-3 Order of Precedence*

| Order | Operator | Description |
|---|---|---|
| First | ( ) | Values in parentheses |
| Second | – | Negative values |
| | + | Positive values |
| Third | * | Multiplication |
| | / | Division |
| Fourth | + | Addition |
| | – | Subtraction |
| Fifth | = | Equal to |
| | <> | Not equal to |
| | < | Less than |
| | > | Greater than |
| | <= | Less than or equal to |
| | >= | Greater than or equal to |
| Sixth | NOT | Reverses the values being compared |
| Seventh | AND | Both values being compared are true |
| | OR | One value being compared is true |

For our sample sheet, follow these steps:

*1.* Click on cell B9 (in which the total will appear).

*2.* Type +.

*3.* Click on cell B6.

*4.* Type +.

*5.* Click on cell B7.

Entering Formulas & Data

Ch. 5

**6.** Type **+**.

**7.** Click on cell B8.

**8.** Press Enter or click on the Confirm button. 1-2-3 completes the formula in the Contents box of the edit line. It also adds the contents of cells B6, B7, and B8, placing the total in B9.

Using the preceding steps, add cells B12 and B13, placing the results in cell B14. Figure 5.5 shows the sample sheet with the results of the preceding formula in B9 and B14.

**FIGURE 5.5** ▶

*The sample sheet with a new total in cells B9 and B14 and a completed formula for cell B14 in the contents box*

**The formula in the current cell**

**The results of computing the formula in this cell**

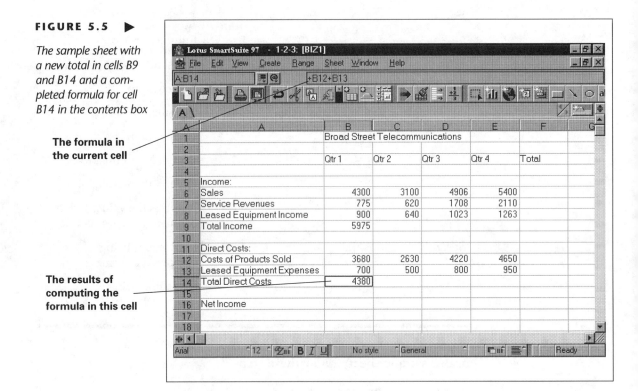

## ▶ *Automatically Copying Formulas*

You need not repeat the preceding steps to copy a formula that is made up of the same cell-mathematical operator combination and that will occur in the same row or column in a sheet. You can use the Copy Down or Copy Right commands or SmartIcons to copy a formula and have 1-2-3 adjust its contents to reflect its new column or row location.

To copy a formula from the cell above the currently selected cell, select both the cell from which you want to copy the formula and the cell to which you want to copy the formula. Then, either click on the Copy the Topmost Row to a Range SmartIcon, choose Copy Down from the shortcut menu (make your selection and click the right mouse button), choose Edit ➤ Copy Down, or press Ctrl+D.

 To copy a formula from the row to the left of the currently selected cell, either click on the Copy the Leftmost Column to a Range Smart-Icon, choose Copy Right from the shortcut menu, choose Edit ➤ Copy Right, or press Ctrl+T.

To copy formulas in our sample sheet, follow these steps:

1. Highlight cell B9 and drag to cell E9.

2. Press down the right mouse button.

3. Choose Copy Right. 1-2-3 copies the formula in cell B9 to cells C9, D9, and E9 and edits the copied formulas so that they reflect the cells that they are to add.

Using the preceding steps, copy the formula from B14 into C14, D14, and E14. Then compute the Net Income for cell B16 using this formula: +B9–B14. Copy the formula to cells C16, D16, and E16. At this point, the sheet should look like Figure 5.6.

## ▶ *Relative Cell References and Absolute Cell References*

You could copy formulas using the preceding steps because you were using *relative cell references*, the default. 1-2-3 found the cells to which the formulas referred by comparing their position relative to the cells holding the formulas. When you copy the formulas to other cells in the same row or column, the relative cells remain in the same position. For example, the ranges B6..B8, C6..C8, D6..D8, and E6..E8 (the two periods between B6 and E6 indicate that you are selecting a range) are in the same position relative to cells B9, C9, D9, and E9, respectively.

*Absolute cell references* do not change when you copy a formula to another cell. For example, if you always calculate interest using the same interest rate, you don't need to use a relative cell reference. To define an absolute cell reference, use the dollar sign prefix. For example, if the

Entering
Formulas & Data

Ch.
5

**FIGURE 5.6** ▶

*The sample sheet with
up-to-date data and
results*

**The formula in the
first cell of the
selection**

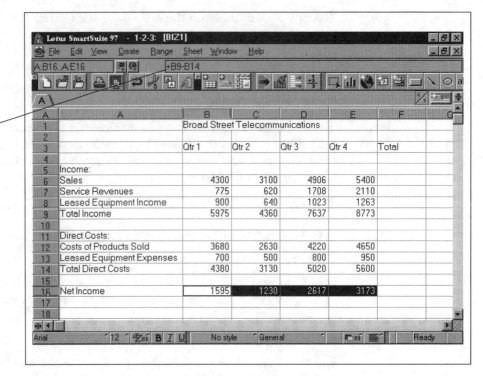

interest rate is stored in cell E16, build a series of formulas in this way:
+E15*$E$16, +F15*$E$16, +G15*$E$16, and so on. When you copy
a formula with an absolute cell reference, although other parts of the
formula may change to reflect relative cell references, the absolute cell
reference remains the same.

# ▶ Introducing @Functions

Rather than build a formula step by step, you can use *@functions*,
which are predefined formulas that automatically perform common
mathematical, statistical, or business calculations. Probably the most
common @function is @SUM, which computes the totals for a list.
For our sample sheet, you'll compute the totals in the Total column
using these steps:

*1.* Move the mouse pointer to cell F6 and click the left mouse
button.

*2.* Click on the @function selector in the edit line.

3. From the list, click on SUM. 1-2-3 displays @SUM(list) in F6.

4. Click in B6 and drag across to E6. Notice that 1-2-3 replaces list with B6..E6.

5. Either click on the Confirm button or press Enter. 1-2-3 sums cells B6, C6, D6, and E6, and places the results in F6 (see Figure 5.7).

**FIGURE 5.7** ▶

*The sample sheet with its first column F total. Note the formula in the contents box.*

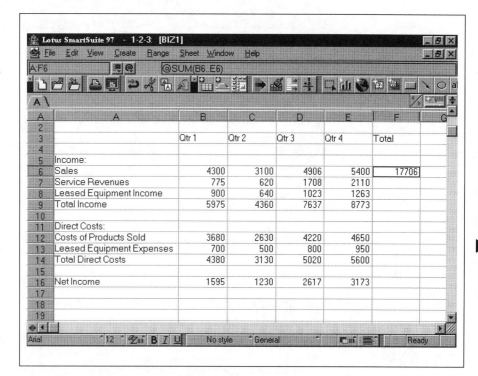

You can compute the sums for rows and columns at the same time by highlighting a range of cells and clicking on the Sum SmartIcon. 1-2-3 builds a set of @SUM formulas to total the contents of the cells above and to the left of the current range. To compute totals for the year in our sample sheet, follow these steps:

1. Highlight cell F7 and drag to cell F9.

2. Click on the Sum SmartIcon. 1-2-3 creates @SUM formulas that calculate the sum of the quarters for each Income row of our sample

sheet. Figure 5.8 shows our sample sheet after the sum of the quarters for the income rows.

**FIGURE 5.8** ▶

*The sample sheet after the income rows have been totaled*

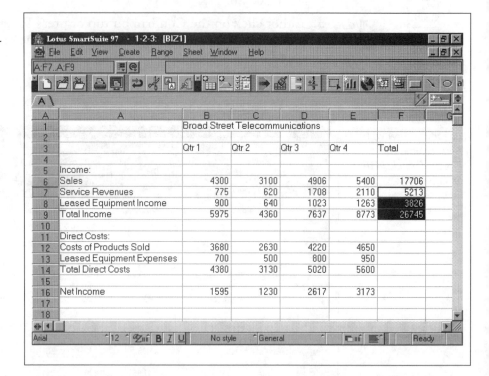

You'll find out about other common @functions at the end of this chapter.

> A quick and easy way to compute totals is to type the label Total or Totals under the last row label or to the right of the last column label in a sheet and press Enter. 1-2-3 inserts @SUM formula in the row of cells under or in the column of cells next to Total or Totals, calculates the totals, and places the results in the appropriate cells. Once the formulas are in place, you can edit the labels any way you want.

## ▶ *Defining Ranges*

Although you have worked with ranges (for example, cells F7 to F9 in the preceding steps) and the Range Fill commands earlier in this chapter, you have not had a formal introduction. Simply put, a *range* is a group of connected cells. A range can be a single cell, one column of cells, one row of cells, or a block of cells several rows by several columns. For example, one of the ranges that you have worked with in this chapter has three cells in a column; another has four cells in a row. You can create ranges that extend the full length or width of a sheet.

## ▶ *Naming Ranges*

If you use the same range often, you can name that range, allowing you to create formulas more easily and quickly than by pointing to cells one at a time. To name a range, select Range ➤ Name. In the Name dialog box (see Figure 5.9), type the name in the Name text box, click on Add to add the name to the list and keep the dialog box open, and either click on OK or press Enter to add the name to the list and close the dialog box. After you name ranges, you'll notice that 1-2-3 changes the formulas containing those ranges. For example, if a formula previously referred to B6..E6 and you named that range SALES_97, 1-2-3 automatically replaces B6..E6 with SALES_97.

FIGURE 5.9 ▶

*The Name dialog box, in which you can name a range of cells*

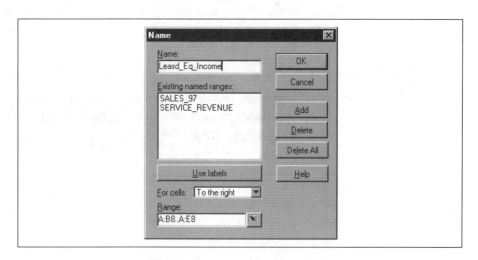

When naming ranges, note that range names can have as many as 15 characters, starting with an alphabetic character.

**▶▶WARNING**

**When you name ranges, don't use spaces, 1-2-3 @function names, key names, cell address names, or any characters that 1-2-3 reserves for mathematical or logical operations: . ; , ! + – * / & > < @ # {.**

You can delete range names using the Name dialog box. To delete a single range name, select it from the Existing Named Ranges list box, click on the Delete button, and either click on OK or press Enter. To delete all the range names for this file, click on Delete All, and either click on OK or press Enter.

You can name a particular range of cells immediately to the right or immediately below a row or a column label by following these steps:

1. Select the label that you want to refer to a cell.

2. Choose Range ➤ Name.

3. In the Name dialog box, click on the Use Labels button.

4. From the For Cells drop-down list box, select the direction that indicates the location of the cell to be named. You can select To the Right or To the Left to refer to directions through rows, or Above or Below to refer to directions through columns.

5. Either click on OK or press Enter.

**▶▶NOTE**

**Before moving on to the following section, in the sample sheet, give the range B13..E13 the name LEASED_EXPS.**

## ▶ *Inserting Named Ranges in Formulas*

When you want to use a named range in a formula, you can use some 1-2-3 shortcuts. You have already used the @function selector to write a simple formula. Now you'll use the @function selector and the navigator to write a more complex formula. To write a formula using an @function and the navigator, follow these steps:

1. Click on the cell in which you want to insert the formula. For the sample sheet, click on F13.

2. Click on the @function selector. 1-2-3 displays the list of common @functions.

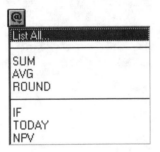

3. Select SUM. 1-2-3 inserts the formula @SUM(list) in the current cell. Notice that list is highlighted.

4. Click on the navigator. 1-2-3 displays a list of all the named ranges (see Figure 5.10) for this file.

**FIGURE 5.10** ▶

*The open navigator list of all the named ranges for this file*

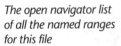

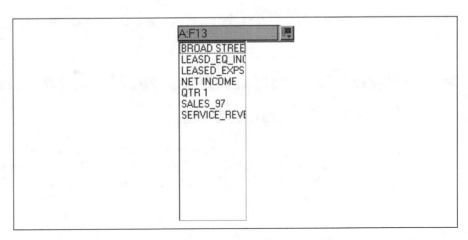

Entering
Formulas & Data

▶▶

*Ch.*
**5**

5. Click on a range name, such as LEASED_EXPS. 1-2-3 replaces list with the name of the range.

6. Either click on the Confirm button or press Enter to indicate that the formula is complete. 1-2-3 calculates the formula and places the results in the current cell.

Figure 5.11 shows the sample sheet completely filled in. Notice that the highlighted cell contains a formula that subtracts the contents of one cell from another.

**FIGURE 5.11** ►

*The sample sheet with all formulas entered and results in place*

**A formula that subtracts one value from another**

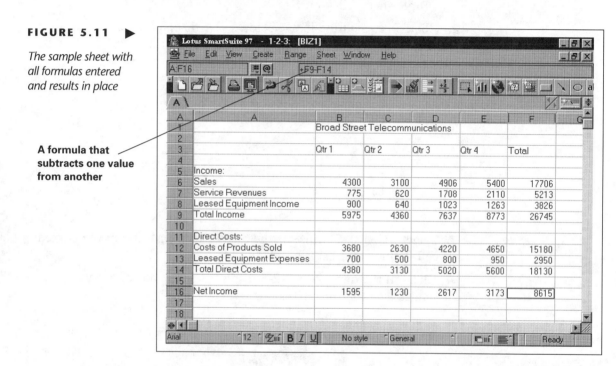

## ►► *Building Formulas with Common 1-2-3 @Functions*

In the preceding sections in this chapter, you learned about creating formulas using the @SUM @function. In this section, you'll learn about several of the common 1-2-3 @functions and how to use them in formulas.

## ▶ Computing an Average

The @AVG function computes the average of a list of values:

```
@AVG(E6..E11)
```

adds the contents of E6, E7, E8, E9, E10, and E11 and then divides by six, the number of cells. If a cell contains a label, 1-2-3 does not add or count it.

## ▶ Identifying Maximum and Minimum Values

Use @MAX and @MIN to identify the maximum and minimum values in a list:

```
@MAX(E6..E11)
```

finds the highest value in the cells E6, E7, E8, E9, E10, and E11 and

```
@MIN(E6..E11)
```

finds the lowest value in the cells E6, E7, E8, E9, E10, and E11.

## ▶ Counting a List of Items

Use @COUNT to count the nonzero items in a list:

```
@COUNT(C2..C7)
```

counts the items in the cells C2, C3, C4, C5, C6, and C7.

## ▶ Returning the Date and Time

You can display the date or time by using date and time functions such as @DATE, @TIME, @TODAY, or @NOW. If you are setting up a new sheet, you can insert a particular date by using @DATE:

```
@DATE(96;8;27)
```

returns 35304, which you can convert to a date format by selecting a date format from the status line.

@TIME works in exactly the same way:

```
@TIME(12;12;12)
```

returns 0.5084722. Select a time format to convert the value to a time. Using @NOW, you can stamp today's date and time into a sheet:

    @NOW

returns a number representing the date and time to which your computer system has been set. 1-2-3 returns a number representing both today's date and time, which you can use in calculations. However, because 1-2-3 does not provide a combination date/time format, you can see either the date or the time, but not both, in the selected format.

## ► Finding the Number of Days between Today and a Future Date

Use @DAYS to calculate the number of days between today (@TODAY) and a date (@DATE(*yy,mm,dd*)), where yy represents the year, *mm* represents the month, and *dd* represents the day. To calculate the number of days between today and May 22, 1997, enter:

    @DAYS(@TODAY,@DATE(97,5,22))

## ► Rounding Values

The @ROUND function rounds a number to a specified number of places:

    @ROUND(956.453964599;2)

looks like 956.45 as displayed in a cell, and

    @ROUND(956.453964599;-2)

looks like 1000. In the formula, the 2 and −2 following the semicolon control the rounding. A positive number rounds the digits to the right of the decimal point, and a negative number rounds to the left of the decimal point.

You can round a value by referring to the cell in which it is located:

    @ROUND(B9,-3)

rounds the integer portion of the contents of cell B9 to three one-hundredths.

## ► *Testing for Conditions*

One of the most important and most used sheet functions is @IF. Use @IF to compare two values; if the first value is true, 1-2-3 returns a particular value, and if the second value is true, 1-2-3 returns another value:

```
@IF(C9>=500;FEE=0;FEE=10)
```

computes a fee for a checking account. If the balance is greater than or equal to $500, the monthly fee is zero; otherwise, the fee is $10.

You can nest @IF statements to test a series of values:

```
@IF(C9>=75000;500;@IF(C9>=50000;350;@IF(C9>=25000;200;
50)))
```

computes a series of bonus amounts.

# ►► *Getting Information about 1-2-3 @Functions*

A comprehensive source of information about all the 1-2-3 @functions is 1-2-3's help facility. You can find out about a particular @function in two ways:

- Choose Help ➤ Help Topics. Click on the Contents tab, double-click on Formulas and @Functions, then go through a series of Help windows until you get to the one for the desired function. Use this procedure if you are not sure of the best @function for the formula.

- Select a cell containing a formula that includes the @function about which you want to learn. Then press F1. This displays the help window about the function. Use this procedure if you have already created a formula and want to get information about syntax or valid *arguments* (variables or expressions that a formula uses to compute the result) or perhaps find a function that better fits the formula. Figure 5.12 shows the @SUM help window.

Entering
Formulas & Data

►►

*Ch.*
**5**

**FIGURE 5.12** ▶

*The @SUM help window, which provides arguments, examples, related SmartIcons, similar @functions, other Help topics, and information about help in the User's Guide.*

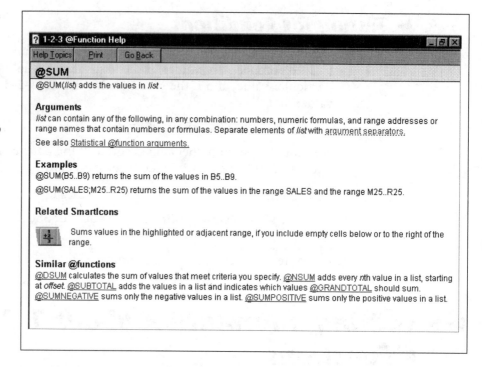

When you choose Help ➤ Help Topics and click on the Contents tab, 1-2-3 displays the Help Contents window (see Figure 5.13) from which you can select from these Formulas and @Functions topics:

**Using Formulas**    Contains a variety of how-to and reference topics on formulas, including entering formulas, using range addresses and range names in formulas, editing formulas, common errors in formulas, and so on.

**Copying and Moving Formulas**    Contains how-to's on copying and moving formulas.

**Using @Functions**    Contains several how-to and reference topics on @functions, including entering @functions; getting help; and adding, changing the order of, or removing an item from the @function menu.

**Alphabetical List of @Functions**    Opens an alphabetically arranged list of all the @functions. Simply click on a letter to go to that portion of the list. If you know the name of an @function, this is the help topic to use.

**@Functions by Category**   Contains a list of @function categories ranging from Calendar to Text. If you know the type of @function but not the specific @function, this is the help topic to use.

**@Function Selector**   To display help information about the @Function Selector in the edit line. From this window, you can return to the @Functions window.

To use the Help menu to display help windows for @functions, follow these steps:

1. Choose Help ➤ Help Topics. 1-2-3 displays the Contents window (see Figure 5.13).

2. Double-click on Formulas and @Functions. 1-2-3 displays five subtopics.

3. Double-click on one of the subtopics.

**FIGURE 5.13** ▶

*The Help Contents window, from which you can select a category of Help topics*

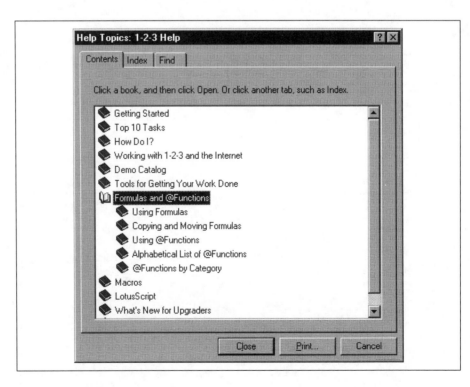

**4.** Once you see the subtopic preceded by a question mark icon, click on the Display button to read the help information.

 ▶▶ N O T E

> **You can print a help topic by clicking on the Print button at the top of the Help window.**

**5.** To return to the current sheet, click on the Close button.

For more information about using Windows help, see your Windows manuals.

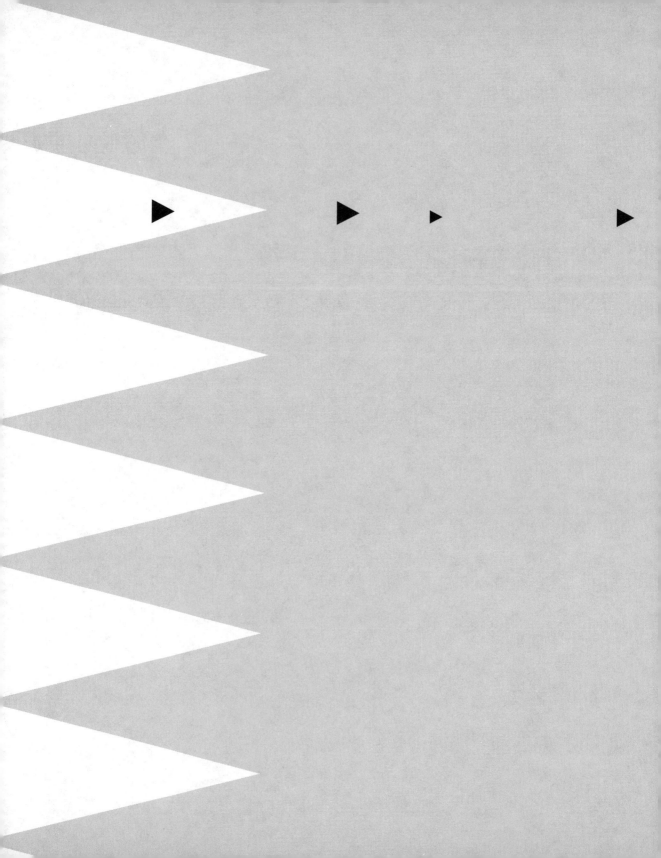

► ► CHAPTER **6**

# Editing and Formatting a Spreadsheet

*I*n the past two chapters, you learned how to fill in a sheet. Now that your sheet is complete, you must think about how to handle future changes and how to present the sheet to other people—in your company and outside.

In this chapter, you'll learn how to edit and format a sheet—from cell by cell to sheetwide. You'll find out how to add new cells, rows, and columns. You'll discover how to search for values and formats and how to replace values and formats. You'll find out how to recalculate automatically and manually, how to add objects (such as logos) to sheets, how to view a sheet before printing it, and how to take advantage of 1-2-3's printing options.

## ▶▶ *Editing and Formatting Cells*

You can edit a cell in two places: in the cell itself and in the edit line. If you type a new value in a cell whose name or contents are part of a formula, 1-2-3 automatically recalculates the formulas and changes appropriate values in other cells.

 ▶▶ WARNING

> If you edit a cell in which 1-2-3 calculated the value, the new value replaces the old, without any warning prompt. To undo the change (if it's the last action performed), click on the Undo the Last Command or Action SmartIcon, choose Edit ➤ Undo, or press Ctrl+Z.

You can use the Edit menu to copy and paste and to cut and paste information from one location to another in a sheet. You can also use the Windows drag-and-drop feature to move data. To learn more about these features, see the *Editing in SmartSuite Applications* chapter.

In the *Editing in SmartSuite Applications* chapter, you also learned how to apply formats to selected parts of a SmartSuite file. Use the same principles to format and/or enhance a 1-2-3 sheet. Simply select one or more cells and click on a SmartIcon, choose a properties command from the Range or Sheet menu, or press a shortcut key or key combination.

In the following sections, you'll learn about editing and formatting techniques that are unique to 1-2-3.

## ▶ *Clearing a Cell's Contents*

To delete the contents of a cell, select the cell and click on the Cut to the Clipboard SmartIcon, choose Edit ➤ Cut (or press Ctrl+X or Shift+Del), right-click and select Cut, or choose Edit ➤ Clear (or press Del). Depending on the command that you choose or the key that you press, there are important differences:

- Clicking on the Cut to the Clipboard SmartIcon, choosing Edit ➤ Cut, right-clicking and selecting Cut, or pressing Ctrl+X or Shift+Del places the contents of the cell in the Clipboard so that you can paste the value into another cell. Remember that the Clipboard keeps only one item at a time; you can retrieve only the last cut you made. You can, however, cut a range of cells to the Clipboard and retrieve them later.

- Clicking on the Delete SmartIcon or pressing Delete permanently deletes the contents of the cell.

- Pressing Ctrl+Del clears both the contents of the cell and its formats.

- Choosing Edit ➤ Clear opens the Clear dialog box (see Figure 6.1) from which you can clear the value in the cell (the default), the formatting styles for the cell, borders, cell comments, and scripts associated with the cell. You learned about some formatting styles in the *Editing in SmartSuite Applications* chapter, and you'll find out about the Style Gallery and Named styles in a following section of this chapter.

Editing a
Spreadsheet

Ch.
6

FIGURE 6.1 ►

*The Clear dialog box, in which you can delete a cell's contents and/or styles*

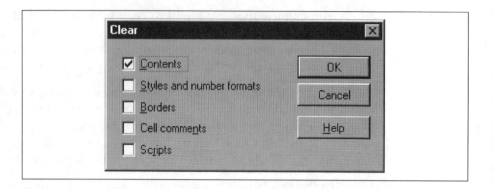

►►► **N O T E**

**You cannot clear the contents of a cell in a protected sheet unless you have "unprotected" a specific range of cells.**

Remember that clicking on the Undo the Last Command or Action SmartIcon, choosing Edit ➤ Undo, or pressing Ctrl+Z undoes only the last action taken.

## ► Clearing a Cell's Formats

In the previous section, you learned how to clear the contents of a cell. If you clear only the contents, any styles or formats remain although the cell looks empty. To clear a selected cell's styles, either click on the Delete Styles from a Range SmartIcon, which automatically deletes the styles, or choose Edit ➤ Clear, which opens the Clear dialog box. Click on Styles and Number Format and either click on OK or press Enter.

## ► Pasting One Cell's Formats to Another

If you have spent time and effort formatting a cell or a range of cells, you can copy the styles to another cell by clicking on a SmartIcon or by selecting commands from the Edit menu.

To use a SmartIcon, click on the cell or select the range whose styles you want to copy. Click on the Copy a Range's Styles to Other Ranges SmartIcon. When the mouse pointer looks like a paint brush, click on the cell or drag across the range to which the styles are to be applied.

To use the Edit menu to copy styles, follow these steps:

1. Select the cell or range whose styles you want to copy.

2. Click on the Copy to the Clipboard SmartIcon, choose Edit ➤ Copy, right-click and select Copy, or press Ctrl+C or Ctrl+Ins.

3. Select the cell or range to which you want to apply the copied styles.

4. Click on the Paste Special SmartIcon or choose Edit ➤ Paste Special.

5. In the Paste Special dialog box (see Figure 6.2), place a checkmark in the Styles and Number Formats checkbox.

6. Either click on OK or press Enter.

**FIGURE 6.2** ▶

*The Paste Special dialog box, in which you can paste data, styles, formulas, comments, and scripts as values in one or more cells*

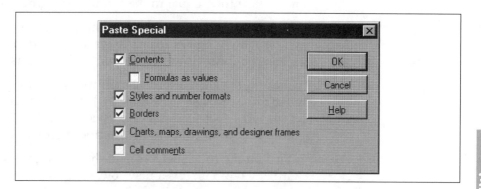

## ▶▶ *Inserting, Deleting, and Moving Rows and Columns*

When you create a sheet, although you can plan in detail, quite often you'll find that you have missed an important element, have included an unnecessary element, or need to move a row or a column to a new location. In this section, you'll find out how to handle these situations.

Editing a Spreadsheet

▶▶

Ch.

**6**

## ► *Inserting New Rows*

You can insert a new row in several ways: using a SmartIcon, a short-cut key combination, or a menu command. Start by clicking anywhere in the row that will be "pushed down" by the new row (for example, if you want to insert a new row 7, click on row label 7). If you select an entire row by clicking on its row label

you can use a set of commands other than those available when you click in a cell.

- Click on the row label to select the entire row and then click on the Insert Rows SmartIcon. 1-2-3 inserts a new row.

- Click on two or more row labels to select two or more rows and then click on the Insert Rows SmartIcon. 1-2-3 inserts two or more new rows equal to the number that you selected.

- Click on the row label to select the entire row and then either choose the Range ➤ Insert Rows command or right-click and select the Insert Rows command. 1-2-3 inserts a new row.

- Click on two or more row labels to select two or more rows and then either choose the Range ➤ Insert Rows command or right-click and select the Insert Rows command. 1-2-3 inserts two or more new rows equal to the number that you selected.

- Click on the row label to select the entire row and then press Ctrl++. 1-2-3 inserts a new row.

- Click on two or more row labels to select two or more rows and then press Ctrl++. 1-2-3 automatically inserts two or more new rows equal to the number that you selected.

- Click anywhere in the row and then click on the Insert Rows SmartIcon, choose the Range ➤ Insert command, right-click and select the Insert command, or press Ctrl++. 1-2-3 opens the Insert dialog box (see Figure 6.3) with which you can specify whether to insert a new row or column and select other options.

**FIGURE 6.3** ▶

*The Insert dialog box with which you can insert columns, rows, or a selection*

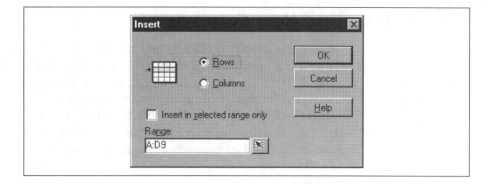

To insert a row using the Insert dialog box, follow these steps:

**1.** Click on the location of the new row within a row but not on the row label.

**2.** Choose Range ➤ Insert, right-click and select Insert, or press Ctrl++ (on the numeric keypad).

**3.** In the Insert dialog box, click on Rows.

**4.** Either click on OK or press Enter. Everything beyond the new row, which is blank, moves down one row. All the formulas in the old rows remain the same; they also move down one row.

▶▶ **N O T E**

> **You might have to edit formulas to include any data that you put into a new row. It depends on whether you used ranges or specific cell addresses in your formulas.**

▶▶ **T I P**

> **To add more than one row at a time, type or select a range in the Insert dialog box. For example, to insert three rows, select a range of three rows, such as A:A7..A:A9.**

**Editing a Spreadsheet**

▶ ▶

Ch.

**6**

## ▶ *Inserting New Columns*

You insert a new column in exactly the same way as you insert a new row; use a SmartIcon, a shortcut key combination, or a menu command. Start by clicking anywhere in the column that will be "pushed over" by the new column (for example, if you want to insert a new column D, click on the column D label). In the same way that you insert a row, if you select an entire column by clicking on its column label, you can use a set of commands other than those available when you click in a cell.

- Click on the column label to select the entire column and then click on the Insert Columns SmartIcon. 1-2-3 inserts a new column.

- Click on two or more column labels to select two or more columns and then click on the Insert Columns SmartIcon. 1-2-3 inserts two or more new columns equal to the number that you selected.

- Click on the column label to select the entire column and then either choose the Range ➤ Insert Columns command or right-click and select the Insert Columns command. 1-2-3 inserts a new column.

- Click on two or more column labels to select the two or more columns and either choose the Range ➤ Insert Columns command or right-click and select the Insert Columns command. 1-2-3 inserts two or more new columns equal to the number that you selected.

- Click on the column label to select the entire column and press Ctrl++. 1-2-3 inserts a new column.

- Click on two or more column labels to select the two or more columns and press Ctrl++. 1-2-3 inserts two or more new columns equal to the number that you selected.

- Click anywhere in the column and click on the Insert Columns SmartIcon, choose the Range ➤ Insert command, right-click and select the Insert command, or press Ctrl++. 1-2-3 opens the Insert dialog box (see Figure 6.3, earlier in this chapter) with which you can specify whether to insert a new row or column and select other options.

To insert a column using the Insert dialog box, follow these steps:

1. Click on the location of the new column within a column but not on the column label.

2. Choose Range ➤ Insert, right-click and select Insert, or press Ctrl++ (on the numeric keypad).

3. In the Insert dialog box, click on Columns.

4. Either click on OK or press Enter. Everything beyond the new column, which is blank, moves one column toward the right side of the screen. All the formulas in the old columns remain the same; they also move over one column.

 ➤➤ **TIP**

> **To add more than one column at a time, in the Insert dialog box, type or select a range.**

## ➤ *Deleting Rows and Columns*

To delete rows and columns, you use the same techniques as you did when inserting rows and columns but slightly different SmartIcons, menu commands, and shortcut key combinations. First, select the rows or columns to be deleted. As with inserting rows and columns, if you select an entire row or column, you can use a set of commands other than those available when you click in a cell. If you click in a cell in a row or column to be deleted, 1-2-3 opens the Delete dialog box (see Figure 6.4) in which you can delete rows, columns, or ranges.

**FIGURE 6.4** ➤

*The Delete dialog box, with which you can delete columns, rows, or a range*

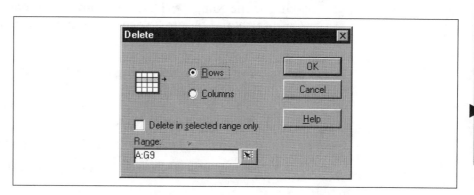

▶▶ **W A R N I N G**

**When deleting rows or columns, be careful not to delete cells that contain important formulas or that are referred to by other formulas. If you inadvertently delete rows or columns, however, choose Edit ➤ Undo DeleteRows or Edit ➤ Undo DeleteColumns or press Ctrl+Z.**

You can delete rows in the following ways:

- Click on the row label to select the entire row and click on the Delete Selected Rows SmartIcon, choose the Range ➤ Delete Rows command, right-click and select the Delete Rows command, or press Ctrl+−. 1-2-3 deletes the row.

- Click on two or more row labels to select two or more rows and click on the Delete Selected Rows SmartIcon, choose the Range ➤ Delete Rows command, right-click and select the Delete Rows command, or press Ctrl+−. 1-2-3 deletes the selected rows.

You can delete columns in the following ways:

- Click on the column label to select the entire column and click on the Delete Selected Columns SmartIcon, choose the Range ➤ Delete Columns command, or right-click and select the Delete Columns command. 1-2-3 deletes the column.

- Click on two or more column labels to select two or more columns and click on the Delete Selected Columns SmartIcon, choose the Range ➤ Delete Columns command, right-click and select the Delete Selected Columns command, or press Ctrl+−. 1-2-3 deletes the columns.

To delete a row or a column using the Delete dialog box, follow these steps:

1. Click in the row or column to be deleted.

2. Choose Range ➤ Delete or press Ctrl+− (on the numeric keypad).

3. If 1-2-3 opens the Delete dialog box, click on Column or Row.

**4.** To delete more than one column or row at a time, type or select a range in the Range box.

**5.** Either click on OK or press Enter. The remaining rows or columns fill in the space formerly taken by the deleted rows or columns.

### ▶ *Moving Rows, Columns, and Ranges*

In the *Editing in SmartSuite Applications* chapter, you learned how to move selections by choosing Edit ➤ Cut and Edit ➤ Paste and by using drag-and-drop. You can use these techniques to edit your sheet. When you move rows, columns, or ranges, however, you may have to reenter data or formulas. Please note that:

- you should not break up ranges of cells that are linked by a formula.

- if you move cells to an area that already contains data, 1-2-3 will overwrite those cells with the moved data. You may then have to edit formulas that contain absolute cell references.

## ▶▶ *Formatting Cells, Ranges, Spreadsheets, and Workbooks*

Earlier in this chapter, you learned a shortcut for applying the style of one cell or range to another cell or range; you simply clicked on a SmartIcon. When you find an appealing combination of formats and enhancements, you can save them as a named style that you can use again and again. In 1-2-3 you can save any combination of number formats, types, type sizes, underlining, text enhancements, colors, and alignment for ranges and sheets—using InfoBoxes and SmartIcons. If you have any questions about SmartSuite formatting in general, refer to the *Editing in SmartSuite Applications* chapter.

 Click on the Range Properties SmartIcon, choose Range ➤ Range Properties (or press Alt+Enter), or right-click on the range and select Range Properties to open the Range Properties InfoBox to change a variety of attributes for a range of cells. Table 6.1 lists and describes formatting and enhancement options for cells and ranges.

Editing a Spreadsheet

▶▶ Ch. 6

▶ **TABLE 6.1:** *1-2-3 Formatting Options—Cells and Ranges*

| InfoBox Tab | Related SmartIcon | Command | Description |
|---|---|---|---|
| | | Range ➤ Range Properties (or press Alt+Enter); click on the Text tab | Allows you to apply text formats: font, size, style, and text color |
| | | Range ➤ Range Properties (or press Alt+Enter); click on the Alignment tab | Allows you to apply alignment options: horizontal alignment, vertical alignment, alignment across columns, wrapping text, and orientation of text within selected cells |
| | N/A | Range ➤ Range Properties (or press Alt+Enter); click on the Format tab | Allows you to change formats of data: add or remove categories from the Status bar, change decimal places, specify currency options, and select date and time formats |
| | | Range ➤ Range Properties (or press Alt+Enter); click on the Lines and Colors tab | Allows you to select colors and patterns: the interior pattern, background color, text color, pattern color, negative values, border type, line style, line color, and designer frame |
| Basics | N/A | Range ➤ Range Properties (or press Alt+Enter); click on the Basics tab | Allows you to name the range, set column width and row height, hide the selected columns and rows, and break the page at the column or at the row |
| | N/A | Range ➤ Range Properties (or press Alt+Enter); click on the Security tab | Allows you to select security options: hiding and/or protecting the contents of a cell or a range |

▶ **TABLE 6.1:** *1-2-3 Formatting Options—Cells and Ranges (continued)*

| InfoBox Tab | Related SmartIcon | Command | Description |
|---|---|---|---|
|  | N/A | Range ➤ Range Properties (or press Alt+Enter); click on the Versions tab | Allows you to name and comment on this version of the range |
| | N/A | Range ➤ Range Properties (or press Alt+Enter); click on the Comments tab | Allows you to include a comment with this cell or range or to date/time stamp it |
| | N/A | Range ➤ Range Properties (or press Alt+Enter); click on the Styles tab | Allows you to create, name, redefine, or manage a style or to access the Style Gallery for this cell or range |

Click on the Sheet Properties SmartIcon, choose Sheet ➤ Sheet Properties (or press Alt+Enter), or right-click and select Sheet Properties to open the Sheet Properties InfoBox to change a variety of attributes for a sheet. Table 6.2 lists and describes formatting and enhancement options for sheets.

## ▶ *Defining and Naming Styles*

Defining and naming a style is easy. Simply format a cell or a range of cells and then follow these steps:

1. Select a cell or a range that has the combination of formats to be saved.

2. Click on the Range Properties SmartIcon, choose Range ➤ Range Properties, or press Alt+Enter. 1-2-3 opens the Range Properties InfoBox.

3. Click on the Styles tab. 1-2-3 opens the Styles section of the Range Properties InfoBox (see Figure 6.5).

Editing a Spreadsheet

Ch.
**6**

▶ **TABLE 6.2:** *1-2-3 Formatting Options—Sheets*

| InfoBox Tab | Related SmartIcon | Command | Description |
|---|---|---|---|
| | | Sheet ▶ Sheet Properties (or press Alt+Enter); click on the Text tab | Allows you to apply text formats: font, size, style, and text color |
| | | Sheet ▶ Sheet Properties (or press Alt+Enter); click on the Alignment tab | Allows you to apply alignment options: horizontal alignment and vertical alignment |
| | N/A | Sheet ▶ Sheet Properties (or press Alt+Enter); click on the Format tab | Allows you to change formats of data: add or remove categories from the Status bar, change decimal places, specify currency options, select date and time formats, and display zeros as a certain character |
| | | Sheet ▶ Sheet Properties (or press Alt+Enter); click on the Lines and Colors tab | Allows you to select colors and patterns: the pattern, pattern color, background color, text color, and negative values in red |
| Basics | N/A | Sheet ▶ Sheet Properties (or press Alt+Enter); click on the Basics tab | Allows you to name the sheet, specify its tab color, and set the default column widths and row height |
| View | N/A | Sheet ▶ Sheet Properties (or press Alt+Enter); click on the View tab | Allows you to select view options: hiding or revealing the labels framing the sheet and hiding or revealing the grid lines |
| Outline | N/A | Sheet ▶ Sheet Properties (or press Alt+Enter); click on the Outline tab | Allows you to hide or reveal the outline frame for rows and/or columns and to specify how summary rows are displayed |

**4.** Click on the Create Style button. The Create Style dialog box (see Figure 6.6) appears.

**5.** In the Style Name text box, type a style name, which can be a maximum of 35 characters. Click on OK or press Enter. 1-2-3 adds the style name to the InfoBox and to the Style button in the Status bar and closes the dialog box.

**FIGURE 6.5** ▶

*In the Styles section of the Range Properties InfoBox, you can create, name, redefine, and manage styles and access the Style Gallery.*

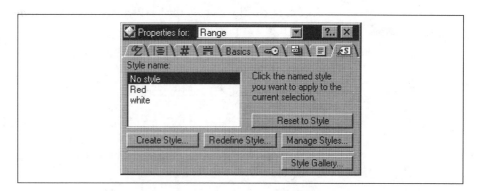

**FIGURE 6.6** ▶

*The Create Style dialog box with a style name filled in*

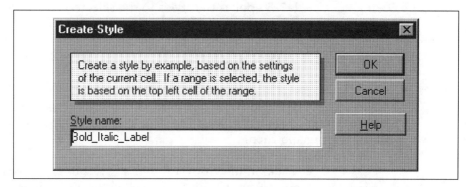

## ▶ *Applying a Style to a Range*

You can apply a named style to a selected cell or a range in two ways: by choosing its name from the Styles section of the Range Properties InfoBox or by selecting it from the Status bar.

Editing a Spreadsheet

▶ ▶

Ch.

**6**

To apply a style using the Range Properties InfoBox, follow these steps:

1. Select the cell or the range of cells to which you want to apply the style.

2. Click on the Range Properties SmartIcon, choose Range ➤ Range Properties, right-click and select Range Properties, or press Alt+Enter.

3. Click on the Styles tab. 1-2-3 displays the Styles section of the Range Properties InfoBox.

4. Select the desired style from the Style Name box. 1-2-3 applies the style.

5. Click on the Close button.

To apply a style using the Status bar, follow these steps:

1. Select the cell or the range of cells to which you want to apply the style.

2. Select a style from the Named Style button on the Status bar. 1-2-3 applies the styles to the selected cell or range.

The two fastest ways to remove the formatting that you have applied by using a named style is to select a cell or a range with the default formatting and then:

• Click on the Copy a Range's Styles to Other Ranges SmartIcon, and select the formatted cell or range. To inactivate the SmartIcon, press Esc.

• Select None from the Named Style button on the Status bar.

## ▶ Removing a Named Style

When you no longer need a named style, delete it by following these steps:

1. Click on the Range Properties SmartIcon, choose Range ➤ Range Properties, right-click and select Range Properties, or press Alt+Enter.

**2.** Click on the Styles tab. 1-2-3 displays the Styles section of the Range Properties InfoBox.

**3.** Click on the Manage Styles button. The Manage Styles dialog box (see Figure 6.7) appears.

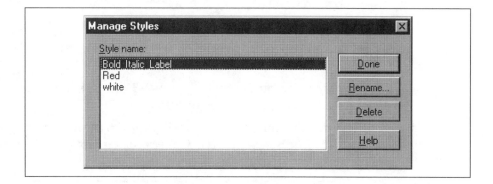

**4.** Select a style in the Style Name box.

**5.** Click on the Delete button.

**6.** Click on the Close button.

▶▶ **N O T E**

**Any cells or ranges that you have already formatted with the named style keep the formats, although the named style has been deleted.**

## ▶ *Formatting with the Style Gallery*

1-2-3 provides predefined styles with which you can format a cell, a range of cells, or even an entire sheet. To use the Style Gallery, follow these steps:

**1.** Select a cell, a range of cells, or the current sheet.

To select the entire sheet, click on the button to the left of column A and above row 1. However, before you do, read the following warning message.

Ch. 6

Editing a Spreadsheet

⊚ ▶▶**W A R N I N G**

**If you format an entire sheet, you may run into memory problems. It is best to select only the columns and rows that will be formatted.**

**2.** Click on the Range Properties SmartIcon, choose Range ➤ Range Properties, right-click and select Range Properties, or press Alt+Enter.

**3.** Click on the Styles tab. 1-2-3 displays the Styles section of the Range Properties InfoBox.

**4.** Click on the Style Gallery button in the lower right corner of the InfoBox. The Style Gallery dialog box (see Figure 6.8) appears.

**FIGURE 6.8** ▶

*The Style Gallery dialog box, from which you can select a predefined style from a selected cell, range, or even the entire sheet*

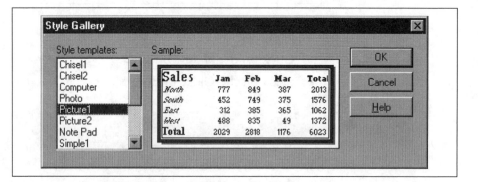

**5.** From the Style Templates scroll box, select a template. Notice that the Sample box shows how your selection will look.

**6.** When you have found the appropriate style, either click on OK or press Enter. Figure 6.9 illustrates our sample sheet formatted using the Picture1 style, with the numbers in the cells changed to Fixed format with no decimal places and with the title aligned across four columns.

**FIGURE 6.9** ▶

*The sample sheet
(with a newly spaced
title) in the Picture1
style from the Style
Gallery*

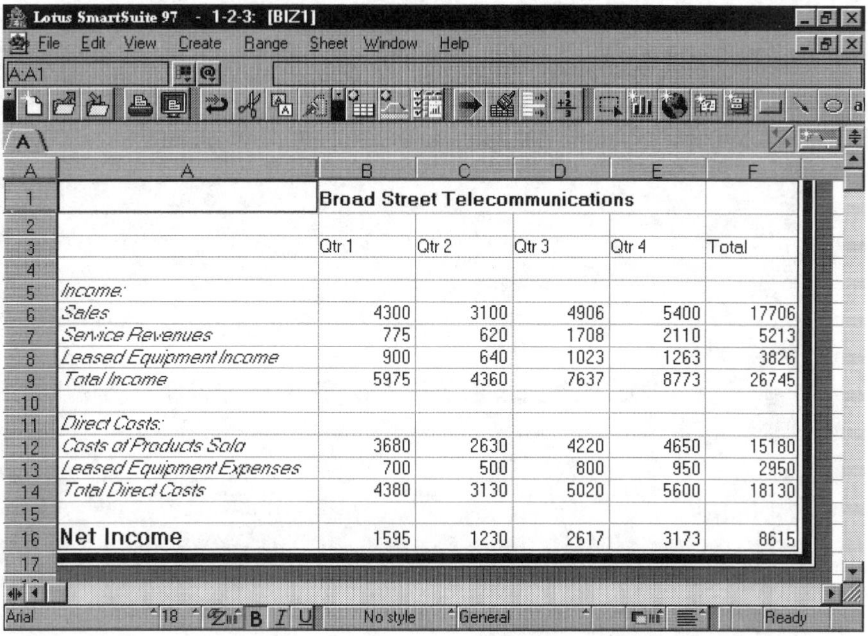

| | A | B | C | D | E | F |
|---|---|---|---|---|---|---|
| 1 | | Broad Street Telecommunications | | | | |
| 2 | | | | | | |
| 3 | | Qtr 1 | Qtr 2 | Qtr 3 | Qtr 4 | Total |
| 4 | | | | | | |
| 5 | Income: | | | | | |
| 6 | Sales | 4300 | 3100 | 4906 | 5400 | 17706 |
| 7 | Service Revenues | 775 | 620 | 1708 | 2110 | 5213 |
| 8 | Leased Equipment Income | 900 | 640 | 1023 | 1263 | 3826 |
| 9 | Total Income | 5975 | 4360 | 7637 | 8773 | 26745 |
| 10 | | | | | | |
| 11 | Direct Costs: | | | | | |
| 12 | Costs of Products Sold | 3680 | 2630 | 4220 | 4650 | 15180 |
| 13 | Leased Equipment Expenses | 700 | 500 | 800 | 950 | 2950 |
| 14 | Total Direct Costs | 4380 | 3130 | 5020 | 5600 | 18130 |
| 15 | | | | | | |
| 16 | **Net Income** | 1595 | 1230 | 2617 | 3173 | 8615 |
| 17 | | | | | | |

▶▶ **T I P**

**To space text, such as a long title, across selected
columns of a sheet, select the title and the columns
over which you want the title to be spaced. Then click
on the Range Properties SmartIcon, choose Range ➤
Range Properties, or right-click and select Range
Properties. Click on the Alignment tab, check the Align
Across Columns checkbox, and click on the Close
button. Adjust column widths where needed.**

**Editing a
Spreadsheet**

▶▶

Ch.

**6**

# MANAGING PROJECTS WITH 1-2-3

A sheet is a great way to track a project from beginning to end. You can list all the details in the row labels and make the column labels dates. Then to schedule your tasks, color-code the cells. In fact, before you get started, define a set of named styles in various colors or patterns. The following illustration shows a sample project management sheet.

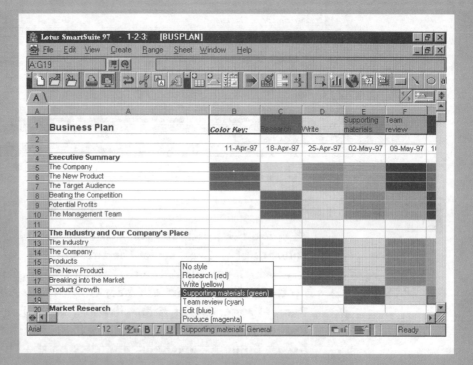

Another way to use a sheet for project management is to color-code cells as you accomplish your goals. The following illustration shows the sheet used to track the progress of this book. The cells with a shaded background show completed tasks, and the cells with deeper shading show tasks that must be done soon.

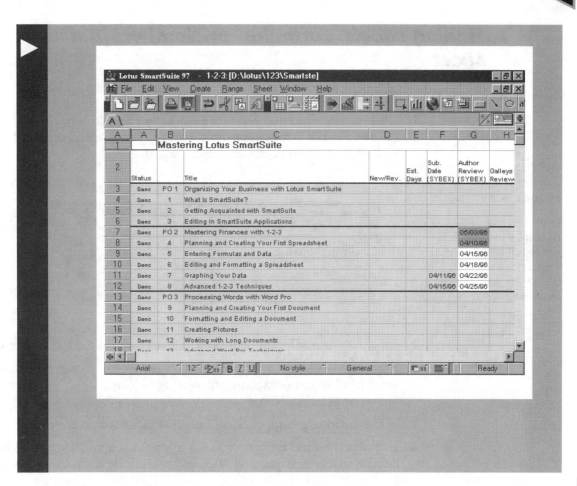

# ▶▶ *Finding and Replacing in 1-2-3*

At the end of the *Editing in SmartSuite Applications* chapter, you read an overview of find and replace. Every SmartSuite application, except for Freelance Graphics, has its own find and replace facility. In 1-2-3 you can find and replace characters in labels and in formulas, and you can find and replace numbers for a selected range, for the current sheet, for the current workbook, or for all workbooks on your computer. You cannot, however, find labels, numbers, and formulas in columns and rows that you have hidden by choosing Hide Column or Hide Row in the Basics section of the Range Properties InfoBox.

Editing a
Spreadsheet

▶▶

Ch.
6

## ▶ Finding Labels, Formulas, or Numbers in a Sheet

To find labels, formulas, or numbers in a sheet, follow these steps:

**1.** Click on the Find and Replace Characters SmartIcon, choose Edit ➤ Find & Replace, or press Ctrl+F. 1-2-3 opens the Find and Replace dialog box (see Figure 6.10).

**FIGURE 6.10** ▶

*In the Find and Replace dialog box, you can search for a search string and optionally replace it with the replace string.*

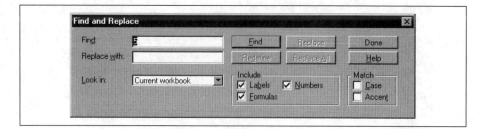

**2.** Type the *search string* (as many as 512 characters) in the Find text box.

**3.** From the Look In drop-down list box, select the area in which to search: All Workbooks, Current Workbook (the default), Current Sheet, or Selected Range.

**4.** In the Include group, click on Labels, Formulas, or Numbers.

**5.** Click on the Find button. If 1-2-3 finds the search string, it highlights the search string and "freezes" all but the buttons in the dialog box.

**6.** To continue the search, click on Find again.

**7.** To change the conditions of the search or to start a new search, click on the Redefine button.

**8.** To end the search, click on Done.

## ▶ *Replacing Labels, Formulas, or Numbers in a Sheet*

To replace labels, formulas, or numbers in a sheet, follow these steps:

1. Click on the Find and Replace Characters SmartIcon, choose Edit ➤ Find & Replace, or press Ctrl+F. 1-2-3 opens the Find and Replace dialog box.

2. Type the *search string* (as many as 512 characters) in the Find text box.

3. Type the *replace string* (as many as 512 characters) in the Replace With text box.

4. From the Look In drop-down list box, select the area in which to search: All Workbooks, Current Workbook (the default), Current Sheet, or Selected Range.

5. In the Include group, click on Labels, Formulas, or Numbers.

6. Click on the Find button. If 1-2-3 finds the search string, it highlights the search string and "freezes" all but the buttons in the dialog box.

7. To replace this occurrence of the search string, click on the Replace button.

8. To replace all occurrences of the search string, click on Replace All.

9. To search for the next occurrence of the search string without replacing this occurrence, click on Find Next.

10. To change the conditions of the search or to start a new search, click on Redefine.

11. Click on Done to end the search.

# ▶▶ *Automatic vs. Manual Recalculation*

By default, whenever you change a value in a cell or edit a formula, 1-2-3 recalculates all the formulas and changes the results in the sheet. If, however, you plan to make many changes to formulas in the sheet, you may want to stop calculation for a while. One reason is that while you're changing formulas, automatic recalculation produces meaning-less error messages because you haven't completed your changes. Another reason is that constant recalculation while you're changing formulas wastes processing time.

To change to manual recalculation for the current sheet, follow these steps:

**1.** Choose File ➤ User Setup ➤ 1-2-3 Preferences. 1-2-3 displays the General section of the 1-2-3 Preferences dialog box (see Figure 6.11).

**FIGURE 6.11** ▶

*In all the sections of the 1-2-3 Preferences dialog box, you can customize 1-2-3 to suit your needs.*

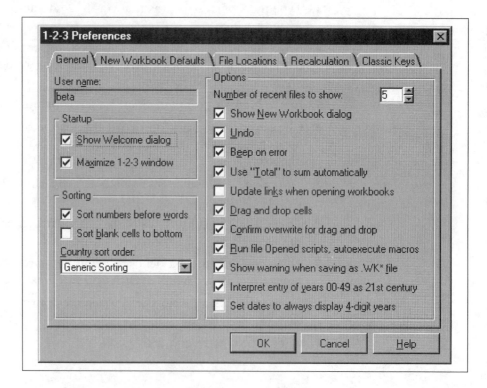

**2.** Click on the Recalculation tab. 1-2-3 displays the Recalculation section of the 1-2-3 Preferences dialog box (see Figure 6.12).

**3.** In the Recalculation group, click on Manual.

**4.** Either click on OK or press Enter.

**FIGURE 6.12** ▶

*In the Recalculation section of the 1-2-3 Preferences dialog box, you can set manual or automatic recalculation and other recalculation options.*

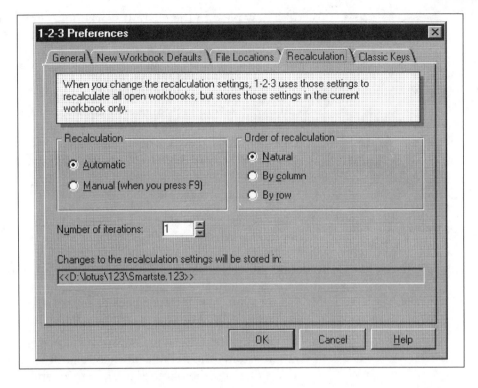

To recalculate a sheet manually, press F9 or click on the Calc button on the Status bar.

To reset recalculation to automatic, repeat the preceding steps, but select Automatic instead of Manual in the Recalculation section.

## ▶▶ *Defining Multiple Sheets in a File*

One of the most powerful features of 1-2-3 is its ability to incorporate multiple sheets in a single workbook. This means that you can save your actual data for this year and budgeted data for next year. In addition, you can keep all related charts and sheets in one file, making it easy to find related information.

You can insert a maximum of 256 sheets (or pages) in a single workbook. Each page is represented on your Desktop with a tab, which you can rename from the default name of A, B, C, and so on.

To add a new page to the current workbook, simply click on the New Sheet button on the right side of your desktop. 1-2-3 inserts a new blank sheet and adds a new tab:

A B

You can insert several new sheets at a time by following these steps:

1. Click on the Create a Sheet SmartIcon or choose Create ➤ Sheet. 1-2-3 displays the Create Sheet dialog box (see Figure 6.13).

2. Select or type a number of sheets (from 1 to 256) in the Number of Sheets text/option box.

3. Either click on OK or press Enter. 1-2-3 displays the new sheets on the Desktop.

To delete a sheet, click on its tab to select it, and follow these steps:

1. Choose Sheet ➤ Delete Sheet or press Ctrl+− (on the numeric keypad). 1-2-3 displays the Delete dialog box.

2. Either click on OK or press Enter. 1-2-3 deletes the sheet and renames only the default tabs (for example, if you remove sheet E, 1-2-3 changes the name *F* to *E*, *G* to *F*, and so on).

**FIGURE 6.13** ▶

*The Create Sheet dialog box with its default settings for one sheet*

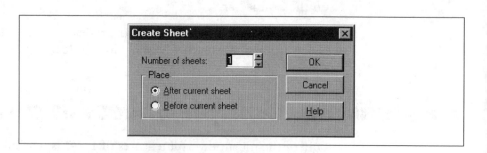

## ▶ Moving among Sheets in a File

To move from one sheet to another, simply click on the tab that represents the desired sheet. When the number of tabs in a file exceeds the width of the Desktop, click on the left-or right-pointing arrow to display more tabs to the left or the right of the current tab. Then click on a tab to display the desired sheet page.

## ▶ Naming a Sheet

To change the name of a tab from the default letter, simply double-click on the tab, type the new name, and either press Enter or click on another part of the sheet.

Monthly    Quarterly

To apply a color to a selected tab, click on the Sheet Properties Smart-Icon or choose Sheet ➤ Sheet Properties. In the Basics section of the Sheet Properties InfoBox (see Figure 6.14), open the Tab Color drop-down palette and select a color. 1-2-3 immediately changes the color of the tab. To apply a color to another tab while the InfoBox is open, double-click on the tab, and select a color from the Tab Color drop-down palette.

## ▶ Using Formulas among Sheets

One of the purposes of a workbook is to keep related sheets together. You can use calculations in one sheet to fill another. For example, you can track monthly revenues in one sheet (see Figure 6.15) and track quarterly revenues in another (see Figure 6.16).

**FIGURE 6.14** ▶

*The Basics section of the Sheet Properties InfoBox with an open Tab Color palette*

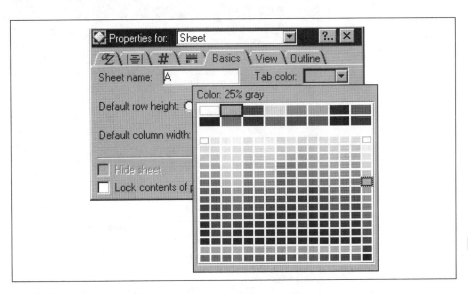

Editing a Spreadsheet

▶ ▶

*Ch.*
**6**

**FIGURE 6.15** ▶

*A sheet with monthly revenues*

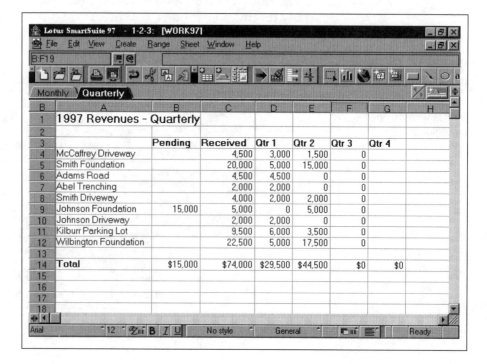

**1997 Revenues – Monthly**

| | A | B | C | D | E | F | G | H |
|---|---|---|---|---|---|---|---|---|
| | | Pending | Received | Jan | Feb | Mar | Apr | May |
| McCaffrey Driveway | | | 4,500 | | 3,000 | | 1,500 | |
| Smith Foundation | | | 20,000 | | | 5,000 | 15,000 | |
| Adams Road | | | 4,500 | | | 4,500 | | |
| Abel Trenching | | | 2,000 | | 500 | 1,500 | | |
| Smith Driveway | | | 4,000 | | | 2,000 | 2,000 | |
| Johnson Foundation | | 15,000 | 5,000 | | | | 5,000 | |
| Johnson Driveway | | | 2,000 | | 500 | 1,500 | | |
| Kilburr Parking Lot | | | 9,500 | | | 6,000 | 3,500 | |
| Wilbington Foundation | | | 22,500 | | | 5,000 | 17,500 | |
| Total | | $15,000 | $74,000 | $0 | $4,000 | $25,500 | $44,500 | $ |

**FIGURE 6.16** ▶

*A related sheet that shows quarterly revenues*

**1997 Revenues – Quarterly**

| | A | B | C | D | E | F | G | H |
|---|---|---|---|---|---|---|---|---|
| | | Pending | Received | Qtr 1 | Qtr 2 | Qtr 3 | Qtr 4 | |
| McCaffrey Driveway | | | 4,500 | 3,000 | 1,500 | 0 | | |
| Smith Foundation | | | 20,000 | 5,000 | 15,000 | 0 | | |
| Adams Road | | | 4,500 | 4,500 | 0 | 0 | | |
| Abel Trenching | | | 2,000 | 2,000 | 0 | 0 | | |
| Smith Driveway | | | 4,000 | 2,000 | 2,000 | 0 | | |
| Johnson Foundation | | 15,000 | 5,000 | 0 | 5,000 | 0 | | |
| Johnson Driveway | | | 2,000 | 2,000 | 0 | 0 | | |
| Kilburr Parking Lot | | | 9,500 | 6,000 | 3,500 | 0 | | |
| Wilbington Foundation | | | 22,500 | 5,000 | 17,500 | 0 | | |
| **Total** | | $15,000 | $74,000 | $29,500 | $44,500 | $0 | $0 | |

To use a formula from one sheet in another sheet, add the prefix of the sheet name; for example, in the Quarterly sheet:

`@SUM(Monthly:D5..Monthly:F5)`

adds the contents of cells D5, E5, and F5 in the Monthly sheet. In other words, the formula adds the contents of particular Jan, Feb, and Mar cells in the Monthly sheet and places the result in a particular Qtr 1 cell in the Quarterly sheet.

> **TIP**
>
> **To insert related formulas in several cells simultaneously, type the formula in one cell, select that cell and others in which you want to insert the formula, choose Range ➤ Fill, select Fill by Example, and click on OK or press Enter. If you check the newly inserted formulas in several cells, you'll find that 1-2-3 has modified the cell address for each cell.**

## ▶ *Viewing Multiple Sheets Simultaneously*

You can view two sheets at the same time. To view two sheets horizontally (to compare rows) or vertically (to compare columns), drag the horizontal or vertical splitter until both sheets are displayed, or choose View ➤ Split. Figure 6.17 shows two sheets, Actual 96 and Budget 97, displayed horizontally.

To return to the display of a single sheet, either drag the horizontal splitter up or down the Desktop or drag the vertical splitter to the left or right. You can also choose View ➤ Clear Split.

# ▶▶ *Viewing a Sheet As It Will Print*

In Preview mode, you can check a file before you print it. When you look at your file in the Print Preview window, you can check page layout, alignment, formatting, and enhancements. You can then correct any problems before you print.

Editing a
Spreadsheet

▶▶

Ch.

6

**FIGURE 6.17** ▶

*Two sheets displayed
horizontally on the
desktop*

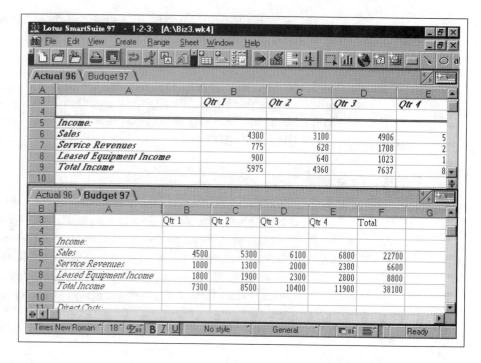

To view all or part of a 1-2-3 sheet as it will print, select all or part of
the sheet. Then, click on the Preview the Print Selection SmartIcon,
choose File ▶ Preview & Page Setup, or click on the Preview & Page
Setup button in the Print dialog box. Figure 6.18 shows the Monthly
sheet in Preview mode.

**▶▶ TIP**

> **To exit Preview mode, click on the Close button for the
> document window—the lower Close button at the top
> right corner of the screen.**

The Print Preview window provides a new set of SmartIcons, the Print
Preview bar, described in Table 6.3.

**FIGURE 6.18** ▶

*1-2-3's Print Preview window displays all or part of a sheet and contains a new set of SmartIcons.*

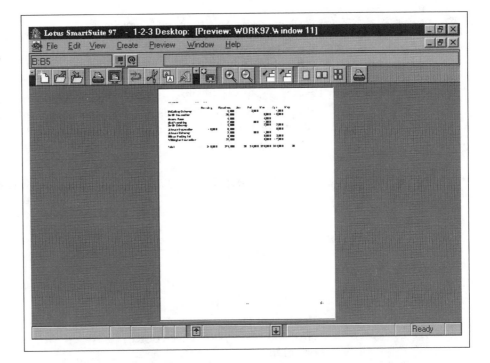

▶▶▶ **N O T E**

While you are viewing your file in the Print Preview window, you can zoom a page and move the page around by pressing the left arrow, the right arrow, the down arrow, and the up arrow. You can display the prior page, if you are not on the first page or are viewing a one-page sheet, by clicking on the upward-pointing arrow in the middle of the Status bar. You can move to the next page, if you are not on the last page or are viewing a one-page sheet, by clicking on the downward-pointing arrow.

Editing a Spreadsheet

▶▶

Ch.

**6**

► **TABLE 6.3:** *SmartSuite Print Preview SmartIcons and Commands*

| SmartIcon | Command (Shortcut Key Combination) | Description |
|---|---|---|
| | Preview ➤ Preview & Page Setup Properties or right-click and select Preview & Page Setup Properties (Alt+Enter) | Opens the Preview & Page Setup Properties InfoBox so that you can modify options such as orientation, margins, and headers and footers |
| | N/A (– [numeric keypad]) | Magnifies the display every time you click with a maximum of five levels of magnification. (Press ★ to unzoom.) |
| | N/A (+ [numeric keypad]) | Reduces the display every time you click with a maximum of five levels of reduction. (Press ★ to unzoom.) |
| | Preview ➤ Next Page or right-click and select Next Page (Enter or PgDn) | Displays the next page |
| | Preview ➤ Previous Page or right-click and select Previous Page (PgUp) | Displays the prior page |
| | Preview ➤ One Page View or right-click and select One Page View | Displays the sheet one page at a time |
| | Preview ➤ Two Page View or right-click and select Two Page View | Displays the sheet two pages at a time |
| | Preview ➤ Four Page View or right-click and select Four Page View | Displays the sheet four pages at a time |
| | File ➤ Print or right-click and select Print (Ctrl+P) | Displays the Print dialog box so that you can modify print options and then print your selection. |

# ▶▶ *Selecting Page Setup Options*

Whether you're viewing your sheet in the Print Preview window or in the work area, or if you're ready to print, you can specify the way the page is set up. You can open the Preview & Page Setup Properties Info-Box (see Figure 6.19) in Preview mode in several ways:

- Click on the Preview & Page Setup Properties SmartIcon from the Print Preview window.
- Choose File ➤ Preview & Page Setup Properties.
- Right-click and select Preview & Page Setup Properties.
- Press Alt+Enter.

In the six sections of the Preview & Page Setup Properties InfoBox, you can change page setup options, such as the orientation of the page, the margins around the border of the page, or the amount of data printed on the page. You can create headers and footers, insert information, show or hide sheet elements, and so on. When you have completed filling in and selecting options in the InfoBox, you can save your settings as a named style so that you can reuse them at a later time. The following sections contain brief descriptions of each Preview & Page Setup Properties InfoBox option.

**FIGURE 6.19** ▶

*1-2-3's Page Setup section of the Preview & Page Setup Properties InfoBox, the default*

**Portrait button**

**Landscape button**

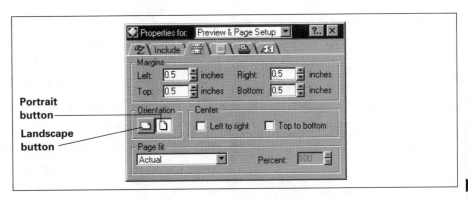

Editing a Spreadsheet

▶▶

*Ch.*
**6**

## ▶ *The Page Setup Section*

The options in the Page Setup section of the Preview & Page Setup Properties InfoBox are:

**Margins**    Set the Top, Bottom, Left, and/or Right margins from 0.5 to 32 inches. The default for each margin is 0.5 inches. When setting margins, be sure to leave enough room for the printed data. For example, if you set wide left and right margins that meet in the center of the page, there will be no space for the data.

**Orientation**    Click on the Portrait button to print the file with the same orientation as a letter or a memo; click on the Landscape button to print the file oriented as a standard sheet. Portrait orientation is longer than it is wide, and landscape orientation is wider than it is long. The default orientation (that is, the button that looks pressed) is Portrait.

**Center**    Check the Left to Right checkbox to center the sheet on the page between the left and right margins. Check the Top to Bottom checkbox to center the sheet on the page between the top and bottom margins. The default is two cleared checkboxes.

**Page Fit**    Click on this drop-down list box to display the choices described in Table 6.4.

▶ **TABLE 6.4**: *1-2-3 Page Setup Size Choices*

| Size | Description |
| --- | --- |
| Actual | Prints the selection, starting at the upper left corner of the page, in its full size. This is the default. |
| Fit All to Page | Fits the entire selection on a single page. |
| Fit Rows to Page | Fits the selection so that all its rows fit a single page. |
| Fit Columns to Page | Fits the selection so that all its columns fit a single page. |
| Custom | Sizes the selection to a percent (from 15 to 1000) that you enter in the Percent text/list box. |

# ▶ *The Text Section*

The options in the Text section of the Preview & Page Setup Properties InfoBox (see Figure 6.20) are:

**Font Properties For**     Open this drop-down list box to select the part of the sheet for which you want to specify font, font size, styles, or color. You can choose from Left Header (the default), Center Header, Right Header, Left Footer, Center Footer, Right Footer, Cell Notes, Formulas and Contents, and Script.

**Font Name**     From this scroll box, select one of the fonts installed on your computer and under Windows.

**Size**     From this scroll box, select a point size for the selected text. You also can type or select a point size from the option box/text box at the bottom of the scroll box.

**Style**     In this scroll box, click on effects with which you can enhance the selection. Styles include Normal, Bold, Italic, Underline, Double Underline, Wide Underline, and Strikethrough.

**Text Color**     Click on any part of this drop-down box to reveal a palette of colors from which you can choose for the selected text—either for display onscreen or for printing on a color printer installed on your computer system.

**FIGURE 6.20** ▶

*1-2-3's Text section of the Preview & Page Setup Properties InfoBox*

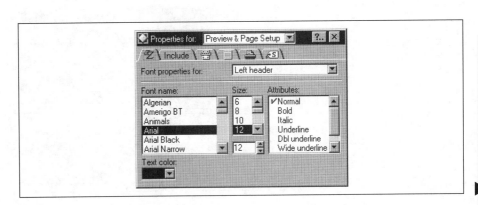

# ► The Include Section

The options in the Include section of the Preview & Page Setup Properties InfoBox (see Figure 6.21) are:

**What to Print**     Click on Current Sheet to print the current sheet in the file, Entire Workbook to print the entire file, or Selected Range (the default) to print a range of cells from either the current sheet or several sheets. Click on the Preview Sheet Selection button to view the range of cells that you have selected.

**Pages**     Click on the All option button to print all pages, or click on Pages to select pages to print. If you have clicked on Pages, select or type a starting page number in the From text/scroll box; the default is 1. Select or type an ending page number in the To text/scroll box; the default is 9999. Select or type the number of the first page to be printed in the Start Page Numbering With text/scroll box; the default is 1.

**Show**     Check or clear these list items to show or hide the Sheet Data; Charts, Maps, and Drawings; Cell Comments; Formulas, Cell Contents; Buttons; Sheet Grid Lines (the boundaries of the cells); Sheet Row and Column Frames (the column and row labels); and the Outline Frame.

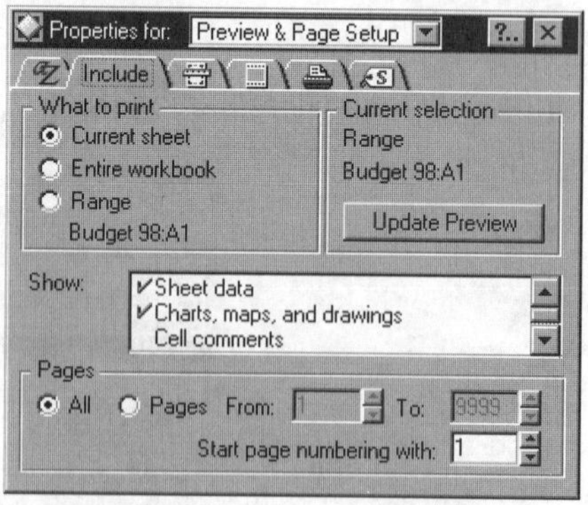

**FIGURE 6.21** ►

*1-2-3's Include section of the Preview & Page Setup Properties InfoBox*

# ▶ *The Headers and Footers Section*

The options in the Headers and Footers section of the Preview & Page Setup Properties InfoBox (see Figure 6.22) are:

**Headers and Footers**   In the Left Header, Center Header, Right Header, Left Footer, Center Footer, and Right Footer text boxes, you can type and insert text. Text in the leftmost boxes will align with the left margin, text in the center boxes will contain centered text, and text in the rightmost box will align with the right margin. The default is no header or footer. Table 6.5 describes the buttons with which you include specific text in a header or footer.

**FIGURE 6.22** ▶

*1-2-3's Headers and Footers section of the Preview & Page Setup Properties InfoBox*

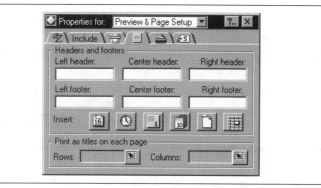

▶▶ **N O T E**

**Don't use | (vertical bar) in a header or footer; it's reserved for 1-2-3 processing. If you need to insert a character (@, +, #, ^, or \) that 1-2-3 uses as a header or footer code, type an apostrophe (') and then type the character.**

**Print As Titles on Each Page**   Select titles for rows and columns. In Columns, specify a cell containing a value displayed to the left of the column labels. In Rows, specify a cell containing a value displayed at the top of the row labels.

Editing a Spreadsheet

▶▶

Ch.

**6**

▶ **TABLE 6.5:** *1-2-3 Insert Buttons*

| Button | Inserted Placeholder Symbol | Click to insert: | Example |
|---|---|---|---|
| 📅 | @ | The current computer system date, formatted *dd/mm/yy* (where *dd* is the day, *mm* is the month, and *yy* is the year) | 12/23/97 |
| 🕐 | + | The current computer system time, formatted *hour:minutes:seconds* | 03:58 PM |
| ▦ | # | The current page number on every page of the workbook | 1 |
| ▦ | % | The current page number on every page of the selected sheet | 1 |
| 📄 | ^ | The name of the current workbook | BIZ3.123 |
| ▦ | \ | The contents of a cell or a range of cells that you type after the inserted backslash symbol (\), for example, \a:b6 | 4300 |

▶▶ **TIP**

**You can combine typed and inserted text. For example, to better identify the page number, type** Page, **press the spacebar to insert a space, and then click on the Page Number button. The result is Page** *n*, **where** *n* **represents the current page number.**

## ▶ *The Printer Section*

The options in the Printer section of the Preview & Page Setup Properties InfoBox (see Figure 6.23) are:

**Paper Size**    Open this drop-down list box and select the paper or envelope on which you'll be printing. Letter 81/2 x 11 in is the default paper size.

**Printer**    Click on this button to open the Windows Printer dialog box in which you can specify the name and set properties for the current printer.

**FIGURE 6.23** ▶

*1-2-3's Printer section of the Preview & Page Setup Properties InfoBox*

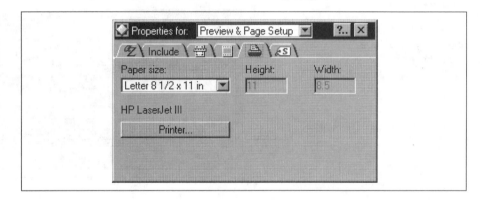

## ▶ *The Styles Section*

The options in the Styles section of the Preview & Page Setup Properties InfoBox (see Figure 6.24) are:

**Print Style Name**    A box in which the names of the saved print styles are displayed. The default print style is Default.

**Reset to Style**    Click on this button to reset the print styles for this print job to the default style.

**Create Style**    Click on this button to open the Create Style dialog box in which you can name and describe a print style based on the current options in the Preview & Page Setup Properties InfoBox. Clicking on OK saves the named style.

Editing a
Spreadsheet

Ch.
**6**

**Redefine Style**    Click on this button to open the Redefine Style dialog box in which you can redefine a previously named print style using the current options in the Preview & Page Setup Properties InfoBox.

**Manage Styles**    Click on this button to open the Manage Styles dialog box in which you can rename, delete, or copy a style from another workbook.

**Retrieve**    Click on this button to fetch a saved named style. In the Retrieve Named Settings dialog box, select the name of the style to be retrieved.

**FIGURE 6.24** ►

*1-2-3's Styles section of the Preview & Page Setup Properties InfoBox*

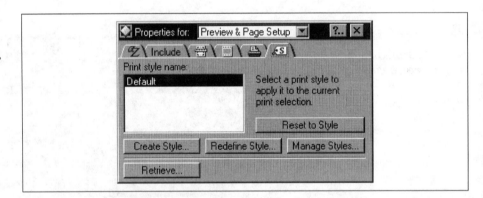

# ►► *Setting Page Breaks*

When you print a 1-2-3 sheet, file, or range, both the way in which you fill out the Page Setup dialog box and 1-2-3 defaults determine where one printed page ends and another begins. The break between pages is a *page break*. A 1-2-3-determined page break is a *soft page break*. When you want to decide the break between pages, you insert a *hard page break*— either horizontally (between rows) or vertically (between columns). You can insert a page break in two ways: by clicking on a SmartIcon or by choosing a menu command and following a few steps.

To insert a hard page break using a SmartIcon, click on a cell before which the break should occur. Then click on the Insert a Vertical Page Break SmartIcon or on the Insert a Horizontal Page Break SmartIcon.

To use a menu command to insert a hard page break, follow these steps:

1. Click on a cell before which the break should occur.

2. Click on the Range Properties SmartIcon, choose Range ➤ Range Properties, right-click and select Range Properties, or press Alt+Enter. 1-2-3 displays the Basics section of the Range Properties InfoBox.

3. Click on Break Page at Column to insert a vertical break, and click on Break Page at Row to insert a horizontal break.

4. Either click on OK or press Enter. 1-2-3 displays a line at the site of a hard page break, as shown in Figure 6.25.

To remove a hard page break, repeat the prior steps but remove the checkmark from the Break Page at Column or Break Page at Row checkbox.

# ▶▶ *Selecting Print Options*

In the "Viewing a Sheet As It Will Print" section of this chapter, you learned how to select print options from the Preview & Page Setup Properties InfoBox. If you have already prepared for printing, you can print the range, sheet, or workbook without returning to the Preview & Page Setup Properties InfoBox. Whether you decide to print from the Print Preview window, choose File ➤ Print, press Ctrl+P, or click on the Display the Print Dialog Box SmartIcon, you have a choice of options for printing in 1-2-3.

## ▶ *Printing from the Print Dialog Box*

This section briefly describes each 1-2-3 print option shown in the Print dialog box (see Figure 6.26). After selecting options in the dialog box, either click on OK or press Enter to start printing.

**FIGURE 6.25** ▶

*The Basics section of the Range Properties InfoBox with the Break Page at Column checkbox checked and a page break between columns G and H*

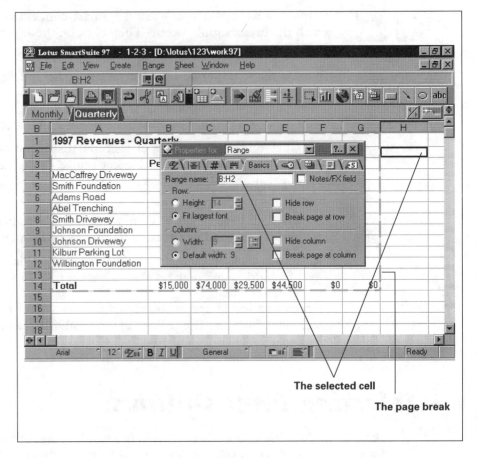

The selected cell

The page break

**Name**    A drop-down list box from which you can select a printer attached to your computer system and installed under Windows.

**Status**    Information about the selected printer and whether it is ready for printing.

**Type**    The name of the selected printer.

**Where**    The port to which the selected printer is attached.

**Comment**    Optional additional information about the selected printer.

**Properties**    A button on which you click to view or change attributes of the selected printer.

**FIGURE 6.26** ▶

*In the Print dialog box you can select options to customize printing of a range, a sheet, or a file.*

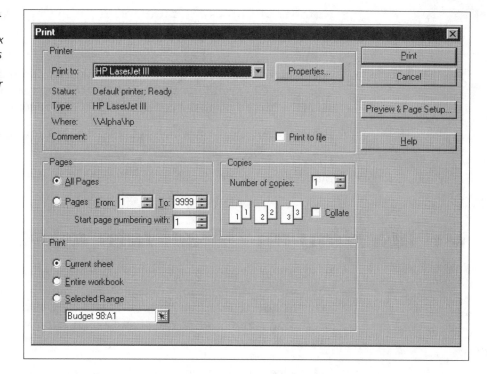

**Print to File**   A checkbox that when checked prints to a named file so that you can print the range, sheet, or workbook later with all its formats intact. A cleared checkbox is the default.

**All Pages**   An option button that when selected prints all the pages in the selection.

**Pages**   An option button that when selected prints a range of pages starting with the From page number in the first text/list box and ending with the page number in the To text/list box. Pages is the default.

**Current Sheet**   An option button that when selected prints only the sheet in which the insertion point is located.

**Entire Workbook**   An option button that when selected prints all the sheets in the current workbook.

**Selected Range**   An option button and range selector box from which you can choose to print a range from the current sheet.

Editing a Spreadsheet

▶▶

Ch.
6

**Number of Copies**     A text/option box in which you select or type the number of copies (from 1 to 9999) that you want to print.

**Collate**     A checkbox that when checked prints all the pages of a document, starting with the first page and ending with the last page before starting to print the next copy. A cleared checkbox prints all the copies of the first page, all the copies of the second page, and so on.

**Print**     A button on which you click to start printing.

**Preview & Page Setup**     A button on which you click to display the range, sheet, or workbook as it will print or to modify the page setup.

# ►► *Inserting an Object into a Sheet*

In the *Creating Pictures* chapter, you will learn how to create a drawing and insert it in a SmartSuite application. In the meantime, this section explains how to insert an object that you have already created into a sheet. For example, after you create a logo using Windows Paint, you can follow these steps:

1. Select the cell or location where the object is to be inserted.

2. Choose Create ➤ Object. 1-2-3 displays the Create Object dialog box (see Figure 6.27).

3. Click on the Create an Object from a File option button.

4. From the Object Type scroll list, select the object to be inserted and then click on OK.

5. In the new version of the Create Object dialog box (see Figure 6.28), click on the Browse button or type the path and filename in the File text box. Then click on OK. The mouse pointer changes to a crosshair.

6. Move the mouse pointer to the top left corner of the cell in which you want to insert the object. Drag to the bottom right corner of the cell. 1-2-3 inserts the object in the cell and adds handles to the cell.

7. Using the handles, adjust the cell height and width to allow for the proportions and dimensions of the object, as shown in Figure 6.29.

**FIGURE 6.27** ▶

*The Create Object dialog box with a bitmap object selected*

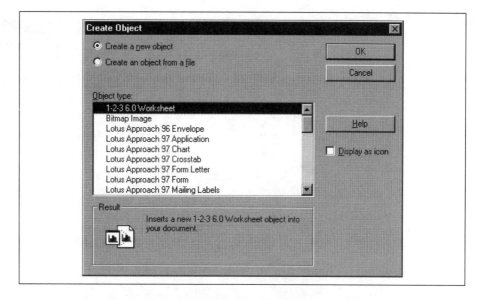

**FIGURE 6.28** ▶

*The Create Object dialog box showing the path and file of the bitmap to be inserted*

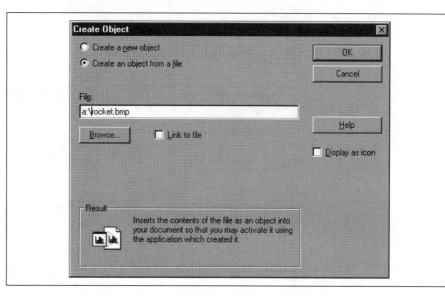

**8.** To move the object, drag it to its new location. Figure 6.30 shows the sample sheet with its new logo, a larger title, no grid lines, and number format changes.

Editing a
Spreadsheet

▶ ▶

*Ch.*

**6**

**FIGURE 6.29** ▶

*An object in the 1-2-3 sheet*

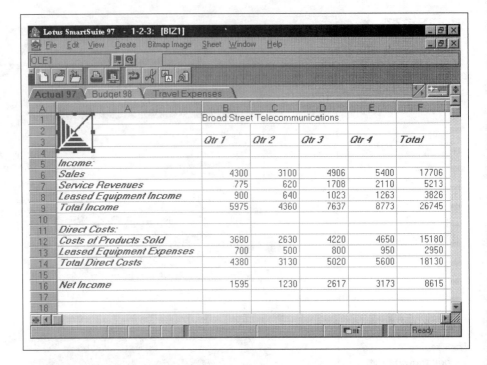

**FIGURE 6.30** ▶

*The sample sheet with a logo, larger title, no grid lines, and changes in number format*

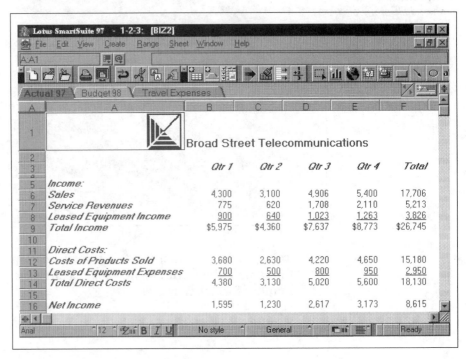

# CHAPTER 7

# Graphing
# Your Data

►► **T**his chapter continues your introduction to 1-2-3 by providing information about important 1-2-3 features: charting and mapping.

In the first part of the chapter, you'll learn how to create *charts*, pictorial representations of your sheet data, and find out about charting features in 1-2-3, Word Pro, Approach, and Freelance Graphics. In the second part, you'll find out how to graph data on a map of a particular region using 1-2-3's Map Assistant.

# ►► *Charting Data*

A sheet application is incomplete without the ability to create and edit charts. For example, our sample sheet is quite small; you can see the entire sheet on your screen. But, if you are working with a very wide sheet, a chart might present the data in a format that's easier to understand. In fact, you might even detect a trend or a relationship between numbers by viewing a chart.

In 1-2-3, you can chart data from a sheet using 12 chart types, including both two- and three-dimensional types. You can also create charts in Word Pro, Approach, and Freelance Graphics and change chart types using the Chart Properties InfoBox. The list below covers the Smart-Suite chart types, shows the SmartIcons that you can use to create them, and describes how best to use each type.

**Line**    Shows one or more series of data points over a period of time. Effective for charting many data points and for showing trends and changes and for comparing series of data points.

Individual values are de-emphasized. Line charts are available in 1-2-3, Word Pro, Approach, and Freelance Graphics. Line with Depth charts and three-dimensional line charts are available in Word Pro, Approach, and Freelance Graphics.

**Area**　Shows one or more series of data points over a period of time. The filled part of the chart emphasizes the total of the series. Individual values are de-emphasized. Area charts are available in 1-2-3, Word Pro, Approach, and Freelance Graphics. Area with Depth charts and 3D Area with Depth charts are available in Word Pro, Approach, and Freelance Graphics.

**Bar**　Shows individual values or magnitudes at a specific time and enables you to compare values easily. A vertical bar chart is the default chart type. A horizontal bar chart places a great emphasis on the flow of time. A stacked bar chart shows the relationship of each value to the whole. A variety of bar charts are available in 1-2-3, Word Pro, Approach, and Freelance Graphics.

**Pie**　Shows the parts of one data range as they compare with the whole. Note that a pie chart can show only positive values. Pie charts and three-dimensional pie charts are available in 1-2-3, Word Pro, Approach, and Freelance Graphics. Multiple pie charts are available in 1-2-3, Word Pro, and Freelance Graphics.

**XY (Scatter)**    Shows points of data drawn from two axes. If two sets of values correlate, data points cluster close to an imaginary line; otherwise, values appear all over the chart. XY (Scatter) charts are available in Word Pro and Freelance Graphics.

**Hi/Low/Close/Open (HLCO)**    Also known as a stock market chart, shows ranges of data and data points over time.

To create HLCO charts, you must arrange data series in this order:

*1.* One data series of high values shown as the top of a vertical line

*2.* One data series of low values shown as the bottom of a vertical line

*3.* One data series of closing values (optional) shown as a tick mark protruding to the right off the vertical line

*4.* One data series of opening values (optional) shown as a tick mark protruding left off the vertical line

*5.* One data series to plot in a bar chart (optional) below the HLCO portion

*6.* Additional data series to plot as lines (optional) below the HLCO portion

HLCO charts are available in 1-2-3, Word Pro, and Freelance Graphics.

**Mixed**    Shows data series in any combination of bar, line, and/or area in order to emphasize particular traits of each series and relationships between them. Choose Chart ➤ Ranges and select the chart type for each data series. Mixed charts are available in 1-2-3 and Freelance Graphics. Mixed with Depth charts and three-dimensional mixed charts are available in Word Pro and Freelance Graphics.

**Radar**    Related to line (unfilled) and area (filled) charts, shows values drawn around a central point on the chart. Emphasizes the symmetry of data. Radar charts are available in Word Pro and Freelance Graphics.

**Table (Number Grid)**    A sheet with the labels in one column and the values in another.

**Donut** (no button)    A version of a pie chart without a center portion.

 ►►**N O T E**

> **Some of the preceding SmartIcons are not on any of the SmartIcon sets added during SmartSuite installation. However, one or more SmartSuite applications make them available for an existing set or a new set. For information on adding a SmartIcon to an existing set or creating a new set, see the Customizing Your SmartSuite Environment appendix.**

Figure 7.1 shows a three-dimensional bar chart, which illustrates two data series over four quarters.

Most charts contain all or most of the elements shown in Table 7.1.

With 1-2-3, creating a chart is easy; all you do is choose one or more rows or columns, optionally choose the type of chart, and edit the chart elements. An extra bonus is that if the charted data change, the chart automatically changes as well; you don't have to re-create the chart with its new values.

**FIGURE 7.1** ▶

*A typical 3-D bar chart showing income and direct costs for one year*

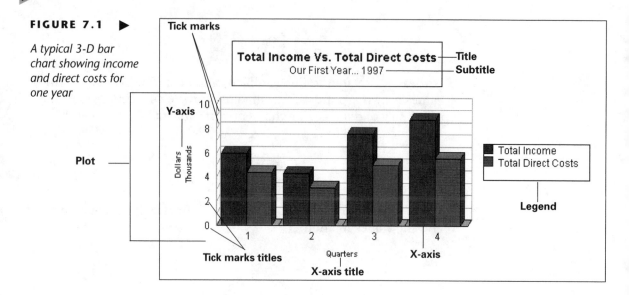

**TABLE 7.1:** *Elements of a Chart*

| Element | Description |
|---|---|
| Title | A chart heading. |
| Subtitle | A chart subheading. |
| X-axis | The horizontal axis, used for time or areas. |
| X-axis title | The title that you give to the x-axis. |
| Y-axis | The vertical axis, used for units of measure, such as years, weights, or currency. You can add a second y-axis to vertical bar charts, line charts, and area charts. |
| Y-axis title | The title that you give to the y-axis. |
| Z-axis | The vertical axis, used for depth on three-dimensional charts. |
| Z-axis title | The title that you give to the z-axis. |
| Plot | The core of the chart; the bars, lines, areas, or slices of pie representing the data series. Each bar, line, area, point, or entire pie chart is based on a single spreadsheet row or column. |
| Legend | The key, which shows each data series and its color and/or pattern. |

▶ **TABLE 7.1:** *Elements of a Chart (continued)*

| Element | Description |
| --- | --- |
| Tick mark | A short line that identifies a value on a chart axis. |
| Tick mark title | A title that identifies a specific tick mark. |
| Grid line | A line that parallels an axis and extends a tick mark across or down the chart. |
| Note | A comment added to a chart. |
| Table | Rows and columns containing the data on which the chart is based. |

▶▶ **N O T E**

**When you create a chart in Word Pro or Freelance Graphics, you fill in the data and let the application draw the chart using the same sets of dialog boxes in each application. To learn how to create a chart in Freelance Graphics, see "Creating a Chart" in the *Planning and Creating a Presentation* chapter. In Approach, the Chart Assistant leads you through the process using data and labels from the current database. Creating a chart using the Chart Assistant is covered in the "Creating a Chart in Approach" sidebar in this chapter.**

## ▶ *Planning a Chart*

Planning a chart involves three important factors: the data, the purpose, and the chart type. Be sure to select appropriate data and leave out unimportant or inappropriate data. For example, don't combine column or row totals with the cell contents that are totaled. Ask yourself what you want to prove with the chart and what you want to show those who will view the chart. Finally, be sure that the chart type matches the selected data and purpose. Once you have created the chart, you can try different chart types to see if they represent the information as accurately as possible.

## ▶ Selecting Data for a Chart

You can select contiguous (adjacent) or noncontiguous rows or columns. To choose contiguous rows or columns, move the cell pointer to the first cell in a selection, press the left mouse button, and drag to the last cell in a selection. To choose noncontiguous data (for example, all totals), drag to select the first applicable cells, press and hold down the Ctrl key, and drag to select the next group of cells. Repeat this process to include additional rows.

 ▶▶**N O T E**

> **Be sure to select the row and column labels that you want the chart to use as its own labels. If you don't select labels, 1-2-3 supplies its own generic labels (for example, Data A, Data B, and so on), and you'll have to edit them.**

## ▶ Creating a Chart

To create a chart, follow these steps:

1. Select one or more rows or columns.

 2. Choose Create ▶ Chart or click on the Create a Chart SmartIcon.

3. Move the mouse pointer to the starting point of the chart, press and hold down the left mouse button, and drag the mouse pointer diagonally to the ending point of the chart. (If necessary, you can always adjust the chart dimensions at a later time.)

 ▶▶**T I P**

> **To use 1-2-3 default chart dimensions, simply click on the top left corner, or starting point, of the chart.**

**4.** Release the mouse button. 1-2-3 draws the chart within the boundaries that you have set. Figure 7.2 shows the resulting chart, with all its defaults.

**FIGURE 7.2** ▶

*A default chart that contains two data series: Total Income and Total Direct Costs*

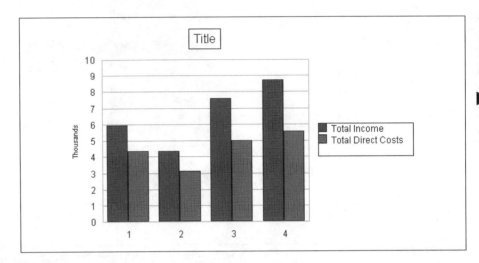

## ▶ *Editing a Chart Using the InfoBox*

As you can see, an unedited 1-2-3 chart is almost good enough to include in a report without further changes. To make a chart's contents more understandable and pleasing, however, it's a good idea to edit and enhance it. This section will review the procedures necessary for adding titles, changing the chart type, and editing other elements.

When you double-click within a chart in 1-2-3, double-click in a chart in Word Pro, or display a chart view in Approach, a context-sensitive Chart menu (see Figure 7.3) appears in the menu bar. Most of the Chart menu commands are identical and behave identically, regardless of the application. Others are specific to their application. Selecting many Chart menu commands opens an InfoBox for the element that you want to change.

To open the Chart Properties InfoBox (see Figure 7.4) in 1-2-3, from which you can edit or enhance any part of the chart, click on the Chart Properties SmartIcon or select a Properties command from the Chart menu. Then select the part of the chart to be changed from the Properties For drop-down list box.

**FIGURE 7.3** ▶

*The 1-2-3 Chart menu and an open submenu*

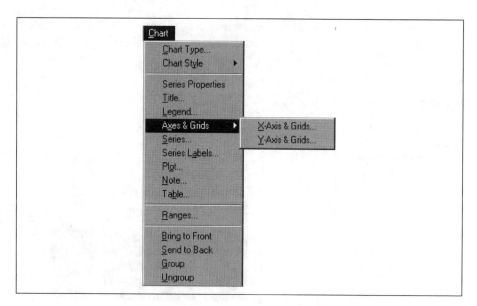

**FIGURE 7.4** ▶

*The 1-2-3 Chart Properties InfoBox with an open Properties For drop-down list box*

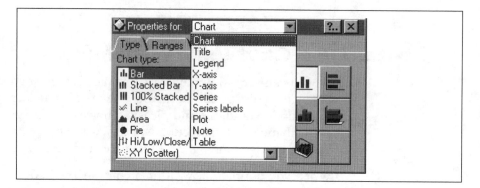

Table 7.2 lists the names of one or more chart elements on which you click, the Chart menu commands you can choose, and the names and sections of the InfoBoxes in which you select options and enter information.

When you click or double-click on a chart (depending on the application), the Chart SmartIcons bar appears onscreen. Like the Chart menu, most Chart SmartIcons bars (see Figures 7.5, 7.6, 7.7, and 7.8) contain the same SmartIcons; a few SmartIcons are related specifically to the applications in which they appear. Table 7.3 illustrates each SmartIcon, names the equivalent Chart menu command, and provides a description.

▶ **TABLE 7.2:** *1-2-3 Chart Elements, Editing Commands, and InfoBoxes*

| Chart Element | Command | InfoBox: Sections |
|---|---|---|
| Title | Chart ➤ Title | Title Properties: Text, Lines and Color, Options |
| Legend | Chart ➤ Legend | Legend Properties: Text, Lines and Color, Options |
| X-axis and X-axis grid | Chart ➤ Axes & Grids ➤ X-Axis & Grids | X-axis Properties: Text, Titles, Ticks, Labels, Grids, Scale |
| Y-axis and Y-axis grid | Chart ➤ Axes & Grids ➤ Y-Axis & Grids | Y-axis Properties: Text, Format, Titles, Ticks, Labels, Grids, Scale |
| Series | Chart ➤ Series | Series Properties: Lines and Color, Options, Pictures |
| Series Labels | Chart ➤ Series Labels | Series Labels Properties: Text, Options |
| Plot | Chart ➤ Plot | Plot Properties: Lines and Color, Options, Layout |
| Note | Chart ➤ Note | Note Properties: Text, Lines and Color, Options |
| Table | Chart ➤ Table | Table Properties: Text, Lines and Color, Format, Options |
| Ranges | Chart ➤ Ranges | Chart Properties: Type, Ranges, Styles, Lines and Color, Basics |

**FIGURE 7.5** ▶

*The 1-2-3 Chart SmartIcons bar*

**FIGURE 7.6** ▶

*The Word Pro Chart SmartIcons bar*

FIGURE 7.7 ►

The Approach Chart
SmartIcons bar

FIGURE 7.8 ►

The Freelance
Graphics Chart
SmartIcons bar

► **TABLE 7.3:** *SmartSuite Chart SmartIcons*

| SmartIcon | Menu Command and Option | Description (application) |
|---|---|---|
| | Create ➤ Chart | Creates a new chart (*all applications*) |
| | Chart ➤ Chart Properties | Opens the Type section of the Chart Properties InfoBox (*1-2-3*) |
| | Chart ➤ Chart Type | Opens the Type section of the Chart Properties InfoBox (*all applications*) |
| | Chart ➤ Chart Type ➤ Apply | Opens the Styles section of the Chart Properties InfoBox (*all applications*) |
| | Chart ➤ Axes & Grids ➤ Y-Axis & Grids; click on the Grids tab; check the Major Intervals checkbox | Inserts horizontal grid lines (*all applications*) |
| | Chart ➤ Axes & Grids ➤ X-Axis & Grids; click on the Grids tab; check the Major Intervals checkbox | Inserts vertical grid lines (*all applications*) |

**TABLE 7.3:** *SmartSuite Chart SmartIcons (continued)*

| SmartIcon | Menu Command and Option | Description (application) |
|---|---|---|
| | Chart ➤ Series; click on the Options tab (if necessary); click on the range selector **or** Chart ➤ Edit Data **or** Chart ➤ Data Source | Returns to the sheet to show the data (*1-2-3*) **or** opens the Edit Data dialog box so that you can edit the data comprising the chart (*Word Pro, Freelance Graphics*) or opens the Chart Data Source Assistant (*Approach*) |
| | Chart ➤ Note; type one to three lines of text in the Options section of the Note Properties InfoBox | Inserts a note or a comment within the borders of the chart (*all applications*) |
| | Chart ➤ Legend; click on the Options tab (if necessary); check the Show Legend checkbox | Displays the legend within the borders of the chart (*all applications*) |
| | Chart ➤ Table; click on the Options tab (if necessary); check the Show Data Table checkbox | Opens the Table Properties InfoBox so that you can replace the legend with a data table under the chart (*all applications*) |
| | Chart ➤ Title | Opens the Options section of the Title Properties InfoBox so that you can edit the chart title (*all applications*) |

## Working with Chart Titles

You can add or edit a chart title in several ways:

- Click on the title and click on the Chart Properties SmartIcon.
- Click on the title and choose Chart ➤ Title Properties.
- Choose Chart ➤ Title.

- From within a Chart Properties InfoBox, open the Properties For drop-down list box, and select Title.

- Double-click on the title in the chart, and type a new title, or select a font, a font size, or a style from the Status bar.

- Right-click on the chart, choose Chart Properties, open the Properties For drop-down list box, and select Title.

Unless you double-click on the title in the chart, the Options section of the Title Properties InfoBox (see Figure 7.9) appears. Type a title in the Line 1 text box, and type subtitle lines in the Line 2 and Line 3 text boxes. In the Text and Lines and Color sections, you can change font and border attributes. For information about using the Text section and Lines and Color section of SmartSuite InfoBoxes, see the *Editing in SmartSuite Applications* chapter.

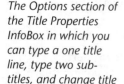

**FIGURE 7.9** ▶

*The Options section of the Title Properties InfoBox in which you can type a one title line, type two subtitles, and change title placement*

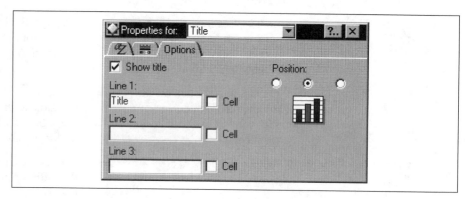

## Working with Legends

You can add or edit a legend in several ways:

- Click on the legend and click on the Chart Properties SmartIcon.

- Click on the legend and choose Chart ➤ Legend Properties.

- Choose Chart ➤ Legend.

- From within a Chart Properties InfoBox, open the Properties For drop-down list box, and select Legend.

- Double-click on a legend label in the chart, and type a new title, or select a font, a font size, or a style from the Status bar.

• Right-click on the chart, choose Chart Properties, open the Properties For drop-down list box, and select Legend.

Unless you double-click on a legend element in the chart, the Options section of the Legend Properties InfoBox (see Figure 7.10) appears. For information about using the Text section and Lines and Color section of SmartSuite InfoBoxes, see the *Editing in SmartSuite Applications* chapter.

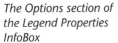

**FIGURE 7.10** ▶

*The Options section of the Legend Properties InfoBox*

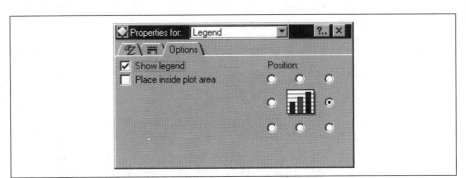

The Options section contains the following options:

**Show Legend**     Check this checkbox to reveal or hide the legend. In some cases, you can hide the legend to reveal a data table instead.

**Place Inside Plot Area**     Check this checkbox to move the legend inside the plot area.

**Position**     Click on one of these option buttons to move the legend to an area above, below, on the left side, or on the right side of the plot. The default legend placement is on the right side of the plot.

## Editing the X-Axis

To edit the x-axis:

• Click on an x-axis label and click on the Chart Properties SmartIcon.

• Click on an x-axis label and choose Chart ➤ X-Axis Properties.

- Choose Chart ➤ Axes & Grids ➤ X-Axis & Grids.

- From within a Chart Properties InfoBox, open the Properties For drop-down list box, and select X-Axis.

- Right-click on the chart, choose Chart Properties, open the Properties For drop-down list box, and select X-Axis.

The X-axis Properties InfoBox is composed of six sections: Text, Titles, Ticks, Labels, Grids, and Scale. For information about using the Text section of SmartSuite InfoBoxes, see the *Editing in SmartSuite Applications* chapter.

The Titles section (see Figure 7.11) contains the following options:

**Show Title**     Check this checkbox to show the x-axis title typed in the text box; clear it to hide the title. A checked checkbox is the default.

**Cell**     Check this checkbox to change either or both the Show Title or Show Subtitle text box to a box with a range selector so that you can use the contents of a cell or a range as the title or subtitle.

**Show Subtitle**     Check this checkbox to show the one- or two-line subtitle typed in the text box; clear it to hide subtitle lines. A checked checkbox is the default.

**Based on Scale**     Rather than using a typed subtitle, if you click on this option button, 1-2-3 automatically displays a subtitle based on the x-axis unit, which must be a number greater than 1,000.

**Subtitle Position**     Open this drop-down list box and select how the subtitle is displayed: On Same Line with Title or On Separate Line.

**Orientation**     The default orientation is horizontal. This drop-down list is not available.

Graphing
Your Data

FIGURE 7.11 ▶

*The Titles section of the X-axis Properties InfoBox*

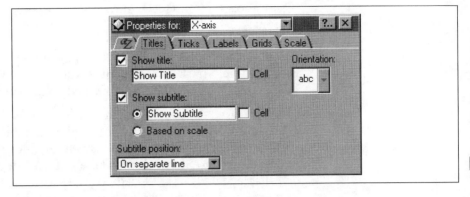

The Ticks section (see Figure 7.12) contains the following options:

**Show Axis Line**   Check this checkbox to display the x-axis line; clear it to hide the x-axis line. (The bottom of the plot can look like the x-axis line, whether the x-axis line is displayed or hidden.)

**Major Intervals**   Check this checkbox to show major intervals using tick marks.

**Position**   From this drop-down list box, select the position of the major interval tick marks: None (the default), Outside, Inside, or Across.

FIGURE 7.12 ▶

*The Ticks section of the X-axis Properties InfoBox*

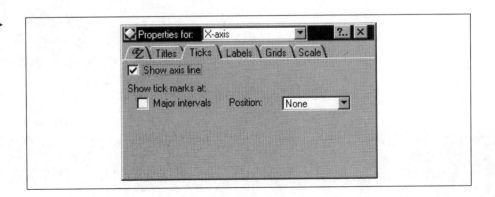

The Labels section (see Figure 7.13) contains the following options:

**Show Labels Every *n* Ticks**     Displays labels with tick marks every *n*th tick mark. If you want to substitute an x-axis title for labels, clear this checkbox. A checked checkbox is the default.

**Overlapping**     From this drop-down list box, select how labels are displayed: Automatic (let the application decide how to display), Stagger (display labels on two lines, alternating from one line to the next), Slant (display labels at a 45-degree angle), Vertical (display labels at a 90-degree angle with the first letter at the bottom), and Down (display labels at a 90-degree angle with the first letter at the top). Automatic is the default.

**Character Limit**     Check this checkbox and type the maximum number of characters for a label.

**Range**     Use the range selector to select a range to be used for labeling.

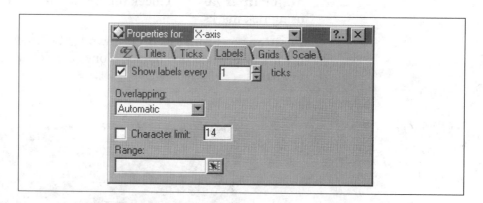

The Grids section (see Figure 7.14) contains the following option:

**Major Intervals**     Check this checkbox to show vertical grid lines at major intervals. Clear it to remove vertical grid lines. A cleared checkbox is the default.

**FIGURE 7.14** ▶

*The Grids section of
the X-axis Properties
InfoBox*

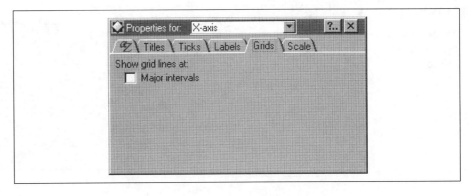

The Scale section (see Figure 7.15) contains the following options:

**Maximum**    Check this checkbox and type the maximum value
for the axis. This is active only for scatter charts.

**Minimum**    Check this checkbox and type the minimum value
for the axis. This is active only for scatter charts.

**Major Ticks**    Check this checkbox and type the value for major interval tick marks on the axis. This is active only for scatter
charts.

**Minor Ticks**    Check this checkbox and type the value for minor tick marks (enabled in the Ticks section of this InfoBox) on
the axis. This is active only for scatter charts.

**Intercept**    Check this checkbox and type the value for the *intercept*, the intersection of the x-axis and the y-axis.

**Direction**    From this drop-down list box, choose an Ascending or Descending direction for the x-axis.

**Position**    From this drop-down list box, choose the position of
the x-axis: Bottom, Top, or Both.

**Type**    From this drop-down list box, choose the type of scale:
Linear, Log, or 100%. This is active only for scatter charts.

**Units**    From this drop-down list box, choose the type of
numeric units, Auto, None, and Other, and from Thousands to
Trillionths. This is active only for scatter charts.

**FIGURE 7.15** ▶

*The Scale section of
the X-axis Properties
InfoBox*

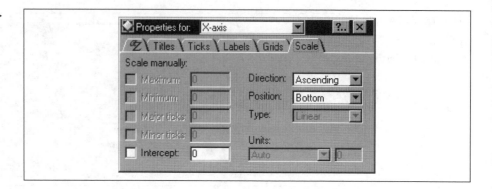

## Editing the Y-Axis

To edit the y-axis:

- Click on a y-axis label and click on the Chart Properties SmartIcon.

- Click on a y-axis label and choose Chart ➤ Y-Axis Properties.

- Choose Chart ➤ Axes & Grids ➤ Y-Axis & Grids.

- From within a Chart Properties InfoBox, open the Properties For drop-down list box, and select Y-Axis.

- Right-click on the chart, choose Chart Properties, open the Properties For drop-down list box, and select Y-Axis.

The Y-axis Properties InfoBox is composed of seven sections: Text, Format, Titles, Ticks, Labels, Grids, and Scale. For information about using the Text section of SmartSuite InfoBoxes, see the *Editing in SmartSuite Applications* chapter. To learn how to use the Format section, see the *Entering Formulas and Data* chapter.

The Titles section (see Figure 7.16) contains the following options:

**Show Title**    Check this checkbox to show the y-axis title typed in the text box; clear it to hide the title. A checked checkbox is the default.

**Cell**    Check this checkbox to change either or both the Show Title or Show Subtitle text box to a box with a range selector so that you can use the contents of a cell or range as the title or subtitle.

**Show Subtitle**   Check this checkbox to show the one- or two-line subtitle typed in the text box; clear it to hide subtitle lines. A checked checkbox is the default.

**Based on Scale**   Rather than using a typed subtitle, if you click on this option button, 1-2-3 automatically displays a subtitle based on the y-axis unit, which must be a number greater than 1,000.

**Subtitle Position**   Open this drop-down list box and select how the subtitle is displayed: On Same Line with Title or On Separate Line.

**Orientation**   From this drop-down list, select the orientation of the title: vertical with the first character of the title at the bottom (the default), horizontal, or vertical with the first character of the title at the top.

**FIGURE 7.16** ▶

*The Titles section of the Y-axis Properties InfoBox with the Orientation drop-down list box open*

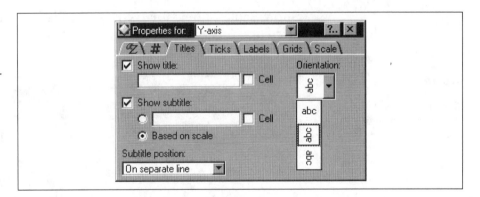

The Ticks section (see Figure 7.17) contains the following options:

**Show Axis Line**   Check this checkbox to display the y-axis line; clear it to hide the y-axis line.

**Major Intervals**   Check this checkbox to show major intervals using tick marks.

**Minor Intervals**   Check this checkbox to show minor intervals using tick marks.

**Position**   From this drop-down list box, select the position of the major and minor interval tick marks: None (the default), Outside, Inside, or Across.

**FIGURE 7.17** ▶

*The Ticks section of
the Y-axis Properties
InfoBox*

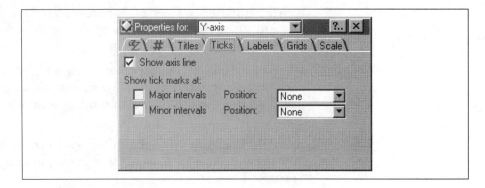

The Labels section (see Figure 7.18) contains the following options:

**Show Labels Every *n* Ticks**     Displays labels with tick marks
every *n*th tick mark. If you want to substitute a y-axis title for labels, clear this checkbox. A checked checkbox is the default.

**Show Scale Labels for Extra Grid Lines**     Displays extra
grid lines. A checked checkbox is the default.

**FIGURE 7.18** ▶

*The Labels section of
the Y-axis Properties
InfoBox*

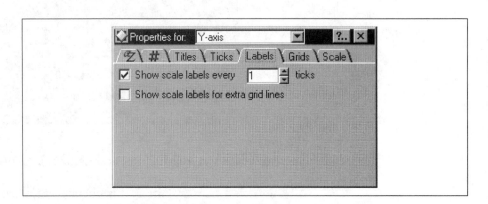

The Grids section (see Figure 7.19) contains the following options:

**Major Intervals**     Shows horizontal grid lines at major intervals. Clear to remove horizontal grid lines. A cleared checkbox is
the default.

**Minor Intervals**     Shows horizontal grid lines at minor intervals. Clear to remove horizontal grid lines. A cleared checkbox is
the default.

**Shown *n* Extra**    Type or select a value representing the number of horizontal grid lines on the chart. Valid values vary depending on the chart.

**Line Number**    Type or select an identifier for a line. Valid values vary depending on the chart.

**Line Value**    Select a starting line value for the number in the Line Number text/option box. Values vary depending on the chart.

**FIGURE 7.19** ▶

*The Grids section of the Y-axis Properties InfoBox*

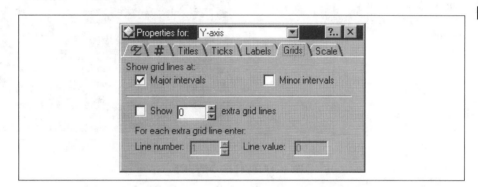

The Scale section (see Figure 7.20) contains the following options:

**Maximum**    Check this checkbox and type the maximum value for the axis.

**Minimum**    Check this checkbox and type the minimum value for the axis.

**Major Ticks**    Check this checkbox and type the value for major interval tick marks on the axis.

**Minor Ticks**    Check this checkbox and type the value for minor tick marks (enabled in the Ticks section of this InfoBox) on the axis.

**Intercept**    This option is available only for the x-axis.

**Direction**    From this drop-down list box, choose an Ascending or Descending direction for the y-axis.

**Position**    From this drop-down list box, choose the position of the y-axis: Left, Right, or Both.

**Type**    From this drop-down list box, choose the type of scale: Linear, Log, or 100%.

**Units**    From this drop-down list box, choose the type of numeric units, Auto, None, and Other, and from Thousands to Trillionths. Accept or type a value in the text box.

**FIGURE 7.20** ►

*The Scale section of the Y-axis Properties InfoBox*

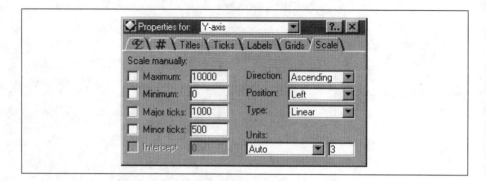

## Working with Series

You can add or edit a series in the chart in several ways:

- Click on a series and click on the Chart Properties SmartIcon.
- Click on a series and choose Chart ➤ Series Properties.
- Choose Chart ➤ Series.
- From within a Chart Properties InfoBox, open the Properties For drop-down list box, and select Series.
- Double-click on a series.
- Right-click on the chart, choose Chart Properties, open the Properties For drop-down list box, and select Series.

The Series Properties InfoBox is composed of three sections: Lines and Color, Options, and Pictures. For information about using the Lines and Color section of SmartSuite InfoBoxes, see the *Editing in SmartSuite Applications* chapter.

The Options section (see Figure 7.21) contains the following options:

**Series**  From this drop-down list box, select the series on which you want to work. If you clicked on a series, its name is selected.

**Show Series**  Check this checkbox to display the series. Clear the checkbox to hide the series. The default is a checked checkbox.

**Plot Against 2nd Y-axis**  Click on this checkbox to plot the series against a second y-axis on the right side of the plot.

**Mixed Type**  From this drop-down list box, select the type of chart with which you would like to plot the selected series. You can choose Area, Bar (the default), or Line.

**Legend Label**  In this text box, type a custom name for the label for the selected series.

► ►
Ch.
7

**FIGURE 7.21** ▶

*The Options section of the Series Properties InfoBox in which you can reveal or hide a series, define a second y-axis, specify a mixed type, or type a custom label*

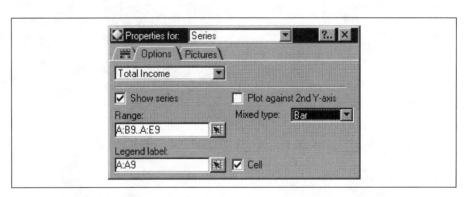

The Pictures section (see Figure 7.22), which is used to specify options for a BMP picture that has replaced a bar (see Figure 7.23), contains the following options:

**Series**  From this drop-down list box, select the series on which you want to work. If you clicked on a series, its name is selected.

**Paste Picture**  Click on this button to paste a picture from the Windows Clipboard to replace the selected series.

**Delete Picture**  Click on this button to replace the picture with the original look of the series.

**Picture Size**    Click on an option button to change the look of the picture.

- **Stretch to Fill Bar** stretches the picture in its original size to fit the bar. This can distort the picture.
- **Preserve Aspect Ratio** keeps the original proportions of the picture. This is the default.
- **One Picture Equals *n* Units** changes the look of the picture from many duplicates (a low number) to a few duplicates (a high number). Selecting this option with the original *n* value is the same as clicking on Preserve Aspect Ratio.

**FIGURE 7.22** ▶

*The Pictures section of the Series Properties InfoBox in which you can edit a picture with which you replaced a bar in a Bar chart*

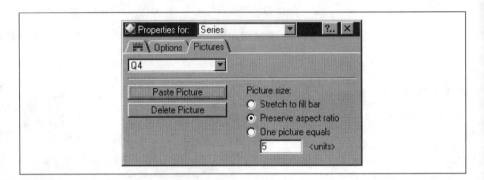

**FIGURE 7.23** ▶

*A plot with the Windows bubbles bitmap picture replacing a bar*

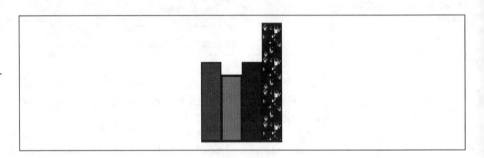

## Adding and Editing Series Labels

You can add or edit series labels in a chart in several ways:

- Click on a series and click on the Chart Properties SmartIcon. Then select Series Labels from the Properties For drop-down list box.

- Click on a series and choose Chart ➤ Series Properties. Then select Series Labels from the Properties For drop-down list box.

- Choose Chart ➤ Series Labels.

- From within a Chart Properties InfoBox, open the Properties For drop-down list box, and select Series Labels.

- Right-click on the chart, choose Chart Properties, open the Properties For drop-down list box, and select Labels.

The Series Labels Properties InfoBox is composed of two sections: Text and Options. For information about using the Text section of Smart-Suite InfoBoxes, see the *Editing in SmartSuite Applications* chapter.

The Options section (see Figure 7.24) contains the following options:

**Series**   From this drop-down list box, select the series that you want to label. If you clicked on a series, its name is selected.

**Show Value Labels**   Check this checkbox to label a series using the data values. A cleared checkbox is the default.

**Show Percent Labels**   Check this checkbox to label a series using the percentages of the data values. A cleared checkbox is the default.

**Show Labels from Range**   Check this checkbox and, using the range selector, select a range with which to label a series.

**Position**   From this drop-down list box, select the location of the series label: above the series or on the series.

**Orientation**   From this drop-down list box, select a label orientation: horizontal, two types of vertical, or two types of slanted. If you choose a vertical orientation, the labels appear on the bars of a Bar chart.

**FIGURE 7.24** ▶

*The Options section of the Series Labels Properties InfoBox in which you can label a series or edit or place the label*

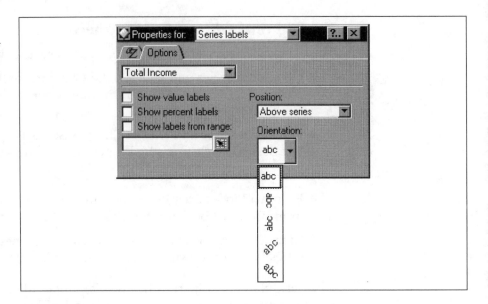

## Working with the Plot

You can work with the plot in several ways:

- Click within the plot and click on the Chart Properties SmartIcon.
- Click within the plot and choose Chart ➤ Plot Properties.
- Choose Chart ➤ Plot.
- From within a Chart Properties InfoBox, open the Properties For drop-down list box, and select Plot.
- Right-click on the chart, choose Chart Properties, open the Properties For drop-down list box, and select Plot.

The Plot Properties InfoBox is composed of three sections: Lines and Color, Options, and Layout. For information about using the Lines and Color section of SmartSuite InfoBoxes, see the *Editing in Smart-Suite Applications* chapter.

The Options section (see Figure 7.25) contains the following options:

**Default Settings**   Click on this option button to return to the default settings for the chart.

**Custom Settings**    Click on this option button to keep custom settings that you have selected for this chart. This is the default.

**Paste Picture**    Click on this button to paste a BMP file into the plot. Note that choosing Edit ➤ Paste or pressing Ctrl+V does *not* paste the file.

**Delete Picture**    Click on this button to delete the pasted BMP file from the plot.

**FIGURE 7.25** ►

*The Options section of the Plot Properties InfoBox in which you can change the position of the plot or paste or delete a BMP file*

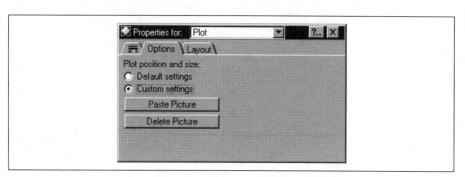

The Layout section (see Figure 7.26) contains the following options:

**Gap %**    From this drop-down list box, select the gap between a series in a Bar chart. Valid values range from 0 to 100. The default is 20. For information about plot options for other types of charts, refer to the help facility.

**Overlap %**    Check this checkbox to overlap the bars in a bar chart by a certain percentage, from 0 (the default) to 100.

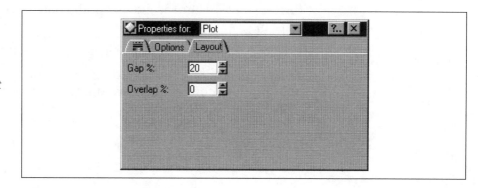

For information about plot options for other types of charts, refer to the help facility.

## Adding Notes to a Chart

You can emphasize a particular part of a chart by adding notes or comments. You can add a note in several ways:

- Click within the chart and click on the Chart Properties SmartIcon. Then choose Note from the Properties For drop-down list box.

- Click within the chart and choose Chart ➤ Chart Properties. Then choose Note from the Properties For drop-down list box.

- Choose Chart ➤ Note.

- From within a Chart Properties InfoBox, open the Properties For drop-down list box, and select Note.

- Right-click on the chart, choose Chart Properties, open the Properties For drop-down list box, and select Note.

The Note Properties InfoBox is composed of three sections: Text, Lines and Color, and Options. For information about using the Text section and the Lines and Color section of SmartSuite InfoBoxes, see the *Editing in SmartSuite Applications* chapter.

The Options section (see Figure 7.27) contains the following options:

**Show Note**   Check this checkbox to reveal the note. Clear the checkbox to hide the note. A checked checkbox is the default.

**Line 1**   Type the first line of the note or comment in this text box.

**Line 2**   Type the second line of the note or comment in this text box.

**Line 3**   Type the third line of the note or comment in this text box.

**Position**   Click on one of these option buttons to place the note at the bottom of the chart, on the left side, in the center, or on the right side (the default).

**FIGURE 7.27** ▶

*The Options section of
the Note Properties
InfoBox in which you
can type a three-line
note and change its
position*

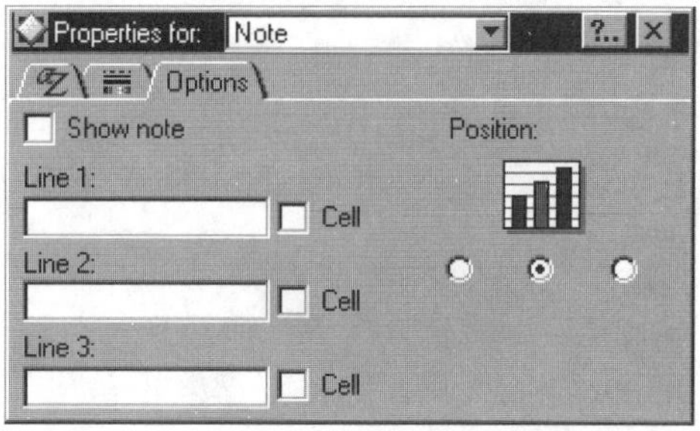

To draw a line and/or an arrow from a text box to another element in
the chart, click on the Draw a Forward-Pointing Arrow, Draw a Double-
Headed Arrow, or Draw a Line SmartIcon, drag a line between the text
box and the chart, and release the left mouse button. You can move or
size the text box or the arrow until the chart looks just the way you
want it.

 ▶▶**T I P**

> **When you have trouble selecting a text box, select
> another part of a chart (for example, the legend), and
> then return to the text box and click on it.**

▶ ## CREATING A CHART WITH THE APPROACH
CHART ASSISTANT

Approach provides the Chart Assistant, which leads you through
the chart creation process. To create a chart, choose Create ➤
Chart and then fill in the sections of the Chart Assistant dialog
box. Approach creates a new view in which it inserts the new chart.

Once you have created a chart, you have plenty of opportunity to
edit and enhance it. If you want to change the chart at a later time,
open the view in which the chart is located and choose a menu
command from the Chart menu or click on Chart SmartIcons.
Approach will open an InfoBox with which you can edit all the elements of the chart.

If the Chart SmartIcons are dimmed or if the message in the Info-Box states that your selection has no properties, double-click on a chart element. This action should reveal an InfoBox for a chart element.

In the first section of the Chart Assistant dialog box, you can type a chart name and select a layout (that is, chart type) and style (two-dimensional or three-dimensional). Click on Next or on the Step 2: X-Axis tab to display the next section of the dialog box. Notice that the Chart Assistant does not "undim" the Done button until you select all the options that make up the chart.

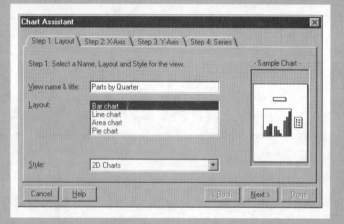

In the second section of the Chart Assistant dialog box, you select the field for the x-axis. The sample chart illustration shows an oval representing the x-axis. Click on Next or on the Step 3: Y-Axis tab to display the next section of the dialog box. If you want to return to the first section of the dialog box to change an option, click on Back.

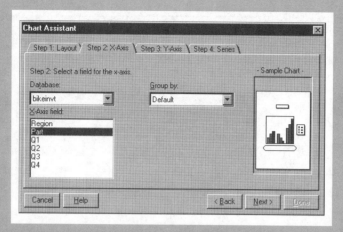

In the third section of the Chart Assistant dialog box, you select
one or more fields for the y-axis. To select a field, click on it and
then click on the Add button. To remove a selected field, click on it
in the box in the middle of the dialog box; then click on the Remove button. To change the mathematical operation performed on
the y-axis fields, select from the Chart The drop-down list box. After you complete the selection, click on Next or on the Step 4: Series tab to display the next section of the dialog box. If you don't
plan on selecting a series, click on the Done button.

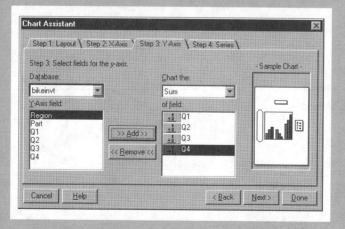

In the fourth section of the Chart Assistant dialog box, you select a series with which the legend will be labeled. Optionally, select a group by which the field will be arranged along the x-axis.

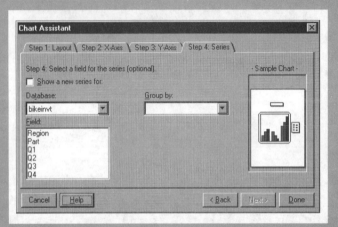

After you click on Done, Approach displays a chart, which you can edit or enhance.

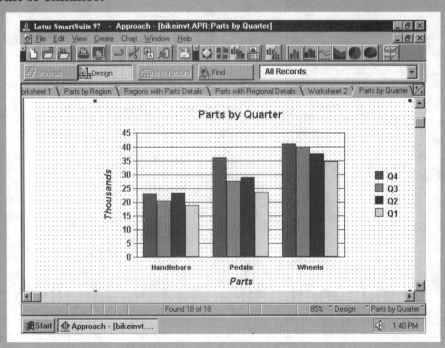

## Adding a Data Table

A data table, with which you can replace the legend, presents numeric information in addition to the column and row labels:

| | 1 | 2 | 3 | 4 |
|---|---|---|---|---|
| ■ Total Income | 5975 | 4360 | 7637 | 8773 |
| ■ Total Direct Costs | 4380 | 3130 | 5020 | 5600 |

To replace the legend with a data table:

- Click within the chart and click on the Chart Properties SmartIcon. Then choose Table from the Properties For drop-down list box.

- Click within the chart and choose Chart ➤ Chart Properties. Then choose Table from the Properties For drop-down list box.

- Click on an existing table and choose Chart ➤ Table Properties.

- Choose Chart ➤ Table.

- From within a Chart Properties InfoBox, open the Properties For drop-down list box, and select Table.

- Right-click on the chart, choose Chart Properties, open the Properties For drop-down list box, and select Table.

The Table Properties InfoBox is composed of four sections: Text, Lines and Color, Format, and Options. For information about using the Text section and Lines and Color section of SmartSuite InfoBoxes, see the *Editing in SmartSuite Applications* chapter. To learn how to use the Format section, see the *Entering Formulas and Data* chapter.

The Options section (see Figure 7.28) contains the following options:

**Show Data Table**    Check this checkbox to replace the legend with a data table; clear it to replace the data table with the legend, if you haven't hidden the legend using the Legend Properties InfoBox. A cleared checkbox is the default.

**Show Row Headers**    Check this checkbox to reveal or hide row headers in a data table. If the Show Data Table checkbox is checked, this checkbox is checked by default.

**Show Column Headers**    Check this checkbox to reveal or hide column headers in a data table. If the Show Data Table checkbox is checked, this checkbox is checked by default.

**Show Column Totals**    Check this checkbox to reveal or hide column totals and a column total header in a data table. The default is a cleared checkbox.

**Column Totals Label**    In this text box, type a column totals label, if you want to change from the default supplied from the sheet. The default is a cleared text box.

**Show Series in Table**    Check this checkbox to show the data series in the table. A checked checkbox is the default.

**Show Series in Chart**    Check this checkbox to show the data series in the chart. A checked checkbox is the default.

**FIGURE 7.28** ▶

*The Options section of the Table Properties InfoBox for a typical data table*

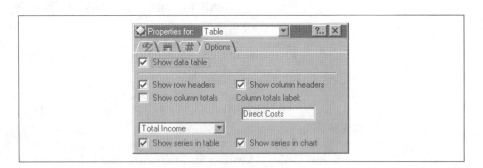

# FREELANCE GRAPHICS SMARTCHARTS

**Freelance Graphics SmartMasters content topic pages include every page style, including charts—some with the standard Click Here to Create Chart block and others with a miniature version of a chart and a Click Here to Create Chart block with specific instructions. A chart with predefined elements, such as labels, legends, and other attributes, is a SmartChart.**

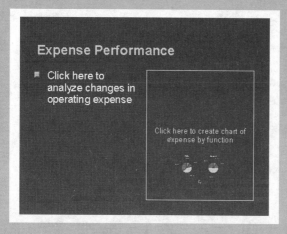

Click on the **Click Here to Create Chart** block to open the Edit
Data dialog box. Simply fill in the data as you would for any other
Freelance Graphics chart, edit the predefined labels if you wish,
and click on OK to close the dialog box.

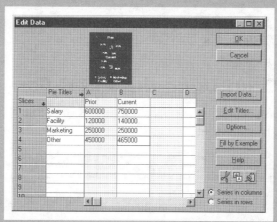

The SmartChart on the presentation page now reflects the data
that you entered. You can continue to edit and enhance the chart
by using the Chart menu and the chart-specific SmartIcons bar.

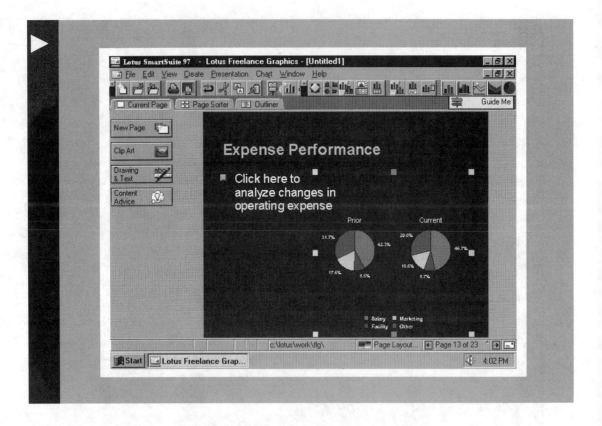

## ▶ *Editing a Chart Using the Status Bar*

When you select a chart in 1-2-3, the Status bar changes. Six chart-specific buttons appear:

Select a background pattern for a chart from this palette:

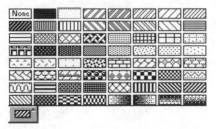

Select a foreground color for the selected pattern from this palette:

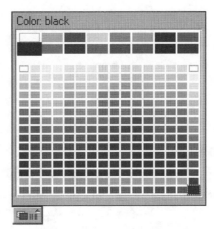

 Select a background color for the selected pattern from this palette:

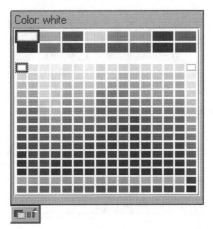

 Select a chart border line pattern from this list:

Select a chart border line thickness from this list:

 ▶▶ **N O T E**

**Selecting a line thickness other than the default changes the current line pattern to a solid line.**

 Select a chart border line color from this palette:

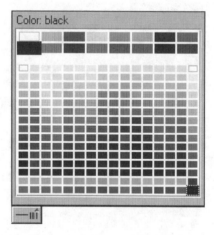

## ▶ *Changing to Another Type of Chart*

When you want to change the chart type, be sure that you select a type that's appropriate to your data. You can change the chart type in several ways:

- Click on the Set Chart Types SmartIcon.
- Click on the Chart Properties SmartIcon.
- Double-click on the area within the axes but outside the plot.
- Choose Chart ➤ Chart Type.
- Click within the chart and click on the Chart Properties SmartIcon. Then choose Chart from the Properties For drop-down list box.
- Click within the chart and choose Chart ➤ Chart Properties. Then, if necessary, choose Chart from the Properties For drop-down list box.
- From within a Chart Properties InfoBox, open the Properties For drop-down list box, and select Chart.
- Right-click on the chart, choose Chart Properties, open the Properties For drop-down list box, and select Chart.

1-2-3 displays the Type section of the Chart Properties InfoBox with the current chart type selected and illustrated. The default chart is Bar.

To change to another type of chart, click on an option button in the Types group. Optionally, click on one of the illustrations to select the best look for your chart.

Figure 7.29 illustrates the Type section of the Chart Properties InfoBox with Bar selected and its equivalent SmartIcons for a Vertical Bar

**FIGURE 7.29** ▶

*The Type section of the Chart Properties InfoBox with Bar selected and the equivalent Bar Chart SmartIcons*

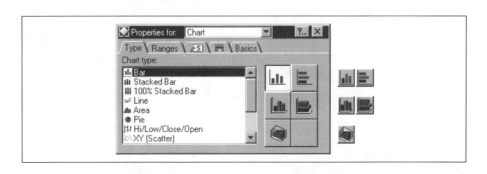

Chart, a Horizontal Bar Chart, a Vertical Bar with Depth Chart, a Horizontal Bar with Depth Chart, and a 3D Bar Chart.

Figure 7.30 illustrates the Type section of the Chart Properties InfoBox with Stacked Bar selected and its equivalent SmartIcons for a Vertical Stacked Bar Chart, a Horizontal Stacked Bar Chart, a Vertical Stacked Bar with Depth Chart, and a Horizontal Stacked Bar with Depth Chart. There is no 1-2-3 SmartIcon for the 3D Stacked Bar Chart.

**FIGURE 7.30** ▶

*The Type section of the Chart Properties InfoBox with Stacked Bar selected and the equivalent Stacked Bar Chart SmartIcons*

Figure 7.31 illustrates the Type section of the Chart Properties InfoBox with 100% Stacked Bar selected. There are no 1-2-3 SmartIcons for the 100% Stacked Bar Chart.

**FIGURE 7.31** ▶

*The Type section of the Chart Properties InfoBox with 100% Stacked Bar selected*

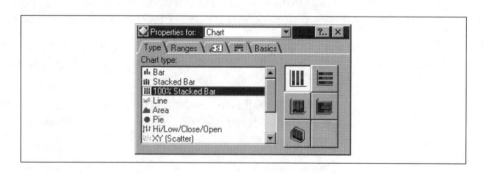

Figure 7.32 illustrates the Type section of the Chart Properties InfoBox with Line selected and its equivalent SmartIcons for a Line Chart, a Line with Depth Chart, and a 3D Line Chart.

Graphing Your Data

Ch. 7

**FIGURE 7.32** ▶

*The Type section of the Chart Properties InfoBox with Line selected and the equivalent Line Chart SmartIcons*

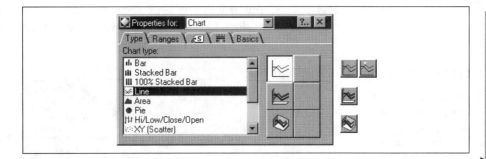

Figure 7.33 illustrates the Type section of the Chart Properties InfoBox with Area selected and its equivalent SmartIcons for an Area Chart, an Area with Depth Chart, and a 3D Area Chart.

**FIGURE 7.33** ▶

*The Type section of the Chart Properties InfoBox with Area selected and the equivalent Area Chart SmartIcons*

Figure 7.34 illustrates the Type section of the Chart Properties InfoBox with Pie selected and its equivalent SmartIcons for a Pie Chart, a Multiple Pie Chart, a 3D Pie Chart, and a Multiple 3D Pie Chart.

**FIGURE 7.34** ▶

*The Type section of the Chart Properties InfoBox with Pie selected and the equivalent Pie Chart SmartIcons*

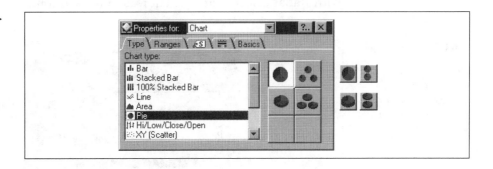

Figure 7.35 illustrates the Type section of the Chart Properties InfoBox with Hi/Low/Close/Open selected and its equivalent SmartIcon.

**FIGURE 7.35 ▶**

*The Type section of the Chart Properties InfoBox with Hi/Low/Close/Open selected and its equivalent SmartIcon*

Figure 7.36 illustrates the Type section of the Chart Properties InfoBox with XY (Scatter) selected and its equivalent SmartIcon.

**FIGURE 7.36 ▶**

*The Type section of the Chart Properties InfoBox with XY (Scatter) selected and its equivalent SmartIcon*

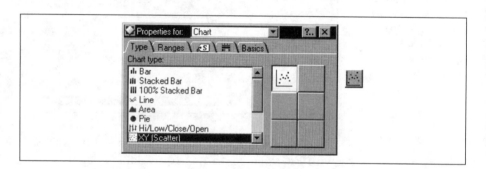

Figure 7.37 illustrates the Type section of the Chart Properties InfoBox with Radar selected and its equivalent SmartIcon.

**FIGURE 7.37 ▶**

*The Type section of the Chart Properties InfoBox with Radar selected and its equivalent SmartIcon*

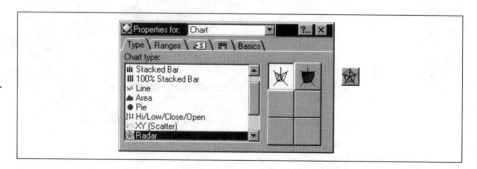

Figure 7.38 illustrates the Type section of the Chart Properties InfoBox with Mixed selected and its equivalent SmartIcons for the Mixed Bar/Line and Mixed Bar/Line with Depth Chart. There is no 1-2-3 SmartIcon for the 3D Mixed Bar/Line Chart.

**FIGURE 7.38** ▶

*The Type section of the Chart Properties InfoBox with Mixed selected and the equivalent Mixed Bar/Line and Mixed Bar/Line with Depth Chart SmartIcons*

▶▶ **N O T E**

**You can specify custom mixed chart elements in the Options section of the Series Properties InfoBox.**

Figure 7.39 illustrates the Type section of the Chart Properties InfoBox with Number Grid selected and the equivalent Word Pro and Freelance Graphics Table Chart SmartIcon.

**FIGURE 7.39** ▶

*The Type section of the Chart Properties InfoBox with Number Grid selected and its equivalent Word Pro and Freelance Graphics SmartIcon*

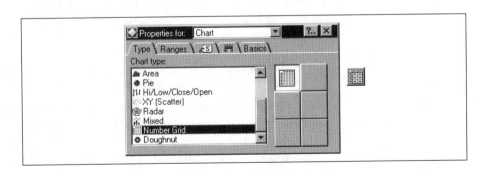

Figure 7.40 illustrates the Type section of the Chart Properties InfoBox with Doughnut selected. There is no equivalent SmartIcon.

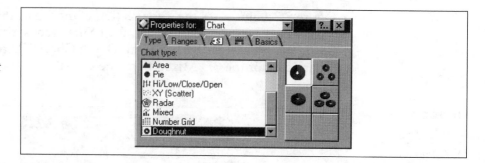

## ▶ Deleting a Chart

To delete a chart, select it (notice the handles around the borders of the chart) and press Delete.

# ▶▶ Charting Data on a Map

You can display regional data on a map of the region using a set of country, state, and city maps. To create and edit maps in 1-2-3, choose Create ➤ Map.

## ▶ Creating a Sheet To Be Mapped

Charting data on a map requires careful preparation and sheet layout, as shown in Figure 7.41. You can't chart all data in this way. To map your data properly, follow these steps:

1. In the leftmost column of the sheet, type the names of regions corresponding with maps. You can find maps in the folder.

2. Type values, map codes (listed in the \MAPDATA subfolder), labels, pin characters (see the help topic, "Adding Pin Characters to a Map"), pin coordinates, or pin character colors in succeeding columns. Do not mix data types in a single column.

Graphing
Your Data

**FIGURE 7.41** ▶

*A sheet from which you can create a chart on a map*

| | A | B | C |
|---|---|---|---|
| 1 | Satellite Dish Sales by State | | |
| 2 | | | |
| 3 | State | Sales | Region |
| 4 | Pennsylvania | 12879 | Mid-Atlantic |
| 5 | New York | 3534 | Mid-Atlantic |
| 6 | Delaware | 705 | Mid-Atlantic |
| 7 | New Jersey | 872 | Mid-Atlantic |
| 8 | Ohio | 1253 | Mid-West |
| 9 | Illinois | 2400 | Mid-West |
| 10 | Indiana | 3270 | Mid-West |
| 11 | Connecticut | 1312 | New England |
| 12 | Rhode Island | 1345 | New England |
| 13 | Massachusetts | 2450 | New England |
| 14 | Vermont | 952 | New England |
| 15 | New Hampshire | 831 | New England |
| 16 | Maine | 674 | New England |

## ▶ Creating a Chart on a Map

To create a chart on a map, follow these steps:

1. Select a range of data to be mapped. Include the region names or region codes in the selection.

2. Choose Create ➤ Map or click on the Create a Map SmartIcon.

3. When the mouse pointer changes to a crosshairs, click in the cell that marks the upper left corner of the map or drag the boundaries of the map. 1-2-3 then creates and displays the map (see Figure 7.42) using default settings.

**FIGURE 7.42** ▶

*A default map showing the selected data*

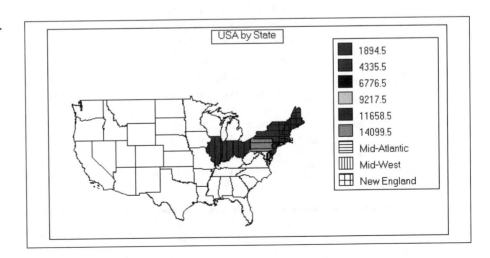

The map is color-coded to show ranges of data (in this case, the contents of column B) and is pattern-coded to show regions (in this case, the company divisions in column C).

## ▶ Editing a Chart on a Map

Once you have created a map, you can use the Map SmartIcons and context-sensitive Map and Drawing menus to edit the map and its components. Table 7.4 shows the Map SmartIcons, lists the equivalent menu commands, and provides descriptions.

▶ **TABLE 7.4:** *1-2-3 Map SmartIcons and Commands*

| SmartIcon | Menu Command | Description |
|---|---|---|
|  | Create ➤ Map | Inserts a new map based on a selected range and in the sheet location that you have indicated |
|  | Map ➤ Map Properties **or** select Map from the Properties For drop-down list box of the Map Properties InfoBox | Opens the Map Properties InfoBox |
| abcd | Map ➤ Title **or** Map ➤ Title Properties **or** Map ➤ Map Properties and select Title from the Properties For drop-down list box **or** select Title from the Properties For drop-down list box of the Map Properties InfoBox | Opens the Title section of the Map Properties InfoBox |
|  | Map ➤ Legend **or** Map ➤ Legend Properties **or** Map ➤ Map Properties and select Legend from the Properties For drop-down list box **or** select Legend from the Properties For drop-down list box of the Map Properties InfoBox | Opens the Legend section of the Map Properties InfoBox |

► **TABLE 7.4:** *1-2-3 Map SmartIcons and Commands (continued)*

| SmartIcon | Menu Command | Description |
|-----------|--------------|-------------|
| | Map ➤ Overlays and click on the Overlays tab **or** Map ➤ Map Properties and click on the Overlays tab | Opens the Overlays section of the Map Properties InfoBox |
| | Map ➤ Plot **or** Map ➤ Plot Properties **or** Map ➤ Map Properties and select Plot from the Properties For drop-down list box **or** select Plot from the Properties For drop-down list box of the Map Properties InfoBox | Opens the Plot section of the Map Properties InfoBox |
| | Map ➤ Zoom In | Zooms in on the map |
| | Map ➤ Zoom Out | Zooms out on the map |
| | Map ➤ Zoom to Original View | Returns the map to its original, unzoomed size |
| | Drawing ➤ Bring to Front | Brings the selected objects to the front of other objects |
| | Drawing ➤ Send to Back | Sends the selected objects to the back of all other objects |
| | Drawing ➤ Group | Groups the selected objects into one object |
| | Drawing ➤ Ungroup | Ungroups the grouped objects |

The Map Properties InfoBox is the focus of map editing just as the Chart Properties InfoBox is for chart editing. Open the Map Properties InfoBox, from which you can edit or enhance the map itself or any part of the map: the Title, the Legend, and the Plot.

## Editing the Map

The Map Properties InfoBox is composed of six sections: Lines and Color, Basics, Ranges, Overlays, Bin Colors, and Bin Patterns. For information about using the Lines and Color section of SmartSuite InfoBoxes, see the *Editing in SmartSuite Applications* chapter.

The Basics section (see Figure 7.43) contains the following options:

**Map Name**   Type the map name in this text box.

**Redraw Map Automatically When Data Changes**   Check this checkbox to have 1-2-3 automatically redraw the map whenever you change the data in the sheet. A checked checkbox is the default.

**Fasten to Cells**   Click on one of these option buttons to anchor the map to the cells at the top left and bottom right cells at its border (the default), to the top left cell only, or not fasten the map to any cells.

**Hide**   Check this checkbox to hide the map. A checked checkbox is the default.

**Lock**   Check this checkbox to make the map read-only. You can, however, size and move the map when it is locked. A checked checkbox is the default.

**FIGURE 7.43** ▶

*The Basics section of the Map Properties InfoBox*

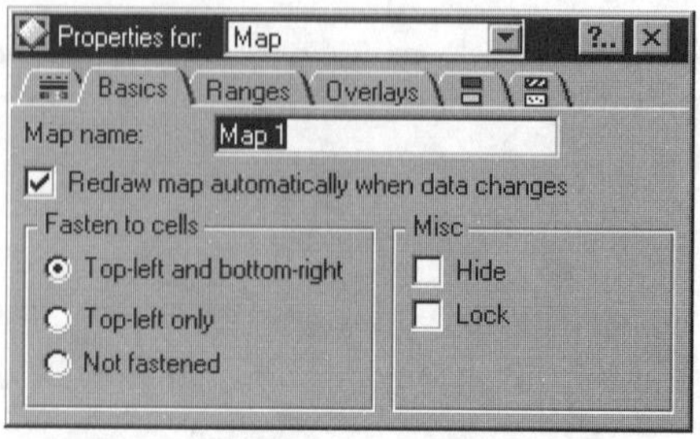

The Ranges section (see Figure 7.44) contains the following options:

**Map Region Names or Codes**    Type the range or select, using the range selector, the part of the sheet from which 1-2-3 will obtain the map region or codes. For example, in the sample map, the selected range is A4 to A16, the state names.

**Data to Map with Colors**    Type the range or select, using the range selector, the labels with which to obtain the data to be color coded. For example, in the sample map, the selected range is B4 to B16, the sales amounts.

**Data to Map with Patterns**    Type the range or select, using the range selector, the labels with which to obtain the data to be pattern coded. For example, in the sample map, the selected range is C4 to C16, the sales regions.

**Pin Characters, Latitude and Longitude**    Type the range or select, using the range selector, the pin characters, latitude, and longitude.

**FIGURE 7.44** ▶

*The Ranges section of
the Map Properties
InfoBox*

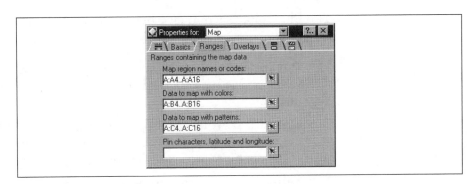

Using the Overlays section, you can add a map overlay to the selected map. *Map overlays* can emphasize a particular area or provide additional information. Map overlay files, which have the TV extension, are stored in the \MAPDATA subfolder if you accepted the suggested folders and subfolders during installation.

The Overlays section (see Figure 7.45) contains the following options:

**Overlays**    This text box contains the names of overlays that have been added to this map.

**Add**    Click on this button to add an overlay to this map.

**Remove**    Click on this button to remove the selected overlay from this map.

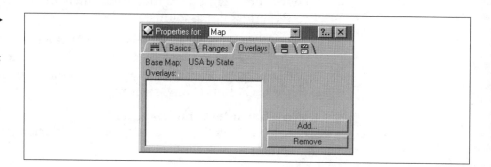

The Bin Colors section (see Figure 7.46) contains the following options:

**Put in Bins By**    From this drop-down list box, select how the values in the bins are determined: by an upper limit or by an exact match.

**Colors**    From this drop-down list box, select Default (the default colors), Manual (you choose a color from a palette for each of the six bins), or From Range.

**Values**    From this drop-down list box, select Computed (the default values), Manual (you type the value for each of the six bins), or From Range (*see above*).

**Colors Range**    If you select From Range, click on the range selector to select a range from the sheet.

**Values Range**    If you select From Range, click on the range selector to select a range from the sheet.

**Legends Range**    If you select From Range, click on the range selector to select a range from the sheet.

**FIGURE 7.46** ▶

*The Bin Colors section
of the Map Properties
InfoBox*

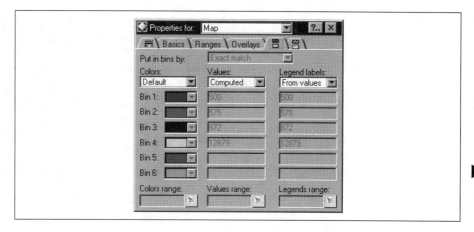

Graphing
Your Data

▶ ▶

Ch.

**7**

The Bin Patterns section (see Figure 7.47) contains the following
options:

**Put in Bins By**     From this drop-down list box, select how the
values in the bins are determined: by an upper limit or by an exact
match.

**Patterns**     From this drop-down list box, select Default (the default patterns), Manual (you choose a pattern from a palette for
each of the six bins), or From Range.

**Values**     From this drop-down list box, select Computed (the
default values), Manual (you type the value for each of the six
bins), or From Range (*see above*).

**Patterns Range**     If you select From Range, click on the range
selector to select a range from the sheet.

**Values Range**     If you select From Range, click on the range selector to select a range from the sheet.

**Legends Range**     If you select From Range, click on the range
selector to select a range from the sheet.

**FIGURE 7.47** ▶

*The Bin Patterns
section of the Map
Properties InfoBox*

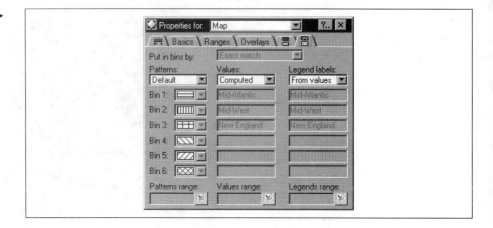

## Editing the Map Title

The Title Properties InfoBox is composed of three sections: Text,
Lines and Color, and Basics. For information about using the Text sec-
tion and the Lines and Color section of SmartSuite InfoBoxes, see the
*Editing in SmartSuite Applications* chapter.

The Basics section (see Figure 7.48) contains the following options:

**Show Title**     Check this checkbox to show the title typed in the
text box; clear it to hide the title. A checked checkbox is the
default.

**Line 1**     Type the first line of the map title in this text box.

**Line 2**     Type the second line of the map title in this text box.

**Line 3**     Type the third line of the map title in this text box.

**Cell**     Check this checkbox to change a Line 1, Line 2, or Line
3 text box to a box with a range selector so that you can use the
contents of a cell or a range as the title or subtitle.

**Position**     Click on one of these option buttons to place the
title in one of five positions. The top center is the default.

**FIGURE 7.48** ▶

*The Basics section of the Title Properties InfoBox*

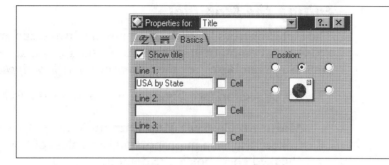

## Editing the Map Legend

The Legend Properties InfoBox is composed of three sections: Text, Lines and Color, and Basics. For information about using the Text section and the Lines and Color section of SmartSuite InfoBoxes, see the *Editing in SmartSuite Applications chapter.*

The Basics section (see Figure 7.49) contains the following options:

**Show Color Legend**   Check this checkbox to show the color portion of the legend; clear it to hide the color portion of the legend. A checked checkbox is the default.

**Show Pattern Legend**   Check this checkbox to show the pattern portion of the legend; clear it to hide the pattern portion of the legend. A checked checkbox is the default.

**Place Inside Plot Area**   Check this checkbox to move the legend inside the plot.

**Position**   Click on one of these option buttons to place the legend in one of eight positions.

**FIGURE 7.49** ▶

*The Basics section of the Legend Properties InfoBox*

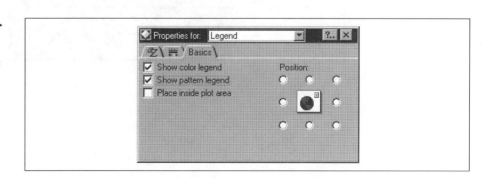

## *Editing the Map Plot*

The Plot Properties InfoBox is composed of two sections: Lines and Color and Basics. For information about using the Lines and Color section of SmartSuite InfoBoxes, see the *Editing in SmartSuite Applications* chapter.

The Basics section (see Figure 7.50) contains the following options:

**Maintain Correct Map Dimensions**    Check this checkbox to keep the map in proportion regardless of how you size it. A checked checkbox is the default.

**Default Settings**    Click on this option button to return to the original map size.

**Custom Settings**    1-2-3 fills in this option button when you move or size the map.

**Rotation**    To rotate the map, type or select a value from 0 to 360 in this text/option box.

**Longitude**    To center the plot along the longitude, type or select a value in this text box.

**Latitude**    To center the plot along the latitude, type or select a value in this text box.

**Zoom**    To zoom in or out on the map, type or select a value from 0 to 10,000 in this text/option box.

**FIGURE 7.50** ▸

*The Basics section of the Plot Properties InfoBox*

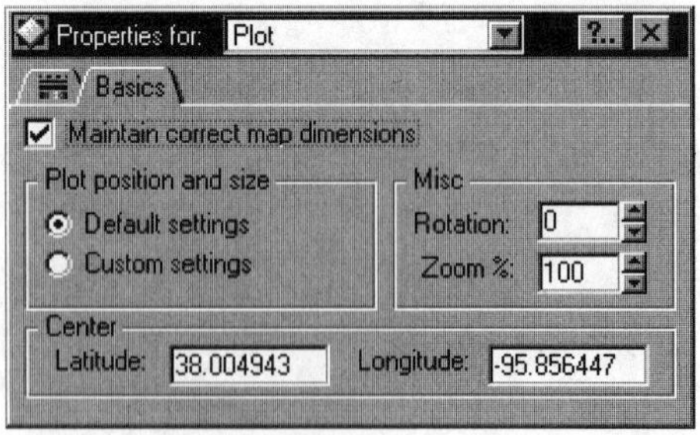

## Editing a Map Using a Shortcut Menu

The map feature also provides shortcut menus (see Figure 7.51) when you click on part of a map and right-click. Commands unique to mapping are:

| | |
|---|---|
| **Map Properties** | Opens the Map Properties InfoBox |
| **Plot Properties** | Opens the Plot Properties InfoBox |
| **Title Properties** | Opens the Title Properties InfoBox |
| **Legend Properties** | Opens the Legend Properties InfoBox |
| **Recenter** | Centers the selected map on the clicked-on location |
| **Copy Code** | Copies the code of the clicked-on region to the Windows Clipboard so that you can copy the code in 1-2-3 or in another Windows application |
| **Copy Name** | Copies the name of the clicked-on region to the Windows Clipboard so that you can copy the name in 1-2-3 or in another Windows application |

**FIGURE 7.51** ▶

*The shortcut menus for editing a map*

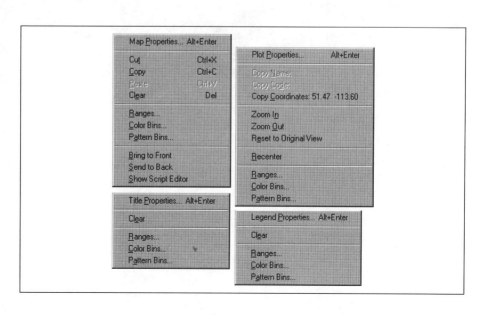

Graphing Your Data

Ch. 7

| Copy Coordinates | Copies the coordinates of the clicked-on region to the Windows Clipboard so that you can copy the coordinates in 1-2-3 to define pin characters or in another Windows application |
|---|---|

## Cropping a Map

When you want to show a particular area on a map, you can crop the extraneous areas. To crop a map, click within the boundary surrounding the map, press and hold down the Ctrl key, and drag a border around the area to be shown. Figure 7.52 shows the cropped sample map.

**FIGURE 7.52** ▶

*The edited sample map, which is cropped to highlight the states in which sales occur*

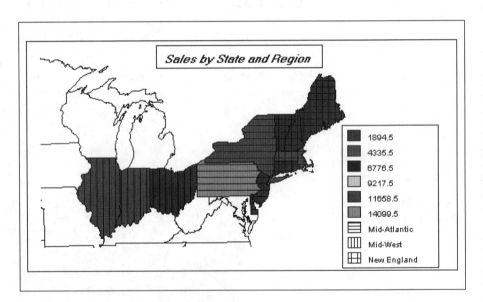

► ► CHAPTER **8**

# Advanced 1-2-3 Techniques

►► **T**his chapter provides information about some of the 1-2-3 advanced features, namely data manipulation, data analysis, 1-2-3 databases, importing and exporting files, using 1-2-3 add-ins, and macros.

## ►► *Transposing Data*

If you want to analyze the numbers in a sheet in a different way, use the Transpose command, which reverses the order of rows and columns: Rows become columns, and columns change to rows. 1-2-3 and other spreadsheet program users often transpose data to set up a matrix that can be multiplied by another matrix. The Transpose command copies data to another range that you specify and transposes the columns and rows.

 You can transpose a block of data and place it in the same location by clicking on the Transpose a Range in Place SmartIcon or by choosing Range ➤ Transpose and keeping the same values in the Transpose dialog box, but you may have to edit the column or row labels. The best way to use the Transpose command is to place the block in a different range.

To transpose data, follow these steps:

1. Select a range of data, including row and column labels (see Figure 8.1) but excluding headings. You can also select totals and other calculated data.

2. Choose Range ➤ Transpose. 1-2-3 opens the Transpose dialog box (see Figure 8.2) with the Transpose the Range box filled in.

Advanced 1-2-3
Techniques

▶ ▶

*Ch.*

**8**

**FIGURE 8.1** ▶

*The selected range to be transposed*

| | Midwest Region | | | | |
|---|---|---|---|---|---|
| 2 | | Q1 | Q2 | Q3 | Q4 | Totals |
| 3 | Handlebars | 3836 | 5928 | 4037 | 5656 | 19457 |
| 4 | Wheels | 5894 | 8056 | 8128 | 8242 | 30320 |
| 5 | Pedals | 3482 | 4886 | 5256 | 7630 | 21254 |
| 6 | Totals | 13212 | 18870 | 17421 | 21528 | 71031 |

**FIGURE 8.2** ▶

*The Transpose dialog box with the range to be transposed already filled in*

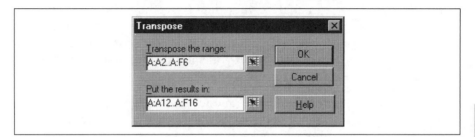

Transpose

Transpose the range:
A:A2..A:F6

Put the results in:
A:A12..A:F16

OK
Cancel
Help

**3.** Either type the range in which you want the transposed data placed, or click on the range selector at the right side of the Put the Results In box and select the range.

**4.** Click on OK or press Enter. 1-2-3 transposes the selected range, recalculates formulas, and places the resulting range in its new location (see Figure 8.3).

**FIGURE 8.3** ▶

*The transposed data with its totals recalculated*

| | Handlebars | Wheels | Pedals | Totals |
|---|---|---|---|---|
| Q1 | 3836 | 5894 | 3482 | 13212 |
| Q2 | 5928 | 8056 | 4886 | 18870 |
| Q3 | 4037 | 8128 | 5256 | 17421 |
| Q4 | 5656 | 8242 | 7630 | 21528 |
| Totals | 19457 | 30320 | 21254 | 71031 |

# ▶▶ Analyzing Your Data

One major advantage of using sheets to hold your data is the ability to "crunch" numbers. For example, if you operate a seasonal business, such as an ice cream store or a ski area, you can estimate the number of employees to be used, not only for an entire season, but even on a day-by-day basis. Or, if you manufacture or sell a line of products, you can analyze your data to see how you can adjust the product mix to maximize income, to minimize expenses, or both. If you are a trainer or a teacher, you can analyze test scores to see if your questions are too easy or to see if you should reteach a topic that most of your students don't seem to understand.

1-2-3 offers frequency distribution, regression analysis, matrix multiplication, and matrix inversion statistical tools as well as what-if analysis and the Backsolver.

- *Frequency distribution* classifies data into specific ranges of values.

- *Regression analysis* shows how much a set of data, a *dependent variable*, is affected by other data, one or more *independent variables*. You can use the results of regression analysis to predict future behavior of the dependent variable.

- *Matrix multiplication* multiplies two *matrices* (tables of data) and places the results in a new matrix used to solve multivariable equations.

- *Matrix inversion* inverts the numbers in one matrix and places the results in a new matrix. You can multiply the inverted matrix by a third matrix to predict future values.

- *What-if analysis* allows you to plug in one, two, or three variables in a formula to produce a table of values that might include the combination of variables for which you are looking.

- The *Backsolver* is an easy-to-use tool with which you can perform what-if analysis to increase or decrease selected values to reach a particular result.

This section simply provides an introduction to 1-2-3 statistical tools. For more information about analyzing your data with 1-2-3, see the 1-2-3 help facility. In addition, you can learn more about these and other mathematical and statistical concepts by studying books on statistics, business mathematics, and linear programming and mathematics.

## ▶ *Frequency Distribution*

Using frequency distribution, a teacher or a trainer can tell how many grades fall between 91 and 100, 81 and 90, and so on. Other uses for frequency distribution are breaking down sales commissions by dollar amounts and analyzing inventory dollar values or counts.

1-2-3 makes a frequency distribution by sorting values, counting the values in each user-defined category, and placing those values in *bins* (the name for ranges in which data are stored) on the sheet. 1-2-3 also places values that are greater than the largest bin value in the cell below the largest bin value. If 1-2-3 finds no value for a particular bin, it places a zero in that bin.

When you change a value, you must run the frequency distribution again. 1-2-3 does not automatically recalculate the frequency distribution when you change the value.

To run a frequency distribution, follow these steps:

*1.* Open a sheet containing a list of values to be analyzed (see Figure 8.4).

**FIGURE 8.4** ▶

*A sample sheet showing a list of values and a bin range*

| Western Region | | | | | |
|---|---|---|---|---|---|
| **Last Name** | **First Name** | **Sales** | **Commission** | | |
| Adams | Mary | $356,892 | $10,707 | | |
| Adamson | Lee | $874,672 | $43,734 | | |
| Bazzulo | Brian | $1,245,243 | $62,262 | | |
| Bryant | Morton | $756,391 | $37,820 | | |
| Chalmers | Tony | $983,289 | $49,164 | | |
| Czymanski | Adam | $874,624 | $43,731 | | |
| Kelly | Michael | $331,953 | $9,959 | | |
| Margino | Margot | $996,783 | $49,839 | | |
| Murphy | Michael | $863,472 | $43,174 | | |
| O'Brien | Thomas | $653,890 | $32,695 | | |
| Peabody | Johnna | $892,463 | $44,623 | | |
| Smith | Samuel | $783,671 | $39,184 | | |
| Smithers | Celia | $874,845 | $43,742 | | |
| Zazner | Jeffrey | $524,458 | $26,223 | | |
| *Totals* | | $11,012,646 | $536,855 | | |

**2.** In an empty part of a column, list bin values ranging from a low value (for example, 10,000) to a high value (for example, 60,000), incremented by a set value (for example, 10,000).

| |
|---|
| 10000 |
| 20000 |
| 30000 |
| 40000 |
| 50000 |
| 60000 |

**3.** Choose Range ➤ Analyze ➤ Distribution. 1-2-3 opens the Frequency Distribution dialog box (see Figure 8.5).

**4.** Click on the Range of Values range selector and select the list of values to be analyzed.

**FIGURE 8.5** ▶

*The Frequency Distribution dialog box with the range of values and the bin range selected for the sample sheet*

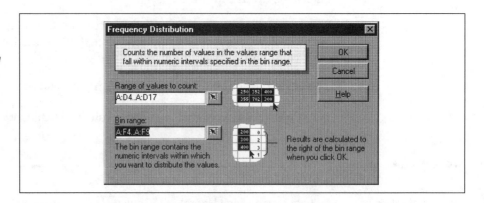

**5.** Click on the Bin Range range selector and select the bin values that you just entered.

**6.** Click on OK. 1-2-3 runs the frequency distribution and places the count to the right of the bin range. Figure 8.6 shows the sheet with the list of values, the bin range, and the results of the frequency distribution.

Figure 8.7 shows a different sheet with the results of a test score frequency distribution and a line chart illustrating the distribution.

**FIGURE 8.6** ▶

*The sample sheet showing the results of the frequency distribution*

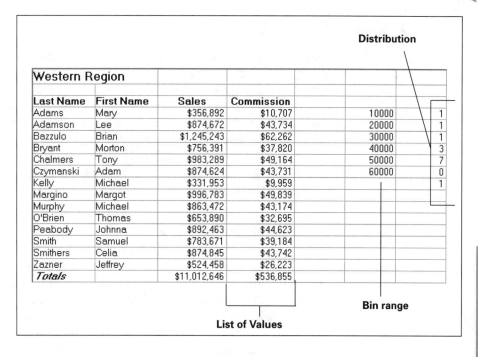

**Distribution**

| Western Region | | | | | | |
|---|---|---|---|---|---|---|
| **Last Name** | **First Name** | **Sales** | **Commission** | | | |
| Adams | Mary | $356,892 | $10,707 | | 10000 | 1 |
| Adamson | Lee | $874,672 | $43,734 | | 20000 | 1 |
| Bazzulo | Brian | $1,245,243 | $62,262 | | 30000 | 1 |
| Bryant | Morton | $756,391 | $37,820 | | 40000 | 3 |
| Chalmers | Tony | $983,289 | $49,164 | | 50000 | 7 |
| Czymanski | Adam | $874,624 | $43,731 | | 60000 | 0 |
| Kelly | Michael | $331,953 | $9,959 | | | 1 |
| Margino | Margot | $996,783 | $49,839 | | | |
| Murphy | Michael | $863,472 | $43,174 | | | |
| O'Brien | Thomas | $653,890 | $32,695 | | | |
| Peabody | Johnna | $892,463 | $44,623 | | | |
| Smith | Samuel | $783,671 | $39,184 | | | |
| Smithers | Celia | $874,845 | $43,742 | | | |
| Zazner | Jeffrey | $524,458 | $26,223 | | | |
| *Totals* | | $11,012,646 | $536,855 | | | |

**Bin range**

**List of Values**

**FIGURE 8.7** ▶

*Another sample sheet showing quiz scores for a small class as well as a chart that illustrates the results*

| Quiz Scores | | | | | | |
|---|---|---|---|---|---|---|
| | **Adams** | **Brown** | **Jones** | **Miller** | **Richards** | **Smith** |
| **03/09/97** | 75 | 90 | 86 | 88 | 93 | 95 |
| **03/16/97** | 76 | 92 | 87 | 86 | 94 | 89 |
| **03/23/97** | 79 | 85 | 92 | 82 | 91 | 95 |
| **03/30/97** | 85 | 91 | 92 | 84 | 98 | 96 |
| **04/06/97** | 83 | 93 | 91 | 87 | 95 | 91 |
| **04/13/97** | 86 | 89 | 92 | 89 | 92 | 94 |

Quiz Scores Distribution

| *Range* | |
|---|---|
| **70** | 0 |
| **75** | 1 |
| **80** | 2 |
| **85** | 5 |
| **90** | 10 |
| **95** | 16 |
| | 2 |

## ▶ *Regression Analysis*

Regression analysis shows the *correlation*, or relationship, of one or more independent variables (typically, the x values), over which you have no control, to a dependent variable (typically, the y value), a value that depends on the value of x. Once you have run a regression analysis and have shown a relationship between the dependent variable and one or more independent variables, you can use the results to predict values of the dependent variable, given other independent variables, thereby estimating business trends, enabling proper distribution of your resources, and so on.

You can use regression analysis to predict sales of a company that is affected by conditions such as weather, the season of the year, and/or national and/or local business indicators. You can also use the results to make hiring decisions, to determine the amount of raw materials to order, to decide on the mix of products to manufacture, and to evaluate new products or services to offer. For example, you can check the birth rate over the past 10 years to decide whether to manufacture cribs or toys or to get into educational software. Or, if you run a ski area, you can analyze the number of lift tickets you sell when the weather is cloudy and 19 degrees versus when the skies are sunny and the temperature is 35 degrees. Using the results, you can decide how many lift operators or slope groomers to bring in on a particular day or to predict how much food to order for the base lodge.

If there is a great deal of correlation between the dependent variable and an independent variable, the lines representing both variables in a chart will touch or almost touch along their lengths or the dots on a scatter chart will follow almost the same path. However, if there is very little correlation between the two variables, the lines and dots will be far apart.

In 1-2-3, the results of running the Regression command creates a table showing values for all the variables you are testing.

1-2-3 does not automatically recalculate the regression analysis when you change the value. When you change a value for a dependent variable or for an independent variable, you must run the regression analysis again.

## Running a Regression Analysis

To run a regression analysis, choose Range ➤ Analyze ➤ Regression. Then, select from these options in the Regression dialog box (see Figure 8.8):

**FIGURE 8.8** ▶

*The Regression dialog box*

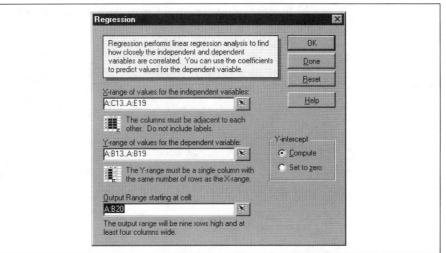

▶▶

*Ch.*

**8**

**X-Range of Values for the Independent Variables**   Click on the range selector and drag a range of up to 75 columns of independent variables. Do not choose the column labels when choosing columns.

**Y-Range of Values for the Dependent Variable**   Click on the range selector and drag a one-column dependent variable. The number of rows in the selection must equal the number of rows selected for the x-range of values. Do not choose the column label when choosing the dependent variable.

**Output Range Starting at Cell**   Click on the cell at the top left corner of the range in which you want to place the results. Be sure to choose a cell in an empty area. When 1-2-3 inserts the results in the output range, it overwrites any data in those cells.

**Compute**    Click on this option button (the default) to compute the *y-intercept*, the point at which a line drawn by the regression formula intercepts the y-axis. In the results, the y-intercept is known as the constant.

**Set to Zero**    Click on this option button to set the y-intercept to 0. Select this option button only if you suspect that if all the independent variables are equal to 0, the dependent variable is also equal to 0.

Figure 8.9 shows sample results of a regression analysis.

**FIGURE 8.9** ▶

*Results of a regression analysis*

| Regression Output: | | | | |
|---|---|---|---|---|
| Constant | | | -62.816282148273 | |
| Std Err of Y Est | | | 187.017712446382 | |
| R Squared | | | 0.97403876779311 | |
| No. of Observations | | | 7 | |
| Degrees of Freedom | | | 3 | |
| | | | | |
| X Coefficient(s) | | -3.42247 | 162.463958844153 | 0.92426866176 |
| Std Err of Coef. | | 33.71596 | 286.589181765499 | 0.1138304514 |

The results are:

**Constant**    The y-axis intercept. If you have clicked on the Set to Zero option button, the y-intercept is equal to 0 1-2-3 has calculated the constant as 0. If you have clicked on the Compute option button, 1-2-3 has calculated the y-intercept and placed the value here.

**Std Err of Y Est**    The *standard error* (the average difference between the dependent value and the line calculated using the regression analysis) of the y values.

**R Squared**    The validity of the regression analysis, with 1 representing the most valid or the highest correlation and 0 being the lowest correlation.

**No. of Observations**    The number of rows selected for the analysis.

**Degrees of Freedom**   The number of observations, minus the number of independent variables, minus 1 if the y-intercept is not equal to 0; or the number of observations, minus the number of independent variables if the y-intercept is equal to 0.

**X Coefficient(s)**   The slope of the line representing the values through the data points representing the values for each independent variable.

**Std Err of Coef.**   The standard error of the x coefficients.

## Predicting Future Values of Dependent Variables

If you enter values for independent variables, you can estimate the future value of a dependent variable. For example, if you can predict lift tickets sold on a Saturday if the weather forecast says that the temperature will be 40 degrees and sunny and if the population for a typical Saturday was 2500, you can decide how many trails to groom, how many lift operators to have onsite, and even how much food to have in the base lodge.

To calculate the value of a dependent variable, add a new row or find an empty row in the sheet. Then, type the estimated values in the cells for each independent variable. Finally, enter a formula, using the following syntax, in the dependent variable cell:

```
+(Ind-var-cell-1*$x-coeff-cell-1)+(Ind-var-cell-2*$x-
coeff-cell-2)+(Ind-var-cell-3*$x-coeff-cell-3)+$Const
```

where:

*Ind-var-cell-1*   The value of the first independent variable, located in cell-1

*$x-coeff-$cell-1*   The absolute reference ($) to the cell in which the x-coefficient for the first independent variable is located

*Ind-var-cell-2*   The value of the second independent variable, located in cell-2

*$x-coeff-$cell-2*   The absolute reference ($) to the cell in which the x-coefficient for the second independent variable is located

*Ind-var-cell-3*   The value of the third independent variable, located in cell-3

*$x-coeff-$cell-3*   The absolute reference ($) to the cell in which the x-coefficient for the third independent variable is located

*$Const*   The y-axis intercept

Of course, if there are more than three independent variables, add them to the formula using the syntax *Ind-var-cell-n\*$x-coeff-$cell-n* within parentheses. Figure 8.10 shows the formula and the results: 1-2-3 estimates that you will sell about 2,436 lift tickets on a Saturday with good weather conditions.

**FIGURE 8.10** ►

*The formula and the results of estimating a dependent variable*

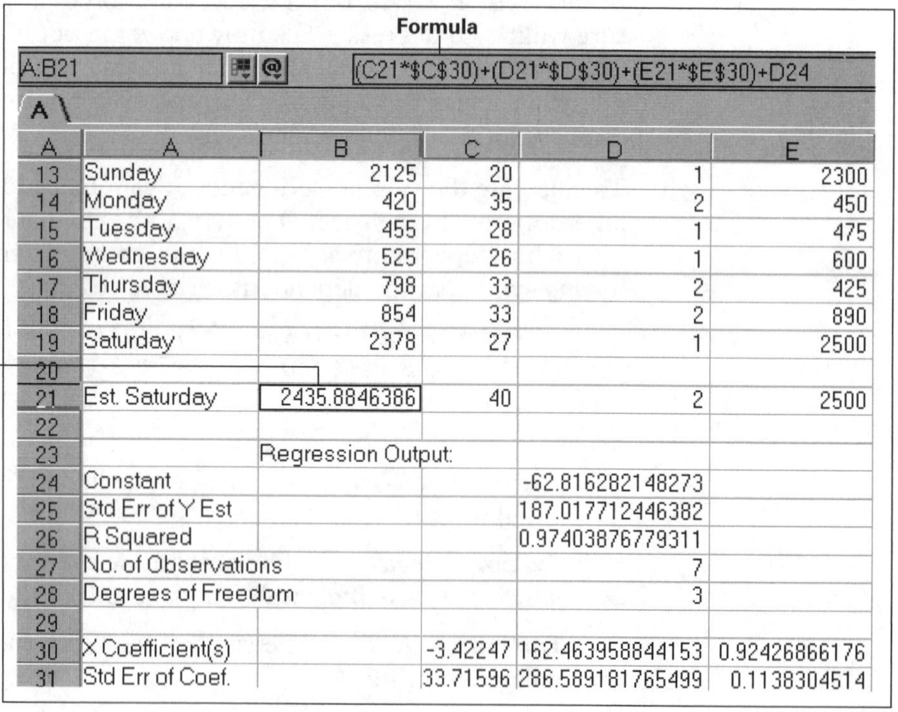

Cell containing formula

| | A | B | C | D | E |
|---|---|---|---|---|---|
| | | | | Formula | |
| A:B21 | | | (C21*$C$30)+(D21*$D$30)+(E21*$E$30)+D24 | | |
| 13 | Sunday | 2125 | 20 | 1 | 2300 |
| 14 | Monday | 420 | 35 | 2 | 450 |
| 15 | Tuesday | 455 | 28 | 1 | 475 |
| 16 | Wednesday | 525 | 26 | 1 | 600 |
| 17 | Thursday | 798 | 33 | 2 | 425 |
| 18 | Friday | 854 | 33 | 2 | 890 |
| 19 | Saturday | 2378 | 27 | 1 | 2500 |
| 20 | | | | | |
| 21 | Est. Saturday | 2435.8846386 | 40 | 2 | 2500 |
| 22 | | | | | |
| 23 | | Regression Output: | | | |
| 24 | Constant | | | -62.816282148273 | |
| 25 | Std Err of Y Est | | | 187.017712446382 | |
| 26 | R Squared | | | 0.97403876779311 | |
| 27 | No. of Observations | | | 7 | |
| 28 | Degrees of Freedom | | | 3 | |
| 29 | | | | | |
| 30 | X Coefficient(s) | | -3.42247 | 162.463958844153 | 0.92426866176 |
| 31 | Std Err of Coef. | | 33.71596 | 286.589181765499 | 0.1138304514 |

# ▶ *Matrix Arithmetic*

In a sheet, a *matrix* (or a table) can be anything from a range of cells in a single row or column to several cells forming a rectangle or a square containing a certain number of rows and a certain number of columns. 1-2-3 provides matrix multiplication, matrix inversion, and a combination of both. You can use matrix arithmetic to multiply many values at once, to evaluate your share of the market, and to determine the best mix of products, and you can use matrix arithmetic in demographics.

**Matrix Multiplication**　Use matrix arithmetic to quickly and simultaneously multiply all the numbers in one matrix by all the numbers in another. Using matrix multiplication, you can quickly automate the multiplication of each number in two matrices, add the products, and place the results in a third matrix.

**Matrix Inversion**　Use matrix arithmetic to find the inverse of the values in a matrix and place the results in a second matrix. Then, when you multiply the original matrix and the new matrix, the result is a third matrix, an *identity matrix*, in which all but one of the elements in a row are equal to 0; the other value is equal to 1.

**Matrix Inversion and Multiplication**　Calculate a matrix inversion, followed by matrix multiplication on the results to compute the mix of products or services that will bring the highest income or to determine how much cost centers or departments will contribute to an advertising campaign or to a research and development budget.

## *Multiplying a Matrix*

Choose Range ➤ Analyze ➤ Multiply Matrix to multiply the values in two matrices to obtain a third matrix. The number of columns in the first matrix and the number of rows in the second matrix must be equal. For example, if you are multiplying five columns in the first matrix, you must choose five rows in the second matrix.

You could use matrix multiplication to calculate costs per project for consultants whose hourly rates and hours worked vary depending on the projects to which they are assigned. Rather than multiply each hourly rate by hours (in our example, 24 separate calculations), have 1-2-3 do it in a few seconds.

To perform matrix multiplication, follow these steps:

1. Create a sheet in which you enter two matrices (see Figure 8.11). In the example, hourly rates for six consultants are listed in a 6-row by 1-column matrix, and project hours are listed in a 4-row by 6-column matrix.

**FIGURE 8.11** ▶

*The original two matrices and another range ready for the calculated matrix*

6-by-1 matrix

| | A | B | C | D | E | F | G |
|---|---|---|---|---|---|---|---|
| 1 | Hourly Rates – Consultants | | | | Consulting Costs | | |
| 2 | Brown | $22 | | | Thurgood | | |
| 3 | Tomas | $25 | | | Jones | | |
| 4 | Margoson | $27 | | | Atlee | | |
| 5 | Smith | $30 | | | DeMarn | | |
| 6 | Elias | $42 | | | | | |
| 7 | Elfred | $50 | | | | | |
| 8 | | | | | | | |
| 9 | | | | Hours | | | |
| 10 | Project | Brown | Tomas | Margoson | Smith | Elias | Elfred |
| 11 | Thurgood | 22 | 19 | 21 | 20 | 16 | 5 |
| 12 | Jones | 18 | 9 | 25 | 22 | 17 | 8 |
| 13 | Atlee | 20 | 17 | 22 | 18 | 16 | 9 |
| 14 | DeMarn | 21 | 12 | 16 | 19 | 15 | 4 |
| 15 | | | | | | | |

4-by-6 matrix

2. Choose Range ➤ Analyze ➤ Multiply Matrix.

3. Then, select from these options in the Multiply Matrix dialog box (see Figure 8.12):

**FIGURE 8.12** ▶

*The Multiply Matrix dialog box with all the ranges selected*

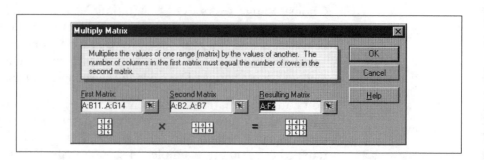

**First Matrix**    Click on the range selector and select a matrix. In the example, select the 4-by-6 matrix in the range B11.. G14.

**Second Matrix**    Click on the range selector and select a matrix. In the example, select the 6-by-1 matrix in the range B2.. B7.

**Resulting Matrix**    Click on the range selector and select the top cell of the resulting matrix. In the example, click on the top cell of a column with at least four empty cells.

**4.** Click on OK. 1-2-3 multiplies the first matrix by the second and places the results (in this case, the total consulting costs for each project) in the resulting matrix range.

| Consulting Costs | |
|---|---|
| Thurgood | $3,048.00 |
| Jones | $3,070.00 |
| Atlee | $3,121.00 |
| DeMarn | $2,594.00 |

## Inverting a Matrix

Matrix inversion creates an inverse of a square matrix (that is, the number of rows that you select must equal the number of selected columns). In most cases, inverting a matrix leads to multiplying the inverted matrix by another matrix—another use for matrix multiplication as described in the following section, "Multiplying an Inverted Matrix."

To invert a matrix, choose Range ➤ Analyze ➤ Invert Matrix. Then, select from these options in the Invert Matrix dialog box (see Figure 8.13):

**FIGURE 8.13** ▶

*The Invert Matrix dialog box with the From and To ranges selected*

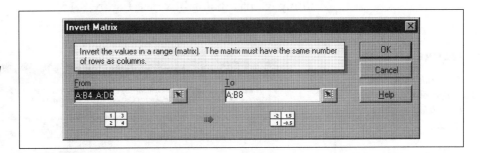

**From**    If you have not specified a range or if you want to change the dimensions of the range, click on the range selector and select a range. A range must be square (that is, three cells by three columns or nine cells by nine columns, and so on).

**To**    Click on the range selector and select the cell that represents the top left corner of the matrix results, or select the range into which the results will be placed. Be sure to choose a cell in an empty area. When 1-2-3 inserts the results in the output range, it overwrites any data in those cells.

After you click on OK, 1-2-3 produces an inverted matrix and places it in the specified output range. Figure 8.14 shows the original matrix and the inverted matrix.

**FIGURE 8.14** ▶

*The original matrix and the inverted matrix*

|  | Trucks | Boats | Trailers |
|---|---|---|---|
| **1996** | 128835 | 136760 | 142451 |
| **1997** | 130894 | 135650 | 146434 |
| **1998** | 129582 | 136732 | 139540 |
|  |  |  |  |
|  | -0.0006188 | 0.00022302 | 0.00039772 |
|  | 0.00040192 | -0.0002724 | -0.0001244 |
|  | 0.00018085 | 0.00005985 | -0.0002403 |
|  | -0.0061539 | 0.00147369 | 0.0070273 |

## Multiplying an Inverted Matrix

To multiply the original matrix by the inverted matrix, choose Range ➤ Analyze ➤ Multiply Matrix. Then, select from these options in the Multiply Matrix dialog box (see Figure 8.15):

**FIGURE 8.15** ▶

*The Multiply Matrix dialog box, which has been filled in with cell ranges*

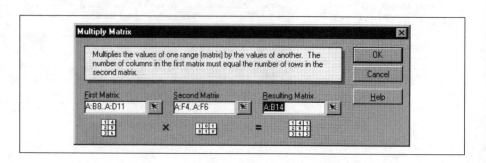

**First Matrix**    Click on the range selector and select the inverted range.

**Second Matrix**    Click on the range selector and, in the example, select the matrix containing the total dollar amounts to be contributed, the four-cell range under the heading Research and Development.

**Resulting Matrix**    Click on the range selector and click on the cell that represents the top of the results (see Figure 8.16). If you have selected and inverted a 4-cell matrix, a column of four cells will result. Be sure to choose a cell in an empty area. When 1-2-3 inserts the results in the output range, it overwrites any data in those cells.

**FIGURE 8.16** ▶

*The sheet, including the first and second matrices, the inverted matrix, and the results formatted as a percentage*

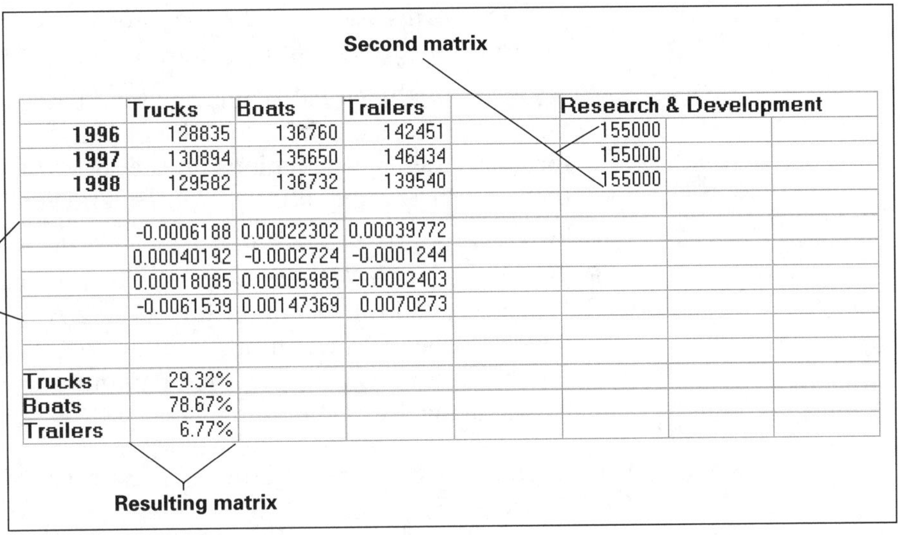

**Inverted range (first matrix)**

| | Trucks | Boats | Trailers | Research & Development | |
|---|---|---|---|---|---|
| **1996** | 128835 | 136760 | 142451 | 155000 | |
| **1997** | 130894 | 135650 | 146434 | 155000 | |
| **1998** | 129582 | 136732 | 139540 | 155000 | |
| | | | | | |
| | -0.0006188 | 0.00022302 | 0.00039772 | | |
| | 0.00040192 | -0.0002724 | -0.0001244 | | |
| | 0.00018085 | 0.00005985 | -0.0002403 | | |
| | -0.0061539 | 0.00147369 | 0.0070273 | | |
| | | | | | |
| Trucks | 29.32% | | | | |
| Boats | 78.67% | | | | |
| Trailers | 6.77% | | | | |

Second matrix

**Resulting matrix**

## ▶ *What-If Tables*

Because it automatically recalculates (unless you have opted for manual recalculation), a sheet always allows you to run an informal what-if analysis any time you change a value. When 1-2-3 recalculates the sheet, your what-if results are onscreen. However, 1-2-3 allows you to formally run a 1-2-3 analysis using a sheet set up for that purpose along with the What-if dialog box.

Perhaps the most popular use of 1-2-3 what-if analysis is in deciding on the size and length of a mortgage and your maximum monthly payments. Simply plug in various values, recalculate the sheet, and get the results. If you want, continue changing values and recalculating until you see the best results. Using a what-if table, you can also predict how your company's income will change based on changes in expenses, number of hours worked, increased production, and so on. You can even use what-if calculations to create a table of varying values, such as a table for computing tips for restaurant servers.

Using 1-2-3's what-if tables, you can calculate formulas in a sheet against one, two, or three variables using one or more holding cells to temporarily store the results of computations.

- A *one-variable table* calculates one or more formulas using one variable. For example, in the formula @PMT(100000,A1/12,25* 12), 1-2-3 performs a series of calculations on the series of variables stored in the cell A1. In this case, A1 holds interest rates.

- A *two-variable table* calculates one formula using two variables. For example, in the formula @PMT(A2,A1/12,25*12), 1-2-3 performs a series of calculations on the series of variables stored in the cells A1 (ranges of interest rates) and A2 (ranges of total loan amounts).

- A *three-variable table* calculates one formula using three variables. For example, in the formula @PMT(A2,A1/12,A3*12), 1-2-3 performs a series of calculations on the series of variables stored in A1 (interest rates), A2 (total loan amounts), and A3 (ranges of terms for the loan).

Setting up a sheet for a what-if table requires entering these elements (see Figure 8.17):

**Input values**    The values that 1-2-3 will use to perform the what-if calculations. In the example, the list of 16 percentages constitutes the input values.

**Formula cell**    A cell in which you enter a formula with one, two, or three variables, depending on the type of what-if table you want 1-2-3 to create. Because you will include the formula cell in the range of values to be calculated, it should be immediately above the list or table of input values.

**FIGURE 8.17** ▶

*A sample sheet showing the elements that set up a one-variable what-if table*

Input cell

Input values

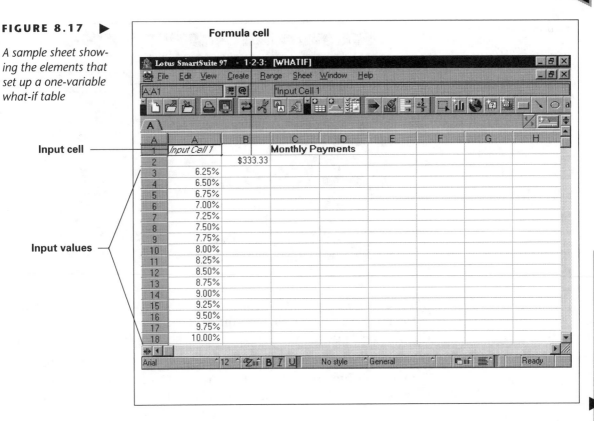

**Input cell**   A cell in which 1-2-3 will temporarily place results as it repeatedly computes the formula. You can label the cell to identify it.

After creating a sheet, run the what-if analysis by choosing Range ➤ Analyze ➤ What-if Table. In the What-if dialog box (see Figure 8.18), select from these options:

**How Many Variables?**   Click on an option button to choose the number of variables: 1, 2, or 3.

**Input Cell 1**   Type the input cell in which 1-2-3 will calculate the first variable, or click on the range selector and click in the cell.

**Input Cell 2**   Type the input cell in which 1-2-3 will calculate the second variable, or click on the range selector and click in the cell. This appears only if you have clicked on the 2 or 3 option button.

**FIGURE 8.18** ▶

*The What-if dialog box showing options for a one-variable what-if table*

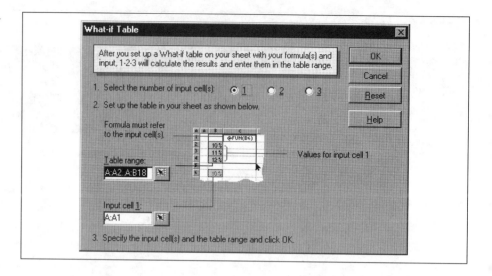

**Input Cell 3**    Type the input cell in which 1-2-3 will calculate the third variable or click on the range selector and click in the cell. This appears only if you have clicked on the 3 option button.

**Table Range**    Type or, using the range selector, select the range in which the input values are located and in which the results will be placed. Be sure to include the cell in which the formula is located.

**Reset**    Click on this button to clear all the what-if tables and to reset all the what-if options in the current workbook.

 ▶▶**N O T E**

> When calculating what-if tables in a multisheet workbook, be sure that all the ranges in the What-if dialog box are preceded with the identifier (for example, the D in D:A1, D:A2, and D:A3..D:H18) for the current sheet.

## Computing a One-Variable What-If Table

To calculate a one-variable what-if table, follow these steps:

1.  Create a sheet in which you enter an input cell, a one-variable formula, and input values (see Figure 8.17, earlier in this chapter).

2.  Choose Range ➤ Analyze ➤ What-if Table. 1-2-3 opens the What-if dialog box (see Figure 8.18, earlier in this chapter).

3.  Click on the 1 option button.

4.  Click on the Input Cell 1 range selector, and click on the cell that you have identified as the input cell.

5.  Click on the Table Range range selector, and drag the range that includes all the input values, the entire range in which 1-2-3 will place the results, and the formula.

6.  Click on OK. 1-2-3 creates the what-if table and places the results in the sheet (see Figure 8.19).

7.  If necessary, apply formats and enhancements to the results.

**FIGURE 8.19** ▶

*The results of running a one-variable what-if calculation*

| A | A | B | C | D |
|---|---|---|---|---|
| 1 | *Input Cell 1* | | Monthly Payments | |
| 2 | | $333.33 | | |
| 3 | 6.25% | $659.67 | | |
| 4 | 6.50% | $675.21 | | |
| 5 | 6.75% | $690.91 | | |
| 6 | 7.00% | $706.78 | | |
| 7 | 7.25% | $722.81 | | |
| 8 | 7.50% | $738.99 | | |
| 9 | 7.75% | $755.33 | | |
| 10 | 8.00% | $771.82 | | |
| 11 | 8.25% | $788.45 | | |
| 12 | 8.50% | $805.23 | | |
| 13 | 8.75% | $822.14 | | |
| 14 | 9.00% | $839.20 | | |
| 15 | 9.25% | $856.38 | | |
| 16 | 9.50% | $873.70 | | |
| 17 | 9.75% | $891.14 | | |
| 18 | 10.00% | $908.70 | | |

Results

Advanced 1-2-3 Techniques

Ch.
8

Remember that you can use multiple formulas in a one-variable what-if analysis. To do so, set up the sheet (see Figure 8.20) with one input cell, input values, and several formulas. In the sample, the formulas

**FIGURE 8.20 ►**

*A tip table resulting from running a what-if analysis using seven formulas*

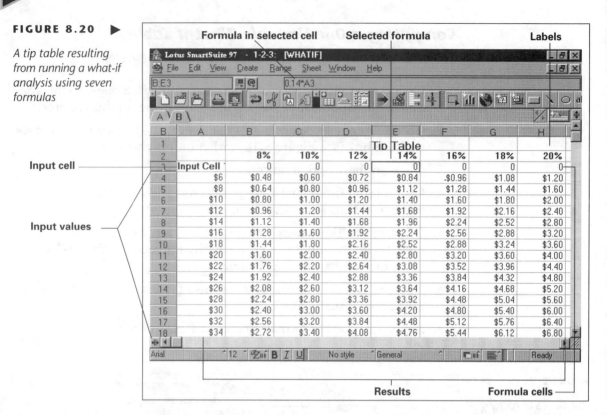

multiply the range of tip percentages by the current input value: 0.08*A3, 0.10*A3, 0.12*A3, 0.14*A3, 0.16*A3, 0.18*A3, and 0.20*A3. To run the analysis, follow the prior steps on the input values in the range A3..H18.

►► **N O T E**

**In the sample table, the formulas are in the range B3..H3. The percentages in B2..H2 are merely labels.**

## Computing a Two-Variable What-If Table

To calculate a two-variable what-if table, follow these steps:

**1.** Create a sheet in which you enter two input cells, a two-variable formula, and input values (see Figure 8.21).

**2.** Choose Range ➤ Analyze ➤ What-if Table. 1-2-3 opens the What-if dialog box (see Figure 8.22).

Advanced 1-2-3
Techniques

**FIGURE 8.21** ▶

*The sheet before running a what-if analysis*

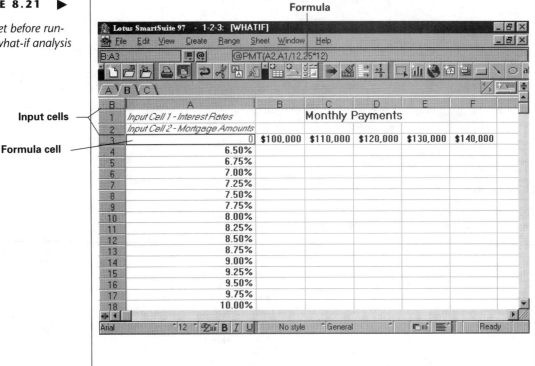

Input cells

Formula cell

Formula

**FIGURE 8.22** ▶

*The What-if dialog box with the ranges selected for the two input cells and the table range*

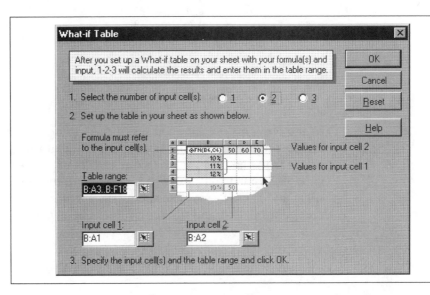

3. Click on the 2 option button.

4. Click on the Input Cell 1 range selector and click on input cell 1.

5. Click on the Input Cell 2 range selector and click on input cell 2.

6. Click on the Table Range range selector, and drag the range that includes all the input values, the range in which 1-2-3 will place the results, and the formula.

7. Click on OK. 1-2-3 creates the what-if table and places the results in the sheet (see Figure 8.23).

**FIGURE 8.23** ►

*The results of running a two-variable what-if calculation*

| Input Cell 1 - Interest Rates | Monthly Payments | | | | |
|---|---|---|---|---|---|
| Input Cell 2 - Mortgage Amounts | | | | | |
| 0 | $100,000 | $110,000 | $120,000 | $130,000 | $140,000 |
| 6.50% | $675.21 | $742.73 | $810.25 | $877.77 | $945.29 |
| 6.75% | $690.91 | $760.00 | $829.09 | $898.18 | $967.28 |
| 7.00% | $706.78 | $777.46 | $848.14 | $918.81 | $989.49 |
| 7.25% | $722.81 | $795.09 | $867.37 | $939.65 | $1,011.93 |
| 7.50% | $738.99 | $812.89 | $886.79 | $960.69 | $1,034.59 |
| 7.75% | $755.33 | $830.86 | $906.39 | $981.93 | $1,057.46 |
| 8.00% | $771.82 | $849.00 | $926.18 | $1,003.36 | $1,080.54 |
| 8.25% | $788.45 | $867.30 | $946.14 | $1,024.99 | $1,103.83 |
| 8.50% | $805.23 | $885.75 | $966.27 | $1,046.80 | $1,127.32 |
| 8.75% | $822.14 | $904.36 | $986.57 | $1,068.79 | $1,151.00 |
| 9.00% | $839.20 | $923.12 | $1,007.04 | $1,090.96 | $1,174.87 |
| 9.25% | $856.38 | $942.02 | $1,027.66 | $1,113.30 | $1,198.93 |
| 9.50% | $873.70 | $961.07 | $1,048.44 | $1,135.81 | $1,223.18 |
| 9.75% | $891.14 | $980.25 | $1,069.36 | $1,158.48 | $1,247.59 |
| 10.00% | $908.70 | $999.57 | $1,090.44 | $1,181.31 | $1,272.18 |

8. If necessary, apply formats and enhancements to the results.

In the previous section, you saw a one-variable tip table that used several formulas to compute tips with a range of tips and a range of meal prices. You can produce the same results with one formula and a two-variable what-if analysis. The differences between the one-variable sheet and the two-variable sheet (see Figure 8.24) are the addition of a second input cell and the replacement of seven formulas with one.

**FIGURE 8.24** ▶

*A tip table resulting from running a two-variable what-if analysis using one formula*

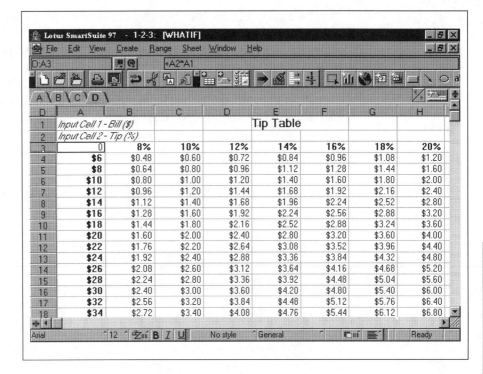

## Computing a Three-Variable What-If Table

Three-variable what-if analysis takes a slightly different tack than one-variable and two-variable analysis:

- You perform the analysis using multiple sheets (that is, this is a three-dimensional analysis).

▶▶ N O T E

**You can perform one-variable and two-variable analyses in three dimensions; however, it is not required.**

- Because all three-dimensional analyses must be symmetrical (that is, all the cells in every sheet must contain like information), the input cells and formula must be located out of the range (that is, they must be located below or to the right of the range of values).

- Only the first sheet in the set of sheets contains input cells and a formula.

In the example, which continues calculating mortgage rates, the formula now contains a third variable: The first variable is the interest rate, the second is the mortgage amount, and the third is the term, the number of years before payment is complete. Figures 8.25 and 8.26 show sheets C, D, E, and F. Note that the only differences among the sheets are that C contains the input cells and formula and that cell A1 in each sheet contains a different term (15, 20, 25, and 30).

**FIGURE 8.25** ▶

*Sheet C with a 15-year term, three input cells, and the formula*

**Third variable**

| C | A | B | C | D | E | F | G | H |
|---|---|---|---|---|---|---|---|---|
| 1 | 15 | 90000 | 100000 | 110000 | 120000 | 130000 | 140000 | 150000 |
| 2 | 6.50% | | | | | | | |
| 3 | 6.75% | | | | | | | |
| 4 | 7.00% | | | | | | | |
| 5 | 7.25% | | | | | | | |
| 6 | 7.50% | | | | | | | |
| 7 | 7.75% | | | | | | | |
| 8 | 8.00% | | | | | | | |
| 9 | 8.25% | | | | | | | |
| 10 | 8.50% | | | | | | | |
| 11 | 8.75% | | | | | | | |
| 12 | 9.00% | | | | | | | |
| 13 | 9.25% | | | | | | | |
| 14 | 9.50% | | | | | | | |
| 15 | | Input Cell 1 | 6.50% | | | | | |
| 16 | | Input Cell 2 | 90000 | | | | | |
| 17 | | Input Cell 3 | 10 | | | | | |
| 18 | | 1021.93179 | | | | | | |

**Input cells** ⟶ (Input Cell 1, Input Cell 2, Input Cell 3)

**Formula cell** ⟶ (row 18)

**FIGURE 8.26** ▶

*Sheets D, E, and F with 20-, 25-, and 30- year terms*

**Third variable**

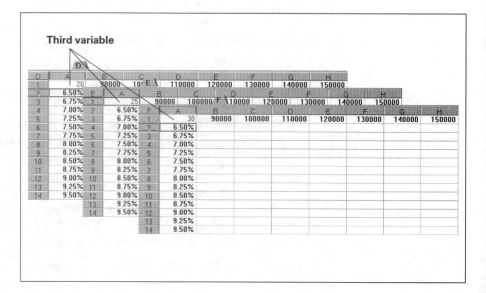

To calculate a three-variable what-if table, follow these steps:

1. Create a sheet in which you enter three input cells, a three-variable formula, and input values for the three variables.

2. Create other sheets in which you enter input values for the three variables.

3. Display the first sheet in the set (that is, the sheet that shows the input cells and formula).

4. Choose Range ➤ Analyze ➤ What-if Table. 1-2-3 opens the What-if dialog box (see Figure 8.27).

**FIGURE 8.27** ▶

*The What-if dialog box with the ranges selected for the three input cells, a formula, and table ranges for four sheets*

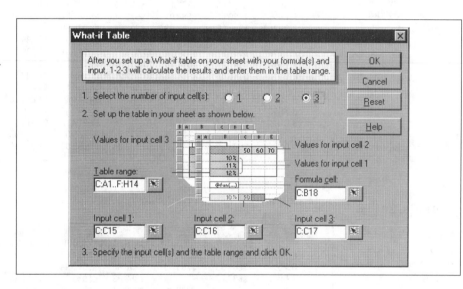

5. Click on the 3 option button.

6. Click on the Input Cell 1 range selector and click on input cell 1.

7. Click on the Input Cell 2 range selector and click on input cell 2.

8. Click on the Input Cell 3 range selector and click on input cell 3.

9. Click on the Formula Cell range selector, and click on the cell in which the formula is located.

10. Click on the Table Range range selector, and drag the range that includes all the input values for the current sheet.

**Advanced 1-2-3 Techniques**

**Ch. 8**

**11.** Edit the contents of the Table Range text box to include the last sheet in the range (for example, change C:A1..C:D7 to C:A1..F:D7).

**12.** Click on OK. 1-2-3 creates the what-if table and places the results in the sheets (see Figures 8.28, 8.29, 8.30, and 8.31).

**13.** If necessary, apply formats and enhancements to the results.

| | A | B | C | D | E | F | G | H |
|---|---|---|---|---|---|---|---|---|
| | 15 | **$90,000** | **$100,000** | **$110,000** | **$120,000** | **$130,000** | **$140,000** | **$150,000** |
| | **6.50%** | $784.00 | $871.11 | $958.22 | $1,045.33 | $1,132.44 | $1,219.55 | $1,306.66 |
| | **6.75%** | $796.42 | $884.91 | $973.40 | $1,061.89 | $1,150.38 | $1,238.87 | $1,327.36 |
| | **7.00%** | $808.95 | $898.83 | $988.71 | $1,078.59 | $1,168.48 | $1,258.36 | $1,348.24 |
| | **7.25%** | $821.58 | $912.86 | $1,004.15 | $1,095.44 | $1,186.72 | $1,278.01 | $1,369.29 |
| | **7.50%** | $834.31 | $927.01 | $1,019.71 | $1,112.41 | $1,205.12 | $1,297.82 | $1,390.52 |
| | **7.75%** | $847.15 | $941.28 | $1,035.40 | $1,129.53 | $1,223.66 | $1,317.79 | $1,411.91 |
| | **8.00%** | $860.09 | $955.65 | $1,051.22 | $1,146.78 | $1,242.35 | $1,337.91 | $1,433.48 |
| | **8.25%** | $873.13 | $970.14 | $1,067.15 | $1,164.17 | $1,261.18 | $1,358.20 | $1,455.21 |
| | **8.50%** | $886.27 | $984.74 | $1,083.21 | $1,181.69 | $1,280.16 | $1,378.64 | $1,477.11 |
| | **8.75%** | $899.50 | $999.45 | $1,099.39 | $1,199.34 | $1,299.28 | $1,399.23 | $1,499.17 |
| | **9.00%** | $912.84 | $1,014.27 | $1,115.69 | $1,217.12 | $1,318.55 | $1,419.97 | $1,521.40 |
| | **9.25%** | $926.27 | $1,029.19 | $1,132.11 | $1,235.03 | $1,337.95 | $1,440.87 | $1,543.79 |
| | **9.50%** | $939.80 | $1,044.22 | $1,148.65 | $1,253.07 | $1,357.49 | $1,461.91 | $1,566.34 |

| | A | B | C | D | E | F | G | H |
|---|---|---|---|---|---|---|---|---|
| | 20 | **$90,000** | **$100,000** | **$110,000** | **$120,000** | **$130,000** | **$140,000** | **$150,000** |
| | **6.50%** | $671.02 | $745.57 | $820.13 | $894.69 | $969.25 | $1,043.80 | $1,118.36 |
| | **6.75%** | $684.33 | $760.36 | $836.40 | $912.44 | $988.47 | $1,064.51 | $1,140.55 |
| | **7.00%** | $697.77 | $775.30 | $852.83 | $930.36 | $1,007.89 | $1,085.42 | $1,162.95 |
| | **7.25%** | $711.34 | $790.38 | $869.41 | $948.45 | $1,027.49 | $1,106.53 | $1,185.56 |
| | **7.50%** | $725.03 | $805.59 | $886.15 | $966.71 | $1,047.27 | $1,127.83 | $1,208.39 |
| | **7.75%** | $738.85 | $820.95 | $903.04 | $985.14 | $1,067.23 | $1,149.33 | $1,231.42 |
| | **8.00%** | $752.80 | $836.44 | $920.08 | $1,003.73 | $1,087.37 | $1,171.02 | $1,254.66 |
| | **8.25%** | $766.86 | $852.07 | $937.27 | $1,022.48 | $1,107.69 | $1,192.89 | $1,278.10 |
| | **8.50%** | $781.04 | $867.82 | $954.61 | $1,041.39 | $1,128.17 | $1,214.95 | $1,301.73 |
| | **8.75%** | $795.34 | $883.71 | $972.08 | $1,060.45 | $1,148.82 | $1,237.19 | $1,325.57 |
| | **9.00%** | $809.75 | $899.73 | $989.70 | $1,079.67 | $1,169.64 | $1,259.62 | $1,349.59 |
| | **9.25%** | $824.28 | $915.87 | $1,007.45 | $1,099.04 | $1,190.63 | $1,282.21 | $1,373.80 |
| | **9.50%** | $838.92 | $932.13 | $1,025.34 | $1,118.56 | $1,211.77 | $1,304.98 | $1,398.20 |

**FIGURE 8.30** ▶

**FIGURE 8.30** ▶

*Sheet E with the results of running the three-variable what-if analysis for a 25-year term*

| 25 | $90,000 | $100,000 | $110,000 | $120,000 | $130,000 | $140,000 | $150,000 |
|---|---|---|---|---|---|---|---|
| **6.50%** | $607.69 | $675.21 | $742.73 | $810.25 | $877.77 | $945.29 | $1,012.81 |
| **6.75%** | $621.82 | $690.91 | $760.00 | $829.09 | $898.18 | $967.28 | $1,036.37 |
| **7.00%** | $636.10 | $706.78 | $777.46 | $848.14 | $918.81 | $989.49 | $1,060.17 |
| **7.25%** | $650.53 | $722.81 | $795.09 | $867.37 | $939.65 | $1,011.93 | $1,084.21 |
| **7.50%** | $665.09 | $738.99 | $812.89 | $886.79 | $960.69 | $1,034.59 | $1,108.49 |
| **7.75%** | $679.80 | $755.33 | $830.86 | $906.39 | $981.93 | $1,057.46 | $1,132.99 |
| **8.00%** | $694.63 | $771.82 | $849.00 | $926.18 | $1,003.36 | $1,080.54 | $1,157.72 |
| **8.25%** | $709.61 | $788.45 | $867.30 | $946.14 | $1,024.99 | $1,103.83 | $1,182.68 |
| **8.50%** | $724.70 | $805.23 | $885.75 | $966.27 | $1,046.80 | $1,127.32 | $1,207.84 |
| **8.75%** | $739.93 | $822.14 | $904.36 | $986.57 | $1,068.79 | $1,151.00 | $1,233.22 |
| **9.00%** | $755.28 | $839.20 | $923.12 | $1,007.04 | $1,090.96 | $1,174.87 | $1,258.79 |
| **9.25%** | $770.74 | $856.38 | $942.02 | $1,027.66 | $1,113.30 | $1,198.93 | $1,284.57 |
| **9.50%** | $786.33 | $873.70 | $961.07 | $1,048.44 | $1,135.81 | $1,223.18 | $1,310.54 |

**FIGURE 8.31** ▶

*Sheet F with the results of running the three-variable what-if analysis for a 30-year term*

| 30 | $90,000 | $100,000 | $110,000 | $120,000 | $130,000 | $140,000 | $150,000 |
|---|---|---|---|---|---|---|---|
| **6.50%** | $568.86 | $632.07 | $695.27 | $758.48 | $821.69 | $884.90 | $948.10 |
| **6.75%** | $583.74 | $648.60 | $713.46 | $778.32 | $843.18 | $908.04 | $972.90 |
| **7.00%** | $598.77 | $665.30 | $731.83 | $798.36 | $864.89 | $931.42 | $997.95 |
| **7.25%** | $613.96 | $682.18 | $750.39 | $818.61 | $886.83 | $955.05 | $1,023.26 |
| **7.50%** | $629.29 | $699.21 | $769.14 | $839.06 | $908.98 | $978.90 | $1,048.82 |
| **7.75%** | $644.77 | $716.41 | $788.05 | $859.69 | $931.34 | $1,002.98 | $1,074.62 |
| **8.00%** | $660.39 | $733.76 | $807.14 | $880.52 | $953.89 | $1,027.27 | $1,100.65 |
| **8.25%** | $676.14 | $751.27 | $826.39 | $901.52 | $976.65 | $1,051.77 | $1,126.90 |
| **8.50%** | $692.02 | $768.91 | $845.80 | $922.70 | $999.59 | $1,076.48 | $1,153.37 |
| **8.75%** | $708.03 | $786.70 | $865.37 | $944.04 | $1,022.71 | $1,101.38 | $1,180.05 |
| **9.00%** | $724.16 | $804.62 | $885.08 | $965.55 | $1,046.01 | $1,126.47 | $1,206.93 |
| **9.25%** | $740.41 | $822.68 | $904.94 | $987.21 | $1,069.48 | $1,151.75 | $1,234.01 |
| **9.50%** | $756.77 | $840.85 | $924.94 | $1,009.03 | $1,093.11 | $1,177.20 | $1,261.28 |

*Advanced 1-2-3 Techniques*

▶ ▶

*Ch.*

**8**

## ▶ *Using the Backsolver*

The Backsolver is an easy-to-use what-if tool, which is ideal for experimenting with single values and lists of values. For example, if you use the what-if tables in the previous section to find a monthly mortgage payment based on a specific mortgage amount, interest rate, and term, you can continue your evaluation by using the Backsolver to see what happens if you increase your monthly payment to a set amount. The Backsolver allows you to "doodle" onscreen, adjusting numbers until you reach a satisfactory conclusion.

What if you are a consultant deciding an appropriate hourly rate for a particular job? List a rate that is standard for your occupation, list your expenses, and at the bottom of the list calculate the surplus dollars that you will end with based on the entered rate. Then use the Backsolver to find the rate that will result in a surplus that makes the job worth taking. Another way to end up with more dollars at the end of the year is to use the Backsolver to reduce each item on a list of expenses by a specific percentage.

To use the Backsolver, prepare a sheet, and choose Range ► Analyze ► Backsolver. In the Backsolver dialog box (see Figure 8.32), select from these options:

**Make the Formula in This Cell**    Type a cell address, or click on the range selector and click on the cell that contains the formula for the value (for example, the year-end surplus) that you would like to optimize.

**Equal to This Value**    In this text box, type the new value (for example, a higher surplus) that you will use to reach the desired amount (for example, a new hourly rate).

**By Changing Cell(s)**    Type a cell address, or click on the range selector and click on the cell that contains the amount to be changed (for example, the hourly rate), or drag over a range of cells to be adjusted by a percentage that the Backsolver computes.

**FIGURE 8.32** ►

*The Backsolver dialog box with options selected to find the hourly rate that will produce an increase in a year-end surplus*

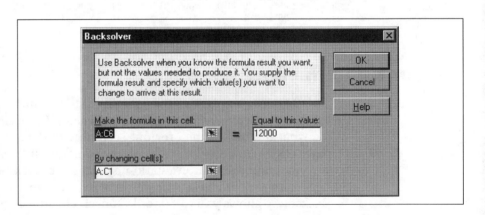

**▶▶▶ T I P**

> **If you want to compare the original values in the sheet with the new values, copy the list to another range of cells.**

Figure 8.33 shows an hourly rate, set expenses, and a surplus. The contents of B1..B6 have been copied to the range C1..C6 so that a comparison can be made after running the Backsolver. Figure 8.34 shows the results of running the Backsolver. If you want to have a surplus of $12,000, the hourly rate must increase to $32.

**FIGURE 8.33** ▶

*A sheet ready to be analyzed using the Backsolver*

| A | A | B | C |
|---|---|---|---|
| 1 | Hourly Rate | 30 | 30 |
| 2 | | | |
| 3 | Annual Pay | 60000 | 60000 |
| 4 | Annual Work Expenses | 10000 | 10000 |
| 5 | Other Expenses | 42000 | 42000 |
| 6 | Surplus (Deficit) | 8000 | 8000 |

**FIGURE 8.34** ▶

*The results of running the Backsolver*

| A | A | B | C |
|---|---|---|---|
| 1 | Hourly Rate | 30 | 32 |
| 2 | | | |
| 3 | Annual Pay | 60000 | 64000 |
| 4 | Annual Work Expenses | 10000 | 10000 |
| 5 | Other Expenses | 42000 | 42000 |
| 6 | Surplus (Deficit) | 8000 | 12000 |

Figure 8.35 shows an original and a copied list of expenses. The range B1..B5 (and C1..C5) shows expenses that are more or less fixed. However, you can run the Backsolver against the contents of the copied cells C7..C11 to decrease the total from $3500 to $3200. Figure 8.36 shows the Backsolver dialog box with options for the sample expense list. Figure 8.37 shows the results of running the Backsolver.

**FIGURE 8.35** ▶

*A sheet with a copied list ready to be analyzed by the Backsolver*

| B | A | B | C |
|---|---|---|---|
| 1 | Mortgage | $1,200.00 | $1,200.00 |
| 2 | Credit Cards | $200.00 | $200.00 |
| 3 | Car Payment | $325.00 | $325.00 |
| 4 | Tuition Loans | $240.00 | $240.00 |
| 5 | Utilities | $120.00 | $120.00 |
| 6 | | | |
| 7 | Food | $275.00 | $275.00 |
| 8 | Entertainment | $260.00 | $260.00 |
| 9 | Gasoline | $230.00 | $230.00 |
| 10 | Clothing | $350.00 | $350.00 |
| 11 | Other | $300.00 | $300.00 |
| 12 | | | |
| 13 | Total | $3,500.00 | $3,500.00 |

**FIGURE 8.36** ▶

*The Backsolver dialog box with options selected to decrease amounts for a list of values*

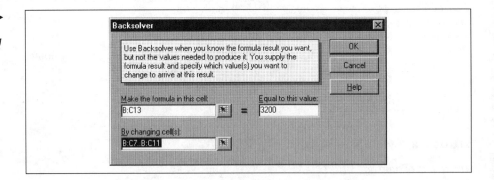

**FIGURE 8.37** ▶

*The results of running the Backsolver*

| B | A | B | C |
|---|---|---|---|
| 1 | Mortgage | $1,200.00 | $1,200.00 |
| 2 | Credit Cards | $200.00 | $200.00 |
| 3 | Car Payment | $325.00 | $325.00 |
| 4 | Tuition Loans | $240.00 | $240.00 |
| 5 | Utilities | $120.00 | $120.00 |
| 6 | | | |
| 7 | Food | $275.00 | $216.70 |
| 8 | Entertainment | $260.00 | $204.88 |
| 9 | Gasoline | $230.00 | $181.24 |
| 10 | Clothing | $350.00 | $275.80 |
| 11 | Other | $300.00 | $236.40 |
| 12 | | | |
| 13 | Total | $3,500.00 | $3,200.00 |

# ▶▶ *Working with 1-2-3 Macros*

Use macros to automate a set of operations on a sheet. For example, you can use a macro to automatically select a range of cells and enhance them with a larger font and boldface. Then, you can change the row height to allow for the increased character size. Or, you can select a range and sort its contents, or you can enter your company name in the top left cell of every sheet you create.

In the remaining pages of this chapter, you'll discover how to create 1-2-3 macros, find out about selected macro commands, and learn how to edit, run, and delete 1-2-3 macros.

1-2-3 macros follow certain rules. Note that:

- A macro command is made up of a left brace ({),an at sign (@), a macro keyword, one or more options, and a closing right brace (}).
- Create a macro command either by selecting a macro keyword from the Macro Keywords dialog box (see Figure 8.38) and filling in the arguments or by typing the command and its arguments.
- When typing a macro command, be sure to type arguments in the order in which they appear in the syntax.
- Place a separator between arguments, by default a semicolon.
- When omitting an optional argument, insert an argument separator in its place.
- Macro commands are case-insensitive: You can use any combination of uppercase and lowercase letters.
- When constructing a macro command, do not insert spaces, except for one between the end of the macro keyword and the beginning of the first argument.
- Enclose text strings, including embedded spaces, within quotation marks. 1-2-3 interprets text not enclosed within quotation marks as range names.
- You can place multiple macro commands one to a cell, within the same cell (with a limit of 512 characters), or in a separate sheet in the workbook.

- To indicate the end of a set of macro commands, either insert an {@QUIT} macro keyword or a blank cell.

- If you plan to use the same macro commands for several workbooks, create a macro library in a separate workbook, which must be open to run one of its macros.

- When placing macro commands in a sheet that also contains data, be sure to place data and macro commands in separate rows and columns. If you then delete a column or a row of data, you will not inadvertently delete macro commands.

- You can name a range of macro commands as you would any other range. If you place macro commands in a separate sheet, you can name that sheet.

**FIGURE 8.38** ▶

*The Macro Keywords dialog box with its default settings*

## ▶ *About the Macro Keywords Dialog Box*

Using the Macro Keywords dialog box, you can create a macro in a cell. To open the Macro Keywords dialog box, type a left brace and, optionally, the at sign ({@) in the selected cell and press the F3 key.

The options in the Macro Keywords dialog box are:

**Category**    From this drop-down list box, select the type of macro keyword that you want to use. The default, All Macros, lists all the 1-2-3 macro keywords.

**@Macro Keywords**    From this scroll list, choose a macro keyword to insert in the selected cell.

**Description**    In this box, view a brief description of the highlighted macro keyword.

# ▶ Selected 1-2-3 Macro Keywords

 1-2-3 provides more than 350 macro keywords, many of which are described in the following section. For detailed information about all 1-2-3 macro keywords, see the 1-2-3 help facility. You can find other 1-2-3 macro information, including a reference guide, on the Lotus support home page. Click on the Go to Lotus Home Page SmartIcon or choose Help ➤ Lotus Internet Support ➤ Lotus Home Page.

### ABS

    {[@]ABS}

Select this keyword to cycle the cell references through absolute (for example, +$C$4), mixed (for example, +$C4 or +C$4), and relative (for example, +C4). This is equivalent to pressing F4.

### ALERT

    {[@]ALERT msg;[1|2];["note"|"caution"|"stop"];
    [results];[x];[y]}

Select this keyword to display a message box that prompts the user to click on OK or Cancel, where:

- *msg* represents the message displayed in the message box.

- 1 displays the OK button or 2 displays both the OK and the Cancel buttons.

- note, caution, or stop indicates the icon in the message box.

- results is the cell in which 1-2-3 returns 1 (OK) or 0 (Cancel), the value of the key on which the user clicks.

- *x* represents the number of pixels from the left side of the screen to the left edge of the message box.

- *y* represents the number of pixels from the top of the screen to the top of the message box.

## ANCHOR

{[@]ANCHOR}

Select this keyword to start a selection of cells at the current cell. This is equivalent to pressing F4 and using arrow keys to increase the number of cells selected.

## APP-ADJUST

{[@]APP-ADJUST *x;y;width;height*}

Select this keyword to adjust the height and position of the 1-2-3 window, where:

- *x* represents the number of pixels from the left side.

- *y* represents the number of pixels from the top of the screen.

- *width* represents the width of the window.

- *height* represents the height of the window.

## BACKSOLVE

{[@]BACKSOLVE *cell;resulting-value;changing-range*}

Select this keyword to run the Backsolver, where:

- *cell* represents the formula used to calculate a specific result.

- *resulting-value* is the value that you want as the result.

- *changing-range* is the range that contains the values to be changed.

## BACKSPACE

{[@]BACKSPACE}

Select this keyword to delete the character to the left of the current cursor location. This is equivalent to pressing the Backspace key. A counterpart command is {DEL} or {DELETE}, with which you can delete the character to the right of the current cursor location or the selection, which is equivalent to pressing the Delete key or choosing Edit ➤ Clear and checking all the checkboxes.

## BACKTAB

{[@]BACKTAB}

Select this keyword to move one sheet to the left. This is equivalent to pressing Ctrl+← or Shift+Tab or using the {BIGLEFT} macro keyword. Counterpart keywords are {BIGRIGHT} and {TAB}, which moves one sheet to the right.

## BRANCH

{[@]BRANCH *location*}

Select this keyword to go to *location*, a cell or a range containing macro instructions, the name of another macro, or subroutine. This is equivalent to a GOTO command in BASIC.

Use {BRANCH} in conjunction with an {IF} command for if-then-else processing.

## CALC

{[@]CALC}

Select this keyword to manually calculate the sheet. This is equivalent to pressing F9.

## CLOSE

{[@]CLOSE}

Select this keyword to close and save the current 1-2-3 file that has been opened with the {OPEN} keyword.

## D

`{[@]D}`

Select this keyword to move down one line. This is equivalent to pressing the down arrow or using the {DOWN} macro keyword. The counterpart keyword is {U} or {UP}, which moves up one line and which is equivalent to pressing the up arrow.

## DELETE-COLUMNS

`{[@]DELETE-COLUMNS [range];["yes"|"no"]`

Select this keyword, which is equivalent to choosing Range ► Delete and clicking on Columns, to delete all or part of a column, where:

- *range* is the name of the cells to be deleted.

- yes indicates that 1-2-3 will delete *range* and fill in the area of deletion with data from the left. If you omit yes or no, 1-2-3 deletes the entire column.

- no indicates that 1-2-3 will delete *range* and fill in the area of deletion with data below. If you omit yes or no, 1-2-3 deletes the entire column.

## DELETE-ROWS

`{[@]DELETE-ROWS [range];["yes"|"no"]`

Select this keyword, which is equivalent to choosing Range ► Delete and clicking on Rows, to delete all or part of a row, where:

- *range* is the name of the cells to be deleted.

- yes indicates that 1-2-3 will delete *range* and fill in the area of deletion with data from the left. If you omit yes or no, 1-2-3 deletes the entire row.

- no indicates that 1-2-3 will delete *range* and fill in the area of deletion with data below. If you omit yes or no, 1-2-3 deletes the entire row.

### EDIT-CLEAR

```
{[@]EDIT-CLEAR [range];["cell-contents"|
"formats"|"both"]}
```

Select this keyword, equivalent to choosing Edit ➤ Clear and checking all or some checkboxes, to delete the selection, its formats, or both, where:

- *range* represents cells to be selected.

- cell-contents indicates that you want to delete the contents of the range but keep the formats.

- formats indicates that you want to delete the formats of the range but keep the contents.

- both indicates that you want to delete both the contents and the formats.

### EDIT-COPY

```
{[@]EDIT-COPY [range];["Clipboard-format"]
```

Select this keyword, equivalent to clicking on the Copy the Current Selection to the Clipboard SmartIcon, choosing Edit ➤ Copy, or pressing Ctrl+C to copy the contents of the selected cells to the Clipboard, where:

- *range* represents cells to be selected.

- *Clipboard-format* is the name of the Clipboard format. If you omit Clipboard-format, 1-2-3 uses the most appropriate format.

### EDIT-CUT

```
{[@]EDIT-CUT [range];["Clipboard-format"]
```

Select this keyword, equivalent to clicking on the Cut the Current Selection to the Clipboard SmartIcon, choosing Edit ➤ Cut, or pressing Ctrl+X to cut the contents of the selected cells to the Clipboard, where:

- *range* represents cells to be selected.

- *Clipboard-format* is the name of the Clipboard format. If you omit Clipboard-format, 1-2-3 uses the most appropriate format.

## EDIT-PASTE

```
{[@]EDIT-CLEAR [range];["clipboard=format"]}
```

Select this keyword, equivalent to clicking on the Paste the Clipboard Contents SmartIcon, choosing Edit ➤ Paste, or pressing Ctrl+V to paste the contents of the Clipboard into the selected range, where:

- *range* represents cells to be selected.
- *Clipboard-format* is the name of the Clipboard format. If you omit Clipboard-format, 1-2-3 uses the most appropriate format.

## FC

```
{[@]FC}
```

Select this keyword to move to the last cell selected in the previous active file or move to the first cell in the first sheet. This is equivalent to pressing Ctrl+Home or using the {FIRSTCELL} macro keyword.

## FILE

```
{[@]FILE}
```

Select this keyword to move to the last cell selected in the next active file. This is equivalent to pressing Ctrl+End.

## FILE-CLOSE

```
{[@]FILE-CLOSE ["yes"|"no"]}
```

Select this keyword, equivalent to choosing File ➤ Close, to close the current file, where:

- yes indicates that you want to close the file without saving it. If you omit yes or no and if you have made no changes, 1-2-3 closes the file without saving. If you omit yes or no and if you have made changes, 1-2-3 opens a dialog box.
- no indicates that you want to close the file if you have made no changes, but want to keep the file open if you have made changes.

### FILE-EXIT

{[@]FILE-EXIT ["yes"|"no"]}

Select this keyword, equivalent to choosing File ➤ Exit or pressing Alt+F4, to end this 1-2-3 session, where:

- yes indicates that you want to exit 1-2-3 without saving the open files. If you omit yes or no and if you have made no changes, 1-2-3 exits without saving. If you omit yes or no and if you have made changes, 1-2-3 opens a dialog box.

- no indicates that you want to exit if you have made no changes, but want to keep 1-2-3 open if you have made changes.

### GOTO

{[@]GOTO}

Select this keyword to open the Go To dialog box with which you can go to a range, sheet, query table, OLE object, chart, map, drawn object, or Notes/FX field. This is equivalent to choosing Edit ➤ Go To or pressing F5 or Ctrl+G.

### HELP

{[@]HELP}

Select this keyword to open a help window. This is equivalent to pressing F1.

### HOME

{[@]HOME}

Select this keyword to move to the top left cell in the current sheet. This is equivalent to pressing Home.

### IF

{[@]IF condition}

Select this keyword to test a condition, which can be a formula, a cell address, a number, or text. If the condition is true, 1-2-3 moves to the next command in the same cell. If the condition is false, 1-2-3 moves to the next cell in the macro.

Advanced 1-2-3 Techniques

Ch.
**8**

If you want to use IF-THEN-ELSE processing, add a {BRANCH} or {RETURN} command to the cell.

### L

    {[@]L}

Select this keyword to move to the previous cell. This is equivalent to pressing the left arrow or using the macro keyword {LEFT}. The counterpart keywords are {R} and {RIGHT}, which you use to move to the next cell and which are equivalent to pressing the right arrow.

### NEXTSHEET

    {[@]NEXTSHEET}

Select this keyword to move to the next sheet in a multisheet workbook. This is equivalent to pressing Ctrl+PgUp or using the {NS} macro keyword. The counterpart keywords are {PREVSHEET} and {PS} with which you can move to the previous sheet in a multisheet workbook and which are equivalent to pressing Ctrl+PgDn.

### PGDN

    {[@]PGDN}

Select this keyword to move down the number of rows currently shown in the window. This is equivalent to pressing PgDn. The counterpart keyword is {PGUP} with which you can move up the number of rows currently shown in the window and which is equivalent to pressing PgUp.

### PRINT

    {[@]PRINT ["all"|"current"|"selection"];
    [from-page];[to-page];[start-page];[num-copies]}

Select this keyword, equivalent to choosing File ➤ Print or pressing Ctrl+P, to print all or part of the current file, where:

- **all** prints the entire current file.
- **current** prints the current worksheet.
- **selection** prints the current selection.

- *from-page* indicates the starting page number.
- *to-page* indicates the ending page number.
- *start-page* indicates the number with which the page numbering starts.
- *num-copies* indicates the number of copies to print.

### PRINT?

```
{[@]PRINT?}
```

Select this keyword, equivalent to choosing File ➤ Print or pressing Ctrl+P, to open the Print dialog box.

### RETURN

```
{[@]RETURN}
```

Select this keyword to return from a subroutine to which you have branched to the macro from which you originally branched in if-then-else processing.

### ROW-HEIGHT-FIT-LARGEST

```
{[@]ROW-HEIGHT-FIT-LARGEST [range]}
```

Select this keyword to set the height of the specified row to fit its highest font, where:

- *range* is the cell or cells whose height you want to change.

### SELECT

```
{[@]SELECT name;[part];
["chart"|"draw"|"query"|"range"]}
```

Select this keyword to select an element in the current sheet but not go to it. You can select cells, a range, a query, a table, a chart, or a graphic, where:

- *name* represents the range name, range address, or element name (enclosed within quotation marks) to be selected.
- *part* represents part of the named element (for example, a cell within a range). If you omit *part*, the entire element is selected.

- *chart, draw, query, <u>range</u>* represents the name of the type of element to be selected.

### SELECT-BIGLEFT

```
{[@]SELECT-BIGLEFT}
```

Select this keyword to select all the cells one sheet to the left. This is equivalent to pressing Shift+Ctrl+←. The counterpart keyword is {SELECT-BIGRIGHT} with which you can select all the cells one sheet to the right and which is equivalent to pressing Shift+Ctrl+→.

### SELECT-DOWN

```
{[@]SELECT-DOWN}
```

Select this keyword to select and move down one line. This is equivalent to pressing Shift+↓. The counterpart keyword is {SELECT-UP} with which you can select and move up one line and which is equivalent to pressing Shift+↑.

### SELECT-HOME

```
{[@]SELECT-HOME}
```

Select this keyword to select all the cells between the current cell and the cell in the upper left corner. This is equivalent to pressing Shift+Home.

### SELECT-LEFT

```
{[@]SELECT-LEFT}
```

Select this keyword to select the current cell and the previous cell. This is equivalent to pressing Shift+←. The counterpart keyword is {SELECT-RIGHT} with which you can select the current cell and the next cell and which is equivalent to pressing Shift+→.

### SELECT-PGDN

```
{[@]SELECT-PGDN}
```

Select this keyword to select from the current cell down the number of rows currently shown in the window. This is equivalent to pressing Shift+PgDn. The counterpart keyword is {SELECT-PGUP} with which you can select from the current cell up the number of rows currently shown in the window and which is equivalent to pressing Shift+PgDn.

### {STYLE-FONT-ALL}

```
{[@]STYLE-FONT-ALL [font];[point-size];
[bold];[italic];[underline];[range];[underline-type];
[font-type];["ansi"|"oem"|"symbol"|"kanji"]}
```

Select this keyword to change the font or font size or to enhance the contents of the specified range, where:

- *font* is the name of a font surrounded by quotation marks.

- *point-size* is a numeric point size.

- bold is a "yes" (apply boldface to the selection) or "no" (remove boldface from the selection) answer.

- italic is a "yes" (apply italics to the selection) or "no" (remove italics from the selection) answer.

- underline is a "yes" (underline the selection) or "no" (remove an underline from the selection) answer.

- *range* indicates the cells that you want to style.

- underline-type is a number: 0 (underline), 1 (double underline), or 2 (wide underline). The default is 0.

- font-type represents a family of fonts: "dontcare" (a relative of *font*, *"decorative" (a symbol font), "modern" (a fixed font), "roman" (a serif body text font), "script" (a script font), or "swiss" (a sans serif headline font)*.

- ansi (the default), oem, symbol, and kanji represent character sets.

## ▶ Creating a Macro

To create a macro, follow these steps:

**1.** Click in the cell in which you want to insert the macro.

**2.** Type a left brace ({).

**3.** Press F3 (NAME). 1-2-3 opens the Macro Keywords dialog box.

4. Select a category or All Macros (the default).

5. Either double-click on a macro keyword, or select the keyword and click on OK. 1-2-3 places the macro keyword and any arguments, in the selected cell.

6. Press Enter. 1-2-3 moves the cursor to the cell below the one in which you inserted the macro keyword.

7. To insert another macro keyword, repeat steps 2 through 6. You can select duplicate commands in a macro.

Figure 8.39 shows a macro with its documented name in cell A3 and the macro commands in cells B3 to B6. The sample macro displays a message box. If you click on OK, the macro changes the contents of the range to Arial 24 bold and adjusts the row height to allow for the larger characters. If you click on No, 1-2-3 ends the macro.

**FIGURE 8.39 ▶**

*A sample macro, which changes the font and font size of the contents and adjusts the row height.*

| LARGEBOLD | {ALERT "You are about to make the contents of this cell large and bold";2;"caution";b:c3} |
| | {IF RESPONSE=0}{QUIT} |
| | {STYLE-FONT-ALL "Arial";24;"yes"} |
| | {ROW-HEIGHT-FIT-LARGEST} |

## ▶ Running a Macro

You can run a macro in several ways:

- To run a named macro, choose Edit ➤ Scripts & Macros ➤ Run or press Alt+F3. In the Run Scripts & Macros dialog box, click on the Macro option button, select the name from the From drop-down list box, select a range, and click on the Run button.

- To run an unnamed macro, click in its first cell and press Alt+F3.

Processing Words
with Word Pro

# PART THREE

# CHAPTER 9

# Planning and Creating Your First Document

►► **I**n this chapter, you'll find out about the elements of the Word Pro application window and certain important word-processing features: the ruler, WYSIWYG, Insert and Typeover modes, the spelling checker, the thesaurus, the grammar checker, and the format checker. The basics of opening and saving files are covered in the *Getting Acquainted with SmartSuite* chapter, and editing concepts are covered in the *Editing in SmartSuite Applications* chapter.

## ►► *Introducing Word Pro*

Word Pro is an easy-to-use and extensive word processor with which you can create a wide range of documents—from a simple one-page memo to a heavily illustrated manual with a table of contents, footnotes, and an index. Regardless of the type of document that you create, you can use the built-in spelling checker, grammar checker, format checker, and thesaurus to proof and refine your work before you send it to the outside world.

Using Word Pro, you can do the following:

- Create a business plan or a report that incorporates 1-2-3 charts and spreadsheet data, drawings and clip art, Approach database information, organizations charts from Freelance Graphics, and even calendars from Organizer.

- Print a handout that accompanies a Freelance Graphics presentation.

# ▶▶ *Viewing the Word Pro Window*

The Word Pro application window (see Figure 9.1) contains many of the elements that you found out about in the *Getting Acquainted with SmartSuite* chapter. Because you are now working in a word-processing application, its window includes unique elements to help make your job easier, as well as common elements about which you have already learned.

**FIGURE 9.1** ▶

*The Word Pro application window provides many helpful elements to help you create and edit documents.*

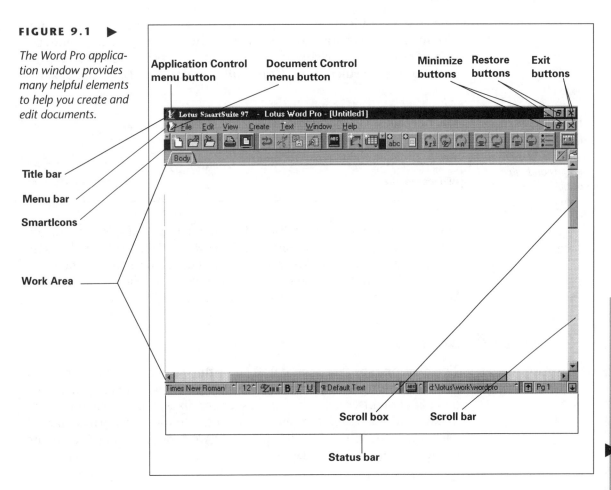

Application Control menu button

Document Control menu button

Minimize buttons

Restore buttons

Exit buttons

Title bar

Menu bar

SmartIcons

Work Area

Scroll box

Scroll bar

Status bar

Creating a Document

▶▶

*Ch.*

**9**

## ▶ Word Pro SmartIcons

To learn how SmartIcons work, see the *Getting Acquainted with Smart-Suite* chapter. When you start Word Pro for the first time, the Universal SmartIcons appear. From then on, the SmartIcons set with which you end a Word Pro session are the same ones that appear when you start a new session.

## ▶ The Ruler

The ruler (see Figure 9.2) displays the current margin and tab settings. Use the ruler to change these settings, to determine paragraph indention (if any), and to widen or narrow columns of text. You'll learn about using the ruler in the *Formatting and Editing a Document* chapter.

**FIGURE 9.2** ▶

*The Word Pro ruler displays and defines margins and tab positions.*

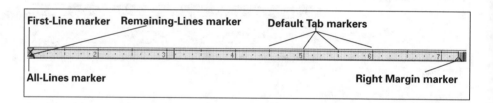

You can display or hide the ruler. To show the ruler, if it is not already on display, choose View ➤ Show/Hide ➤ Ruler. If the ruler appears in the application window, Word Pro places a checkmark before the ruler command. To hide the ruler, choose View ➤ Show/Hide ➤ Ruler again. Word Pro removes the checkmark preceding the Ruler command.

## ▶ Division Tabs

The division tabs (see Figure 9.3) show the parts of a document. When you are working with a long document, separating its parts (such as the table of contents, chapters, sections, appendixes, the index, and so on) makes working easier. Simply click on a tab to move to a particular part of the document. You'll learn about working with long documents in the *Working with Long Documents* chapter.

**FIGURE 9.3** ▶

*The Word Pro division tabs identify each part of a longer document.*

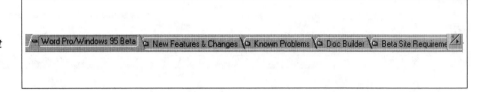

## ▶ *The Document Area*

The document area (see Figure 9.4) displays your document as you work. The vertical blinking line is the *insertion point,* which shows the location of the next character that you type. Don't confuse the insertion point with the I-beam mouse pointer; use the I-beam to point to the area in a page of text to which you want to move the insertion point. Notice that the document area includes both a vertical and a horizontal scroll bar.

**FIGURE 9.4** ▶

*In the document area, you can type and edit each document.*

## ▶ *The Word Pro Status Bar*

You use the Word Pro Status bar (see Figure 9.5) to change paragraph style, font, or point size; check the current date and time, the current path, or current location of the insertion point; check for mail (if cc:Mail or Notes is installed); switch typing modes; display a set of SmartIcons; and display the current page number (if you are in Layout mode) or go to a specific page or screen.

Creating a
Document

▶ ▶

*Ch.*
**9**

**FIGURE 9.5** ▶

*The Word Pro Status bar consists of various buttons with which you can change styles, fonts, and point sizes, and check your current status.*

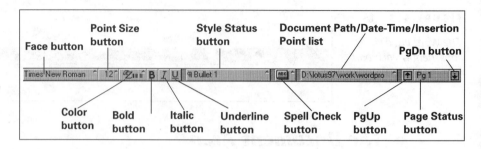

The Word Pro Status bar provides these buttons:

**Face**   Click on this button to reveal a list of the installed fonts on your computer system (see Figure 9.6).

**Point Size**   Click on this button to display a list of point sizes for the selection.

▶▶ N O T E

**The available point sizes depend on the fonts that are installed on your system and which one you select. For instance, if you choose the Fixedsys font, only these point sizes are available: 5, 10, 14, 19, 24, 29, 34, and 38.**

**FIGURE 9.6** ▶

*A list of some of the fonts installed on one computer system. The highlighted font is the current font.*

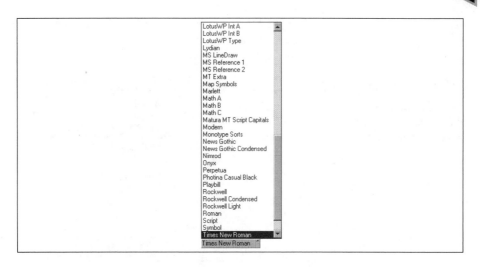

**Color**    Click on this button to reveal a palette from which you can choose a color for the selected text.

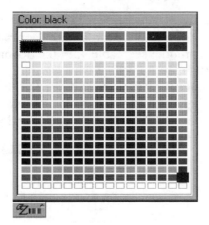

 **Bold**    Click on this button to apply or remove boldface from selected text.

 **Italic**    Click on this button to italicize or remove italics from selected text.

 **Underline**    Click on this button to underline or remove the underline from selected text.

Creating a Document

▶ ▶

*Ch.*

**9**

**Style Status**    Click on this button to reveal a list of paragraph styles (see Figure 9.7).

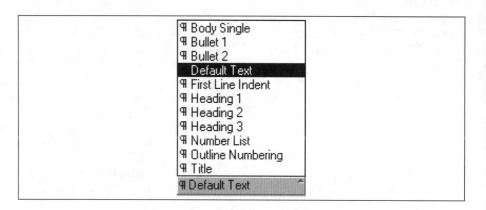

**Spell Check**    Click on this button, if it is highlighted, to add this word to the dictionary.

**Document Path/Date-Time/Insertion Point list**    Click on this button to cycle through the computer system time and date; the typing mode (see Table 9.2); the document path; the editor of this file (usually the person who registered this copy of Word Pro); the language used to write and/or edit this document; the current line number, column number, and position (using the current unit of measure) of the insertion point; and version of this file.

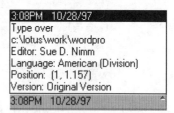

**Mail Notification**    If you have cc:Mail or Notes and you see an envelope on this button, click on it to read your mail.

**PgUp Arrow**    Click this button to go to the previous page.

**Page Status**    Click on this button, which shows the current page number, to display the Go To dialog box (see Figure 9.8).

**PgDn**    Click on this button to move to the next page, unless you are on the last page or screen.

▶ **TABLE 9.2:** *Word Pro Typing Modes*

| Mode | Description |
|------|-------------|
| Insert | As you type a character or a space, all characters and spaces to the right of the insertion point are pushed ahead; no text is deleted as you type. Insert mode is the default typing mode. To switch between Insert mode and Typeover mode, press the Insert key. To cycle through all typing modes, click on the Typing Mode button. |
| Typeover | As you type a character or a space, the character or space to the right of the insertion point is erased. |
| Markup Edits | As you type a character or a space, Word Pro marks it with the attributes or colors that you specify. This means that you can more easily identify the text that you edit during a particular Word Pro session. |

**FIGURE 9.8** ▶

*The Go To dialog box, which allows you to move to a particular page or item in the current document*

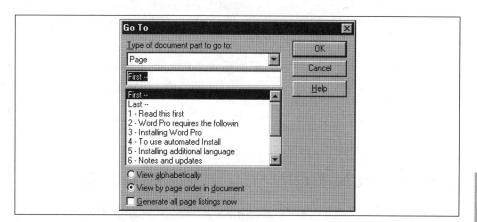

▶▶ **TIP**

**You can also open the Go To dialog box by choosing Edit ➤ Go To or by pressing Ctrl+G.**

## ▶▶ *What Is WYSIWYG?*

With Word Pro you can view a document as it will look when printed. This technology is known as WYSIWYG (What You See Is What You Get).

## ▶▶ *Creating a Document*

Once you start Word Pro, you can just start typing in the document window after selecting a SmartMaster stylesheet (see the *Getting Acquainted with SmartSuite* chapter). You can modify or select a new stylesheet if desired.

As you type, the text seems to push the insertion point along the line toward the right margin. This is known as *Insert mode.* When the text reaches the end of the line, you don't have to press Enter to start a new line. Word Pro has *word wrap*, which means that if a word that you are typing won't fit on the line, Word Pro moves the word to the beginning of the next line.

By default, Word Pro is in Insert mode. To replace each existing character or space with a new character or space, press the Insert key. This switches to *Typeover mode.* Typeover mode is useful when you want to replace an entire block of text without explicitly deleting it.

## ▶▶ *Checking Your Document*

Part of the editing process is running Word Pro's spelling checker, thesaurus, and grammar checker.

As you learned in the *Getting Acquainted with SmartSuite* chapter, four of the five SmartSuite applications have access to the central spelling checker. To learn how to use the spelling checker, see the *Getting Acquainted with SmartSuite* chapter. These are the proofing tools that are unique to Word Pro:

- A thesaurus, which helps you find the best synonym (and sometimes antonym) for a selected word.

• A grammar checker, which you can set to different levels of formality and which can display readability statistics. The grammar checker is available only if you install Word Pro using the Custom Install program. To learn about using the Custom Install program, see the *Installing Lotus SmartSuite* appendix.

## ▶ *Using the Thesaurus*

Use the thesaurus to substitute synonyms for overused words in a document. You can also use the thesaurus to find a better word—one that conveys your meaning with greater clarity.

 Place the insertion point immediately before or after the first or last character in the word, or click on any character within the word, and choose Edit ➤ Check Thesaurus or click on the Thesaurus SmartIcon. Word Pro displays the Thesaurus dialog box (see Figure 9.9).

**FIGURE 9.9** ▶

*The Thesaurus dialog box displays words from which you can choose.*

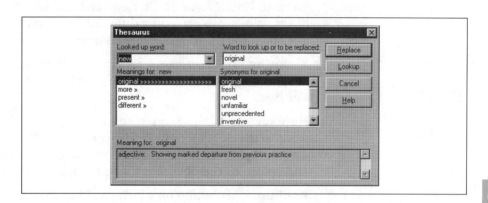

The Thesaurus dialog box provides these options:

**Looked Up Word** Displays the word or phrase that you selected. If there is no synonym for a selected word (or if you have misspelled it), Word Pro displays a dialog box (see Figure 9.10). To return to a previous looked-up word, open the drop-down list box and select it.

**Word To Look Up or To Be Replaced** A text box that displays the suggested replacement word.

Creating a
Document

▶ ▶

*Ch.*
**9**

**FIGURE 9.10** ▶

*If you select a word that is not in the thesaurus, Word Pro opens the Can't Find Word inThesaurus dialog box from which you can select the word for which you are looking.*

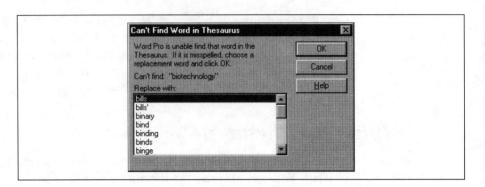

**Meanings for:** *looked-up word*    A text box that displays a list of replacement words. When you click on a word in this list, the Word To Look Up or To Be Replaced text box also displays the word.

**Synonyms for** *word to look up or to be replaced*    A scroll box that displays a list of synonyms starting with the word in the Word to Look Up or To Be Replaced and Meanings for: *word* boxes. When you click on a different word in the Meanings for: *word* box, the list of synonyms changes.

**Meaning for:** *looked-up word*    A box that displays the part of speech and definition of the highlighted word in the Meanings For box.

**Replace**    A button on which you click to replace the selected word in the document with the word in the Word To Look Up or To Be Replaced text box. Click on Cancel to close the dialog box and return to the document with the replacement word in place.

**Lookup**    A button on which you click to change the looked-up word and all the other words, lists, and meanings in the dialog box, to the word in the Word To Look Up or To Be Replaced text box.

## ▶ Checking Your Grammar

An important step in editing your document is to check its grammar—following a set of stringent or casual rules or somewhere in between. You can also specify that the grammar checker produce a list of readability statistics after it evaluates the document.

▶▶ **N O T E**

> **The grammar checker is available only if you use the Custom Install program to install Word Pro. For more information, see the *Installing Lotus SmartSuite* appendix.**

Choose Edit ➤ Check Grammar or click on the Grammar Check SmartIcon to display the Grammar Check bar (see Figure 9.11).

**FIGURE 9.11** ▶

*When the grammar checker finds potential problems with your document, it highlights the affected part of the document, gives a reason, and sometimes suggests a solution.*

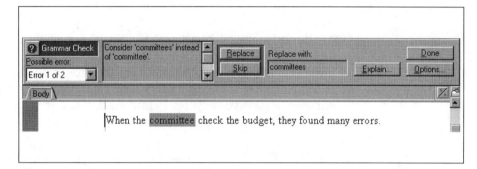

After you start the grammar checker, it runs until it finds a sentence to be brought to your attention. At this point, the grammar checker highlights the word, phrase, or sentence in question, displays the reason for the highlight, and sometimes suggests a replacement.

These are the options in the Grammar Check bar:

**Possible Error**     The number of errors found in the highlighted word, phrase, or sentence.

**Suggestions**     A scroll box containing a suggestion.

**Questionable Item / Replace With**     The type of item that may or may not be in error or an optional replacement word, phrase, or sentence. If the grammar checker does not have a questionable item or suggested replacement, the box is empty.

**Replace**     A button on which you click to replace the selected sentence with a replacement word, phrase, or sentence in the Replace With box.

**Skip**    A button on which you click to ignore the selected word, phrase, or sentence and find the next problem.

**Continue**    A button on which you click to return to running the grammar checker after you have edited in the document.

**Explain**    Opens the Rule Explanation dialog box in which a more detailed explanation of the problem appears. To close this dialog box and return to the grammar checker, click on OK.

**Options**    Opens the Grammar Options dialog box in which you can select and set the level of rules and can specify the grammatical style. (See the following section.)

**Done**    Closes the Grammar Check bar.

At the end of its evaluation, the grammar checker displays the Readability Statistics dialog box (see Figure 9.12), which provides document statistics (for example, the number of words, sentences, paragraphs, and syllables; words per sentence and sentences per paragraph; and the number of passive sentences) and readability statistics (showing the grade level at which you are writing).

**FIGURE 9.12** ▶

*The Readability Statistics dialog box shows the word, sentence, paragraph, and syllable count and the grade level for the document.*

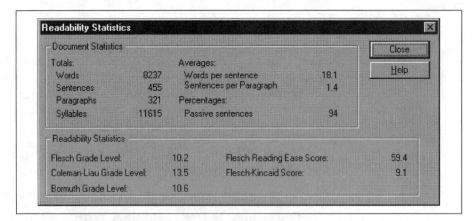

## *Specifying Options for the Grammar Checker*

You can customize the grammar checker to change the rules in order to inform you of occurrences that either don't meet the rules or grammatical styles. To customize the grammar checker, choose Edit ➤ Check Grammar. When the grammar check bar appears, click on the Options button.

The Grammar Options dialog box is composed of the Rules section (see Figure 9.13) and the Grammatical Style section (see Figure 9.14).

**FIGURE 9.13** ▶

*In the Rules section of the Grammar Options dialog box, you can select a set of rules, set the formality, and customize a set of rules.*

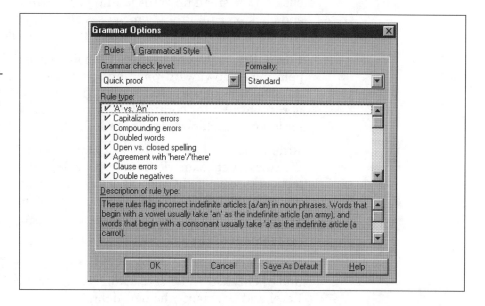

**FIGURE 9.14** ▶

*In the Grammatical Style section of the Grammar Options dialog box, you can select options such as the number of words per sentence, the number of spaces between sentences, and the number of consecutive prepositional phrases or nouns.*

Creating a Document

▶ ▶

*Ch.*
**9**

The Rules section contains these options:

**Grammar Check Level**     Open this drop-down list box and click on the small upward-pointing or downward-pointing arrow and click on Full Proof, which uses all 42 rules, or Quick Proof (the default), which is less stringent, with 26 rules.

**Formality**     Open this drop-down list box and click on the upward-pointing or downward-pointing arrow and click on an option for the strictness of the rules: Formal (all the rules), Standard (ignores the rules for contractions), and Informal (ignores the rules for jargon, stock phrases, and wordiness). Standard is the default.

**Rule Type**     This scroll box contains short descriptions for all the rules. A checkmark preceding a rule indicates that it is in effect for the selected Grammar Check Level and Formality. Click on the Rule Type to insert or clear the checkmark.

**Description of Rule Type**     When you select a Rule Type, an explanation of the rule is displayed here.

**Save As Default**     Click on this button to make this combination of checked and cleared Rule Types for this Grammar Check Level and Formality the new default.

▸▸ **W A R N I N G**

**Clicking on the Save As Default button changes a set of rules permanently. The only way to return to the original settings is to keep a record of them, manually change the Rule Types, and click on Save As Default.**

The Grammatical Style section contains these options:

**Maximum Number of Words per Sentence**     In this text/option box, type or select the maximum number of words that you want any sentence to have (the intent here is to prevent overly complex sentences). Valid values range from 25 to 75. The default is 35.

**Number of Spaces Between Sentences**    In this text/option box, type or select the number of spaces after a period ending a sentence and before the first character in the following sentence. Valid values are 1 (which is the default and which is also the acceptable spacing for typeset documents) or 2.

**Flag Consecutive Prepositional Phrases**    From this drop-down list box, select Never (the default), If 3 or More in a Row, If 4 or More in a Row, or If 5 or More in a Row.

**Flag Consecutive Nouns**    From this drop-down list box, select Never (the default), If 3 or More in a Row, If 4 or More in a Row, or If 5 or More in a Row.

**Flag Split Infinitives**    From this drop-down list box, select Never (the default), Always, If 2 or More Intervening Words, If 3 or More Intervening Words, or If 4 or More Intervening Words.

**Maximum Number of Identical Sentence Openers**    From the text/option box, type or select the number of consecutive sentences (For Consecutive Sentences) and the number of sentences within 10 sentences (Within 10 Sentences) that can start with the same words. Valid values for both options range from 0 to 9. The default for both is 3.

**Save As Default**    Click on this button to make the specified options the new default.

## Customizing Grammar Checker Rules

You can adjust the grammar checker rules to fit your grammatical strengths and weaknesses. When you have finished checking or clearing Rule Types, you can select another Grammar Check Level and/or Formality and repeat the process. If you have a question about any of the options, click on it and read the text in the Description of Rule Type box. When you have finished, click on Save As Default to save the set as the new default.

To customize rules for the grammar checker, follow these steps:

1.  Choose Edit ➤ Check Grammar. Word Pro displays the Grammar Check bar immediately below the SmartIcons toolbar and starts checking the open document's grammar.

Creating a
Document

➤ ➤

*Ch.*
**9**

2. Click on the Options button. Word Pro opens the Rules section of the Grammar Options dialog box.

3. If the selection in the Grammar Check Level drop-down list box is not your choice, choose Quick Proof or Full Proof from the list.

4. If the selection in the Formality drop-down list box is not your choice, choose Formal, Standard, or Informal from the list.

5. Check or clear Rule Types to ease or tighten the rules. When you select a Rule Type in order to check or clear it, Word Pro explains the option in the Description of Rule Type box.

6. To specify the grammatical style of sentences and paragraphs, click on the Grammatical Style tab.

7. To save the selected options as the new default, click on the Save As Default button.

8. Select OK or press Enter. Word Pro returns to the document with the Grammar Check bar remaining on the screen.

9. Click on Done to close the Grammar Check bar.

## ▶ Checking Document Information

Word Pro automatically tracks your document by keeping information such as the date and time of creation, the date and time of your last revision, the total number of revisions, and the time that you have spent working on the document. You can also see the number of pages, words, and characters and the size of the document (in kilobytes).

To open the Document Properties dialog box (see Figure 9.15), choose File ➤ Document Properties ➤ Document. If you want to make your future job of locating the document easier, type a description and keywords in the Description and Keywords text boxes.

## ▶ Checking Your Document Format

In Word Pro you can check your document for particular formats:

● Do one or two spaces follow the period at the end of a sentence? (If you are preparing documents for typesetting, the standard is one space.)

**FIGURE 9.15** ▶

*The Document Proper-*
*ties dialog box displays*
*and allows you to add*
*information about the*
*current document.*

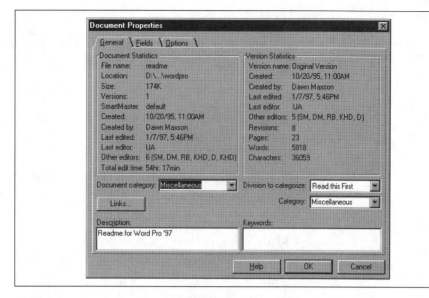

- How are bulleted lists formatted? For example, if you have created them using asterisks as bullets, the format checker will automatically convert them to standard bulleted lists.

- What do abbreviations, such as AM, PM, and EST, look like? The format checker will change them from uppercase letters to 10% smaller uppercase letters.

- When you type quotation marks and single quotes, the format checker can change them to typographically correct symbols. Or if you create arrows or trademark and copyright symbols using combinations of characters, the format checker can change them to the proper symbols.

- If you type two commas or spaces or underline the space following a word, the format checker can correct them.

To check document formats, click on the Check Format SmartIcon or choose Edit ➤ Check Format. Word Pro opens the Format Check bar and runs the format checker. When a formatting error is found, the checker highlights it and adds a set of buttons to the Format Check bar (see Figure 9.16).

Creating a
Document

**Ch.**
**9**

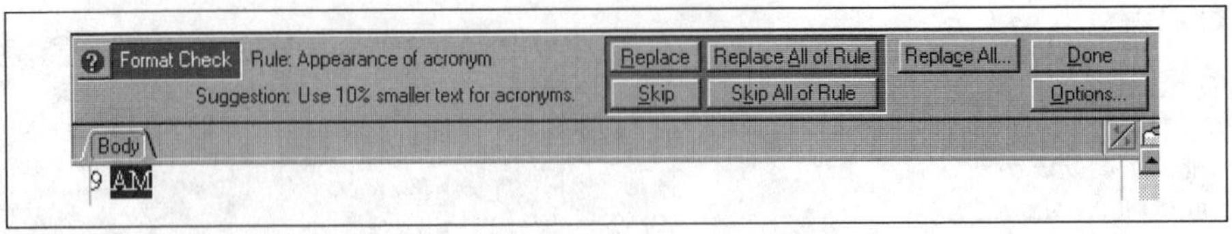

**FIGURE 9.16** ▶

*The Format Check bar after finding a format error*

These are the options in the Format Check bar:

**Rule**   The rule that governs the highlighted characters.

**Suggestion**   The solution to the format error.

**Replace**   A button on which you click to replace the selected format with a replacement format.

**Skip**   A button on which you click to ignore the selected word, phrase, or sentence and find the next problem.

**Replace All of Rule**   A button on which you click to replace all similar formats with a replacement format.

**Skip All of Rule**   A button on which you click to ignore all similar formats and find the next problem.

**Continue Format Check**   A button on which you click to return to running the format checker after the format checker says that it is complete.

**Replace All**   A button on which you click to accept all corrections that the format checker suggests, except for those that you already skipped.

**Options**   Opens the Grammar Options dialog box in which you can select rules for the format checker. (See the following section.)

**Done**   Closes the Format Check bar.

## Specifying Format Checker Options

You can change the format checker options. If you have a question about any of the options, simply click on the Help button. When you have finished, click on OK to save the options.

To specify options for the format checker, follow these steps:

**1.** Choose Edit ➤ Check Format. Word Pro displays the Format Check toolbar immediately below the SmartIcons toolbar and starts checking the open document's format.

**2.** Click on the Options button. Word Pro opens the Format Check Options dialog box (see Figure 9.17).

**3.** To check the number of spaces between sentences, check the Check Spacing Between Sentences checkbox, and select 1 Space or 2 Spaces.

**4.** To automatically format bullets, check the Improve Format of Bulleted Lists checkbox.

**5.** To change particular abbreviations or acronyms to smaller size uppercase letters, check the Improve the Appearance of Acronyms checkbox.

**6.** To replace certain typed characters with typographical characters, scroll through the Replace with Proper Character scroll box, checking those characters and combinations of characters to be replaced.

**7.** To correct trailing space underlines, double spaces, or double commas, check the options in the Mis-typed Correction Options text box.

**8.** To save the selected options and to close the dialog box, click on OK.

**9.** To close the Format Check bar, click on Done.

**FIGURE 9.17** ▶

*The Format Check Options dialog box showing its starting options*

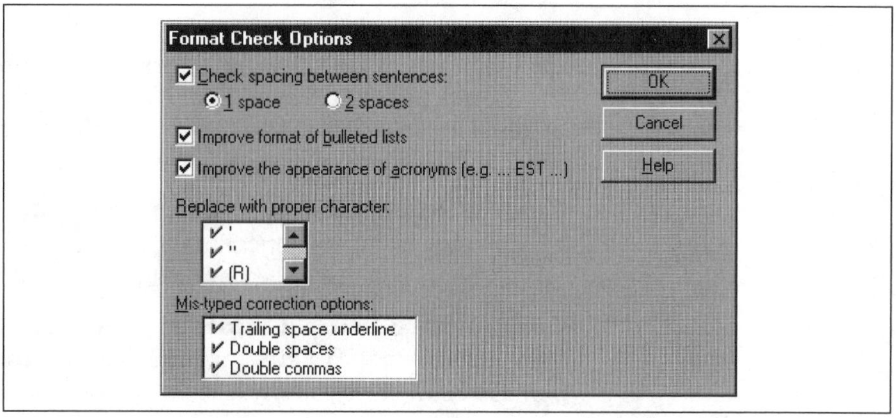

Ch.
**9**

## ▶ *Using the SmartCorrect Feature*

If you constantly mistype certain words (for example, *teh* instead of *the* or *recieve* instead of *receive*), you can have Word Pro correct the typos automatically using the SmartCorrect feature. Or you can type a few characters (for example, LDC) and have Word Pro replace them with a longer word or words (for example, Lotus Development Corporation). The Word Pro programmers have selected words that are commonly typed incorrectly, and you can add to or delete from that list. Smart-Correct runs as you type; you don't have to start it.

To add or delete a word from the list or change a SmartCorrect option, choose Edit ▶ SmartCorrect, and work in the SmartCorrect dialog box (see Figure 9.18).

**FIGURE 9.18** ▶

*The SmartCorrect dialog box with its default options*

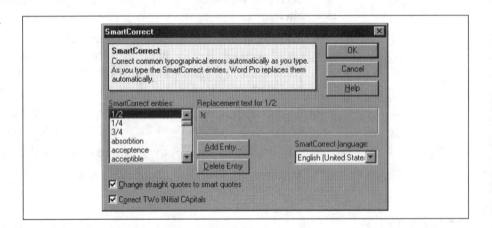

These are the options in the SmartCorrect dialog box:

**SmartCorrect Entries**    A scroll box containing a list of entries that will be corrected when encountered in a document

**Change Straight Quotes to Smart Quotes**    A checkbox in which you can place a checkmark to automatically change straight quotes (that is, ") to smart quotes (that is, "")

**Correct TWo INitial CApitals**    A checkbox in which you can place a checkmark to automatically change the second of two uppercase characters to lowercase (for example, Two Initial Capitals)

**Replacement Text for** *word*    A box in which you can see the entry that will replace the selected mistyped entry in the Smart-Correct Entries scroll box

**Add Entry**    A button on which you click to open the Add Smart-Correct Entry dialog box to add an entry to the list in the SmartCorrect Entries scroll box

**Delete Entry**    A button on which you click to delete an entry from the list in the SmartCorrect Entries scroll box

▶▶ **W A R N I N G**

**Word Pro does not ask you to confirm a deletion from the SmartCorrect Entries scroll box. You cannot undo a deletion once it has occurred.**

**SmartCorrect Language**    A list of languages for SmartCorrect entries

## Adding a Word to the SmartCorrect List

To add a word to the SmartCorrect list, follow these steps:

1. Choose Edit ➤ SmartCorrect. Word Pro opens the SmartCorrect dialog box.

2. Click on the Add Entry button. The Add SmartCorrect Entry dialog box (see Figure 9.19) appears.

3. In the SmartCorrect Entry text box, type the incorrect version of a word or character.

4. In the Replacement Text text box, type the correct version.

5. Click on OK.

**FIGURE 9.19** ▶

*The filled-in Add SmartCorrect Entry dialog box*

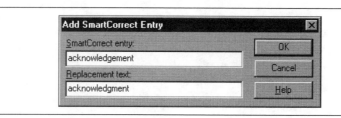

*Ch.* **9**

▶▶ **N O T E**

**To replace typed characters with a symbol, use the instructions in the Adding Special Characters section of the *Formatting and Editing a Document* chapter.**

## Deleting a Word from the SmartCorrect List

To delete a word from the SmartCorrect list, follow these steps:

1. Choose Edit ➤ SmartCorrect. Word Pro opens the SmartCorrect dialog box.

2. From the SmartCorrect Entries scroll box, select a word to be deleted.

3. Click on the Delete Entry button. Word Pro removes the word without your confirming the deletion and closes the dialog box.

► ► CHAPTER 10

# Formatting and Editing a Document

▶▶ **O**nce you have typed a document, your work is far from done. You'll want to highlight and possibly change the type face (font) and size of some text, such as headings and special terms. You may decide to center or justify the alignment of selected paragraphs. You might even add page numbers and headers and footers.

In this chapter, you'll find out about many of Word Pro's formatting and editing functions (and some special shortcuts). Remember that if you have any questions about editing features common to most Smart-Suite applications, you can turn to the *Editing in SmartSuite Applications* chapter.

# ▶▶ *Formatting Text*

Word Pro has three basic levels of formatting: document-wide (page layout), paragraph, and character. *Document-wide formatting* encompasses the entire document page by page; *paragraph formatting* changes the appearance of one or more selected paragraphs; and *character formatting* determines the appearance of selected characters, words, lines, or sentences. You change document-wide formats using the Page Layout Properties InfoBox, and you format paragraphs and characters using the Text Properties InfoBox. For information about the InfoBox panels that are available for several SmartSuite programs, see the *Getting Acquainted with SmartSuite* chapter.

Document-wide formatting controls margins, paper dimensions and orientation, the insertion of headers and footers, page and line numbering, and other attributes that apply to every page of a document.

► ► **T I P**

**Choose File ➤ Document Properties ➤ Document and
click on the Options tab to change default document-
wide attributes for the current document. For example,
you can specify several hyphenation options, control
widow and orphan lines, and set the look of review
and comment options if several people work on the
document. For information about customizing the
environment for each of the SmartSuite applications, see
the *Customizing Your SmartSuite Environment* appendix.**

Paragraph formatting controls selected text, as short as a one-word
heading or as long as the entire document, ending with a paragraph
mark. Using paragraph formatting, you can align text against the left or
right margin, both margins, or from the center point between the margins; you can control indention—of the first line of a paragraph, of all
but the first line, or of all lines—and you can control the spacing between lines in the selection.

Character formatting changes the way that selected text looks. With
Word Pro you can enhance characters (with **boldface**, *italics*, single underlines, or color), apply special effects (such as superscript, subscript,
double underlines, and strikethroughs), and modify the design and size
of the characters (by changing the font or point size).

## ► *Enhancing Text*

You use several Text menu commands to enhance text in a document.
To change the look of text in a Word Pro document, select it, and click
on a SmartIcon, choose a menu command, or press a shortcut key.
Some commands open a particular section of the InfoBox for Text; others take immediate effect. Table 10.1 presents Word Pro's text enhancement options.

▶▶ **N O T E**

Some of the SmartIcons in Table 10.1 are available only if you add them to a SmartIcons toolbar. To do this, choose File ➤ *n filename* ➤ SmartIcons Setup (where *n* represents the number of an open document and *filename* represents its name) or click on a small downward-pointing arrow to the left of a SmartIcons toolbar. Then choose SmartIcons Setup and insert these custom SmartIcons in a set. For instructions on customizing your SmartIcons, see the *Customizing Your SmartSuite Environment* appendix.

▶ **TABLE 10.1:** *Word Pro's Text Enhancement Options*

| Smart-Icon | Enhancement | Command | Shortcut Key |
|---|---|---|---|
| | Change the font, point size, or color | Text ➤ Font & Color; then select from the Font Name or Size scroll boxes, or select a color from the Text Color drop-down list box | N/A |
| | Cycle through the font options | Text ➤ Font & Color; then select from the Font Name scroll box | N/A |
| | Cycle up the point sizes | Text ➤ Attributes ➤ Enlarge Text | F4 |
| | Decrease the point size | Text ➤ Attributes ➤ Reduce Text | Shift+F4 |
| | Apply or remove boldface | Text ➤ Attributes ➤ Bold, or right-click and choose Bold | Ctrl+B |
| | Apply or remove italics | Text ➤ Attributes ➤ Italic, or right-click and choose Italic | Ctrl+I |
| | Apply or remove single underline | Text ➤ Attributes ➤ Underline, or right-click and choose Underline | Ctrl+U |
| N/A | Remove all text formats | Text ➤ Normal, or right-click and choose Normal | Ctrl+N |

▶ **TABLE 10.1:** *Word Pro's Text Enhancement Options (continued)*

| Smart-Icon | Enhancement | Command | Shortcut Key |
|---|---|---|---|
| | Cycle through enhancements: bold, italics, and underline | Text ➤ Attributes ➤ Bold, Text ➤ Attributes ➤ Italic, Text ➤ Attributes ➤ Underline | Ctrl+B, Ctrl+I, Ctrl+U |
| | Apply or remove an underline from selected words | Text ➤ Attributes ➤ Other; select Word Underline from the Attributes scroll box | Ctrl+W |
| | Apply or remove a double underline from selected words | Text ➤ Attributes ➤ Other; select Dbl Underline from the Attributes scroll box | N/A |
| | Display selected characters in uppercase | Text ➤ Attributes ➤ Other; select Upper Case from the Attributes scroll box | N/A |
| N/A | Display selected characters in lowercase | Text ➤ Attributes ➤ Other; select Lower Case from the Attributes scroll box | N/A |
| N/A | Display selected characters in small uppercase | Text ➤ Attributes ➤ Other; select Small Caps from the Attributes scroll box | N/A |
| | Display selected characters either above or on the baseline | Text ➤ Attributes ➤ Other; select Superscript from the Attributes scroll box | N/A |
| | Display selected characters either below or on the baseline | Text ➤ Attributes ➤ Other; select Subscript from the Attributes scroll box | N/A |
| N/A | Apply or remove a line through the selection | Text ➤ Attributes ➤ Other; select Strikethrough from the Attributes scroll box | N/A |
| | Apply the format of the prior selection to the next selection | Text ➤ Fast Format | Ctrl+T |

Figure 10.1 shows an informal memorandum with some character enhancements that emphasize the message.

**FIGURE 10.1** ▶

*A sample memorandum with several kinds of character enhancements*

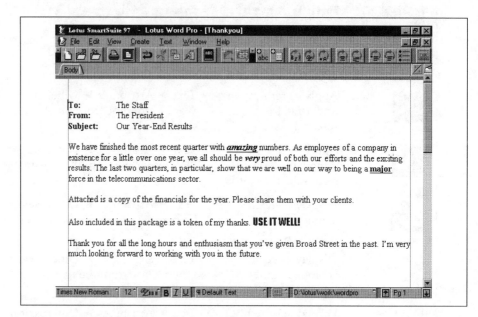

## ▶ *Using the Fast Format Feature*

Using a SmartIcon, menu command, or shortcut key, you can copy all the formats from a selection to another selection in any open Word Pro document. Note that:

- if your selection contains separate formats (for example, the first word selected is boldfaced, and the second word is italicized), Fast Format uses the formats of the first word selected.

- if you click in a paragraph, sometimes Word Pro displays a dialog box (see Figure 10.2).

**FIGURE 10.2** ▶

*A dialog box that prompts you to make the proper selection for fast formatting*

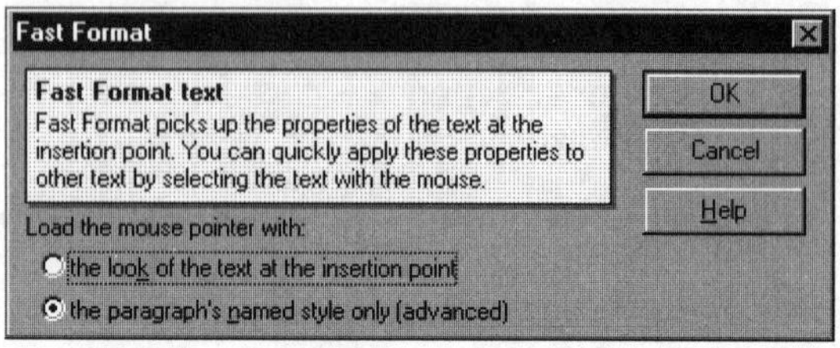

To use the Fast Format feature, simply follow these steps:

*1.* Select a word that has formats to be copied.

*2.* Click on the Fast Format SmartIcon, choose Text ➤ Fast Format, or press Ctrl+T.

*3.* Drag the paint brush mouse pointer across any text that you want to reformat. You can repeat this as often as you wish.

*4.* When you are finished, click on the Fast Format SmartIcon or press Esc to turn off fast formatting.

# ▶ *Adding Special Characters*

In many documents, you'll need to add a character that you won't find on your keyboard. For example, three very common special characters are the copyright symbol, the trademark, and the registered trademark. If you are self-publishing a book or writing a technical manual, you'll need to embed at least one of these symbols—the copyright. Another reason for inserting special characters in a document is for emphasis. For example, you might want to point to an important paragraph by placing a symbol, such as a Windows Wingdings arrow, to its left.

In Word Pro you can add special characters in three ways: by using the Windows Character Map, by inserting an ANSI (American National Standards Institute) symbol via the numeric keypad, or by using the SmartCorrect feature (for the copyright symbol, the registered trademark, and for three common fractions).

## *Inserting Special Characters with SmartCorrect*

You can use the Word Pro SmartCorrect feature to correct commonly misspelled or incorrectly formatted words as well as convert certain typed characters to special characters. You can use SmartCorrect to convert (c) to ©, (r) to ®, 1/2 to ½, 1/4 to ¼, and 3/4 to ¾. Additionally, you can check a checkbox, and Word Pro automatically converts straight quotes to typographically correct smart quotes. If you want SmartCorrect to convert typed characters to special characters or automatically correct commonly misspelled words, you can do so in the SmartCorrect dialog box.

To use SmartCorrect to replace typed characters with special characters, simply type the characters (for example, **(c)**). When you press the spacebar or press Enter, SmartCorrect automatically replaces the characters that you have typed with the special character (for example, ©).

SmartCorrect is part of the spelling checker. When the spelling checker finds a misspelled word (or a word that is missing from the main or custom dictionary), you can automatically add it to the SmartCorrect list by clicking on the SmartCorrect button in the spelling check bar.

To add entries to SmartCorrect, follow these steps:

**1.** Choose Edit ➤ SmartCorrect. Word Pro opens the SmartCorrect dialog box, as shown in Figure 10.3.

**2.** Click on the Add Entry button. The Add SmartCorrect Entry dialog box, as shown in Figure 10.4, appears.

**3.** Type the word to be replaced in the SmartCorrect Entry text box.

**FIGURE 10.3** ▶

*The SmartCorrect dialog box in which you can define typed characters that Word Pro automatically converts to special characters*

**FIGURE 10.4**

*The Add SmartCorrect Entry dialog box in which you can add a SmartCorrect entry and its replacement text or characters*

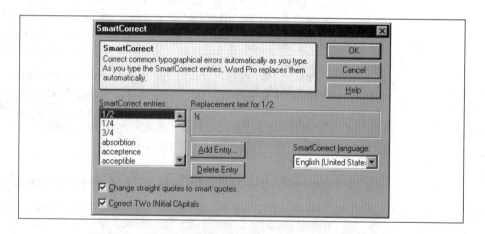

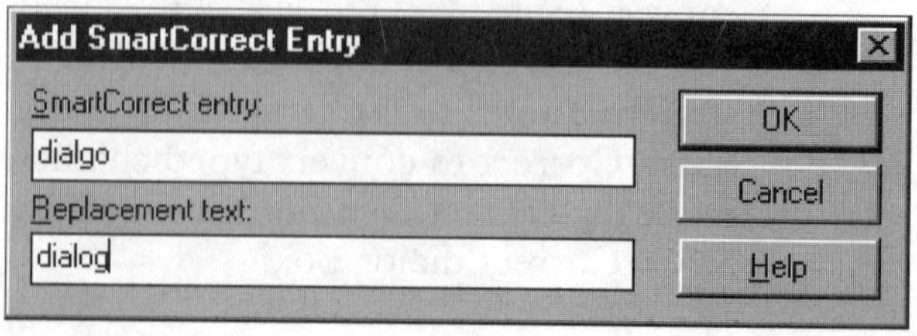

**4.** Type the replacement word in the Replacement Text text box. Then click on OK.

**▶▶ TIP**

**To add a special character to the SmartCorrect list, copy the character to the Clipboard using the information in the "Inserting Special Characters with the Windows Character Map" section or the "Inserting Special Characters Using the Numeric Keypad" section. Then follow the preceding steps until you reach step 4. Instead of using step 4, paste the special character by choosing Edit ➤ Paste, by clicking on the Paste SmartIcon, or by pressing Ctrl+V.**

## Inserting Special Characters with the Windows Character Map

With Character Map, Windows provides as many groups of special characters as you have fonts installed on your computer system.

To insert a special character in a document, follow these steps:

**1.** Click on the Start button. (For information about running Windows, see the insert *Sybex's Quick Tour of Windows 95.*) Windows opens the Start menu.

**2.** Move the mouse pointer to Programs. Windows opens another menu.

**3.** Move the mouse pointer to Accessories. Windows opens another menu.

**4.** Click on Character Map. Windows opens the Character Map application window (see Figure 10.5).

**5.** Select the desired font from the Font drop-down list box. Whenever you select a different font, some of the characters displayed in the application window disappear and new characters appear, because not every font supports every special character.

**FIGURE 10.5** ►

*The Character Map window from which you can select one or more symbols to be copied to the Clipboard and then pasted into a Windows application document*

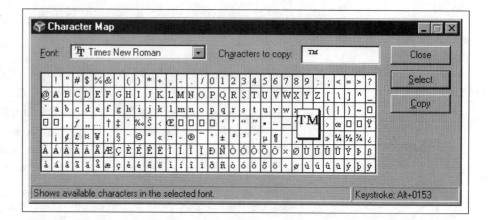

► ► **T I P**

**One of the best ways of ensuring that the symbol that you select in Character Map is the same one that will be inserted in the document is to choose a text font (for example, Times New Roman, which is the Word Pro default font) from the Font drop-down list box. Choosing a font such as Symbol or Wingdings may result in odd characters placed in your document.**

**6.** Double-click on the special character, or click on the character and then click on the Select button. (To see an enlarged view of a character, move the mouse pointer to the desired character and then click the left mouse button.) Windows moves the character into the Characters to Copy text box.

► ► **T I P**

**To see the keystroke equivalent and ANSI code of the character, look at the bottom right side of the screen. You can refer to this code when embedding characters with the numeric keypad.**

**7.** Repeat step 6 to accumulate as many characters as you want.

▶▶ **W A R N I N G**

**If you change to a different font after selecting one or more characters, all the accumulated characters in the Characters to Copy text box disappear.**

**8.** Select the Copy button to copy the characters to the Clipboard.

**9.** Click on the Close button to close the Character Map window and return to the document.

**10.** Move the insertion point to the location where you want the characters placed.

**11.** Choose Edit ➤ Paste, click on the Paste SmartIcon, or press Ctrl+V.

## Inserting Special Characters Using the Numeric Keypad

Most standard text fonts have their own unique set of ANSI symbols. When you find an ANSI chart with the symbol that you want to embed, be sure that you change the surrounding text to that font (otherwise, you may embed a different symbol) and then follow these steps:

**1.** Press the NumLock key (because the number keys on the numeric keypad must be active).

**2.** Press and hold down the Alt key.

**3.** On the numeric keypad, press the three- or four-digit ANSI code for the special character (for example, the ANSI code for the trademark symbol is Alt+0153).

**4.** Release the Alt key. Word Pro displays the symbol that you entered.

**5.** Press the NumLock key again to turn off the numeric keypad number keys.

# ▶▶ *Viewing and Hiding Nonprinting Symbols*

With Word Pro you can show nonprinting symbols such as paragraph marks, tab settings, page breaks, and embedded headers, footers, and rulers. For example, Figure 10.1 (earlier in this chapter) shows a document as it will print; no nonprinting symbols are in evidence. Figure 10.6 shows the same document with nonprinting symbols turned on. When you display nonprinting symbols, you can verify where a page has ended and another started or find the location of one or more new formats. Table 10.2 illustrates each nonprinting symbol and how it is embedded in the document.

**FIGURE 10.6** ▶

*The sample memorandum with nonprinting symbols displayed*

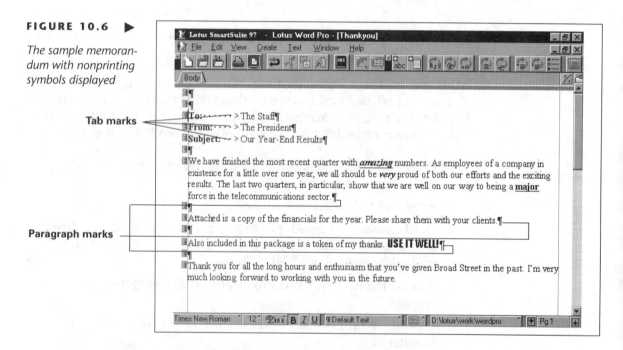

To reveal or hide nonprinting symbols, either choose View ➤ Set View Preferences or click on the View Preferences SmartIcon. In the View Preferences dialog box (see Figure 10.7), open the Show Marks drop-down list box and either check All to show all nonprinting

Editing a
Document

Ch.
**10**

▶ **TABLE 10.2:** *Word Pro Nonprinting Symbols*

| Symbol | Type of Mark | How It's Inserted |
|---|---|---|
| ¶ | Paragraph | Press ↵. |
| . . . . > | Tab | Press Tab. |
| (ruler icon) | Inserted ruler | Select a paragraph and change a margin setting or tab stop on the ruler. |
| Page Break | Page break | Select a location for the break, choose Text ➤ Insert Page Break, or press Ctrl+Enter. |
| Column Break | Column break | Select a location for the break, choose Text ➤ Insert Other ➤ Column Break. |
| ⚓ | DDE link | In another Windows application, select an object to be linked, choose Edit ➤ Copy, and minimize or keep the application running. In Word Pro, select a location for the link, choose Edit ➤ Paste Special, click on Paste Link to Source, and click on OK. |

**FIGURE 10.7** ▶

*The View Preferences dialog box in which you can customize many viewing options*

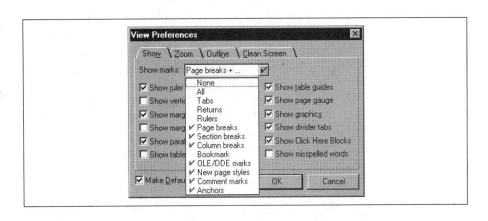

symbols or select certain marks, such as Returns (paragraph marks), Tabs, Rulers, Page Breaks, and Column Breaks. A checkmark preceding the option indicates a type of nonprinting symbol that will appear in a document; no checkmark indicates that that type of non-printing symbol will be hidden. For additional information about setting view preferences, see the *Customizing Your SmartSuite Environment* appendix.

If you want to display tabs and paragraph returns, click on the Show/Hide Tabs & Returns SmartIcon. If you want to display other marks (column breaks, page breaks, inserted page layouts, inserted rulers, floating headers and footers, and DDE text links), click on the Show All Marks/Hide All Marks SmartIcons.

# ►► *Formatting a Paragraph*

Paragraph formatting determines the alignment of text between the left and right margins, the space between the lines of text in the paragraph, page breaks that occur within the paragraph, paragraph indentions, and paragraph enhancements (borders, lines, and shading).

To format one paragraph, place the insertion point anywhere in the paragraph. To format multiple paragraphs, be sure that you select all or part of all of them using either the mouse or the keyboard. In Word Pro you can apply paragraph formats in several ways: with the Ruler, with SmartIcons, using keyboard shortcuts, or from the Text menu.

## ► *Aligning Paragraphs*

Unless you specifically change settings, Word Pro aligns text along the left margin and does not align it with the right margin. Figure 10.8 shows you a sample of each type of paragraph alignment. You can click on a SmartIcon or select a menu command to align paragraphs. Choose Text ➤ Text Properties (or press Alt+Enter), Text ➤ Attributes ➤ Other, or right-click and choose Text Properties; then click on the Alignment tab. In the Alignment panel of the Text Properties InfoBox (see Figure 10.9), click on an Alignment button. Table 10.3 summarizes Word Pro's paragraph alignments.

**FIGURE 10.8** ►

*A sample document
showing the four
types of paragraph
alignment*

**Left-aligned
text**

**Centered
text**

**Right-aligned
text**

**Justified
text**

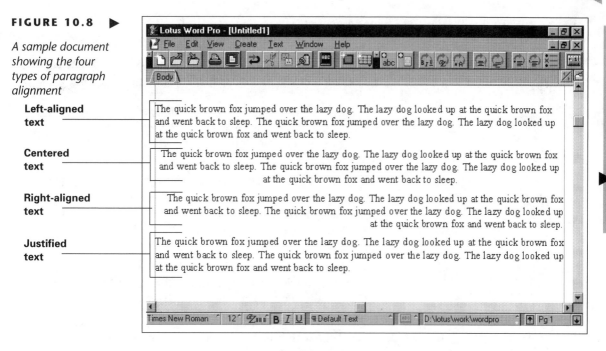

**FIGURE 10.9** ►

*The Alignment panel
of the Text Properties
InfoBox*

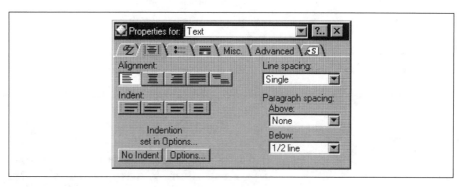

 You also can cycle through the alignment choices (centered, right-aligned,
justified, and left-aligned) by repeatedly clicking on the Alignment
Options SmartIcon.

► **TABLE 10.3:** *Word Pro's Paragraph Alignment Options*

| Smart-Icon | InfoBox Button | Formatting | Command | Shortcut Key |
|---|---|---|---|---|
| ▤ | ▤ | Align the text in the selected paragraphs with the left margin, leaving the text at the right margin ragged. | Text ➤ Alignment ➤ Left | Ctrl+L |
| ▤ | ▤ | Align the text in the selected paragraphs along the center point of the page, leaving the text at both the left and right margins ragged. | Text ➤ Alignment ➤ Center | Ctrl+E |
| ▤ | ▤ | Align the text in the selected paragraphs with the right margin, leaving the text at the left margin ragged. | Text ➤ Alignment ➤ Right | Ctrl+R |
| ▤ | ▤ | Align the text in the selected paragraphs with both the left and right margins | Text ➤ Alignment ➤ Full Justify | Ctrl+J |
| N/A | ▤ | Indent all lines of text in the selected paragraphs from the left margin, and aligns numbers using the current setting. | N/A | N/A |

►►**NOTE**

Some of the SmartIcons in Table 10.3 are available only if you add them to a SmartIcon bar. To do this, choose File ➤ *n filename* ➤ SmartIcons Setup (where *n* represents the number of an open document and *filename* represents its name), or click on a small downward-pointing arrow to the left of a SmartIcon bar. Then choose SmartIcons Setup and insert these custom SmartIcons in a set. For instructions on customizing your SmartIcons, see the *Customizing Your SmartSuite Environment* appendix.

# ▶ *Changing the Spacing between Lines*

In this section, you'll find out how to adjust the *leading*, which is the spacing between the lines within a paragraph. Leading not only includes the text on an imaginary line on which the characters rest (this is known as the *base line*) but also the white space between the top of the characters in the line to the bottom of the characters in the previous base line. As you increase the point size of selected characters, Word Pro adds extra white space.

For most business documents, you'll use single spacing, which is the default, but for manuscripts, double spacing is the rule. You can use line spacing to emphasize a particular paragraph within a document. For example, if you are quoting a reviewer or introducing a new product, inserting extra space above and below the selected paragraph almost forces the reader to look at the important text.

 Choose Text ➤ Text Properties (or press Alt+Enter or click on the Text Properties InfoBox SmartIcon), Text ➤ Attributes ➤ Other (or right-click and choose Text Properties); then click on the Alignment tab to choose line spacing. In the Alignment panel of the Text Properties Info-Box (see Figure 10.9), choose from one of these line spacing options:

| | |
|---|---|
| Single | Single spacing, determined by the point size of the largest character on the line. |
| $\frac{1}{2}$ | One-half line, determined by the point size of the largest character on the line. |
| $1\frac{1}{2}$ | An extra half-line between the selected lines of text, determined by the point size of the largest character on the line. |
| Double | An extra line between the selected lines of text, determined by the point size of the largest character on the line. |

| Multiple | A multiple number of lines that you type, determined by the point size of the largest character on the line. The default is 0.72 lines. |
| Leading | A specified measurement to be added to the current font size and to be calculated between the base line of one line and the base line of the next. The default is 0 pica. |
| Custom | A measurement that you set (0 to 2730.583 picas). The default is 1.18 picas. |

Word Pro provides four units of measure from which you can choose for Leading or Custom line spacing. Table 10.4 shows Word Pro's units of measures, the abbreviation, and the equivalent in inches.

**TABLE 10.4:**   *Word Pro's Units of Measure*

| Type of Measure | Abbreviation | Equivalent in Inches |
|---|---|---|
| inches (the default) | in | N/A |
| centimeters | cm | 0.3937 inch |
| picas | pi | 1/6 inch |
| points | pts | 1/72 inch |

## ▶ *Spacing between Paragraphs*

Paragraph spacing inserts space above and/or below selected paragraphs. Choose Text ➤ Text Properties (or press Alt+Enter or click on the Text Properties InfoBox SmartIcon), Text ➤ Attributes ➤ Other, or right-click and choose Text Properties; then click on the Alignment tab to choose paragraph spacing. In the Alignment panel of the Text Properties InfoBox (see Figure 10.9 earlier in this chapter), choose from one of these paragraph spacing options:

| None | No extra spacing, the default. |
| 1/2 Line | One-half line extra. |

| One Line | One line extra. |
| $1^1/_2$ Lines | One-and-one-half lines extra. |
| Two Lines | Two lines extra. |
| Multiple | A multiple number of lines that you specify (0 to 16959). The default is 0 lines. |
| Custom | A measurement that you set (0 to 2730.583 picas). The default is 0 picas. |

 ►►**N O T E**

> You can determine when paragraph spacing is applied. Doing so allows you to maintain the integrity of page layout from page to page. Choose Text ► Text Properties (or press Alt+Enter or click on the Text Properties InfoBox SmartIcon), choose Text ► Attributes ► Other, or right-click and choose Text Properties and then click on the Advanced tab. From the Add Paragraph Spacing drop-down list box, select Always to always add paragraph spacing, or choose When Not at Break to add paragraph spacing only when the paragraph is *not* at the beginning (for paragraph spacing Above) or end (for paragraph spacing Below) of a page break, column break, cell break, or column block break.

## ► Indenting Paragraphs

Paragraph indention moves either the entire paragraph or the first line away from the left and/or right margin. The default indention is 0; that is, no indention.

In Word Pro you can indent paragraphs in four ways: with SmartIcons, from the Text menu, from two shortcut menus, and with the Ruler. Table 10.5 describes three paragraph indention types: block indents, first line indents, and hanging indents.

►►**N O T E**

The SmartIcons in Table 10.5 are available only if you add them to a SmartIcon bar. To do this, choose File ➤ *n filename* ➤ SmartIcons Setup (where *n* represents the number of an open document and *filename* represents its name), or click on a small downward-pointing arrow to the left of a SmartIcon bar. Then choose SmartIcons Setup and insert these custom SmartIcons in a set. For instructions on customizing your SmartIcons, see the *Customizing Your SmartSuite Environment* appendix.

### Indenting Paragraphs with SmartIcons

Use the SmartIcons documented in Table 10.5 to indent in 0.5-inch increments. Select a paragraph and repeatedly click on a SmartIcon to increase the indention setting.

You also can cycle through the indention choices by repeatedly clicking on the Indent Options SmartIcon.

### Indenting Paragraphs with a Menu Command

Choose Text ➤ Text Properties (or press Alt+Enter or click on the Text Properties InfoBox SmartIcon), choose Text ➤ Attributes ➤ Other, right-click on the paragraph and choose Text Properties, or right-click on the Ruler and choose Set Indents; then, if needed, click on the Alignment tab (see Figure 10.9 earlier in the chapter). In the InfoBox, click on an indent button and then to precisely adjust the measurements using the Indent Options dialog box (see Figure 10.10), click on the Options button.

▶ **TABLE 10.5:** *Word Pro's Paragraph Indention*

| Smart-Icon | InfoBox Button | Name | Description | Example of Usage |
|---|---|---|---|---|
| N/A | [icons] | Block Indent | Indents all the lines in a paragraph from the left margin and/or right margin | Use block indents to emphasize the selected paragraph and make it stand out from the rest. |
| [icon] | [icon] | First Line Indent | Indents just the first line in a paragraph | Use the first-line indent for documents in which there is little or no spacing between paragraphs and you want to differentiate between paragraphs. |
| [icon] | [icon] | Hanging Indent | Indents the first line in a paragraph closer to the left margin than the rest of the lines | Hanging indents are ideal for bulleted and numbered lists. (To insert a bullet at the beginning of the paragraph in which the insertion point is located, choose Edit ➤ Insert ➤ Bullet, select a bullet from the dialog box, and click on OK.) |

**FIGURE 10.10** ▶

*In the Indent Options dialog box, you can fine-tune indention measurements, in this instance for a hanging indent.*

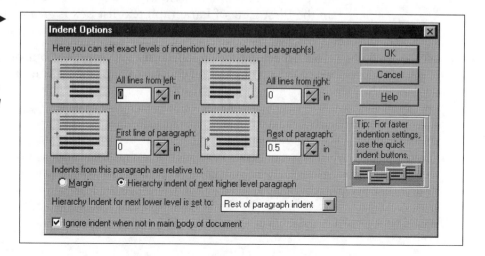

▶▶ **T I P**

**Using an InfoBox button to indent a selected paragraph fills in the All Lines from Left, First Line of Paragraph, All Lines from Right, and Rest of Paragraph text/list boxes in the Indent Options dialog box. Thus, you can open the dialog box, read the current values, and figure out how to change the settings for the desired type of indention.**

To create a block indent from the left margin, select or type a value from 0 to the page width in the All Lines from Left text/list box. (You can also set a block indent by selecting or typing identical numbers in the First Line of Paragraph and Rest of Paragraph text/list boxes.) The higher the number you type, the farther the indent is from the left margin.

To create a block indent from the right margin, type or select a value from 0 to the page width in the All Lines from Right text/list box. The higher the number you type, the farther the indent is from the right margin. You can create a block indent from both the left margin and the right margin by typing numbers in the All Lines from Left and All Lines from Right text/list boxes.

To create a hanging indent, be sure that the number you select or type in the Rest of Paragraph text/list box is greater than the value in the First Line of Paragraph text/list box.

To create a first line indent, be sure that the number you select or type in the First Line of Paragraph text/list box is *greater* than the value in the Rest of Paragraph text/list box.

To turn off indention, click on the No Indent button at the bottom of the Alignment panel of the Text Properties InfoBox.

## Indenting Paragraphs with the Ruler

The quickest (and most visual way) to indent paragraphs is to use the ruler (see Figures 10.11, 10.12, and 10.13). Move the mouse pointer on the ruler and drag the small markers until you set the selected indents as desired.

**FIGURE 10.11** ▶

*The Word Pro ruler showing margin and indent markers for a hanging indent as well as the affected paragraph*

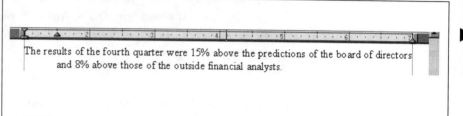

The results of the fourth quarter were 15% above the predictions of the board of directors and 8% above those of the outside financial analysts.

**FIGURE 10.12** ▶

*The Word Pro ruler showing margin and indent markers for a first-line indent along with the affected paragraph*

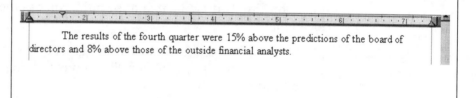

The results of the fourth quarter were 15% above the predictions of the board of directors and 8% above those of the outside financial analysts.

**FIGURE 10.13** ▶

*The Word Pro ruler showing margin and indent markers for a block indent from the left and right margins as well as the affected paragraph*

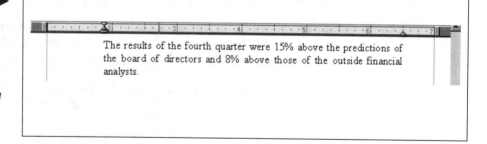

The results of the fourth quarter were 15% above the predictions of the board of directors and 8% above those of the outside financial analysts.

►►TIP

**If the ruler is not displayed between the SmartIcons and the document area, make sure that you are in Layout or Page Sorter mode, and choose View ➤ Show/Hide ➤ Ruler or click on the Show/Hide Ruler SmartIcon. (To hide the ruler, choose View ➤ Show/Hide ➤ Ruler or click on the Show/Hide Ruler SmartIcon.) If the Show/Hide Ruler is dimmed, choose View ➤ Set View Preferences and check the Show Ruler checkbox.**

At the left margin of the ruler are three markers—the downward-pointing marker is the first-line indent marker, the upward-pointing marker is for all lines except the first line, and the bottom marker shows the indention of all lines. To indent paragraphs from the left or the right, simply drag the markers on the ruler to the desired indention location.

To set a block indent from the left margin, point to the bottom rectangular marker and drag. The first-line and remaining-lines markers move simultaneously.

To set a hanging indent, first set a block indent that marks the indention of all the lines except the first line in the paragraph. Then point to the first-line marker and drag to the left (toward the left margin).

To set a first line indent, first set a block indent that marks the indention of all the lines except the first in the paragraph. Then point to the first-line marker and drag to the right (away from the left margin).

At the right margin is a single right margin marker. To indent paragraphs from the right, move the right margin marker.

**►►NOTE**

**You can also set a first-line indent for a selected paragraph using the current tab settings by pressing the Tab key.**

# ▶ *Setting and Using Tabs*

Although you can indent paragraphs by pressing the Tab key, the most important use for tabs is to align text within paragraphs. For example, you can use tabs to align the To, From, and Subject lines in a memo. To insert a tab, move the insertion point to the desired location and press the Tab key. You work with tabs in three ways: using the ruler, a Ruler shortcut menu, or the Text Properties InfoBox. Table 10.6 describes each tab type and shows its marker on the ruler.

▶ **TABLE 10.6:** *Word Pro's Tab Types*

| | Tab Type | Description |
|---|---|---|
| ▐▶ | Left-aligned tab | The first character in the character string following the tab symbol aligns with the tab position; the remaining characters flow toward the right margin. |
| ◀▌ | Right-aligned tab | The last character in the character string preceding the tab symbol aligns with the tab position; the remaining characters flow toward the left margin. |
| ↓ | Centered tab | The character string is centered on the tab stop. |
| ▐▶. | Numeric (decimal) tab | Any decimal point is aligned with the tab position. The remaining digits flow both left and right from the decimal point. If there is no decimal point, the character string is aligned as if the numeric tab were a right tab. |

**T I P**

> If the ruler is not displayed between the SmartIcons and the document area, choose View ➤ Show/Hide ➤ Ruler or click on the Show/Hide Ruler SmartIcon. (To hide the Ruler, choose View ➤ Show/Hide ➤ Ruler or click on the Show/Hide Ruler SmartIcon.)

## Setting and Clearing Tabs with the Ruler

To set and clear tab positions, use the ruler.

- To set a tab position, click on the ruler at the desired tab position.
- To clear a tab position, drag it off the ruler.
-  To change the location of a tab position, drag it to another part of the ruler using the mouse cursor that has the double-headed arrow tail.

## Setting, Clearing, and Adjusting Tabs with a Shortcut Menu

A fast yet thorough way of working with tabs is to use the Ruler shortcut menu. With the menu commands, you can specify the tab alignment, set and modify tabs using the Set Tabs on ruler dialog box, and clear all tabs from the ruler. To open the shortcut menu (see Figure 10.14), move the mouse pointer to the ruler and right-click.

The tab-related commands on the Ruler shortcut menu are:

**Set Tabs**  Opens the Set Tabs on Ruler dialog box in which you can set and clear tabs, specify tab alignment, select a leader, specify a ruler to which the chosen options apply, and set default tabs for every document.

 **Create Left Tabs**  Selects left alignment for any tab positions that you specify until you select a different alignment. When you select this command, a tail is added to the mouse pointer.

 **Create Right Tabs**  Selects right alignment for any tab positions that you specify until you select a different alignment. When you select this command, a tail is added to the mouse pointer.

**FIGURE 10.14** ▶

*The Ruler shortcut menu with which you can open a dialog box, specify tab alignment, and clear tabs*

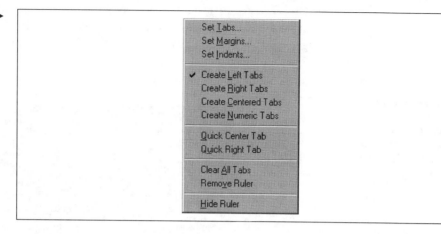

Set Tabs...
Set Margins...
Set Indents...

✓ Create Left Tabs
Create Right Tabs
Create Centered Tabs
Create Numeric Tabs

Quick Center Tab
Quick Right Tab

Clear All Tabs
Remove Ruler

Hide Ruler

 **Create Centered Tabs**     Selects centered alignment for any tab positions that you specify until you select a different alignment. When you select this command, a tail is added to the mouse pointer.

 **Create Numeric Tabs**     Selects numeric alignment for any tab positions that you specify until you select a different alignment. When you select this command, a tail is added to the mouse pointer.

 **Quick Center Tab**     Sets a centered tab halfway between the left margin and the right margin. To set a centered tab, you can click on the Quick Center Tab SmartIcon.

 **Quick Right Tab**     Sets a right-aligned tab at the right margin. To set a right-aligned tab, you can click on the Quick Right Tab SmartIcon.

**Clear All Tabs**     Removes all tabs from the ruler, which restores all default tab settings.

## Setting, Clearing, and Adjusting Tabs using a Dialog Box

 To set and clear tab positions, specify tab alignment, and determine the type of *leader* (the dotted lines between a title and a page number in some tables, for example), use the Set Tabs on Ruler dialog box (see Figure 10.15). To open the dialog box, either choose Text ▶ Text Properties (or press Alt+Enter or click on the Text Properties

InfoBox SmartIcon), click on the Misc tab, and click on the Set Tabs button in the Misc panel of the Text Properties InfoBox (see Figure 10.16); or right-click on the ruler and select the Set Tabs command.

**FIGURE 10.15** ▶

*Select from a variety of tabs options in the Set Tabs on Ruler dialog box.*

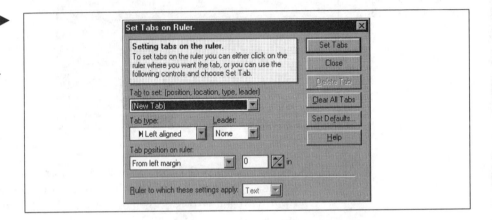

**FIGURE 10.16** ▶

*The Misc panel of the Text Properties InfoBox enables you to choose from miscellaneous options, including tab settings.*

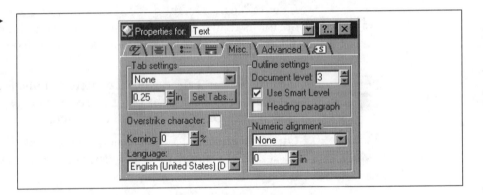

To set tab positions using the Set Tabs on Ruler dialog box, follow these steps:

*1.* Choose Text ➤ Text Properties, or press Alt+Enter. Word Pro opens the Text Properties InfoBox.

*2.* Click on the Misc tab. Word Pro displays the Misc panel of the Text Properties InfoBox.

*3.* Click on the Set Tabs button.

**T I P**

A shortcut for opening the Set Tabs on Ruler dialog box is to right-click on the ruler and select the Set Tabs command.

**4.** From the Tab Type drop-down list box, choose a tab alignment: Left Aligned, Right Aligned, Centered, or Numeric.

**5.** From the Tab Position on the Ruler drop-down list box, select a tab position as related to the left margin, right margin, or spaced along the ruler.

**6.** Click on the Set Tabs button.

**7.** Repeat steps 4, 5, and 6 to insert additional tabs.

**8.** To view the previously set tabs, open the Tab to Set drop-down list box.

**9.** To clear all the tabs, click on the Clear All Tabs button.

**10.** When you have completed defining tabs, click on the Close button.

# ▶ Using Paragraph Styles

Word Pro provides predetermined paragraph styles, as shown in Table 10.7, and allows you to create your own styles and modify styles. For detailed information on Word Pro styles, not only for paragraphs but also for other Word Pro elements (such as characters, pages, frames, tables, and table cells), see "Using SmartMasters" in the *Getting Acquainted with SmartSuite* chapter, the Word Pro user's guide, the introductory Help topic "Overview: Paragraph Styles," and other Style topics. In this section, you'll learn how to apply Word Pro styles, create a style, and modify a style.

## Applying Paragraph Styles

To apply a paragraph style, follow these steps:

**1.** Select the paragraph and click on the Style Status button. Word Pro opens the Style Status button list.

**2.** Click on a style name. Word Pro changes the style for the selected paragraph, closes the Style Status button list, and displays the name of the style on the Style Status button.

▶ **TABLE 10.7:**    *Word Pro Predefined Paragraph Styles*

| Style | Attributes |
| --- | --- |
| Body Single | Times New Roman, 12 point type, left aligned |
| Bullet 1 | bulleted list item having a round bullet, Times New Roman, 12 point type |
| Bullet 2 | bulleted list item having a checkmark bullet, Times New Roman, 12 point type |
| Default Text | Times New Roman, 12 point type, left aligned (the default) |
| First Line Indent | Times New Roman, 12 point type, left aligned, first line indented 0.5 inch |
| Heading 1 | Arial Black, 14 point type, boldface, left aligned |
| Heading 2 | Arial, 12 point type, boldface, left aligned |
| Heading 3 | Times New Roman, 12 point type, boldface, left aligned |
| Number List | numbered list item (for example, 1.), Times New Roman, 12 point type |
| Outline Numbering | outline list item (for example, I) Times New Roman, 12 point |
| Title | Arial Black, 24 point type, boldface, centered |

### Creating a Style

To create a style based on formatted text, follow these steps:

1. Format the text on which you'd like to define the new style.

2. Select the newly formatted text.

3. Choose Text ➤ Named Styles ➤ Create. Word Pro opens the Create Style dialog box (see Figure 10.17).

4. Type the new style name in the Style Name text box.

5. Type a description in the Description text box.

6. Click on OK. Word Pro adds the new style name to the Style Status button list and closes the dialog box.

**FIGURE 10.17** ▶

*In the Create Style dialog box, you can name a new style based on either an existing style or selected text.*

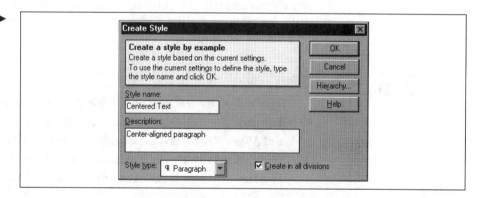

  You also can open the Create Style dialog box from the Text Properties InfoBox. Choose Text ➤ Text Properties, press Alt+Enter, or click on the Text InfoBox SmartIcon. In the Text Properties InfoBox, click on the Style tab.

# ▶▶ Formatting a Document

Document-wide (page layout) formatting controls the look of all the pages in a document. You can specify document-wide formats by using SmartIcons, the File menu, and in many cases the ruler. In this section, you'll learn about specifying margins, paper dimensions, the

orientation of a page, and page and column breaks. Then you'll find
out about Word Pro's page differentiation, headers and footers, and
page numbers.

## ▶ Specifying Margins

Margins determine the space between the edge of the page and the text
on the page. Word Pro's initial margin settings for all four margins—
top, bottom, left, and right—are 1 inch. The total of the left and right
margin settings cannot be greater than the width of the paper, and the
total of the top and bottom margin settings cannot be greater than
the length of the paper.

 In Word Pro, you can set all four margins by choosing File ➤ Document Properties ➤ Page and working in the Page Layout Properties
InfoBox. You can use the ruler to set the left and right margins. Turn on
the ruler by clicking on the Ruler SmartIcon or by choosing View ➤
Show/Hide ➤ Ruler.

 ▶▶ T I P

> The ruler, by default, is hidden. To permanently display
> the ruler (until you decide to hide it), choose View ➤
> Set View Preferences, check the Show Ruler checkbox,
> click on Make Default (otherwise, the ruler is displayed
> for the current document only), and click on OK.

### Setting Margins with a Menu Command

You can change margins whether or not there is a document in the
document area. To change margins using File ➤ Document Properties ➤
Page, follow these steps:

 **1.** Choose File ➤ Document Properties ➤ Page or click on the
Page InfoBox SmartIcon. Word Pro opens the Page Layout Properties InfoBox (see Figure 10.18).

**FIGURE 10.18** ▶

*The Page Layout
Properties InfoBox in
which you can specify
a variety of document-
wide settings*

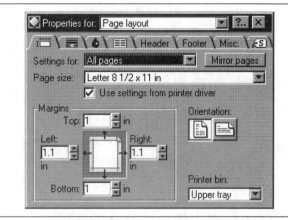

 ▶ ▶ **T I P**

**You can quickly open the Page Layout Properties
InfoBox in two ways: (1) Move the mouse pointer to
the ruler, right-click, and choose Set Margins; (2) move
the mouse pointer to the work area, right-click, and
choose Page Properties.**

**2.** In the Margins group, type or select a measurement in the Left,
Right, Top, and/or Bottom text/list boxes. As you change any margin setting, the document, if there is one in the work area, changes
its appearance. As you change the left or right margin, the markers on the ruler, if it is displayed onscreen, move.

**3.** Click on the Close button.

## Setting Margins with the Ruler

If you have a document in the document area, you can change the left
and right margins and see how the document looks as a result. On the
ruler, you'll find the black left and right margin markers below the blue
tab and indent markers. (To show the ruler, either click on the Ruler
SmartIcon or choose View ➤ Show/Hide ➤ Ruler.)

 To adjust the left margin, drag the left margin marker along the
ruler. To change the right margin, drag the right margin marker on
the ruler. As you point to margin markers, Word Pro adds an

appropriate tail to the mouse pointer (first-line, remaining-line, all-line, and right margin). As you drag, Word Pro shows a vertical line representing the current margin location and moves the tab markers. After you release the mouse button, your document changes to reflect the new margins.

 ▶▶ **N O T E**

> If you can't see the ruler in the application window, choose View ▶ Show Ruler.

## ▶ Setting Page Dimensions

You can adjust page size to match the dimensions of the paper on which you are printing and, of course, the capacity of your printer. Simply follow these steps:

1. Choose File ▶ Document Properties ▶ Page; click on the Page InfoBox SmartIcon; right-click on the ruler, and choose Set Margins; or right-click in the work area, and choose Page Properties. Word Pro opens the Page Layout Properties InfoBox (see Figure 10.18 earlier in this chapter).

2. From the Page Size drop-down list box, select one of the predefined sizes or select Custom from the bottom of the list. If you choose Custom, Word Pro opens the Custom Page Size dialog box (see Figure 10.19).

3. Type or select the page width from the Width text/option box. Valid values are 0.05 to 44 inches. The default is 8.5 inches.

4. Type or select a page height from the Height text/option box. Valid values are 0.05 to 44 inches. The default is 11 inches.

5. Click on OK.

6. Click on the Close button.

## ▶ Setting Page Orientation

Page orientation enables you to print on a page that is longer than it is wide (this is called *portrait*) or wider than it is long (that is, *landscape*). Examples of portrait orientation are reports, letters, and memoranda. A spreadsheet is the most common landscape document.

**FIGURE 10.19** ▶

*In the Custom Page
Size dialog box, you
can select or type the
page dimensions:
width and height.*

To change the page orientation for the current document, follow these
steps:

***1.*** Choose File ➤ Document Properties ➤ Page; click on the Page
InfoBox SmartIcon; right-click on the ruler, and choose Set Margins; or right-click in the document area, and choose Page Properties. Word Pro opens the Page Layout Properties InfoBox (see
Figure 10.18 earlier in this chapter).

***2.*** Click on an orientation button: for portrait (the default) or landscape. Word Pro changes the look of the sample page in the lower
right corner of the dialog box.

***3.*** When you have completed filling in the InfoBox, click on the
Close button.

## ▶ *Laying Out All, Right, or Left Pages*

In Word Pro you can lay out all pages in a document identically, or you
can specify separate page layouts for left (even-numbered) pages and
right (odd-numbered) pages. Thus, you can change margins on a left
page and keep the original settings on a right page, or insert borders of
different colors on each type of page. In fact, you can differentiate between left and right pages in every way except page size and orientation. Probably the most important use for page differentiation is to
create unique headers and footers for left and right pages.

▶▶**N O T E**

Word Pro numbers the pages of a document internally whether or not you insert printed page numbers. Therefore, when you identify left or right pages for headers and/or footers, you need not insert page numbers.

To differentiate between left and right pages, follow these steps:

1. Choose File ➤ Document Properties ➤ Page; click on the Page InfoBox SmartIcon; right-click on the ruler, and choose Set Margins; or right-click in the document area, and choose Page Properties. Word Pro opens the Page Layout Properties InfoBox (see Figure 10.18 earlier in this chapter).

2. Click on the Mirror Pages button.

3. To adjust the settings for specific pages, open the Settings For drop-down list box and select All Pages (the default), Left Pages, or Right Pages.

4. When you have completed the InfoBox, click on the Close button.

▶▶**T I P**

To view two pages at a time (that is, two facing pages) onscreen, which is a great help when specifying page layout options, choose View ➤ Zoom To ➤ Other. In the View Preferences dialog box, click on the View to Show Multiple Pages button, and select 2 Pages Across Screen. Then click on OK or press Enter.

# ▶▶ *Using Headers and Footers*

A header is an area containing text or graphics within the top margin, and a footer is an area containing text or graphics within the bottom margin. For a longer document, headers and footers aid the reader in identifying the page or chapter and even the date and/or time of printing.

Headers and footers can appear on every page, on only left (even-numbered) pages, on only right (odd-numbered) pages, on left and right pages (with different text on each), or on all except the first page of a document. Clicking on the Mirror Pages button and then selecting All Pages, Left Pages, or Right Pages in the Page Size and Margins panel of the Page Layout Properties InfoBox determines the pages on which a header or a footer appears.

You can produce different headers and footers for different parts of a document. For example, for a long document with several chapters, you can produce different headers and footers for the beginning of every chapter. Simply click in the document area and choose Create ➤ Section. This adds a new section, which inserts a new page layout, including headers and footers that you can edit.

## ▶ *Inserting Headers and Footers*

Inserting headers and footers on every page of the current document is an easy operation. To insert a header or a footer on every page of a document, move the insertion point within the top or bottom margin and type one or two lines of header or footer text (see Figure 10.20). You can click on SmartIcons to insert Quick Tabs, the page number, the time, and/or the date.

**FIGURE 10.20** ▶

*A sample header, two Quick Tabs on the ruler, and added header-related SmartIcons*

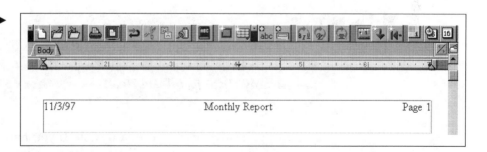

If you plan to have different headers or footers on left or right pages, be sure that you have selected mirror pages (see the preceding section, "Laying Out All, Right, or Left Pages"). If you will have identical headers and footers on all pages or will not start them on the first page, you don't need to choose mirror pages. Move the insertion point inside the header or footer and follow these steps:

1. Click on the Header or Footer InfoBox SmartIcon, choose Text ▶ Text Properties and select Header or Footer from the Properties For drop-down list box, right-click and choose Header Properties or Footer Properties, or press Alt+Enter. Word Pro opens the Header Properties InfoBox (see Figure 10.21) or the Footer Properties InfoBox.

**FIGURE 10.21** ▶

*The Header Properties InfoBox, from which you can specify header margins and dimensions as well as the first page on which the header appears*

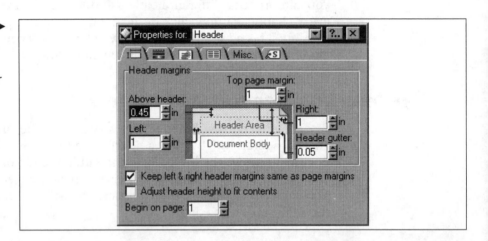

  **TIP**

**If the Page Layout Properties InfoBox is open, you can go to the Header or Footer Properties InfoBox by simply clicking on the Header or Footer tab.**

2. Edit the header or footer as you wish. If you have selected mirror pages, editing one header or footer for the right or left page erases the contents of the other (left or right) page.

3. To eliminate the header or footer from the first page of the document, in the Header or Footer Properties InfoBox, type or select page 2 or later from the Begin on Page text/list box.

4. Click on the Close button to close the InfoBox.

Once you have inserted a header or footer, type one or two lines of text using the same methods you use for any other part of a document. (You can also edit and format headers and footers just as you would any other text in a document.) In the following sections, you'll learn how to insert page numbers and the date and time in a header or a footer.

## ▶ *Numbering Pages*

When you add a page number to a header or a footer (or to another part of your document), Word Pro automatically inserts the correct number on each page. You can indicate the page on which the first page number is to be printed and specify the beginning number. You can also include a text prefix with the page number.

To insert page numbers in a document, follow these steps:

1. Move the insertion point to the desired page number location.

2. Choose Text ➤ Insert Page Number, or if the insertion point is located in the header or footer, click on the Insert Page Number SmartIcon. Word Pro opens the Insert Page Number dialog box (see Figure 10.22).

3. If you want to precede or follow the page number with text, type text in the Text Before or Text After text box.

4. To select a style for page numbers, open the Number drop-down list box, and choose None, 1 (the default), A, a, I, or i.

5. To start page numbering with a number other than 1, type or select it from the Start At text/option box.

6. To specify page numbering options for a long document made up of more than one section or division, click on the Options button. Word Pro opens the Page Number Options dialog box (see Figure 10.23).

7. When you have completed selecting page number options, click on OK or press Enter to close each dialog box.

## ▶ *Inserting Hard Page Breaks*

As you add text to a document, Word Pro inserts page breaks (known as *soft page breaks*) by computing the length of a page and the space

**FIGURE 10.22** ▶

*In the Insert Page Number dialog box, you can set the style of the number, specify the starting page number, and the text (for example, Page) that precedes the number.*

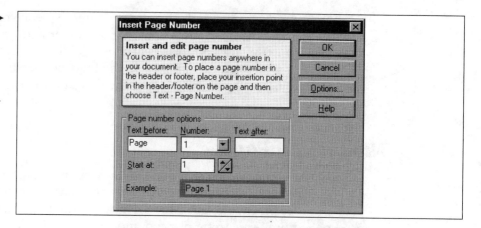

**FIGURE 10.23** ▶

*In the Page Number Options dialog box, you can select options for multiple-section or multiple-division documents.*

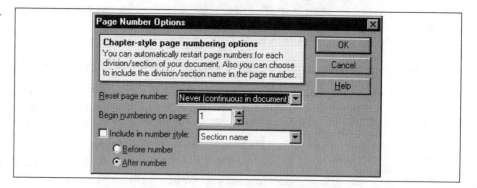

taken by the top and bottom margins. When you want to end a page at a particular place in the text (for example, at the end of a section or chapter, or before the next paragraph begins), you can insert a page break (a *hard page break*).

To embed a hard page break, follow these steps:

**1.** Move the insertion point to the exact point in the body of the document where you would like the break.

**2.** Choose Text ➤ Insert Page Break, press Ctrl+Enter, or click on the Page Break SmartIcon. Word Pro inserts the page break and closes the dialog box. In Draft view, a page break looks like this:

In Layout view, a page break looks like the separation between two pages:

▶▶**T I P**

To replace a soft page break with a hard page break, move the insertion point above the soft page break and insert the break. The only way to fit more text on a particular page is to decrease one or more margins, decrease line spacing, change to a more condensed font, or reduce the point size.

▶▶**N O T E**

For information about parallel columns and column breaks, see the Word Pro user's guide or the help system.

## ▶ *Removing Hard Page Breaks*

You can remove a page break by placing the insertion point after the last character and before the page break symbol on the prior page and pressing Delete.

## ▶ *Controlling Page Breaks within Paragraphs*

A page break sometimes splits a paragraph between two pages. When the break occurs in the middle of a paragraph, usually there's no problem. When a single line is left at the bottom of a page (an *orphan*) or at the top of a page (a *widow*), however, it's best to adjust the break.

To prevent widows and orphans in all documents, follow these steps:

*1.* Choose File ➤ Document Properties ➤ Document. Word Pro opens the General section of the Document Properties dialog box (see Figure 10.24).

**FIGURE 10.24** ▶

*The General section of the Document Properties dialog box provides document and version statistics about the current Word Pro environment.*

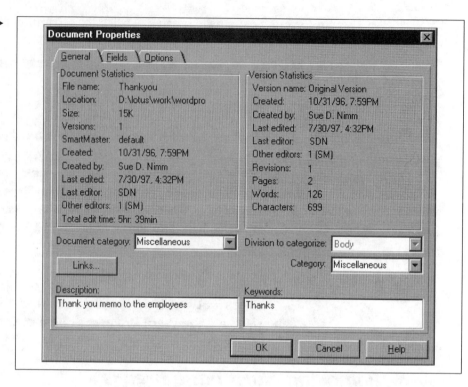

**2.** Click on the Options tab. Word Pro displays the Options section of the Document Properties dialog box (see Figure 10.25).

**3.** Check the Widow/Orphan Control checkbox. A checked checkbox is the default.

**4.** Either click on OK or press Enter.

# ▶▶ *Going to Pages and Items*

On the Edit menu, Word Pro offers a navigation command, common to many Windows applications. If you choose Edit ➤ Go To, click on the Go To SmartIcon, click on the page number at the bottom right of the screen, or press Ctrl+G, Word Pro opens the Go To dialog box (see Figure 10.26).

Editing a Document

**FIGURE 10.25** ▶

*You use the Options section of the Document Properties dialog box to control hyphenation, revision comments, widow/orphan lines, and more.*

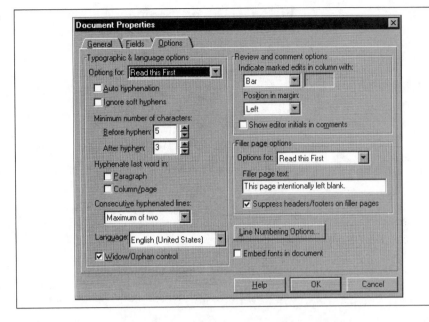

Ch.
**10**

**FIGURE 10.26** ▶

*In Word Pro's Go To dialog box, you can specify either an option for going to a page or any one of 13 items in a document.*

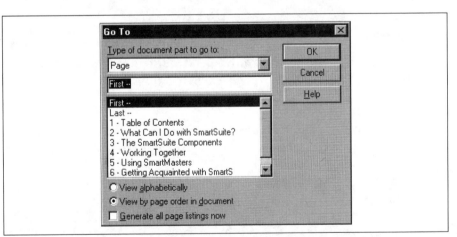

The options in this dialog box are:

**Type of Document Part to Go To**   Open this drop-down list box to choose a document element to which to go. Page is the default element.

**First**    Click on this option button to go to the top of the first page of the document. This is the default.

**Last**    Click on this option button to go to the top of the last page of the document.

**Text**    Click on an item in this scroll box to go to the top of a specific page *n*, which contains the text *text* (for example, selecting 3 - The SmartSuite Components goes to the top of page 3, which happens to start with the text *The SmartSuite Components*).

**View Alphabetically**    Click on this option button to rearrange the list in the scroll box alphabetically.

**View by Page Order in Document**    Click on this option button to rearrange the list in the scroll box by page number. This is the default.

**Generate All Page Listings Now**    Automatically generates updated page descriptions (for example, 1 - Table of Contents) whenever you add or delete pages from the document.

▶▶**N O T E**

**The vertical lines in the list (for example, preceding Grammar Checking) represent a nonprinting symbol— in this case, a bullet.**

Double-click on the item in the scroll box, click on OK, or press Enter to go to the next page or item that you specified.

▶▶**T I P**

**To go to the top of the first page of the current document, press Ctrl+Home; to go to the end of the last page of the current document, press Ctrl+End.**

# ▶▶ *Finding and Replacing*

You use find and replace features to make wholesale changes to text and formats in a document. For example, if you move to another state, you can go through all your documents, searching for your old address and replacing it with the new address automatically. In Word Pro, you can also find and replace characters not on your keyboard and paragraph styles. In this section, you'll learn all about finding and replacing.

Whether you are performing a search or a search and a replace, you'll use the same opening steps.

To begin, place the insertion point in the area of the document in which you want to search. Choose Edit ➤ Find & Replace Text, click on the Find & Replace SmartIcon, or press Ctrl+F to display the Find & Replace bar (see Figure 10.27). Type the *search string*, the characters for which you are looking, in the Find text box. If you want to replace the search string, type a *replace string* in the Replace With text box. You can search for entire words (for example, *theater* but not *the*) or words starting with (for example, specifying *or* will find *or*, *orange*, and *orifice*), ending with (for example, specifying *ity* will find *city*, *fluidity*, and *sorority*), or containing the search string (for example, specifying *on* will find *on*, *pony*, and *front*). In addition, you can search from the insertion point toward the top or toward the bottom of the document.

▶▶**N O T E**

> **If you have more than one document open, and switch from the document in which the Find & Replace bar is open, the document to which you go does not have a Find & Replace bar on display—unless you have opened it in that document.**

Click on the Options button in the Find & Replace bar to open the Find & Replace Text Options dialog box (see Figure 10.28), in which you can specify enhancements for the search. For example, you can search for a boldfaced or an italicized search string, or you can look in a specific part of the document. You can search and optionally replace the search string if it matches uppercase or lowercase letter by letter, and you can search and optionally replace special characters.

**FIGURE 10.27** ▶

*The Find & Replace bar is the starting point for finding and optionally replacing text, nonprinting characters, and formats.*

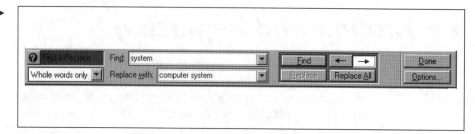

**FIGURE 10.28** ▶

*In the Find and Replace Text Options dialog box, you can specify the combination of enhancements for which you are searching and optionally replacing.*

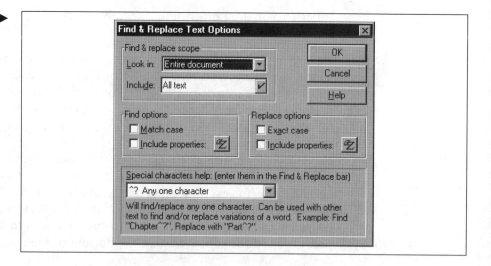

These are the options in this dialog box:

**Look In**    Open this drop-down list box to look in either the entire document (the default) or the current division, if you have broken the document into divisions.

**Include**    Open this drop-down list box to select one or more areas of the document in which to search: All Text (the default), Main Document Text, Headers & Footers, Tables, Frames, and Footnotes.

**Match Case**    Check this checkbox to search for an exact match of upper- and lowercase characters (for example, if *MaTcH* is the search string, Word Pro only finds *MaTcH*, not *match* or *MATCH*).

**Include Properties**    Check this checkbox and click on the button to define properties for the search string or replace string. You can search for and replace with a particular font name, font size, attribute, text or background color, or style.

## ▶ *Finding Text*

To find text, follow these steps:

*1.* Move the insertion point to the location in which you want to search.

*2.* Choose Edit ➤ Find & Replace, click on the Find & Replace SmartIcon, or press Ctrl+F. Word Pro displays the Find & Replace bar.

*3.* Type the search string in the Find text box.

*4.* Click on the Find button. If Word Pro finds the search string, it highlights it in the document. You can click on Find to continue the search, or you can click on Done to end it. After Word Pro has found the last occurrence of the search string, it displays an information box with the results of the search.

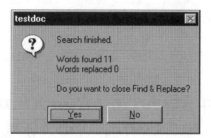

*5.* Click on Yes to close the Find & Replace bar; click on No to start another search. If you continue the search, the Find button becomes the Continue Find and Replace button.

## ▶ *Finding and Replacing Text*

To find and replace text, follow these steps:

*1.* Move the insertion point to the location in which you want to search.

2. Choose Edit ➤ Find & Replace, click on the Find & Replace SmartIcon, or press Ctrl+F. Word Pro displays the Find & Replace dialog box.

3. Type the search string in the Find text box.

4. Type the replace string in the Replace With text box.

5. To replace every occurrence of the search string with the replace string, click on Replace All. Word Pro displays the results in an information box.

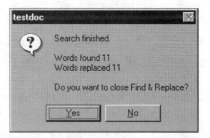

6. To search and replace one occurrence at a time, click on Find.

7. To replace this occurrence with the replace string, click on Replace. Word Pro automatically continues the search.

8. To replace all occurrences of the search string with the replace string, click on Replace All.

9. To end the search and replace process, click on Done.

## ► Finding and Replacing Nonprinting Characters and Paragraph Styles

You can search for and replace nonprinting characters in your document. Table 10.8 provides examples of Word Pro nonprinting character codes that you can insert in the Find and/or Replace With text boxes in the Find & Replace bar. In the Find & Replace Text Options dialog box is a list of special characters that can help you perform searches. Other than the special codes, the find and replace processes are exactly the same as those for text.

▶ **TABLE 10.8:** *Examples of Word Pro Nonprinting Character Find and Replace Codes*

| Code | Nonprinting Character |
|------|----------------------|
| *<ANSI symbol>* | an ANSI symbol |
| ^? | any single character |
| ^* | any characters |
| ^+ | the entire current document |
| ^p | an entire paragraph |
| ^t | a tab symbol |
| ^r | a return symbol |
| ^ | a ^ character in the document |
| <*> | an asterisk |
| <?> | a question mark |

# ▶▶ *Selecting Print Options*

Whether you decide to print by choosing File ➤ Print, pressing Ctrl+P, or clicking on the Print SmartIcon, you have a choice of options that are tailored for printing a Word Pro document. This section briefly describes each Word Pro print option shown in the Print dialog box (see Figure 10.29). After selecting options in the dialog box, either click on OK or press Enter.

▶▶ **N O T E**

> The Print dialog box provides "gateways" to the Print Setup dialog box (click on Setup) for the active printer and to the Print Options dialog box (click on Options).

**FIGURE 10.29** ►

*The Print dialog box, in which you select options to customize printing of a document*

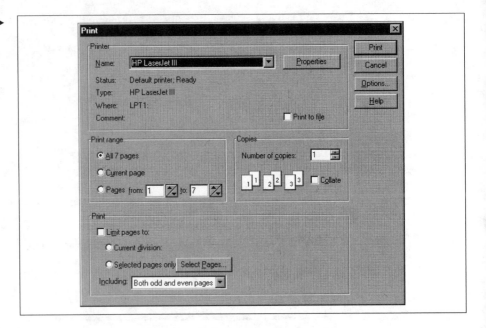

**Name**      A drop-down list box from which you can select a printer attached to your computer system and installed under Windows.

**Status**      Information about the selected printer and whether it is ready for printing.

**Type**      The name of the selected printer.

**Where**      The port to which the selected printer is attached.

**Comment**      Optional additional information about the selected printer.

**Properties**      A button on which you click to view or change attributes of the selected printer.

**Print to File**      A checkbox that when checked prints to a named file so that you can print the document later with all its formats intact. A cleared checkbox is the default.

**All**      An option button that when selected prints all the pages in the document. This is the default.

**Current Page**      An option button that when selected prints only the page in which the insertion point is located.

**Pages**    An option button that when selected prints a range of pages starting with the From page number in the first text/list box and ending with the page number in the To text/list box.

**Current Division**    An option button that when selected (along with the Limit Pages To checkbox) prints only the division in which the insertion point is located.

**Selected Pages Only**    An option button that when selected (along with the Limit Pages To checkbox) prints selected pages or divisions. Click on the Select Pages button to open the Select Pages dialog box in which you can select a list of pages: individual pages (such as 5, 6, 9, 34) and ranges (2-18); or entire divisions (in the box, check the divisions to be printed).

**Including**    A drop-down list from which you can choose to print both odd and even pages, only even pages, or only odd pages.

**Number of Copies**    A text/option box in which you select or type the number of copies (from 1 to 9999) that you want to print.

**Collate**    A checkbox that when checked prints all the pages of a document, starting with the first page and ending with the last page before starting to print the next copy. A cleared checkbox prints all the copies of the first page, all the copies of the second page, and so on.

**Options**    A button on which you click to display the Print Options dialog box (see Figure 10.30). In this dialog box, you can select six print options and three update options.

**FIGURE 10.30** ▶

*The Print Options dialog box with which you can select additional print options*

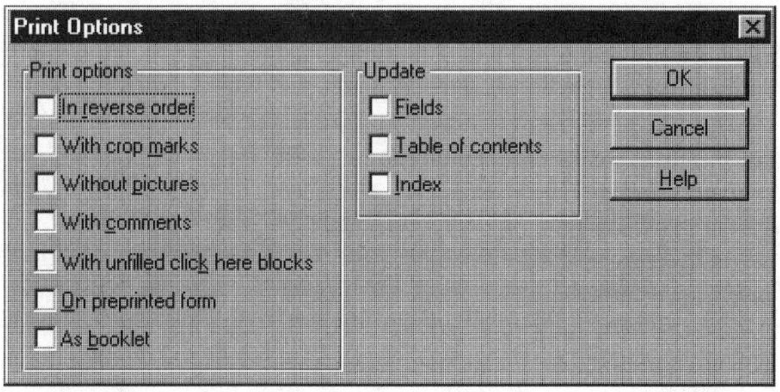

**Print Options**

Print options:
- [ ] In reverse order
- [ ] With crop marks
- [ ] Without pictures
- [ ] With comments
- [ ] With unfilled click here blocks
- [ ] On preprinted form
- [ ] As booklet

Update:
- [ ] Fields
- [ ] Table of contents
- [ ] Index

[ OK ]  [ Cancel ]  [ Help ]

The Print Options dialog box contains these print options:

**Reverse Order**     Check this checkbox to print the last page in the document, followed by the next to last page, and so on, until the first page is printed. This is useful for printers in which pages are sent through in a straight line, resulting in a last page-first page order.

**Crop Marks**     Check this checkbox to print lines that indicate the finished dimensions of the page when cropped for binding.

**Without Pictures**     Check this checkbox to print frames but not the pictures within the frames.

**With Comments**     Check this checkbox to print the document and the notes (both initialed and numbered) inserted in the document.

**With Unfilled Click Here Blocks**     Check this checkbox to print Click Here blocks that are not filled in with text that prompts for input.

**On Preprinted Form**     Check this checkbox to print all the text in the document stripped of lines and patterns.

**As Booklet**     Check this checkbox to print a booklet.

**Update**     Check these three checkboxes to update all power fields, those used to create a table of contents, and/or those used to create an index.

# CHAPTER 11

# Creating
# Pictures

▶▶ **I**n the last two chapters, you learned how to create, edit, and format documents using Word Pro. In this chapter, you'll find out how to create drawings and import pictures from other Windows applications in order to enhance your documents. This chapter provides an overview of drawing in Word Pro but can be applied in many ways to 1-2-3, Approach, and Freelance Graphics. For more detailed information about drawing, either see the user's guide or search for graphics and drawing topics in Word Pro's Help facility. To get drawing help quickly, double-click on a drawing and press F1.

 ▶▶ **N O T E**

**To create Word Pro drawings, you must have a mouse installed and working. Although you can modify drawings using menu commands, drawing tools are only available through clicking on SmartIcons and buttons.**

Whether you create or import them, drawings in Word Pro are *objects*—individual parts of an application or a file. Other examples of objects are fields in Approach, charts and pieces of charts in 1-2-3, dialog boxes, SmartIcons, boxes, and buttons.

1-2-3, Freelance Graphics, and Approach have drawing features and share many of the same drawing tools; you can apply the information in this chapter to other SmartSuite applications. And because you are running under Windows, you can create a drawing in one application (whether or not it's a SmartSuite application) and use it in another. Table 11.1 illustrates and describes common SmartSuite drawing tools and shows examples of using each.

**TABLE 11.1:** *SmartSuite Drawing Tools*

| SmartIcon | Description | Applications | Example |
|---|---|---|---|
| | Selects an object in a drawing (Press Shift and click to add the next object to the selection.) | Word Pro, Approach, Freelance Graphics | |
| | Selects all the drawn objects | Word Pro, 1-2-3, Approach | |
| | Draws a straight line | Word Pro, 1-2-3, Approach, Freelance Graphics | |
| | Draws a polyline made up of segments | Word Pro, 1-2-3, Freelance Graphics | |
| | Draws a polygon | Word Pro, 1-2-3, Freelance Graphics | |
| | Draws a rectangle or a square | Word Pro, 1-2-3, Approach, Freelance Graphics | |
| | Draws a rectangle or a square with rounded corners | Word Pro, 1-2-3, Approach | |
| | Draws an ellipse or a circle | Word Pro, 1-2-3, Approach, Freelance Graphics | |
| | Draws an arc | Word Pro, 1-2-3, Freelance Graphics | |
| abc | Inserts text in a drawing | Word Pro, 1-2-3, Approach, Freelance Graphics | text |
| | Draws an arrow pointing forward | 1-2-3, Freelance Graphics | |
| | Draws freehand | 1-2-3, Freelance Graphics | |
| OK | Draws a macro button in a drawing | 1-2-3 | Button |
| | Draws an open curve | Freelance Graphics | |

Drawing in Word Pro involves using SmartIcons; Word Pro's Draw menu provides drawing editing commands only. In Freelance Graphics and Approach, drawing tools are located on a palette (see Figures 11.1 and 11.2); 1-2-3 has drawing SmartIcons and its own set of drawing commands that are available after you choose Create ▶ Drawing. Table 11.2 presents the list of 1-2-3 drawing commands.

**FIGURE 11.1** ▶

*The palette from which you select Free-lance Graphics drawing, text shapes, and connector tools*

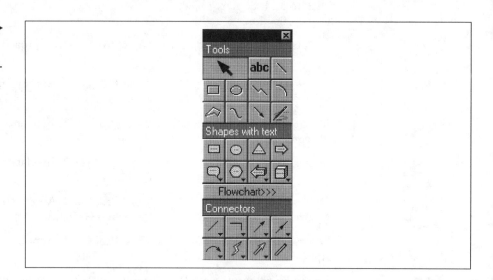

**FIGURE 11.2** ▶

*Approach's drawing tool palette*

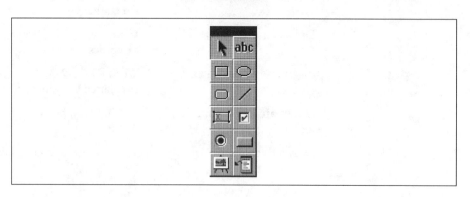

▶ **TABLE 11.2:** *1-2-3 Drawing Menu Commands*

| SmartIcon | Menu Command | Description |
|---|---|---|
| | Create ➤ Drawing ➤ Line | Draws a straight line |
| | Create ➤ Drawing ➤ Polyline | Draws a line made up of segments |
| | Create ➤ Drawing ➤ Arrow | Draws an arrow pointing forward |
| | Create ➤ Drawing ➤ Rectangle | Draws a rectangle or a square |
| | Create ➤ Drawing ➤ Rounded Rectangle | Draws a rectangle or a square with rounded corners |
| | Create ➤ Drawing ➤ Arc | Draws an arc |
| | Create ➤ Drawing ➤ Ellipse | Draws an ellipse or a circle |
| | Create ➤ Drawing ➤ Polygon | Draws a polygon |
| | Create ➤ Drawing ➤ Freehand | Draws freehand |

*Creating Pictures*

Ch.
**11**

# ▶▶ *Creating Pictures in Word Pro*

 To start the Drawing feature, click on the Drawing SmartIcon or choose Create ➤ Drawing. Word Pro inserts a frame at the insertion point,

adds the Drawing Tools toolbar,

and adds the Drawing Actions toolbar (by default, arranged vertically, but here changed to a floating toolbar, so that all the tools are visible onscreen):

 ▶▶ **T I P**

> If the Drawing Tools and Drawing Actions toolbars do not appear, double-click within the frame.

 ▶▶ **N O T E**

> Some Drawing Action tools are dimmed. They are available only if you take a particular action. For example, some tools are not available unless you select at least two drawing objects; others are not available if more than one object is selected.

The frame has handles at each corner and on each side so that you can change its dimensions. It also contains margin guides, the gray vertical lines on the left and right sides. Changing the size of the frame has no effect on the size of the objects enclosed. When you move the sides of a frame over an object, however, the object remains in its original location; that section just seems to disappear. To avoid this, move the sides of the frame away from the object.

► ► **T I P**

> **To keep the dimensions of the frame in their original proportions, drag a corner handle rather than one of the handles on the sides, top, or bottom.**

To move from a frame to a document, click outside the frame. The handles disappear, the Text toolbar appears, and the insertion point is outside the frame. Sometimes, the frame disappears. Although you can't see it, it is there.

To select the frame, click within its borders; eight handles appear at the corners and in the middle of each side, and the border around the frame is heavier (see Figure 11.3). The Frame toolbar appears.

**FIGURE 11.3** ►

*A selected frame contains eight handles.*

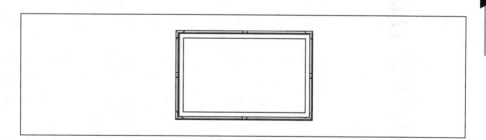

To create or edit a drawing within a frame, double-click within its borders; the frame's handles remain, but the border is dimmed. The Drawing Tools and Drawing Actions toolbars appear.

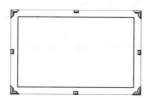

Creating Pictures

► ►

*Ch.*
**11**

When you start the drawing feature, Word Pro also adds the Draw menu to the menu bar. The Draw menu provides editing commands for drawings, listed in Table 11.3.

▶ **TABLE 11.3:** *Word Pro Draw Menu Commands*

| SmartIcon | Menu Command | Description |
| --- | --- | --- |
| | Draw ➤ Draw Properties | Opens the Drawing InfoBox or an InfoBox related to the selected object so that you can edit the drawing or object |
| | Draw ➤ Extract Properties | Copies the line style, line color, fill color, pattern, pattern color, and/or text attributes from the selected object |
| | Draw ➤ Apply Properties | Applies the copied line style, line color, fill color, pattern, pattern color, and/or text attributes to the selected object |
| | Draw ➤ Import Drawing | Imports a drawing from another source into the current document |
| | Draw ➤ Save As Drawing | Saves the entire drawing or selected objects as a Word Pro drawing |
| | Draw ➤ Rotate | Rotates the selected object 10 degrees clockwise |
| | Draw ➤ Align ➤ Top | Aligns the selected objects with the top of the frame |
| | Draw ➤ Align ➤ Bottom | Aligns the selected objects with the bottom of the frame |
| | Draw ➤ Align ➤ Left | Aligns the selected objects to the left border of the frame |
| | Draw ➤ Align ➤ Right | Aligns the selected objects to the right border of the frame |
| | Draw ➤ Align ➤ Center Vertically | Aligns the selected objects with the center of the frame and places them vertically |

▶ **TABLE 11.3:** *Word Pro Draw Menu Commands (continued)*

| SmartIcon | Menu Command | Description |
|---|---|---|
| | Draw ➤ Align ➤ Center Horizontally | Aligns the selected objects with the center of the frame and places them horizontally |
| | Draw ➤ Align ➤ Center on Centers | Clusters the selected objects in the center of the frame |
| | Draw ➤ Flip ➤ Top to Bottom | Flips the selected object on the horizontal axis (for example, the sample car ends on its roof) |
| | Draw ➤ Flip ➤ Side to Side | Flips the selected object on the vertical axis (for example, a car that is facing to the right now faces to the left) |
| | Draw ➤ Priority ➤ Bring to Front | Moves the selected object to the front of the layers of objects |
| | Draw ➤ Priority ➤ Send to Back | Moves the selected object to the back of the layers of objects |
| | Draw ➤ Priority ➤ Bring Forward One | Moves the selected object to the front of the layers of objects |
| | Draw ➤ Priority ➤ Send Back One | Moves the selected object to the back of the layers of objects |
| | Draw ➤ Group | Groups the selected objects |
| | Draw ➤ Ungroup | Ungroups the selected group |
| N/A | Draw ➤ Curved Text | Curves the selected text |
| | Draw ➤ Select All | Selects all the drawing objects within the frame |

Creating Pictures

▶▶ *Ch.* **11**

## ▶ *Using the Drawing Tools*

To use a drawing tool, click on it. Doing so selects the tool and deselects any other tool. Then place the mouse pointer inside the frame and start working. Word Pro provides several mouse pointers, depending on the selected tool. Table 11.4 shows each mouse pointer and its associated tools.

► **TABLE 11.4:** *Word Pro Drawing Tool Mouse Pointers*

| Mouse Pointer | Associated Tools |
|---|---|
| ↖ | Select tool |
| ✋ | Hand tool |
| ┼ | Line tool, segmented line tool, polygon tool, rectangle tool, rounded rectangle tool, ellipse tool, arc tool |
| I | Text block tool |

## ► Selecting Objects

There are two Word Pro selection tools: the Selection Arrow tool and the Select All tool. To select an object in the drawing, click on the Selection Arrow or choose Draw ➤ Select All; then click on the object. Word Pro displays handles around the outside of the object. Once you have selected an object, you can delete it (press Delete) or move it (drag it within the borders of the frame). To add another object to the selection, press and hold down the Shift key and click on the object. You can continue this until every object is selected (that is, every selected object has handles). To "deselect" a selection, click outside the object.

To select every object within the frame, click on the Select All tool.

►► N O T E

**To select the frame and its contents, move the mouse pointer to the left of the frame and press Shift+→. You can also move the mouse pointer to the right of the frame and press Shift+←.**

## ▶ Cropping Drawings

 Use the Hand tool to select and move the entire picture within the frame. Moving the picture shows only part of the picture (that is, the picture is *cropped*). You can start with a picture that looks like this:

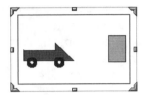

and ends up looking like:

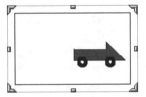

You can recover the cropped part of the picture—even if you have saved your document and exited Word Pro—by clicking on the Hand tool again and moving the picture back to its original position.

## ▶ Drawing Lines and Arcs

Word Pro provides two line-drawing tools—Line and Polyline—and one arc-drawing tool.

 To draw a straight line, click on the Line tool. Move the cross-hatch mouse pointer to one end of the line, hold down the left mouse button, drag to the other end of the line, and release the mouse button. To draw a line horizontally, vertically, or at a 45-degree angle, press the Shift key while you are drawing.

 To draw a segmented line, click on the Polyline tool and draw the first segment as you did the straight line. To draw a new segment, move the mouse pointer to the ending point and click. Word Pro joins the end of the previous segment with the end of this segment. As long as the Polyline tool is active ("pressed down"), you will continue to add segments. To inactivate the tool, click on another button. Your best choice is the Selection Arrow, since it does not add more objects to your drawing, nor does it change the drawing.

 Drawing an arc is very similar to drawing a straight line; in fact, you can draw a straight line using the Arc tool. To draw an arc, click on the Arc tool. Move the cross-hatch mouse pointer to where you want the arc to begin, hold down the left mouse button, drag to where you want the arc to end, and release the mouse button. If you drag directly horizontally or vertically from the starting point, you'll draw a straight line. If you drag diagonally from the starting point, however, you'll form the arc. To adjust the arc's curve, click on a section of the curve and drag it one way if you want more curve and the other way if you want less.

## ▶ Drawing Polygons

 To draw a polygon, which is a closed object with three or more straight lines, click on the Polygon tool and move the cross-hatch mouse pointer to the starting point in the drawing. Draw the polygon using the same techniques you used to draw the segmented line. The only difference is that after you have drawn at least two sides of the polygon, Word Pro will close the object with a final line for you. All you have to do is signal that you are finished with the other sides: Click on another drawing tool, or click outside the borders of the frame.

## ▶ Drawing Rectangles, Rounded Rectangles, and Ellipses

 Drawing rectangles, rounded rectangles, and ellipses involves almost identical procedures. Click on the drawing tool, move the mouse pointer to a starting point, and drag diagonally until the object is the desired size. To draw a square or a circle, hold down the Shift key while dragging. To draw a square, hold down the Shift key, click on the Rectangle tool or rounded rectangle tool, and Word Pro always keeps the sides of the object the same length. To draw a circle, hold down the Shift key, and click on the Ellipse tool. As you draw, Word Pro always keeps the object a circle.

## ▶ *Inserting Text in a Drawing*

To insert text, click on the Text drawing tool, move the mouse pointer to the drawing, click, and start typing as you would in a regular document. To change text attributes, click on the Draw InfoBox SmartIcon, choose Draw ▶ Draw Properties, or right-click and choose Draw Properties. In the Draw Text Properties InfoBox (see Figure 11.4), change the font, point size, attributes, rotation, or text color of the selected text object. You also can click on the Bold, Italics, and Underline buttons in the Status bar or press shortcut keys such as Ctrl+B, Ctrl+I, or Ctrl+U to enhance text in a drawing.

**FIGURE 11.4** ▶

*In the Draw Text Properties InfoBox, you can change the attributes of text in a drawing.*

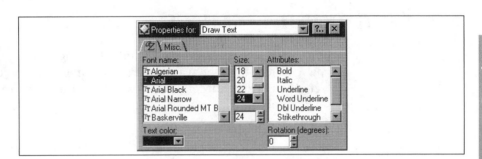

## ▶ *Copying, Cutting, and Pasting Objects*

You can use the Copy, Cut, and Paste commands on the Edit menu (or press Ctrl+C, Ctrl+X, or Ctrl+V) to copy, cut, and paste a selected object. (You can also use SmartIcons to copy, cut, and paste.) Simply select the object, either copy or cut it to the Clipboard, and then paste it back into the drawing. Word Pro will paste the copy on top of the original object. To move the copy to another location in the drawing, drag it.

To learn more about copying, cutting, and pasting, see the *Editing in SmartSuite Applications* chapter.

▶▶**W A R N I N G**

**Deleting a character or a block of text is different from cutting the same character or text. A cut selection of text can be pasted back into the document, as long as no other Cut or Copy operation has been performed. You can undo a deletion as long as you haven't performed another action, but after that, a deleted selection is gone forever.**

# ▶▶ *Modifying Pictures*

Once you have inserted objects in a drawing, you'll probably want to change them in some way. Before you can edit an object, you must select it by clicking directly on it. Word Pro places handles around the selected object:

In this section, you'll learn how to use the editing buttons on the Drawing toolbar.

## ▶ *Grouping and Ungrouping Objects*

When you group objects, you can define several objects as a single object. This command is very useful when you must move several objects that form one part of a drawing (see Figure 11.5).

**FIGURE 11.5** ▶

*The polygon and circles that make up the car look like a single unit, but are actually three objects.*

Before grouping all the objects in a drawing, click on the Select All tool or choose Draw ➤ Select All. Word Pro selects all the objects (and places handles on each selected object):

 ▶▶ **N O T E**

> **To select a few of the objects in a drawing, click on the Selection Arrow, press and hold down the Shift key, and click on each object.**

Then click on the Group tool or choose Draw ➤ Group. The Group tool is dimmed, the Ungroup tool is now available, and the grouped object now has just eight handles:

When you want to work with one part of a grouped object (for example, to change its color or to delete it), click on the Ungroup tool or choose Draw ➤ Ungroup. This separates the group into the individual objects with which you started.

## ▶ *Using the Bring to Front and Send to Back Tools*

As you add objects to the same general location in a drawing, you'll find that the new objects partially or completely overlap older objects:

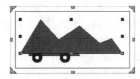

Creating Pictures

▶▶

Ch.
**11**

To send a selected object to the bottom layer of the drawing, click on the Send to Back tool or choose Draw ➤ Priority ➤ Send to Back.

 Another way to change the order of objects in a drawing is to select an object that you want to bring to the front of the drawing and click on the Bring to Front tool, or choose Draw ➤ Priority ➤ Bring to Front.

  If you have several layers of objects, you can select an object to be moved one layer at a time. Then either click on the Bring Forward One or Send Back One tool, or choose Draw ➤ Priority ➤ Bring Forward One or Draw ➤ Priority ➤ Send Back One.

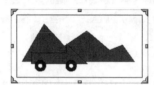

  **T I P**

**You can press Ctrl+Z or choose Edit ➤ Undo to reverse your last action. If things really look desperate and the drawing is a total mess, you can choose File ➤ Close and answer No to the save prompt. (This works only if you've previously saved a successful version of your work. If you haven't saved your work, you won't have anything left to work with.)**

## ▶ *Rotating an Object*

 To rotate a selected object, click on the Rotate tool or choose Draw ➤ Rotate. Each click on the Rotate tool or selection of the command rotates the object 10 degrees. So, to rotate an object completely around to its starting position, click 36 times.

If you choose Draw ➤ Draw Properties or right-click and choose Draw Properties, Word Pro opens the Misc panel of the Drawn Objects (or the name of the object) Properties InfoBox (see Figure 11.6). In the Info-Box, you can set the degree of each rotation (the default is 10) and click on the Clockwise or Counterclockwise button to set the direction for the selected object.

**FIGURE 11.6** ▶

*The Drawn Objects Properties InfoBox with the default settings*

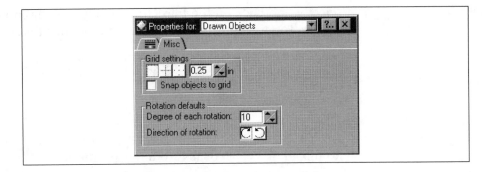

You can also rotate an object by double-clicking on it after selecting it. Word Pro displays the center point around which you can rotate the object and which you can move to change the path of rotation (see Figure 11.7). To rotate an object, point to one of the small double-pointed arrows and drag. As you rotate the object, a "shadow" image of the object shows you the current degree of rotation.

**FIGURE 11.7** ▶

*An object about to be rotated around a center point by dragging on one of four arrows*

## ▶ *Flipping an Object*

To flip an object horizontally from this position:

select it and click on the Flip Horizontally tool, or choose Draw ➤ Flip ➤ Top to Bottom. The end result looks like this:

To flip an object vertically from this position:

 select it and click on the Flip Vertically tool, or choose Draw ➤ Flip ➤ Side to Side. The end result looks like this:

## ▶ Using the Grid

As you draw an object, you may not be able to control its final size; the lines may seem to *snap* (jump) to another point in the frame. This seeming lack of control is caused by *snapping to the grid*. In this section, you'll find out how to control snapping to the grid, how to view or hide the grid, and how to change grid attributes. Figure 11.8 shows two drawing objects: one snapped to the grid and the other not.

**FIGURE 11.8** ▶

*Two drawing objects: one snapped to the grid and the other not*

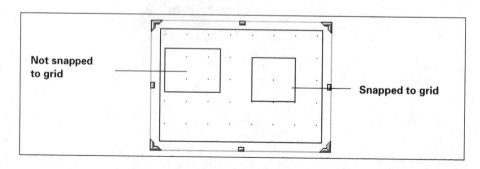

## Snapping to the Grid

If you need to line up several objects in a flow chart or pictures on a catalog page, the Snap to Grid option is a great help. If you are making a drawing in which you create an object, size it, and then place it, however, Snap to Grid could be a disadvantage.

To turn on or off the Snap to Grid feature, click on the Snap To tool, choose Draw ➤ Draw Properties, or right-click and choose Draw Properties to open the Misc panel of the Drawing Properties InfoBox. If the Snap To tool looks pressed down, the Snap to Grid feature is turned on.

The advantage of using the Drawing Properties InfoBox is that you can not only turn on Snap to Grid but you can also select the type of grid and specify the number of dots within the frame. You can click on one of three buttons to set the look of the grid: no dots, dots that are close together, and dots that are far apart (the default). You can set the distance between the dots (from 0.05 to 455.097 inches). The default is 0.25 inches.

## Viewing the Grid

After you have turned on Snap to Grid, it's a good idea to actually see the grid within the frame. To show (or hide) the grid, click on the Show/Hide Grid tool. When the grid appears (with its default settings), the frame looks like this:

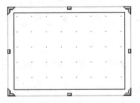

# ▶ Specifying Line Style, Fill Pattern, and Color

Use the Drawing Properties InfoBox to define the following aspects of a Word Pro drawing:

- line or border style (dashed, solid, or none)
- line endings (arrow heads, and so on)

- line or border color
- fill (interior of an object) color
- fill pattern

## Copying Line and Fill Attributes from One Object to Another

Copying the line and fill attributes from one object to another is a two-step process.

 Select the object whose attributes you wish to copy and click on the Extract Properties tool, or choose Draw ➤ Extract Properties.

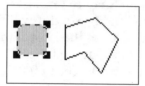

 Select the object whose attributes you want to change and click on the Apply Properties tool, or choose Draw ➤ Apply Properties. The end result looks like this:

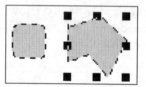

## Modifying Line, Border, and Pattern Attributes

 You can change line, border, and pattern attributes for selected and future drawn objects. To do so, click on the Draw InfoBox tool, choose Draw ➤ Draw Attributes, right-click and select Draw Properties, or press Alt+Enter. Word Pro displays the Draw Properties InfoBox (see Figure 11.9) for the selected object or for the drawing. (The selected object in Figure 11.7, earlier in this chapter, is a polygon.) If needed, click on the Lines & Color tab to display the Lines & Color panel of the Draw Properties InfoBox.

The Draw Properties InfoBox for various drawn objects offers these options:

**Arrowheads**   Choose from the drop-down list box on the left side of the InfoBox and one on the right side. You can select one type of ending for the left side of a line and another type for the right side. (Arc, Line, Polyline)

**Fill Color**   Click on a box in the color palette. If you have selected a pattern, this is the background color behind the pattern. (Oval, Polygon, Rectangle, Rounded Rectangle)

**Line Color**   Click on a box in the color palette. The current color is named at the top of the palette. (Arc, Line, Oval, Polygon, Polyline, Rectangle, Rounded Rectangle)

**Line Style**   Open this drop-down list box and click on your choice: None, a dashed line, and lines of various thicknesses. (Arc, Line, Oval, Polygon, Polyline, Rectangle, Rounded Rectangle)

**Pattern**   Click on a box in the pattern palette: None (which results in a transparent object), one of six patterns, and a solid. (Oval, Polygon, Rectangle, Rounded Rectangle)

**Pattern Color**   Click on a box in the color palette. If you have selected a pattern, this is the color of the pattern itself; if you have selected the solid box, this is the only color of the object. (Oval, Polygon, Rectangle, Rounded Rectangle)

**FIGURE 11.9** ▶

*In the Draw Properties InfoBox, you can define the line or border style, line color, fill color, pattern, and pattern color.*

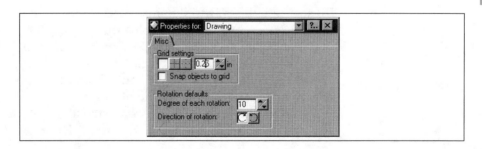

## ▶ *Scaling an Object*

Word Pro provides two ways to *scale* (increase or decrease the size of) an object: dragging on its handles, or clicking on a SmartIcon and then filling in an InfoBox.

## Scaling with Handles

To scale a selected object using its handles, it's a good idea to move the object to a part of the frame that will accommodate the final size.

In many applications, when you click on a handle, the mouse pointer changes to a double-headed arrow. In Word Pro, a "shadow" image of the object that you want to scale appears, and the mouse pointer remains as an upward-pointing arrow:

When you release the mouse button, the object changes size to fill the area defined by the final size of the sizing border:

## Scaling with the Frame Properties InfoBox

To scale an object by the numbers (that is, using its measurements as a guide), select the frame that holds the graphic. Then click on the Scaling SmartIcon, choose Frame ➤ Graphics Scaling, or right-click and choose Graphics Scaling. You also can choose Frame ➤ Frame Properties or right-click and choose Frame Properties and click on the Misc tab. You don't have to select the object if it's the only object in the drawing. In the Graphic Scaling drop-down list box in the Misc panel of the Frame Properties InfoBox (see Figure 11.10), select from these options:

**Original Size**    Choose this option to return to the starting size of the selected object. This is the default.

**Fit in Frame**    Choose this option to fit the object within the frame. If you change the dimensions of the frame, the object changes as well.

**Percentage**     Choose this option and then scroll through the choices (from 0 to 2304) in the text/list box. The default is 100%.

**Custom**     Click on this option button to specify a custom width and height for the object. Valid values for both width and height are from 0.05 to 22 inches. If you check the Scale Proportionately checkbox, you'll ensure that the original proportions of the object are maintained.

**FIGURE 11.10** ▶

*The Misc panel of the Frame Properties InfoBox with an open Graphic Scaling drop-down list box and part of the Scale Proportionately checkbox underneath*

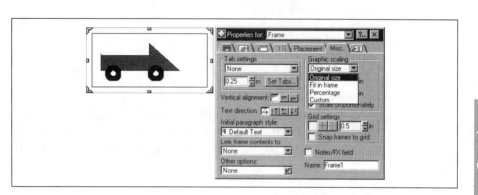

*Creating Pictures*

# ▶▶ *Creating and Editing Frames*

When you start the Drawing feature, Word Pro inserts a frame in which you can draw objects. In the previous section, you learned how to create and edit the contents of a frame but not how to edit the frame itself. You can use frames to allow text to wrap close to all four sides but separate the contents of the frame from the text outside the frame. You can insert objects, such as completed drawings and text, into a frame, or you can keep it empty as a placeholder for later use. You can add a frame to an empty or a text-filled document.

▶▶

Ch.
**11**

## ▶ *Adding a Frame to a Document*

To insert a frame in a document, either click on the Frame SmartIcon or choose Frame ➤ Create Frame. Then move the mouse pointer, which changes to a miniature frame, into the document. Click at the starting corner, and drag diagonally toward the opposite corner.

When the bounding box reaches the desired dimensions, release the mouse button.

## ▶ Modifying a Frame

In this section, you'll learn about the four versions of the Modify Frame Layout dialog box and their options.

 To modify a frame, click on the Frame InfoBox SmartIcon, choose Frame ➤ Frame Properties, or right-click in the frame and select Frame Properties. Word Pro opens the Size and Margins panel of the Frame Properties Info-Box (see Figure 11.11).

**FIGURE 11.11** ▶

*The Size and Margins panel of the Frame Properties InfoBox in which you can specify line and shadow styles and colors*

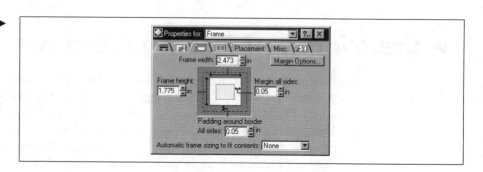

| Click on: | To select: |
|---|---|
|  | the look of the borders around the frame and the look of an optional shadow |
|  | a watermark (such as Draft, Confidential, or Internal, and so on) for inside the frame |
|  | the frame size, the size of the margins, and the way that the frame will grow to fit its contents |

| Click on: | To select: |
|---|---|
| ▦ | the number of columns in a frame, column attributes, and column margins |
| Placement | the placement of the frame on a page, the way in which text wraps around the frame, and the page element to which the frame is anchored (or attached) |
| Misc. | tab settings, the style of the text within the frame, graphic scaling, and grid settings |
| ⟨S⟩ | the frame's styles—defined, created, redefined, and managed |

## Modifying Frame Size and Position

These are the options in the Size and Margins panel of the Frame Properties InfoBox:

**Frame Width**    Type or select a value for the width of the frame. A frame can be almost as wide as the paper on which it is printed. Valid values depend on the defined paper size.

**Frame Height**    Type or select a value for the length of the frame. A frame can be almost as long as the paper on which it is printed. Valid values depend on the defined paper size.

**Margin All Sides**    Type or select a value for the measurement between the border and contents of the frame. The default value is 0.05 inches.

**Margin Options**    Click on this button to specify the measurement between the border and the closest text, the border and the contents of the frame, or around the layout.

**Padding around Border**    Type or select a value for the measurement between the frame and its border.

**Automatic Frame Sizing to Fit Contents**    Select the way in which you want the frame to be resized to fit its contents: None, Grow Down, Grow Up, or Fit Graphic.

Creating Pictures

►► Ch. **11**

## Modifying Frame Lines and Shadows

These are the options in the Lines and Color panel of the Frame Properties InfoBox (see Figure 11.12):

**Lines Around Frame**    Click on a button to specify the type of border: None, square corners (the default), shadowed square corners, rounded corners, or shadowed rounded corners.

**Designer Borders**    Choose from one of 13 custom frame borders or None, the default.

**Line Style**    From this drop-down list box, select a style for the lines around the frame.

**Line Width**    From this drop-down list box, select a width (in points) for the lines around the frame, or select Other to specify a line width (in points).

**Line Color**    From this drop-down list box, select a color for the border. The default color is black.

**Background Color**    From this drop-down palette, select a color for the background of the frame. The default color is white.

**Pattern**    From this drop-down palette, select a pattern for the inside of the frame. The default pattern is solid white.

**Pattern Color**    From this drop-down list box, select a color for the pattern within the frame. The default color is black.

**Shadow**    From this drop-down list box, select no shadow (None, the default) or the location of the shadow: Top Left, Top Right, Bottom Left, or Bottom Right.

**Shadow Depth**    From this drop-down list box, select the size of the shadow: Shallow (0.04 inch), Normal (0.07 inch, the default), Deep (0.12 inch), or Other, which opens the Shadow Depth dialog box in which you can specify the depth in inches.

**Shadow Color**    From this drop-down list box, select a color for the shadow. The default color is black.

**Show Sides**    From this drop-down list box, you can check the border sides that you wish to show: All Sides (the default), Left, Right, Top, or Bottom.

**Corners** From this drop-down list box, you can select rounded corners for the border of the frame: three degrees of rounding, Other (you can set the rounding from 0% to 100%), or None (a 90-degree angle corner).

**FIGURE 11.12** ▶

*The Lines and Color panel of the Frame Properties InfoBox*

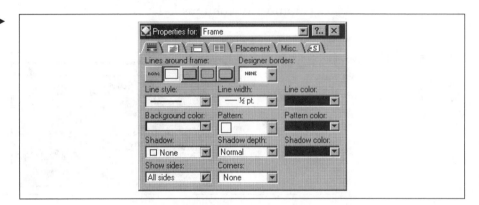

## Modifying Frame Columns and Tabs

These are the options in the Columns panel of the Frame Properties InfoBox (see Figure 11.13):

**Number of Newspaper Columns** Type or select the number of columns in the frame (from 1 to 9). The default is 1. If you set the number of columns to 1, the Space Between Columns, Vertical Line Between Columns, and Column Balance options are not available.

**Space Between Columns** Select the width of the space between columns. Valid values are 0 to 0.25 inches. The default is 0.17 inches, unless the number of columns is 1 and this option is not available.

**Line Style** From this drop-down list box, select None (no vertical line between the columns) or a line type or pattern. This option is not available if the number of columns is 1.

**Line Width** From this drop-down list box, select the width of the vertical line between the columns or Other, which opens the Line Width dialog box in which you can specify a line width, in points. The default is $\frac{1}{2}$ point. This option is not available if the number of columns is 1.

**Line Color**    From this drop-down list box, select a color for the vertical line between the columns. The default color is black. This option is not available if the number of columns is 1.

**Column Balance**    Check this checkbox to make the length of the columns as equal as possible. This option is not available if the number of columns is 1.

**FIGURE 11.13** ▶

*The Columns panel of the Frame Properties InfoBox*

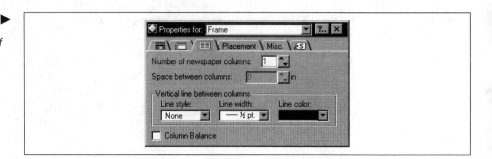

## Modifying Frame Placement

These are the options in the Placement panel of the Frame Properties InfoBox (see Figure 11.14):

**Quick Alignment**    Click on a button to align the frame to the left margin, between the left margin and the right margin, to the right margin, from the left margin to the right margin, or from the top of the page to the bottom of the page. These buttons are available only if you select On All Pages, On Left/Right Pages, With Paragraph Above, or On Current Page.

**Wrap Options**    Click on a button to wrap text around all sides of the frame (the default), to not wrap to the left or right of the frame, or to cover the frame. These buttons are available only if you select On All Pages, On Left/Right Pages, Same Page As Text, On Current Page, or In Text—Vertical.

**Place Frame**    From this drop-down list box, select the page element to which this frame will be anchored and how the frame can move because of editing around the frame and throughout the document.

**Offset from Anchor Point to Frame**    Select or type values in the Vertical and Horizontal text/option boxes to indicate the distance, both vertically and horizontally, from the place at which the frame is anchored. Click on Clear to reset the Vertical and Horizontal measurement to 0.05 inches. Both Vertical and Horizontal options are available if you select On All Pages, On Left/Right Pages, Same Page As Text, On Current Page, or In Text—Vertical. If you choose With Paragraph Above, only the Horizontal option is available.

**Placement and Anchoring Options**    Click on this button to open the Placement Options dialog box in which you can fine-tune the location of the frame in relation to the place on the page on which it is anchored.

**FIGURE 11.14** ▶

*The Placement panel of the Frame Properties InfoBox*

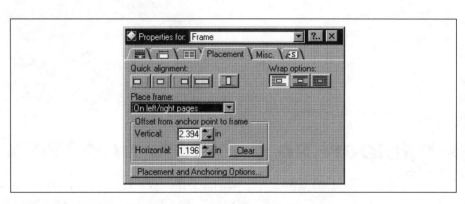

## Other Frame Attributes

For information about options in the Misc and Style panels of Smart-Suite InfoBoxes (see Figures 11.15 and 11.16), see the *Getting Acquainted with SmartSuite* chapter.

Creating Pictures

Ch.
**11**

**FIGURE 11.15** ▶

*The Misc panel of
the Frame Properties
InfoBox*

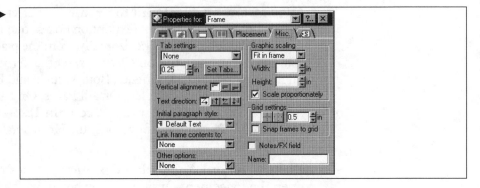

**FIGURE 11.16** ▶

*The Style panel of
the Frame Properties
InfoBox*

# ▶▶ *Importing a Picture into Word Pro*

In Word Pro, you can import a variety of pictures into your documents. You can import pictures that have any of the following file types:

| | |
|---|---|
| DrawPerfect 1 (*.WPG) | CGM (*.CGM) |
| DrawPerfect 2 (*.WPG) | CorelDraw (*.CDR) |
| Equations (*.TEX) | EPS (*.EPS) |
| GIF (*.GIF) | Freelance (*.DRW) |
| JPEG (*.JPG) | HPGL (*.PLT) |
| PCX (*.PCX) | Kodak Photo CD (*.PCD) |
| TIFF (*.TIF) | LotusPIC (*.PIC) |
| PNG (*.PNG) | |

Windows Bitmap (*.BMP)      Word Pro Draw (*.SDW)

Windows Metafile
(*.WMF, *.EMF)

You can also use the Edit menu in most Windows applications to copy and paste pictures into Word Pro or from Word Pro into another Windows application. Whether you paste or import a picture, pictures must be inserted into frames in Word Pro. You can either create a frame or have Word Pro create the frame while the picture is being pasted or imported.

To import a picture into a Word Pro document, follow these steps:

1. Either click on the Import a Picture SmartIcon or choose File ➤ Import Picture.

2. In the Import Picture dialog box (see Figure 11.17), select a file type from the Files of Type scroll box.

3. If no list appears in the scroll box, you may need to change folders (for example, the DRAWSYM folder contains Word Pro Draw files).

4. Select a file from the scroll box. (When you select the filename, you can see a preview of the picture at the bottom of the dialog box—if the Preview checkbox is checked.)

**FIGURE 11.17** ➤

*In the Import Picture dialog box, you can select a picture to be imported.*

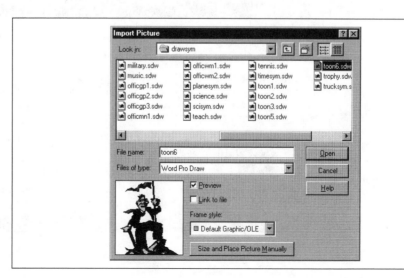

**5.** Either click on Open or press Enter. If you have not created a drawing frame, Word Pro creates one and imports the picture into it.

Figure 11.18 shows the top of a document with three frames: one with a logo drawn in Windows Paint, one holding the company name, and the third with a piece of Word Pro Draw clip art.

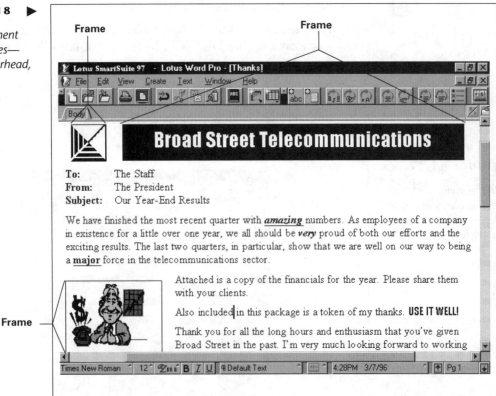

► ►  CHAPTER **12**

# Working with Long Documents

▶▶ **T**his chapter covers all aspects of working with long documents, usually those with at least one table of contents and an index and that include several portions of body text, broken into chapters, sections, or both. This chapter begins with a discussion of Word Pro divisions, sections, and master documents and shows how to use them to assemble a long document or to break a long document into smaller portions. You'll also learn how to define table of contents and index entries and how to generate and update tables of contents and indexes. Then, you'll find out how to use footnotes and endnotes in a Word Pro document of any size. Finally, you'll learn how to use Word Pro's outlining feature to build a long document from a foundation of headings.

## ▶▶ *Sections versus Divisions*

When you are creating and editing a long document, such as a manual or a long report or proposal, an efficient work method is to divide the document into chunks. In Word Pro, you can work with sections, divisions, and master documents.

A section is a portion of a document, ranging in size from a paragraph to an entire document. Each section in a document includes its own page layout formats, which start out as the defaults specified for the entire document. By changing the page layout for a particular section, you can embed a two-column section within a one-column document. Or, you can create unique header and footer text or assign special page numbers within the section. Several sections can appear on one document page. After you create a section, Word Pro inserts a section divider tab in the tab bar. Once the section divider tab is in place, you can drag an entire section from one location in a document to another.

A division, which is made up of one or more sections, is considered a document within a file. Divisions, which can range in size from a small section to many pages, can be composed of text or can contain other divisions, external files (even files from the Internet), or OLE objects. Each division that you define can use a different SmartMaster template and must always start on a new page. After you create a division, Word Pro inserts a division divider tab in the tab bar. Once the division divider tab is in place, you can drag an entire division from one location in a document to another.

A master document, which comprises one or more divisions, must contain a division that contains a link to an external file.

# ►► *Specifying Document Sections*

In Word Pro, you can use commands from the menu bar and from short-cut menus as well as SmartIcons to create, manipulate, and edit sections in a document. Almost every command or click on a SmartIcon opens a dialog box with which you can specify attributes for a section.

## ► *Creating a New Section*

Create a new section using the Create Section dialog box (see Figure 12.1), which includes these options:

> **Start Section**     From this drop-down list box, select the page or part of a page on which this section will start: within the page (that is, the new section starts immediately after the prior section ends), on the next page, on the next odd-numbered page, or on the next even-numbered page.
>
> **Initial Page Layout Style**     From this list box, select the page style for this section. The default is Default Page.

▶▶ **N O T E**

**To create and save a new style, click on the Page InfoBox SmartIcon, choose Text ➤ Text Properties and select Page Layout from the drop-down list box, or right-click and choose Page Properties. Change properties in the Page Properties InfoBox, and then click on the Styles tab, click on the Create Style button, name the style, and click on OK. Word Pro adds the new named style to the Create Section dialog box the next time you open it.**

**Show Divider Tab**    Check this checkbox to show the divider tab. Clear this checkbox to hide the divider tab. A checked checkbox is the default.

**Use Header Text from Previous Page**    Check this checkbox to use the header text from the previous section in this section. If you clear this checkbox, you can enter new header text for this section. A checked checkbox is the default.

**Use Footer Text from Previous Page**    Check this checkbox to use the footer text from the previous section in this section. If you clear this checkbox, you can enter new footer text for this section. A checked checkbox is the default.

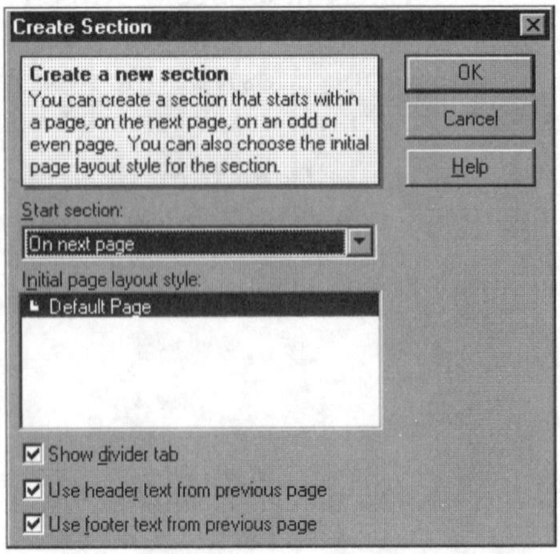

**FIGURE 12.1** ▶

*The Create Section dialog box with its default settings*

Create Section

**Create a new section**
You can create a section that starts within a page, on the next page, on an odd or even page. You can also choose the initial page layout style for the section.

OK
Cancel
Help

Start section:
On next page

Initial page layout style:
┗ Default Page

☑ Show divider tab
☑ Use header text from previous page
☑ Use footer text from previous page

To create a new section, follow these steps:

1. Move the insertion point to the location at which you want to create the section.

2. Click on the Create Section SmartIcon, choose Create ➤ Section, or right-click on the section divider tab and select New Section. Word Pro opens the Create Section dialog box.

3. From the Start Section drop-down list box, select whether the section will start within the page, on the next page, on the next odd-numbered page, or on the next even-numbered page.

4. If you want to change the page style and you have defined additional page styles, click on a page style in the Initial Page Layout Style list box.

5. If you want to show the divider tab, check the Show Divider Tab checkbox.

6. To use the header text from the previous section, check the Use Header Text from Previous Page checkbox.

7. To use the footer text from the previous section, check the Use Footer Text from Previous Page checkbox.

8. Click on OK or press Enter to close the dialog box. Word Pro inserts a new section divider tab in the tab bar and a section break at the end of the section.

- - - - - - - - - - - - - - - - - - - - - - - - - - - - Section: Sample Section - - - - - - - - - - - - - - - - - - - - - - - - - - - - -

▶▶**N O T E**

**After you create the first section in a document, you can create a section without opening the Create Section dialog box. Simply right-click on the section divider tab and choose the Quick Section command. Word Pro creates a copy of the current section.**

**Long Documents**

▶▶

*Ch.*
**12**

## ► *Editing a Section*

To edit a section, use the Section Properties dialog box (see Figure 12.2), which includes these options:

**Section Name**    In this text box, type the name that will appear on the divider tab.

**Page Style for Section**    From this drop-down list box, select the page style for this section. You can define page styles in the Styles section of the Text Properties InfoBox.

**Start Section**    From this drop-down list box, select the page or part of a page on which this section will start: within the page (that is, the new section starts immediately after the prior section ends), on the next page, on the next odd-numbered page, or on the next even-numbered page.

 ►► N O T E

> If you are laying out the pages for a book, remember that the odd-numbered pages are on the right side of a two-page layout and the even-numbered pages are on the left side.

**Show Divider Tab**    Check this checkbox to show the divider tab, the default. Clear this checkbox to hide the divider tab.

**Divider Tab Color**    Click on the downward-pointing arrow to open a drop-down palette from which you can choose a divider tab color.

 ►► N O T E

> Editing a section is not the same as editing text, which you can do with the Page Layout Properties InfoBox. Editing a section involves changing its name, selecting a particular predefined page style, and controlling the appearance of the section divider tab.

**FIGURE 12.2** ▶

*The Section Properties dialog box showing the current attributes for the selected section*

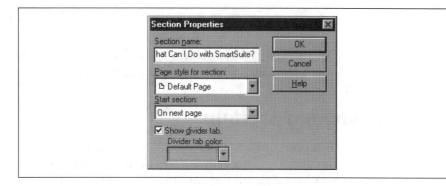

To edit a section, follow these steps:

**1.** Click in front of or on the Page icon on the section break line.

**2.** Click on the Section Properties SmartIcon, choose File ➤ Document Properties ➤ Section, or right-click on the section divider tab and choose Section Properties.

▶▶ **T I P**

> **If you have defined multiple sections in the same area of a document, the best way to edit a particular section is to right-click on the section divider tab and choose Section Properties.**

**3.** To change the name on the section divider tab, type a new name in the Section Name text box.

▶▶ **T I P**

> **The fastest way to change the name on a tab in the tab bar is to double-click on the tab and type the new name.**

**4.** To change to a different page style if you have defined any named styles, select from the Page Style for Section drop-down list box.

**5.** To change the part of the document at which this section will start, select an option from the Start Section drop-down list box.

Long Documents

▶▶
Ch.
**12**

6. To display or hide the divider tab, check or clear the Show Divider Tab checkbox.

7. To change the divider tab color, click on the downward-pointing arrow and select from the palette.

## ▶ Combining Sections

You can combine selected sections when you no longer need them to be separate (for example, two sections have the same page attributes or you have deleted the contents of a section). To combine sections in a document, right-click on a section divider tab and choose Combine Section. In the Combine Sections dialog box (see Figure 12.3), click on sections to select them. A checkmark preceding a section indicates that it has been selected. The new section uses the page layout and other attributes of the first section that you selected.

**FIGURE 12.3** ▶

*The Combine Sections dialog box with its default settings*

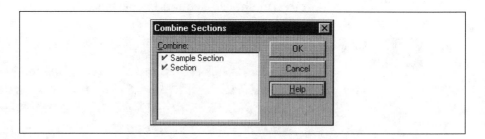

## ▶ Selecting, Copying, and Moving Sections

In Word Pro, you use the Select Section command to select a section for copying or moving. To select a section, right-click on a section divider tab and choose Select Section.

To copy a section and paste the copy in a new location, right-click on a section divider tab and choose Select Section. To copy the section to the Windows Clipboard, click on the Copy to the Clipboard SmartIcon (shown top left), choose Edit ➤ Copy, right-click and choose Copy, or press Ctrl+C. To paste the section, click on the division or section in which you want it to be located, click on the Paste the Clipboard Contents SmartIcon (shown bottom left), choose Edit ➤ Paste, right-click and choose Paste, or press Ctrl+V.

To move (cut) the contents of a section to a new location, right-click on a section divider tab and choose Select Section. To cut the section to the Windows Clipboard, click on the Cut to the Clipboard Smart-Icon, choose Edit ➤ Cut, right-click and choose Cut, or press Ctrl+X. To paste the section, click on the division or section in which you want it to be located, click on the Paste the Clipboard Contents SmartIcon, choose Edit ➤ Paste, right-click and choose Paste, or press Ctrl+V.

## ▶ Deleting a Section Mark

When you delete a section mark, Word Pro erases the section mark and removes the section divider tab, leaving the contents of the section in the division in which the section was located. To delete a section mark, right-click on a section divider tab and choose Delete Section Mark.

# ▶▶ Specifying Document Divisions

Use commands from the menu bar and in shortcut menus as well as SmartIcons to create, manipulate, and edit divisions. In almost the same way that you create and change sections, you can use various dialog boxes to specify attributes for a division.

## ▶ Creating a New Division

In Word Pro, you can create a new division in several ways: from an existing document, a SmartMaster, or an Internet file; using a plain division, OLE, or the Internet. In addition, after you create a division, you can copy it using the Quick Division command.

**Creating a Division from an Existing Document**    If you have already created documents (for example, chapters) that you want to combine into a single document, you can create divisions by choosing Creating a Division from an Existing Document. You can create a division using Word Pro documents and documents from other word processors and applications.

**Creating a Division Using a SmartMaster**    Take advantage of professionally designed Word Pro SmartMaster templates to create a division.

**Creating a Plain Division**     Create an empty division in which you can type and edit new material.

**Creating an OLE Division**     If you create an OLE division, you can start an OLE server when you click on the division divider tab. This enables you to edit a linked or embedded OLE object without explicitly opening the application in which the object was created.

**Creating an Internet Division**     Access the Internet and download a file into its own division. For example, you can insert expert information to support the data in a report.

## Creating a Division from an Existing Document

To create a division from an existing document, follow these steps:

1. If you have created previous divisions in the current document, click on the division divider tab before or after the location into which you want to insert the new division. However, if you click on an OLE division divider tab, you will start the application in which the OLE object was created.

2. Click on the Create Division SmartIcon, choose Create ➤ Division, or right-click on a division divider tab and choose New Division. Word Pro opens the Create Division dialog box (see Figure 12.4).

3. If you have recently used the document that you want to insert into the new division, select it from the scroll box and click on OK. Go to step 6.

4. If you want to find another document on your hard drive, on a floppy disk, or on a CD-ROM, click on the Browse for More Files button. Word Pro opens the Document to Insert As Division dialog box (see Figure 12.5).

5. Select a file as you would in a typical Windows Open dialog box, and then click on the Open button. Word Pro opens the Insert Division dialog box (see Figure 12.6).

6. To place the division before the current division, after the current division, or at the insertion point (which splits the current division into two divisions), click on an Insert Division option button. Inserting the new division after the current division is the default.

**FIGURE 12.4** ▶

*The Create a Division from an Existing Document section of the Create Division dialog box*

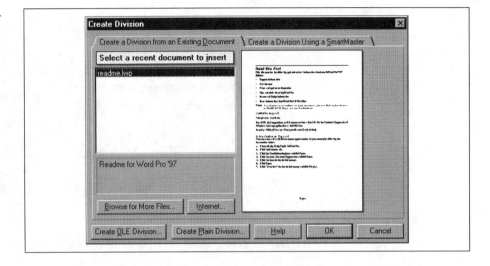

**FIGURE 12.5** ▶

*The Document to Insert as Division dialog box with the documents in the Word Pro folder*

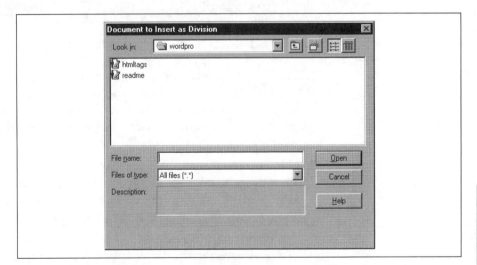

**7.** To insert a copy of the file or to link the file, leaving the original in its starting location, click on a Selected File Will Be option button.

**8.** Click on OK. Word Pro inserts the new division in the current document and creates a division divider tab.

**FIGURE 12.6** ►

*The Insert Division dialog box with its default settings*

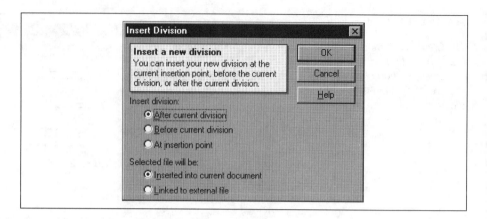

## Creating a Division Using a SmartMaster

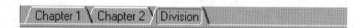

To create a division from a SmartMaster, follow these steps:

1. If you have created previous divisions in the current document, click on the division divider tab before or after the location into which you want to insert the new division. However, if you click on an OLE division divider tab, you will start the application in which you created the OLE object.

2. Click on the Create Division SmartIcon, choose Create ➤ Division, or right-click on a division divider tab and choose New Division. Word Pro opens the Create Division dialog box.

3. Click on the Create a Division Using a SmartMaster tab. Word Pro displays the Create a Division Using a SmartMaster section of the Create Division dialog box (see Figure 12.7).

4. If you have recently used the SmartMaster that you want to insert into the new division, select it from the scroll box and click on OK. Go to step 7.

5. If you want to find another document on your hard drive, on a floppy disk, or on a CD-ROM, click on the Browse for More Files button. Word Pro opens the New Division dialog box.

**6.** Select a file as you would in a typical Windows Open dialog box. Then click on the OK button. Word Pro opens a new version of the Insert Division dialog box (see Figure 12.8).

**7.** To place the division before the current division, after the current division, or at the insertion point (which splits the current division into two divisions), click on an Insert Division option button. Inserting the new division after the current division is the default.

**8.** Click on OK. Word Pro inserts the new division in the current document and creates a division divider tab. The first division in a document is named Body by default; otherwise, it is named Division.

**FIGURE 12.7** ▶

*The Create a Division Using a SmartMaster section of the Create Division dialog box with the most recently used SmartMasters on display*

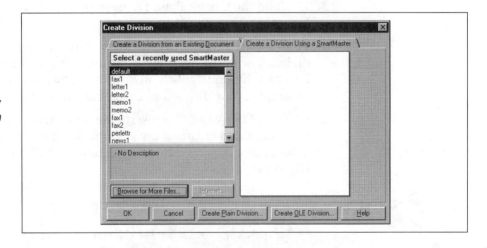

**FIGURE 12.8** ▶

*A new version of the Insert Division dialog box*

Long Documents

▶ ▶

*Ch.*
**12**

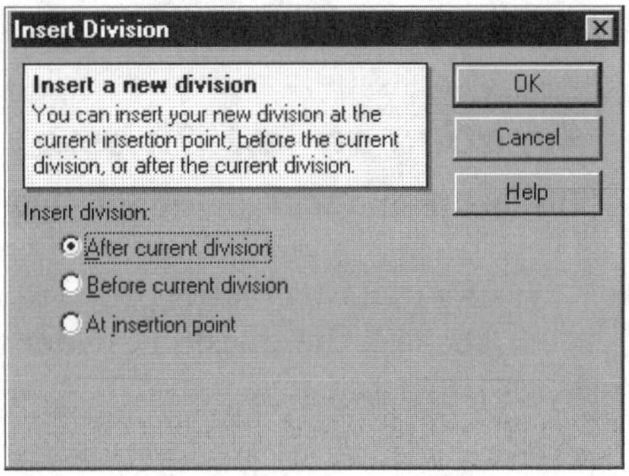

### Creating a Plain Division

To create a plain division, follow these steps:

1. If you have created previous divisions in the current document, click on the division divider tab before or after the location into which you want to insert the new division. However, if you click on an OLE division divider tab, you will start the application in which you created the OLE object.

2. Click on the Create Division SmartIcon, choose Create ▶ Division, or right-click on a division divider tab and choose New Division. Word Pro opens the Create Division dialog box.

3. Click on the Create Plain Division button. Word Pro displays the Insert Division dialog box.

4. To place the division before the current division, after the current division, or at the insertion point (which splits the current division into two divisions), click on an Insert Division option button. Inserting the new division after the current division is the default.

5. Click on OK. Word Pro inserts the new division in the current document and creates a division divider tab. The first division in a document is named Body by default; otherwise, it is named Division.

 ▶▶ **T I P**

> **To quickly create a plain division after the current division, right-click on its division divider tab and choose Quick Division.**

### Creating an OLE Division

To create an OLE division, follow these steps:

1. If you have created previous divisions in the current document, click on the division divider tab before or after the location into

which you want to insert the new division. However, if you click on an OLE division divider tab, you will start the application in which you created the OLE object.

**2.** Click on the Create Division SmartIcon, choose Create ➤ Division, or right-click on a division divider tab and choose New Division. Word Pro opens the Create Division dialog box.

**3.** Click on the Create OLE Division button. Word Pro displays the Insert OLE Division dialog box (see Figure 12.9).

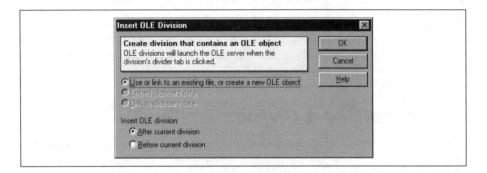

 ▶▶**TIP**

**To skip step 2 and open the Insert OLE Division dialog box immediately, click on the Create OLE Division SmartIcon.**

**4.** To embed the contents of the Clipboard, click on the Embed Clipboard Data option button. Word Pro starts the server application so that you can paste the Clipboard contents.

**5.** To link to the contents of the Clipboard, click on the Link to Clipboard Data option button. Word Pro starts the server application so that you can update the Clipboard contents.

**6.** To use or link to an existing file or create a new OLE object, click on the Use or Link to an Existing File option or on the Create a New OLE Object option. Word Pro opens the Create Object dialog box, from which you can create a new object or create an object from an existing file. For additional information about using the Create Object dialog box, see the "Inserting an Object into a Sheet" section in the *Getting Acquainted with SmartSuite* chapter.

**Long Documents**

▶▶

*Ch.*
**12**

**7.** To place the division before or after the current division, click on an Insert OLE Division option button. Inserting the new division after the current division is the default.

**8.** Click on OK. Word Pro inserts the new division in the current document and creates a division divider tab.

Word Pro starts the OLE server whenever you click the division's divider tab.

### Creating an Internet Division

The Internet is full of data with which you can support or enhance the information in a proposal or report. You can embed Internet data in a new division. For information on doing so, see the *SmartSuite and the Internet* appendix.

## ► Editing a Division

The Division Properties dialog box (see Figure 12.10) is the center-piece of division editing. In it are these options:

**Division Name**　In this text box, type the name that will appear on the division's divider tab.

**FIGURE 12.10** ►

*The Division Properties dialog box showing the current attributes for the selected section*

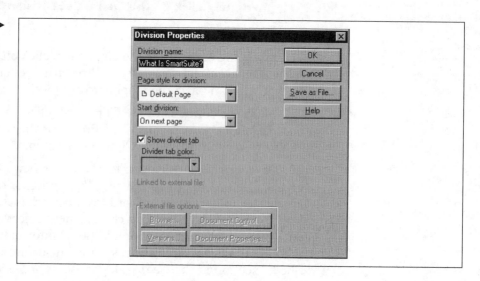

**Page Style for Division**    From this drop-down list box, select the page style for this section.

**Start Division**    From this drop-down list box, select the page on which this division will start: on the next page, on the next odd-numbered page, or on the next even-numbered page.

 ▶▶ **N O T E**

> If you are laying out the pages for a book, remember that the odd-numbered pages are on the right side of a two-page layout and the even-numbered pages are on the left side.

**Show Divider Tab**    Check this checkbox to show the division divider tab, the default. Clear this checkbox to hide the division divider tab.

**Divider Tab Color**    Click on the downward-pointing arrow to open a drop-down palette from which you can choose a division divider tab color.

To edit a division, follow these steps:

*1.* Click on the division divider tab. However, if you click on an OLE division divider tab, you will start the application in which the OLE object was created.

 *2.* Click on the Division Properties SmartIcon, choose File ➤ Document Properties ➤ Division, or right-click on the division divider tab and choose Division Properties.

*3.* To change the name on the division divider tab, type a new name in the Division Name text box.

 ▶▶ **T I P**

> The fastest way to change the name on a tab in the tab bar is to double-click on the tab (except for OLE division divider tabs) and type the new name. If you double-click or click on the OLE division divider tab, the application in which you created the OLE object starts.

*Ch.*
**12**

**Long Documents**

4. To change to a different page style if you have defined any named styles, select from the Page Style for Division drop-down list box.

5. To change the page on which this division will start, select an option from the Start Division drop-down list box.

6. To display or hide the divider tab, check or clear the Show Divider Tab checkbox.

7. To change the divider tab color, click on the downward-pointing arrow and select from the palette.

## ▶ Combining Divisions

You can combine selected divisions when you no longer need them to be separate (for example, two divisions have the same page attributes or you have deleted some or all the contents of a division).

 ▶▶**N O T E**

> **You can only combine divisions that are immediately next to each other, and you cannot combine OLE divisions.**

To combine divisions in a document, right-click on a division divider tab and choose Combine Division. In the Combine Divisions dialog box (see Figure 12.11), click on sections to select them. A checkmark preceding a division name indicates that it has been selected. The new division uses the page layout and other attributes of the first division that you selected. After the divisions have been combined, Word Pro inserts page breaks at the location of the end of each former division and the start of the next.

## ▶ Deleting a Division

When you delete a division, Word Pro erases the invisible division mark, deletes the contents of the division, and removes the division divider tab without prompting you for confirmation. To delete a division, right-click on a division tab and choose Delete Division.

**FIGURE 12.11** ▶

*The Combine Divisions
dialog box with two
adjacent divisions
selected*

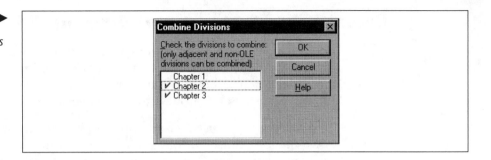

 If you have inadvertently deleted a division, you can undo the deletion by clicking on the Undo the Last Command or Action SmartIcon or by choosing Edit ➤ Undo - Delete Division.

# ▶▶ *Working with Sections and Divisions*

Once you have broken a document into sections and divisions, you can move through its pages much more easily than you could when the document was composed of pages only.

## ▶ *Showing or Hiding Sections*

Because the space on the view tab bar is limited by the size of the monitor screen, you can view a division without its sections or a division and its sections.

 A plus sign on a division divider tab indicates a division with hidden sections.

 A minus sign on a division divider tab indicates a division with displayed sections.

 A division divider tab with nothing but its name indicates a division with no sections.

- To display hidden sections for a division, click on the plus sign on the division divider tab.

- To hide all sections in a division, click on the minus sign on the division divider tab.

## ▶ *Rearranging Sections and Divisions*

One of the main advantages of working with sections and divisions is that you can move chunks of text from one location to another rather than selecting text, cutting it, and pasting it elsewhere. You can use Word Pro's drag-and-drop feature to move sections and divisions.

To move a section or a division, point to its divider tab, press and hold down the left mouse button, and move the mouse pointer to an empty space or a space between divisions or sections on the tab bar. If the mouse pointer looks like this:

Word Pro will not allow you to drop the section or division.

However, if the mouse pointer looks like this:

you can release the left mouse button to drop the section or division in its new location.

# ▶▶ *Moving through a Long Document*

To move up or down the pages of a long document, you can drag the scroll box in the vertical scroll bar. While you drag, Word Pro shows you exactly where the insertion point will be when you release the left mouse button to stop dragging. For example, if you want to go to page 4, which is in Chapter 1, drag until a marker in the right margin looks like this:

Or, if you want to go to page 76, which happens to be in the index division, drag until the marker looks like this:

# ▶▶ *Creating a Master Document*

A master document contains external files (that is, files to which you create a link within the current document). You can build a master document only with external linked files or with a combination of external linked files and files created and edited in the current file.

You can use master documents to allow each individual in a workgroup to be responsible for a single portion of a document. For example, a team under a heavy deadline can put together a set of technical manuals in a very short time. Or, representatives of the accounting, legal, and marketing departments and upper management can work together to write a business plan. Use the Master Document—(*filename*) dialog box (see Figure 12.12) to create a master document.

**FIGURE 12.12** ▶

*The Master Document—(filename) dialog box*

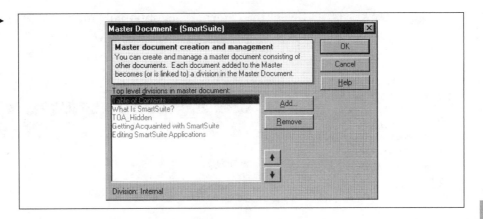

The options in this dialog box are:

**Top Level Divisions in Master Document**    In this box is a list of top-level divisions in the document. To move a division up the list, click on the upward-pointing arrow button; to move a division down the list, click on the downward-pointing arrow button.

**Add**    Click on this button to open a dialog box with which you can add an external file to be inserted into the current division or a new division.

**Remove**    Click on this button to remove the selected division. Be careful about using this button; you are not prompted to confirm the deletion. If you have inadvertently deleted a division, click on Cancel to close the dialog box without taking any actions.

To create a master document, follow these steps:

1. Click on the Create Master Document SmartIcon or choose Create ➤ Master Document. Word Pro opens the Master Document—(*filename*) dialog box.

2. Click on the Add button. Word Pro opens the Browse dialog box (see Figure 12.13).

3. Select file type, location, and the file that you want to add to the master document. Then click on Open. Word Pro adds the file to the list in the Master Document—(*filename*) dialog box.

4. Select the external file, optionally move it to its proper location in the list of divisions, and click on OK. Word Pro creates a new division divider tab.

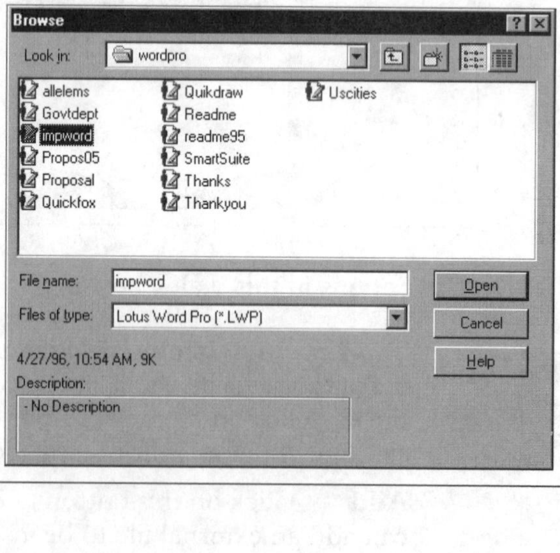

**FIGURE 12.13** ▶

*The Browse dialog box, from which you can select an external file to copy into a master document*

| Browse | ? ✕ |
|--------|-----|

Look in: 📁 wordpro

🗎 allelems  🗎 Quikdraw  🗎 Uscities
🗎 Govtdept  🗎 Readme
🗎 **impword**  🗎 readme95
🗎 Propos05  🗎 SmartSuite
🗎 Proposal  🗎 Thanks
🗎 Quickfox  🗎 Thankyou

File name: impword                    Open

Files of type: Lotus Word Pro [*.LWP]    Cancel

4/27/96, 10:54 AM, 9K           Help
Description:
· No Description

# ▶▶ *Creating a Table of Contents*

In a document such as a technical manual or a long proposal, readers can benefit by being able to refer to a table of contents to discover what's within the document. For a particularly long document, you can further aid the reader by providing multiple tables of contents—one at the beginning of each chapter. Word Pro makes it easy to specify table of content entries and to generate one or more tables of contents.

## ▶ *Specifying a Table of Contents Entry*

A standard table of contents shows document headings at several levels. Headings typically include chapter titles, division headings, and section headings. Tables of contents can also include table and figure headings, incorporated into standard tables or as separate tables.

Choose Text ➤ Mark Text As ➤ TOC Entry to open the Mark Text bar (see Figure 12.14), which you use to specify table of contents entries. You can keep the Mark Text bar open to insert both index and table of contents entries.

**FIGURE 12.14** ▶

*The Mark Text bar with its starting defaults*

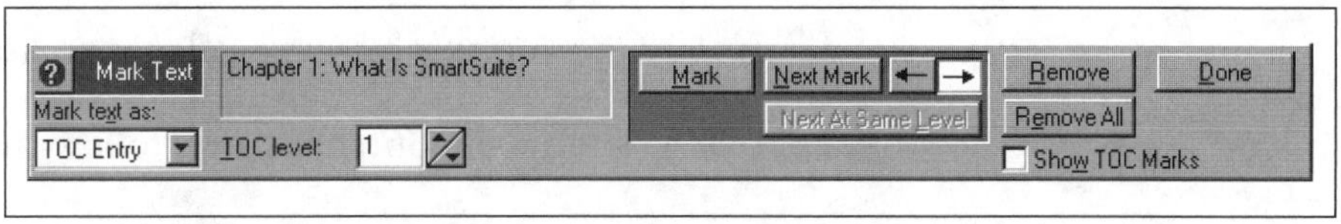

Options on the Mark Text bar for table of contents entries are:

**Mark Text As**    From this drop-down list box, choose whether the selected text will be marked as a table of contents entry or as an index entry. If you choose TOC Entry, Word Pro removes index options from and adds table of contents options to the Mark Text bar.

**TOC Level**    In this text/option box, type or select a table of contents level. Valid values include 0 and range from 1 (the highest level) to 9 (the lowest level); the default value is 1.

**Mark**    Click on this button to mark the selected text as a table of contents entry.

**Next Mark**   Click on this button to go to the next table of contents mark.

 **Left Arrow**   Click on this button to find the prior valid table of contents mark when you click on the Next Mark or Next At Same Level button. A button that looks pressed shows the current direction.

 **Right Arrow**   Click on this button to find the next valid table of contents mark when you click on the Next Mark or Next At Same Level button. A button that looks pressed shows the current direction.

**Next at Same Level**   Click on this button to move to the next or prior table of contents mark at the same level as the current mark.

**Remove**   Click on this button to remove the current table of contents mark.

**Remove All**   Click on this button to remove all the table of contents marks from this document.

**Show TOC Marks**   Check this checkbox to show table of contents marks. A cleared checkbox, the default, hides table of contents marks.

**Done**   Click on this button to close the Mark Text bar.

To mark text as a table of contents entry, follow these steps:

 **1.** Click on the Mark Text As a TOC Entry SmartIcon or choose Text ➤ Mark Text As ➤ TOC Entry.

**2.** Select all the text in a heading to be included in the table of contents. Word Pro displays the selected text in the Mark Text bar.

 ▶▶ **T I P**

**If all the sections you have created start with a heading, a quick way to move through a document is to click on section divider tabs.**

**3.** Type or select the TOC level for the text. Word Pro automatically selects the TOC level of the previous entry that you marked until you change the level for the current entry.

**4.** Click on the Mark button. If you have checked the Show TOC Marks checkbox, Word Pro displays the TOC mark.

```
<TOC 1 "SmartSuite Features">SmartSuite Features
```

**5.** Continue to scroll through the document to find the next heading to add to the table of contents. Repeat steps 2, 3, and 4 when you find an entry.

**6.** If you want to correct marked entries, click on an arrow button; then click on the Next Mark or Next At Same Level button to go to the marked text. To remove the entry, click on the Remove button. If Word Pro doesn't find an entry, it goes either to the top of the document or to the bottom of the document, depending on the direction of the search.

▶▶ **TIP**

**A foolproof way of changing the level of entries is to check the Show TOC Marks checkbox. Then when you go to an entry, you can actually edit the TOC mark (for example, TOC 1, TOC 2, and so on). You can also generate the table of contents, change the entries using the styles in the Status bar, and then update the table of contents.**

**7.** When you have finished adding entries, click on Done to close the Mark Text bar.

▶▶ **TIP**

**If you don't want to show TOC marks in a document, remove the checkmark from the Show TOC Marks checkbox.**

## ▶ *Generating a Table of Contents*

Once you define all the entries for a table of contents, you can generate the table of contents using the Table of Contents Assistant dialog box, which is composed of three sections: Step 1: Look (see Figure 12.15), Step 2: Scope and Placement (see Figure 12.16), and Step 3: Contents (see Figure 12.17).

**Long Documents**

▶▶

*Ch.*
**12**

**FIGURE 12.15** ▶

*The Step 1: Look section of the Table of Contents Assistant dialog box*

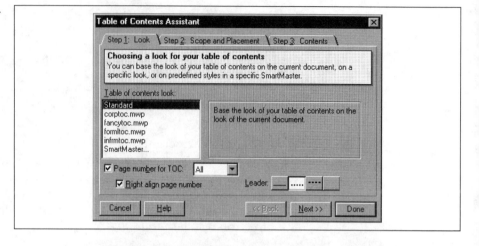

**FIGURE 12.16** ▶

*The Step 2: Scope and Placement section of the Table of Contents Assistant dialog box*

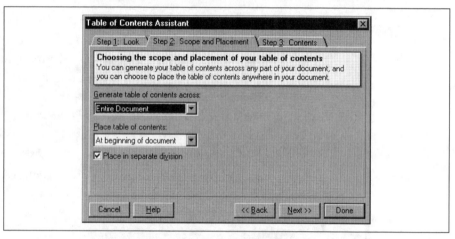

**FIGURE 12.17** ▶

*The Step 3: Contents section of the Table of Contents Assistant dialog box*

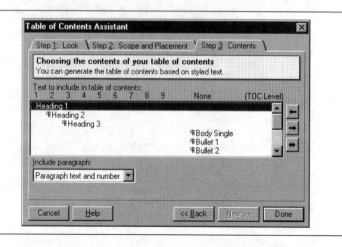

The options in the Step 1: Look section of the dialog box are:

**Table of Contents Look** From this list, select the look of this table of contents. Figures 12.18, 12.19, 12.20, 12.21, and 12.22 show examples of the standard, corporate, formal, informal, and fancy looks. If you select SmartMaster, you can choose a look from one of the Word Pro SmartMasters.

**▶▶ NOTE**

**If you are also creating an index for this document, it's a good idea to choose identical looks for both the table of contents and the index.**

**Page Number for TOC** Check this checkbox to insert page numbers for all entries or selected entries in the table of contents. If you check the checkbox, open the drop-down list box and choose a level or All levels. A cleared checkbox indicates that the table of contents will contain no page numbers. A checked checkbox and All are the defaults.

**Right Align Page Number** Check this checkbox to align the page number with the right margin. The default is a checked checkbox.

**Leader** Click on a button to choose the *leader*, the line that extends from the end of the table of contents entry to the page number. The default is a dotted line.

**FIGURE 12.18 ▶**

*A portion of a table of contents with the Standard look and the dotted line leader*

| | |
|---|---|
| Chapter 1: What Is SmartSuite? . . . . . . . . . . . . . . . . . . . . . . . . . . . . | 2 |
| What Can I Do with SmartSuite? . . . . . . . . . . . . . . . . . . . . . . . . . . . . | 3 |
| SmartSuite Features . . . . . . . . . . . . . . . . . . . . . . . . . . . . . . . . | 5 |
| The SmartSuite Components . . . . . . . . . . . . . . . . . . . . . . . . . . . . | 7 |
| 1-2-3 . . . . . . . . . . . . . . . . . . . . . . . . . . . . . . . . . . . . . . . | 7 |

**FIGURE 12.19** ▶

*A portion of a table of contents with the Corporate look and the dashed line leader*

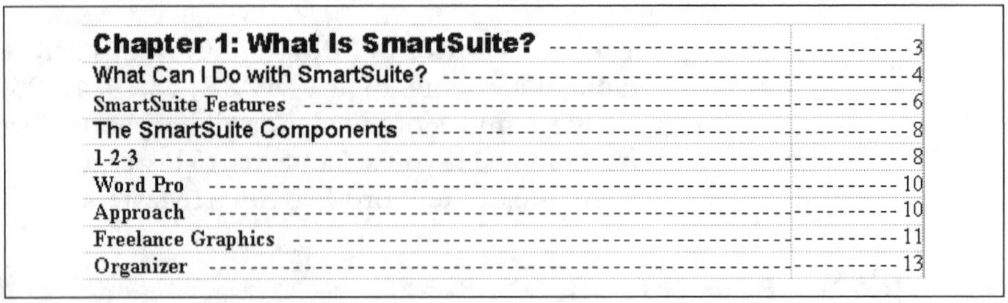

Chapter 1: What Is SmartSuite? ---------- 3
What Can I Do with SmartSuite? ---------- 4
SmartSuite Features ---------- 6
The SmartSuite Components ---------- 8
1-2-3 ---------- 8
Word Pro ---------- 10
Approach ---------- 10
Freelance Graphics ---------- 11
Organizer ---------- 13

**FIGURE 12.20** ▶

*A portion of a table of contents with the Formal look and the solid line leader*

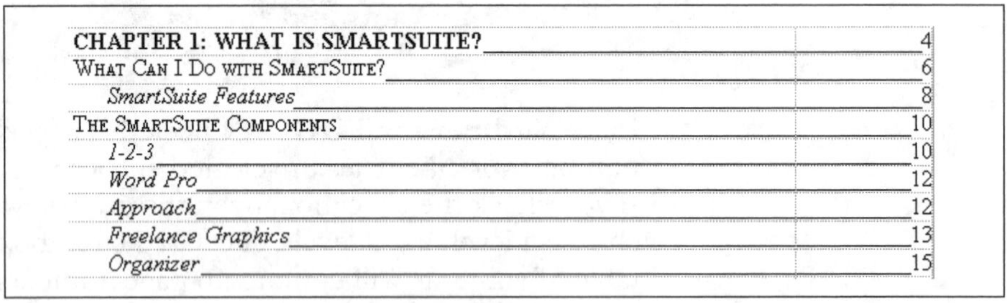

CHAPTER 1: WHAT IS SMARTSUITE? 4
WHAT CAN I DO WITH SMARTSUITE? 6
*SmartSuite Features* 8
THE SMARTSUITE COMPONENTS 10
*1-2-3* 10
*Word Pro* 12
*Approach* 12
*Freelance Graphics* 13
*Organizer* 15

**FIGURE 12.21** ▶

*A portion of a table of contents with the Informal look and no leader*

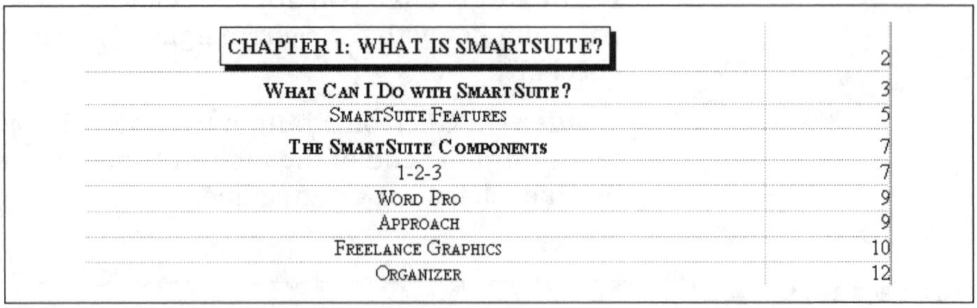

CHAPTER 1: WHAT IS SMARTSUITE? 2
WHAT CAN I DO WITH SMARTSUITE? 3
SMARTSUITE FEATURES 5
THE SMARTSUITE COMPONENTS 7
1-2-3 7
WORD PRO 9
APPROACH 9
FREELANCE GRAPHICS 10
ORGANIZER 12

**FIGURE 12.22** ▶

*A portion of a table of contents with the Fancy look and the dotted line leader*

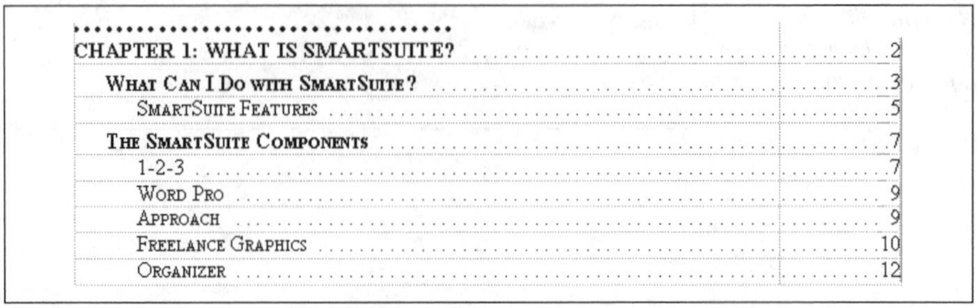

CHAPTER 1: WHAT IS SMARTSUITE? .......... 2
WHAT CAN I DO WITH SMARTSUITE? .......... 3
SMARTSUITE FEATURES .......... 5
THE SMARTSUITE COMPONENTS .......... 7
1-2-3 .......... 7
WORD PRO .......... 9
APPROACH .......... 9
FREELANCE GRAPHICS .......... 10
ORGANIZER .......... 12

The options in the Step 2: Scope and Placement section of the dialog box are:

**Generate Table of Contents Across**     From this drop-down list box, select the scope of the table of contents: over the entire document (the default), over the current grouped divisions, or for the current division.

**Place Table of Contents**     From this drop-down list box, select the location of the table of contents: at the beginning of the document (the default), at the beginning of this division, at the beginning of this group of divisions, or at the insertion point.

**Place in Separate Division**     Check this checkbox to place the table of contents in a separate division. A checked checkbox is the default.

The options in the Step 3: Contents section of the dialog box are:

**Text to Include in Table of Contents**     To include additional text styles in the table of contents, select a style and click on a TOC Level button. The left-pointing button moves the selected style to the next higher level, the right-pointing button moves the selected style to the next lower level, and the double-right-pointing arrow moves the selected style under the None column. Not including these styles (that is, having them in the None column) is the default.

**Include Paragraph**     From this drop-down list box, choose to include the selected paragraph and its number, the number, or the paragraph.

To generate a table of contents, follow these steps:

1. Click on the Generate Table of Contents SmartIcon or choose Create ➤ Other Document Part ➤ Table of Contents. Word Pro opens the Step 1: Look section of the Table of Contents Assistant dialog box.

2. Select a look, page number options, and a leader.

3. Click on Next or Step 2: Scope and Placement. Word Pro opens the Step 2: Scope and Placement section of the dialog box. (If you want to return to the first section of the dialog box, click on the Back button.)

4. Select the part of the document that will provide the entries for the table of contents, and choose its location.

5. Click on Next or Step 3: Contents. Word Pro opens the Step 3: Contents section of the dialog box. (During any of these steps, you can click on Done to run the table of contents using the defaults and the options that you have selected thus far.)

6. Select other styles and specific paragraph styles to be included in the table of contents. Click on Done. Word Pro generates the table of contents.

▶▶ **T I P**

**After you generate a table of contents, you can change the level of an entry by selecting it and then choosing from the styles in the Status bar.**

## ▶ *Updating a Table of Contents*

After you edit headings or add text to a document, it's likely that you should edit the table of contents too. Word Pro enables you to automatically update a table of contents—its headings as well as changed page numbers. To update a table of contents, follow these steps:

1. Click on the Generate Table of Contents SmartIcon or choose Create ➤ Other Document Part ➤ Table of Contents. Word Pro opens the Update or Create Table of Contents dialog box (see Figure 12.23).

**FIGURE 12.23** ▶

*The Update or Create Table of Contents dialog box with a selected table of contents*

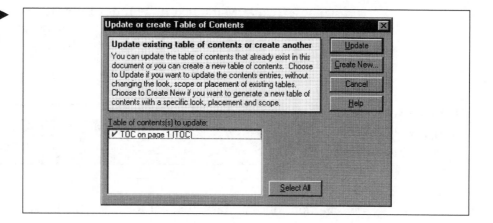

2. To update a single table of contents, select it from the list, and click on Update.

3. To update all tables of contents, click on the Select All button, and click on Update.

# ▶▶ *Creating an Index*

An index makes it much easier for a reader to access the contents of a book, especially a technical manual or a long report with new terms, company names, proper names, and so on. Using Word Pro's indexing feature, you can identify index entries and generate indexes on one or multiple levels.

## ▶ *Specifying an Index Entry*

A standard index shows one or two levels of entries, alphabetically arranged, sometimes under symbols that start each letter's entries. Index entries typically include terms, how-to's, proper names, company names, and abbreviated headings. The index is a very important part of a long book. Although Word Pro does a good job of generating an index, the index entries that you identify can make or break an index. Consider spending some time learning how to identify index terms, how to cross-reference terms for multiple index entries, and how to format indexes.

**Long Documents**

▶▶

Ch.

**12**

Choose Text ➤ Mark Text As ➤ Index Entry to open the Mark Text bar (see Figure 12.24), which you use to specify index entries. You can keep the Mark Text bar open to insert both index and table of contents entries.

**FIGURE 12.24** ►

*The Mark Text bar for indexing with its starting defaults*

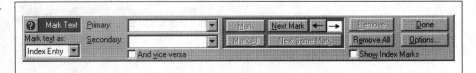

Options on the Mark Text bar for index entries are:

**Mark Text As**     From this drop-down list box, choose whether the selected text will be marked as an index entry or a table of contents entry. If you choose Index Entry, Word Pro removes table of contents options from and adds index options to the Mark Text bar.

**Primary**     In this text/drop-down list box, type or select the first-level index entry (that is, the entry closest to the left margin). For example, in the entry ***Page, Internet,*** *Page* is the primary index entry. You can edit the text in this text box.

**Secondary**     In this text/drop-down list box, type or select the second-level index entry (that is, an entry subordinate to the primary entry). For example, in the entry ***Page, Internet,*** *Internet* is the secondary index entry. You can edit the text in this text box.

**And Vice Versa**     Check this checkbox to have Word Pro automatically create an index entry that reverses the primary and secondary entries. For example, for the ***Page, Internet*** entry, the vice versa entry is ***Internet, Page.***

**Mark**     Click on this button to mark the selected text as an index entry.

**Next Mark**     Click on this button to go to the next index mark.

**Left Arrow**     Click on this button to find the prior valid index mark when you click on the Next Mark or Next At Same Level button. A button that looks pressed shows the current direction.

**Right Arrow**    Click on this button to find the next valid index mark when you click on the Next Mark or Next At Same Level button. A button that looks pressed shows the current direction.

**Next Same Mark**    Click on this button to move to the next or prior index mark at the same level as the current mark.

**Remove**    Click on this button to remove the current index mark.

**Remove All**    Click on this button to remove all the index marks from this document.

**Show Index Marks**    Check this checkbox to show index marks. A cleared checkbox, the default, hides index marks.

**Done**    Click on this button to close the Mark Text bar.

**Options**    Click on this button to open the Index Mark Options dialog box with which you can select cross-reference options for the current entry.

To mark text as an index entry, follow these steps:

*1.* Click on the Mark Text for Index SmartIcon or choose Text ➤ Mark Text As ➤ Index Entry.

*2.* Select a word or phrase to be included in the index. Word Pro displays the selected text in the Primary text/drop-down list box. Optionally, type a word or phrase in the Secondary text/drop-down list box. You can edit freely in both the Primary and Secondary text/drop-down list boxes.

*3.* Click on the Mark button. If you have checked the Show Index Marks checkbox, Word Pro displays the index mark.

```
<Index "SmartCenter bar" # "" >
```

*4.* Continue to scroll through the document to find and create other index entries. Repeat steps 2 and 3 when you find an entry.

*5.* To correct marked entries, click on an arrow button; then click on the Next Mark or Next Same Mark button to go to the marked text. To remove the entry, click on the Remove button. If Word Pro doesn't find an entry, it goes either to the top of the document or to the bottom of the document, depending on the direction of the search.

Long Documents

➤ ➤

*Ch.*
**12**

> **T I P**
>
> **If the Show Index Marks checkbox is checked, you can edit the index entries within the document. For example, you can change uppercase to lowercase or remove extra commas. Showing index marks also allows you to see whether you have already created an index mark for a particular word or phrase. Before you close the Mark Text bar, remove the checkmark from the Show Index Marks checkbox so that the index marks are hidden. Then, when Word Pro inserts page breaks at the end of each page, index marks are not included.**

**6.** To select cross-reference entries, click on the Option button. For more information, see the following section, "Inserting Cross-References in Indexes."

**7.** When you finish adding entries, remove the checkmark from the Show Index Marks checkbox, and click on Done to close the Mark Text bar.

## ▶ *Inserting Cross-References in Indexes*

In the best indexes, you'll find cross-references to other index entries. For example, if you always call a computer application an *application*, your index entries will refer to applications (such as, Starting applications, Exiting applications, Backing up applications, and so on). However, it's a good idea to plan for those readers who think of applications as *programs*. If so, you can use the Index Mark Options dialog box to include a *See* or *See also* reference—with or without a page number.

- *See* references point to an entry that is a synonym for the current entry (for example, application and program, or starting and launching).

- *See also* references direct the reader to an entry that can help him or her understand the current entry or that is related in some way (for example, saving files and backing up files, or printing and printers).

To insert a cross-reference, select or type a primary index entry, and then follow these steps:

***1.*** Click on the Options button in the Mark Text bar.

***2.*** To add a page number reference to the cross-reference entry, check the Page Number checkbox. A checked checkbox is the default.

***3.*** To add a "See also" reference and optional text, check the See Also checkbox and optionally type text in the text/drop-down list box. Figure 12.25 shows the Index Mark Options dialog box with the checked Page Number checkbox, a checked See Also checkbox, and the sample entry in the box at the bottom of the dialog box. Figure 12.26 shows the Index Mark Options dialog box with a cleared Page Number checkbox, the checked See Also checkbox, and the results in the box at the bottom of the dialog box.

**FIGURE 12.25** ▶

*The Index Mark Options dialog box with the checked Page Number checkbox*

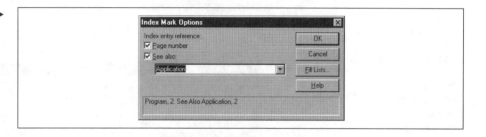

**FIGURE 12.26** ▶

*The Index Mark Options dialog box with the checked See Also checkbox*

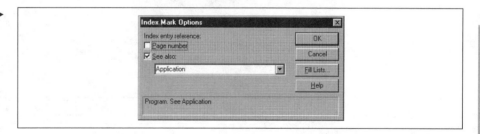

## ▶ *Generating an Index*

After you insert a number of index entries in a document, generate an index—to be sure that you have inserted the appropriate index entries and to be able to mark index entries for correction. Generate the index using the Index Assistant dialog box, which is composed of two sections: Step 1: Look (see Figure 12.27) and Step 2: Scope and Placement (see Figure 12.28).

FIGURE 12.27 ▶

*The Step 1: Look section of the Index Assistant dialog box*

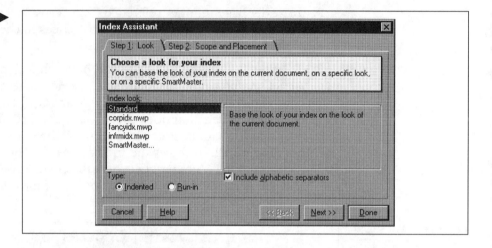

FIGURE 12.28 ▶

*The Step 2: Scope and Placement section of the Index Assistant dialog box*

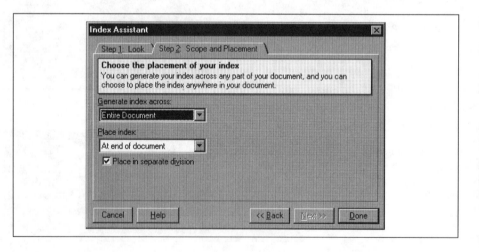

The options in the Step 1: Look section of the dialog box are:

**Index Look**     From this list, select the look of this index. Figures 12.29, 12.30, and 12.31 show examples of the Corporate, Informal, and Fancy looks. If you select SmartMaster, you can choose a look from one of the Word Pro SmartMasters.

**FIGURE 12.29** ▶

*A portion of an index with the Corporate look and an Indented type*

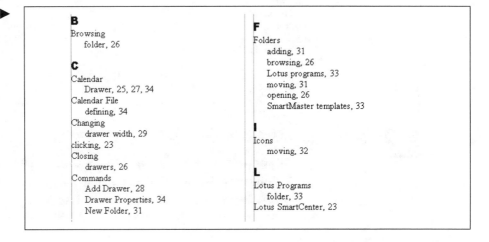

**B**
Browsing
    folder, 26

**C**
Calendar
    Drawer, 25, 27, 34
Calendar File
    defining, 34
Changing
    drawer width, 29
clicking, 23
Closing
    drawers, 26
Commands
    Add Drawer, 28
    Drawer Properties, 34
    New Folder, 31

**F**
Folders
    adding, 31
    browsing, 26
    Lotus programs, 33
    moving, 31
    opening, 26
    SmartMaster templates, 33

**I**
Icons
    moving, 32

**L**
Lotus Programs
    folder, 33
Lotus SmartCenter, 23

**FIGURE 12.30** ▶

*A portion of an index with the Informal look and a Run-in type*

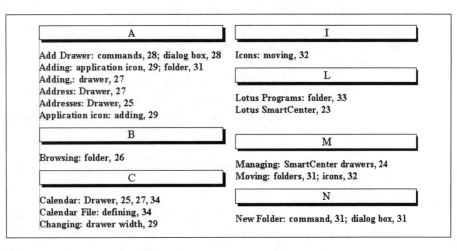

**A**

Add Drawer: commands, 28; dialog box, 28
Adding: application icon, 29; folder, 31
Adding,: drawer, 27
Address: Drawer, 27
Addresses: Drawer, 25
Application icon: adding, 29

**B**

Browsing: folder, 26

**C**

Calendar: Drawer, 25, 27, 34
Calendar File: defining, 34
Changing: drawer width, 29

**I**

Icons: moving, 32

**L**

Lotus Programs: folder, 33
Lotus SmartCenter, 23

**M**

Managing: SmartCenter drawers, 24
Moving: folders, 31; icons, 32

**N**

New Folder: command, 31; dialog box, 31

**Long Documents**

▶▶

*Ch.*
**12**

**FIGURE 12.31** ▶

*A portion of an index with the Fancy look and an Indented type*

B

Browsing
    folder, 26

C

Calendar
    Drawer, 25, 27, 34
Calendar File
    defining, 34
Changing
    drawer width, 29
clicking, 23
Closing
    drawers, 26

▶▶ **N O T E**

**If you are also creating a table of contents for this document, it's a good idea to choose identical looks for both the table of contents and the index.**

**Type**   Click on the Indented option button to indent secondary entries on the line after their primary entries, or click on the Run-in option button to follow each primary entry with all associated secondary entries. Indented is the default.

**Include Alphabetic Separators**   Check this checkbox to have Word Pro insert a separator symbol between the end of each letter's entry and the beginning of the next letter's entry. A checked checkbox is the default.

The options in the Step 2: Scope and Placement section of the dialog box are:

**Generate Index Across**   From this drop-down list box, select the scope of the index: over the entire document (the default), over the current grouped divisions, or for the current division.

**Place Index**   From this drop-down list box, select the location of the index: at the end of the document (the default), at the end of this division, at the end of this group of divisions, or at the insertion point.

**Place in Separate Division**    Check this checkbox to place the index in a separate division. A checked checkbox is the default.

To generate an index, follow these steps:

*1.* Click on the Generate Index SmartIcon or choose Create ➤ Other Document Part ➤ Index. Word Pro opens the Step 1: Look section of the Index Assistant dialog box.

*2.* Select a look, a type, and an alphabetic separator.

*3.* Click on Next or Step 2: Scope and Placement. Word Pro opens the Step 2: Scope and Placement section of the dialog box. (If you want to return to the first section of the dialog box, click on the Back button.)

*4.* Select the part of the document that will provide the entries for the index, and choose its location.

*5.* Click on Done. Word Pro generates the index.

## ▶ *Updating an Index*

After you generate an index, there is no doubt that you will have to correct it. For example, you'll find extra commas, secondary entries that you'll want to standardize under one primary entry, misspellings, and entries that you want to eliminate. Rather than correct the index, which you can easily do since it is a text document, it is best to change the original entries in the document, and update the index. This means that the next time you add text, sections, and divisions to the document, you need work only on index entries for the new portions.

You only need to generate an index once for a document. In fact, the first time you add index entries to a document, consider generating an index based on a few entries—perhaps chapter by chapter. Correct those, add new entries for the next chapter, update the index, and repeat the process until you have completed the index for the entire document.

To update an index, follow these steps:

**1.** Choose Create ➤ Other Document Part ➤ Index. Word Pro opens the Update or Create Index dialog box (see Figure 12.32).

**FIGURE 12.32** ▶

*The Update or Create Index dialog box showing a selected index*

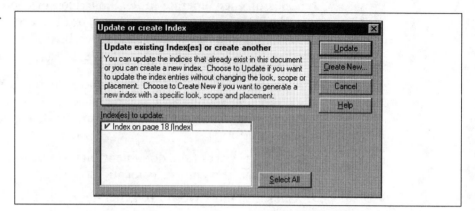

**2.** To select one index to update, click on its entry in the list. Word Pro precedes the index with a checkmark.

**3.** To update all indexes, click on the Select All button. Word Pro precedes all the indexes with checkmarks.

**4.** Click on Update. Word Pro closes both the Index Assistant and the Update Index dialog boxes and regenerates the index.

► ► ► CHAPTER **13**

# Advanced Word Pro Techniques

———

►► **T**his chapter, which concludes the Word Pro part of this book, covers tables and fields—both useful tools for producing documents. Using tables, you can organize text in rows and columns. Use fields to insert and automatically update information in a document. You can use fields to always insert the current date or time or to customize particular information in a form letter.

## ►► Using Tables

Word Pro tables are word-processing worksheets; they are made up of grids of rows and columns. The *rows* run horizontally, and the *columns* run vertically. Where a row and column meet is a *cell*, which holds one piece of text or even a graphic. Each cell is a miniature document with its own margins and its own formats. Thus, you can use a table as a grid in which tolay out a page or to display columns of text.

### ► Creating a Table

In Word Pro you can create a table in two ways: with the Create a Table Grid SmartIcon and with a dialog box. In addition, you can convert selected text to a table.

#### Creating a Table Using a SmartIcon

To create a table using a SmartIcon, follow these steps:

1. Move the insertion point to the location at which you will create the table.

**2.** Click on the Create a Table Grid SmartIcon. Word Pro opens a table grid with no cells selected:

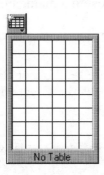

**3.** Drag the number of rows and columns that you want in the table. You can drag from 1 to 21 columns and from 1 to 26 rows. Figure 13.1 shows a 5 (rows) × 3 (columns) table grid, and Figure 13.2 shows the resulting table in the document.

**FIGURE 13.1** ▶

*The table grid below the Create a Table Grid SmartIcon shows a 5 × 3 table*

**FIGURE 13.2** ▶

*A 5 × 3 table in a document and, in the first cell, the insertion point, the left margin guide, and the right margin guide*

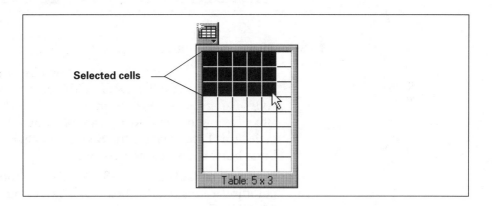

## Creating a Table Using a Dialog Box

To create a table using a dialog box, follow these steps:

**1.** Move the insertion point to the location at which you will create the table.

**2.** Choose Create ➤ Table or click on the Create Table SmartIcon. Word Pro opens the Create Table dialog box (see Figure 13.3).

**FIGURE 13.3** ▶

*The Create Table dialog box with a 5 × 3 table selected*

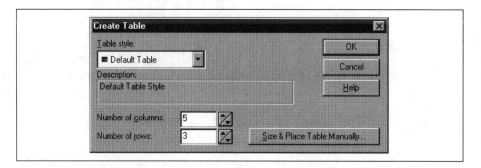

**3.** Select from these options:

**Table Style**   From this drop-down list box, select a table style. The default is Default Table. You can create table styles using the Styles section of the Table Properties Info-Box. To enhance and format a table, open the Table Properties InfoBox, click on the Styles tab, click on the Create Style button, and name the style.

**Number of Columns**   Type or select the number of columns in this text/list box. Valid values range from 1 to 255. The default value is 4.

**Number of Rows**   Type or select the number of rows in this text/list box. Valid values range from 1 to 8192. The default value is 4.

**Size & Place Table Manually**   Click on this button to be able to drag the table dimensions. Word Pro closes the dialog box and changes the mouse pointer.

**4.** If you have not clicked on Size & Place Table Manually, click on OK. Word Pro closes the dialog box and inserts the table.

## Converting Text to a Table

To get the best results when converting text to a table, set up the text in multiple columns. For example, type a last name, press the Tab key, type a first name, press Tab, and so on. Don't add extra spaces between blocks of text. Be prepared to remove extra spaces and adjust column width after Word Pro creates the table.

To convert text to a table, follow these steps:

**1.** Type the text to be converted, pressing Tab each time you want to separate a text block to be placed in a cell from the text that goes into the next cell.

**2.** Select the text to be converted.

**3.** Click on the Create Table SmartIcon or choose Create ➤ Table. (Since Word Pro automatically creates a table with the appropriate number of rows and columns, this is preferable to clicking on the Create a Table Grid SmartIcon and dragging table dimensions.) Word Pro prompts you to confirm the conversion (see Figure 13.4).

**FIGURE 13.4** ▶

*Selected text, a table grid, and the text-to-table confirmation message*

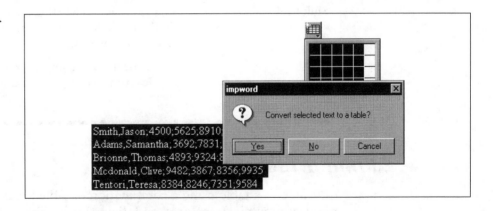

**4.** Click on Yes. Word Pro converts the text selection to a table.

**5.** To undo the table, choose Edit ➤ Undo - Text to Table, press Ctrl+Z, or click on the Undo the Last Command or Action SmartIcon.

## ▶ *Moving around a Table*

You can move from cell to cell in a table either to add or to edit text. Because each cell is a miniature document, you can add text just as you would in a regular document.

To move around a table, either click in a specific cell or use the keys listed in Table 13.1.

▶ **TABLE 13.1:** *Word Pro Table Navigation Shortcut Keys*

| Shortcut Key(s) | Moves |
| --- | --- |
| ↓ | to the cell below |
| ← | to the previous cell |
| → | to the next cell |
| ↑ | to the cell above |
| Ctrl+Shift+Tab | to the next tab stop within the cell |
| End, End | to the last cell in the row |
| Home, Home | to the first cell in the row |
| Shift+Tab | to the previous cell (If you are in the first cell in the first row in a table, pressing Shift+Tab creates a new row.) |
| Tab | to the next cell (If you are in the last cell in the last row in a table, pressing Tab creates a new row.) |

## ▶ *Editing a Table*

You can edit a table using a combination of table SmartIcons and menu commands, InfoBoxes, and dialog boxes. Table 13.2 summarizes the SmartIcons and menu commands that you can use for table editing.

▶ **TABLE 13.2:** *Word Pro Table Editing SmartIcons and Commands*

| SmartIcon | Command | Description |
|---|---|---|
| | Table ➤ Text Properties | Opens the Text Properties InfoBox from which you can enhance selected text. |
| | Table ➤ Cell Properties | Opens the Cell Properties InfoBox from which you can change attributes of the selected cell. |
| | Table ➤ Table Properties | Opens the Table Properties InfoBox from which you can change attributes of the current table. |
| | Table ➤ Insert ➤ Row (Ctrl++), or Table ➤ Insert ➤ Row/Column | Inserts one or more rows in the current table, depending on the number of rows that you have selected. |
| | Table ➤ Insert ➤ Column, or Table ➤ Insert ➤ Row/Column | Inserts one or more columns in the current table, depending on the number of columns that you have selected. |
| | Table ➤ Delete ➤ Row (Ctrl+-), or Table ➤ Delete ➤ Row/Column | Deletes one or more rows from the current table, depending on the number of rows that you have selected. |
| | Table ➤ Delete ➤ Column, or Table ➤ Delete ➤ Row/Column | Deletes one or more columns from the current table, depending on the number of columns that you have selected. |
| | Table ➤ Delete ➤ Entire Table | Deletes the current table |
| | Table ➤ Connect Cells | Merges the selected cells into one cell. (To split the merged cells into the original cells, choose Table ➤ Disconnect Cell.) |

▶ **TABLE 13.2:** *Word Pro Table Editing SmartIcons and Commands (continued)*

| SmartIcon | Command | Description |
|---|---|---|
| | Table ▶ Connect Row | Merges all the cells in the row containing the insertion point. (To split the merged cells into the original cells, choose Table ▶ Disconnect Cell.) |
| | Table ▶ Split Entire Table | Splits the selected row and prior rows from the remaining rows in the current table. (To return the split row[s] to the table, choose Edit ▶ Undo - Split Table or press Ctrl+Z.) |
| N/A | Table ▶ Size Row/Column | Opens the alignment section of the Table Cell Properties InfoBox so that you can change column and/or row dimensions for the selected column or row. |
| | Table ▶ Alignment ▶ Top Align Contents | Aligns the contents of the cell with the top border (the default). |
| | Table ▶ Alignment ▶ Center Align Contents | Aligns the contents of the cell between the top border and the bottom border. |
| | Table ▶ Alignment ▶ Bottom Align Contents | Aligns the contents of the cell with the bottom border. |
| N/A | Table ▶ Alignment ▶ Left Align Table | Aligns the entire table with the left margin. |
| N/A | Table ▶ Alignment ▶ Center Table | Centers the entire table between the left margin and the right margin. |
| N/A | Table ▶ Alignment ▶ Right Align Table | Aligns the entire table with the right margin. |

► **TABLE 13.2:** *Word Pro Table Editing SmartIcons and Commands (continued)*

| SmartIcon | Command | Description |
|---|---|---|
| N/A | Table ➤ Alignment ➤ Span Margin to Margin | Aligns the entire table with both the left margin and the right margin. |
| (icon) | Table ➤ Insert SmartSum ➤ Column | Uses the SmartSum feature to calculate the total of the numbers in the cells in the selected column. |
| (icon) | Table ➤ Insert SmartSum ➤ Row | Uses the SmartSum feature to calculate the total of the numbers in the cells in the selected row. |
| (icon) | Table ➤ Edit Formula | Enables you to edit a formula in the selected cell. |
| N/A | Table ➤ Lines & Fill Color; click on the Lines & Color tab, and select line options | Shows or hides the grid lines for the current table. |
| (icon) | View ➤ Set View Preferences; click on the Show tab, check or clear the Show Table Row/Col. Headings checkbox | Shows or hides table headings (that is, A, B, C,... above the top row of the table and 1, 2, 3,... to the left of the leftmost column) when the insertion point is within the table. A cleared checkbox is the default. |
| (icon) | Table ➤ Select ➤ Row Contents | Selects the contents of the current row. |
| (icon) | Table ➤ Select ➤ Column Contents | Selects the contents of the current column. |
| (icon) | Table ➤ Select ➤ Entire Table Contents | Selects the contents of the entire table. |
| (icon) | Table ➤ Select ➤ Cell Contents | Selects the contents of the current cell. |

▶ **TABLE 13.2:** *Word Pro Table Editing SmartIcons and Commands (continued)*

| SmartIcon | Command | Description |
|---|---|---|
| ▦ | Table ➤ Select ➤ Cells | Selects the entire current cell and its contents. |
| ▦ | Table ➤ Select ➤ Entire Table | Selects the entire current table and its contents. |
| ▦ | Table ➤ Mark As Repeated Heading | Enables you to display the heading in the current table at the top of every page on which it continues. |
| N/A | Table ➤ Named Styles ➤ Create | Opens the Create Style dialog box in which you can create a style based on the current styles. |
| N/A | Table ➤ Named Styles ➤ Redefine | Opens the Redefine Style dialog box in which you can redefine a style based on the current styles. |
| N/A | Table ➤ Named Styles ➤ Apply | Applies a style from the list of styles to the selection. |
| N/A | Table ➤ Named Styles ➤ Manage | Opens the Manage Style dialog box in which you can rename, copy a style from, or delete one of the listed styles. |
| N/A | Table ➤ Named Styles ➤ Reset to Style | Resets the current style to the original style. |

## Selecting a Table, Its Elements, or Its Contents

You can select an entire table, elements of a table, and the contents of a table using the following variety of menu commands and SmartIcons.

- To select the contents of the current cell, choose Table ➤ Select ➤ Cell Contents, click on the Select Cell Contents SmartIcon, or select the appropriate command from the submenu after choosing Text ➤ Select.

- To select the entire current cell and its contents, choose Table ➤ Select ➤ Cells or click on the Select Cells SmartIcon.

For more information about selecting in SmartSuite, see the "Making a Selection" section in the *Editing in SmartSuite Applications* chapter.

- To select the contents of the current row, click on the Select Row Contents SmartIcon or choose Table ➤ Select ➤ Row Contents.

- To select the contents of the current column, click on the Select Column Contents SmartIcon or choose Table ➤ Select ➤ Column Contents.

- To select the contents of the entire table, click on the Select Entire Table SmartIcon or choose Table ➤ Select ➤ Entire Table Contents

- To select the entire current table and its contents, choose Table ➤ Select ➤ Entire Table.

You can also use the mouse pointer to select parts of a table. To do so, follow these steps:

*1.* Select a table to make it active.

*2.* To select a column, move the mouse pointer over or below the column that you want to select. When the mouse pointer changes to a downward-pointing or upward-pointing arrow, click the left mouse button.

*3.* To select a row, move the mouse pointer to the left or to the right of the row that you want to select. When the mouse pointer changes to a leftward-pointing or rightward-pointing arrow, click the left mouse button.

Another way to select all or part of a table is to drag over it. Move the mouse pointer to one end of the range that you want to select, hold down the left mouse button, and drag diagonally to the other end of the range. Word Pro highlights the cells that you have selected.

### Inserting and Deleting Columns and Rows

You can insert and delete columns and rows in a table or delete an entire table.

- To insert one row, move the insertion point to the location of the new row, click on the Insert Row in a Table SmartIcon, choose Table ➤ Insert ➤ Row, or press Ctrl++ (use the + key on the numeric keypad).

- To insert one row, move the insertion point to the location of the new row, choose Table ➤ Insert ➤ Row/Column, click on the Row option button, click on the Before or After option button, and click on OK.

- To insert two or more rows, move the insertion point to the location of the new row, choose Table ➤ Insert ➤ Row/Column, click on the Row option button, type or select the Number to Insert, click on the Before or After option button, and click on OK.

- To insert one column, move the insertion point to the location of the new column, click on the Insert Column in a Table SmartIcon, or choose Table ➤ Insert ➤ Column.

- To insert one column, move the insertion point to the location of the new column, choose Table ➤ Insert ➤ Row/Column, click on the Column option button, click on the Before or After option button, and click on OK.

- To insert two or more columns, move the insertion point to the location of the new columns, choose Table ➤ Insert ➤ Row/Column, click on the Column option button, type or select the Number to Insert, click on the Before or After option button, and click on OK.

- To delete one row, select the row, click on the Delete Selected Rows in a Table SmartIcon, choose Table ➤ Delete ➤ Row, or press Ctrl+- (on the numeric keypad).

- To delete one row, select the row, choose Table ➤ Delete ➤ Row/Column, click on the Row option button, and click on OK.

- To delete two or more rows, select the rows to be deleted, click on the Delete Selected Rows in a Table SmartIcon or choose Table ➤ Delete ➤ Row.

- To delete two or more rows, select the rows to be deleted, choose Table ➤ Delete ➤ Row/Column, click on the Row option button, and click on OK.

- To delete one column, select the column, click on the Delete Selected Columns in a Table SmartIcon or choose Table ➤ Delete ➤ Column.

- To delete one column, select the column, choose Table ➤ Delete ➤ Row/Column, click on the Column option button, and click on OK.

- To delete two or more columns, select the columns to be deleted, click on the Delete Selected Columns in a Table SmartIcon or choose Table ➤ Delete ➤ Column.

- To delete two or more columns, select the columns to be deleted, choose Table ➤ Delete ➤ Row/Column, click on the Column option button, and click on OK.

- To delete the entire table, click on the Delete Table SmartIcon or choose Table ➤ Delete ➤ Entire Table.

## Changing Column Width, Row Height, and Cell Margins

To change column or row dimensions or cell margins using an Info-Box, follow these steps:

1. Click in the column, row, or cell that you want to change.

2. Choose Table ➤ Size Row/Column. Word Pro opens the Table Cell Size & Margins section of the Table Cell Properties InfoBox (see Figure 13.5).

**FIGURE 13.5** ▶

*The Table Cell Size & Margins section of the Table Cell Properties InfoBox with its default settings*

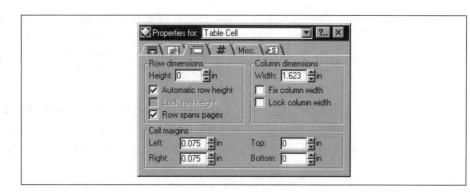

3. Select from these options:

   **Height**    Type or select the height for the selected row. The default value varies with the dimensions of the current table.

   **Automatic Row Height**    Check this checkbox to have Word Pro increase the row height when necessary for text with larger font sizes. A checked checkbox is the default.

**Lock Row Height**     Check this checkbox to prevent dragging to change the height. A cleared checkbox is the default.

**Row Spans Pages**     Check this checkbox to enable text that overflows from the last table row on a page to appear on the next page without moving the entire row to the next page. A checked checkbox is the default.

**Width**     Type or select the width for the selected column. The default value varies with the dimensions of the current table.

**Fix Column Width**     Check this checkbox to prevent a change to the current width in a table that stretches from the left margin to the right margin, regardless of width changes to other columns in the table. A cleared checkbox is the default.

**Lock Column Width**     Check this checkbox to prevent a change to the width, using the InfoBox or the mouse. A cleared checkbox is the default.

**Cell Margins**     Type or select the margins for the selected cell. The default value for Left and Right is 0.075 inches; the default value for Top and Bottom is 0.

You can change the width of a column using the mouse. To do so, move the mouse pointer to the border to the right of the cell that you want to adjust. When the mouse pointer changes to a double-headed arrow, drag the colunm border to its new location.

## Moving and Copying Columns, Rows, and Cells

You can move or copy the contents of columns, rows, and cells in Word Pro tables by using the Cut, Copy, and Paste commands in the Edit menu. For information about using these commands, see the "Copying and Pasting a Selection" and "Cutting and Pasting a Selection" sections in the *Editing in SmartSuite Applications* chapter.

You can also use the mouse pointer to drag column, row, or cell contents from one part of a table to another. To drag table contents to another location, follow these steps:

*1.* Select the column, row, or cell whose contents you want to move.

*2.* Move the mouse pointer until it looks like a hand. The best locations for this change are near the borders of a selection.

3. Hold down the left mouse button and drag. The mouse pointer changes to a hand holding a group of cells.

4. Release the mouse button when you have dragged to the desired location.

## Adding and Editing Table Borders

The Lines and Color section of the Table Properties InfoBox (see Figure 13.6) provides many ways in which you can change the look of table borders and table interiors. You can change the line style, color, and width; the shadow depth and color; and corners, including designer borders.

**FIGURE 13.6** ▶

*The Lines and Color section of the Table Properties InfoBox with the Designer Borders drop-down palette open*

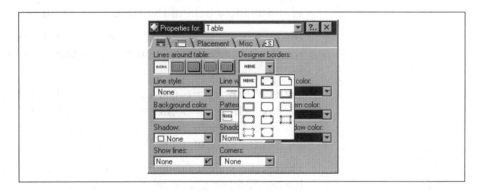

To open this InfoBox, click in the table, and use one of the following methods:

- Click on the Table Cell InfoBox SmartIcon, choose Table ➤ Cell Properties, or right-click and choose Cell Properties, select Table from the Properties For drop-down list box, and select the Lines and Color tab.

- Click on the Table InfoBox SmartIcon or choose Table ➤ Table Properties, and select the Lines and Color tab.

- Choose Table ➤ Lines & Fill Color.

The options in the Lines and Color section of the Table Properties InfoBox are:

**Lines Around Table**     Click on a button to select the look of the lines around the table. The default is None.

**Designer Borders**     From this drop-down list box, select a special border around the table. The default is None.

**Line Style**     From this drop-down list box, select from 19 line styles and None, the default.

**Background Color**     Open this color palette and select a background color for the table. The default color is white.

**Shadow**     From this drop-down list box, select the placement of the shadow behind the table. The default is None.

**Show Lines**     Open this drop-down list box and click on any of the line display options: on one or more sides, on all sides, or None, the default.

**Line Width**     From this drop-down list box, select the width of the line—from 1/4 point to 8 points, with a default of 1/2 point. Click on Other to open a dialog box in which you can specify a line width ranging from 0.1 to 720 points.

**Pattern**     From this drop-down palette, select a pattern for the background of the table. The default is None.

**Shadow Depth**     From this drop-down list box, select the depth of the shadow: Shallow, Normal, or Deep. Click on Other to open a dialog box in which you can specify a shadow depth ranging from 0 to 0.2 inches. The default is 0.07 inches.

**Corners**     From this drop-down list box, select the type of corner for the table. You can choose from a right angle to a very curved corner. Click on Other to open a dialog box in which you can set the percentage of roundedness ranging from 0 to 100. The default is None.

**Line Color**     From this drop-down palette, select the color of the border line. The default is black.

**Pattern Color**     From this drop-down palette, select the color of the pattern foreground. The default is black.

**Shadow Color**     From this drop-down palette, select the color of the shadow behind the table. The default is black.

# ▶▶ *Using Fields*

Use Word Pro, fields to insert and automatically update information in a document. For example, you can insert the date that you most recently edited a document in its header so that your readers will be able to see its timeliness. Or, you can automatically increment numbers in a numbered list or create a filled-in letter or fax cover sheet. The table of contents and index mark entries covered in the previous chapter are good examples of common Word Pro fields.

Word Pro provides two categories of fields—power fields and document fields:

**Power fields**     Show dynamic information about the current document or calculated information. Examples include word and character counts, string manipulation statements, and programming calls. Word Pro power fields are very similar to 1-2-3 @functions.

**Document fields**     Provide information about you and the current document. A document field inserted in a document is a word, a phrase, or a block of text that you can edit as you would edit text. Examples include your name, your company name, other company and personal information, and bookmarks. Updated information categorized as document fields are the Number of Pages, Number of Words, and so on.

 ▶▶ **N O T E**

> **Word Pro provides power fields and document fields that display a word count, page count, and so on for a document. The difference between the two types of fields is that you can update a power field with the latest count, but once you have inserted a document field in the document, the count cannot be updated.**

## ▶ Inserting a Power Field

To insert a power field in the current document, follow these steps:

**1.** Move the insertion point to the location at which you want to insert the field.

**2.** Click on the Insert Power Fields SmartIcon or choose Text ➤ Insert Other ➤ Power/Doc. Field. Word Pro opens the Power Field section of the Document Fields dialog box (see Figure 13.7).

**FIGURE 13.7** ▶

*The Document Fields dialog box with a field ready for insertion*

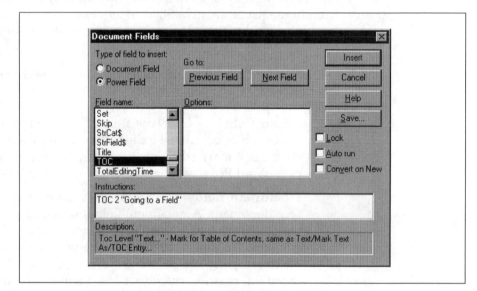

**3.** From the Field Name scroll box, select a field name. Word Pro inserts the field in the Instructions text box and a description in the Description box.

**4.** If the Options box displays a list of formats, select the most appropriate one.

**5.** Edit the field attributes in the Instructions text box.

**6.** Click on OK. Word Pro inserts the field, surrounded by angle brackets, or the results in the document at the insertion point.

To learn more about inserting power fields, see "Inserting a Power Field" and "Details: Inserting a Power Field" in the Word Pro help facility.

## ▶ *Displaying a Power Field or Its Results*

 By default, Word Pro inserts the results of a power field (for example, the creation date, a text string, numeric string, or filename) at the insertion point. You can toggle between viewing the results and the field itself by clicking on the Show/Hide Power Fields SmartIcon, by choosing View ➤ Show/Hide ➤ Power Field Formulas, or by right-clicking on the field or results and choosing Show Power Field Formulas. If Power Field Formulas or Show Power Field Formulas is not preceded by a checkmark, Word Pro displays results of fields:

$9,899.50 taxes

If the Power Field Formulas command is preceded by a checkmark, Word Pro displays fields:

<FormatNum$("$"," taxes",2,9899.5)>

## ▶ *Going to a Power Field*

You can go to each field in a document to edit or to update selectively. Word Pro provides several ways of going to fields—toward the top of the document or toward the bottom:

- To go to the previous field, right-click on a field or results and choose Previous Field.

- To go to the next field, right-click on a field or results and choose Next Field.

 - To go to the previous field, click on the Go to Previous Power Field SmartIcon.

 - To go to the next field, click on the Go to Next Power Field SmartIcon.

- To go to the previous field, choose Text ➤ Insert Other ➤ Power/Doc. Field. In the Document Fields dialog box, click on the Previous Field button.

- To go to the next field, choose Text ➤ Insert Other ➤ Power/Doc. Field. In the Document Fields dialog box, click on the Next Field button.

## ▶ Editing a Power Field

If you want to change a number, a word, or a phrase or part of the instructions that constitute a field, follow these steps:

*1.* Move the insertion point to the field that you want to edit.

*2.* Click on the Insert Power Fields SmartIcon, choose Text ➤ Insert Other ➤ Power/Doc. Field, or right-click on the field and choose Edit Field. Word Pro opens the Document Fields dialog box (see Figure 13.7, earlier in this chapter) with the selected field displayed.

*3.* Edit the field in the Instructions text box.

*4.* Click on Insert. Word Pro recomputes the field and displays the new results or edited field in the document.

*5.* Click on Cancel to close the dialog box.

## ▶ Updating Power Fields

If you have changed an index or a table of contents entry, if you have added new text, if you have changed values in the Word Pro Preferences dialog box, or if you have edited a document on a new date, the old fields in the document may need to be updated. For example, if you created a document on May 6, 1997, and edited it for the first time on May 7, any CreateDate field is set to May 6, and any EditDate field is set to May 7. If you next edit the document on September 15, you should update the EditDate fields, which should change to September 15.

**NOTE**

When you attempt to update one or all fields in a document, Word Pro does not update locked fields. To learn more about locking and unlocking fields, see the "Locking or Unlocking a Power a Field" section, which follows this section.

Ch. 13

In Word Pro you can update unlocked fields in several ways:

- To update one field, select it, and click on the Update Selected Power Fields SmartIcon.

- To update one field, right-click on it, and choose Update Field.

- To update one field whenever you open the document that contains the field, click on the Insert Power Fields SmartIcon, choose Text ➤ Insert Other ➤ Power/Doc. Field, or right-click on the field and choose Edit Field. In the Document Fields dialog box, place a checkmark in the Auto Run checkbox, click on Insert, and click on Cancel.

- To update one field in all new documents based on a particular SmartMaster, click on the Insert Power Fields SmartIcon, choose Text ➤ Insert Other ➤ Power/Doc. Field, or right-click on the field and choose Edit Field. In the Document Fields dialog box, place a checkmark in the Convert on New checkbox, click on Insert, and click on Cancel.

- To update all fields in the current document, click on the Update All Power Fields SmartIcon, or right-click on a field, and choose Update All Fields.

## ▶ Locking or Unlocking a Power Field

In Word Pro, you can lock a field so that updates do not change it. For example, if several people will work on the document but you want the creator's initials to remain with the document, lock the Initials field. Or, if you are working on a long document with many fields, including a multiple-page index, you may not want Word Pro to update the index, and waste time and computing resources, whenever you update other fields.

To lock a field, select it, click on the Insert Power Fields SmartIcon, choose Text ➤ Insert Other ➤ Power/Doc. Field, or right-click on the field and choose Edit Field. In the Document Fields dialog box, place a checkmark in the Lock checkbox, click on Insert, and click on Cancel.

To unlock a locked field, open the Document Fields dialog box, remove the checkmark from the Lock checkbox, click on Insert, and click on Cancel.

## ► Removing a Power Field

 To delete a field from a document, right-click on it, and choose Delete Field. Deleting a field does not delete the text associated with it. For example, deleting a date field deletes the field, but a text version of the date remains. To undo the deletion, click on the Undo the Last Command or Action SmartIcon, choose Edit ➤ Undo - Deletion, or press Ctrl+Z.

## ► Inserting a Document Field

To insert a document field, follow these steps:

1. Move the insertion point to the location at which you want to insert the document field.

 2. Click on the Insert Power Fields SmartIcon, choose Text ➤ Insert Other ➤ Power/Doc. Field, or right-click on the field and choose Edit Field. Word Pro opens the Document Fields dialog box.

3. Click on the Document Field option button. Word Pro changes the options in the dialog box (see Figure 13.8).

4. Select a field name from the scroll box.

5. Click on the Insert button. Word Pro closes the dialog box and inserts the contents of the field at the insertion point.

## ► Word Pro Power Fields

This portion of the chapter lists and briefly describes most of the Word Pro power fields. Under a field, you'll also find the syntax; in most cases, one or two examples; and cross-references to entries in the Word Pro help facility.

**FIGURE 13.8** ▶

*The Document Field options of the Document Fields dialog box*

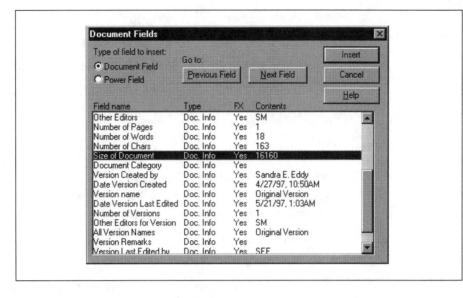

These fields are covered in the following sections.

| | | |
|---|---|---|
| Address1 | Index | PhoneNumber |
| Address2 | Initials | PostalCode |
| Address3 | Lcase$ | PrintEscape |
| Bookmark | Left$ | Query$ |
| Call | Len | Right$ |
| Company | MergeField | SectionName |
| CreateDate | MergeRec | Seq |
| Decide | Message | Set |
| Defined | Mid$ | Skip |
| Description | NextRec | StrCat$ |
| DivisionName | Now | StrField$ |
| EditDate | NumChars | Title |
| Email | NumEdits | TOC |
| Exec | NumPages | TotalEditingTime |
| ExecuteScript | NumWords | UCase$ |

| FaxNumber | PageRef | User |
|-----------|---------|------|
| FileSize | PersonalData1 | UserName |
| FormatNum$ | PersonalData2 | Void |
| IF | PersonalData3 | |
| Include | PersonalData4 | |

## Address1

This field returns the contents of the Address 1 text box in the Personal section of the Word Pro Preferences dialog box. (Choose File ➤ User Setup ➤ Word Pro Preferences.)

**Syntax:**

```
Address1
```

For more information, see the "Address1" or "Fields, Address1" topic in the Word Pro help facility.

## Address2

This field returns the contents of the Address 2 text box in the Personal section of the Word Pro Preferences dialog box. (Choose File ➤ User Setup ➤ Word Pro Preferences.)

**Syntax:**

```
Address2
```

For more information, see the "Address2" or "Fields, Address2" topic in the Word Pro help facility.

## Address3

This field returns the contents of the Address 3 text box in the Personal section of the Word Pro Preferences dialog box. (Choose File ➤ User Setup ➤ Word Pro Preferences.)

**Syntax:**

```
Address3
```

For more information, see the "Address3" or "Fields, Address3" topic in the Word Pro help facility.

## Bookmark

This field inserts the contents of a bookmark into the current document at the insertion point. This field is case-sensitive.

**Syntax:**

```
bookmark
```

For more information, see the "Bookmark Fields" or "Fields, Bookmark" topic in the Word Pro help facility.

## Call

This field runs and optionally returns a value from an Ami Pro 3.*x* macro.

**Syntax:**

```
Call [path] filename[!macroname](parameters)
```

**Example:**
This example runs the lwpdbasw.smm macro in C:\LOTUS\WORDPRO.

```
<call c:\lotus\wordpro\lwpdbasw.smm()>
```

For more information, see the "Call" or "Fields, Call" topic in the Word Pro help facility.

## Company

This field returns the contents of the Company text box in the Personal section of the Word Pro Preferences dialog box. (Choose File ➤ User Setup ➤ Word Pro Preferences.)

**Syntax:**

```
Company
```

For more information, see the "Company, Power Fields" or "Fields, Company" topic in the Word Pro help facility.

## CreateDate

This field inserts the creation date or creation time of the current document, using the format that you selected from the Document Fields dialog box. When you select a format, Word Pro inserts a code in the command.

**Syntax:**

```
CreateDate [%Dx]¦[%Tx]
```

**Examples:**

This example inserts the default creation date, using the mm/dd/yy format, at the insertion point.

```
<CreateDate>
```

This example inserts the default creation date, using the *mm/dd/yy* format, at the insertion point.

```
<CreateDate %Da>
```

For more information, see the "CreateDate" or "Fields, CreateDate" topic in the Word Pro help facility.

## Decide

This field, which must be inserted within another field, opens a dialog box displaying a message that prompts the user to click on Yes or No. The answer triggers an action.

**Syntax:**

```
Decide("message")[,"titlebartitle"]
```

**Example:**

This example, which would be part of another field, would prompt the user to display the edit date for this document.

```
<Decide("Display the edit date?"),"Date Request"
EditDate>
```

For more information, see the "Decide Power Fields" or "Fields, Decide" topic in the Word Pro help facility.

## Defined

This field, usually used with another field (such as an IF field), ensures that a bookmark name, merge field name, or global variable name has been defined before it is used in another field.

**Syntax:**

```
Defined variable
```

For more information, see the "Defined Power Field" or "Fields, Defined" topic in the Word Pro help facility.

## Description

This field displays the description of the current document in the General section of the Document Properties dialog box. (Choose File ➤ Document Properties ➤ Document.)

**Syntax:**

```
Description
```

For more information, see the "Description Power Fields" or "Fields, Description" topic in the Word Pro help facility.

## DivisionName

This field inserts the name of the division in which the insertion point is located into the document. The default division name is Body.

**Syntax:**

```
DivisionName
```

For more information, see the "DivisionName Power Fields" or "Fields, DivisionName" topic in the Word Pro help facility.

## EditDate

This field inserts the date or time at which the current document was last edited, using the format that you selected from the Document Fields dialog box. When you select a format, Word Pro inserts a code in the command.

**Syntax:**

```
EditDate [%Dx]¦[%Tx]
```

**Examples:**
This example inserts the default edit date, using the *day, Month dd, yyyy* format, at the insertion point.

```
<EditDate %Dd>
```

For more information, see the "EditDate Power Fields" or "Fields, EditDate" topic in the Word Pro help facility.

## Email

This field returns the contents of the E-mail text box in the Personal section of the Word Pro Preferences dialog box. (Choose File ➤ User Setup ➤ Word Pro Preferences.)

**Syntax:**

```
Email
```

For more information, see the "Email Power Fields" or "Fields, Email" topic in the Word Pro help facility.

## Exec

This field runs an application from a DOS window.

**Syntax:**

```
Exec("[path]application.ext",
parameters¦""[,0|1|2 |3|4|5|6|7|8|9]
```

where:

| | |
|---|---|
| **0** | Hides the window in which the application runs |
| **1** | Starts the application in its default window |
| **2** | Starts the application in an active minimized window |
| **3** | Starts the application in a maximized window |
| **4** | Starts the application in an inactive window |
| **5** | Starts the application using the defaults |
| **6** | Starts the application in an inactive minimized window |
| **7** | Starts the application in an inactive minimized window |
| **8** | Starts the application in its default window |
| **9** | Starts the application in a restored window |

**Example:**

This example runs Windows Cardfile in an active minimized window.

```
<exec("c:\windows\cardfile.exe","",2)
```

For more information, see the "Exec Power Fields" or "Fields, Exec" topic in the Word Pro help facility.

## ExecuteScript

This field executes a LotusScript function.

**Syntax:**

```
ExecuteScript "filename.lss!LSfunction"
```

For more information, see the "ExecuteScript Power Fields" or "Fields, ExecuteScript" topic in the Word Pro help facility.

## FaxNumber

This field returns the contents of the Fax text box in the Personal section of the Word Pro Preferences dialog box. (Choose File ➤ User Setup ➤ Word Pro Preferences.)

**Syntax:**

```
FaxNumber
```

For more information, see the "FaxNumber Power Fields" or "Fields, FaxNumber" topic in the Word Pro help facility.

## FileSize

This field displays the size of the current document, found in the Size of Document entry in the Fields section of the Document Properties dialog box (choose File ➤ Document Properties ➤ Document.)

**Syntax:**

```
FileSize
```

For more information, see the "FileSize Power Fields" or "Fields, File-Size" topic in the Word Pro help facility.

## FormatNum$

This field applies a format to a number and adds a prefix or a suffix.

**Syntax:**

```
FormatNum$("prefix"|""|"text_or_spaces","suffix
"|""|"text_or_spaces",decplaces,plain_number)
```

**Examples:**

This example adds a dollar sign and two decimal places to the number 864.5 (that is, $864.50).

```
<FormatNum$("$","",2,864.5)>
```

This example adds a text suffix and no decimal places to 999.

```
<FormatNum$(""," pages",0,999)>
```

For more information, see the "FormatNum$ Power Fields" or "Fields, FormatNum$" topic in the Word Pro help facility.

## IF

This field determines whether a condition is true or false and then returns a value or performs an action if it branches to a "true" expression and another value or action if it goes to a "false" expression.

**Syntax:**

```
IF condition expression [ELSEIF truecondition
expression] [ELSE expression] ENDIF
```

**Example:**

This example evaluates a quiz grade and displays a specific message for someone with a grade greater than 85 and a different message for someone with a lower grade.

```
<IF Grade > 85 ELSEIF "Excellent" ELSE "Better luck
next time" ENDIF >
```

For more information, see the "IF Power Fields" or "Fields, IF" topic in the Word Pro help facility.

## Include

This field inserts the contents of a file or a bookmark into the current document at the insertion point.

**Syntax:**

```
include "[path]filename.exe[!bookmarkname]
```

**Example:**

This example inserts the QUICKFOX.LWP file into the current document.

```
<include "quickfox.lwp">
```

For more information, see the "Include Power Fields" or "Fields, Include" topic in the Word Pro help facility.

## Index

This field inserts an index entry and an optional number for the page in which the entry is located at the insertion point.

**Syntax:**

```
index "primaryentry" [#][ "secondaryentry"] ["cross-
ref"]
```

**Example:**
This example inserts a primary entry, a secondary entry, and a page number at the insertion point.

```
<index "point" # "insertion">
```

For more information, see the "Marking, Index Entries," "Details: Marking Index Entries," or "Fields, Index" topic in the Word Pro help facility. Also see the previous chapter, *Working with Long Documents*.

## Initials

This field returns the contents of the Initials text box in the Personal section of the Word Pro Preferences dialog box. (Choose File ➤ User Setup ➤ Word Pro Preferences.)

**Syntax:**

```
Initials
```

For more information, see the "Initials, Power Fields" or "Fields, Initials" topic in the Word Pro help facility.

## Lcase$

This field converts mixed-case letters to all lowercase.

**Syntax:**

```
Lcase$("TEXT")
```

**Example:**
This example converts the word *oRaNGe* to *orange*.

```
<Lcase$("oRaNGe")>
```

For more information, see the "Lcase$ Power Fields" or "Fields, Lcase$" topic in the Word Pro help facility.

## Left $

This field returns the leftmost *n* characters, alphabetic or numeric, from the string.

**Syntax:**

```
Left$("string",n)
```

**Examples:**
This example returns the first three characters from the word *command*. The result is *com*.

```
<Left$("command",3)>
```

This example returns the first two characters from the number *9753*. The result is *97*.

```
<Left$("9753",2)>
```

For more information, see the "Left$ Power Fields" or "Fields, Left$" topic in the Word Pro help facility.

## Len

This field counts the number of characters, alphabetic or numeric, in a string.

**Syntax:**

```
Len("string")
```

**Example:**
This example counts the number of characters (7) in the word command.

```
<Len("command")>
```

For more information, see the "Len Power Fields" or "Fields, Len" topic in the Word Pro help facility.

## MergeField

This field inserts a merge field at the insertion point.

**Syntax:**

```
MergeField mfieldname
```

**Example:**
This example inserts the merge field, City, at the insertion point.

```
<MergeField CITY>
```

For more information, see the "MergeField Power Fields" or "Fields, MergeField" topic in the Word Pro help facility.

## MergeRec

This field inserts the record number at the insertion point at the time of a merge.

**Syntax:**

```
MergeRec
```

For more information, see the "MergeRec Power Fields" or "Fields, MergeRec" topic in the Word Pro help facility.

## Message

This field, which may or may not be inserted within another field, opens a dialog box displaying a message. To close the dialog box, the user must click on OK or press Esc.

**Syntax:**

```
Message("message"[,"titlebartitle"])
```

**Example:**
This example opens a message box with New Day in its title bar and containing the message "Good morning."

```
<Message("Good morning","New Day")
```

For more information, see the "Message Power Fields" or "Fields, Message" topic in the Word Pro help facility.

## Mid$

This field returns a certain number of characters, starting with a particular position, from the string.

**Syntax:**

```
Mid$("string",startnum,length)
```

**Examples:**
This example returns the three characters, starting with m, from the word *command*. The result is *mma*.

```
<Mid$("command",3,3)>
```

For more information, see the "Mid$ Power Fields" or "Fields, Mid$" topic in the Word Pro help facility.

## NextRec

This field indicates the end of a record. Insert this field at the end of the fields for a particular record.

**Syntax:**

```
NextRec
```

For more information, see the "NextRec Power Fields" or Fields, NextRec" topic in the Word Pro help facility.

## Now

This field inserts the current computer system date or time, using the format that you selected from the Document Fields dialog box. When you select a format, Word Pro inserts a code in the command.

**Syntax:**

```
Now() [%Dx]¦[%Tx]
```

**Examples:**
This example inserts the current date, using the *dd month yyyy* format, at the insertion point.

```
<Now() %Dc>
```

For more information, see the "Now Power Fields" or "Fields, Now" topic in the Word Pro help facility.

## NumChars

This field displays the number of characters in the current document. This is the same count as the Number of Chars in the Fields section of the Document Properties dialog box. (Choose File ➤ Document Properties ➤ Document.)

**Syntax:**

    NumChars

For more information, see the "NumChars Power Fields" or "Fields, NumChars" topic in the Word Pro help facility.

## NumEdits

This field displays the number of times that the current document has been opened, edited, and saved. This is the same number as the Number of Revisions in the Fields section of the Document Properties dialog box (choose File ➤ Document Properties ➤ Document).

**Syntax:**

    NumEdits

For more information, see the "NumEdits Power Fields" or "Fields, NumEdits" topic in the Word Pro help facility.

## NumPages

This field displays the number of pages in the current document. This is the same count as the Number of Pages in the Fields section of the Document Properties dialog box. (Choose File ➤ Document Properties ➤ Document).

**Syntax:**

    NumPages

For more information, see the "NumPages Power Fields" or "Fields, NumPages" topic in the Word Pro help facility.

## NumWords

This field displays the number of words in the current document. This is the same count as the Number of Words entry in the Fields section of the Document Properties dialog box. (Choose File ➤ Document Properties ➤ Document.)

**Syntax:**

```
NumWords
```

For more information, see the "NumWords Power Fields" or "Fields, NumWords" topic in the Word Pro help facility.

## PageRef

This field inserts a page number of a bookmark on that page. This field is case-sensitive.

**Syntax:**

```
pageref bookmark
```

**Example:**
This example inserts the number 45 if the bookmark Printing is located on page 45 in the current document.

```
<pageref Printing>
```

For more information, see the "Fields, PageRef" topic in the Word Pro help facility.

## PersonalData1

This field returns the contents of the Data 1 text box in the Personal section of the Word Pro Preferences dialog box. (Choose File ➤ User Setup ➤ Word Pro Preferences.)

**Syntax:**

```
PersonalData1
```

For more information, see the "PersonalData1 Power Fields" or "Fields, PersonalData1" topic in the Word Pro help facility.

## PersonalData2

This field returns the contents of the Data 2 text box in the Personal section of the Word Pro Preferences dialog box. (Choose File ➤ User Setup ➤ Word Pro Preferences.)

**Syntax:**

```
PersonalData2
```

For more information, see the "PersonalData2 Power Fields" or "Fields, PersonalData2" topic in the Word Pro help facility.

## PersonalData3

This field returns the contents of the Data 3 text box in the Personal section of the Word Pro Preferences dialog box. (Choose File ➤ User Setup ➤ Word Pro Preferences.)

**Syntax:**

```
PersonalData3
```

For more information, see the "PersonalData3 Power Fields" or "Fields, PersonalData3" topic in the Word Pro help facility.

## PersonalData4

This field returns the contents of the Data 4 text box in the Personal section of the Word Pro Preferences dialog box. (Choose File ➤ User Setup ➤ Word Pro Preferences.)

**Syntax:**

```
PersonalData4
```

For more information, see the "PersonalData4 Power Fields" or "Fields, PersonalData4" topic in the Word Pro help facility.

## PhoneNumber

This field returns the contents of the Phone text box in the Personal section of the Word Pro Preferences dialog box. (Choose File ➤ User Setup ➤ Word Pro Preferences.)

**Syntax:**

```
PhoneNumber
```

For more information, see the "PhoneNumber Power Fields" or "Fields, PhoneNumber" topic in the Word Pro help facility.

## PostalCode

This field returns the contents of the Post Code text box in the Personal section of the Word Pro Preferences dialog box. (Choose File ➤ User Setup ➤ Word Pro Preferences.)

**Syntax:**

```
PostalCode
```

For more information, see the "PostalCode Power Fields" or "Fields, PostalCode" topic in the Word Pro help facility.

## PrintEscape

This field issues an Esc keystroke and sends instruction codes to the default printer. Refer to your printer manual for information about valid codes.

**Syntax:**

```
PrintEscape"[27]|[0x1b]printercode"
```

**Example:**

This example issues a manual envelope feed command to an HP Laser-Jet III printer.

```
<PrintEscape"[27]l3H">
```

For more information, see the "PrintEscape Power Fields" or "Fields, PrintEscape" topic in the Word Pro help facility.

## Query$

This field, which may or may not be inserted within another field, opens a dialog box displaying a question and a text box in which there may be suggested text. To close the dialog box, the user must click on OK or Cancel or press Enter or Esc.

**Syntax:**

```
Query$("question"[,"suggestedtext"])
```

**Example:**

This example asks the user his or her favorite word processor. He or she can overtype Word Pro, the suggested answer.

```
<Query$("What is your word processing
preference?"[,"Word Pro"])>
```

For more information, see the "Query$ Power Fields" or "Fields, Query$" topic in the Word Pro help facility.

## Right$

This field returns the rightmost *n* characters, alphabetic or numeric, from the string.

**Syntax:**

```
Right$("string",n)
```

**Examples:**

This example returns the last three characters from the word *command*. The result is *and*.

```
<Right$("command",3)>
```

For more information, see the "Right$ Power Fields" or "Fields, Right$" topic in the Word Pro help facility.

## SectionName

This field inserts the name of the section in which the insertion point is located into the document. If the insertion point is not in a section, the field does not return any value.

**Syntax:**

```
SectionName
```

For more information, see the "SectionName Power Fields" or "Fields, SectionName" topic in the Word Pro help facility.

## Seq

This field inserts a positive sequential number, formatted as you specify, at the insertion point. The first Seq field sets the starting number, and the remaining Seq fields increase or decrease by 1 or a value that you specify. In the Document Fields dialog box, click on a format to insert it in the field.

**Syntax:**

```
seq numname[=[numberval]]|[-[numberval]]|
[+numberval]%Format
```

**Examples:**

This example sets the starting number, using the defaults. Copy and paste this field to increment the starting number by 1.

```
<seq name %N1>
```

This example increments the starting number by two and uses lower-case roman numerals.

```
<seq name +2%N3>
```

For more information, see the "Fields, Seq" topic in the Word Pro help facility.

## Set

This field specifies the value of a variable that is available to all documents until the current document is closed.

**Syntax:**

```
set globalvariable "value"
```

**Example:**

This example specifies that the variable *department* is equal to Research and Development for all documents until you close the current document.

```
<set department "Research and Development">
```

For more information, see the "Set Power Fields" or "Fields, Set" topic in the Word Pro help facility.

## Skip

This field skips a record during a merge. Insert this field in another field (for example, as a condition in an IF field).

**Syntax:**

```
Skip
```

For more information, see the "Skip Power Fields" or "Fields, Skip" topic in the Word Pro help facility.

## StrCat$

This field joins (that is, concatenates) two or more text strings into one string. You can also insert spaces into the new string.

**Syntax:**

```
StrCat$("string1","string2"[,"string3"[,..."stringn"]]
```

**Example:**

This example concatenates the two text strings, Fred and Rogers.

```
<StrCat$("Fred"," ","Rogers")>
```

For more information, see the "StrCat$" or "Fields, StrCat$" topic in the Word Pro help facility.

## *StrField$*

This field extracts a string from a long string. In the long string, the same separator symbol must indicate the place at which each smaller string is separated from the next. Separators can include commas, spaces, periods, slashes, and so on.

**Syntax:**

```
StrField$("longstring","fieldno","separator")
```

**Example:**

This example extracts the string, oranges, from a long string.

```
<StrField$("apples,oranges,peaches,pears",2,",")>
```

For more information, see the "StrField$ Power Fields" or "Fields, StrField$" topic in the Word Pro help facility.

## *Title*

This field returns the contents of the Title text box in the Personal section of the Word Pro Preferences dialog box. (Choose File ➤ User Setup ➤ Word Pro Preferences.)

**Syntax:**

```
Title
```

For more information, see the "Title Power Field" or "Fields, Title" topic in the Word Pro help facility.

## TOC

This field marks a table of contents entry.

**Syntax:**

```
TOC TOClevel "TOC_text"
```

**Example:**

This example marks a second level table of contents entry, *Printing Documents*.

```
<TOC 2 "Printing Documents">
```

For more information, see the "Creating a Table of Contents Entry from Selected Text," "Details: Creating A Table of Contents Entry from Selected Text," or "Fields, TOC" topic in the Word Pro help facility. Also see the previous chapter, *Working with Long Documents*.

## TotalEditingTime

This field displays the time spent on creating and editing the current document. This is the same count as Total Editing Time in the Fields section of the Document Properties dialog box. (Choose File ➤ Document Properties ➤ Document.)

**Syntax:**

```
TotalEditingTime
```

For more information, see the "TotalEditingTime Power Fields" or "Fields, TotalEditingTime" topic in the Word Pro help facility.

## UCase$

This field converts mixed-case letters to all uppercase.

**Syntax:**

```
Ucase$("text")
```

**Example:**

This example converts the word *oRaNGe* to *ORANGE*.

```
<Ucase$("oRaNGe")>
```

For more information, see the "UCase$ Power Fields" or "Fields, UCase$" topic in the Word Pro help facility.

### User

This field inserts anything the user types within the field.

**Syntax:**

```
user[,][ ]any value
```

For more information, see the "User Power Fields" or "Fields, User" topic in the Word Pro help facility.

### UserName

This field returns the contents of the User Name text box in the Personal section of the Word Pro Preferences dialog box. (Choose File ➤ User Setup ➤ Word Pro Preferences.)

**Syntax:**

```
UserName
```

For more information, see the "UserName Power Fields" or "Fields, UserName" topic in the Word Pro help facility.

### Void

This field performs an action but does not return a value.

**Syntax:**

```
void powerfield
```

**Example:**

```
<void call c:\lotus\wordpro\lwpdbasw.smm( )>
```

For more information, see the "Void Power Fields" or "Fields, Void" topic in the Word Pro help facility.

Organizing Information
with Approach

# PART FOUR

# CHAPTER 14

# Planning and Creating
# Your First Database

►► **I**n this chapter, you'll get acquainted with Approach. First, you'll find out some basic facts about databases. Then you'll learn how to plan, create, edit, and delete a database. Remember that you can learn the basics of opening and saving files by reviewing the *Getting Acquainted with SmartSuite* chapter, and you can review editing concepts in the *Editing in SmartSuite Applications* chapter.

## ►► *Introducing Approach*

Approach is an easy-to-use and powerful relational database. *Relational databases* allow you to work simultaneously with multiple database files to get to and report on the information you require. For example, you can retrieve name and address information from one file, inventory items from another file, and vendor data from a third file.

Relational databases form their relationships on common fields. For example, in a database of employee names and addresses and another database of employee travel information, the common field might be an employee identification number. Or in an inventory system, one database might list parts and another database might contain detailed warehouse address information. The common field might be a warehouse name or number.

Using Approach, you can do the following:

- Print reports of customer or employee names, addresses, and telephone numbers.

- Track all goods sold or not sold, including length of time on the market, asking price, and so on.

- Match a vendor's database with your inventory database to find out from whom to order.

- Retrieve a list of employees who meet certain criteria. For example, you could retrieve a list of salespeople located in one region and experienced in selling a particular item.

- Create a mail merge to all customers who meet income, education, or residence criteria.

- Print inventory reports based on the entire inventory or categories of items. You can age the inventory or find out how popular certain items are.

## ▶ *Reading and Writing Common File Formats*

Approach reads and writes file formats from many database programs and other programs.

Approach reads 1-2-3 Ranges (*), All Files (*.*), dBASE III+ (*.DBF), dBASE IV (*.DBF), Excel (*.XLS), Foxpro (*.DBF), INTERSOLV 2.10 32-BIT SQL Server (*), INTERSOLV OEM 2.12 32-BIT Paradox (*), Lotus 1-2-3 (*.123, *WK*), Lotus Approach (*.APR, *.VEW, *.APT), ODBC Data Sources (*), ODBC INTERSOLV 2.10 32-BIT Oracle7 (*), ODBC INTERSOLV 2.12 32-BIT TextFile (*), Oracle (*), Paradox (*.DB), Query (*.QRY), SmartMaster (*.MPR), SQL Server (*), SQL Server6 (*), Sybase System 10 & 11 (*), Text - Delimited (*.TXT), and Text - Fixed-Length (*.TXT) files.

 ▶▶ N O T E

> **There are some restrictions on field definitions and limits on files, records, and fields. Some file formats may not be available.**

Approach writes to Approach (*.APR) and SmartMaster (*.MPR) files.

# ▶▶ *Viewing the Approach Window*

The Approach application window (see Figure 14.1) contains many of the elements that you found out about in the *Getting Acquainted with Smart-Suite* chapter. Because you are now working in a database application, its window includes unique elements to help make your job easier, as well as common elements about which you have already learned. In this section, you'll get an overview of all the elements of the application window.

**FIGURE 14.1** ▶

*The Approach application window provides many helpful elements to assist you in creating and editing databases.*

## ▶ Approach SmartIcons

To learn how SmartIcons work, see the *Getting Acquainted with Smart-Suite* chapter.

## ▶ Action Bar

You use the Approach Action bar (see Figure 14.2) to switch between the Browse environment, in which you can add, modify, and delete records; the Design environment, in which you can change the look of the form in which you are currently working; and the Find environment, in which you can find a subset of records. Also on the Action bar is the New Record button; click on this button to insert a blank form on

**FIGURE 14.2 ▶**

*The Approach Action bar consists of buttons with which you can change the view, add a record, or find records.*

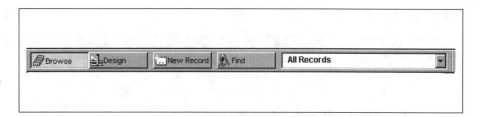

which you can insert information for a new record. To reveal or hide the Action bar, choose View ➤ Show Action Bar. To hide the Action bar using a shortcut menu, point to an empty space on the Action bar, right-click, and choose Hide.

 Go to Browse view (the default) in which you can add, edit, and delete records. Other ways to go to Browse view are choosing View ➤ Browse & Data Entry, pressing Ctrl+B, or selecting Browse after pressing the Environment button on the Status bar.

 Go to Design view in which you can change the design or enhance elements of the current form. Other ways to go to Design view are choosing View ➤ Design, pressing Ctrl+D, or selecting Design after pressing the Environment button on the Status bar.

 Display a new record to be filled in. Other ways to display a new record are choosing Browse ➤ New Record or pressing Ctrl+N.

Go to Find view in which you can look for a subset of records that meet certain criteria. Other ways to go to Find view are choosing Browse ➤ Find ➤ Find, pressing Ctrl+F, or choosing Find after pressing the Environment button on the Status bar.

Run a named Find, including finding all records in the current database.

## ▶ *View Tabs*

Click on any of the tabs immediately below the Action bar (see Figure 14.3) to switch to another view, or input form. If you have defined more views than can show on your computer screen, click on the left-pointing or right-pointing arrow at the right side of the tab bar to reveal additional tabs. To reveal or hide the view tabs, choose View ➤ Show View Tabs.

Creating a Database

▶ ▶

*Ch.*
**14**

*You use the Approach tabs to switch among views (forms).*

| Lead Information | Fax | Letter | Select Callbacks | Follow-up Schedule | Forecast Report | List | Mailing Labels |

## ► The Work Area

The work area displays records and views as you work. Notice that the work area includes both a vertical and a horizontal scroll bar.

## ► The Approach Status Bar

You use the Approach Status bar (see Figures 14.4 and 14.5) to change to a different view or environment. Depending on the current environment (in particular, Browse or Design), you might be able to magnify or reduce the form on the screen, enhance parts of a form, see the location of your mouse pointer, select a style, see the page or record number, or go to a specific record. To reveal or hide the Status bar, choose View ► Show Status Bar.

*The Approach Status bar for the Browse environment consists of buttons with which you can change the record, the environment, or the view.*

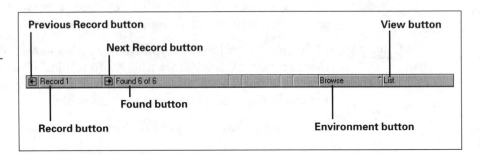

*The Approach Status bar for the Design environment consists of buttons with which you can change the font size, enhance part of the view, select a style, zoom the view, or change the environment or view.*

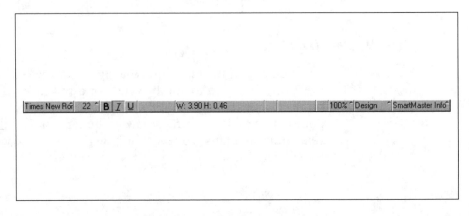

The Approach Status bar provides these buttons:

**Previous Record**    In the Browse and Print Preview environments, click on this button to move to the previous record, unless you are on the first record.

Record 1

**Record Status**    In the Browse and Print Preview environments, click on this button, which shows the current record number, to display the Go to Record dialog box (see Figure 14.6).

**Next Record**    In the Browse and Print Preview environments, click on this button to move to the next record, unless you are on the last page or screen.

Found 6 of 6

**Found**    In the Browse and Print Preview environments, this button displays the number of records you have found. If you have not explicitly found any records, Approach states that all the records are found.

**Environment**    In the Browse, Design, and Print Preview environments, click on this button to reveal a list of the environments (see Figure 14.7) to which you can go.

**View**    In the Browse, Design, and Print Preview environments, click on this button to reveal a list of views for the current database (see Figure 14.8).

Creating a Database

▶ ▶
Ch.
**14**

**FIGURE 14.6** ▶

*Use the Go to Record dialog box to move to a particular record in the current database.*

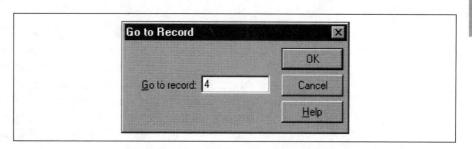

**FIGURE 14.7** ▶

*A list of the Approach environments*

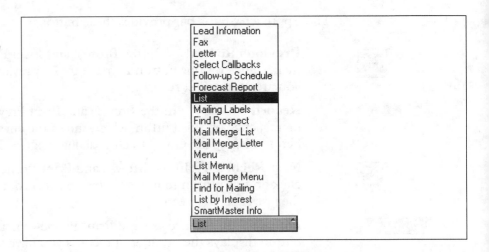

**Zoom**    In the Design and Print Preview environments, this button displays the size at which you are currently viewing a record, form, report, or page. For example, if you see 50% on this button, you are viewing at half the size of the printed page. Click on this button to choose from a list of percentages.

**Dimensions**    In the Design environment, you can always be aware of the current cursor location and size of the page or an object that you are drawing. The number after W shows the location of the mouse pointer between the left and right margins. The number after the H shows the location of the mouse pointer between the top and bottom margins.

W: 6.22 H: 0.31

**Size**    In the Design environment, this button displays the font or point size of the selected text. Click on this button to choose from a list of font sizes (see Figure 14.9).

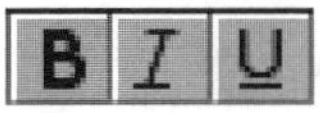

**Enhancements** In the Design environment, click on any of these buttons to apply or remove boldface, italics, or underlines from the selected text.

**Style** In the Design environment, click on this button to reveal a list of styles (see Figure 14.10) from which you can select to apply attributes to the selected element.

**FIGURE 14.9** ▶

*A list of the font sizes for a particular computer*

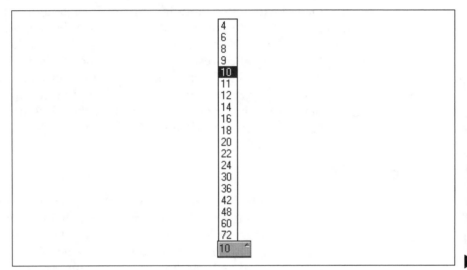

**FIGURE 14.10** ▶

*A list of styles from which you can select to apply different attributes to the selected design element*

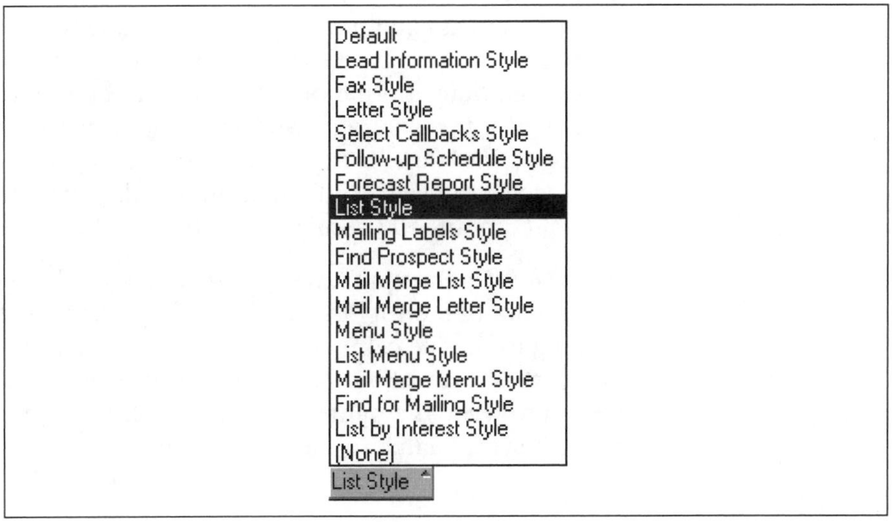

# ▶▶ Learning about the Elements of a Database

A *database* contains groups of organized information, which can be sorted, retrieved, reported on, and/or copied into letters and mailing labels. To make an analogy, a database is like a file cabinet drawer loaded with letters and documents. If each folder in the drawer is arranged in some sort of order, you'll be able to find the information you are looking for almost instantaneously. On the other hand, if you have high stacks of correspondence and reports piled on your desk and waiting to be filed, you won't be able to find a crucial document when your manager urgently needs it. So one of the most important elements of a database is organization—ensuring that each drawer and folder is just so. A database is made up of fields and records.

## ▶ Field

A *field*, which is the smallest piece of a database, is the area into which you type a single piece of information. A field is one piece of information on a form or letter in the file drawer. For example, one field on an employment application includes the name of the college that an applicant attended and another field holds the applicant's first name.

To describe the contents of a field and tell Approach how it can use the information, assign a *field type*. For example, you can define a Date field as a *date* field type(especially if you calculate the difference between that date and the date of hire to track the weeks, months, or years that it takes for a prospective employee to become an actual employee). Last Name, First Name, Street, City, and Zip are all text fields. Approach can use the information in a date field for computation but cannot compute the contents of a text field.

A *field label* is the name that you give to a field; it helps the person entering data to identify the kind of information the field contains. Returning to the file cabinet analogy, examples of field labels are College or University and First Name. It's very clear that the applicant is expected to write the name of his or her alma mater in the first field and his or her first name in the second field.

## ▶ *Record*

A *record* contains a group of related fields. In other words, one application for employment is a record, and as you remember, every piece of information on the application is a field. It's a record of the meaningful information about an individual. Examples of other records are a time card, a trip report, and a passport application.

## ▶ *Form*

A *form* is a record layout that allows for easy and efficient data entry. For example, you'll place name and address information so that you can type information in the order with which you are most comfortable. In most cases, you'll type the first and last name, then the street address, followed by the city, state, and zip code.

# ▶▶ *Planning and Designing a Database*

In this section, you'll plan, design, and create a sample database, Staff, which contains employee information. In many cases, you'll be able to use one of the Approach SmartMaster templates rather than designing and creating your own.

If you plan to create a database based on your design, devote some time to planning. Although Approach makes it easy to fine-tune and redesign an existing database on the fly, it is a good idea to develop the habit of using pencil and paper to plan. All you have to do is write down the name of each field and its length. After you learn about field types in "Specifying Field Types" later in this chapter, you'll add the appropriate type next to each field label. You'll learn how to design a form later in this chapter; so all you need at this point is a list of fields—nothing more.

As you plan any database, ask the following questions:

- What are the main reasons for creating this database? Will you create mailing labels, are you gathering information for reports, or both?

Creating a Database

▶▶

*Ch.*
**14**

- Which fields does this database need? When developing your list of fields, are you thinking about your company or department's growth and plans for the future? For example, do you have room for several telephone numbers: for voice, fax, and modem?

- Do you need to reserve space for new fields, or is it more practical to create a new database?

- Are the fields arranged so that data entry is easy? Are related fields grouped together?

- Which information types should you assign to each field? Which fields are used for calculations? for sorting? for indexes?

- How many ways do you need to sort the information in the database? How many subsets of records do you want to be able to retrieve?

- Should the database include room for addresses outside your home country?

Other factors to consider:

- Give a database an easy-to-remember name. For example, the names Travel or even Emp_Trav are better reminders that a database contains travel information than Emp_09AB.

- Keep it simple and small! You can add complex computations and multiple pages of fields after you spend time learning Approach. In fact, because Approach is a relational database, there is never a need for a gigantic database; it's much easier to work with a set of small interrelated databases instead.

- For better sorting and retrieving, each field should be the smallest possible component of the database. For example, instead of a Name field containing Mr. Thomas Jones, Jr., define Title (Mr.), First Name (Thomas), and Last Name (Jones). In fact, if your database will include many names (for example, a list of registered voters or licensed drivers), consider adding a suffix field for Jrs, IIIs, and so on.

- It is a good idea to include a field with a unique identifier for each record. If you are building a company database, you can use the employee's identification number. But if you are compiling a list of clients, consider combining the last name with the year and date (for example, SMIL950712). An ID field makes it more difficult to duplicate records accidentally—especially if you make the ID field unique (see "Validating Values in a Field" in the *Entering Data* chapter). When you create the Staff database, you'll see two built-in identifiers: the employee number and the key name.

# ▶▶ *Specifying Approach Field Types*

When you design an Approach database, the two important pieces of information you'll provide for a field are its name and its type. Selecting the correct field type ensures that you see the contents of a field in a familiar format (for example, a typical date field looks like *Apr 17, 1998*, or a zip code field for a state of the northeastern United States keeps its leading zeros), that you'll be able to calculate numbers when needed (for example, to determine an employee's years of service or to compute a commission in dollars for a paycheck), and that you can define a field so that it contains a graphic (for example, to display your company logo on a report or a mailing label).

The list below summarizes the Approach field types.

**Text**　Alphanumeric information, such as names, addresses, cities, and company names

**Memo**　Alphanumeric information, such as notes, descriptions, and supplemental information

**Numeric**　Numeric information, such as percentages, currency, quantities, units, discount rates, multipliers, bonus factors, measures, zip codes, telephone numbers, and Social Security numbers

**Date**　Date information, for date formatting

**Time**　Time information, for time formatting

**Calculated**　Formulas; the results appear in the field

**Boolean**　Answers to Yes/No, True/False, or 0/1

**PicturePlus**　Objects, such as graphics, charts, spreadsheet ranges, and sound files from Windows applications that support OLE

**Variable**　Information stored temporarily for any field type that you define

## ► Text Field Type

The most common field type is text, which is the default. Text fields accept any combination of characters—alphabetic, numeric, punctuation, or special symbols—and can have a maximum of 255 characters. (For longer fields, such as those for which you do not want to set a character limit, use the memo field type instead.) Use the text field type for any data that you either won't use for calculations or don't want Approach to format as money, a date, or a time. Other examples of text fields are identification numbers, last name, address, city, and state. In the Staff database, every field that does not fall into another field type category is a text type. To see how to specify a format for a text field, see "Selecting a Format for a Field," later in this chapter.

## ► Memo Field Type

A close, but much larger, relative of the text field is the memo field type. Like a text field, a memo field accepts any combination of characters. A memo field can be up to 5 (dBASE III) or 64 (dBASE IV) kilobytes in length. When you enter information in a memo field, Approach stores it in a separate file. A memo field is ideal for a long description of an item in a catalog database or a movie in a movie database.

## ► Numeric Field Type

The numeric field type is the all-purpose field type for numbers that will be calculated or numerically sorted but cannot be categorized as date or time. Approach does not accept nonnumeric characters typed in a numeric field, except for negative signs and decimal points, which indicate negative numbers and numbers that are not integers (for example, –101.34). Don't type commas or currency symbols; you'll select a format to have Approach do that for you. Typing commas into a number field is not necessary because Approach removes or adds them depending on the format defined for that number field. Normally, Approach does not accept leading zeros (for example, 0566.80) in a number field; after you type a leading zero, Approach removes it (for example, 566.80). However, if you format a numeric field as a zip code, for example, Approach allows leading zeros. Examples of number fields are percentages, quantities, units, discount rates, multipliers, bonus factors, measures, zip codes, currency, telephone numbers, and Social Security numbers. The Commission field in the

Staff database, which is a percentage, is a numeric field. To see how to specify a format for a numeric field, see "Selecting a Format for a Field," later in this chapter.

## ▶ *Date Field Type*

Selecting the date field type ensures that appropriate numbers and characters typed in a field are converted to a date format. The default date format is the current Windows date format. (To change the default Windows date format, select the Regional Settings icon in the Control Panel. You can have Approach automatically enter the date in date fields. Your choices are the date on which the record was created or the date on which it was modified.

Approach can calculate date fields. For example, you can have Approach compute the number of years that an employee has worked for your company by subtracting the date of hire from today's date, or you can calculate someone's age by subtracting a birthday field from the current date. To see how to specify a format for a date field, see "Selecting a Format for a Field," later in this chapter.

## ▶ *Time Field Type*

The time field type ensures that Approach formats numbers typed in the field as a time. The only nonnumeric characters that you can type in a time field are AM and PM. You can have Approach automatically enter the time in time fields. Your choices are the time at which the record was created or the time at which it was modified.

Approach can calculate time fields. For example, an employee can track his or her hours by having Approach subtract a login time from a logout time. The Staff database does not have a time field. To see how to specify a format for a time field, see "Selecting a Format for a Field," later in this chapter.

## ► Calculated Field Type

Use a calculated field type to hold the results of a formula written in the field at the same time you define the field. Approach formulas can hold *constants* (items that keep the same value in contrast to *variables*, which can change through calculations) or references to another field (for example, Price $^X$.07).

## ► Boolean Field Type

You can use the Boolean field type to answer questions to which the answer is Yes or No, True or False, or 0 or 1. For example, in the Staff database, a Yes/No field shows whether an employee travels or not. *Yes, y, True, T,* or *1* indicates that the employee travels; otherwise, the answer is *No, n, False, F,* or *0*. If you use a checkbox or an option box for a Boolean field, the person entering data can simply click on a choice.

## ► PicturePlus Field Type

Approach uses the PicturePlus field type to define a field in which you will embed or paste a graphic or an object from an application that supports Object Linking and Embedding (OLE). In addition to pictures, PicturePlus fields can hold charts, spreadsheet ranges, and sound files. Supported picture formats are none, 1-2-3, Bitmap, Lotus Freelance Graphics96 Drawing and Presentation, Lotus Screencam Movie 2.1, WordPro Media Clip, Packager, Paintbrush Picture, TvMap Doc, Video Clip, and WordPad Doc. Approach supports any sound files for which you have an OLE server.

## ► Variable Field Type

Approach uses the variable field type to temporarily store information. The contents of a variable field are very similar to the contents of the Windows Clipboard; a variable field is a temporary storage place for information. When you turn off your computer, the contents of the variable field, like those of the Clipboard, disappear permanently. When you define a variable field, identify the field type of the information that it will hold.

# ▶▶ *Creating a Database*

In this section, you can create a database. If you want, you can use the sample database STAFF.DBF:

| Field Name | Description | Field Type | Field Length (if applicable) |
|---|---|---|---|
| SS Number | Employee Social Security number | Numeric | 9.0 |
| Hire Date | Date employee started work | Date | Fixed |
| First Name | Employee's first name | Text | 30 |
| Last Name | Employee's last name | Text | 30 |
| Address 1 | First line of employee's street address | Text | 30 |
| Address 2 | Second line of employee's street address (for example, apartment number or post office box number) | Text | 30 |
| City | City or town in which the employee resides | Text | 30 |
| State | State in which the employee resides | Text | 2 |
| ZIP | Zip code | Numeric | 9.0 |

| Field Name | Description | Field Type | Field Length (if applicable) |
|---|---|---|---|
| Department | The department to which the employee is assigned | Text | 10 |
| Title | The employee's job title or position | Text | 40 |
| Extension | The employee's telephone extension | Text | 4 |
| Salary | The employee's current gross salary | Numeric | 10.2 |
| Commission | A computed percentage of sales for which the employee is totally or somewhat responsible | Numeric | 1.2 |
| Calc_ Commission | The calculated dollar commission | Calculated | Fixed |
| Travel | A yes or no answer to whether the employee travels for the company | Boolean | Fixed |

Once you have decided on the fields and their field types, the next step is to create the database. To create a new database, start Approach and follow these steps:

1.  In the Welcome dialog box, double-click on Blank Database. (If you have turned off the Welcome dialog box, choose File ➤ New Database.) Approach then opens the Welcome to Lotus Approach dialog box (see Figure 14.11).

2.  Click on the Create a New File Using a SmartMaster tab. Approach changes to a new section of the Welcome to Lotus Approach dialog box (see Figure 14.12).

3.  Select Blank Database and click on OK. Approach opens the New dialog box (see Figure 14.13).

4.  To store the new file in a different location, select from the choices in the Create In drop-down box.

5.  In the File Name text box, type a filename (for example, STAFF).

**FIGURE 14.11** ▶

*The Welcome to Lotus Approach dialog box*

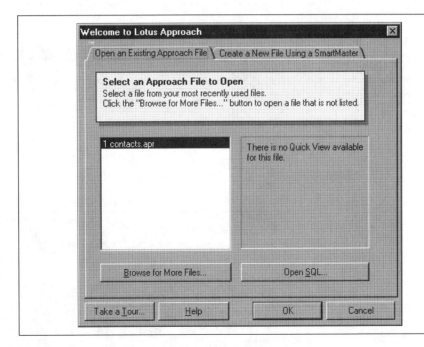

**FIGURE 14.12** ▶

*The Welcome to Lotus Approach dialog box with the Blank Database selected*

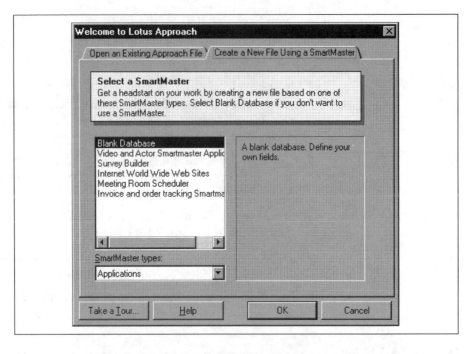

**FIGURE 14.13** ▶

*The New dialog box with the name of a new database already filled in*

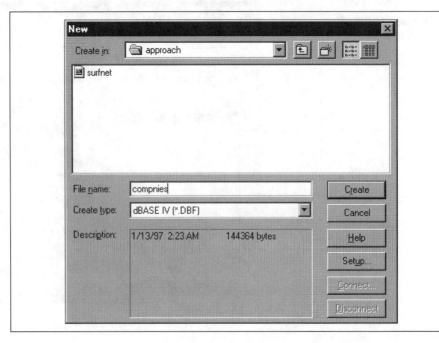

**6.** Click on the Create button or press Enter. You don't have to type an extension after the filename; Approach assigns the DBF (dBASE IV) extension. Approach then opens the Creating New Database dialog box (see Figure 14.14), in which you define the fields in the database.

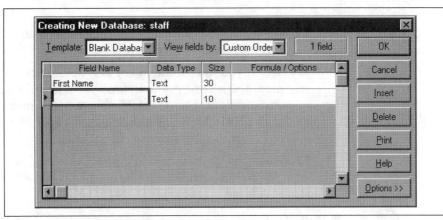

**7.** Type a field name in the Field Name column.

**8.** Assign a field type by clicking in the Data Type text box, clicking on the downward-pointing arrow to the right of the Type drop-down list box, and clicking on your choice. For instructions on entering a formula in a calculated field, see the following section.

 ▶▶ **TIP**

> **You can select a field type quickly by highlighting the Type drop-down list box and typing the first character of the type name.**

**9.** Fill in a field length in the Size column. Try to be accurate in determining length, but don't underestimate.

▸▸ **N O T E**

**If you are filling in a numeric field, the number to the left of the decimal point in the Length text box represents the number of digits to the left of the decimal point, not the total length of the number.**

**10.** After clicking in the next empty Field Name cell, repeat steps 7 through 9 to add the next fields.

**11.** When you have defined the last field, click on OK. Approach displays the record in the default format and changes to the Browse environment. Figure 14.15 shows the almost completed database in the Field Definition dialog box. Figure 14.16 shows the database form in the Browse environment.

**12.** Save the database by clicking on the Save SmartIcon, by choosing File ➤ Save Approach File, or by pressing Ctrl+S.

▸▸ **N O T E**

**You can use the preceding steps to add a field to a database at any time.**

**FIGURE 14.15** ▸

*The Field Definition dialog box with several fields in Staff displayed in the Database Fields box*

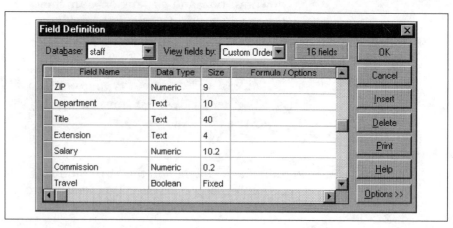

**FIGURE 14.16** ▶

*The new Staff database as it is displayed in the Browse environment. If you want, you can start typing data in the first field.*

![Screenshot of Lotus SmartSuite 97 Approach Blank Database in Browse environment, showing fields: SS Number, Hire Date, First Name, Last Name, Address 1, Address 2, City, State, ZIP, Department, Title, Extension, Salary, Commission, Travel]

## ▶ *Defining a Calculated Field*

Defining a calculated field in the Creating New Database dialog box (if you are creating a database) or in the Field Definition dialog box (if you are editing a database that you have created and saved) is very similar to defining any other field, until you select the field type. (Assuming that you have already saved the database, choose Create ▶ Field Definition to reopen the Field Definition dialog box.) When you select Calculated, Approach adds another section to the Field Definition dialog box (see Figure 14.17). Assemble the formula by clicking on fields, operators, and functions. For example, to create the Calc_Commission formula, double-click on Salary, double-click on the multiplication operator, and double-click on Commission.

Notice that the flag graphic to the left of the Formula text box changes its look as you add new elements to the formula; a red X indicates an invalid formula. When the X is removed, to show that the formula is valid, click on OK. Approach switches to the Design environment and displays the Add Field dialog box. Notice that Approach differentiates between calculated fields and all others by displaying the calculated field in *italics*. Simply drag the new field from the dialog box onto the form, and then the new field looks like all the other fields. Approach closes the Add Field dialog box and asks if you want to remain in the Design environment (click on the Design button) or change to the Browse environment (click on the Browse button).

**FIGURE 14.17** ▶

*The Creating New Database dialog box with the Calc_Commission formula defined*

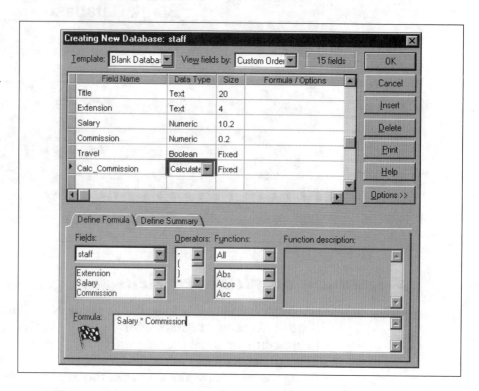

## ▶ *Selecting a Format for a Field*

You can ensure that the value entered in a field looks like a date, time, money, or one of three text formats. Simply click on Design in the Action bar or Status bar, double-click on a field, choose Object ▶ Object Properties, or press Alt+Enter or Ctrl+E. Fill in the InfoBox (see Figure 14.18) and click on OK. For detailed information about the Info-Boxes that are common to most SmartSuite applications, refer to the *Editing in SmartSuite Applications* chapter.

**FIGURE 14.18** ▶

*The Format section of the Approach InfoBox, in which you can change a number format for a selected field*

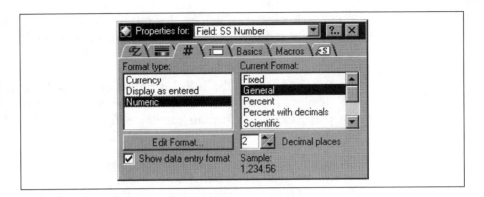

These are the categories in the InfoBox:

**Text**     Click on this tab to change the font, style, font size, alignment, text color, and text relief for data or a label. For detailed information about this InfoBox, refer to the *Editing in SmartSuite Applications* chapter.

**Lines and Colors**     Click on this tab to change the border width, border color, fill color, shadow color, type of frame, and border lines. For detailed information about this InfoBox, refer to the *Editing in SmartSuite Applications* chapter.

**Format**     Click on this tab to change the format for the current field. See the following section for information about date, time, numeric, and text formats.

**Dimensions**     Click on this tab to change the width, height, position of the object in the work area or when printing. For detailed information about this InfoBox, refer to the *Editing in SmartSuite Applications* chapter.

**Basics**     Click on this tab to select a field, open the Field Definition dialog box, select or define a data entry type, check field attributes, and name a style. For more information, see the "Using Forms" section in this chapter and in the *Entering Data* chapter.

**Macros**     Click on this tab to specify what triggers the running of a macro attached to the selected field or to define a macro. For more information about macros in Approach, see the *Advanced Approach Techniques* chapter.

▶▶

*Ch.*

**14**

**Styles**     Click on this tab to specify a named style for the selected field. For more information about styles in Approach, see the *Advanced Approach Techniques* chapter.

When you open the InfoBox and click on the Format tab, Approach displays *Display as Entered* or the format type for the selected field. Display as Entered formats the value in the selected field just as you entered it. This is the default for any field.

Approach data formats are as follows:

**Date Format**     Click on this option button to select a custom date format or create a custom date format after you click on the Other option button. The list below shows each date format.

> **Format**
> 04/05
> 04/05/58
> 05.04
> 05.04.58
> 05/04/58
> 05-Apr
> 05-Apr-58
> 1958-04-05
> 1058Q2
> 2nd Qtr. 1958
> 2nd Qtr. 58
> 2nd Quarter, 58
> 2Q1958
> 2Q58
> 5 Apr
> 5 Apr 58
> 5/04/58
> 58Q2
> Apr
> Apr 58
> Apr-58

April

Q2

Q2 1958

Q2, 1958

Sat

Sat, Apr 5, 1958

Saturday

Saturday, Apr 5

Saturday, April 5, 1958

Second Quarter, 1958

**Time Format**    Click on this option button to select a time format. The list below shows each time format:

17 h

17:05 h

17:05:07 h

17:05:07.84 h

5 PM

5:05 PM

5:05:07 PM

5:05:07.84 PM

**Numeric Formats**    Approach numeric format types are Fixed, General, Percent, Percent with Decimals, Scientific, Social Security, Telephone, and Zip Code. You use the General, Percent with Decimals, and Scientific formats to select the number of decimal points, from 0 to 8. A sample of the numeric formats is shown at the bottom right of the dialog box, under the Samples header. The format also shows in the selected field box, if the box isn't hidden by the dialog box. To move a dialog box out of the way, simply drag it by its title bar.

The list below illustrates each numeric format:

**#,##0;(#,##0)**    For the Fixed format, Approach inserts commas to indicate thousands. Digits following decimal points are not included in the display. Negative numbers are enclosed in parentheses.

**#,##0.00;(#,##0.00)**    For the General format, Approach inserts commas to indicate thousands. Digits following decimal points are included in the display. Negative numbers are enclosed in parentheses.

**0%**    For the Percent format, Approach inserts a percent sign following the number. Digits following decimal points are not included in the display. Negative numbers are preceded by minus signs.

**0.00%**    For the Percent with Decimals format, Approach inserts a percent sign following the number. Digits following decimal points are included in the display. Negative numbers are preceded by minus signs.

**0.00e+00**    For the Scientific format, Approach formats the number as an exponent.

**000-00-000**    For the Social Security format, Approach formats the number as a Social Security number (for example, 555-55-5555).

**>7 (###)" "000-0000 or =7 000-0000**    For the Telephone format, Approach formats the number as a U.S. telephone number; for example, (555) 555-5555 or 555-5555.

**>5 00000-0000 or 00000**    For the Zip Code format, Approach formats the number as a 9- or 5-digit zip code.

**Currency Formats**    You can select a Currency format for many countries—from Australia to the United States. To view and optionally edit a Currency format for a country, follow these steps:

1. Double-click on a currency field. Approach opens the InfoBox.

2. Click on the Format (#) tab.

3. Select Currency in the Format Type box.

4. Select the name of a country in the Current Format scroll box.

5. Click on the Edit Format button.

6. In the Edit Format dialog box, view or edit the Format Code.

7. Click on OK to close the Edit Format dialog box.

8. Click on the Close button to close the InfoBox.

The list below presents the syntax used for Approach numeric formats.

**#**      A placeholder for an optional number. If the number isn't large enough to include a digit other than 0, Approach omits the digit.

**0**      A placeholder for a required number. If the number isn't large enough to include a digit other than 0, Approach inserts a 0.

**.**      A decimal point.

**,**      A comma, which separates thousands. If a number isn't large enough to include a thousands separator, Approach omits it.

**;**      A semicolon, which separates two related syntaxes. For example, a semicolon separates positive and negative syntaxes in some numeric formats.

**$**      A dollar sign, which is inserted in the place it appears in the syntax.

**%**      A percent sign, which is inserted in the place it appears in the syntax.

**+**      A plus sign, which is inserted in the place it appears in the syntax, if the number is positive.

**-**      A minus sign, which is inserted in the place it appears in the syntax, if the number is negative.

**()**      A Parentheses, which are inserted in the places they appear in the syntax, if the number is negative.

**:**      A colon, which is inserted in the place it appears in the syntax; normally used to separate digits in a date or time.

**Text Format**      Click on this option button to select a text format: ALL CAPITALIZED, all lowercase, First Capitalized (the first letter in every word in the field is uppercase), or Lead capitalized (the first letter in the first word in the field is uppercase).

You'll learn more about using the InfoBox later in this chapter. In the meantime, go through the sample database and format the fields (for example, format ZIP as a Zip Code field and format SS Number as a Social Security field).

# ▶▶ *Using Forms*

Once you have created a database, you can start typing information into the form. Approach provides a better way, however: You can design and create a customized form, which should make data input a much more pleasant experience.

## ▶ *Planning and Designing a Form*

Although you can accept the default form, arranging the fields in the order in which you would add information is important. For example, most people are so accustomed to filling out forms in a "name, address, city, state, zip code" order that it makes sense to arrange fields in the same order.

In sketching out your own database design on paper, plan for easy data entry by spreading fields out (from the left margin to the right margin, and from the top of the screen to the bottom). Is there room for adding lines and boxes? Use white space (areas that don't contain text or graphics), boxes, and lines to group similar or related fields and to separate dissimilar fields. Be sure that you leave enough room to add a new field to groups of related fields.

When you design a form, you can use all the fields in the database or only a few. If you plan to use several types of information from a database (for example, to create special mailing labels or a unique report), create a form for each purpose.

## ▶ *Creating a Form*

When you create a form, you'll start working with the Form Assistant. First, you'll select a form, and then you'll identify the fields that you want in the form, clicking on the Add button after selecting the fields. (If you want to remove any selection, click on it and then click on the Remove button.) After you have selected the last field for the form, click on the Done button.

To create a new form for your new database, open the Staff database (or the database with which you are working) and follow these steps:

1. Choose Create ➤ Form. Approach displays the Form Assistant dialog box (see Figure 14.19).

2. Type the name of the form in the View Name & Title text box. Select Standard from the Layout list box. Click on the Next button. Approach changes to Step 2 in the Form Assistant dialog box (see Figure 14.20).

3. Select a field to be added to the form.

4. Click on the Add button to add the selected field to the form. Approach automatically selects the next field on the list.

**TIP**

**A fast way to select a field is to double-click on it. This combines steps 3 and 4.**

5. To remove a field from the form, select it and click on the Remove button.

**FIGURE 14.19 ▶**

*The Form Assistant dialog box with Step 1 filled in*

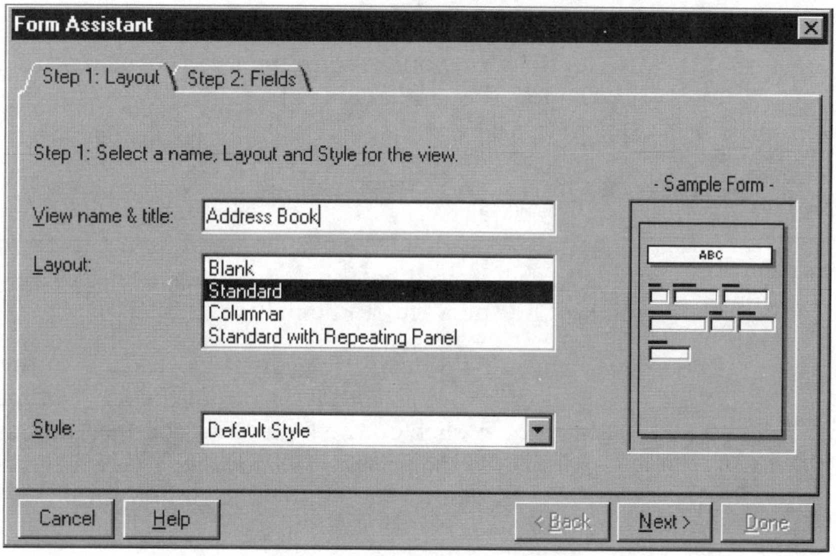

Ch.
**14**

---

**Form Assistant** ☒

Step 1: Layout \ Step 2: Fields \

Step 1: Select a name, Layout and Style for the view.

- Sample Form -

View name & title:  Address Book

Layout:
Blank
Standard
Columnar
Standard with Repeating Panel

ABC

Style:  Default Style  ▼

Cancel    Help    < Back    Next >    Done

6. Repeat steps 3 and 4 to add more fields to the new form.

7. When you have added all the desired fields to the new form, click on Done. Approach closes the dialog box, displays the selected fields arranged in the work area as you specified, and displays the form name on a tab and on the view button.

**FIGURE 14.20** ►

*The Form Assistant dialog box with Step 2 filled in*

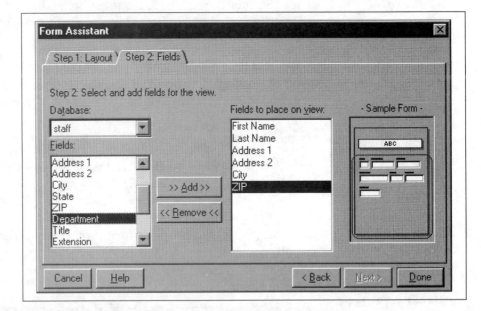

If you wish, you can edit the form by using the InfoBox or by changing the location and/or size of fields.

## ► Enhancing a Form

Approach provides a great deal of flexibility in form design. After you add the desired fields to a form, you can change their sizes, move them around the form, and enhance them.

Sizing a field box is quite easy. First, click on the Design button on the Action bar, or select Design from the Environment list on the Status bar. Then click on the field to be changed. (Be sure not to double-click; double-clicking opens the InfoBox.) When Approach adds handles to the field, point to a handle and drag it until the field reaches the desired size.

It's easy to rearrange the form so that objects, such as fields, are logically placed and that data entry is as easy as possible. To move an object, press and hold down the mouse button anywhere within the object's boundaries. When the mouse pointer looks like a hand, drag the object to its new location, and release the mouse button. When you drag a field, you also drag its field label.

Before moving the first object, particularly for a very crowded form, review these notes:

- If an object is one of the last to be moved, temporarily drag it to an empty space, preferably at the bottom of the form. Doing so gets it out of the way, leaving you with more workspace.

- Before starting to move objects around the form, turn the grid on by choosing View ➤ Show Grid. (Since this is the default, the grid is probably already turned on.)

- To have objects align with, or *snap to*, the grid, choose View ➤ Snap to Grid, or press Ctrl + Y.

- You can refine the grid so that fine adjustments in movement are possible. Choose File ➤ User Setup ➤ Approach Preferences, and click on the Display tab, if needed. Open the Grid Width drop-down list box, select values from $\frac{1}{16}$ to $\frac{1}{2}$ inch, and either click on OK or press Enter. The default value is $\frac{1}{12}$.

- If you know that you will be increasing the length of a field in its final location, be sure to leave extra room on the form. In fact, if the field will be quite long, don't drag another object to the same horizontal grid line.

- If you know that you will shorten the length of a field, you can squeeze more objects in the same area and adjust the length later.

- Although it's very useful to group related objects (by selecting the objects and then choosing Object ➤ Group or pressing Ctrl+G), there is a disadvantage. Before you can add or remove room from an object in a group, you must ungroup. There is enough fine-tuning to each field and field label on a form that grouping can be counterproductive. Therefore, it is good to do your grouping as one of your later steps.

Creating a Database

Ch.
**14**

To enhance fields, use the InfoBox. Table 14.1 lists and describes the InfoBox elements used to enhance objects, including fields, and provides examples.

▶ **TABLE 14.1:** *Approach InfoBox Styles and Enhancements*

| InfoBox Tab | InfoBox Element | Description |
|---|---|---|
| Text | Font Name drop-down list box | Specifies the font for the selected data or label |
| Text | Attributes box | Specifies the style (that is, Bold, Italic, Underline, or Strikethrough) of the selected data or label |
| Text | Size scroll box | Specifies the font size of the selected data or label |
| Text | Size option box | Specifies the font size of the selected data or label |
| Text | Alignment buttons | Specify the alignment (that is, left-aligned, center-aligned, or right-aligned) of the selected data or label |
| Text | Text Color drop-down list box | Applies a color to the selected data or label |
| Text | Text Relief drop-down list box | Specifies whether the selected text or label looks flat, embossed, or carved into the surface |
| Text | Label Text text box | Specifies the name of the label on the form—not in the database itself |
| Text | Label Position drop-down list box | Specifies the alignment of the label in relationship to the field box (that is, to the left, right, above, or below the field box or having no label at all) |
| Lines and Colors | Style drop-down list box | Specifies the look of the border of an object (for example, the box that contains the contents of a field) |

▶ **TABLE 14.1:** *Approach InfoBox Styles and Enhancements (continued)*

| InfoBox Tab | InfoBox Element | Description |
|---|---|---|
| Lines and Colors | Fill Color drop-down list box | Specifies the color within the borders of an object (for example, the box that contains the contents of a field) |
| Lines and Colors | Shadow Color drop-down list box | Specifies the color of the shadow above or below an object |
| Lines and Colors | Width drop-down list box | Specifies the thickness of the defined border |
| Lines and Colors | Borders checkboxes | Specify whether left, right, top, bottom, and baseline borders are present or absent, whether the baseline at the bottom of the label is present or absent, or whether the field label is enclosed |
| Lines and Colors | Color drop-down list box | Specifies the color of the border of the box enclosing the contents of a field |

Figure 14.21 shows the completed Address Book form for the Staff database.

## ▶ Specifying Cursor Movement in a Form

Normally, as you press the Tab key in an input form, the cursor moves from field to field in a left-to-right, top-to-bottom pattern. However, sometimes this does not happen or you want to change the order. For example, as you drag fields around a form, their old tab order remains with them. To change tab order, in Design, choose View ➤ Show Tab Order and type new numbers on the tab symbols.

**FIGURE 14.21** ►

*The Staff Address Book form with fields enhanced and in new positions*

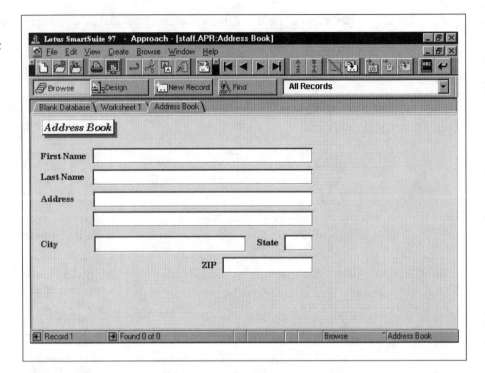

 ►►**N O T E**

**You can have different tab orders for different input forms within the same database file.**

When you show the tab order for a specific input form, tab symbols are superimposed over the fields on the input form (see Figure 14.22). As you press Tab during data entry, the cursor travels from 1 to 2 to 3 and so on. You can view and/or change tab order for the current input form by following these steps:

*1.* Go to the Design environment by clicking on the Design button on the Action bar, selecting Design from the Environment list on the Status bar, choosing View ► Design, or pressing Ctrl+D.

*2.* Choose View ► Show Tab Order. Approach overlays tab symbols on the input form.

**3.** Select the number on the tab symbol you want to change, and type a new number.

▶▶**NOTE**

**Sometimes Approach fills in the new number as you highlight the old; if you have eliminated a number and have created a gap between numbers, Approach fills in the missing number as you highlight the next number.**

**4.** Repeat step 3 until you have made all the desired changes.

**5.** Choose View ➤ Show Tab Order, click on the OK button on the Action bar, or select Browse from the Environment list on the Status bar. Approach removes the tab symbols from the form and implicitly saves the new tab order.

**Creating a Database**

**Ch.**
**14**

**FIGURE 14.22** ▶

*A form showing the slightly out of order default tab order*

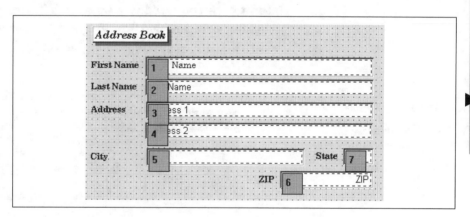

## ▶ *Renaming a Form*

Sometimes it's necessary to rename a view to better explain the purpose of the form. For example, you might have accepted the default name of Blank Database, or now you have two versions of a mailing label, one named Label and the other Form 6. To rename a view, be sure that you are in the Design environment, and follow these steps:

**1.** Select the view that you want to rename by clicking on the View button on the Status bar and selecting from the list or by clicking on the appropriate View tab.

**2.** Click on the form title at the top of the form.

**3.** Open the InfoBox by clicking on its SmartIcon, by choosing Object ➤ Object Properties, or by pressing Alt+Enter or Ctrl+E.

**4.** Click on the Basics tab, if needed.

**5.** Open the Properties For drop-down list box, and select Form: *form name*.

**6.** In the Form Name text box, type the new name. Figure 14.23 shows the InfoBox as a view is renamed.

**7.** Close the InfoBox by clicking on the Close button.

**8.** Save the Approach file.

▶▶**NOTE**

**To change the title text at the top of the form, click on the title until it's surrounded by a blue border. (However, don't click too rapidly. If Approach interprets your clicking as a double-click, it opens the InfoBox.) Then edit the title as you would any text.**

**FIGURE 14.23** ▶

*The InfoBox as a view being renamed*

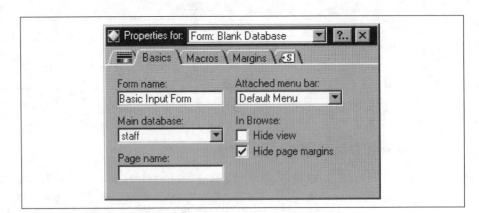

## ▶ *Deleting a Form*

When you decide to move to a better form design or you change a database in such a way that a form is obsolete, it's better to remove it than to keep it. To remove a form, change to the Design environment, and follow these steps:

**1.** Make active the soon-to-be-deleted form by clicking on its View tab or on the Environment button on the Status bar.

**2.** Choose Form ➤ Delete Form. (If you're deleting a report, form letter, envelope, or mailing label, this command changes to Delete Report, Delete Form Letter, Delete Envelope, or Delete Mailing Label.) Approach displays a message box that prompts you to confirm the deletion.

**3.** To delete the form, click on Yes. If you change your mind, click on No.

**4.** Save the Approach file.

# ▶▶ *Using the Worksheet Assistant*

When you create a new database, Approach creates two default views: an input form and a worksheet, both of which include all the fields in the database. In earlier sections of this chapter, you have learned how to create and edit input forms with selected fields. In this section, you will find out how to create and edit worksheets, which are spreadsheetlike input forms.

## ▶ *Creating a Worksheet*

Creating a worksheet is just like creating any input form. Simply select the fields and let Approach take care of the rest of the work. To create an Approach worksheet, follow these steps:

**1.** Start Approach and open the database for which you will create the worksheet.

**2.** Choose Create ➤ Worksheet. Approach opens the Worksheet Assistant dialog box (see Figure 14.24).

**3.** Select a field to be added to the worksheet.

**4.** Click on the Add button to add the selected field to the worksheet.

**FIGURE 14.24** ▶

*The Worksheet Assistant dialog box with the fields already selected*

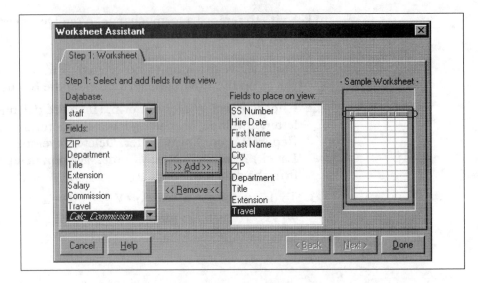

  **T I P**

> **A fast way to select a field is to double-click on it. This combines steps 2 and 3.**

**5.** To remove a field from the worksheet, select it and click on the Remove button.

**6.** Repeat steps 3 and 4 to add more fields to the new worksheet.

**7.** When you have added all the desired fields to the new worksheet, click on Done. Approach closes the dialog box, displays the selected fields arranged in the work area as you specified, and displays the worksheet name on a tab in the View bar. If you want to add new records and you are not in Browse mode, click on the Browse button on the Action bar, choose View ▶ Browse & Data Entry, or press Ctrl+B.

## ▶ *Adding a Column to a Worksheet*

What if you have forgotten to add an important field? You can add a new column using your mouse or a menu command. To add a new column using a mouse, follow these steps:

1. In either the Browse or the Design environment, click on the column to the right of the location in which you want to add the new column. Approach highlights the selected column.

2. Move the mouse pointer until it looks like a downward-pointing arrow.

3. Click the left mouse button. Approach adds the column and opens the Formula dialog box, in which you can enter a formula, which can be a field (see Figure 14.25).

4. Select a field or enter a formula. Then click on OK. Approach closes the dialog box.

5. Click three times at the top of the column. Type the name of the column label, and then press Enter.

6. To delete a column, select it, and press the Delete key on your keyboard.

To add a new column using a menu command, follow these steps:

1. In either the Browse or the Design environment, click on the column to the left of the location in which you want to add the new column. Approach highlights the selected column.

2. Choose Worksheet ➤ Add Column. Approach adds the column and opens the Formula dialog box, in which you can enter a formula, which can be a field.

3. Select a field or enter a formula, and then click on OK. Approach closes the dialog box.

Creating a Database

▶ ▶
*Ch.*
**14**

**4.** Click three times at the top of the column. Type the name of the column label, and then press Enter.

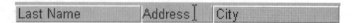

**5.** To delete a column, select it, and press the Delete key on your keyboard.

**FIGURE 14.25** ▶

*The Formula dialog box with a field defined as a formula*

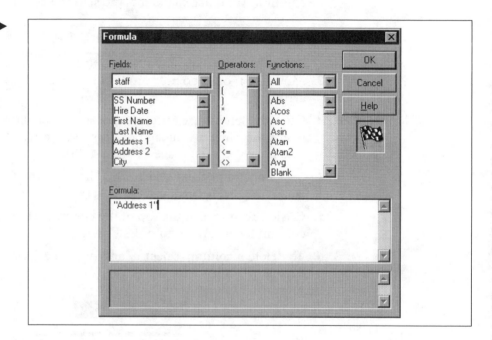

## ▶ *Enhancing a Worksheet*

You can enhance a worksheet in the Browse or Design environment using the Text and the Lines and Colors sections of the InfoBox. You also can change the width or location of columns in a worksheet whether you are in the Browse or the Design environment.

To enhance the label at the top of a column, select the column and click on the InfoBox SmartIcon, choose Worksheet ▶ Worksheet Properties, or press Alt+Enter or Ctrl+E. Then select options from either the Text or Lines and Colors section. For more information about using the InfoBox, see the *Editing in SmartSuite Applications* chapter.

### Adjusting the Width of a Column

Sometimes, changing a font or font size means that you must change the width of a worksheet column. To do this, move the mouse pointer to the border between the column that you want to widen and the column to its right. When the mouse pointer changes to a double-pointed arrow, simply drag the column border to the left or right.

### Moving a Column

If it makes sense to move a column to a different location in a worksheet, you can do so easily in Approach. To move a column, follow these steps:

1. Click on the column to be moved. Approach highlights it.
2. Move the mouse pointer within the column until it changes to a hand.
3. Drag the column toward its new location. The hand mouse pointer will close and appear to carry the column label. As you move the mouse, Approach emphasizes column borders with a heavy vertical line. This shows you the current destination of the column.
4. When the mouse pointer reaches the desired destination, release the left mouse button. Approach places the column in its new location.

## ▶ Deleting a Worksheet

To delete a worksheet, make active the worksheet to be deleted, go to the Design environment, and choose Worksheet ➤ Delete Worksheet. When Approach prompts you to confirm the deletion, click on the Yes button.

# ▶▶ Adding Fields to a View

If you have been working with a particular view for a while and would like to add a field, it's easy to do. For example, if you want to display the date on which a field was added or edited or identify the person who is entering particular records, add the fields to the view. If the field is already defined to the database, all you have to do is choose the Form ➤ Add Field command and drag the field onto the view. You can edit the newly entered field using the InfoBox. If you want to add a new field to the database, you can do so in one of two ways:

- Choose Create ➤ Field Definition and add the field to the Field Definition dialog box.

- Choose Form ➤ Add Field, click on the Field Definition button, and add the field to the Field Definition dialog box.

## ▶ Adding an Existing Field to a View

To add an existing field to a view, follow these steps:

1. Go to the Design environment.

2. Choose Form ➤ Add Field. Approach opens the Add Field dialog box (see Figure 14.26).

3. Drag the desired field onto the view.

4. Click on the Close button to close the dialog box.

**FIGURE 14.26** ▶

*The Add Field dialog box from which you can drag a field onto a view*

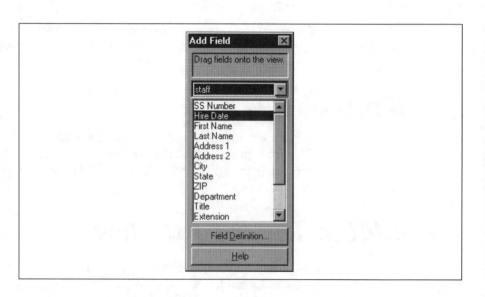

### ▶ *Adding a New Field to a View*

To add a new field to a view, follow these steps:

1. In the Browse or Design environment, choose Create ➤ Field Definition, or in the Design environment, choose Form or Worksheet ➤ Add Field, and click on the Field Definition button. Approach opens the Field Definition dialog box.

2. Click on the field before which you want to insert the new field and click on the Insert button, or go to the bottom of the list and click in the empty Field Name cell.

3. Type the name of the new field in the Field Name cell.

4. Select a data type.

5. Enter the field size for Text or Numeric fields. (All others are a fixed size.)

6. Click on OK. Approach opens the Add Field dialog box with only the new field listed.

7. Drag the new field to the view. Approach automatically closes the Add Field dialog box.

# ▶▶ *Deleting Fields from a View*

To delete a field from a view, go to the Design environment, select the field, and either choose Edit ➤ Cut, or press Ctrl+X, Shift+Del, or the Delete key. Approach deletes the field without prompting for confirmation. (To restore the deleted field, choose Edit ➤ Undo or press Ctrl+Z.)

Creating a
Database

▶▶
*Ch.*
**14**

# CHAPTER 15

# Entering Data

▶▶ ***A**lthough* you can retrieve records, create reports, design input forms, and change a database's structure in Approach, most of your time is spent entering data—either by adding new records or by editing existing records. In this chapter, you'll find out all about entering data—preparing to enter data, entering data in different types of fields, and special methods by which you can save time.

# ▶▶ *Displaying Records*

You can view a record in two ways: as a form or as a worksheet. As you learned in the last chapter, in a form you see all or part of one record at a time. A form displays the fields in various locations in the work area. A worksheet shows you several records at once, in a format that is very similar to a spreadsheet. A worksheet has one record per row and one field per column. Regardless of how you view your database, you enter data in the same way. The only difference is the layout of fields and records.

A newly created Approach database starts with two basic views: Blank Database, which is your first form, and Worksheet 1, the first worksheet. To choose one of these views, either click on the View button in the Status bar and select or click on one of the View tabs.

## ▶ *Displaying a Database As a Form*

When you display a form, you can move fields to any location on the form. As you learned in the previous chapter, you can move the fields with the mouse and alter their fonts and field box sizes through the

InfoBox. You can design and create several forms for a database—each for its own purpose. Figure 15.1 displays an employee information form from Approach's sample Contacts database. Notice that there is only one record on display.

**One record**

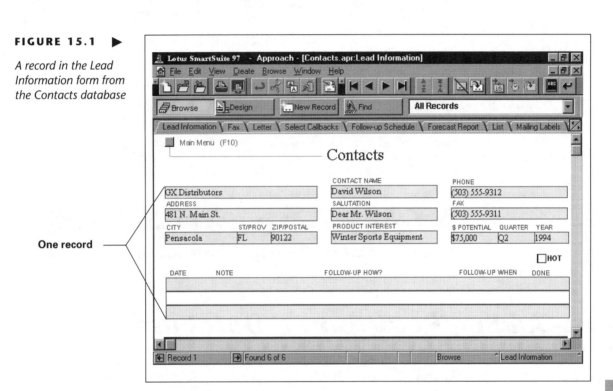

## ▶ *Displaying a Database As a Worksheet*

Worksheet view displays fields as columns in a spreadsheet or a table, and each record of the database is displayed as a row. Since you can see more than one record at a time, Worksheet view is a more complete look at your database. Figure 15.2 shows a list form from the Contacts database.

Entering Data

▶ ▶
*Ch.*
**15**

**FIGURE 15.2** ►

*The List form from the
Contacts database*

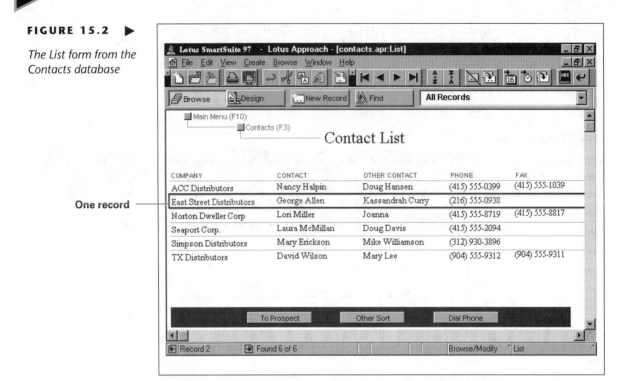

One record

## ►► *Adding Records to a Database*

A carefully designed form is the best way to add records to a database. When you work with a form, you can see the overall record before starting to fill in the next one. You can also add records in Worksheet view. For example, if you are entering many records at once and the contents of many fields will be the same (for example, the same city, state, and zip code), simply select a worksheet or form and start typing. You can add records to a database in either Form view or Worksheet view by following these steps:

**1.** If you are not in the Browse environment, click on the Browse button on the Action bar, click on the Environment button in the Status bar and select Browse from the list, choose View ► Browse & Data Entry, or press Ctrl+B.

**2.** Click on the New Record button on the Action bar, choose Browse ➤ New Record, or press Ctrl+N. This displays a blank form in Form view or a blank row in Worksheet view and places your cursor in the first field of the new record.

**3.** Add the appropriate data in the new record. To move through the record, either click on each new field or press Tab or Shift+Tab.

**4.** Repeat steps 2 and 3 until you have completed the last record. As you enter information in a record, Approach automatically saves it. Whenever you change to a different mode or start to add another record, Approach automatically saves your changes or additions up to that point.

## ▶ *Duplicating a Record*

When the current record contains much of the information in the previous record, an easy way to enter data is to duplicate the last active record and then change the appropriate fields. To add a new duplicate record, click on the Duplicate Record SmartIcon, select Browse ➤ Duplicate Record, or press Ctrl+Alt+D. Approach copies the data from the most recently added or edited record to the current one.

## ▶ *Duplicating the Value in a Field*

As you add new records to a database, you can have Approach copy the contents of the record that you just added into the next record. For example, if you have been operating with paper files of customer records, which are sorted by date, some of the records might have duplicate dates. Rather than type the same date over and over again, simply choose Browse ➤ Insert ➤ Previous Value or press Ctrl+Shift+P.

 ▶▶**N O T E**

> The Previous Value command is available for only the last record that you entered or edited; however, you can duplicate any record in a database. To duplicate a record, display it and then click on the Duplicate Record SmartIcon, select Browse ➤ Duplicate Record, or press Ctrl+Alt+D.

## ▶ *Setting Initial Values for a Field*

You can tell Approach to automatically fill in the data in a field or fields when you add a record. For example, if you add a record for every new contact, Approach can enter today's date for you. This ensures that the date is accurate (if your computer system date is accurate) and also saves time. Or if most records in the database will have the same city, state, and zip code, Approach can insert those values automatically, and you can edit them as needed. You can also tell Approach to insert a value that automatically increases for each new record. This is a good way of inserting a unique identifier, such as a contact ID, for each record in a database.

To insert initial values, choose Create ▶ Field Definition to open the Field Definition dialog box. Click on the Options button, and Approach adds a new section to the dialog box (see Figure 15.3).

**FIGURE 15.3** ▶

*The extended Field Definition dialog box*

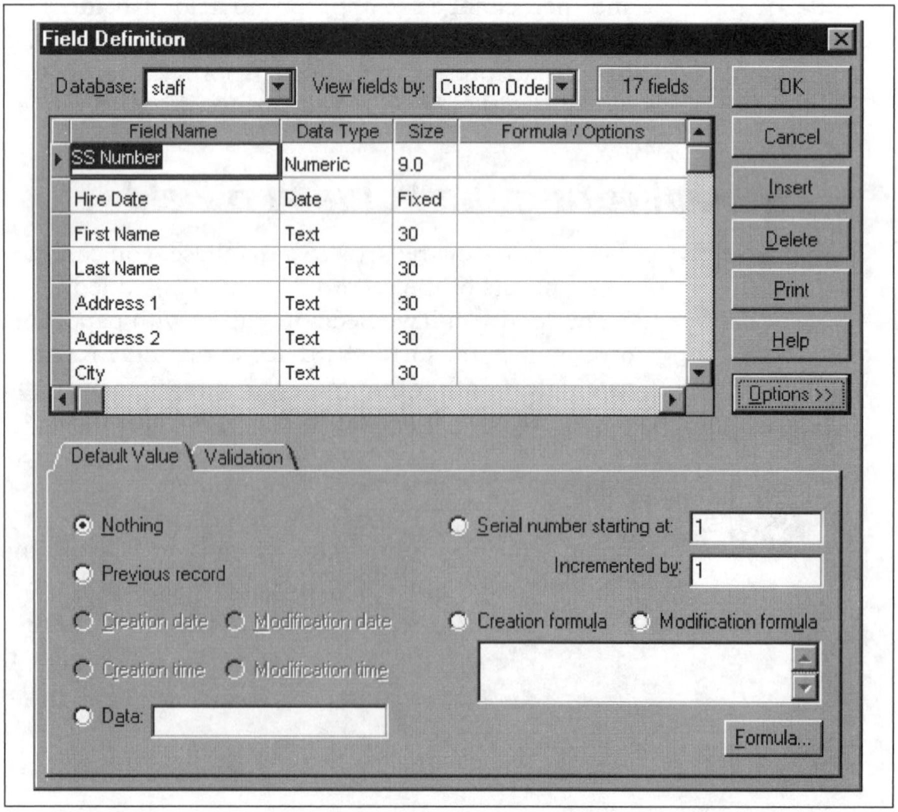

You can specify a value or a formula for a selected field by clicking on one of these option buttons:

**Nothing**   Leave the field blank.

**Previous Record**   Insert the contents of the previous active record in the selected field.

**Creation Date**   Insert the system date in the selected field when you add the record. Use this initial value only with date fields (although other field types accept this value).

**Modification Date**   Insert the system date in the selected field when you modify the record. Use this initial value only with date fields (although other field types accept this value).

**Creation Time**   Insert the system time in the selected field when you add the record. Use this initial value only with time fields (although other field types accept this value).

**Modification Time**   Insert the system time in the selected field when you modify the record. Use this initial value only with time fields (although other field types accept this value).

**Data**   Insert the data that you type in the text box in the selected field.

▶▶**TIP**

> **You can use the Data option to automate data entry. For example, if you know that you will add 50 records that have identical values in the City and State fields, set the values using the Data option. When you finish adding these records, remove these initial values.**

**Serial Number Starting At**   Insert a number *incremented* (increased) or *decremented* (decreased) by the positive or negative number in the Incremented By text box. This initial value is a *counter* (a number that is changed by a certain value each time it is used). If you start numbering at 1 and increment by 1, the first record that you add has 1 in the selected field, the second record has 2, and so on. You can increment a number by a value up to

**Entering Data**

▶▶

*Ch.*
**15**

2147483647 or decrement a number by a value up to –2147483647.

**T I P**

**You cannot increment a number by 0; so if you want to insert the same number in a field in every new record, enter the value in the Data option button and text box.**

**Creation Formula**    Insert the results of a formula when you create any new record. For example, if a school district gets transportation aid, a city code could be calculated and inserted in a code field whenever a new pupil is added. The school district could then easily prepare reports sorted by aid and sent to the agency responsible for dispensing the aid.

**Modification Formula**    Insert the results of a formula whenever you edit a record. For example, if a pupil in the prior example moves, a new city code could be calculated. Or if employees are given certificates to mark anniversaries, a formula could compute the length of service by subtracting the date of hire from today's date and insert the number of years in an Anniversary field.

To create initial values for a field, follow these steps:

1. In either the Browse or the Design environment, choose Create ➤ Field Definition. Approach displays the Field Definition dialog box.

2. Click in the Formula/Options column for the field for which you want to define the initial value.

3. Click on the Options button. Approach adds a section to the dialog box.

4. If needed, click on the Default Value tab in the extra section.

5. Click on an option button in the Default Value section. If you click on Data or Serial Number Starting At, enter values in the appropriate text boxes (see Figure 15.4). Approach adds information to the Formula/Options column for the selected field.

6. Click on OK to close the dialog box.

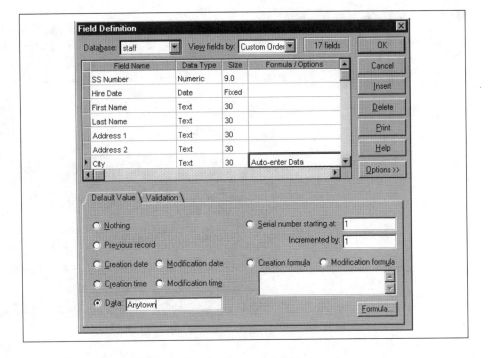

**FIGURE 15.4** ▶

*The Field Definition dialog box with an initial city value*

 **7.** Save the database by clicking on the Save Approach File Smart-Icon, choosing File ➤ Save Approach File, or pressing Ctrl+S.

## ▶ Validating Values in a Field

You can also use the Field Definition dialog box to check information as you enter it. You can check to see if a value is unique in the database, if it is one of a list of values, if it fits within a range of values, or if it exists at all.

To check entered data, open the Field Definition dialog box (see Figure 15.5), click on the Options button, click on the Validation tab, and check or select an option:

**Unique**   Ensures that the value in the selected field is unique in the database.

**From/To**   Ensures that the value in the selected field is within the values entered in the From text box and the To text box.

**Filled In**   Ensures that there is a value in the selected field.

Entering Data

▶▶

Ch.
**15**

**FIGURE 15.5 ▶**

*This extended Field Definition dialog box shows a validation value for the SS Number field.*

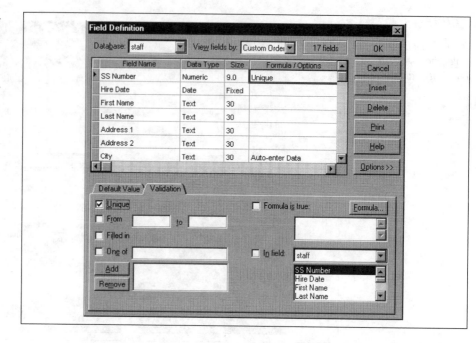

**One Of**     Ensures that the value in the selected field is one of the values listed in the text list box. To add another value to the text box, click on the Add button. To remove a value, select it and click on Remove.

**Formula Is True**     Ensures that the value in the selected field is true when the formula in the text box is calculated. To enter a formula, click on the Formula button.

**In Field**     Ensures that the value in the selected field matches the value in the selected field in the database that you selected from the drop-down list box.

To validate values in a field, follow these steps:

1. In either the Browse environment or the Design environment, choose Create ➤ Field Definition. Approach displays the Field Definition dialog box.

2. Click in the Formula/Options column for the field for which you want to define the initial value.

**3.** Click on the Options button. Approach adds a section to the dialog box.

**4.** If needed, click on the Validation tab in the extra section.

**5.** Click on a checkbox in the Validation section. Approach adds information to the Formula/Options column for the selected field.

**6.** If you click on From, One Of, or Formula Is True, enter values in the appropriate text boxes.

**7.** If you click on In Field, select a field from the list box.

**8.** Click on OK to close the dialog box

 **9.** Save the database by clicking on the Save Approach File SmartIcon, choosing File ➤ Save Approach File, or pressing Ctrl+S.

## ▶ *Creating a List of Values for a Field*

You can limit the choices that can be entered in a field by creating a list of values from which the person entering data must choose. For example, you can list only the current departments in your company, the states in which your company is located, or even chapters and sections in a book. This prevents entering invalid information and can also speed up data entry. It's much easier to select from a list than to type the information character by character.

 ▶▶▶ N O T E

> The Approach database in this section and the next is a real-life example—used to compile the thousands of entries in *The Internet Business-to-Business Directory*, written by Sandra E. Eddy, Michael M. Swertfager, and Margaret M. E. Cusick, and published by SYBEX.

To create a list of values, follow these steps:

**1.** From the Design environment, select the field for which you want the list.

 **2.** Open the InfoBox by clicking on its SmartIcon, by double-clicking on the selected field, by choosing Object ➤ Object Properties, or pressing Alt+Enter or Ctrl+E.

Entering Data

▶▶
*Ch.*
**15**

3. Click on the Basics tab, if needed.

4. From the Data Entry Type drop-down list box, select Drop-Down List (see Figure 15.6). Approach displays the Drop-Down-List dialog box. Figure 15.7 shows the Drop-Down List dialog box with a list already filled in.

**FIGURE 15.6** ▶

*In the InfoBox, select Drop-Down List and click on the Define Buttons button to open the Drop-Down List dialog box.*

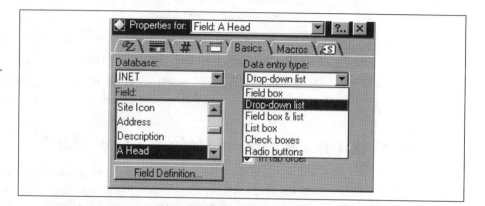

**FIGURE 15.7** ▶

*The Drop-Down List dialog box with a list of chapter headings coded and ready to use*

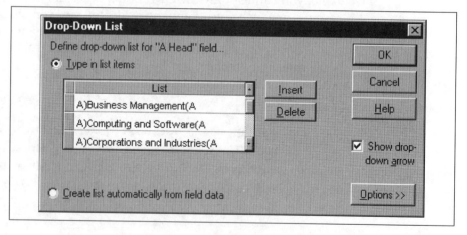

5. Type a list in the List scroll box.

6. To insert a new item at a particular place on this list, click on the value before which you want the new item, click on the Insert button, and type the new value.

7. To delete an item, select it, and click on the Delete button.

8. To always display an arrow button in the field box, check the Show Drop-Down Arrow checkbox. To display the arrow button only when you have clicked in the field box, clear the Show Drop-Down Arrow checkbox.

9. Click on OK to close the dialog box.

10. Click on the X button to close the InfoBox.

11. Save the Approach file by clicking on the Save Approach File SmartIcon, choosing File ➤ Save Approach File, or pressing Ctrl+S. Figure 15.8 shows part of a value list in a form in the Browse environment. Notice all the other value lists in the form.

**FIGURE 15.8** ▶

*The A Head (chapter) field with an open value list in a form filled with lists, checkboxes, text boxes, and a large memo field*

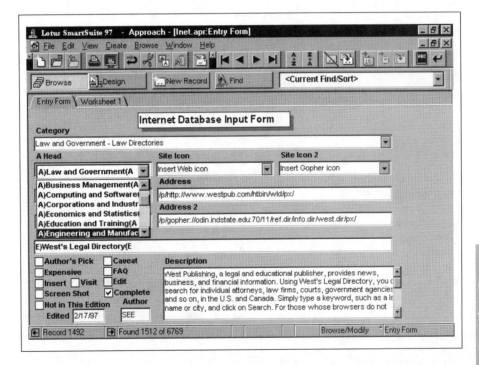

▶▶**NOTE**

**The next time you need to edit the list, open the InfoBox and click on the Define List button under the Data Entry Type drop-down list box.**

Entering Data

▶▶

Ch.

**15**

## ▶ Using Checkboxes for Boolean Fields

Remember that Boolean data types accept only two values: On or Off, Yes or No, or 1 or 0. Checkboxes, common Windows elements, are also Boolean: They are either checked (On) or cleared (Off). In Approach, you can use checkboxes for Boolean fields.

To create a checkbox, follow these steps:

*1.* From the Design environment, select the field for which you want the checkbox.

*2.* Open the InfoBox by clicking on its SmartIcon, by double-clicking on the selected field, by choosing Object ▶ Object Properties, or by pressing Alt+Enter or Ctrl+E.

*3.* Click on the Basics tab, if needed.

*4.* From the Data Entry Type drop-down list box, select Check Boxes (see Figure 15.9). Approach displays the Define Check Box dialog box. Figure 15.10 shows the Define Check Box dialog box with the Complete field values filled in.

**FIGURE 15.9** ▶

*In the InfoBox, select Check Boxes, and click on the Define Buttons button to open the Define Check Box dialog box.*

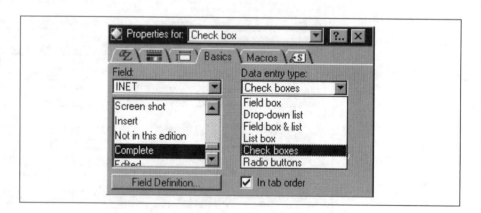

*5.* In the first row of the dialog box, type values:

• In the Checked Value column, type the value for a checked checkbox.

• In the Unchecked Value column, type the value for a cleared checkbox.

• In the Check Box Label column, type the name of the label for this field.

**FIGURE 15.10** ▶

*The Define Check Box dialog box showing the values for a check-box field*

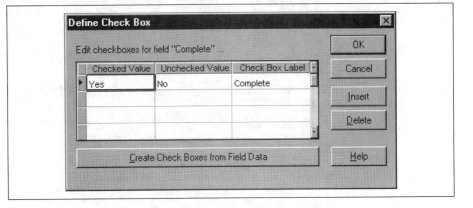

6. Click on OK.

7. Close the InfoBox by clicking on the Close button.

8. Save the Approach file by clicking on the Save Approach File SmartIcon, choosing File ➤ Save Approach File, or pressing Ctrl+S. Figure 15.11 shows several checkboxes in a form in the Browse environment.

## ▶ Using Radio Buttons to Display Your Choices

If you want a field to allow a limited set of choices, you can use either a drop-down list, as described in a prior section, or a set of radio buttons. *Radio,* or *option,* buttons are analagous to the station buttons on a car radio; you can only choose one at a time. In the Staff database, the Department field is ideal for radio buttons; using the proper labeling, each button is a reminder of the available choices.

To create a set of radio buttons, follow these steps:

1. From the Design environment, select the field for which you want the set of radio buttons.

2. Open the InfoBox by clicking on its SmartIcon, by double-clicking on the selected field, by choosing Object ➤ Object Properties, or by pressing Alt+Enter or Ctrl+E.

Entering Data

▶▶

*Ch.*
**15**

**FIGURE 15.11** ▶

*An input form with checked and cleared checkboxes*

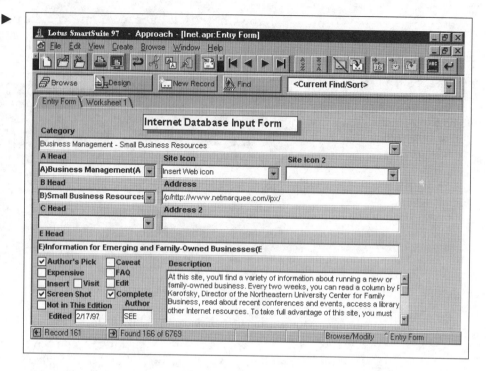

**3.** Click on the Basics tab, if needed.

**4.** From the Data Entry Type drop-down list box, select Radio Buttons (see Figure 15.12). Approach displays the Define Radio Buttons dialog box (see Figure 15.13).

**5.** In each row of the dialog box, type the value for the radio button and the name of the button label. It's a good idea to include the value in the label name.

**6.** To insert a value, select the row that will follow the new value, and then click on the Insert button.

**7.** To delete a row, select it, and click on the Delete button.

**8.** Click on OK to close the dialog box. Approach inserts the new radio buttons on the form.

**9.** Click on the Close button to Close the InfoBox.

**FIGURE 15.12** ▶

*In the InfoBox, select Radio Buttons, and click on the Define Buttons button to open the Define Radio Buttons dialog box.*

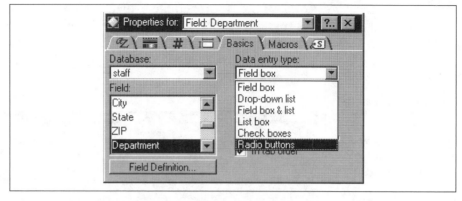

**FIGURE 15.13** ▶

*The Define Radio Buttons dialog box with several values filled in*

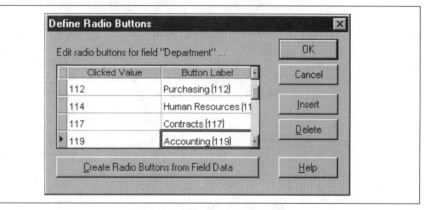

**10.** Drag the set of radio buttons to its final location. (You may have to move other fields too.)

**11.** To change the position of the radio button set, click inside the group and then drag the sizing handles. You can move the radio button items closer together or display them in multiple columns.

 ▶▶**TIP**

> **If the tools palette gets in the way, close it by choosing View ➤ Show Tools Palette or by pressing Ctrl+L. To redisplay it, choose View ➤ Show Tools Palette or press Ctrl+L again.**

**Entering Data**

▶▶
Ch.
**15**

**12.** Save the Approach file by clicking on the Save Approach File SmartIcon, by choosing File ➤ Save Approach File, or by pressing Ctrl+S. Figure 15.14 shows a set of radio buttons in a form in the Browse environment.

**FIGURE 15.14** ▶

*The Staff input form with a set of radio buttons for selected company departments*

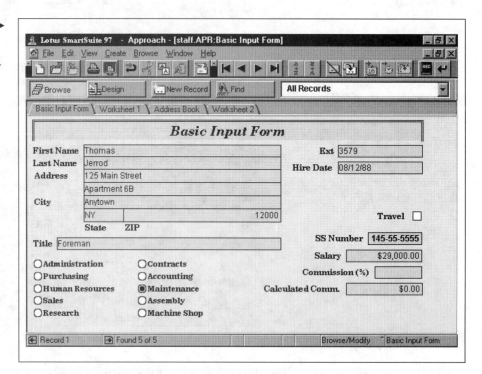

# ▶▶ *Entering Data into Different Types of Fields*

As you enter data, the data is accepted differently for each field type. If you type a number with a leading zero in a number field, Approach removes the leading zero from the data. If you type a number with a leading zero in a text field, however, the leading zero remains. For example, in the Staff database, if you type **02139** in the ZIP field, which is a numeric field with a Zip Code format, Approach will not remove the leading zero.

## ▶ *Entering Data in Text and Memo Fields*

When you type text, numbers, and dates into a text field, the data is not changed from the way in which you entered it. These entries are no longer considered dates, times, and numbers, however, and will probably not calculate properly. If you select ALL CAPITALIZED, all lowercase, First Capitalized, or Lead capitalized for a field, you can type data any way you want, and Approach will format it as you have defined. For example, if you select ALL CAPITALIZED and type **indy** in the First Name field, Approach changes the entry to **INDY**.

## ▶ *Entering Data in Numeric Fields*

You can type only numeric values in a number field; Approach issues an error message if you type any other characters. Remember that Approach removes leading zeros from numbers, unless you specifically choose a format that allows them. If you enter numbers with values to the right side of the decimal point, you must enter the decimal points. If you choose a numeric format that adds comma separators, Approach adds commas automatically; otherwise, comma separators are not inserted. If you enter numbers that you want to be formatted as currency, select an appropriate numeric format.

> **If you installed SmartSuite from a CD-ROM, you can use the ZIP zip code database, which is in the \EXTRA\ DBASES folder. Because of its very large size, consider using it from the CD-ROM rather than copying it onto your hard drive. You can join this database to a main database so that you can look up zip codes and insert them in your records. Note that the ZIP database works well with small towns that have only one zip code. Cities with multiple zip codes still require your looking up exact codes in a zip code directory**

## ▶ *Entering Data in Date Fields*

You can type a value in a date field using *mm*/*dd*/*yy*|*yyyy*, where *mm* represents the number of the month from 01 or 1 to 12, *dd* represents the number of the day from 01 or 1 to 28, 29, 30, or 31 (depending on the month), *yy* or *yyyy* represents the year—either the last two digits or the full four digits. Separate each element of a date with a nonnumeric character, such as a dash, a slash, or a comma. You can type as many as 10 characters in a date field. An invalid value in a date field triggers an error message.

## ▶ *Entering Data in Time Fields*

When you type a time (or have Approach automatically enter a time) in a time field, Approach automatically converts your data to the time format set in the InfoBox. You can type in *h*, *hh*, *hh*:*mm*, *hh*:*mm*:*ss*, or *hh*:*mm*:*ss*.*00* format. You can type a time value in either military (for example, 1700) or standard (for example, 5:00 [PM]) format. If you type a time in standard format, Approach defaults to AM. You can type as many as 12 characters in a time field.

## ▶ *Entering Data in Calculated Fields*

Approach calculates formulas and places the results in calculated fields. Therefore, you cannot enter data in calculated fields.

## ▶ *Entering Data in Boolean Fields*

In Boolean fields you can use only a few affirmative and negative entries: Yes, No, Y, N, 1, and 0. Any entries besides these and any entry starting with the letter *N* put a Yes in the field.

## ▶ *Entering Data in PicturePlus Fields*

PicturePlus fields can contain only graphical images—those with the extensions BMP, EPS, GIF, PCX, TGA, TIF, and WMF—sound files, Lotus ScreenCam movies, video clips, and other OLE objects pasted from the Windows Clipboard or imported from other Windows applications. To place a picture in a PicturePlus field, copy and paste it just as you learned in the *Editing in SmartSuite Applications* chapter. If you choose the Edit ➤ Paste Special command, you can embed the picture as an OLE object (when the source application supports OLE). If the picture is an OLE object, you can edit the picture using the source application while you remain in Approach.

▶▶ **T I P**

**You can use drag and drop to copy a picture from the Windows Explorer, a My Computer window, a Find window, and so on to a PicturePlus field. First, display both the window containing the icon that represents the picture file and the Approach PicturePlus field on the desktop; then drag the picture icon to the PicturePlus field.**

## ► Entering Data in Variable Fields

Remember that variable fields are temporary fields of any type. To enter data in a variable field, follow the instructions in this section for that type of field.

## ► Entering Data in Restricted Fields

When you restrict input in a field using the extended Field Definition dialog box, the condition of the option buttons, checkboxes, and text boxes in the Default Value and Validation sections determine whether you can type certain data in a field. For example, if you check the Unique checkbox for the SS Number field and try to type a duplicate Social Security number, Approach will not allow you to do so.

# ►► Deleting a Record

Whether you have just added a record, the record has been in your database for years, or you are in the middle of adding the record, you can delete it by clicking on the Delete Record SmartIcon, by choosing Browse ► Delete Record, or by pressing Ctrl+Del. Answer Yes to the prompt, and Approach permanently deletes the record. Once you have responded to the prompt, you cannot undo the deletion.

# CHAPTER 16

# Retrieving and Sorting Data and Joining Databases

**L***ike* any good filing system, Approach can search for and update the records already entered into a database. With Approach, you can easily select the specific records you want to retrieve for viewing, printing, or editing.

You can use the Approach Find process to specify particular records to be viewed, edited, or included in a report. For example, you can find all active employees who have worked for you for more than three years and who have a salary less than $30,000. Or you can find all ex-employees who were hired in a particular year for a particular position. With a paper filing system, these tasks probably require going through each record—a lengthy process if the database contains many records. With Approach, the retrieval is immediate.

# ►► *Finding Records in a Database*

When you want to get records to view, print, or edit, you must find them by comparing them against criteria that you define. The records that Approach then retrieves are called a *Found Set*. The Status bar shows the number of records you have found out of the total number of records in the database. Typically, when you are working in the database (that is, you have not performed a Find), the Status bar shows that you have found all the records in the database (for example, Found 350 of 350). To retrieve records, follow these steps:

*1.* If you are not in the Browse environment, click on the Browse button on the Action bar, click on the Environment button on the Status bar and select Browse from the list, choose View ➤ Browse & Data Entry, or press Ctrl+B.

**2.** Click on the Find button, click on the Environment button on the Status bar and choose Find, choose Browse ➤ Find, or press Ctrl+F. Approach displays a Find request form (see Figure 16.1) and a new group of SmartIcons.

**FIGURE 16.1** ▶

*The Approach Find request form with two Find fields: City equals Anytown, and Department equals Purchasing.*

**A text Find request**

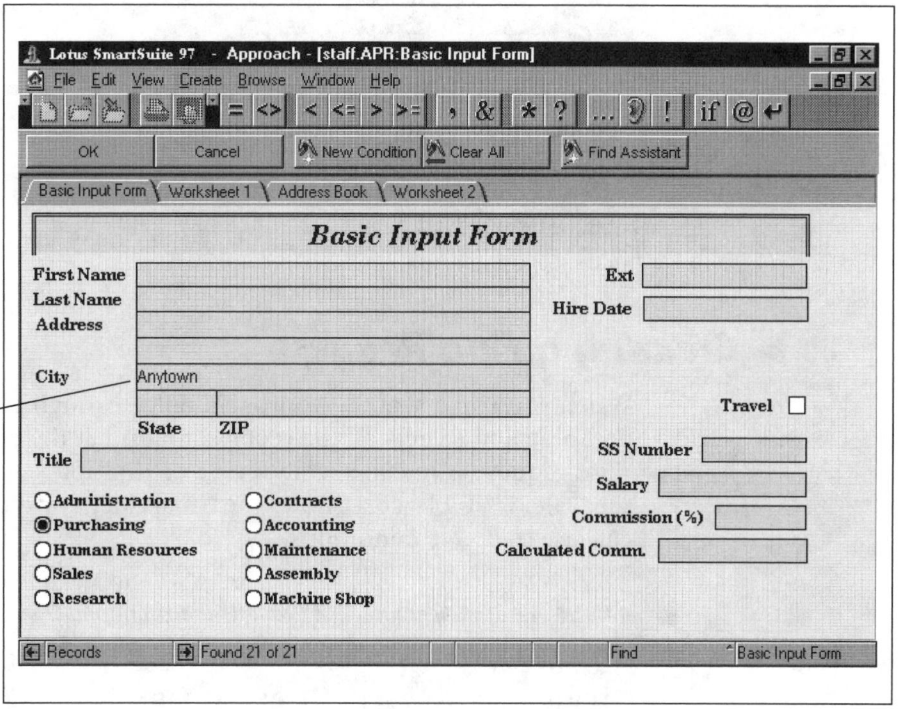

**3.** Type the Find criteria you want into the appropriate fields.

**4.** Click on the Enter button or press Enter. The Status bar reports the number of records that have been found and the total number of records in the database. Record 1 of the Found Set appears in the work area.

Found 1 of 21

If Approach does not find any records, it displays a prompt:

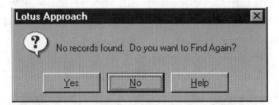

To return to the full database, choose Browse ➤ Find ➤ Find All, press Ctrl+A, or select All Records from the drop-down list on the Action bar.

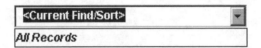

## ▶ Creating a Find Request

When you run a search, Approach looks through every record in the database and selects all the records that meet the conditions in the Find request. You can specify single or multiple conditions in one or more fields. Table 16.1 shows the SmartIcons and operators that you can use to create conditions.

▶ **TABLE 16.1:** *Approach Find Request SmartIcons and Operators*

| Smart-Icon | Key(s) | Description | Example |
|---|---|---|---|
| = | = | Finds items that are equal to the Find request, or when entered by itself, finds blank fields. | The Find request **=99** (or **99**) finds a record when the selected field contains *99.* |
| <> | <> | Finds items that are not equal to the Find request, or when entered by itself, finds nonblank fields. | The Find request **<>99** finds a record when the selected field contains every value except 99. |

▶ **TABLE 16.1:** *Approach Find Request SmartIcons and Operators (continued)*

| Smart-Icon | Key(s) | Description | Example |
|---|---|---|---|
| < | < | Finds items that are less than the Find request. | The Find request <99 finds a record when the selected field contains *98, 97, 96, 95,* and so on. |
| <= | <= | Finds items that are less than or equal to the Find request. | The Find request <=99 finds a record when the selected field contains *99, 98, 97, 96, 95,* and so on. |
| > | > | Finds items that are greater than the Find request. | The Find request >99 finds a record when the selected field contains *100, 101, 102, 103,* and so on. |
| >= | >= | Finds items that are greater than or equal to the Find request. | The Find request **>=99** finds a record when the selected field contains *99, 100, 101, 102, 103,* and so on. |
| , | , | Retrieves a record when the item matches condition 1 *or* condition 2. | The Find request **VT, NY** finds a record when the selected field contains *VT* or *NY*. |
| & | & | Retrieves records when the item matches condition 1 *and* condition 2. | The Find request **\*computer\*&\*table\*** finds a record when the selected field contains the words *computer* and *table* in any order or location. |

▶ **TABLE 16.1:** *Approach Find Request SmartIcons and Operators (continued)*

| Smart-Icon | Key(s) | Description | Example |
|---|---|---|---|
| ✱ | * | Finds items with any character(s) at the location of the asterisk in the Find request. You can use a combination of asterisks and question marks in the Find request. If you enclose text with asterisks, Approach finds records that contain the word in any location in the search field. | The Find request **th★** finds a record when the selected field contains *the, them, those, thesaurus, thanksgiving,* and so on. |
| ? | ? | Finds an item with any character at the location of the question mark in the Find Request. You can search using a combination of asterisks and question marks. | The Find request **the?** finds a record when the selected field contains *thee, them, then,* and *they.* |
| ... | ... | Finds items within the range specified in the Find request. | The Find request *A...S* finds a record when the selected field contains *Alfred, Don, Monty, Stuart,* and so on. |
| 👂 | ~ | Finds items that sound like the Find request. | The Find request ~Manetenince finds a record when the selected field contains *Maintenance.* |

Ch.
16

▶ **TABLE 16.1:** *Approach Find Request SmartIcons and Operators (continued)*

| Smart-Icon | Key(s) | Description | Example |
|---|---|---|---|
| ! | ! | Finds items that match by case in the Find request. | The Find request **!Bart** finds a record when the selected field contains *Bart*, but not *BART*, *bart*, *bArT*, and so on. |
| if | if | Retrieves a record when the expression in the Find request is true. | The Find request If(Bonus>Salary) finds a record when the contents of the Bonus field are greater than the contents of the Salary field. |
| @ | @ | Retrieves a record when the value returned by the function in the Find request is not equal to 0. | The Find request >@Pi() finds a record when the selected field contains a value greater than 3.14159. |
| ← | ↵ | Enters the new record in the database or starts the Find. | N/A |

The Action bar in the Find environment provides these buttons:

OK

Clicking on the OK button is just the same as clicking on the Enter SmartIcon or pressing the Enter key. Clicking on OK starts the Find.

Cancel

Clicking on the Cancel button is the same as pressing Esc. When you click on Cancel, you move from the Find environment to the Browse environment without completing the current search.

Clicking on the New Condition button opens another Find window so that you can enter a set of new conditions in addition to the previous conditions. When you press Enter, click on the Enter SmartIcon, or click on OK, Approach searches for the search conditions in all the Find windows and returns to the Browse window. Clicking on New Condition is the equivalent of choosing Browse ➤ Find ➤ Find More.

Clicking on the Clear All button removes all the Find criteria from the fields so that you can begin a new search.

Clicking on the Find Assistant button opens the Find/Sort Assistant window, which you can use as a guide for complex searches or sorts. For information on the Find/Sort Assistant, see the "Using the Find/Sort Assistant" section of this chapter.

## ▶ Setting Conditions for a Search

You request certain records in Approach the same way that you might request a set of paper records. For example, to get all the records in which *Tom* is the value in the First Name field, simply type:

    =Tom

or

    Tom

in the First Name field of the Find request.

## ▶ Finding Text and Memo Fields

Text fields are the most straightforward of the field types. The information that you type in a text field for a retrieval is the information that Approach retrieves.

### Using Wildcards to Find Text

In Approach you can use the wildcard characters * and ? to find groups of similar records or to Find records containing words whose spelling you don't remember completely. Use *wildcards* as a placeholder for one character or several characters at the beginning, middle, and/or end of a word in a Find request.

Manipulating Data

Ch. **16**

To find any number of unknown characters, use the asterisk. Here are some examples:

| Find request | Finds | Examples |
|---|---|---|
| *s* | text that begins with any number of unknown characters or no characters, includes an *s*, and ends with any number of unknown characters or no characters | baseball, O*s*lo, sati*s*faction, *s* |
| s*o | text that begins with an *s*, includes any number of unknown characters or no characters, and ends with an o | *s*o, *s*ol*o*, *s*cenari*o*, *s*tilett*o* |
| s* | text that begins with an *s* and ends with any number of unknown characters or no characters | *s*, *s*o, *s*olo, *s*cenario, *s*tiletto *s*atisfaction, *s*erious |
| *s | text that begins with any number of unknown characters or no characters and ends with an *s* | *s*, *s*eriou*s*, haras*s*, video*s* |

To find a set number of unknown characters, use the question mark. Here are some examples:

| Find request | Finds | Examples |
|---|---|---|
| s??? | text that begins with *s* and ends with three unknown characters | *s*olo, *s*ans, *s*ole, *s*ale |
| s?le | text that begins with *s*, includes one unknown character, and ends with *le* | *s*ole, *s*ale |

| Find request | Finds | Examples |
|---|---|---|
| ?ale? | text that begins with one unknown character, includes *ale*, and ends with one unknown character | *sales*, S*ale*m, m*ale*s |

### Finding Sounds-Like Text

You can use a special operator that finds values that sound similar to the Find request. Simply type a tilde (~) in front of what you think the value sounds like. For example, to find all records with Last Name fields that sound something like Donovan, type any of the following:

```
~donvan
~donvin
~donvn
~donovan
```

and you will find records with the Last Name value of *Donovan*.

## ▶ Finding Numeric Fields

Finding numeric fields is almost as easy as searching for text fields. Simply type a number (without format characters such as dollar signs, commas, dashes, slashes, and so on) into the numeric field, and Approach retrieves only the records that contain that value. For example, to retrieve the records with the value of *80,000.00*, type the following:

```
80000
```

You enter only the numbers for which you are searching because field formats, such as the dashes between numeric Social Security numbers (for example, 123-45-6789) are not saved with the data (for example, 123456789) in a field. Therefore, when Approach searches for data in this type of field, it searches only for the numbers, not for the combination of numbers and characters. So, if you fill in a Find request and include the separator characters, Approach will not find your data. However, if you define a Social Security number as a text field and enter a combination of numbers and dashes, you must type the numbers and the dashes as entered to search successfully.

## ▶ *Finding Date Fields*

When finding dates, you can use any numeric date format typed using your current Windows short date default (that is, *mm/dd/yy*). For example, you could find the following:

```
01/01/95
1-1-1995
```

You cannot use a search string such as:

```
January 1, 1995
```

Approach also carefully checks the numbers that you type. For example, typing a month greater than 12 or a day greater than 31 produces an error message. In fact, Approach even checks the month against the day, so you can't type 2/29 except in leap years.

## ▶ *Finding Time Fields*

You can enter time in a Find request using either military or standard format:

```
18:00
6:00 PM
```

## ▶ *Finding Exact Matches*

An exact match finds records that strictly match the conditions entered in a Find request. For example, if you enter either of these lines:

```
=123 Main Street
123 Main Street
```

Approach finds only records that contain exactly that text. Notice that the equal sign is not required in an exact match Find request.

## ▶ *Finding Ranges of Information*

Use range Find requests to retrieve records that contain values that fall within a range specified in the Find environment. For example, you can find all the cities between Albuquerque and Boston in an alphabetic list by typing this:

Albuquerque...Boston

or you can find salaries greater than $16,000 but less than $70,000 by typing this:

16000...70000

 ▶▶ **N O T E**

**You can also find ranges of dates and times.**

## ▶ *Specifying More Than One Condition in a Search*

There are several ways to search using more than one condition. You can combine search criteria in one Find request by entering values in several fields at once. For example, you can find all the records that have a value of **VT** in the State field and a value less than *$25,000* in the Salary field. Simply type the two search criteria in the appropriate fields; type **VT** in the State field and **>25000** in the Salary field.

You can combine search criteria in a single field by separating the values with commas. For example, you can find all the records that have a value of VT or NY in the State field by typing **VT, NY** in the State field.

Another way to combine several search criteria is to create several Find requests *before* pressing Enter, clicking on the Enter SmartIcon, or clicking on the OK button. First, fill in the first Find request as you learned earlier. Then either choose Browse ➤ Find ➤ Find More or press Ctrl+F, and create the next Find request. You can repeat this as many times as necessary. (Note that you won't see the Find More command on the Find submenu until you start the second search; it replaces the Find command at that point.) When you have finished filling in the last Find request, either press Enter, click on the Enter SmartIcon, or click on the OK button.

You can also create multiple Find requests by clicking on the New Condition button on the Action bar in the Find environment to display a new empty Find window. When you have filled in the last Find window, press Enter, click on the Enter SmartIcon, or click on the OK button.

You can use an If statement to create a Find request. An If statement tests conditions and returns either Yes or No. A value of Yes adds a record to the Found Set. Following are some examples of If statements:

**If(Bonus>Salary)**   Tests whether the value in the Bonus field is greater than the value in the Salary field. If Bonus is greater than Salary, Approach returns Yes, thereby adding the record to the Found Set.

**If((State=VT) And (Last Name=A...L))**   Tests whether the value in the State field is *VT* and whether the value in the Last Name field starts with A–L. If both these conditions are true, Approach returns Yes, thereby adding the record to the Found Set.

**If((State=VT) Or (Last Name=A...L))**   Tests whether the value in the State field is *VT* or whether the value in the Last Name field starts with A–L. If either of these conditions is true, Approach returns Yes, thereby adding the record to the Found Set.

## ▶ Repeating a Search

During this work session, you can repeat a search using the same criteria and conditions that you used in the last search. Simply choose Browse ➤ Find ➤ Find Again. Approach displays the most recent Find request, which you can edit. Then go to the Browse environment or press Enter.

# ▶▶ Sorting Records

Now that you know about finding records, you are ready to learn about displaying records in a sorted order. Ordinarily, Approach presents records in the order in which they were entered. However, Approach can arrange records in a database in various orders depending on the field type. Text, memo, and Boolean fields are sorted in alphabetic order; numeric fields are sorted in numeric order; and dates and times are sorted in chronological order. You can sort records as follows:

- in a simple *ascending* (A to Z or 0 to 9) order on one field
- in a simple *descending* (Z to A or 9 to 0) order on one field
- in a complex sort of two or more fields in ascending and/or descending order

You cannot sort PicturePlus or memo fields. All sorts are temporary; when you exit Approach and restart it, the records return to the order in which you added them.

▸▸**N O T E**

> **To permanently keep records in their sorted order, export them to a new database. Choose File ➤ Export Data, specify a new filename, choose a database file type, select whether to export the Found records or all the records, move the fields to be exported, and click on OK. For more information about exporting Approach data, see the *Advanced Approach Techniques* chapter.**

## ▶ Sorting on One Field

To perform a simple Sort on one field, follow these steps:

1. In the Browse environment, click on the field on which you want the records in the database or in the Found Set sorted.

2. To sort in ascending order, either click on the Sort in Ascending Order SmartIcon or choose Browse ➤ Sort ➤ Ascending.

3. To sort in descending order, either click on the Sort in Descending Order SmartIcon or choose Browse ➤ Sort ➤ Descending.

## ▶ Sorting on Multiple Fields

Complex sorts may seem complicated at first, but they are actually quite easy. To sort on more than one field, choose Browse ➤ Sort ➤ Define or press Ctrl+T. Then choose fields and other options in the Sort dialog box (see Figure 16.2).

**FIGURE 16.2** ▶

*This example of a filled-in Sort dialog box shows four sort fields—all ascending.*

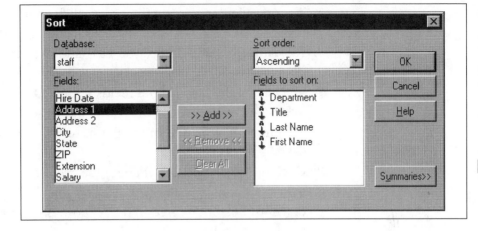

Note that:

- All fields are sorted in ascending order unless you deliberately choose Descending.

- Select the fields in the order in which you want the Sorts to occur—from the largest (such as department), to the next largest (for example, job title within department), to a lower level (for example, last name within job title within department), and so on.

- To add a field to a Sort, either select it in the Fields scroll box and click on the Add button, or double-click on the field.

- To delete a field from a Sort, select it in the Fields to Sort On list and click on the Remove button.

- To delete all fields and start over, click on the Clear All button.

- If you change your mind about the Sort order, delete all the fields below the field that you want to change. Then add the deleted fields in the proper order.

To sort on two or more fields, follow these steps:

1. Choose Browse ➤ Sort ➤ Define or press Ctrl+T. Approach opens the Sort dialog box.

2. In the Fields scroll box, select a field and click on Add to add it to the Fields to Sort On list.

3. To sort a field in descending order, click on it, and then select Descending from the drop-down list box.

4. Repeat steps 2 and 3 until you have added all the desired fields to the Sort.

5. To clear all the fields in the Fields to Sort On box, click on Clear All.

6. To remove one field from the Fields to Sort On box, select it and click on Remove.

7. Click on OK. Approach changes the order of the records.

8. To return to the original order, select All Records from the drop-down list box on the Action bar, choose Browse ▶ Find ▶ Find All, or press Ctrl+A.

# ▶▶ *Using the Named Find/Sort Feature*

If you are working on a complicated Find and/or Sort involving many Find criteria and sorting on several fields, you might want to save the Find or Sort rather than reconstruct it at a later time. You follow the same steps to save a Find/Sort: Run a Find, optionally sort it, choose Create ▶ Named Find/Sort, and in the Named Find/Sort dialog box, name and save it. Saved Find/Sorts are not "carved in stone." Simply use the Named Find/Sort dialog box to edit it, or copy it using a new name and then edit. You can even keep a long list of both Finds and Sorts that you can retrieve and run at any time.

 ▶▶**N O T E**

**A saved Find/Sort is only available for the database in which it was created, named, and saved.**

The Named Find/Sort dialog box (see Figure 16.3) provides the following options:

**Name**  A column showing 20 or more characters of the names of the previously saved Finds and Sorts.

**Find**  A column with checkmarks indicating saved Finds.

**FIGURE 16.3** ▶

*The Named Find/Sort dialog box with several saved Finds and/or Sorts*

**Sort**   A column with checkmarks indicating saved Sorts. Note that checkmarks can appear in both the Find and Sort columns, indicating a Find/Sort combination.

**Edit Name**   A text box in which you type the name for a Find/Sort.

**Edit Find**   A button on which you click to display the Find window in which you can specify additional Find criteria. Clicking on Cancel or pressing Esc closes the window and returns to the Named Find/Sort dialog box.

**Edit Sort**   A button on which you click to display the Sort dialog box in which you can specify additional Sort criteria. Clicking on Cancel or pressing Esc closes the dialog box and returns to the Named Find/Sort dialog box.

**New**   A button on which you click to further define a Find using the current view or using the Find/Sort Assistant (see the following section).

**Copy** A button on which you click to display the Name Find/Sort dialog box in which you can type a name for the Find. You can then edit one copy and keep the other in its original condition.

**Delete** A button on which you click to delete a named Find/Sort. The button is not available for an unnamed Find/Sort. After you click on the Delete button, Approach asks you to confirm the deletion.

**Run** Closes the dialog box and runs the Find and/or Sort.

## ▶ Saving a Find/Sort

To save a new or edited Find/Sort, follow these steps:

1. Choose Create ➤ Named Find/Sort. Approach opens the Named Find/Sort dialog box.

2. Select <Current Find/Sort>, which is the name of an unnamed Find/Sort.

3. In the Edit Name text box, replace <Current Find/Sort> with a unique, descriptive name. It is best, but not required, to keep the name to 35 characters or fewer. You can then see the entire name in the list of Find/Sorts on the right side of the Action bar.

4. Click on Done to save the Find/Sort and close the dialog box.

## ▶ Running a Saved Find/Sort

The quickest way to run a saved Find or Sort is to open the drop-down list box on the right side of the Action bar and select the name of the Find/Sort to be run. Another way to run a saved Find or Sort is to follow these steps:

1. Choose Create ➤ Named Find/Sort.

2. Select the name of a named Find/Sort in the box in the center of the Named Find/Sort dialog box.

3. Click on the Run button. Approach closes the dialog box and runs the Find/Sort.

## ▶ *Editing a Saved Find*

If you have spent some time setting conditions for a Find, have saved it, and then remember another condition to be added or a change from one operator (for example, an equal sign) to another (for example, the less-than or equal sign), you don't have to recreate the Find from scratch; you can edit it instead. To edit a saved Find or the Find part of a Find/Sort, follow these steps:

*1.* Choose Create ➤ Named Find/Sort.

*2.* Select the named Find to be edited. (Remember that there will be a checkmark in the Find column in the Named Find/Sort dialog box.)

*3.* Click on the Edit Find button. Approach opens the Find window with the conditions that you have specified in their fields.

*4.* Add conditions to fields using the instructions in the "Finding Records in a Database" section at the beginning of this chapter.

*5.* Click on OK. Approach displays the Named Find/Sort dialog box.

*6.* If you want to rename the Find, follow the instructions in the "Saving a Find/Sort" section.

*7.* Click on Done to save the Find and close the dialog box.

## ▶ *Editing a Saved Sort*

You also can edit a saved Sort by adding another field to be sorted, removing a sort field, or changing from ascending to descending or from descending to ascending. To edit a saved Sort or the Sort part of a Find/Sort, follow these steps:

*1.* Choose Create ➤ Named Find/Sort.

*2.* Select the named Sort to be edited. (Look for the checkmark in the Sort column in the Named Find/Sort dialog box.)

*3.* Click on the Edit Sort button. Approach opens the Sort dialog box with the previously set Sort options in place.

*4.* Add conditions to fields using the instructions in the "Sorting Records" section in this chapter.

*5.* Click on OK. Approach displays the Named Find/Sort dialog box.

6. If you want to rename the Sort, follow the instructions in the "Saving a Find/Sort" section.

7. Click on Done to save the Sort and close the dialog box.

## ▶ Deleting a Saved Find or Sort

It's a simple matter to delete a saved Find or Sort. Follow these steps:

1. Choose Create ➤ Named Find/Sort.

2. Select the named Find/Sort to be deleted.

3. Click on the Delete button. Approach asks you to confirm the deletion.

4. Click on Yes to delete the named Find/Sort.

# ▶▶ Using the Find/Sort Assistant

The Find/Sort Assistant guides you through the Find process and allows you to sort and/or name a Find. You can use the Find/Sort Assistant to:

- perform a simple search, which can include logical operators such as AND and OR.

- find records with duplicate values in selected fields. Approach sorts the records by the selected fields in order to find the duplicate values.

- find unique records. Approach sorts the records by the selected fields in order to find the unique records.

- find a group of records with either the top or lowest numeric values in selected fields. Approach sorts the records by the selected fields in order to find the desired values.

- find using Query by Box, which enables complex graphical searches and which can include logical operators such as AND and OR.

To open the Find/Sort Assistant dialog box, click on the Find button on the Action bar and click on the Find Assistant button on the Find Action bar, choose Browse ➤ Find ➤ Find Assistant, or press Ctrl+I. When Approach opens the dialog box, select from the Type of Find list. Your choice determines the names on the tabs in the dialog box and the text in the Description box.

## ▶ *Performing a Basic Find with the Find/Sort Assistant*

To perform a basic Find using the Find/Sort Assistant, follow these steps:

1. Click on the Find button on the Action bar and click on the Find Assistant button on the Find Action bar, choose Browse ➤ Find ➤ Find Assistant, or press Ctrl+I. Approach opens the Find/Sort Assistant dialog box (see Figure 16.4).

**FIGURE 16.4** ▶

*The Find/Sort Assistant dialog box with the Basic Find option selected*

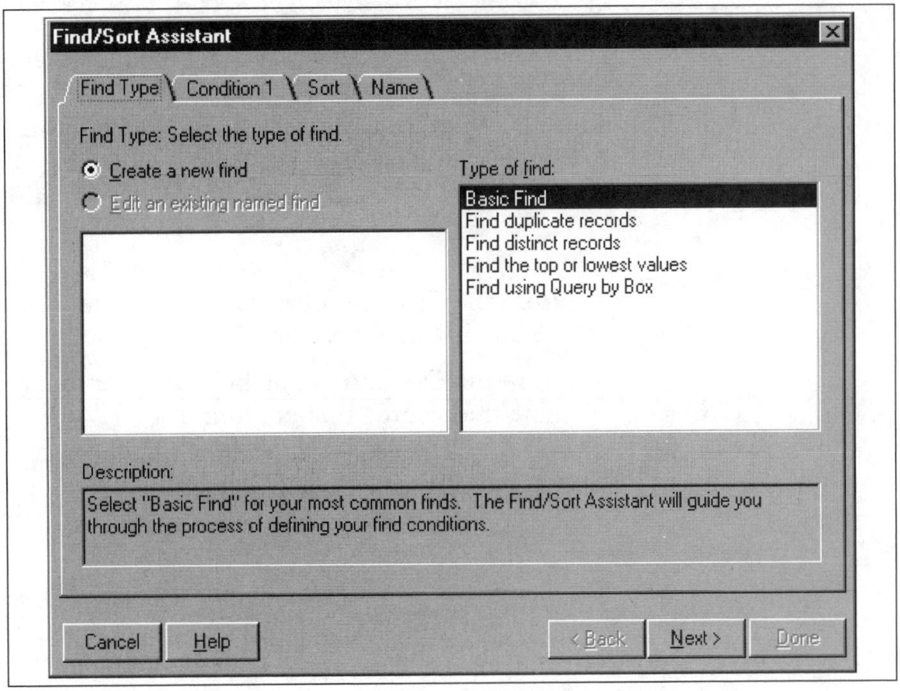

[Figure 16.4 — Find/Sort Assistant dialog box]

**Find/Sort Assistant**

Find Type \ Condition 1 \ Sort \ Name \

Find Type: Select the type of find.

◉ Create a new find
○ Edit an existing named find

Type of find:

Basic Find
Find duplicate records
Find distinct records
Find the top or lowest values
Find using Query by Box

Description:
Select "Basic Find" for your most common finds. The Find/Sort Assistant will guide you through the process of defining your find conditions.

Cancel   Help                    < Back   Next >   Done

2.  Click on the Next button or the Condition 1 tab. Approach opens the Condition 1 section of the Find/Sort Assistant dialog box (see Figure 16.5).

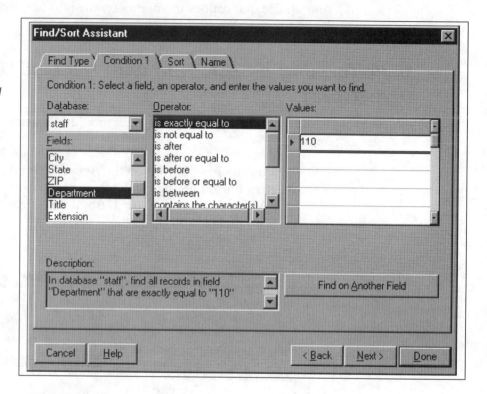

3.  From the Fields scroll box, select a field that will be used to set the conditions for the search.

4.  From the Operator scroll box, select an operator that will determine the records that are found.

5.  In the Values scroll box, type a value for which Approach will search. In the Description box, you will find a query that Approach has created based on your selections.

▶▶▶ **N O T E**

**If you have created radio buttons for a field included in a Find, look for the clicked value of the field (for example, a cost code of 110) rather than the button label (for example, Administration). If the field name is Department and the field label of Department 110 is Administration, specifying "Department is exactly equal to Administration" is incorrect; instead, specify "Department is exactly equal to 110" (see Figure 16.6).**

**6.** To add another condition to the search, click on the Find on Another Field button. Approach adds another Condition section to the dialog box (see Figure 16.6).

**FIGURE 16.6** ▶

*The Find/Sort Assistant dialog box with a second condition specified*

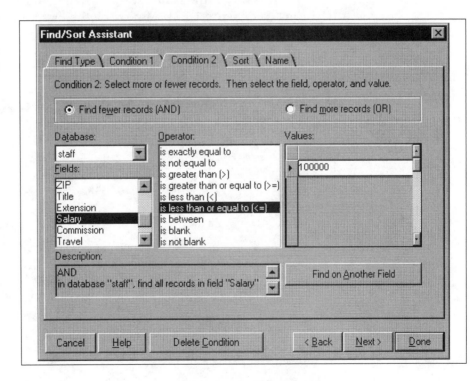

7. Select a logical operator: AND to search for Condition 1 *and* Condition 2, or OR to search for Condition 1 or Condition 2.

8. Select other options (see steps 3, 4, and 5).

9. To add another condition, click on Find on Another Field.

10. To end adding conditions, click on Next or the Sort tab (to specify the conditions for sorting the Found records), click on the Name tab (to name and save the Sort), or click on Done (to run the Find).

11. If you have chosen to sort the Find, fill in the Sort section of the Find/Sort Assistant dialog box in exactly the same way that you would fill in the Sort dialog box (see the "Sorting Records" section in this chapter). Then click on the Name tab (to name and save the Sort), or click on Done (to run the Find).

12. If you have chosen to name the Find, type the name of the Find in the text box in the Name section of the Find/Sort Assistant dialog box (see Figure 16.7). Also check the Description to be sure that you have specified the proper conditions, operators, and values.

13. Click on Done to run the Find.

**FIGURE 16.7** ▶

*The Name section of the Find/Sort Assistant dialog box with the Find name specified*

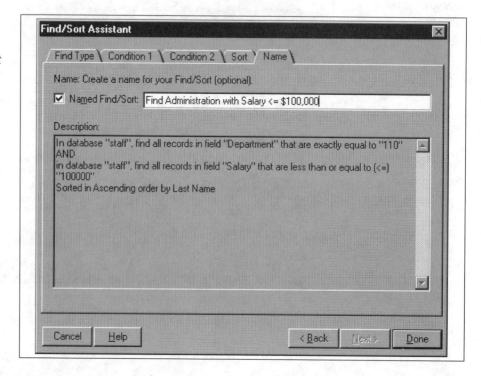

# ▶ *Finding Records with Duplicate Values*

Using the Find/Sort Assistant, you can search through all active records (that is, every record in the database or every Found record) and find records with duplicate values in selected fields. This is especially useful for large databases and for those to which you are constantly adding records. It's a part of good database housekeeping to periodically check for duplicate records.

Note that:

- One way of avoiding records with duplicate values is to make one or two fields unique (for example, a Social Security number or a customer identifier).

- Do not search for duplicate records using a field that may legitimately contain duplicate values (for example, a last name of Smith or Jones, a creation or edit date, or nearby towns).

- Do not use a Boolean field, which has only two values (Yes or No, 1 or 0, and so on), to search for duplicate records.

- You cannot use Memo, PicturePlus, or Variable fields in a search for duplicate records.

To search for duplicate values, follow these steps:

1. Click on the Find button on the Action bar and then click on the Find Assistant button on the Find Action bar, choose Browse ➤ Find ➤ Find Assistant, or press Ctrl+I. Approach opens the Find/Sort Assistant dialog box.

2. Click on Find Duplicate Records in the Type of Find box.

3. Click on the Next button or the Find Duplicates tab. Approach opens the Find Duplicates section of the Find/Sort Assistant dialog box (see Figure 16.8).

4. Select a field and click on the Add button.

5. To exclude the first record in a group of duplicate records from the final results, check the Exclude First Record Found in Each Set of Duplicates checkbox.

**FIGURE 16.8** ►

*The Find Duplicates section of the Find/ Sort Assistant dialog box with a field selected*

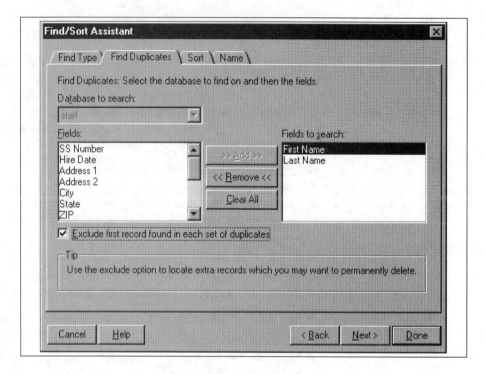

6. To move on, click on Next or on the Sort tab (to specify the conditions for sorting the Found records), click on the Name tab (to name and save the Sort), or click on Done (to run the Find).

7. If you have chosen to sort the Find, fill in the Sort section of the Find/Sort Assistant dialog box in exactly the same way that you would fill in the Sort dialog box (see the "Sorting Records" section in this chapter). Then click on the Name tab (to name and save the Sort), or click on Done (to run the Find).

8. If you have chosen to name the Find, type the name of the Find in the text box in the Name section of the Find/Sort Assistant dialog box. Also check the Description to be sure that you have specified the desired fields and sort conditions.

9. Click on Done to run the Find and optionally sort the results. If Approach finds duplicates, it creates a Found Set. If Approach does not find duplicates, it prompts you to find again.

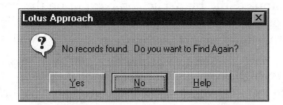

## ▶ *Finding Unique Records Using the Find/Sort Assistant*

In Approach you can search for unique records. For example, if a local government has one database that combines voting, volunteer, school population, and tax record information, there may be several records for each resident—but each resident might not be covered in each category. To prepare and send announcements about a summer festival to as many residents as possible but to avoid duplication, finding unique records based on the street address might be the best way to compile the master list.

To search for records with unique values, follow these steps:

1. Click on the Find button on the Action bar and click on the Find Assistant button on the Find Action bar, choose Browse ➤ Find ➤ Find Assistant, or press Ctrl+I. Approach opens the Find/Sort Assistant dialog box.

2. Click on Find Distinct Records in the Type of Find box.

3. Click on the Next button or the Find Distinct tab. Approach opens the Find Distinct section of the Find/Sort Assistant dialog box (see Figure 16.9).

4. Select a unique field, and click on Add.

5. Add fields by repeating step 4 until you have filled in the Fields To Search list with all the fields by which you want to restrict the search. Every time you add a field, you narrow the scope of the Find.

6. To complete the Find, click on Next or on the Sort tab (to specify the conditions for sorting the Found records), click on the Name tab (to name and save the Sort), or click on Done (to run the Find).

7. If you have chosen to sort the Find, fill in the Sort section of the Find/Sort Assistant dialog box in exactly the same way that you would fill in the Sort dialog box (see the "Sorting Records" section in this chapter). Then click on the Name tab (to name and save the Sort), or click on Done (to run the Find).

8. If you have chosen to name the Find, type the name of the Find in the text box in the Name section of the Find/Sort Assistant dialog box. Also check the Description to be sure that you have specified the desired fields and sort conditions.

9. Click on Done to run the Find and optionally sort the results. If Approach finds unique records, it creates a Found Set. If Approach does not find unique records, it prompts you to find again.

**FIGURE 16.9** ▶

*The Find Distinct section of the Find/Sort Assistant dialog box with two fields selected*

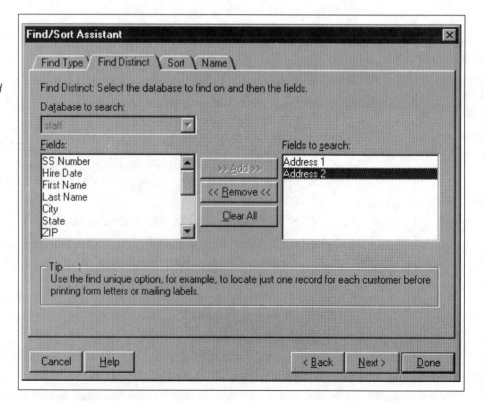

# ► *Finding Highest and Lowest Values Using the Find/Sort Assistant*

You can find the highest or lowest valued fields in a database using the Find/Sort Assistant. You can look for the highest- or lowest-paid employees, those with the earliest or most recent hiring dates, those with the top commissions, or even those with last names beginning with letters near the beginning or the end of the alphabet.

To search for records with the highest or lowest values, follow these steps:

1. Click on the Find button on the Action bar and click on the Find Assistant button on the Find Action bar, choose Browse ➤ Find ➤ Find Assistant, or press Ctrl+I. Approach opens the Find/Sort Assistant dialog box.

2. Click on Find the Top or Lowest Values in the Type of Find box.

3. Click on the Next button or the Find Top/Lowest tab. Approach opens the Find Top/Lowest section of the Find/Sort Assistant dialog box (see Figure 16.10).

4. From the drop-down list box, select Top, Top(%), Lowest, or Lowest(%).

5. If you have chosen Top or Lowest, select or type a value in the Values text/option box. Valid values range from 1 to 1000.

6. If you have chosen Top(%) or Lowest(%), open the drop-down list box and select a value from 10% to 100%.

7. Select a field containing the values that will determine the top or lowest records found.

8. To complete the Find, click on Next or on the Sort tab (to specify the conditions for sorting the found records), click on the Name tab (to name and save the Sort), or click on Done (to run the Find).

9. If you have chosen to sort the Find, fill in the Sort section of the Find/Sort Assistant dialog box in exactly the same way that you would fill in the Sort dialog box (see the "Sorting Records" section in this chapter). Then click on the Name tab (to name and save the Sort), or click on Done (to run the Find).

**FIGURE 16.10** ►

*The Find Top/Lowest section of the Find/Sort Assistant dialog box with Salary selected*

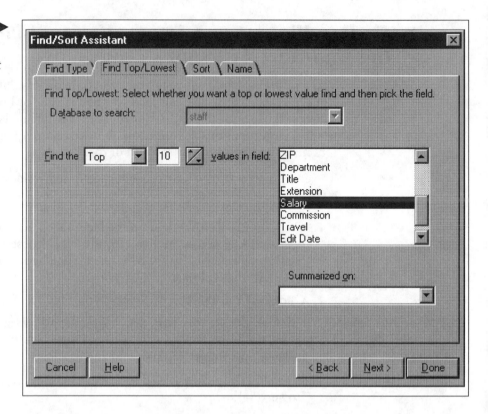

10. If you have chosen to name the Find, type the name of the Find in the text box in the Name section of the Find/Sort Assistant dialog box. Also check the Description to be sure that you have specified the desired fields and sort conditions.

11. Click on Done to run the Find and optionally sort the results.

## ► Using the Query by Box Feature of the Find/Sort Assistant

Query by Box is a simple way to build a Find with several conditions linked by ANDs (which narrow the search by testing multiple conditions and finding only those that match) and/or ORs (which widen the search by testing multiple conditions and finding any of those that match). Just select a field and an operator, type a value, add a logical

Manipulating Data

operator (that is, AND or OR), add other conditions linked by logical operators, optionally sort and name, and then run the Find. To build a Find using Query by Box, follow these steps:

1. Click on the Find button on the Action bar and click on the Find Assistant button on the Find Action bar, choose Browse ➤ Find ➤ Find Assistant, or press Ctrl+I. Approach opens the Find/Sort Assistant dialog box.

2. Click on Find Using Query by Box in the Type of Find box.

3. Click on the Next button or the Query by Box tab. Approach opens the Query by Box section of the Find/Sort Assistant dialog box (see Figure 16.11).

4. From the Field drop-down list box, select a field on which the condition will be tested.

Ch. **16**

**FIGURE 16.11** ▶

*The Query by Box section of the Find/Sort Assistant dialog box with two Find conditions linked by an AND logical operator*

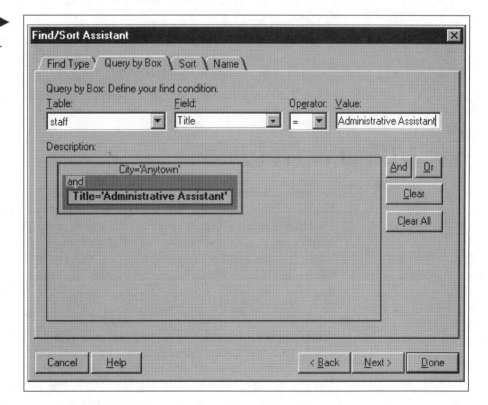

5. From the Operator drop-down list box, select an operator to tell Approach how to test the condition.

6. In the Value text box, type a value.

7. Click on the And button to add an AND logical operator, or click on the Or button to add an OR logical operator.

8. Repeat steps 4, 5, and 6 to add another statement to the Find, following each statement but the last with an And or an Or selection.

9. To complete the Find, click on Next or on the Sort tab (to specify the conditions for sorting the found records), click on the Name tab (to name and save the Sort), or click on Done (to run the Find).

10. If you have chosen to sort the Find, fill in the Sort section of the Find/Sort Assistant dialog box in exactly the same way that you would fill in the Sort dialog box (see the "Sorting Records" section in this chapter). Then click on the Name tab (to name and save the Sort), or click on Done (to run the Find).

11. If you have chosen to name the Find, type the name of the Find in the text box in the Name section of the Find/Sort Assistant dialog box. Also check the Description to be sure that you have specified the desired fields and sort conditions.

12. Click on Done to run the Find and optionally sort the results.

# ▶▶ Filling a Field

A very useful but potentially dangerous Approach feature is the Browse ➤ Fill Field command. Use Fill Field to add the same value to a selected field in a Found Set or in every record in the active database. Keep in mind, however, that when you use this command, any value currently in the field is replaced. For example, if you want to insert a comment in a memo field or a bonus in a currency field, all contents of that field (including other comments and previous bonuses, respectively) will be overwritten. Once you fill a field, you cannot undo it.

A useful way to use the Fill Field command is to put an initial value in a field that you have just added to a database in which you have been working for some time. For example, if you add a creation date field some time after creating the database and after you have added many records, you can specify an initial value of Creation Date for new records created after adding the field. For all those existing records, however, you can use Fill Field to insert the date on which you created the database or even the date on which you added the creation date field. In the following steps, we will insert author's initials in a field that is used to credit the author of a record.

To fill a field in the active database, follow these steps:

1. Choose Browse ➤ Fill Field. Approach opens the Fill Field dialog box (see Figure 16.12).

2. Select the field in which you want to insert a fill value.

3. In the To the Following scroll box, type the fill value.

4. To add a fill formula, click on the Formula button and fill in the Formula dialog box.

**FIGURE 16.12** ▶

*The Fill Field dialog box with a field selected and a fill value typed in the To the Following scroll box*

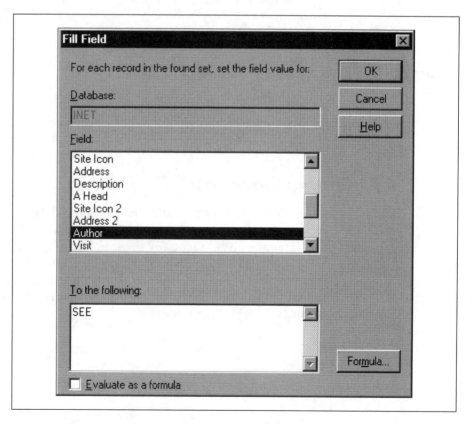

**5.** To evaluate the fill value as a formula, check the Evaluate As a Formula checkbox.

**6.** Click on OK to close the dialog box. Approach starts filling records, showing you the status along the way.

 ▶▶**T I P**

> **To delete the contents of a field (that is, to fill it with spaces), choose Browse ➤ Fill Field. In the Fill Field dialog box, select a field from the Field scroll box. Leave the To the Following scroll box empty and click on OK. Approach opens a message box asking if you want to delete all data for the selected field. If you click on Yes, Approach fills the selected field with spaces. If you click on No, Approach closes the message box and returns to the Fill Field dialog box.**

# ▶▶ *Joining Two Databases*

As you learned in the *Planning and Creating Your First Database* chapter, Approach is a relational database in which several databases can work together to produce reports, mailing labels, and form letters.

## ▶ *Designing Databases for Joining*

Before joining databases and designing the databases that will form a related set of databases, determine the *join field*, the field that connects the databases; it is essentially the same field in the joined databases. For example, in the STAFF database, the join field should be SS Number, the Social Security number. Even though employees can have the same first and last names or the same address, each employee's Social Security number is unique.

Let's say that you will design a database that holds travel information for any employees who travel for the business. Other than adding SS Number, the join field, you don't need to duplicate any other fields. For example, if you periodically send a travel report to your employees, you can incorporate the name and address from the main database STAFF with the information in the *detail database* TRAVEL.

There are three possible types of relationships between the main database and detail databases: one-to-one, one-to-many, and many-to-one.

- The *one-to-one* relationship associates one record from each database. This enables you to look up and possibly display the contents of the looked-up record in a database when you type an identifier in a field in the other database.

- The *one-to-many* relationship associates one record in one database and several records in the other database.

- The *many-to-one* relationship associates several records in one database with one record in the other.

Figure 16.13 shows a filled-in data-entry form for the detail database TRAVEL. Notice that this database has one field, SS Number, in common with the main database STAFF.

**FIGURE 16.13** ▶

*The detail database TRAVEL form*

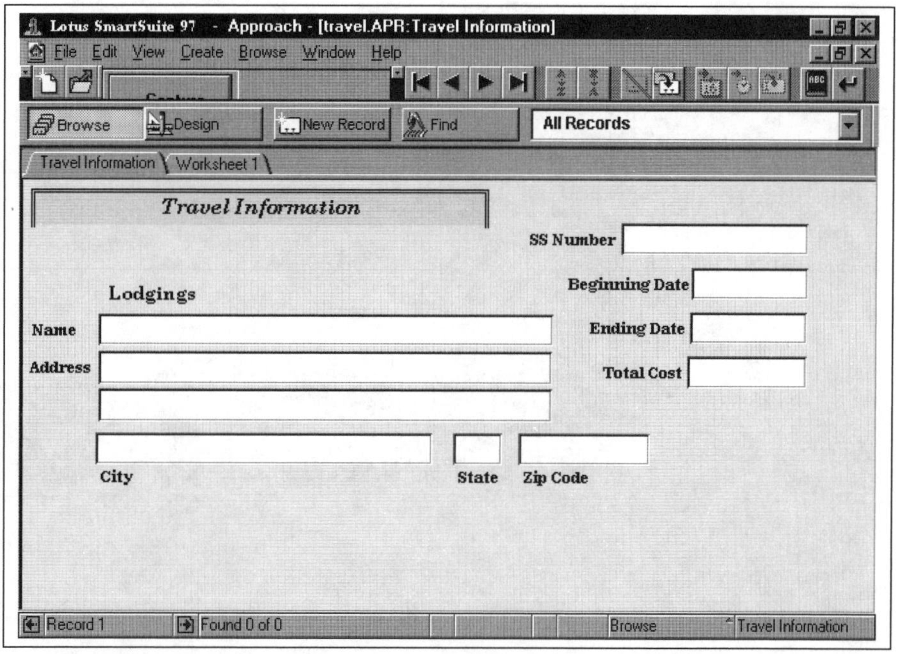

Manipulating Data

▶▶

*Ch.*
**16**

## ► Joining Databases

Approach allows you to join a maximum of 10 databases to a view file. To join two database files, follow these steps:

1. Open the main database and go to Design.

2. Choose Create ➤ Join. Approach displays the Join dialog box (see Figure 16.14), which shows the name of the main database and lists its fields.

3. Either click on Open or press Enter. Approach displays the Open dialog box (see Figure 16.15), which lists the available database files.

**FIGURE 16.14** ►

*The Join dialog box, in which you join two or more databases*

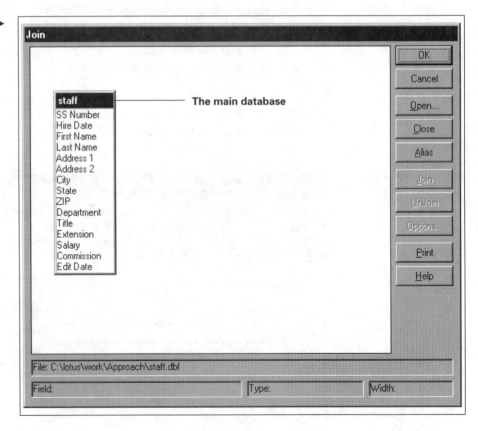

**FIGURE 16.15** ▶

*The Open dialog box, from which you select a detail database to be joined to the main database*

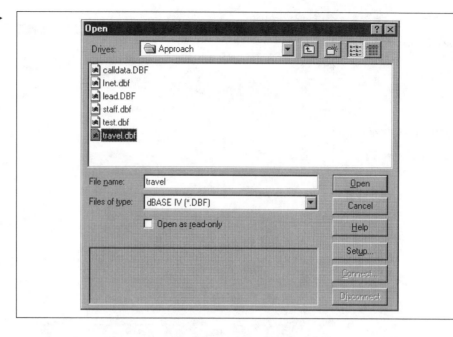

**4.** Double-click on a database name in the box in the center of the dialog box. Approach adds the list of detail database fields to the Join dialog box.

**5.** In the Join dialog box, click on the join fields in both lists and click on the Join button. Approach draws a line between the join fields (see Figure 16.16).

**6.** To join more databases, repeat steps 3, 4, and 5.

**7.** When you have finished joining databases, click on OK. (If OK is dimmed, the joins are not valid.)

## ▶ Adding a Repeating Panel to a Form

Once you have joined databases, you can display the data from the detail database in a repeating panel in the main database. A *repeating panel* displays records in a one-to-many relationship. Once you display

**FIGURE 16.16** ▶

*The Join dialog box, with the detail database added*

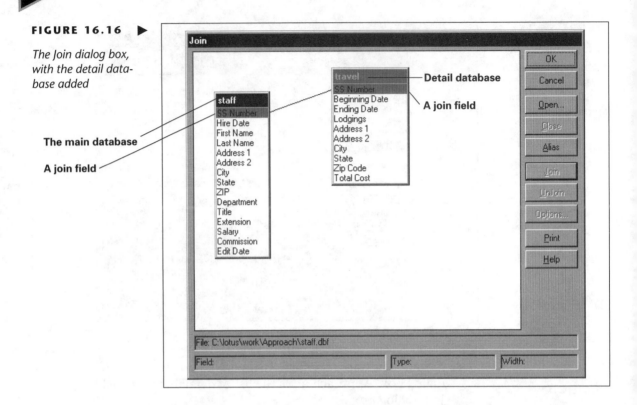

a record on your desktop, the repeating panel displays one of possibly many records related to the current record. To add a repeating panel, follow these steps:

1. Open the main database and go to Design.

2. Choose Create ➤ Add Repeating Panel. Approach displays the Add Repeating Panel dialog box (see Figure 16.17).

3. In the Number of Lines text box, type the number of records (as individual lines) to be displayed in the repeating panel at one time. It's a good idea not to go above the default of 5.

4. Choose the name of the detail database from the Database drop-down list box. This step is necessary when more than one detail database is joined to the main database.

5. Select a field to be included in the repeating panel and click on Add (or simply double-click on the field name). Approach adds the field name to the Fields to Place in Panel box (see Figure 16.18).

**FIGURE 16.17** ▶

*The Add Repeating Panel dialog box, in which you create a repeating panel*

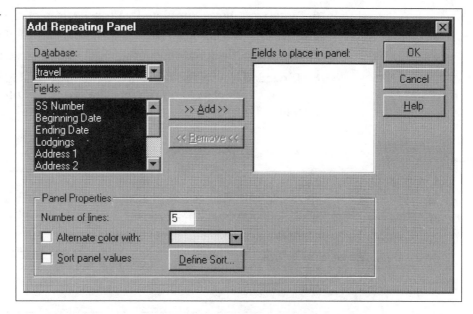

**FIGURE 16.18** ▶

*The Add Repeating Panel dialog box with fields selected for the repeating panel*

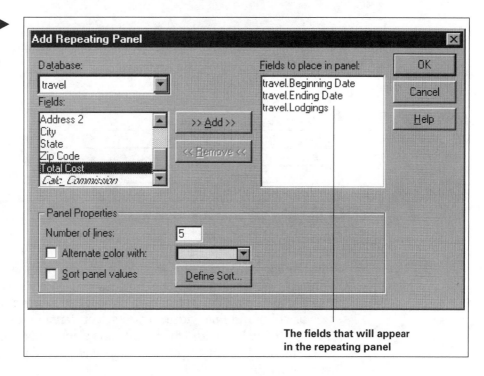

**The fields that will appear in the repeating panel**

6. When you have completed your selection, click on OK. Approach adds the repeating panel to the main database form.
7. If needed, drag the repeating panel to a new location on the form.
8. If needed, resize the repeating panel by pressing and holding down the Ctrl key and moving the mouse pointer to the top of the panel. Drag the side of the panel until it's the desired size (see Figure 16.19).

**FIGURE 16.19** ▶

*You can drag the edge of a repeating panel to change its dimensions.*

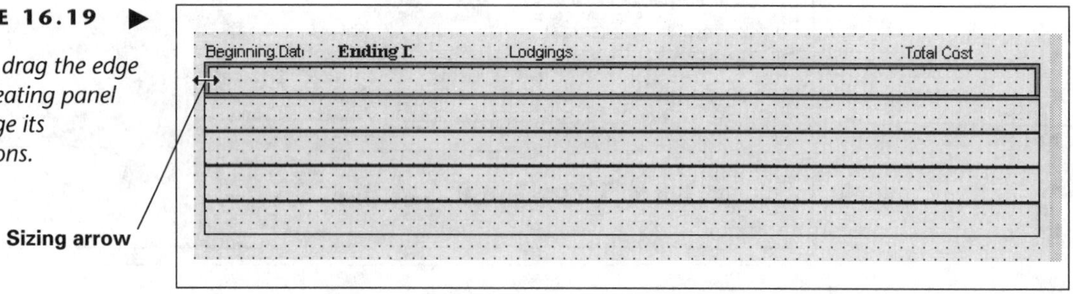

Beginning Dat
Ending I
Lodgings
Total Cost
Sizing arrow

9. If needed, format the fields in the repeating panel using Style menu commands. Figure 16.20 shows an example of a repeating panel in the STAFF database.

**FIGURE 16.20** ▶

*The STAFF repeating panel in the Design environment*

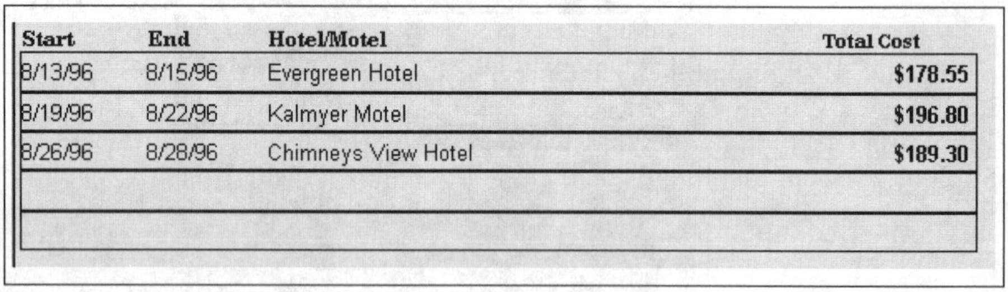

Start
End
Hotel/Motel
Total Cost
8/13/96
8/15/96
Evergreen Hotel
$178.55
8/19/96
8/22/96
Kalmyer Motel
$196.80
8/26/96
8/28/96
Chimneys View Hotel
$189.30

You can edit or change the appearance of a repeating panel by pointing within the borders of the panel and clicking with the right mouse button. This reveals a menu from which you can select editing options such as color and line width. If you select Panel Options, Approach opens a dialog box with which you can select fields from another database, change the number of lines displayed, and change the color on every other line of the panel.

# CHAPTER 17

# Reporting on Your Database

►► **S**o far, we've covered entering, finding, and sorting Approach data, all of which provide a useful background for creating reports and mail merge documents. In this chapter you'll find out how to create Standard and Columnar reports and how to edit and format them. Next, you'll learn about calculating in Approach reports, creating a summary report using calculations, and creating and manipulating crosstab reports. Finally, you'll learn about mail merge documents: form letters and mailing labels.

## ►► Approach Reports

In Approach, a variety of reports are available to you: Blank (for custom reports), Standard, Columnar, Summary, Repeating Panel, and Crosstab. The Report Assistant and the Crosstab Assistant provide help with creating reports. The most common report types are described below.

### ► The Standard Report

The Standard report shows selected data from the current database with fields from each record in their own section. The contents of each record are separated by a heavy horizontal line.

The Standard report looks like a form and is actually an Approach view. Figure 17.1 shows you an unformatted page from a standard report.

### ► The Columnar Report

In a Columnar report fields are arranged in columns; each column holds the contents of the same field from different records. Rows hold all the selected fields from individual records. Figure 17.2 displays an unsorted and unformatted Columnar report.

**FIGURE 17.1** ▶

*A Standard report displays selected fields a few records at a time.*

Header ——

Footer ——

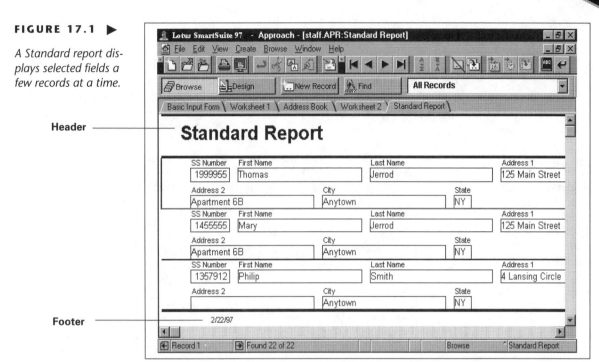

**FIGURE 17.2** ▶

*A Columnar report displays fields in columns and records in rows.*

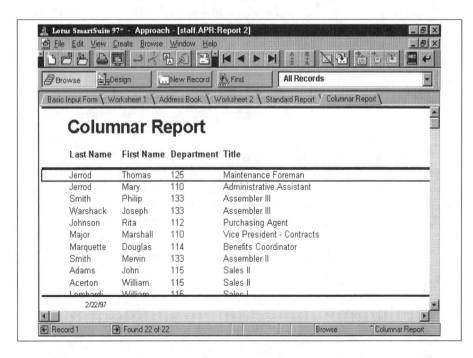

## ▶ The Summary Report

Summary reports display summary information for a group of records. Depending on the type of report you select, Approach shows or does not show other details from the database. Figure 17.3 displays a Summary report.

**FIGURE 17.3 ▶**

*A Summary report displays summary information and optionally other details from the current database.*

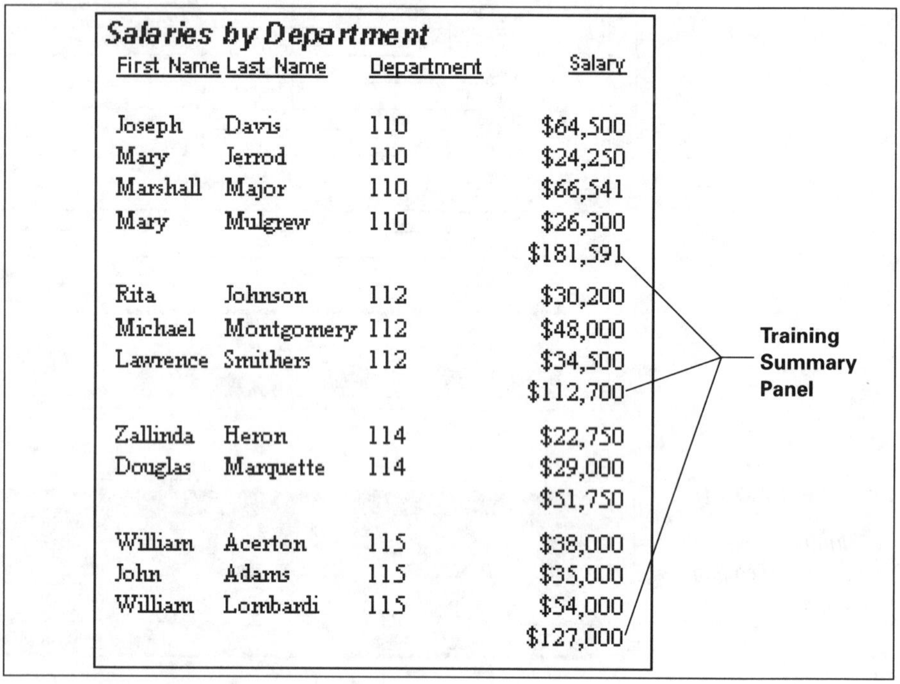

**Salaries by Department**

| First Name | Last Name | Department | Salary |
|------------|-----------|------------|--------|
| Joseph | Davis | 110 | $64,500 |
| Mary | Jerrod | 110 | $24,250 |
| Marshall | Major | 110 | $66,541 |
| Mary | Mulgrew | 110 | $26,300 |
| | | | $181,591 |
| Rita | Johnson | 112 | $30,200 |
| Michael | Montgomery | 112 | $48,000 |
| Lawrence | Smithers | 112 | $34,500 |
| | | | $112,700 |
| Zallinda | Heron | 114 | $22,750 |
| Douglas | Marquette | 114 | $29,000 |
| | | | $51,750 |
| William | Acerton | 115 | $38,000 |
| John | Adams | 115 | $35,000 |
| William | Lombardi | 115 | $54,000 |
| | | | $127,000 |

**Training Summary Panel**

## ▶ The Custom Report

Most of the time you'll use the Standard or Columnar layout when you create a report. If you want to start out with a blank page and build from there, however, use a Custom report. You can then add fields, a header, a footer, and a title page using commands on the Report menu. Figure 17.4 displays a Custom report from the Approach Contacts database.

FIGURE 17.4 ▶

*This Custom report displays a summary report with many customized features.*

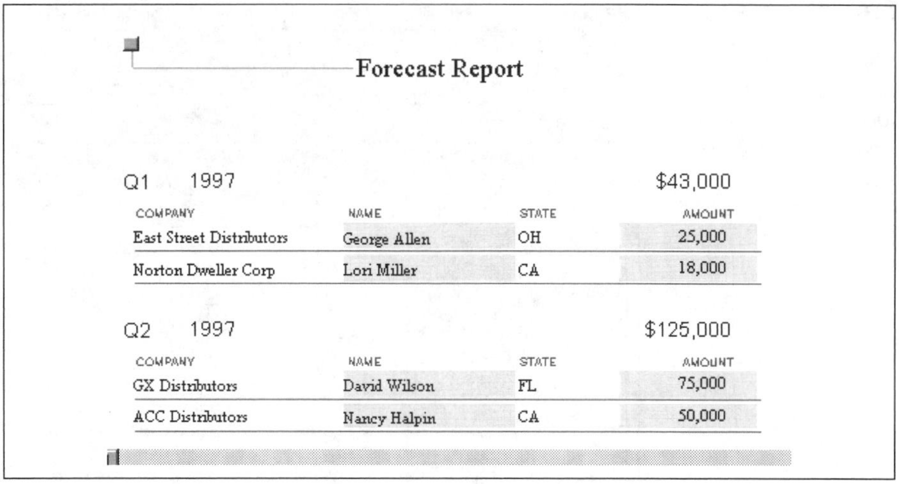

## ▶ *The Crosstab Report*

Crosstabulations, or crosstabs, are sophisticated worksheets that analyze or summarize data from many records. A crosstab typically shows data using at least three variables: one for the rows, another for the columns, and a third for the contents of the crosstab. You can rearrange Approach crosstabs by dragging row and column labels to new locations: to new row or column locations, from row to column, or from column to row. Figure 17.5 shows part of a sample Crosstab report.

# ▶ ▶ *Creating a Standard Report with the Report Assistant*

To create a Standard report, follow these steps:

*1.* Open the database for which you want to create a report and go to Design.

*2.* Choose Create ➤ Report. Approach displays the Report Assistant dialog box (see Figure 17.6).

*3.* Type the report name in the View Name & Title text box.

*4.* Click on Standard in the Layout scroll box.

Database
Reporting

▶ ▶
Ch.
**17**

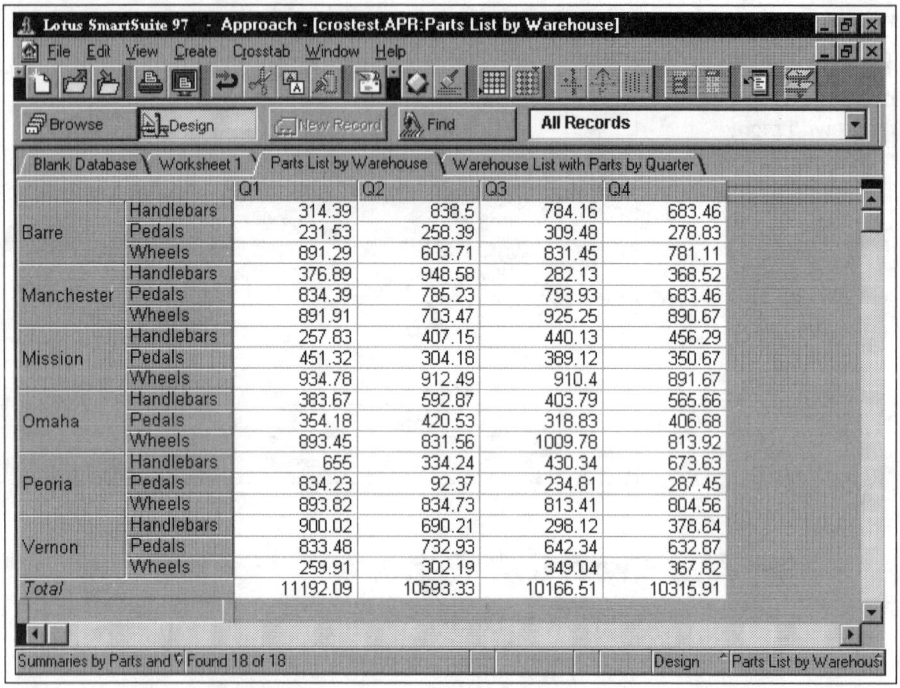
Lotus SmartSuite 97 - Approach - [crostest.APR:Parts List by Warehouse]
File Edit View Create Crosstab Window Help
Browse
Design
New Record
Find
All Records
Blank Database
Worksheet 1
Parts List by Warehouse
Warehouse List with Parts by Quarter
Q1 Q2 Q3 Q4
Barre Handlebars 314.39 838.5 784.16 683.46
Pedals 231.53 258.39 309.48 278.83
Wheels 891.29 603.71 831.45 781.11
Manchester Handlebars 376.89 948.58 282.13 368.52
Pedals 834.39 785.23 793.93 683.46
Wheels 891.91 703.47 925.25 890.67
Mission Handlebars 257.83 407.15 440.13 456.29
Pedals 451.32 304.18 389.12 350.67
Wheels 934.78 912.49 910.4 891.67
Omaha Handlebars 383.67 592.87 403.79 565.66
Pedals 354.18 420.53 318.83 406.68
Wheels 893.45 831.56 1009.78 813.92
Peoria Handlebars 655 334.24 430.34 673.63
Pedals 834.23 92.37 234.81 287.45
Wheels 893.82 834.73 813.41 804.56
Vernon Handlebars 900.02 690.21 298.12 378.64
Pedals 833.48 732.93 642.34 632.87
Wheels 259.91 302.19 349.04 367.82
Total 11192.09 10593.33 10166.51 10315.91
Summaries by Parts and
Found 18 of 18
Design
Parts List by Warehous

**FIGURE 17.5 ▶**

*This Crosstab report displays warehouse locations, a parts list, and the value of the parts.*

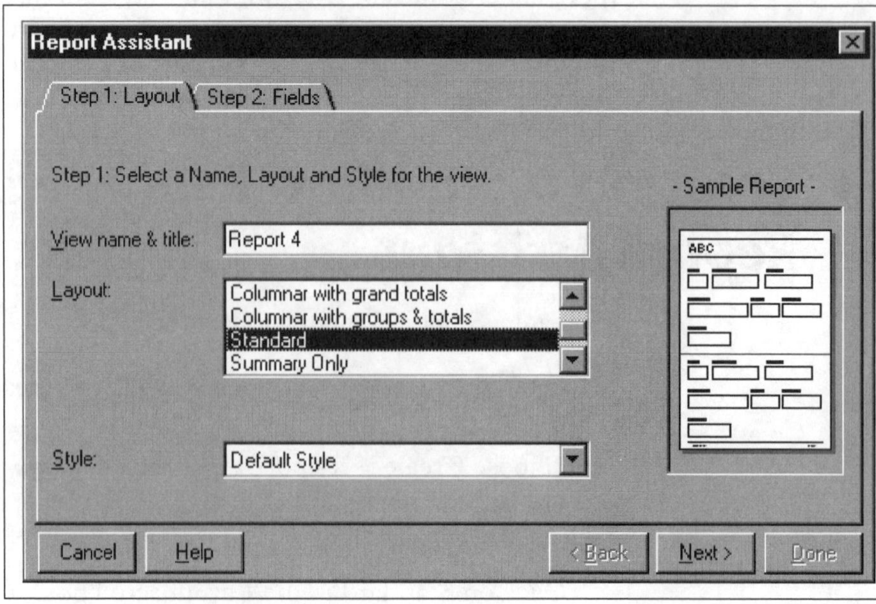
Report Assistant
Step 1: Layout
Step 2: Fields
Step 1: Select a Name, Layout and Style for the view.
- Sample Report -
View name & title:
Report 4
Layout:
Columnar with grand totals
Columnar with groups & totals
Standard
Summary Only
Style:
Default Style
Cancel
Help
< Back
Next >
Done

**FIGURE 17.6 ▶**

*Using the Report Assistant dialog box, you can create Custom, Columnar, Standard, and Summary reports.*

5. Select a style from the Style drop-down list box. The Sample Report box shows the general appearance of the report.

6. Click on the Next button. Approach displays the Step 2: Fields section (see Figure 17.7) of the Report Assistant dialog box.

**FIGURE 17.7** ▶

*Define report fields in the Step 2: Fields section of the Report Assistant dialog box.*

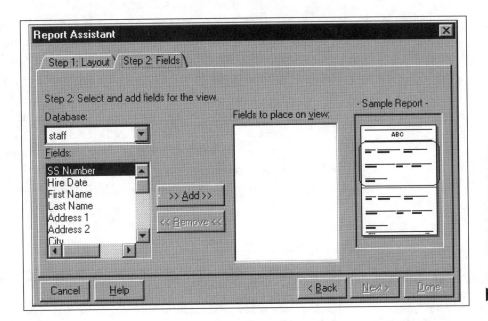

7. In the Fields scroll box, click on a field to be displayed, and then click on Add to insert a field in the Fields to Place on View box. (You can also insert a field in the Fields to Place on View box by double-clicking on it.) The sample box shows the area of the report in which the fields will be inserted.

8. Select the remaining fields for the report, in the order in which you want them to appear, from left to right and from top to bottom of the report page.

9. Click on Done. Approach closes the dialog box, displays the report in the Design environment, and inserts the report name on the View list on the Status bar and on a tab right below the SmartIcons. Figure 17.8 shows a formatted Standard report in the Print Preview environment.

10. Save the Approach file.

**Database Reporting**

**Ch. 17**

▶▶ **T I P**

> Most people like to see reports that are sorted in some way. If you forget to sort the database or the Found Set before creating the report, don't worry. After the report appears on your screen, choose Report ➤ Sort ➤ Define or press Ctrl+T. Fill in the Sort dialog box, as you learned in the *Retrieving and Sorting Data and Joining Databases* chapter, and then click on OK to run the Sort. Remember that if you have saved the Sort in an earlier Approach session, you can select it from the drop-down list box at the right side of the Action bar. Unless you saved it, a Sort lasts only as long as the current Approach session; the next time you start Approach, the report will be "sorted" in the order in which you added records to the database.

**FIGURE 17.8** ▶

*Part of a formatted Standard report in the Print Preview environment*

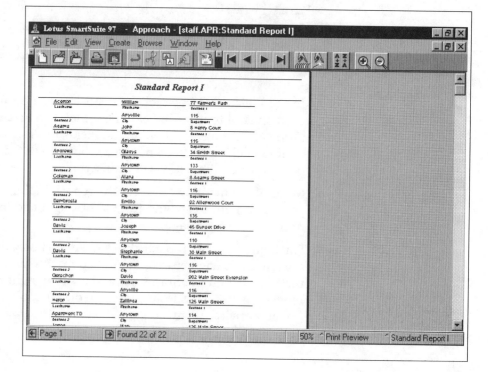

# ▶▶ *Creating a Columnar Report with the Report Assistant*

To create a Columnar report, follow these steps:

1. Open the database for which you want to create a report and go to Design.

2. Choose Create ➤ Report. Approach displays the Report Assistant dialog box (see Figure 17.9).

**FIGURE 17.9 ▶**

*The Report Assistant dialog box with a report name, layout, and style selected*

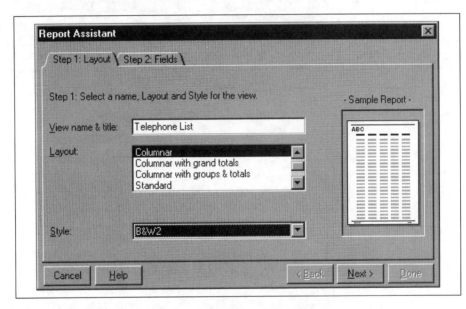

3. Type the report name in the View Name & Title text box.

4. Click on Columnar in the Layout scroll box.

5. Select a style from the Style drop-down list box.

6. Click on the Next button. Approach displays the Step 2: Fields section of the dialog box.

7. From the Database Fields scroll box, click on a field to be displayed, and then click on Add to insert a field in the Fields to Place on View box. (You can also insert a field in the Fields to Place on View box by double-clicking on it.)

**8.** Select the remaining fields for the report, in the order in which you want them to appear, from left to right.

**9.** Click on Done. Approach closes the dialog box, displays the report in the Design environment, and inserts the report name on the View list on the Status bar and on a tab in the View bar. Figure 17.10 shows a formatted columnar report in the Print Preview environment.

**10.** Save the Approach file.

FIGURE 17.10 ▶

*An example of a formatted Columnar report in the Print Preview environment*

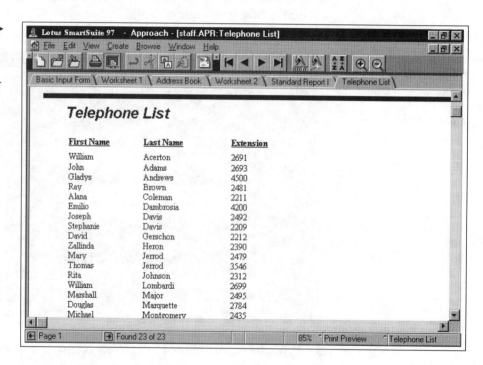

## ▶▶ *Editing a Report*

You can add information to reports by using headers, footers, and title pages. You can also add columns to a Standard report, adjust the spacing between columns, and fill in or remove blank spaces. In this section, you'll learn how to edit reports. In a following section, you'll find out how to create a Custom report.

> **T I P**
>
> **To enhance a report (for example, to change the font, apply boldface, reduce the point size, and so on), use the InfoBox. For a synopsis of Approach InfoBox options, see the *Planning and Creating Your First Database* chapter. For general InfoBox information, refer to the *Editing in SmartSuite Applications* chapter.**

## ▶ *Inserting Headers and Footers*

In Standard and Summary Only reports, Approach adds headers and footers. In Columnar reports, Approach adds column headers. The *header*, which is an area at the top of each page, and the *footer*, which is an area at the bottom of the page, contain information that appears on every page (for example, the date, your name, report name, page number, or your company name).

To customize, turn off, or turn on a header or a footer, follow these steps:

1. Open the database for which you have created a report and go to Design.

2. Click on the tab for the report and choose Report ➤ Add Header to add or remove a header, or choose Report ➤ Add Footer to add or remove a footer. (A checkmark preceding the menu command indicates that Approach has added a header and/or a footer.)

3. To insert an object in a header or a footer, click on a button in the tools palette. (If the tools palette is not on your computer screen, choose View ➤ Show Tools Palette or press Ctrl+L.) Draw a box in the header or footer pane by clicking one side of the box and dragging diagonally to the other side. For more information about SmartSuite drawing tools, see the *Creating Pictures* chapter.

4. To enter text, click twice (but not as fast as a double-click) within the text box and start typing.

5. To insert the page number in the header or the footer, click within the text box, and choose Text ➤ Insert ➤ Page Number.

▶▶**N O T E**

Text is a context-sensitive menu name. So whether the name of the menu between Create and Window is Text, Report, Panel, or something else, you'll find the Insert command and the Page Number subcommand when you open the menu.

▶▶**T I P**

Because you can also type normal text in the text box, you can type the word *Page* and then insert the page number.

**6.** To insert your current computer system clock date, click within the text box and choose Text ➤ Insert ➤ Today's Date.

**7.** To embed an object such as a Paintbrush picture, copy and paste using the Clipboard and the Copy, Cut, and/or Paste commands from the Edit menu. (Remember that you can double-click on an embedded object to edit it in the application in which it was created while remaining in the current application.)

## ▶ Adding a Title Page

You can create a unique first page for a report. The page looks like every other page in the report, but can contain its own header and/or footer and report information. To add a title page to a report, follow these steps:

**1.** Open the database for which you want to create a report and go to Design.

**2.** Choose Report ➤ Add Title Page to insert a new header pane, entitled Title Page Header, and a footer pane, entitled Title Page Footer, on the first page of the report. Approach places a checkmark in front of the Add Title Page command.

**3.** Follow steps 3 through 7 in the preceding section to embed text, the page number, today's date, or a graphic in the header and/or footer pane.

Choose Report ➤ Add Title Page to remove a title page. Approach removes the checkmark that precedes the Add Title Page command.

# ▶ *Moving and Resizing Fields or Parts of a Report*

Blank spaces occur in an Approach report when you decrease font size, when the body panel is too large, or when the data in a field is much shorter than the maximum size of a field.

To move fields or parts of a report, go to Design, click on the field, and drag it to its new location.

You can change the size of a section only by moving its bottom border up or down. To change the size of a section in a report, click within the section, and move the mouse pointer to the bottom border. Move the mouse pointer until it changes to a double-headed arrow, and then drag the bottom border until the size of the section is appropriate.

To adjust the size of a field box so that its contents fit properly, click on the field and move the mouse pointer to a handle. When the mouse pointer changes to a double-headed arrow, drag the handle to change the dimensions of the field box.

To adjust the size of a column in a Columnar report, click anywhere within the column. Move the mouse pointer to the right side of the selected column. When the mouse pointer changes to a double-headed arrow, drag to reduce or increase the width of the column. Approach adjusts the position of the columns to the right of the column that you changed.

To move a column in a Columnar report, click anywhere within the column. Move the mouse pointer within the column. When the mouse pointer looks like a hand, drag the column to the left or to the right. Approach adjusts the position of the columns to the right of the column that you changed.

## ► Changing the Number of Columns in a Standard or a Columnar Report

You can change the number of columns on a page for a Standard or a Columnar report. For example, if the report extends only from the left margin to the center of the page, you might be able to print two columns and save paper.

 ►► N O T E

> Do not confuse the columns in a Columnar report with the columns on a page, which you are changing using the instructions in this section. By default, a page is composed of one column, stretching from the left margin to the right margin. Even a Columnar report, made up of one or more columns, takes up one page column. So, when you change to multiple columns on a page, you are not changing the format of the Columnar report; you are changing the number of columns on which that report appears.

To change the number of columns in a report, follow these steps:

1. Open the database, click on the tab for the report, and go to Design.

2. Double-click on a report element. Approach opens the InfoBox.

3. Select Report: *reporttitle* from the Properties For drop-down list box (see Figure 17.11).

4. Click on the Basics tab.

5. Select the number in the Number of Columns text box and overtype a new number.

6. Close the InfoBox. Approach converts the report to a two-column format. Figure 17.12 shows a three-column Columnar report in two columns.

**FIGURE 17.11** ▶

*In the Basics section of the InfoBox, you can change the number of columns in a report.*

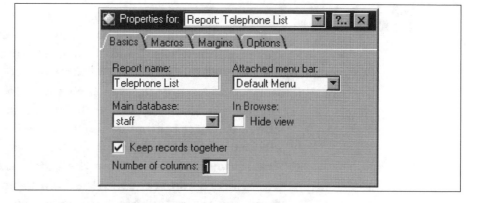

**FIGURE 17.12** ▶

*A three-column Columnar report displayed in two columns with new column labels in a text block*

**A text block containing column labels**

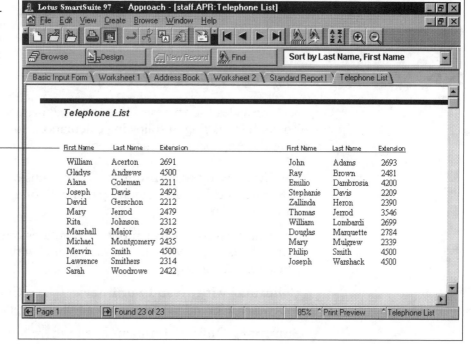

▶▶**N O T E**

**The second column in a two-column layout does not have column labels. To label both sets of columns, click on the Text Block tool in the tools palette. Draw a long horizontal text block, type the column labels, and format or enhance as you wish. Then remove the labels above the first column by opening the InfoBox, clicking on the Label option button in the Text section, and removing the text from the Label Text text box. If you want to adjust the newly added column labels, move the entire text block down toward the fields. (You cannot remove or reduce the space that the labels occupied.)**

# ▶▶ *Summarizing Your Data*

Approach provides four types of Summary reports. Summary reports can also contain leading or following calculations for numeric fields. These are the Approach summary reports:

> **Leading Grouped Summary**   Contains one or more groups of like fields led by a Summary panel with one or more field labels for each group.

> **Trailing Grouped Summary**   Contains one or more groups of like fields followed by a Summary panel with one or more field labels for each group.

> **Columnar with Grand Summary**   Is a Columnar report with a single grand calculation in a following position.

> **Summary Only**   Contains one or more Summary panels without detail lines.

You can use the Report Assistant (in either the Browse or the Design environment) to create a basic summary report, or you can choose Create ▶ Summary (in the Design environment) to open the Summary dialog box (see Figure 17.13), in which you can select options to produce customized Summary reports.

**FIGURE 17.13** ▶

*The Summary dialog box, in which you can create a customized Summary report*

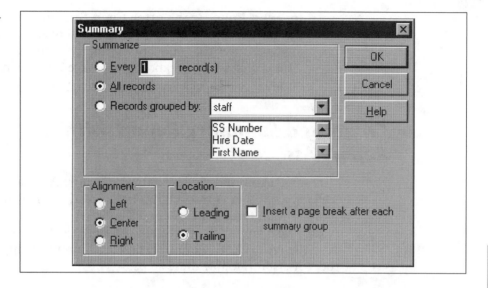

In the Summarize group are three option buttons:

> **Every *n* Records**    Click on this option button to summarize the values before or after every *n*th record in the database or to create a group of *n* records, where *n* represents a number from 1 (the default) to 999.

> **All Records**    Click on this option button to summarize the values before or after the active group of records—either the entire database or those in the Found Set. This is the default.

> **Records Grouped By**    Click on this option button to either group values without a summary or summarize the values before or after each group of records sorted by a selected field. You can select a field from a selected main or detail database.

At the bottom of the dialog box are two sets of option buttons and a checkbox:

> **Left, Center, Right**    Click on one of these option buttons to indicate the location to display the panel on the report page. Center is the default.

> **Leading, Trailing**    Click on one of these option buttons to indicate whether to diplay the panel before or after the group being summarized. Trailing is the default.

**Insert a Page Break after Each Summary Group**   Check this checkbox to insert a page break between summary items. Doing so ensures that only one summary occurs on a page. The default is a cleared checkbox, or no page break between summary items.

## ▶ Creating a Summary Report with the Report Assistant

Creating a summary report with the Report Assistant is a lot like producing any other Approach report. Instead of the two steps used to make a Standard or a Columnar report, Approach adds a third step with which you select a grouping and/or select a field to be calculated and the type of calculation. To create a summary report with the Report Assistant, follow these steps:

1. Open the database for which you want to create a report.

2. Choose Create ➤ Report. Approach displays the Report Assistant dialog box.

3. Type the report name in the View Name & Title text box.

4. Click on Columnar with Grand Totals, Columnar with Groups & Totals, or Summary Only in the Layout scroll box. The Sample Report box shows the layout.

5. Select a style from the Style drop-down list box.

6. Click on the Next button or on the Step 2: Fields tab. Approach displays the Step 2: Fields section of the dialog box for all but the Summary Only report. For the Summary Only report, skip to step 10.

7. In the Fields scroll box, click on a field to be displayed and click on Add to insert a field in the Fields to Place on View box. (You can also insert a field in the Fields to Place on View box by double-clicking on it.)

8. Select the remaining display fields (see Figure 17.14) for the report, in the order in which you want them to appear, from left to right.

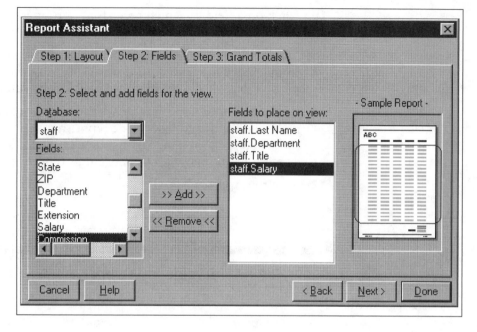

**9.** Click on the Next button or on the Step 3: Grand Totals tab. Approach displays the Step 3: Grand Totals (for Summary Only reports, Step 2: Fields) section (see Figure 17.15).

**FIGURE 17.15** ▶

*The Step 3: Grand Totals section of the Report Assistant dialog box*

10. Click on a field by which records are grouped. Approach inserts the field, preceded by an operator symbol, in the Summary Fields list.

11. In the Calculate The drop-down list box, select a calculation, and in the Field scroll box, click on a field to be calculated.

12. Click on Done. Approach closes the dialog box, displays the report in Design, and inserts the report name on the View list on the Status bar and on a tab right below the SmartIcons. Figure 17.16 shows a Columnar with Grand Totals report.

13. Save the Approach file.

**FIGURE 17.16** ►

*A Columnar with Grand Totals report with the Revenue Potential field formatted as currency*

## Potential Business Summary

| Company | Contact | Revenue Potential |
|---------|---------|------------------:|
| ACC Distributors | Nancy Halpin | $50,000 |
| East Street Distributors | George Allen | $25,000 |
| GX Distributors | David Wilson | $75,000 |
| Norton Dweller Corp | Lori Miller | $18,000 |
| Seaport Corp. | Laura McMillan | $100,000 |
| Simpson Distributors | Mary Erickson | $28,000 |
| | *Total:* | $296,000 |

►► **N O T E**

You can view a Summary Only report in Print Preview, Find, and Design environments. You cannot view it in the Browse environment.

> ▶▶ **T I P**
>
> **To sort a Summary report by one or two fields within each group, press Ctrl+T, choose Browse ➤ Sort ➤ Define in the Browse or the Print Preview environment, or choose Report ➤ Sort ➤ Define in the Design environment. In the Sort dialog box, you'll find the field by which the report is grouped in the Fields to Sort on box. To add other fields, simply click on the field in the Fields scroll box and click on the Add button. When you have completed specifying the fields on which to sort and have selected sort orders, click on OK. You also can select a saved Sort from the drop-down list box on the right side of the Action bar.**

## ▶ Adding a Summary to a Report

You can add a summary to an Approach report in three ways:

- Choose Create ➤ Summary and fill in the Summary dialog box.
- Click in a column to be calculated, choose Column ➤ Groups & Totals, and either select a calculation type or the placement of the summary.
- Click in a column to be calculated, and click on the appropriate PowerClick Reporting SmartIcons.

Table 17.1 illustrates and describes the PowerClick SmartIcons and commands. Not all these SmartIcons appear on the Default Report SmartIcons toolbar. To learn more about adding SmartIcons to SmartIcons toolbars, refer to the *Customizing Your SmartSuite Environment* appendix.

### Adding a Report Summary Using the Summary Dialog Box

To add a report summary using the Summary dialog box, follow these steps:

**1.** Open the database containing the report and go to Design.

**2.** Open a report for which you want to add a summary.

► **TABLE 17.1:** *Approach PowerClick SmartIcons and Commands*

| SmartIcon | Command | Description |
|---|---|---|
| | Column ➤ Groups & Totals ➤ Sum | Sums the values in a group of numeric fields |
| | Column ➤ Groups & Totals ➤ Average | Calculates the average of the values in a group of numeric fields |
| | Column ➤ Groups & Totals ➤ Count | Counts the fields in a group |
| | Column ➤ Groups & Totals ➤ Minimum | Finds the minimum value in a group of numeric fields |
| | Column ➤ Groups & Totals ➤ Maximum | Finds the maximum value in a group of numeric fields |
| | Column ➤ Groups & Totals ➤ Standard Deviation | Calculates the standard deviation of the values in a group of numeric fields |
| | Column ➤ Groups & Totals ➤ Variance | Calculates the variance of the values in a group of numeric fields |
| | Column ➤ Groups & Totals ➤ Leading Summary | Places a summary panel before a group of records |
| | Column ➤ Groups & Totals ➤ Trailing Summary | Places a summary panel after a group of records |

**3.** Choose Create ➤ Summary. Approach displays the Summary dialog box (see Figure 17.17).

**4.** In the Summarize group, choose whether you want to summarize for every record, all records, or by a group of fields.

**5.** In the Alignment group, select the alignment for the Summary panel.

**FIGURE 17.17** ▶

*The Summary
dialog box*

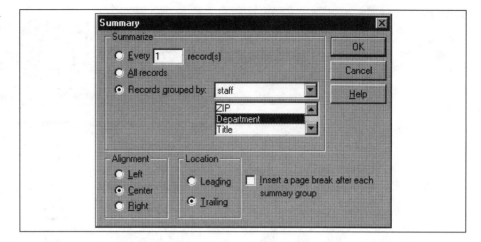

6. In the Location group, choose whether the summary leads or follows the group(s) of records.

7. Check or clear the Insert Page Break after Each Summary Group checkbox to specify whether a page break is inserted after each summary group.

8. When you have filled in the dialog box, click on OK or press Enter. Approach adds Summary panels to the report (see Figure 17.18) and marks the parts of the report.

## Adding a Report Summary Using the PowerClick Feature

To add a report summary using PowerClick SmartIcons, follow these steps:

1. Open the database containing the report and go to Design.

2. Create a Columnar report without totals. (For more information, see "Creating a Columnar Report," earlier in this chapter.)

3. Click in the column that holds the field by which you want to group the report records. Click on the Trailing Summary SmartIcon. Approach sorts and groups the records by the selected field, leaving a space between groups and placing panel labels after each group.

⟮Trailing summary by staff.Department⟯

**FIGURE 17.18** ▶

*A zoomed portion of a Columnar report with Trailing Summary panels*

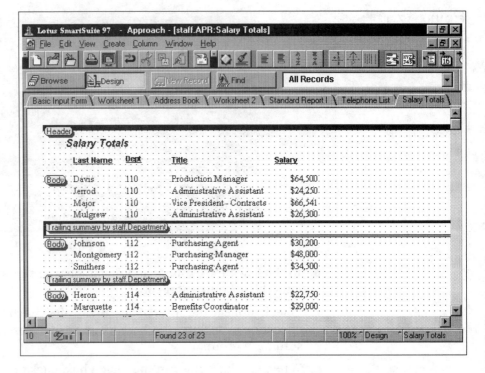

4. Optionally, choose Column ➤ Sort ➤ Define or press Ctrl+T. In the Sort dialog box, select fields by which you can further sort the report. Or choose a Sort from the drop-down list box at the right side of the Action bar. Approach sorts the records within the group.

5. Click in the field for which you want a summary.

6. Click on the Calculate the Total SmartIcon. Approach calculates a total for each group in the report. Figure 17.19 shows part of a formatted report in Print Preview.

7. Save the Approach file.

# ▶▶ *Creating a Crosstab Report with the Crosstab Assistant*

Crosstabs are reports that summarize multiple variables. Using crosstab reports, you can rearrange information to analyze it or view it in different ways. For example, for the Inventory database used as the

## Salaries by Department

| First Name | Last Name | Department | Salary |
|---|---|---|---|
| Joseph | Davis | 110 | $64,500 |
| Mary | Jerrod | 110 | $24,250 |
| Marshall | Major | 110 | $66,541 |
| Mary | Mulgrew | 110 | $26,300 |
| | | | $181,591 |
| Rita | Johnson | 112 | $30,200 |
| Michael | Montgomery | 112 | $48,000 |
| Lawrence | Smithers | 112 | $34,500 |
| | | | $112,700 |
| Zallinda | Heron | 114 | $22,750 |
| Douglas | Marquette | 114 | $29,000 |
| | | | $51,750 |
| William | Acerton | 115 | $38,000 |
| John | Adams | 115 | $35,000 |
| William | Lombardi | 115 | $54,000 |
| | | | $127,000 |

example in this section, you can arrange data by region, by part, or by both region and part—simply by dragging field labels from row to column, from column to row, or from one part of a row or column to another.

You can use Approach crosstabs in 1-2-3. To learn more about using Approach crosstabs in 1-2-3, see the *Advanced 1-2-3 Techniques* chapter.

In planning a crosstab, take note of the following:

- Use short field labels. You should be able to view as much of a crosstab as possible on your computer screen.

- Using rows and columns, you can group data from like locations or from a specific time period.

- The best data to analyze in a crosstab is numeric: expenses, manufacturing costs, income, and so on.

- Make your first crosstab reports simple, with one field each for rows and columns.

- You can drag field labels from one part of a crosstab to another, thereby changing the view. Before dragging labels, consider making several copies of the basic crosstab by choosing Edit ➤ Duplicate Crosstab. You'll then always have the original.

- Dragging field labels involves learning a few techniques. For more information, see "Formatting a Crosstab" on a following page.

- You can chart the crosstab by choosing Crosstab ➤ Chart This Crosstab. To edit the chart, follow the instructions in the *Graphing Your Data* chapter.

To create a crosstab report, follow these steps:

**1.** Open the database for which you want to create a report and go to Design.

**2.** Choose Create ➤ Crosstab. Approach displays the Step 1: Rows section of the Crosstab Assistant dialog box (see Figure 17.20).

**FIGURE 17.20** ▶

*In the first section of the Crosstab Assistant dialog box, select one or more fields for the rows.*

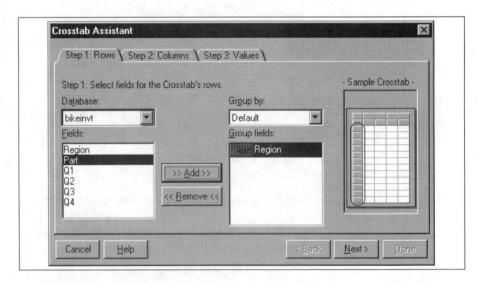

**3.** Select one or more fields for the rows.

**4.** Click on the Next button. Approach displays the Step 2: Columns section of the Crosstab Assistant dialog box (see Figure 17.21).

**5.** Select one or more fields for the columns.

**FIGURE 17.21** ▶

*In the second section of the Crosstab Assistant dialog box, select one or more fields for the columns.*

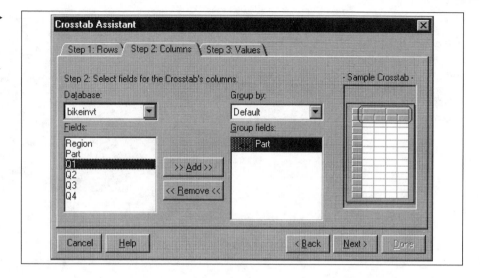

6. Click on the Next button. Approach displays the Step 3: Values section of the Crosstab Assistant dialog box (see Figure 17.22).

7. Select one or more fields for the values in the body of the crosstab.

8. To change from Sum, the default calculation for a summary field, click on the field in the Summary Fields box. When the box listing calculation types opens, click on an item on the list.

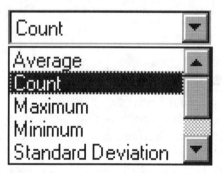

9. Click on Done. Approach closes the dialog box and displays the report in Design. Figure 17.23 shows an unformatted part of a crosstab in Print Preview.

10. Save the Approach file.

**FIGURE 17.22** ▶

*In the third section of
the Crosstab Assistant
dialog box, select one
or more fields for the
values in the body of
the crosstab.*

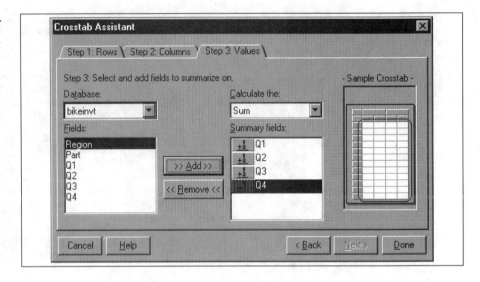

**FIGURE 17.23** ▶

*An unformatted part
of a crosstab in the
Print Preview
environment*

|  | Handlebars | | | | Pedals | | | |
|---|---|---|---|---|---|---|---|---|
|  | Q4 | Q3 | Q2 | Q1 | Q4 | Q3 | Q2 | Q1 |
| Midwest | 5656 | 4037 | 5928 | 3836 | 7630 | 5256 | 4886 | 3482 |
| Mountain | 4125 | 4380 | 4291 | 4592 | 5935 | 6249 | 6225 | 6490 |
| Northeast | 3685 | 2821 | 4246 | 3768 | 5683 | 4666 | 6682 | 4782 |
| Pacific | 3683 | 3784 | 3832 | 3143 | 4835 | 6243 | 6245 | 5546 |
| Southeast | 4562 | 4401 | 4071 | 2578 | 9346 | 3989 | 4023 | 2678 |
| Southwest | 1289 | 994 | 1002 | 989 | 2582 | 1200 | 859 | 689 |
| *Total* | 23000 | 20417 | 23370 | 18906 | 36011 | 27603 | 28920 | 23667 |

## ▶ *Formatting a Crosstab*

You can format parts of a crosstab as you would any Approach view.
Select a row or column, including its label, and click on the InfoBox
SmartIcon, choose Crosstab ▶ Crosstab Properties, press Ctrl+E, or
press Alt+Enter to open the InfoBox. For a synopsis of Approach Info-
Box options, see the *Planning and Creating Your First Database* chapter.
For general InfoBox information, refer to the *Editing in SmartSuite Ap-
plications* chapter.

**TIP**

> If a field appears under several categories, you only
> have to format it once. For example, in the sample
> report choose the Q3 column, which appears under
> Handlebars, Pedals, Wheels, and Total. Apply the Fixed
> numeric format to the selected column and all Q3
> columns are formatted in the same way.

## ▶ *Modifying Crosstab Rows and Columns*

Crosstabs are unique in that you can move row and column labels
around to improve a report or to change the results altogether.

**TIP**

> Before moving rows and columns around, it's a good
> idea to make a duplicate and change the copy. To do
> so, go to the Design environment and choose Edit ➤
> Duplicate Crosstab.

You can move row and column labels within the same row or column
or from the row to column or column to row. Simply follow these
instructions:

- To change the position of a single column label (and its contents)
  to the last place in a row, first drag the label above the border
  between the body (details) and the label. When you see a heavy
  horizontal line, release the left mouse button. Then drag the label
  down into the body of the crosstab to its new position. When the
  body is surrounded by a blue border, release the left mouse
  button.

- When changing the positions of several column labels, select them
  in the order in which you want them to appear (in our example,
  first move Q1, then Q2, followed by Q3 and Q4).

- To change a column label into a row label, drag the column label
  toward the row label area of the crosstab. When you see a heavy
  vertical line, release the left mouse button.

- To change a row label into a column label, drag the row label toward the column label area of the crosstab. When you see a heavy horizontal line, release the left mouse button.

- To undo a change of location, choose Edit ➤ Undo or press Ctrl+Z.

Figure 17.24 shows a crosstab with the Parts field dragged to the right of the Region column. Notice that the totals differ from those in the previous crosstab.

**FIGURE 17.24** ►

*This crosstab shows the data rearranged by Parts under Region.*

| | | | Q1 | Q2 | Q3 | Q4 |
|---|---|---|---|---|---|---|
| Midwest | Handlebars | | 3836 | 5928 | 4037 | 5656 |
| | Pedals | | 3482 | 4886 | 5256 | 7630 |
| | Wheels | | 5894 | 8056 | 8128 | 8242 |
| Mountain | Handlebars | | 4592 | 4291 | 4380 | 4125 |
| | Pedals | | 6490 | 6225 | 6249 | 5935 |
| | Wheels | | 9024 | 8998 | 9244 | 9002 |
| Northeast | Handlebars | | 3768 | 4246 | 2821 | 3685 |
| | Pedals | | 4782 | 6682 | 4666 | 5683 |
| | Wheels | | 7348 | 8422 | 7848 | 7620 |
| Pacific | Handlebars | | 3143 | 3832 | 3784 | 3683 |
| | Pedals | | 5546 | 6245 | 6243 | 4835 |
| | Wheels | | 5924 | 6278 | 6444 | 6728 |
| Southeast | Handlebars | | 2578 | 4071 | 4401 | 4562 |
| | Pedals | | 2678 | 4023 | 3989 | 9346 |
| | Wheels | | 5208 | 4216 | 6682 | 6894 |
| Southwest | Handlebars | | 989 | 1002 | 994 | 1289 |
| | Pedals | | 689 | 859 | 1200 | 2582 |
| | Wheels | | 1200 | 1658 | 1486 | 2690 |
| *Total* | | | 77171 | 89918 | 87852 | 100187 |

Figure 17.25 shows part of a version of the crosstab with the Parts field dragged to the left of the Region column. In this version, subtotals are inserted into the body of the crosstab, and a grand total ends the crosstab.

# ► *Drilling Down for Data*

You can review the underlying records for a selected row header, column header, individual cell, or contiguous cells in a crosstab. For example, in

| | | Q1 | Q2 | Q3 | Q4 |
|---|---|---|---|---|---|
| Handlebars | Midwest | 3836 | 5928 | 4037 | 5656 |
| | Mountain | 4592 | 4291 | 4380 | 4125 |
| | Northeast | 3768 | 4246 | 2821 | 3685 |
| | Pacific | 3143 | 3832 | 3784 | 3683 |
| | Southeast | 2578 | 4071 | 4401 | 4562 |
| | Southwest | 989 | 1002 | 994 | 1289 |
| | *Total* | 18906 | 23370 | 20417 | 23000 |
| Pedals | Midwest | 3482 | 4886 | 5256 | 7630 |
| | Mountain | 6490 | 6225 | 6249 | 5935 |
| | Northeast | 4782 | 6682 | 4666 | 5683 |
| | Pacific | 5546 | 6245 | 6243 | 4835 |
| | Southeast | 2678 | 4023 | 3989 | 9346 |
| | Southwest | 689 | 859 | 1200 | 2582 |
| | *Total* | 23667 | 28920 | 27603 | 36011 |
| Wheels | Midwest | 5894 | 8056 | 8128 | 8242 |
| | Mountain | 9024 | 8998 | 9244 | 9002 |
| | Northeast | 7348 | 8422 | 7848 | 7620 |
| | Pacific | 5924 | 6278 | 6444 | 6728 |
| | Southeast | 5208 | 4216 | 6682 | 6894 |

our example, if you click on the cell at the intersection of Q4 and Midwest in the Handlebars section:

| | | Q1 | Q2 | Q3 | Q4 |
|---|---|---|---|---|---|
| Handlebars | Midwest | 3836 | 5928 | 4037 | 5656 |
| | Mountain | 4592 | 4291 | 4380 | 4125 |
| | Northeast | 3768 | 4246 | 2821 | 3685 |
| | Pacific | 3143 | 3832 | 3784 | 3683 |
| | Southeast | 2578 | 4071 | 4401 | 4562 |
| | Southwest | 989 | 1002 | 994 | 1289 |
| | *Total* | 18906 | 23370 | 20417 | 23000 |

and either click on the Drill Down to Data SmartIcon or choose Crosstab ▶ Drill Down to Data, Approach creates a new view that looks like this:

| Region | Part | Q1 | Q2 | Q3 | Q4 |
|---|---|---|---|---|---|
| Midwest | Handlebars | 3836 | 5928 | 4037 | 5656 |

You can either keep the view or press Esc to delete it.

# ▶▶ *Creating and Editing Mail Merge Documents*

One of the most important reasons for maintaining a database is that you can use it to send out mass mailings. In Approach, you can prepare both form letters and mailing labels. In addition to names and addresses, mail merge documents can contain almost any other information that you can direct to a specific individual. By using Approach's mail merge feature, you can automate yet personalize a large mailing.

The basic components of mail merge are database fields, which are merged into the finished form letter, and a form letter. For the most part, the starting form letter is like any other letter. It contains text for your entire audience, but omits unique information, such as the name, address, city, state, and zip code of the recipient. You can create a letter from scratch either in Approach or in a word processor, such as Word Pro, or you can edit an existing document.

The database fields, from Approach or even another database program, contain the unique information about the recipient of each letter. In addition to the name and address information previously mentioned, other typical fields merged into a form letter are amount owed, credit and sales history, and date of last contact.

## ▶ *Creating a Form Letter*

The Form Letter Assistant guides you through writing a form letter and selecting the fields to be inserted in the letter. To create a form letter, follow these steps:

1. Open the database for which you want to create a form letter.
2. Choose Create ➤ Form Letter. Approach displays the Step 1: Layout section of the Form Letter Assistant dialog box (see Figure 17.26).
3. Type the form letter name in the View Name & Title text box.
4. Choose a layout from the Layout box.
5. Select a style from the Style drop-down list box.

**FIGURE 17.26** ▶

*In the Step 1: Layout section of the Form Letter Assistant dialog box, choose a name, a layout, and a style.*

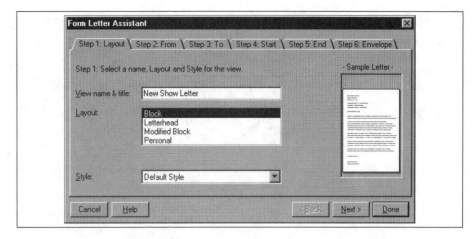

6. Click on the Next button. Approach displays the Step 2: From section of the Form Letter Assistant dialog box (see Figure 17.27).

**FIGURE 17.27** ▶

*In the Step 2: From section, either type your return address or click on None.*

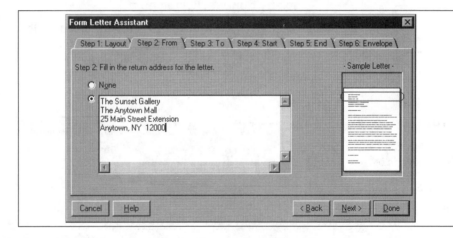

7. Type the return address. (If you use letterhead stationery, click on None to leave the box blank.) Click on Next. Approach displays the Step 3: To section of the Form Letter Assistant dialog box (see Figure 17.28).

8. Select the number of lines or a layout from the Address Layout drop-down list box. Notice that Approach changes the look of the Fields for the Address box.

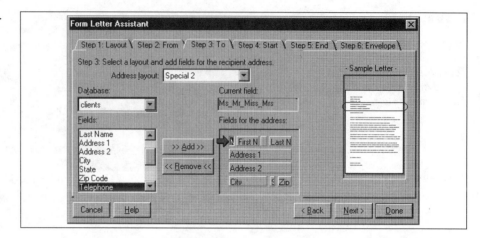

9. From the Fields scroll box, click on the first field of the inside address and click on Add to insert a field in the Fields for the Address box. (You can also insert a field in the Fields for the Address box by double-clicking on it.)

10. Select the remaining fields for the inside address, in the order in which you want them to appear. Click on Next. Approach displays the Step 4: Start section of the Form Letter Assistant dialog box (see Figure 17.29).

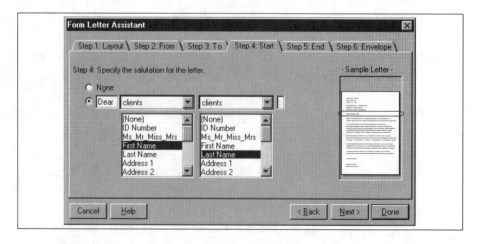

11. If desired, type another salutation in the Dear text box. Click on a field, such as First Name, in the first scroll box. Optionally, click

on a field, such as Last Name, in the second scroll box. Optionally, change the punctuation in the small text box to the right of
the second scroll box. Then click on Next. Approach displays the
Step 5: End section of the Form Letter Assistant dialog box (see
Figure 17.30).

**FIGURE 17.30** ▶

*The Step 5: End sec-
tion of the Form Letter
Assistant dialog box
with the defaults*

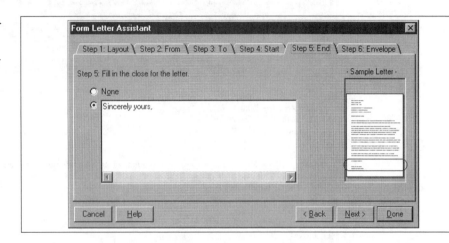

**12.** Fill in the close for your letter, and click on Next. Approach displays the Step 6: Envelope section of the Form Letter Assistant
dialog box (see Figure 17.31).

**FIGURE 17.31** ▶

*The section of the
Form Letter Assistant
dialog box in which
you specify options for
an envelope*

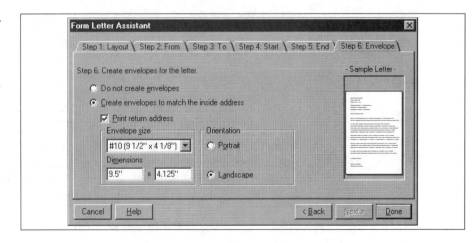

Database
Reporting

▶ ▶

*Ch.*
**17**

Approach displays the form letter with the address, fields, salutation, and close (see Figure 17.32).

**FIGURE 17.32** ▶

*A form letter ready to
be filled in with its
body text*

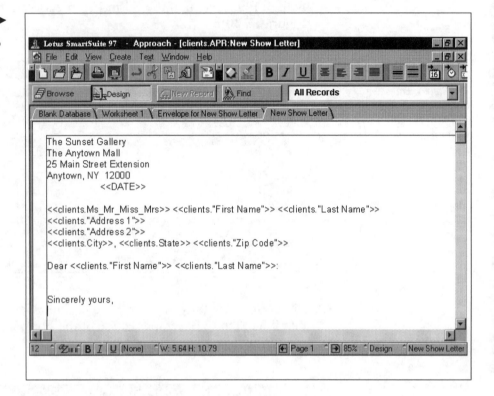

## Inserting Text in a Form Letter

To write a form letter, follow these steps:

1. In the Design environment, select the desired form letter from the
   View list on the Status bar or by clicking on its View tab.

2. Repeatedly click on the text box if it is not active. When a blue
   border appears, you can start typing. (Remember not to click too
   rapidly. If Approach senses a double-click, the InfoBox appears.)

3. Type the letter just as you would any letter.

4. Either type around the fields, or insert fields into the letter.

When working on a form letter, note the following:

- You can use a field more than once in a letter.

- When inserting two fields side by side (for example, First Name and Last Name), insert a space between the fields. If you forget to insert the space, the second field will begin immediately after the last character in the first field.

- Periodically check the appearance of the form letter by looking at it in Browse view and editing or formatting as needed. For example, you may have to add or remove spaces. Approach will have already filled in the letter with the results of the fields.

- To switch between viewing the data or the fields in the Design environment (if you don't want to switch between Design and Browse), choose View ➤ Show Data. A checked Show Data command indicates that you will view the data. A Show Data command without the preceding checkmark indicates that you will view the fields.

- To copy a field to another part of the letter, select the field, choose Edit ➤ Copy (or press Ctrl+C), move the insertion point to the desired location, and choose Edit ➤ Paste (or press Ctrl+V).

- To move a field to another part of the letter, select the field, choose Edit ➤ Cut (or press Ctrl+X), move the insertion point to the desired location, and choose Edit ➤ Paste (or press Ctrl+V).

- To delete a field from the letter, select the entire field (for example, <<clients."First Name">>) and press Delete.

- To insert a field into the letter, point to the location in which you want to insert the field, choose Text ➤ Insert ➤ Field Value, select the field from the Insert Field dialog box, and click on OK.

- To insert today's date (from your computer system clock) into the letter, point to the location in which you want to insert the date, and choose Text ➤ Insert ➤ Today's Date.

- To insert a picture into the upper left corner of the letter, choose Edit ➤ Picture ➤ Import, select the picture format (BMP, WMF, TIF, PCX, GIF, TGA, EPS, or JPG), optionally change to the folder in which the picture is located, and double-click on the filename.

- To format the entire letter at one time, choose Edit ➤ Select All.

Figure 17.33 shows a completed form letter.

**FIGURE 17.33** ▶

*The completed form letter in Print Preview*

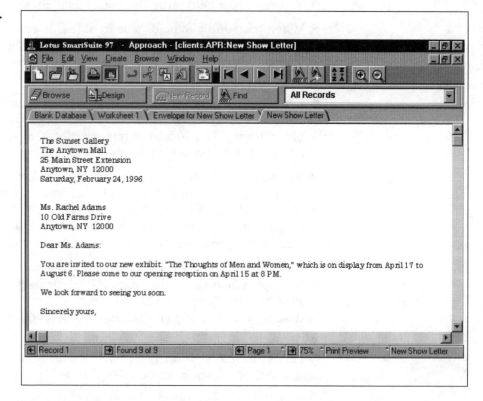

## ▶ *Creating Mailing Labels*

Using almost the same techniques that you use to produce a form letter, you can create mailing labels. Approach provides predefined label formats, or you can create your own. To create mailing labels, follow these steps:

1. Open the database for which you want to create a mailing label and go to Design.

2. Choose Create ➤ Mailing Label. Approach displays the Mailing Label Assistant dialog box (see Figure 17.34).

3. Type the mailing label name in the Mailing Label Name text box.

**FIGURE 17.34** ▶

*In the Mailing Label
Assistant dialog box,
you can name a mail-
ing label and select
the fields to be
merged into it.*

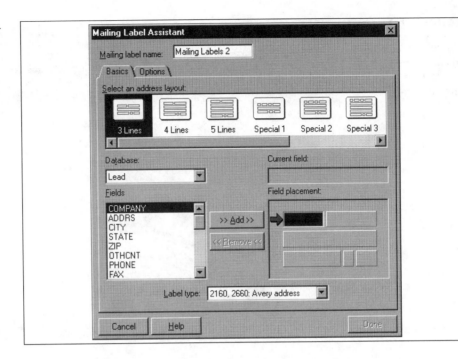

4. Select a database from the Database drop-down list box. You can create a mailing label using fields from several joined databases.

5. In the Fields scroll box, double-click on fields for the label in the order in which you want them to appear. As you double-click, Approach adds the fields in the Field Placement box.

6. To remove a field from the mailing label, select it in the Field Placement box and click on Remove.

7. Open the Label Type drop-down list box, and select an Avery label code that matches the mailing labels on which you will print.

8. Either click on OK or press Enter when you have completed your selection. Approach closes the dialog box and displays the mailing label (see Figure 17.35).

9. If needed, format the fields on the mailing label, periodically going to Browse view to check your progress or choosing View ➤ Show Data. Figure 17.36 illustrates several completed mailing labels in Print Preview. Notice that Approach moves lines on labels to fill in empty Address 2 fields.

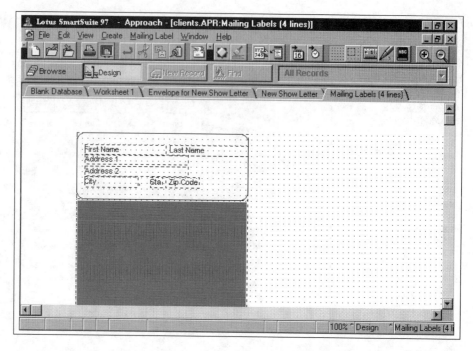

**FIGURE 17.36** ►

*Some completed mailing labels in Print Preview*

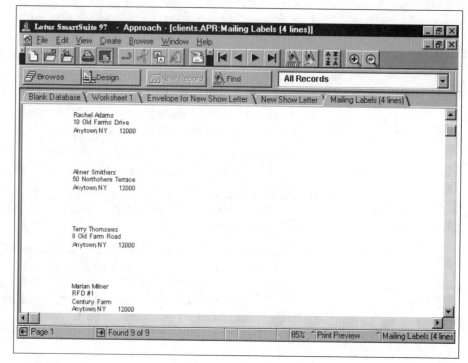

# CHAPTER 18

# Advanced Approach Techniques

▶▶ **I**n this final Approach chapter, you'll learn about two important features: importing and exporting files from and to Approach and other Windows applications, and using macros to automate your work.

Although Approach works well as a standalone application, you can take advantage of the Windows environment by importing "foreign" files into Approach and exporting Approach records to other Windows applications. This feature can save you a great deal of time. Simply create a file once and use it in different formats. You'll learn about importing and exporting in the first pages of this chapter.

Another time-saver is the Approach macro feature. Using macros, you can automate finding, sorting, filling records, printing, spell checking, and much more. The second part of this chapter describes macros and the commands used to create them.

# ▶▶ *Importing and Exporting*

As you learned in previous chapters, you do not have to manually enter all the records in an Approach database. Sometimes, you can import many records at once from a word processor or from a spreadsheet program. For example, if your department keeps a long list of names and addresses in a word-processing document, your manager might assign you to convert the document to a database, which will allow for better data manipulation—for example, finding specific records or creating and sending form letters. Or, if you have maintained an inventory sheet, you might want to import it into Approach and add information such as company and contact names, addresses, telephone numbers that you can actually dial from a record, and tracking data.

Exporting data from Approach to another application allows you to manipulate the database information in other ways. For example, you can export selected records to a word processor to create catalog pages or to a spreadsheet to analyze numeric data.

In this section, you will learn how to import from and export to a word processor and a spreadsheet—to show the similarities in the processes.

## ▶ Importing a Text File

A text file to be imported to Approach should have certain characteristics:

- The first line in the file should contain field labels, separated by a separator symbol. Although this is not required, it is easier to match fields during the final stage of importing if you have field labels.

- Each line of text, including the first line, should contain the same number of potential fields, separated by a separator symbol. If a line has a missing field, insert two separator symbols, each of which indicates the end of a field.

- Use the same symbol to separate each field in every line of text. During the import, Approach will ask you to identify one separator symbol. If you intend to import text that includes commas, consider using the semicolon (or a character used less frequently than a comma in a standard file) as the separator symbol.

- Save the file in ASCII or text delimited (TXT) format. This means that any word-processing codes, which might inadvertently be imported, are removed as part of the save process. (The text delimited format enables you to import fields of varying lengths.)

- Once imported into Approach, each line of text in the file is a record.

Figure 18.1 shows part of a Word Pro-based text file that is ready to be imported by Approach.

Advanced
Approach

▶ ▶
Ch.
**18**

**FIGURE 18.1** ▶

*Part of a Word Pro-based text file with semicolon field separators*

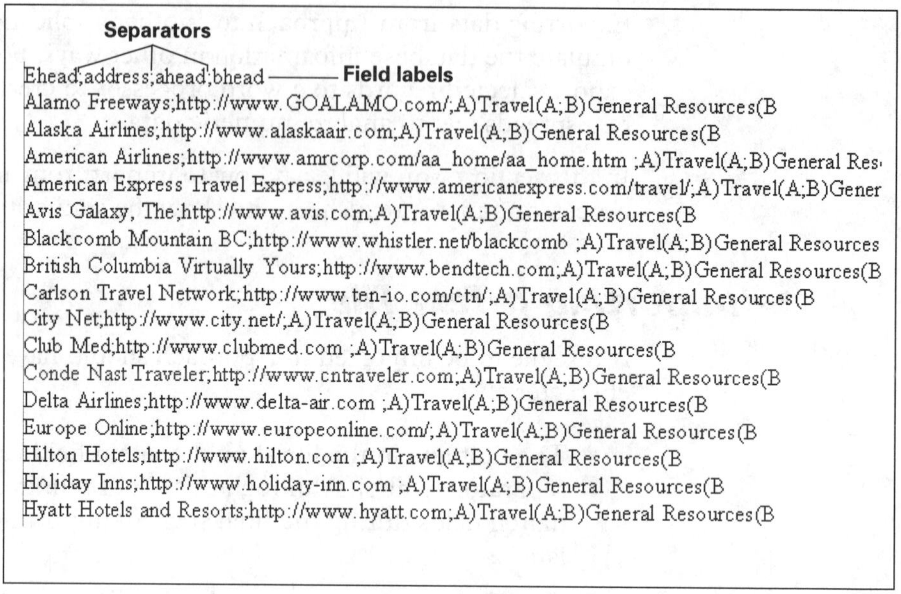

**Separators**

Ehead,address,ahead,bhead ——— **Field labels**
Alamo Freeways;http://www.GOALAMO.com/;A)Travel(A;B)General Resources(B
Alaska Airlines;http://www.alaskaair.com;A)Travel(A;B)General Resources(B
American Airlines;http://www.amrcorp.com/aa_home/aa_home.htm ;A)Travel(A;B)General Res·
American Express Travel Express;http://www.americanexpress.com/travel/;A)Travel(A;B)Gener
Avis Galaxy, The;http://www.avis.com;A)Travel(A;B)General Resources(B
Blackcomb Mountain BC;http://www.whistler.net/blackcomb ;A)Travel(A;B)General Resources
British Columbia Virtually Yours;http://www.bendtech.com;A)Travel(A;B)General Resources(B
Carlson Travel Network;http://www.ten-io.com/ctn/;A)Travel(A;B)General Resources(B
City Net;http://www.city.net/;A)Travel(A;B)General Resources(B
Club Med;http://www.clubmed.com ;A)Travel(A;B)General Resources(B
Conde Nast Traveler;http://www.cntraveler.com;A)Travel(A;B)General Resources(B
Delta Airlines;http://www.delta-air.com ;A)Travel(A;B)General Resources(B
Europe Online;http://www.europeonline.com/;A)Travel(A;B)General Resources(B
Hilton Hotels;http://www.hilton.com ;A)Travel(A;B)General Resources(B
Holiday Inns;http://www.holiday-inn.com ;A)Travel(A;B)General Resources(B
Hyatt Hotels and Resorts;http://www.hyatt.com;A)Travel(A;B)General Resources(B

To import a file into Approach, switch to the Approach Browse environment, and follow these steps:

1. In the application in which you created it, prepare a file for importing. Separate each field in the file with a separator character. Add a top line of field names to the file. Save the file as you would any file, making sure that you select a file type of Text Only, Text - ASCII, Text - ANSI, or another text or ASCII format.

2. In Approach, click on the Import SmartIcon or choose File ➤ Import Data. Approach opens the Import Data dialog box (see Figure 18.2).

3. Select a text type of Text - Delimited (*.TXT).

4. Select the file to be imported. You may have to go to another folder or drive to find it.

5. Click on Import. Approach displays the Text File Options dialog box (see Figure 18.3).

6. Either click on an option button to indicate the character that separates fields or type the separator in the Other text box.

7. If the first row contains field names (which is recommended), place a checkmark in the First Row Contains Field Names checkbox. A checked checkbox is the default.

8. Click on OK. Approach opens the Import Setup dialog box (see Figure 18.4).

9. Drag the fields on the right side of the dialog box to match the related fields on the left side. Figure 18.5 shows two matching fields with two more to go, and Figure 18.6 is the completed dialog box.

10. Click on OK. After a few seconds of processing, Approach imports the data into records at the end of the file.

11. Edit the new records as needed. Figure 18.7 shows an edited record, ready for further work.

**FIGURE 18.2** ▶

*The Import Data
dialog box*

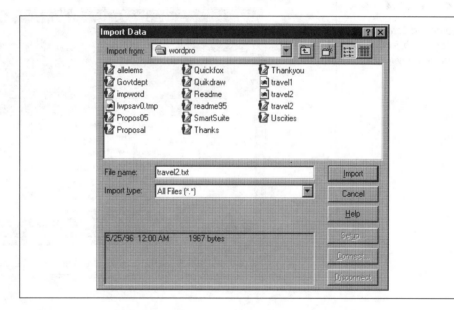

## ▶ *Importing a Sheet*

Importing a sheet into an Approach database is very similar to importing a text file. Instead of using separators to mark the end of one field and the beginning of another, a cell contains a field. To prepare a sheet for importing, at the top of the sheet, add a new row in which you type field names to be used to match the receiving fields in the database.

**FIGURE 18.3** ►

*The Text File Options dialog box with the semicolon selected*

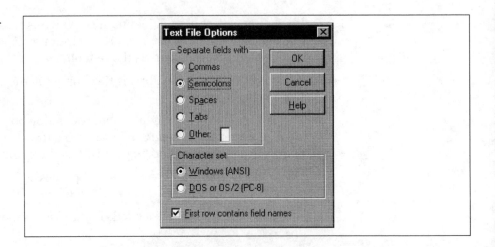

**FIGURE 18.4** ►

*The Import Setup dialog box before matching any fields*

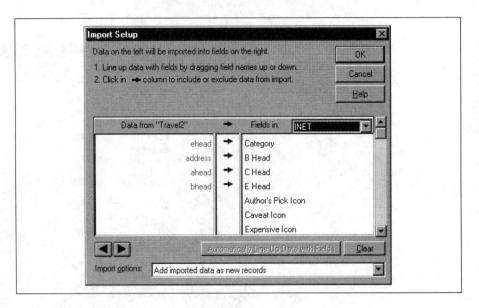

**FIGURE 18.5**  ▶

*Two matching fields in the Import Setup dialog box*

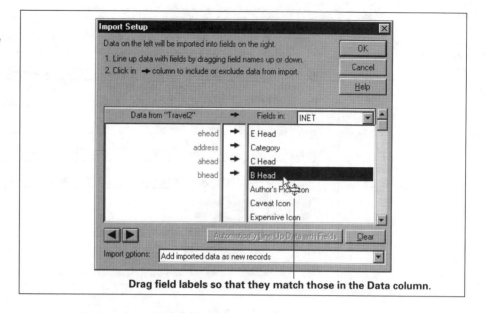

**Drag field labels so that they match those in the Data column.**

**FIGURE 18.6**  ▶

*The Import Setup dialog box with all text file fields matched with Approach fields*

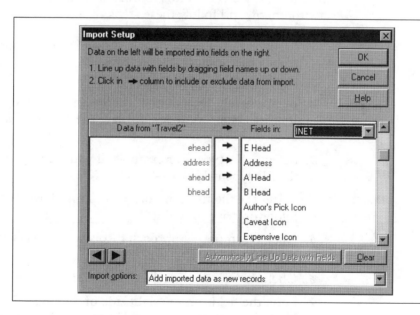

**FIGURE 18.7** ▶

*A record with im-
ported data in some
of its fields*

| Internet Business-to-Business Directory |
|---|

**Category**

| | ▼ |

**A Head**                    **Site Icon**              **Site Icon 2**

| A)Travel(A ▼ | Insert Web icon ▼ | ▼ |

**B Head**                    **Address**

| B)General Resources(B ▼ | http://www.ual.com/ |

**C Head**                    **Address 2**

| ▼ | |

**E Head**

| United Airlines |

☐ Author's Pick     ☐ Caveat     **Description**
☐ Expensive         ☐ FAQ
☐ Insert  ☑ Visit   ☐ Edit
☐ Screen Shot       ☐ Complete
☐ Not in This Edition  **Author**

**Edited** | 5/27/97 |   | SEE |

To import a 1-2-3 file into Approach, switch to the Approach Browse environment, and follow these steps:

1. Prepare a file for importing. Be sure to add a top line of field names to the sheet. Figure 18.8 shows the sample sheet containing data to be imported.

2. In Approach, click on the Import SmartIcon or choose File ➤ Import Data. Approach displays the Import Data dialog box (see Figure 18.9).

3. Select a file type. For example, if you are importing from 1-2-3, the file type is Lotus 1-2-3 (*.WK*).

4. Select the file to be imported. You may have to go to another folder or drive to find it.

5. Click on Import. Approach displays the Select Range dialog box (see Figure 18.10).

6. Click on OK. Approach opens the Import Setup dialog box.

7. Drag the fields on the right side of the dialog box to match the related fields on the left side. Figure 18.11 shows a completed dialog box with the mouse pointer ready to move fields.

**8.** Click on OK. Approach imports the data into the database. Figure 18.12 shows a sample record.

**FIGURE 18.8** ▶

*A sample sheet containing data to be imported*

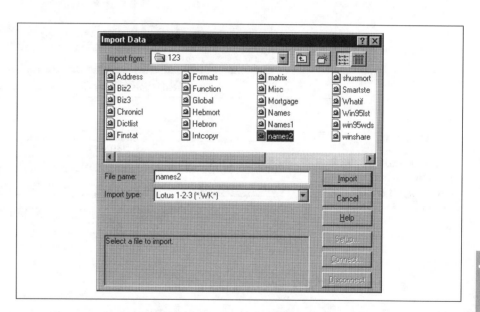

**FIGURE 18.10** ▶

*The Select Range dialog box*

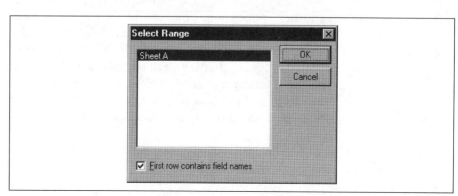

Advanced Approach

▶ ▶

*Ch.*
**18**

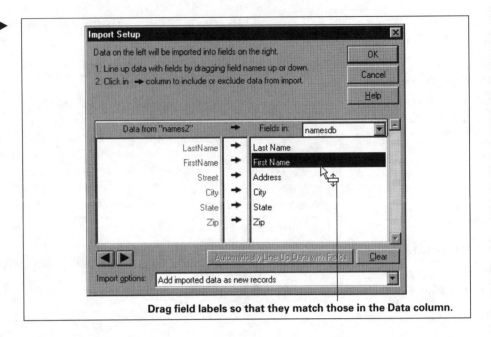

Drag field labels so that they match those in the Data column.

## ▶ Exporting Records

You can export records, a group of records, or selected fields for use in another application. For example, my co-authors and I produced *The Internet Business-to-Business Directory* (also published by SYBEX) using an Approach database of more than 8,000 records. When the records for a particular chapter were complete, I "found" the set of records, sorted them by a heading field, and exported selected fields to a text file. I opened the text file using a word processor and edited the contents into the appropriate manuscript format.

Using a database to contain entries meant that moving a record from one chapter to another involved changing only one field. In contrast, the same move in a word processor would have required cutting the entry from one file and pasting it into another. In addition, sorting the selected records before exporting them guaranteed that all entries were in alphabetic order. Using an Approach database to write a large book or a much smaller catalog or inventory list is a very efficient and easy way to work.

The centerpiece of exporting records from Approach to another application is the Export Data dialog box (see Figure 18.13).

**FIGURE 18.13** ▶

*The Export Data dialog box*

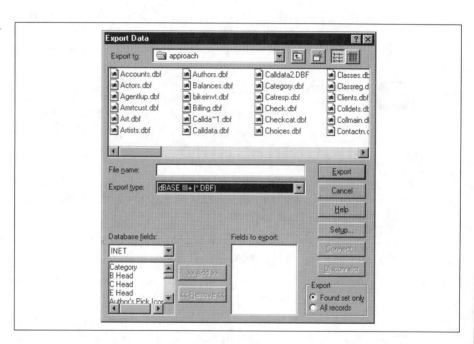

The Export Data dialog box contains these options:

**Export To**   Open this drop-down list box to select a drive and/or a folder in which Approach will save the exported file.

**Up One Level**   Click on this button to move to the folder that is the "parent" of or is one level higher than the current folder.

**Create New Folder**   Click on this button to create a new folder in which Approach will store the exported file.

**List/Details**    Click on the List button (the default) to have Approach display a list of files, or click on the Details button to have Approach display filenames, size, type, and the last date modified.

**File Name**    In this text box, type the name of the file to which the records will be exported.

**Export Type**    From this drop-down list box, select the type of file format in which the records will be saved.

**Database Fields**    From the drop-down list box, select the main database or joined database from which you will export the records. From the scroll box, select the fields to be exported.

**Add**    Click on this button to indicate that the selected field in the Database Fields scroll box will be exported. Approach copies the field name to the Fields to Export box.

  **T I P**

**You can also add a field to the Fields to Export box by double-clicking on it.**

**Remove**    Click on this button to indicate that the selected field in the Fields to Export box will be removed from the box and not exported.

**Fields to Export**    Approach displays the fields to be exported in this box.

**Export**    After selecting options in the dialog box, click on this button to start the export process.

**Setup**    Click on this button to open a dialog box in which you can select options for a particular database application. This button is not available for most export types.

**Connect**    Click on this button to open a dialog box in which you can connect to a selected application. This button is not available for most export types.

**Disconnect**    Click on this button to disconnect from the application to which you are connected. This button is not available for most export types.

**Found Set Only**     Click on this option button (the default) to export the Found Set, if you have chosen one.

**All Records**     Click on this option button to export all the records in the database.

## Exporting Records to a Text File

To export selected records to a text file, follow these steps:

**1.** Optionally, find a set of records to be exported by clicking on the Find button, selecting search fields, and clicking on OK. Figure 18.14 shows a selection of three fields and one checkbox.

**2.** Optionally, click in a field and sort it by clicking on the Sort Field in Ascending Order SmartIcon or the Sort Field in Descending Order SmartIcon.

**3.** Click on the Export Database SmartIcon or choose File ➤ Export Data. Approach opens the Export Data dialog box.

**4.** Select options from the dialog box, making sure to type a name in the File Name text box. Figure 18.15 shows a filled-in dialog box.

**5.** Click on the Export button to start the process. Approach opens the Text File Options dialog box.

**6.** Select a separator character, and check the First Row Contains Field Names checkbox. Click on OK. Approach exports the data to the specified file.

## Exporting Records to a Sheet

To export selected records to a sheet, follow these steps:

**1.** Optionally, find a set of records to be exported by clicking on the Find button, selecting search fields, and clicking on OK.

**2.** Optionally, click in a field and sort it by clicking on the Sort Field in Ascending Order SmartIcon or the Sort Field in Descending Order SmartIcon.

**3.** Click on the Export Database SmartIcon or choose File ➤ Export Data. Approach opens the Export Data dialog box.

**4.** Select options from the dialog box, making sure to type a name in the File Name text box. To export data in 1-2-3 format, select the

Lotus 1-2-3 (*.WK1) export type. Figure 18.16 shows the filled in Export Data dialog box.

**5.** Click on the Export button to start the process. Approach exports the data to the specified file.

**FIGURE 18.14**   ▸

*Three fields and one checkbox identified for exporting*

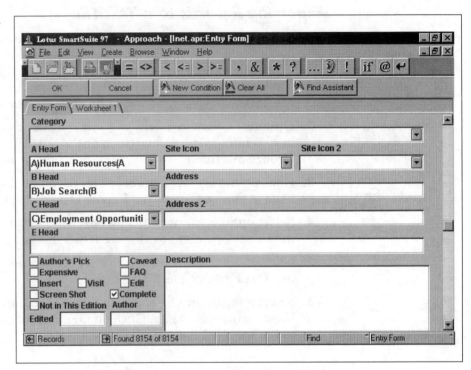

## ▸▸ *Automating Tasks with Macros*

You use macros to automate a set of operations on a database. For example, Approach provides a command with which you can fill in a field with a particular value throughout a database or in a set of Found records. With a macro, you can fill in the fields, find and sort a different set of records, fill in another set of fields, export and/or import records, run the spell checker, and so on, without issuing a command for each action. In the remaining pages of this chapter, you'll learn about the dialog boxes that you use to create and manipulate macros, find out about macro commands, and discover how to create, edit, run, and delete Approach macros.

**FIGURE 18.15** ▶

*An Export Data dialog box, which is filled-in and ready for exporting data to a text file*

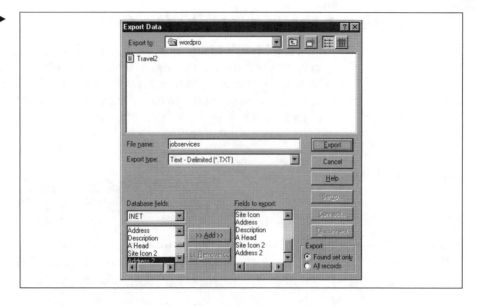

**FIGURE 18.15** ▶

*An Export Data dialog box, which is filled-in and ready for exporting data to a text file*

**FIGURE 18.16** ▶

*The Export Data dialog box, which is filled-in and ready for exporting data in 1-2-3 format*

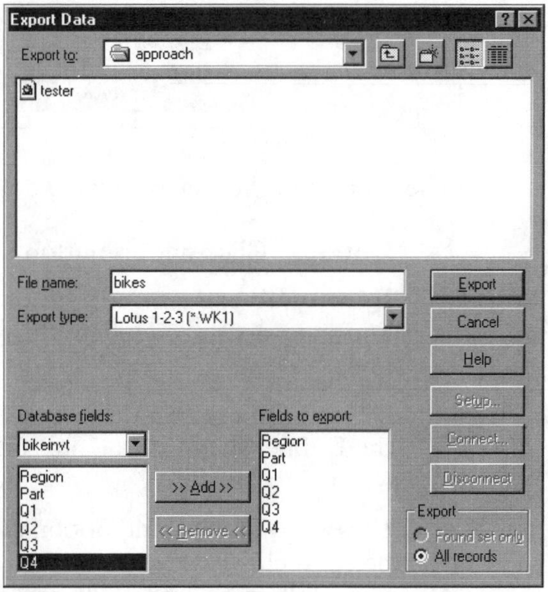

## ▶ *About the Macros Dialog Box*

Using the Macros dialog box (see Figure 18.17), you can run or delete a macro or open the Define Macro dialog box (see the following section) in which you can create, edit, or copy a macro. In the Macros dialog box, you'll also see a list of the macros that you have created, and you can run a macro from a submenu of the Edit menu. To open the Macros dialog box, choose Edit ➤ Macros.

**FIGURE 18.17** ▶

*This Macros dialog box lists two macros which you can edit, copy, delete, or run—from the dialog box.*

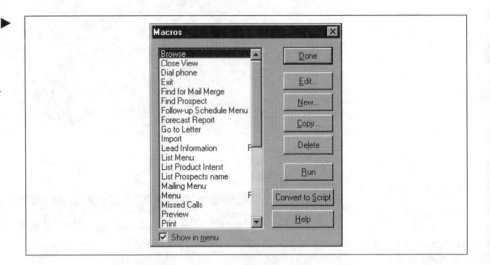

The options in the Macros dialog box are:

**Done**   Click on this button to close the dialog box.

**Edit**   To edit a macro, select it from the box and click on this button to open the Define Macro dialog box. See a following section, "Editing a Macro."

**New**   To create a macro, click on this button. Approach opens the Define Macro dialog box. See a following section, "Creating a Macro."

**Copy**   To copy and optionally edit a macro, select it from the box and click on this button to open the Define Macro dialog box. See a following section, "Copying a Macro."

**Delete**     To delete one or more macros, select them from the box, click on this button, and confirm the deletion. See a following section, "Deleting Macros."

**Run**     To run a macro, click on this button. See a following section, "Running a Macro."

**Show in Menu**     Check this checkbox to insert the name of the macro in a submenu of the Edit menu. If you do so, you can run a macro without opening the Macros dialog box.

## ▶ *About the Define Macro Dialog Box*

In the Define Macro dialog box (see Figure 18.18), you can create and edit a macro or copy a macro. Use this dialog box in the same way that you use the Field Definition dialog box to add fields to a database. Rather than adding new fields one line at a time, insert or delete macro commands line by line.

**FIGURE 18.18** ▶

*The Define Macro dialog box showing sample settings*

**Command** ⎯⎯⎯

**Options for the selected command** ⎯⎯

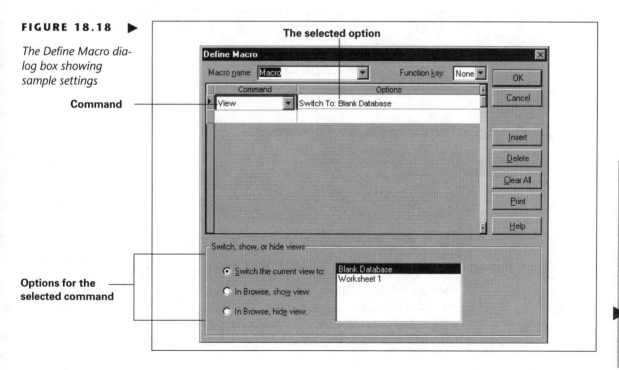

▶▶

*Ch.*
**18**

The options in the Define Macro dialog box are:

**Macro Name**    In this text box/drop-down list box, type or select the name of the macro you are creating, editing, or copying.

**Command**    From this drop-down list box, select a macro command. Approach inserts the command name in the first column of the scroll box. The following sections describe each macro command and its options.

**Options**    After you select a command, Approach automatically inserts the default option information in the second column of the scroll box. If you select another option, Approach replaces the original information. The following sections describe each macro command and its options.

**Insert**    Click on this button to insert a new line above the selected line.

**Delete**    Click on this button to delete the selected line.

**Clear All**    Click on this button to delete all but one of the lines in the macro, leaving a blank line with which you can start creating a macro.

**Print**    Click on this button to open the Print dialog box with which you can print the commands in the current macro.

## ▶ Approach Macro Commands

Approach provides 28 macro commands, each of which is described in the following sections.

### Browse

Select this command to switch to the Browse environment. This is equivalent to clicking on the Go to Browse to Review or Modify Data SmartIcon, clicking on the Browse button, selecting Browse from the Environment drop-down list box in the Status bar, choosing View ▶ Browse & Data Entry, or pressing Ctrl+B. Approach provides no options for this command. For more information, see the "Browse, Macro Command" topic in the Approach help facility.

## Close

Select this command to close the current Approach file. This is equivalent to clicking on the Close a File SmartIcon or choosing File ➤ Close. You can set this option for the Close command:

**Automatically Disconnect from Server**     Check this checkbox to have the macro automatically disconnect from the server when it closes the file.

For more information, see the "Close, Macro Command" topic in the Approach help facility.

## Delete

Select this command to delete the current record, the current set of found records, or the current Approach file. You can select from these options for the Delete command:

**Current Record**     Click on this option button to delete the current record. This is the default. Selecting this option is equivalent to clicking on the Delete the Current Record SmartIcon or choosing Edit ➤ Delete Form.

**Found Set**     Click on this option button to delete all the records in the Found Set.

**File**     Click on this option button to delete an entire file. Selecting this option is equivalent to choosing File ➤ Delete Approach File.

**Files**     Click on this button to open the Macro Delete File dialog box with which you can select a file to be deleted.

**Don't Show Warning Dialog before Deleting**     Check this checkbox to bypass the display of a message box with which you can confirm the deletion. If the checkbox is cleared, the macro pauses until you or the user responds to the confirmation message. A cleared checkbox is the default.

For more information, see the "Delete, Macro Command" topic in the Approach help facility.

## Dial

Select this command to dial the telephone number in the current field using the settings in the Dialer tab of the Approach Preferences dialog box. This is equivalent to clicking on the Dial a Phone Number Smart-Icon or choosing Browse ➤ Dial or Worksheet ➤ Dial in the Browse environment. You can select from these options for the Dial command:

**Using Database**     From this drop-down list box, select the database file from which you will dial.

**Dial the Number in This Field**     From this list box, select the field that contains the telephone number that the macro will dial.

For more information, see the "Dial, Macro Command" topic in the Approach help facility.

## Edit

Select this command to use a command from the Edit menu. You can select from these options for the Edit command:

**Cut**     Click on this option button (the default) to cut selected data to the Windows Clipboard. This is equivalent to clicking on the Cut the Current Selection to the Clipboard SmartIcon, choosing Edit ➤ Cut, or pressing Ctrl+X.

**Copy**     Click on this option button to copy selected data to the Windows Clipboard. This is equivalent to clicking on the Copy the Current Selection to the Clipboard SmartIcon, choosing Edit ➤ Copy, or pressing Ctrl+C.

**Paste**     Click on this option button to paste the contents of the Windows Clipboard. This is equivalent to clicking on the Paste the Clipboard Contents SmartIcon, choosing Edit ➤ Paste, or pressing Ctrl+V.

**Select All**     Click on this option button to select all the data. This is equivalent to choosing Edit ➤ Select All.

**Open Paste Special Dialog and Wait for Input**     Click on this option button to open the Paste Special dialog box. This is equivalent to clicking on the Paste Special SmartIcon or choosing Edit ➤ Paste Special. If you select this option button, the macro pauses until you or the user clicks on OK to close the dialog box.

For more information, see the "Edit, Macro Command" topic in the Approach help facility.

### Enter

Select this command to enter the current record into the database. This is equivalent to clicking on the Enter the Record or Perform the Find SmartIcon or pressing the Enter key. For more information, see the "Enter, Macro Command" topic in the Approach help facility.

### Exit

Select this command to exit Approach. This command is equivalent to clicking on the Exit Approach SmartIcon, choosing File ➤ Exit Approach, or pressing Alt+F4. Approach provides no options for this command. For a brief explanation, see the "Exit, Macro Command" topic in the Approach help facility.

### Export

Select this command to open the Export Data dialog box in which you can choose options or export the current record or the current set of found records to a file. This command is equivalent to clicking on the Export Database SmartIcon or choosing File ➤ Export Data. You can select from these options for the Export command:

**When Macro Is Run, Open Export Data Dialog and Wait for Input**    Click on this option button to open the Export Data dialog box. If you select this option, the macro pauses until you or the user clicks on OK to close the dialog box. This is the default.

**Set Export Data Options Now and Automatically Export When Macro Is Run**    Click on this option button to specify the export options now so that the macro will run the export process without opening the Export Data dialog box and waiting for you or the user to click on OK.

**Edit Export**    Click on this button to open the Export Data dialog box from which you can select export options.

For more information, see the "Export, Macro Command" topic in the Approach help facility.

## Find

Select this command to run, create, or edit a named Find using the Find Assistant. This command is equivalent to clicking on the Find button, choosing Browse ➤ Find ➤ Find, pressing Ctrl+F, or selecting a named Find from the drop-down list box on the right side of the action bar. You can select from these options for the Find command:

**Perform Stored Find When Macro Is Run**    Click on this option button to indicate that the macro will run a saved Find during processing.

**New Find**    Click on this button to create a saved Find. This button is available only if you select the Perform Stored Find When Macro Is Run option button.

**Edit Find**    Click on this button to edit a saved Find. This button is available only if you have saved a named Find and have selected the Perform Stored Find When Macro Is Run option button.

**Named Find/Sort**    Type or select a named Find from this text box/drop-down list box.

**Refresh the Found Set**    Click on this option button to update the found named Find with new data.

**Go to Find and Wait for Input**    Click on this option button to open a Find window and wait for the user to specify options on which to find.

**Find Again and Wait for Input**    Click on this option button to find the next occurrence of the Find and wait for the user to specify options on which to find.

**Go to Find Assistant and Wait for Input**    Click on this option button to open the Find Assistant and wait for the user to specify options on which to find.

**Find All Records**    Click on this option button to run the Find.

**When No Records Are Found, Run Macro**    Click on this checkbox and provide an action that Approach will take if the Find doesn't find records. Either fill in the text box or select an action from the drop-down list box. This checkbox and text box/drop-down list box are available only if you select the Perform Stored Find When Macro Is Run option button.

For more information, see the "Find, Macro Command" topic in the Approach help facility.

### Import

Select this command to open the Import Data dialog box in which you can choose options or import a file into the current database. This is equivalent to clicking on the Import SmartIcon or choosing File ➤ Import Data.

> **When Macro Is Run, Open Import Data Dialog and Wait for Input**    Click on this option button to open the Import Data dialog box. If you select this option, the macro pauses until you or the user clicks on OK to close the dialog box. This is the default.

> **Set Import Data Options Now and Automatically Import When Macro Is Run**    Click on this option button to specify the import options now so that the macro will run the import process without opening the Import Data dialog box and waiting for you or the user to click on OK.

> **Define Import File**    Click on this button to open the Import Data dialog box to start defining import conditions.

> **Edit Import Setup**    Click on this button to open the Import Setup dialog box in which you can change export options. This button is active only if you have defined an import file first.

For more information, see the "Import, Macro Command" topic in the Approach help facility.

### Mail

Select this command to open the TeamMail dialog box so that you can send a message or attachment(s) or specify TeamMail options. This is equivalent to clicking on the New Message SmartIcon or choosing File ➤ TeamMail ➤ Send New Message.

> **When Macro Is Run, Open TeamMail Dialog and Wait for Input**    Click on this option button to open the TeamMail Data dialog box. If you select this option, the macro pauses until you or the user clicks on OK to close the dialog box. This is the default.

**Set Mail Options Now and Automatically Send Mail when Macro Is Run**    Click on this option button to specify the TeamMail options now so that the macro will send mail without opening the TeamMail dialog box and waiting for you or the user to click on OK.

**Edit TeamMail**    Click on this button to open the TeamMail dialog box from which you can select mail options.

For more information, see the "Mail, Macro Command" topic in the Approach help facility.

## Menu Switch

Select this command to switch to the default menu, to the short menu, or to a user-defined menu, which is available in the Browse environment.

**Switch the Menu Bar to**    From this drop-down list box, select the Default Menu (the default) or Short Menu.

**Customize Menus**    Click on this button to open a dialog box in which you can create and edit custom menus. You must have created a custom menu before this button is available.

For more information, see the "Menu Switch, Macro Command" topic in the Approach help facility.

## Message

Select this command to open a user-defined message box with one or two buttons on which you can click to run a macro, continue running the current macro, or stop running the macro.

**Title**    Type the message box title in this text box.

**Text**    Type the text of the message in this text box.

**Button 1 Name**    Type the name of the first button in this text box. The default button name is OK.

**Button 1 Macro**    From this drop-down list box, select a saved macro, the **CONTINUE** command to keep running the current macro, or the **STOP** command to stop running the current macro. The default selection is **CONTINUE**.

**Button 2 Name**    Type the name of the second button, if you want to define one, in this text box. If you do not type a button name, the message box will not contain a second button.

**Button 2 Macro**    From this drop-down list box, select a saved macro, the \*\*CONTINUE\*\* command to keep running the current macro, or the \*\*STOP\*\* command to stop running the current macro.

For more information, see the "Message, Macro Command" topic in the Approach help facility.

## Open

 Select this command to open the Open dialog box in which you can specify a file to be opened. This is equivalent to clicking on the Open a File SmartIcon, choosing File ➤ Open, or pressing Ctrl+O.

**When Macro Is Run, Open the File Open Dialog and Wait for Input**    Click on this option button to open the Open dialog box. If you select this option, the macro pauses until you or the user clicks on OK to close the dialog box. This is the default.

**Define the File to Automatically Open When Macro Is Run**    Click on this option button to specify the Open options now so that the macro will open a file without opening the Open dialog box and waiting for you or the user to click on OK.

**File Name**    In this text box, type the name of the file that you want the macro to open.

**Files**    Click on this button to open the Macro Open File dialog box so that you can choose the file that the macro will run.

For more information, see the "Open, Macro Command" topic in the Approach help facility.

## Page To

Select this command to go to a particular page in the current record.

**Go to First Page**    Click on this option button to go to the first page of the current record. This is the default.

**Go to Last Page**     Click on this option button to go to the last page of the current record.

**Go to Previous Page**     Click on this option button to go to the previous page of the current record.

**Go to Next Page**     Click on this option button to go to the next page of the current record.

**Go to Page Number**     Click on this option button to go to particular page number in the current record.

For more information, see the "Page To, Macro Command" topic in the Approach help facility.

## Print

Select this command to open the Print dialog box from which you can print the current record or Approach file or define print and printer properties. This is equivalent to clicking on the Print the Current Selection SmartIcon or choosing File ➤ Print.

**When Macro Is Run, Open the Print Dialog and Wait for Input**     Click on this option button to open the Print dialog box. If you select this option, the macro pauses until you or the user clicks on OK to close the dialog box. This is the default.

**Set Print Options Now and Automatically Print When Macro Is Run**     Click on this option button to specify the Print options now so that the macro will open a file without opening the Print dialog box and waiting for you or the user to click on OK.

**Edit Print**     Click on this button to open the Print dialog box so that you can select options that this command will use when the macro runs.

For more information, see the "Print, Macro Command" topic in the Approach help facility.

## Print Preview

Select this command to switch to the Print Preview environment. This is equivalent to clicking on the Print Preview SmartIcon, selecting Print Preview from the Environment drop-down list box in the Status bar, choosing File ➤ Print Preview, or pressing Ctrl+Shift+B. Approach provides no options for this command. For a short explanation of this command, see the "Print Preview, Macro Command" topic in the Approach help facility.

## Records

Select this command to perform an action on a record: go to, hide, duplicate, or create a record.

> **Current Record**     Click on this option button to go to the current record.

> **First Record**     Click on this option button to go to the first record in the current database. This is equivalent to clicking on the Go to the First Record or Page SmartIcon; or clicking on the Record button, typing 1 in the Go to Record text box, and clicking on OK.

> **Previous Record**     Click on this option button to go to the previous record in the current database. This is equivalent to clicking on the Go to the Previous Record or Page SmartIcon; clicking on the Previous Record button in the Status bar; or clicking on the Record button, typing the number that is one less than that displayed in the Go to Record text box, and clicking on OK.

> **Next Record**     Click on this option button to go to the next record in the current database. This is equivalent to clicking on the Go to the Next Record or Page SmartIcon; clicking on the Next Record button in the Status bar; or clicking on the Record button, typing the number that is one greater than that displayed in the Go to Record text box, and clicking on OK.

> **Last Record**     Click on this option button to go to the last record in the current database. This is equivalent to clicking on the Go to the Last Record or Page SmartIcon; or clicking on the Record button, typing the number of the last record (look at the Found *m* of *n* button, where *n* represents the last record number) in the Go to Record text box, and clicking on OK.

Advanced Approach

▶ ▶

Ch.

**18**

**Record Number**    Click on this option button to go to the record whose number you type in the text box. This is equivalent to clicking on the Record button, typing the desired record number in the Go to Record text box, and clicking on OK.

**Create a New Record**    Click on this option button to create a record. This is equivalent to clicking on the New Record button, choosing Browse ▶ New Record, or pressing Ctrl+N.

**Hide Record**    Click on this option button to hide the current record. This is equivalent to choosing Browse ▶ Hide Record or pressing Ctrl+H.

**Duplicate Record**    Click on this option button to make a copy of the current record. This is equivalent to clicking on the Duplicate Current Record SmartIcon, choosing Browse ▶ Duplicate Record, or pressing Ctrl+Alt+D.

For more information, see the "Records, Macro Command" topic in the Approach help facility.

## Replicate

Select this command to replicate a Notes database on your hard drive, if Notes is installed on your network.

**When Macro Is Run, Open the Replicate Dialog and Wait for Input**    Click on this option button to open the Replicate dialog box. If you select this option, the macro pauses until you or the user clicks on OK to close the dialog box. This is the default.

**Set Replication Options Now and Automatically Replicate When Macro Is Run**    Click on this option button to specify the replication options now so that the macro will open a file without opening the Replicate dialog box and waiting for you or the user to click on OK.

**Edit Replicate**    Click on this button to open the Replicate dialog box so that you can select options that this command will use when the macro runs.

For more information, see the "Replicate, Macro Command" topic in the Approach help facility.

## Run

Select this command to go to another macro and optionally return to the current macro from which you have issued the Run command.

**Run Macro**    Click on this option button (the default) and select a macro to run from the drop-down list box.

**Return to the Next Line in This Macro**    Check this checkbox to return to the next line of the current macro after going through the steps in the embedded macro. A checked checkbox is the default.

**If**    Check this option button to specify a condition for running the macro from within the current macro.

**Formula**    Click on this button to open the Formula dialog box in which you can build a formula from fields, operators, and functions. This button is available only if you have selected the If option button.

**Is True**    From this drop-down list box, select an action that the macro performs if the If statement is true. This drop-down list box is available only if you have selected the If option button. List entries are Run & Return from Macro (the default), Run Macro, Continue This Macro, and End This Macro.

**Else**    From this drop-down list box, select an action that the macro performs if the If statement is false. This drop-down list box is available only if you have selected the If option button and have placed a checkmark in the Else checkbox. List entries are Run & Return from Macro (the default), Run Macro, Continue This Macro, and End This Macro.

For more information, see the "Run, Macro Command" topic in the Approach help facility.

## Save

Select this command to choose File ➤ Save to automatically save the current Approach file using the defaults or to choose File ➤ Save As to open the Save As dialog box in which you can select save options for the current Approach file.

**When Macro Is Run, Open the Save As Dialog and Wait for Input**    Click on this option button to open the Save As dialog box. This is equivalent to clicking on the Save As New File Smart-Icon or choosing File ➤ Save As. If you select this option, the macro pauses until you or the user clicks on OK to close the dialog box.

 **Save Approach File**    Click on this option button to save the Approach file without opening the Save As dialog box and waiting for you or the user to click on OK. This is equivalent to clicking on the Save the Current Approach File SmartIcon, choosing File ➤ Save Approach File, or pressing Ctrl+S. This is the default.

For more information, see the "Save, Macro Command" topic in the Approach help facility.

## Send Key

Select this command to insert keystrokes in the current macro. So, if you want to have the macro perform an action using shortcut keys or key combinations, simply enter them in the Keystroke Sequence text box. To enter a key that you can print in a document, press the key. To enter a key that will not print in a document (for example, Alt, Ctrl, Backspace, and so on), type a key code surrounded by braces. For more information about nonprinting keystrokes, see the "Send Key Keystrokes" topic in the Approach help facility. For a short explanation of the Send Key command, see the "SendKey, Macro Command" topic in the Approach help facility.

## Set

Select this command to set the selected field to a particular value or to insert a formula in the field. This is equivalent to choosing Browse ➤ Fill Field.

**Using Database**    From this drop-down list box, select the database in which the field that you want to fill is located.

**Set This Field**    From this scroll box, select the field in which you want to specify the value or insert the formula.

**To This Value**    In this text box, type the value to be inserted in the selected field.

**Formula**    Click on this button to open the Formula dialog box in which you can create a formula using fields, operators, and functions.

For more information, see the "Set, Macro Command" topic in the Approach help facility.

## Sort

Select this command to open the Sort dialog box in which you can select sort options. This is equivalent to clicking on the Open the Sort Dialog SmartIcon, choosing Browse ➤ Sort ➤ Define, or pressing Ctrl+T.

**When Macro Is Run, Open the Sort Dialog and Wait for Input**    Click on this option button to open the Sort dialog box. If you select this option, the macro pauses until you or the user clicks on OK to close the dialog box. This is the default.

**Set Sort Now and Automatically Sort the Records when the Macro Is Run**    Click on this option button to specify the sort options now so that the macro will not have to wait for you or the user to click on OK. If you click on this option button, select the database from the drop-down list box, select a sort field by clicking on it and clicking on the Add button, and select an Ascending (the default) or Descending sort. To remove a selected field, click on it, and click on the Remove button. To remove all selected fields, click on a field, and click on the Clear All button.

**Summaries**    Click on this button to display an additional part of the dialog box in which you can select summary fields from the Summary Fields box.

▶▶ **N O T E**

> **To include a summary field in the Summary Fields box, you must have selected it in the Sort dialog box.**

For more information, see the "Sort, Macro Command" topic in the Approach help facility.

## Spell Check

Select this command to open the Spell Check dialog box in which you can specify spell check options or from which you can check spelling in the current Approach file. This is equivalent to clicking on the Check Spelling SmartIcon, choosing Edit ➤ Check Spelling, or pressing Ctrl+F2. Approach provides no options for this command. For a short explanation of this command, see the "Spell Check, Macro Command" topic in the Approach help facility.

## Tab

Select this command to move to a particular field in the current record.

> **Tab to Position *n* of the Current View's Tab Order**   In this text box, type the number of the tab to which you want the macro to go.

For more information, see the "Tab, Macro Command" topic in the Approach help facility.

▶▶ **N O T E**

> **To view the tab orders of the current form, go to the Design environment, and choose View ➤ Show Tab Order.**

## View

Select this command to go to another view, display the current view, or hide the current view. This is the default macro command.

**Switch the Current View To**    Click on this option button to switch to the view that you select from the box to the right of the option button. This is equivalent to clicking on a tab in the View Tabs bar or clicking on the View button in the Status bar and selecting a view. This is the default.

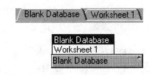

 **In Browse, Show View**    Click on this option button to display the hidden view that you select from the box to the right of the option button. This is equivalent to switching to the Design environment, clicking on the background of the form, and either clicking on the Change the Properties of the Selected Object SmartIcon, choosing Form ➤ Form Properties, or pressing Alt+Enter. Then, click on the Basics tab and clear the checkmark from the Hide View checkbox.

 **In Browse, Hide View**    Click on this option button to hide the view that you select from the box to the right of the option button. This is equivalent to switching to the Design environment, clicking on the background of the form, and either clicking on the Change the Properties of the Selected Object SmartIcon, choosing Form ➤ Form Properties, right-clicking on the form and choosing Form Properties, or pressing Alt+Enter. Then, click on the Basics tab and place a checkmark in the Hide View checkbox.

For a short explanation, see the "View, Macro Command" topic in the Approach help facility.

## Zoom

Select this command to zoom in or out within the current window in the Design environment.

 **Zoom In**    Click on this option button to zoom in to see the details of part of the form. This is equivalent to clicking on the Zoom In for a Closer Look SmartIcon or choosing View ➤ Zoom In.

 **Zoom Out**    Click on this option button to zoom out to a wider view of the form. This is equivalent to clicking on the Zoom Out to See More SmartIcon or choosing View ➤ Zoom Out.

Advanced
Approach

➤ ➤

*Ch.*
**18**

**Actual Size (100%)**    Click on this option button to view the form at its actual size. This is equivalent to clicking on the Zoom to 100% SmartIcon, choosing View ➤ Zoom To ➤ 100%, or pressing Ctrl+1.

 **Zoom to 200%**    Click on this option button to view the form at double its actual size. This is equivalent to clicking on the Zoom In to 200% SmartIcon or choosing View ➤ Zoom To ➤ 200%.

 **Zoom to 85%**    Click on this option button to view the form at 85% of its actual size. This is equivalent to clicking on the Zoom Out to 85% SmartIcon or choosing View ➤ Zoom To ➤ 85%. Other options are 75%, 50%, and 25%.

For a short explanation, see the "Zoom, Macro Command" topic in the Approach help facility.

## ► Creating a Macro

To create a macro, follow these steps:

1. Choose Edit ➤ Macros. Approach displays the Macros dialog box.

2. Click on the New button. Approach opens the Define Macro dialog box with the default View command selected.

3. To name the macro, overtype Macro in the Macro Name text box.

4. To assign a function key from F1 to F12, select from the Function Key drop-down list box.

5. To choose a macro command, open the Command drop-down list box, and click on a command name. Select an appropriate option, if the command offers options.

6. To insert another command and select an option, click on the next line, and repeat step 5. You can select duplicate commands in a macro.

7. To insert a line between other command lines, click on the line that will follow the new line, and click on Insert.

8. To delete a line, click on the line to be deleted, and click on Delete.

9. To delete all lines but one blank line, click on Clear All.

**10.** To print the current lines in the macro, click on the Print button, select options from the Print dialog box, and click on Print.

**11.** When you have completed the macro, click on OK. Figure 18.19 shows a sample macro.

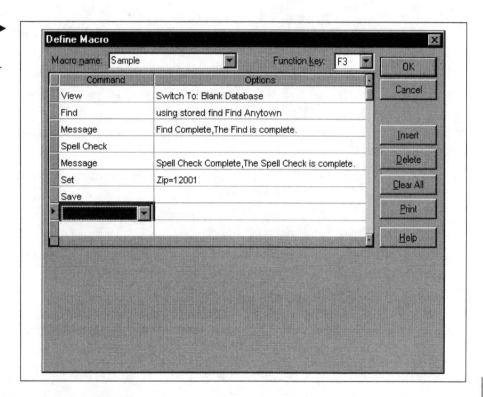

## ▶ *Running a Macro*

You can run a macro in several ways:

- If you have assigned a function key, press it.
- If the Show in Menu checkbox in the Macros dialog box is checked, choose Edit ➤ Run Macro and click on a macro name.
- Choose Edit ➤ Macros, click on a macro name, and click on the Run button.

## ▶ *Editing a Macro*

To edit a macro, follow these steps:

1. Choose Edit ➤ Macros. Approach displays the Macros dialog box.

2. Select the macro to be edited and click on the Edit button. Approach opens the Define Macro dialog box with the macro command lines displayed.

3. To rename the macro, overtype the name in the Macro Name text box.

4. To assign a function key from F1 to F12, select from the Function Key drop-down list box.

5. To edit a command line, click on it, and select a command and/or option.

6. To insert a new line, click on the Insert button, and select a command and an option.

7. To delete a line, click on the line to be deleted, and click on Delete.

8. When you have completed editing, click on OK.

## ▶ *Copying a Macro*

You can create a new macro based on an existing one by copying the macro and editing it. To copy a macro, follow these steps:

1. Choose Edit ➤ Macros. Approach displays the Macros dialog box.

2. Select the macro to be copied and click on the Copy button. Approach opens the Define Macro dialog box with the command lines of the copied macro displayed.

3. Give the copied macro a new name by overtyping the name in the Macro Name text box.

4. To assign a function key from F1 to F12, select from the Function Key drop-down list box.

5. To edit a command line, click on it, and select a command and/or option.

6. To insert a new line, click on the Insert button, and select a command and an option.

**7.** To delete a line, click on the line to be deleted, and click on Delete.

**8.** When you have completed editing, click on OK.

## ▶ Deleting a Macro

You can delete a macro that you no longer need. For example, you might have created a macro to fill in fields that you have added to a database to improve it. Once you have added the new fields, you no longer have a reason to keep the macro.

▶▶ **N O T E**

> You can delete more than one macro at a time. To select a range of macros, click on a macro name at one end of the range, press and hold down the Shift key, and click on the macro name at the other end of the range. Then, release the Shift key. To select noncontiguous macros, click on the first macro name to be selected, press and hold down the Ctrl key, and repeatedly click on other macro names to be selected. Then, release the Ctrl key.

To delete a macro permanently, follow these steps:

**1.** Choose Edit ➤ Macros. Approach displays the Macros dialog box.

**2.** Select the macro to be deleted and click on the Delete button. Approach asks you to confirm the deletion.

**3.** To delete the macro, click on Yes.

▶▶ **T I P**

> If you have inadvertently deleted a macro, you can recover it by exiting Approach without saving. Of course, this means that other changes that you have made, other than adding new records, will also be reversed.

**Advanced Approach**

▶ ▶
*Ch.*
**18**

Presenting Information
with Freelance Graphics

# PART FIVE

# CHAPTER 19

# Planning and Creating a Presentation

►► **I**n this chapter, you'll learn about creating a Freelance Graphics presentation. First, you'll learn about the elements of the Freelance Graphics window. You'll then find out about the tools that help you create a presentation quickly and easily. With all the basics in hand, you'll plan and create a presentation. Remember that you can learn the fundamentals of opening and saving files by reviewing the *Getting Acquainted with SmartSuite* chapter.

## ►► *Introducing Freelance Graphics*

Freelance Graphics is an easy-to-use application with which you can produce a professional-looking presentation almost as soon as you install the program.

Using Freelance Graphics, you can do the following:

- create a presentation from an outline. Simply write the outline and convert it into a presentation.

- create a presentation using help from experts and consultants for a particular topic.

- build a bulleted list.

- create and rehearse a *screen show*, an automated on-screen presentation.

- enhance your presentation with symbols, charts, and tables.

- draw or import pictures into your presentations—on selected pages or all pages.

- produce speaker notes and handouts.

- post a presentation to the Internet's World Wide Web.

# ►► *Viewing the Freelance Graphics Window*

The Freelance Graphics application window (see Figure 19.1) contains many of the elements that you found out about in the *Getting Acquainted with SmartSuite* chapter. Because you are now in a presentation application, however, some of the elements focus on helping you create a presentation. In this section, you'll get an overview of all the elements of the application window and find out about the Freelance Graphics Status bar.

**FIGURE 19.1** ►

*The Freelance Graphics application window provides many elements that help you create and edit presentations.*

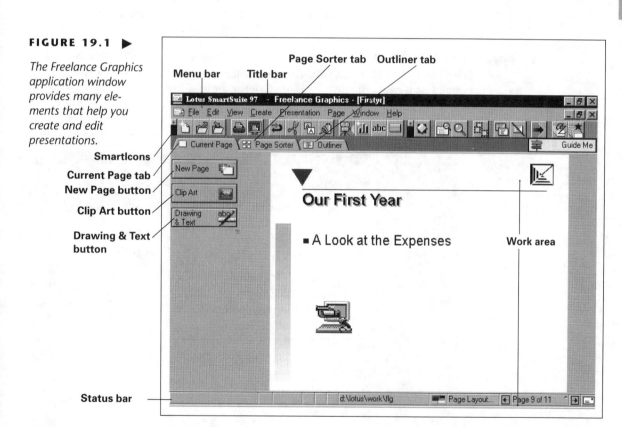

## ► *Freelance Graphics SmartIcons*

To learn how SmartIcons work, see the *Getting Acquainted with SmartSuite* chapter.

## ► *View Tabs*

Click on any of the tabs immediately below the SmartIcons to switch to another way of viewing your presentation pages or to get step-by-step help in creating and/or editing a Freelance Graphics presentation.

☐ Current Page    Click on this tab (which is the same as choosing View ➤ Current Page) to view one page of your presentation at a time. Figure 19.2 shows a preliminary presentation page in Current Page view.

⊞ Page Sorter    Click on this tab (which is the same as choosing View ➤ Page Sorter) to view a screenful of presentation pages. Figure 19.3 shows the first pages of a presentation in Page Sorter view.

**FIGURE 19.2** ►

*A preliminary presentation page in Current Page view*

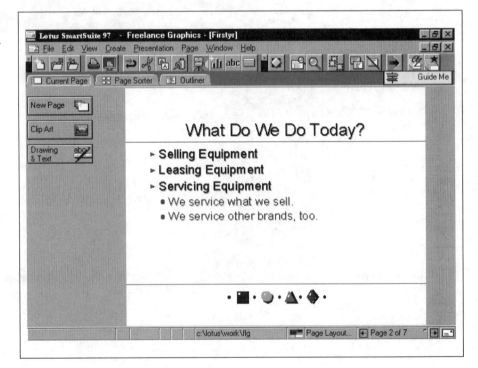

**FIGURE 19.3** ▶

*The first seven pages of a presentation in Page Sorter view*

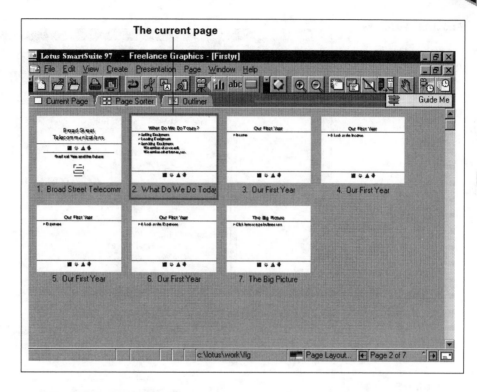

| | |
|---|---|
| [Outliner] | Click on this tab (which is the same as choosing View ➤ Outliner) to view an outline of the presentation. Figure 19.4 shows an outline of a new presentation. |
| [Guide Me] | Click on this button (which is the same as choosing Help ➤ Guide Me) to get help in working on a presentation. Figure 19.5 shows a Guide Me window. Click on a button to access a useful help topic. |

## ▶ *The Work Area*

The work area displays a presentation as you work. On the left side of the work area are three buttons:

[New Page]   Click on the New Page button to open the New Page dialog box from which you can select a page layout for a new page. Clicking on this button is equivalent to choosing Create ➤ Page, right-clicking and selecting New Page, or pressing F7.

**FIGURE 19.4** ▶

*A rough outline for a new presentation*

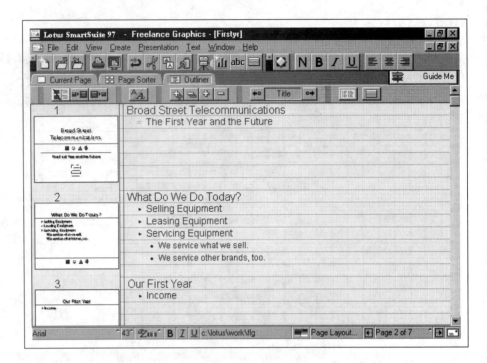

**FIGURE 19.5** ▶

*The Guide Me window that results from selecting a bulleted list and clicking on the Guide Me button*

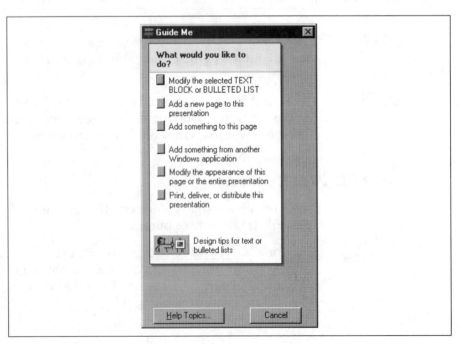

Click on the Clip Art button to open the Add Clip Art or Diagram to the Page dialog box from which you can select clip art or a diagram from a library of objects. Clicking on this button is equivalent to choosing Create ➤ Add Clip Art.

Click on the Drawing & Text button to open a drawing and text tools palette (see Figure 19.6). There is no equivalent command. Table 19.1 describes the tools on the tool palette.

**FIGURE 19.6 ▶**

*The Freelance Graphics drawing and text Tools palette*

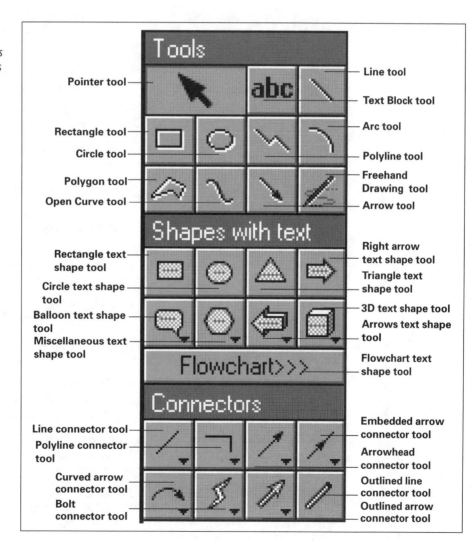

▶ **TABLE 19.1:** *Freelance Graphics Drawing Tool Palette*

| Tool | Name | Description |
| --- | --- | --- |
| | Pointer tool | Selects an object in a drawing. (Press Shift and click to add the next object to the selection.) |
| | Text Block tool | Inserts text in a drawing. |
| | Line tool | Draws a line or, if you press and hold down the Shift key, a line at a multiple of 45 degrees. |
| | Rectangle tool | Draws a rectangle or, if you press and hold down the Shift key, a square. |
| | Circle tool | Draws an ellipse or, if you press and hold down the Shift key, a circle. |
| | Polyline tool | Draws a line made up of segments. |
| | Arc tool | Draws an arc, or part of a circle. |
| | Polygon tool | Draws a polygon. |
| | Open Curve tool | Draws a curve from point to point. |
| | Arrow tool | Draws an arrow. |
| | Freehand Drawing tool | Draws freehand. |
| | Rectangle text shape tool | Draws a rectangle or, if you press and hold down the Shift key, a square on which you can type text. |
| | Circle text shape tool | Draws an ellipse or, if you press and hold down the Shift key, a circle on which you can type text. |
| | Triangle text shape tool | Draws a triangle or, if you press and hold down the Shift key, a symmetrical triangle on which you can type text. |

▶ **TABLE 19.1:** *Freelance Graphics Drawing Tool Palette (continued)*

| Tool | Name | Description |
|------|------|-------------|
| | Right arrow text shape tool | Draws a right arrow (or, if you press and hold down the Shift key, an arrow within a transparent square) on which you can type text. |
| | Balloon text shape tool | Opens a palette of text shape tools from which you can select to type spoken text on the current page. |
| | Miscellaneous text shape tool | Opens a palette of text shape tools from which you can select to type text on the current page. |
| | Arrows text shape tool | Opens a palette of three arrow text shape tools from which you can select to type text on the current page. |
| | 3D text shape tool | Opens a palette of 3D text shape tools from which you can select to type text on the current page. |
| Flowchart>> | Flowchart text shape tool | Opens a palette of text shape tools from which you can select to type text in a flowchart on the current page. |
| | Line connector tool | Opens a palette of line tools from which you can select to connect two objects or to draw on the current page. |
| | Polyline connector tool | Opens a palette of polyline tools from which you can select to connect two objects or to draw on the current page. |
| | Arrowhead connector tool | Opens a palette of single- and double-headed arrow tools from which you can select to connect two objects or to draw on the current page. |
| | Embedded arrow connector tool | Opens a palette of embedded-head arrow tools from which you can select to connect two objects or to draw on the current page. |

▶ **TABLE 19.1:** *Freelance Graphics Drawing Tool Palette (continued)*

| Tool | Name | Description |
|---|---|---|
| | Curved arrow connector tool | Opens a palette of curved arrow tools from which you can select to connect two objects or to draw on the current page. |
| | Bolt connector tool | Opens a palette of two lightning bolt tools from which you can select to connect two objects or to draw on the current page. |
| | Outlined arrow connector tool | Opens a palette of outlined arrow tools from which you can select to connect two objects or to draw on the current page. |
| | Outlined line connector tool | Draws an outlined line on the current page or, if you press and hold down the Shift key, an outlined line at a multiple of 45 degrees. |

Click on the Content Advice button to open the Content Advice for Current Page dialog box (see Figure 19.7) from which you can obtain help for filling in a page for a SmartMaster content topic presentation. This button is available only when you are working with this type of presentation.

**FIGURE 19.7**

*The context-sensitive Content Advice for Current Page dialog box*

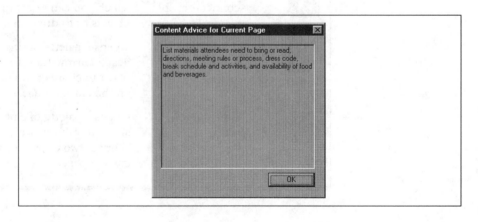

## ▶ *The Freelance Graphics Status Bar*

You can use the Freelance Graphics Status bar at the bottom of the
screen (see Figure 19.8) to go to a different page, open the Page Layout dialog box, view your presentation in color or black and white, select a font or a point size, or send a message over the local network to
which your computer is attached.

**FIGURE 19.8** ▶

*The Freelance Graphics
Status bar consists of
buttons with which
you can change the
look of a presentation
or send a message over
your local network.*

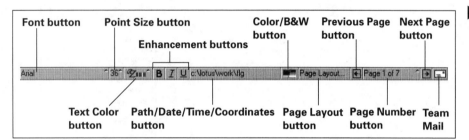

These are the buttons on the Status bar:

**Font**     Click on this button to open the list (see Figure 19.9) of
some of the fonts installed on your computer. To open this list,
you must have selected some text. Click on More Fonts to display
the More Fonts dialog box, from which you have the choice of all the
fonts installed under Windows.

**Point Size**     Click on this button to display the list of some of
the point sizes for the current font. To open this list, you must
have selected some text. Click on Custom Size to display the Custom Text Size dialog box, in which you can type a point size in the
Size in Points text box. If you have selected text with varying font
sizes, the word *Mixed* appears in the Size in Points text box.

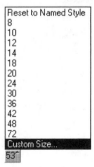

**FIGURE 19.9** ▶

*The installed fonts on one computer system*

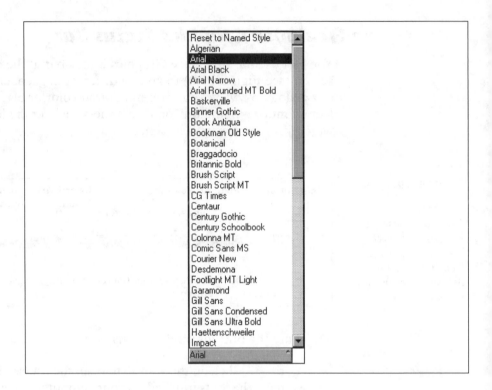

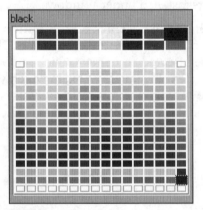

**Text Color** Click on this button to open a palette with which you can change the color of the selected text.

**Enhancement** Click on any of these buttons to apply or remove boldface, italics, or underline from the selected text.

**Path/Date/Time/Coordinates**    Click on this button to cycle through a display of the current path and folder, the computer system date and time, and coordinates of the current mouse pointer position.

**Color/B&W**    Click on this button to switch between displaying the presentation in color or black and white.

**Page Layout**    Click on this button to open the Switch Page Layout dialog box (see Figure 19.10), from which you can select a page layout for the current page.

**Previous Page**    Click on this button to move to the previous page, unless you are viewing the first page.

**Page Number**    Click on this button, which shows the current page number, to display the names of all the pages in the presentation. The checkmark indicates the current page. If you are in Outliner view, the button displays the word *Outliner*. If you are editing a page layout, this button reads *Layout*. If your presentation is greater than 20 pages, Freelance Graphics opens the Go to Page dialog box instead of listing all the pages in the presentation.

```
1.  Broad Street Telecommunications
2.  What Do We Do Today?
3.  Our First Year
4.  Our First Year
5.  Our First Year
6.  Our First Year
7.  The Big Picture
```

**Next Page**    Click on this button to move to the next page, unless you are viewing the last page.

**TeamMail**    Click on this button to open the TeamMail for Lotus Freelance dialog box (see Figure 19.11), from which you can send mail from your networked computer to another computer on the network. Clicking on this button is the equivalent of choosing File ➤ TeamMail.

Creating a
Presentation

▶▶

*Ch.*
**19**

**FIGURE 19.10** ▶

*The Switch Page Layout dialog box, from which you can select a layout for the current page*

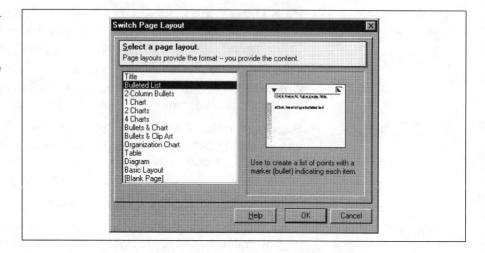

**FIGURE 19.11** ▶

*The TeamMail for Lotus Freelance dialog box, from which you can create and send mail to others on your network*

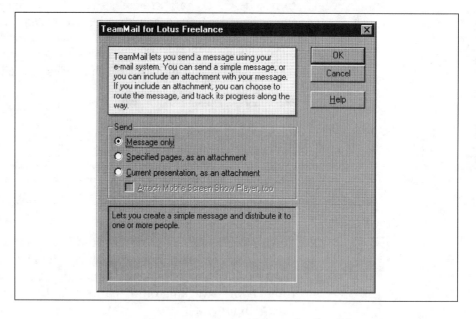

## ▶▶ *Planning a Presentation*

Although Freelance Graphics makes it very easy to write a presentation on the fly, it's best to plan it. When planning a presentation, consider these important points:

**Audience Profile and Environment**     Tailor the presentation to your audience and their surroundings. Consider such factors as the meeting time and day, the meeting location, professional and educational backgrounds of the attendees, their knowledge of the topic, and the amount of time you've been assigned.

**Your Objectives**     What do you want to happen as a result of giving the presentation? Is it purely educational? Do you want your audience to remember or have a positive feeling about certain topics? The three basic purposes for giving a presentation are education, information, and selling. Although you can combine all three into a single presentation, you'll probably want to emphasize one of the three.

After determining your audience and objectives, you can get into the details of the presentation by writing an outline.

- Plan an introduction, which is an overview of the presentation and a preface to the topic. You are preparing your audience for the rest of the presentation.

- Write down the major topics, and then fill in with four or five subtopics for each. Consider ending each major topic with a short summary and an introduction to the next topic.

- Briefly summarize the presentation.

## ▶▶ *Creating a Presentation*

With Freelance Graphics, you can develop a presentation in two basic ways: by creating a page-by-page presentation in Current Page view or by writing an outline in Outliner view and having Freelance Graphics convert it to a presentation.

- If you are creating a presentation from scratch, using the Outliner is a good choice. It is probably the fastest way to create a presentation. Once Freelance Graphics completes the pages, you'll be able to edit them on your desktop.

- If you are editing a presentation or have a little more time, using Current Page view works well because you can spend your time working on each page. When you start Freelance Graphics, the program steps you through creating a new presentation and selecting the style and page on which you want to work. You can also use these opening dialog boxes to open an existing presentation.

Typing and editing the text on a presentation page or in an outline is just about the same as creating and editing a word-processing document. The main difference between working on a presentation and working on a document is the length of sentences; presentation sentences are usually short and sweet.

## ▶ Getting Started

When you start Freelance Graphics, the Welcome to Lotus Freelance Graphics dialog box (see Figure 19.12) prompts you to create a new presentation, open an existing presentation, or take the Freelance Graphics tour.

To work on an existing presentation, select it in the Open an Existing Presentation section of the dialog box, and then click on OK. Freelance Graphics opens the presentation and you can start work right away.

To create a new presentation, click on the Create a New Presentation Using a SmartMaster tab, and Freelance Graphics displays a new section (see Figure 19.13) with two steps: Select a Content Topic and Select a Look.

 If you have been working in Freelance Graphics, start a new presentation by clicking on the Create a New File SmartIcon or by choosing File ➤ New Presentation. Freelance Graphics opens the New Presentation dialog box, which contains the same options as the Create a New Presentation Using a SmartMaster section of the Welcome to Lotus Freelance Graphics dialog box.

**FIGURE 19.12** ▶

*The Open an Existing Presentation section of the Welcome to Lotus Freelance Graphics dialog box*

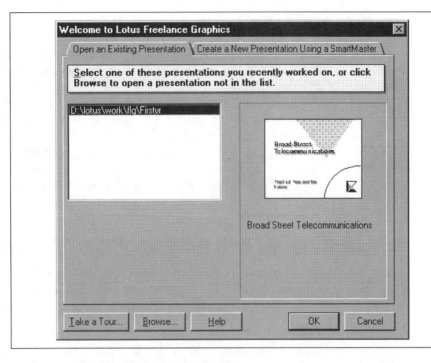

**FIGURE 19.13** ▶

*The Create a New Presentation Using a SmartMaster section of the Welcome to Lotus Freelance Graphics dialog box*

## ▶ Selecting the Content Topic

The first step in starting a new presentation is to select the *content topic*: the types of pages making up the presentation and the content of each page. In either the New Presentation dialog box or the Create a New Presentation Using a SmartMaster section of the Welcome to Lotus Freelance Graphics dialog box, you can choose No Content Topic, which enables you to design the presentation page by page, or you can select one of the SmartMaster sets of titled pages that you can fill in using content advice from consulting firms and experts. (For information about using SmartMaster templates, see the section entitled "Using SmartMaster Templates," on a following page.) In this section, we will select No Content Topic.

## ▶ Selecting a Look for Your Presentation

In the Select a Look scroll box, you choose the format and background for each page of the presentation. Freelance Graphics displays the SmartMaster set with which you worked most recently.

To view looks before choosing, click on the name in the scroll box and look at the sample on the lower right side of the dialog box. Keep selecting files and viewing the samples until you find a set that you like. Click on OK to select the set and close the dialog box.

## ▶ Choosing a Page Layout

Freelance Graphics displays the New Page dialog box (see Figure 19.14), with which you can select the type of page on which to work. The sample box shows the look of the selected page and describes it.

When you have selected a page type, click on OK. Freelance Graphics displays the page that you have chosen (see Figure 19.15).

## ▶ Creating a Presentation in Outliner View

An Outliner view outline is very similar to any document outline. You work with four levels. Level 1, which is the highest level, is the presentation or page title line, and each of the three additional levels is indented slightly under the one above it. As you change to Level 2, 3, or 4, the bullet symbol in front of the line changes, and the line moves away from the left margin.

**FIGURE 19.14** ▶

*The New Page dialog box with the Title page layout selected*

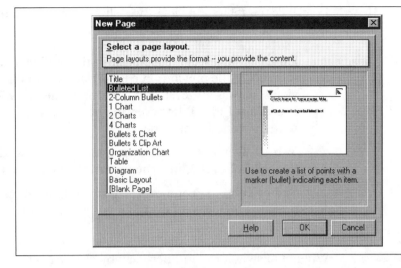

**FIGURE 19.15** ▶

*The first page of a new Freelance Graphics presentation ready for you to edit*

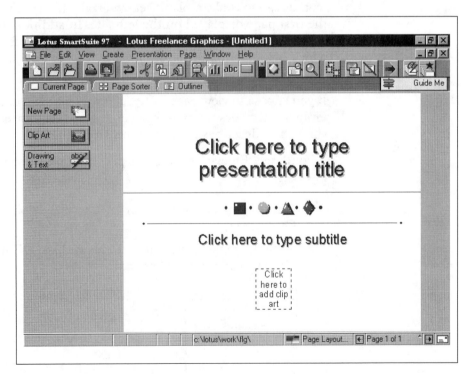

Freelance Graphics provides two shortcut keys and one key combination for use in Outliner view:

**Enter**      Creates the next line in the outline. Except for Level 1, the level of the previous line is carried over to this line. If the previous line was at Level 2, the new line is also Level 2. If the previous line was at Level 1, however, the new line is at Level 2. A page can have only one Level 1 line.

**Tab**      Demotes the current line. In other words, if the previous line was a Level 3 line, the current line becomes a Level 4 line.

**Shift+Tab**      Promotes the current line. In other words, if the previous line was a Level 3 line, the current line becomes a Level 2 line.

When you switch to Outliner view by clicking on the Outliner tab, the work area looks like a blank yellow legal pad (see Figure 19.16), with the first page displayed on the left side. In addition, Freelance Graphics adds a button bar to the window. Table 19.2 describes these buttons, which help you to move from level to level in an outline or collapse or expand pages or the entire presentation.

If you choose to view page icons rather than a page image, Freelance Graphics provides symbols representing certain page elements. Table 19.3 shows and describes page icons on an Outliner view page.

To outline a Freelance Graphics presentation using Outliner view, follow these steps:

**1.** Click on the Outliner tab or choose View ➤ Outliner to switch to Outliner view.

**2.** Type the presentation title (Title) and press Enter. Freelance Graphics adds a new line.

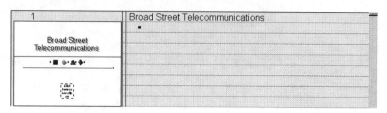

**FIGURE 19.16** ▶

*The Freelance Graphics
work area in Outliner
view*

The first page of
a presentation in
Outliner view

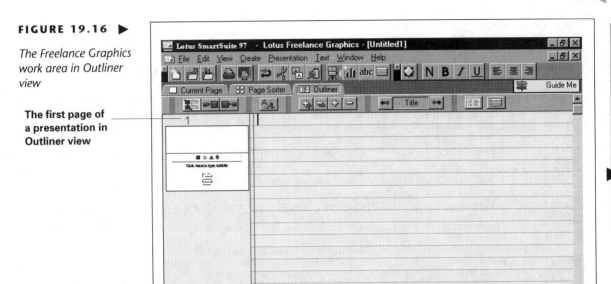

▶ **TABLE 19.2:** *Freelance Graphics Outliner Buttons*

| Button | Button Name | Menu Command;<br>Shortcut Key | Description |
|---|---|---|---|
| | Show Page Picture/Page Icon | View ➤ Show Pictures of Pages; N/A | Toggles between pictures of the presentation pages and icons representing page types. |
| | Increase Page Size | View ➤ Page Size ➤ Medium or View ➤ Page Size ➤ Large; N/A | Increases the sizes of pictures of pages. (This is available only if you are showing pictures of pages.) |
| | Decrease Page Size | View ➤ Page Size ➤ Small or View ➤ Page Size ➤ Medium; N/A | Decreases the sizes of pictures of pages. (This is available only if you are showing pictures of pages.) |

▶ **TABLE 19.2:** *Freelance Graphics Outliner Buttons (continued)*

| Button | Button Name | Menu Command; Shortcut Key | Description |
|---|---|---|---|
| | Formatted/ Unformatted Text | View ➤ Draft Mode; N/A | Toggles between displaying formatted text as it is formatted or not. |
| | Expand Outline | View ➤ Expand All; N/A | Displays all levels of the outline of the entire presentation. |
| | Collapse Outline | View ➤ Collapse All; N/A | Displays the highest levels only in the outline of the entire presentation. |
| | Expand Page | View ➤ Expand; + | Displays all levels of the outline of the current page. |
| | Collapse Page | View ➤ Collapse; – | Displays the title, the highest level only, in the outline of the current page. |
| | Promote | N/A; Shift+Tab | Increases the selected line of text to the next higher level. If you promote from Level 1 to a Title, Freelance Graphics starts a new page with the new title. |
| Title | Page Type | N/A; N/A | Displays the current page type. |
| | Demote | N/A; Tab | Decreases the selected line of text to the next lower level unless its level is already Level 5. |
| | Columns | Text ➤ Make Second Columns; N/A | Inserts a column break to start a second column. |
| | Speaker Note | Create ➤ Speaker Note; N/A | Creates speaker notes for the current page. |

Creating a
Presentation

Ch.
**19**

▶ **TABLE 19.3:** *Freelance Graphics Outliner Symbols*

| Symbol | The page contains: |
|--------|--------------------|
| | Text (no graphics or symbols, charts, tables, or organization charts) |
| | Chart(s) |
| | Table, graphics, or symbols |
| | Organization chart |

*3.* Type the subtitle and press Enter.

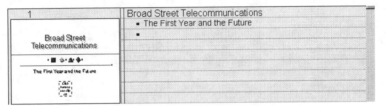

*4.* Press Shift+Tab or click on the Promote button. Freelance Graphics promotes the new line to a Title and starts a new page.

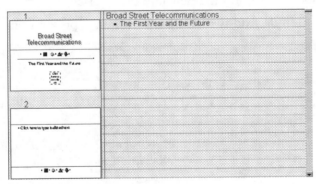

*5.* Type the title of the second page and press Enter.

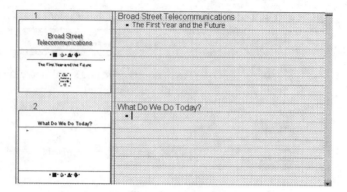

**6.** Add three bulleted items, pressing Enter after each.

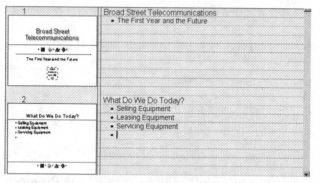

**7.** Press Tab or click on the Demote button. Freelance Graphics demotes the new line to Level 2.

**8.** Add two new bulleted items, pressing Enter after each.

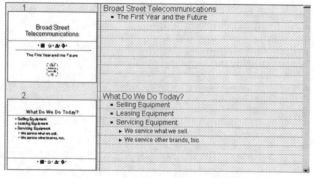

**9.** Click on the Show Page Picture/Page Icon button to show page icons rather than pictures of each page, allowing more pages on your desktop.

*10.* Press Shift+Tab or click on the Promote button two times. Free-lance Graphics starts a new page.

*11.* Continue filling in the presentation, page by page. Save the presentation at any time. Figure 19.17 shows the first part of a presentation in Outliner view.

Ch.
**19**

▶▶

**FIGURE 19.17** ▶

*The first part of a presentation in Outliner view*

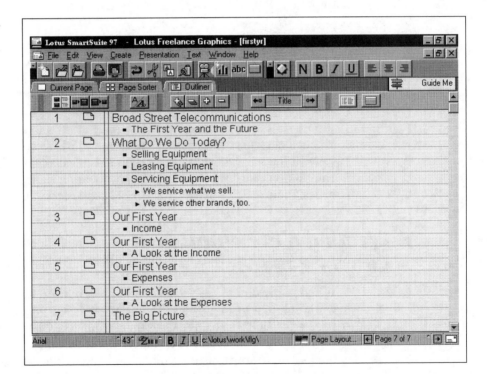

You can click on the Current Page tab or choose View ➤ Current Page to view the current page of the presentation. Once in Current Page view, you can either edit or view other pages. Figure 19.18 shows the second page of the presentation in Current Page view.

**FIGURE 19.18** ▶

*The second page of the sample presentation in Current Page view*

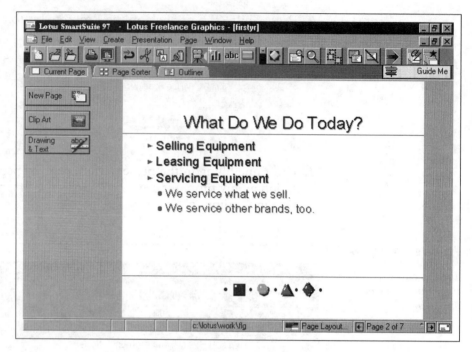

You can click on the Page Sorter tab or choose View ➤ Page Sorter to view all the pages of the presentation and to rearrange the pages in a presentation by dragging a page to its new location between two current pages. Figure 19.19 shows the sample presentation in Page Sorter view.

## ▶ Creating a Presentation in Current Page View

When you want to see the look of a presentation page immediately, work in Current Page view. To add to or edit a page, select part of the page and click. Freelance Graphics displays a Click Here text box (see Figure 19.20) in which you can type and format text. At the top of the box is a set of buttons on which you can click to change formats or get help. Table 19.4 describes the buttons.

To add more pages to the sample presentation, follow these steps:

*1.* Click on the Current Page tab or choose View ➤ Current Page to switch to Current Page view.

**FIGURE 19.19** ▶

*All the pages of the sample presentation in Page Sorter view*

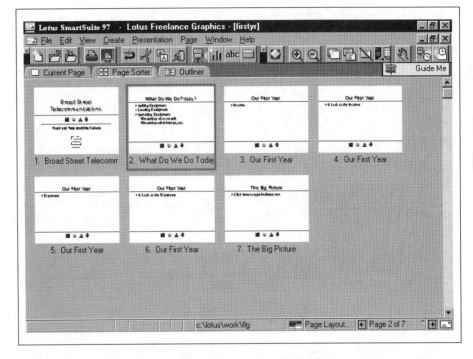

**FIGURE 19.20** ▶

*A new page in Current Page view*

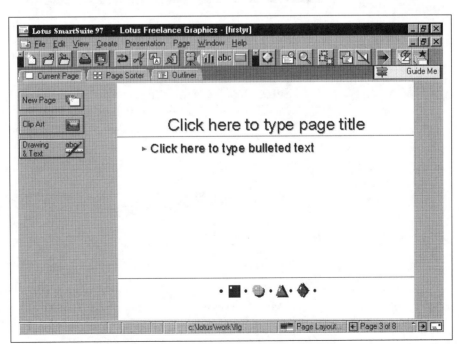

▶ **TABLE 19.4:** *Click Here Text Box Elements*

| Element | Description |
|---------|-------------|
| ←○ | Click on the Promote button to increase the selected line of text to the next higher level, from Level 1 to Level 5. |
| Level 2 | Current Level displays the level of the current selection. |
| ○→ | Click on the Demote button to decrease the selected line of text to the next lower level. |
| A▸A | Click on the Decrease Font button to decrease the font of the selected line of text to the next lower size. (Look at the font size button in the status bar to see the current size.) |
| A▸A | Click on the Increase Font button to increase the font of the selected line of text to the next higher size. (Look at the font size button in the status bar to see the current size.) |
| Tips... | Click on the Tips button to reveal a dialog box with lists of tasks and the shortcut keys, SmartIcons, or menu commands with which you complete a task. |

**2.** Click on the New Page button, choose Create ➤ Page, right-click and select New Page, or press F7. Freelance Graphics displays the New Page dialog box.

**3.** Select a page layout (our sample page is a Bulleted List) from the Choose a Page Layout box and either click on OK or press Enter. Freelance Graphics displays a new page on the desktop (see Figure 19.21).

**FIGURE 19.21** ▶

*A text box in which you can type text for a presentation page*

**4.** Click on Click Here to Type Page Title. Freelance Graphics opens a box in which you can type. (To close the box without typing a title, press Esc.)

5. Type the page title, **Our Future**, and click on OK. Freelance Graphics closes the dialog box and puts the new text in the former location of Click Here to Type Page Title. Click anywhere on the window to remove the handles from the title.

6. Click on Click Here to Type Bulleted Text. Freelance Graphics displays a box in which you can type.

7. Type **Retail Stores** and press Enter. Freelance Graphics adds a new bullet in the box.

8. Press Tab or click on the Demote button. Freelance Graphics demotes the bullet to Level 2 from Level 1.

9. Type **Selling our goods**, press Enter, type **Selling our services**, and click on OK. Freelance Graphics closes the box and displays the new bulleted items.

10. Repeat the preceding steps to add new pages. Be sure to save the presentation from time to time.

## ▶ *Getting Guidance and Tips*

Freelance Graphics provides two unique help features: Guide Me and Tips. Guide Me provides step-by-step help for standard Freelance Graphics tasks, such as modifying pages or page elements, adding new pages, printing and distribution, and more. When you are adding elements to a page, you can access Tips, which are lists of shortcut keys, SmartIcons, or menus containing the commands that you can use to fill in a text box.

### *Guide Me Help*

When you need help working with a Freelance Graphics feature or function, click on the Guide Me button to open a window listing common tasks (see Figure 19.22). Click on a button to reveal another window, which either displays a list related to the selected task (see Figure 19.23) or instructions (see Figure 19.24). For additional information about using the SmartSuite help system, see the *Getting Acquainted with SmartSuite* chapter.

**FIGURE 19.22** ▶

*A Guide Me window with a list of tasks for which you can get help*

**Click on a button to open another help window.**

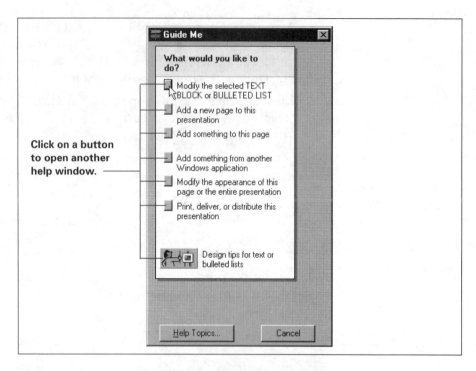

**FIGURE 19.23** ▶

*Layers of Guide Me windows, which narrow the search for particular help*

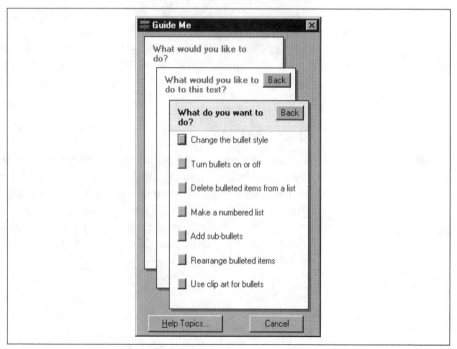

**FIGURE 19.24** ▶

*A Freelance Graphic
Help window*

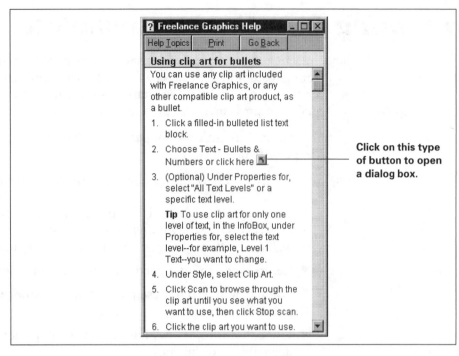

**Click on this type
of button to open
a dialog box.**

## Tips

When filling in a Click Here text box, you can access a "cheat sheet" that has a list of tasks and the shortcut key, SmartIcon, or menu command. Simply click on the Tips button to open a context-sensitive Tips dialog box (see Figure 19.25).

**FIGURE 19.25** ▶

*A context-sensitive
Tips dialog box*

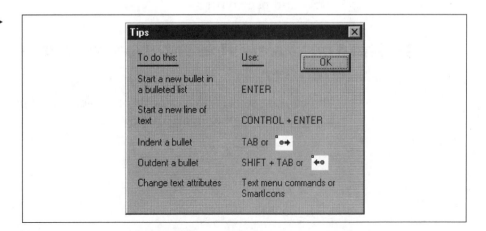

# ▶▶ *Using SmartMaster Templates*

Freelance Graphics provides several sets of presentation page designs from consultants and experts. SmartMaster templates cover business plans, competitor analysis, market research, market strategy, meetings, quality improvement, sales, training, and more.

You can use an entire set of pages on which to create a presentation or a page or two as a start.

You can use a SmartMaster content topic for several purposes:

- Learn how to create an effective presentation by seeing how the experts do it. Study individual pages and the elements on them as well as the flow of pages from the beginning to end.

- Learn more about a particular business practice from experts.

- Use elements from these pages to make your presentations more effective.

- Use content topics to plan meetings and projects within your own department or business.

- Use content topics as the basis for reports and proposals: business plans, annual reports, project reports, employee handbooks, and so on.

This section is composed of two portions. The first explains how to start a new presentation using a set of SmartMaster content topics; the second briefly describes each SmartMaster content topic, and lists its pages and page types.

## ▶ *Starting a New Presentation with a SmartMaster*

You can use selected pages or the complete set of pages to create a presentation based on a SmartMaster.

To use a SmartMaster template, follow these steps:

1. If you have just started Freelance Graphics, click on the Create a New Presentation Using a SmartMaster tab in the Welcome to Lotus Freelance Graphics dialog box.

2. If you have been working in Freelance Graphics, start a new presentation by clicking on the Create a New File SmartIcon or by choosing File ➤ New Presentation. Freelance Graphics opens the New Presentation dialog box (see Figure 19.26), which contains the same options as the Create a New Presentation Using a Smart-Master section of the Welcome to Lotus Freelance Graphics dialog box.

3. From the content topic scroll box, select one of the SmartMaster sets of titled pages.

4. From the Select a Look scroll box, either accept the Look Stored with Content Topic or another look.

**FIGURE 19.26** ▶

*The New presentation dialog box with the pre-designed Meeting—Standard SmartMaster and the look stored with it*

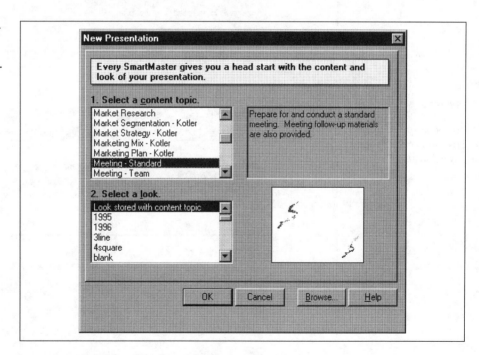

**5.** Click on OK. If Freelance Graphics opens a dialog box that describes the content topic (see Figure 19.27), read the message, and click on OK. Freelance Graphics opens the New Page dialog box (see Figure 19.28).

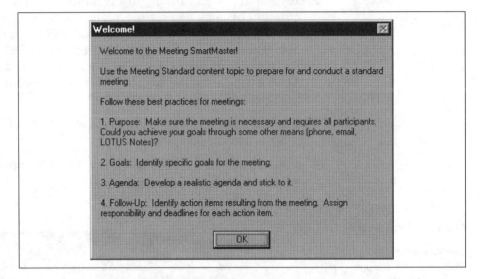

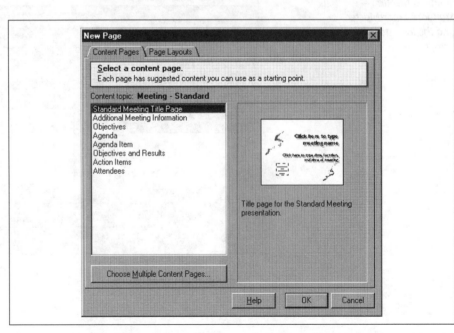

6. To select a single page from the list, click on it and click on OK. Freelance Graphics displays the new page in the work area (see Figure 19.29).

**FIGURE 19.29** ▶

*The Standard Meeting Title Page for the Meeting—Standard SmartMaster*

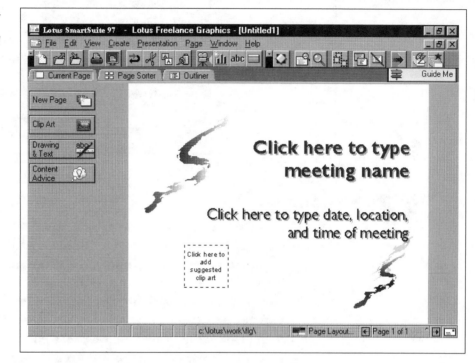

7. To select all the pages from the list, click on Choose Multiple Content Pages. In the New Page—Choose Multiple Content Pages dialog box, click on the Select All button, and click on OK. Freelance Graphics displays the new page in the work area.

8. To select multiple pages from the list, click on Choose Multiple Content Pages. In the New Page—Choose Multiple Content Pages dialog box, choose pages, following the directions in the yellow box. Click on OK. Freelance Graphics displays the new page in the work area.

9. Using the content of the Content Advice for Current Page (see Figure 19.30) as a guide, add text, graphics, a table, symbols, or an organization chart to the current page. You'll find that many SmartMaster pages automatically include bulleted items.

**FIGURE 19.30** ▶

*One of the Content
Advice message boxes
for the Meeting—
Standard SmartMaster*

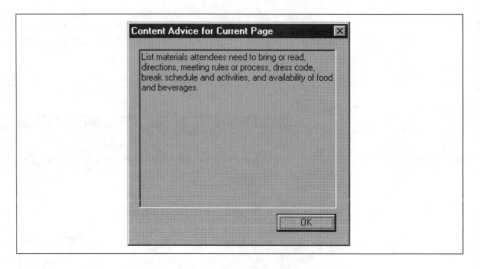

**Content Advice for Current Page**

List materials attendees need to bring or read,
directions, meeting rules or process, dress code,
break schedule and activities, and availability of food
and beverages.

OK

▶▶ **T I P**

**An efficient way of using the Content Advice for
Current Page dialog box to "build" a page is to print it
as you would a help window. Unfortunately, a Print
button is not included in the message box. To prepare
to print the message box, open Word Pro, another
word processor, or the Windows Wordpad word
processor (open WordPad by pressing the Start button,
choosing Programs, selecting Accessories, and clicking
on WordPad). Then, press Alt+Print Screen to copy the
message box into the Windows Clipboard. Finally, go
to the open word processor, press Ctrl+V or choose
Edit ➤ Paste to paste the message box into the work
area, and print by choosing File ➤ Print. To print more
pages, keep the word or text processor open and
repeat the copy/paste/print instructions.**

**10.** Continue to add pages by clicking on the New Page button and
following steps 7, 8, and 9.

**11.** At any time, save the presentation.

# ▶▶ *SmartMaster Content Topics*

Freelance Graphics provides 30 SmartMaster content topics—the basis for presentations on a variety of subjects—with which you can present information to your employees and customers and plan for the growth of your business. Each of the following sections describes a particular content topic, lists its page titles, and identifies its page types.

## *Business Plan*

This content topic includes all the components of a business plan presentation. It could be converted to a business plan proposal. Page titles and page types are:

| Page Title | Page Type |
| --- | --- |
| Business Plan Title Page | Title |
| Agenda | Bulleted List |
| Executive Summary | Bulleted List |
| Company Background—Section Title | Title |
| Mission Statement | Bulleted List |
| Product/Service Positioning | Bulleted List |
| Competitive Advantage | Bulleted List |
| Market Overview—Section Title | Title |
| Target Market Description | Bullets & Clip Art |
| Target Market Profile | Bulleted List |
| Purchase Criteria | Bullets & Clip Art |
| Target Market Growth Rates | 1 Chart |

| Page Title | Page Type |
|---|---|
| Product Overview—Section Title | Title |
| Products/Services | Table |
| Pricing | Bulleted List |
| Revenue Forecast | Bullets & Chart |
| Business Strategy—Section Title | Title |
| Marketing Channels | Diagram |
| Marketing Mix | Bullets & Chart |
| Selling | Bullets & Clip Art |
| Value Added | Bulleted List |
| Suppliers | Bulleted List |
| Competition—Section Title | Title |
| Key Competitors | Bulleted List |
| Competitor Evaluation | Table |
| Competitor Positioning | Diagram |
| Risks—Section Title | Title |
| Barriers to Entry | Bullets & Clip Art |
| Substitutes | Bulleted List |
| Other Risks | Table |
| Business Team—Section Title | Title |
| Organizational Structure | Organization Chart |
| Management Profile | Table |
| Board of Directors | Table |

| Page Title | Page Type |
|---|---|
| Company Ownership | 2 Charts |
| Funding Request—Section Title | Title |
| Total Funding Required | Table |
| Exit Strategy | Bulleted List |
| Timeline of Events | Diagram |
| Financial Statements—Section Title | Title |
| Financial Summary | Table |
| Financial Statements | Bulleted List |

## Business Review

This content topic reviews business performance, including goals and achievements, the state of the industry, and a prediction of the company's future. Page titles and page types are:

| Page Title | Page Type |
|---|---|
| Business Review Title Page | Title |
| Agenda | Bulleted List |
| Executive Summary | Bulleted List |
| Goals & Accomplishments—Section Title | Title |
| Goals | Bullets & Clip Art |
| Accomplishments | Bulleted List |
| Significant Events | Diagram |
| Performance—Section Title | Title |

| Page Title | Page Type |
| --- | --- |
| Market Share | Bullets & Chart |
| Market Share by Segment | Table |
| Revenue Performance | Bullets & Chart |
| Gross Margin Performance | Bullets & Chart |
| Expense Performance | Bullets & Chart |
| Income Performance | Bullets & Chart |
| Capital Structure | Bullets & Chart |
| Cash Flow | Bullets & Chart |
| Productivity Indicators | Bullets & Chart |
| Benchmark Analysis | Table |
| Business Outlook—Section Title | Title |
| Industry Trends | Bullets & Clip Art |
| Internal Responses | Bulleted List |
| Business Goals | Bullets & Chart |
| Summary | Bulleted List |

## Corporate Overview

This content topic describes a company in great detail. Many pages could become part of a comprehensive business plan. Page titles and page types are:

| Page Title | Page Type |
| --- | --- |
| Corporate Overview Title Page | Title |
| Agenda | Bulleted List |

| Page Title | Page Type |
| --- | --- |
| Company Overview—Section Title | Title |
| Business Definition | Bulleted List |
| Product Line Description | Bulleted List |
| Competitive Advantage | Bullets & Clip Art |
| Significant Events | Diagram |
| Financial Performance | 2 Charts |
| Additional Performance Measures | Table |
| Stock Price Performance | 1 Chart |
| Segment Overview—Section Title | Title |
| Segment Structure | Diagram |
| Segment Definition | Table |
| Sales by Segment | 1 Chart |
| Profitability by Segment | 1 Chart |
| Outlook by Segment | Diagram |
| Industry Overview—Section Title | Title |
| Industry Landscape | Diagram |
| Industry Size and Growth | 1 Chart |
| Industry Trends | Bulleted List |
| Impact of Industry Trends | Table |
| Competitor Landscape—Section Title | Title |
| Market Share | 1 Chart |

| Page Title | Page Type |
|---|---|
| Competitor Profile | Bullets & Chart |
| Strengths and Weaknesses | Table |
| Summary and Outlook—Section Title | Title |
| Summary | Bulleted List |
| Corporate Outlook | Bullets & Chart |
| Recommendations | Bulleted List |

## Industry Analysis

This content topic provides an analysis of a particular industry, including competing companies, customers, and industry trends. Page titles and page types are:

| Page Title | Page Type |
|---|---|
| Industry Analysis Title Page | Title |
| Agenda | Bulleted List |
| Background—Section Title | Title |
| Industry Definition | Bulleted List |
| Industry History | Bullets & Clip Art |
| Significant Changes | Bulleted List |
| Industry Sales and Growth | 1 Chart |
| Sales Growth by Segment | 1 Chart |
| Industry Patterns | Bullets & Clip Art |

Creating a Presentation

Ch. **19**

| Page Title | Page Type |
| --- | --- |
| Barriers to Entry and Exit | 2-Column Bullets |
| Critical Success Factors | Bulleted List |
| Customers—Section Title | Title |
| Customer Categories | Bulleted List |
| Customer Motivation | Bulleted List |
| Customer Profile | Bulleted List |
| Customer Influence | Bullets & Clip Art |
| Competitors—Section Title | Title |
| Competitive Products | Diagram |
| Competitor Strategies | Table |
| Market Share | Bullets & Chart |
| Performance | 2 Charts |
| Strengths and Weaknesses | Table |
| Market Signals | Bulleted List |
| Suppliers—Section Title | Title |
| Supplied Products | Diagram |
| Supplier Influence | Bulleted List |
| Trends—Section Title | Title |
| Innovation | Bullets & Clip Art |
| Complements | Bulleted List |
| Substitutes | Bulleted List |
| Summary | Bulleted List |
| Next Steps | Bullets & Clip Art |

## IT Strategy—Gemini Consulting

This content topic helps your company evaluate and make plans for an information technology strategy. Page titles and page types are:

| Page Title | Page Type |
| --- | --- |
| IT Strategy Title Page | Title |
| Agenda | Bullets & Clip Art |
| IT Strategy Development—Section Title | Title |
| Need for IT Strategy | Diagram |
| The IS Organization | Diagram |
| Organization Input | Organization Chart |
| The Foundation for the IT Strategy | Diagram |
| IT Vision and Strategy | Diagram |
| Corporate IT Strategy—Section Title | Title |
| Corporate IT Initiatives | Table |
| Corporate IT Initiative Description | Bulleted List |
| Business Unit IT Strategy—Section Title | Title |
| Value Delivery System | Diagram |
| Business IT Opportunities | Table |
| Business Unit Initiative Description | Bulleted List |
| Technology Deliverables—Section Title | Title |

| Page Title | Page Type |
| --- | --- |
| Business Critical Technologies | Table |
| IT Products & Services Deliverables | Bulleted List |
| Governance | Diagram |
| Accountability for Deliverables | Table |
| Conclusions—Section Title | Title |
| Summary | Bulleted List |
| Next Steps | Bullets & Clip Art |

## Market Research

This content topic proposes or presents a market research program for your company. Page titles and page types are:

| Page Title | Page Type |
| --- | --- |
| Market Research Title Page | Title |
| Agenda | Bulleted List |
| Objectives—Section Title | Title |
| Background | Bulleted List |
| Objectives | Diagram |
| Executive Summary | Bulleted List |
| Methods—Section Title | Title |
| Research Approach | Bulleted List |
| Sample | Bulleted List |
| Results—Section Title | Title |

| Page Title | Page Type |
|---|---|
| Detailed Findings | Bullets & Chart |
| Recommendations—Section Title | Title |
| Conclusions | Bulleted List |
| Next Step | Bullets & Clip Art |

## Market Segmentation—Kotler

This content topic covers the market segmentation part of a marketing plan. This is part two of a four-part series of presentations. Page titles and page types are:

| Page Title | Page Type |
|---|---|
| Market Segmentation Title Page | Title |
| Executive Summary | Bulleted List |
| Overview: Segmentation Analysis | Blank Page with an illustration |
| Agenda | Bulleted List |
| Market Background—Section title | Title |
| Product Driven View of the Market | Table |
| Product Fact Book | Table |
| Customer Base View of the Market | Table |
| Customer Fact Book | Table |

| Page Title | Page Type |
| --- | --- |
| Segment Development— Section Title | Title |
| Segmentation Variable Selection | Table |
| Market Segments | Diagram |
| Segment Requirements Statement | Table |
| Segment Targeting— Section Title | Title |
| Segment Attractiveness Analysis | Table |
| Business Strength Analysis | Table |
| Segment Strategy Map | Diagram |
| Segment Product Fit Strategies | Table |
| Segment Product Selection | Table |
| Segment Targeting Statement | Table |
| Segment Positioning— Section Title | Title |
| Quality/Price Differentiation | Diagram |
| Competitive Differentiation | Diagram |
| Product/Attribute Differentiation | Table |
| Benefit Differentiation | Table |
| User Differentiation | Table |

| Page Title | Page Type |
|---|---|
| Use Differentiation | Table |
| Positioning Strategy Selection | Table |
| Segment Positioning Strategies | Table |
| Next Steps | Bulleted List |

## Market Strategy—Kotler

This content topic presents the market strategies for a business. It is part one of a four-part series of presentations. Page titles and page types are:

| Page Title | Page Type |
|---|---|
| Market Strategy Title Page | Title |
| Executive Summary | Bulleted List |
| Overview: Market Strategy Analysis | Blank Page with an illustration |
| Agenda | Bulleted List |
| The Business Vision— Section Title | Title |
| Business Definition | Table |
| Stakeholder Needs | Table |
| Stakeholder Issues | Table |
| Stakeholder Tradeoffs | Table |
| Core Customers | Table |
| Core Products/Services | Table |
| Core Competences | Table |

| Page Title | Page Type |
|---|---|
| Mission Statement | Bulleted List |
| Vision Statement | Bulleted List |
| Estimate Planning Gap—Section Title | Title |
| External Trend Assessment | Table |
| Internal Trend Assessment | Table |
| Core Competences Gap | Table |
| Opportunities | Table |
| Threats | Table |
| Business Strengths & Weaknesses | Table |
| Competitor Strengths & Weaknesses | Table |
| Total Net Adjustment | Table |
| Projected Baseline Trends | Table |
| Strategic Planning Gap Chart | 2 Charts |
| Close Planning Gap—Section Title | Title |
| Market Attractiveness Analysis | Table |
| Business Strength Analysis | Table |
| Strategy Map | Diagram |
| Strategy Statement | Table |
| Unadjusted Revenue Baseline | Table |

| Page Title | Page Type |
|---|---|
| Unadjusted ROI Baseline | Table |
| Strategy Impacts | Table |
| Planned Growth and Changes | Table |
| Planned Baseline Trends | Table |
| Implement Market Strategy—Section Title | Title |
| Business Programs | Table |
| Program Implementation | Diagram |
| Management and Control | Table |
| Next Steps | Bulleted List |

## Marketing Mix—Kotler

This content topic covers the marketing mix part of a marketing plan. It is part three of a four-part series of presentations. Page titles and page types are:

| Page Title | Page Type |
|---|---|
| Marketing Mix Title Page | Title |
| Executive Summary | Bulleted List |
| Overview: Marketing Mix Analysis | Blank Page with an illustration |
| Agenda | Bulleted List |
| Estimate Planning Gap—Section Title | Title |
| External Trend Assessment | Table |
| Internal Trend Assessment | Table |

| Page Title | Page Type |
| --- | --- |
| Core Competences Gap | Table |
| Opportunities | Table |
| Threats | Table |
| Marketing Strengths & Weaknesses | Table |
| Competitor Strengths & Weaknesses | Table |
| Total Net Adjustment | Table |
| Projected Baseline Trends | Table |
| Marketing Mix Planning Gap Chart | 2 Charts |
| Closing the Marketing Planning Gap— Section Title | Title |
| Price Plan | Table |
| Product Plan | Table |
| Channel Plan | Table |
| Promotion Plan | Table |
| Strategy Statement | Table |
| Unadjusted Revenue Baseline | Table |
| Unadjusted Market Share Baseline | Table |
| Strategy Impacts | Table |
| Planned Growth and Changes | Table |
| Planned Baseline Trends | Table |

| Page Title | Page Type |
|---|---|
| Implement Marketing Plan—Section Title | Title |
| Marketing Campaigns | Table |
| Campaign Implementation | Diagram |
| Campaign Budget | Table |
| Marketing Budget | Table |
| Management and Control | Table |
| Next Steps | Bulleted List |

## Marketing Plan—Kotler

This content topic incorporates market segmentation, market strategy, and marketing mix results for a marketing plan. It is part four of a four-part series of presentations. Page titles and page types are:

| Page Title | Page Type |
|---|---|
| Marketing Plan Title Page | Title |
| Executive Summary | Bulleted List |
| Agenda | Bulleted List |
| Business Orientation—Section Title | Title |
| Market Characteristics | Table |
| Key Stakeholders | Diagram |
| Stakeholder Issues and Tradeoffs | Table |
| Core Competences | Bulleted List |
| Enabling Capabilities | Diagram |
| Business Vision | Table |

| Page Title | Page Type |
|---|---|
| Customers and Products—Section Title | Title |
| Prime Customer Groups | Diagram |
| Principal Products | Diagram |
| Toughest Competitors | Diagram |
| Marketing Challenges—Section Title | Title |
| Opportunities and Threats | Table |
| Strengths and Weaknesses | Table |
| Marketing Planning Gap | 2 Charts |
| Target Markets—Section Title | Title |
| Market Segments | Table |
| Product Fit Strategies | Table |
| Product Enhancements | Diagram |
| New Products | Table |
| Segment Positioning Strategy | Table |
| Marketing Campaigns—Section Title | Title |
| Marketing Mix Strategy | Bulleted List |
| Campaign Plans | Diagram |
| Campaign Implementation | Diagram |
| Management and Control | Table |
| Marketing Budget | Bullets & Chart |
| Planned Results | 2 Charts |

| Page Title | Page Type |
|---|---|
| Next Steps | Bulleted List |

## Meeting—Standard

This content topic provides the structure for a standard meeting and includes information to be used to create the agenda for the next meeting. Page titles and page types are:

| Page Title | Page Type |
|---|---|
| Standard Meeting Title Page | Title |
| Additional Meeting Information | Bullets & Clip Art |
| Objectives | Diagram |
| Agenda | Table |
| Agenda Item | Bulleted List |
| Objectives and Results | Table |
| Action Items | Table |
| Attendees | Table |

## Meeting—Team

This content topic provides presentation pages and handouts for a regularly scheduled team meeting. Page titles and page types are:

| Page Title | Page Type |
|---|---|
| Team Meeting Title Page | Title |
| Agenda | Bulleted List |
| Company News | Bulleted List |

| Page Title | Page Type |
|---|---|
| Team Member Updates | Bulleted List |
| Other Discussion Topics | Bulleted List |
| Current Events Discussion | Bullets & Clip Art |
| Action Items | Table |
| Summary | Bullets & Clip Art |

## New Market Entry

This content topic aids in the evaluation of the industry, competing companies, and customers in a market that you may enter. Page titles and page types are:

| Page Title | Page Type |
|---|---|
| New Market Entry Title Page | Title |
| Agenda | Bulleted List |
| Executive Summary | Bulleted List |
| Market Analysis— Section Title | Title |
| Market Definition | Bullets & Clip Art |
| Market Landscape | Diagram |
| Customers | Bulleted List |
| Competition | Bullets & Clip Art |
| Competitor Market Share | Bullets & Chart |
| Suppliers | Table |
| Substitutes | Bulleted List |
| Barriers to Entry | Bulleted List |

| Page Title | Page Type |
| --- | --- |
| Market Opportunity Summary | Bulleted List |
| Entry Strategy— Section Title | Title |
| Overall Strategy | Bulleted List |
| Specific Strategies | Bulleted List |
| Fit with Core Competencies | Bulleted List |
| Competitor Reactions | Table |
| Forecast Market Share | Bullets & Chart |
| Milestones | Diagram |
| Financial Summary— Section Title | Title |
| Capital Investment | Table |
| Projected Sales and Earnings | Bullets & Chart |
| Return on Investment | Bullets & Chart |
| Opportunities | Bulleted List |
| Potential Risks | Table |
| Summary—Section Title | Title |
| New Market Entry Summary | Bulleted List |
| Recommendations | Bulleted List |
| Next Steps | Bullets & Clip Art |

## Positioning Proposal—Trout & Ries

This content topic helps you to analyze your company's current market position and enables you to develop a unique strategy for your company and products or services. Page titles and page types are:

| Page Title | Page Type |
| --- | --- |
| Positioning Proposal Title Page | Title |
| Agenda | Bullets & Clip Art |
| Our Current Position—Section Title | Title |
| Current Customer Profile | Bullets & Clip Art |
| Current Position | Bulleted List |
| Focus Group Results | Bulleted List |
| Key Attribute Findings | Diagram |
| Research Findings | 1 Chart |
| Third Party Quotations | Basic Layout |
| Market Share | 1 Chart |
| The Competition—Section Title | Title |
| Key Competitors | Bulleted List |
| Competitor Strengths/Weaknesses | 2-Column Bullets |
| Our Desired Position—Section Title | Title |

| Page Title | Page Type |
|---|---|
| Desired Position | Bullets & Clip Art |
| Benefit of Desired Position | Bulleted List |
| Support for Desired Position | Bullets & Clip Art |
| Alternative Positions Considered | Table |
| Implementation—Section Title | Title |
| Program Elements | Bulleted List |
| Program Timetable | Diagram |
| Competitive Reaction | Table |
| Follow-up Programs | Bulleted List |
| Communication—Section Title | Title |
| Possible Messages | Bullets & Clip Art |
| Possible Communication Conflicts | Bulleted List |
| Internal Programs | Bullets & Clip Art |
| Budget—Section Title | Title |
| Competitive Spending Comparison | 1 Chart |
| Marketing Budget | 1 Chart |
| Alternative Spending Plans | 1 Chart |
| Summary | Bulleted List |

## Product/Service Briefing

This content topic presents your business and its products and/or services to companies and individuals who may support your company in some way. Page titles and page types are:

| Page Title | Page Type |
| --- | --- |
| Product/Service Briefing Title Page | Title |
| Agenda | Bulleted List |
| Briefing Overview | Bulleted List |
| Market—Section Title | Title |
| Market Overview | Bulleted List |
| Market Size and Growth | 1 Chart |
| The Competition | Table |
| Market Share | Bullets & Chart |
| Product/Service Review— Section Title | Title |
| Original Need | Bulleted List |
| Competitive Advantage | Bulleted List |
| Key Features | Bullets & Clip Art |
| Positioning Strategy— Section Title | Title |
| Messaging | Bulleted List |
| Proposed Budget | Bullets & Chart |
| Schedule | Diagram |
| Next Steps | Bullets & Clip Art |

## Product/Service Launch

This content topic enables you to launch a new product or service in its market. Page titles and page types are:

| Page Title | Page Type |
|---|---|
| Product/Service Launch Title Page | Title |
| Agenda Page | Bulleted List |
| Product Overview—Section Title | Title |
| Product/Service Description | Bulleted List |
| Positioning | Bullets & Clip Art |
| Primary Target Market | Bullets & Clip Art |
| Key Messages | Bulleted List |
| Features and Benefits | Table |
| Target Market Demographics | Bulleted List |
| Customer Requirements | Diagram |
| Competitors: Strategy Analysis | Table |
| Competitors: Product Comparison | Table |
| Pricing Comparisons | Table |
| Suppliers | Bulleted List |

| Page Title | Page Type |
|---|---|
| Launch Objectives— Section Title | Title |
| Sales Goals | 2 Charts |
| Market Share Goals | 1 Chart |
| Additional Objectives | Diagram |
| Launch Plans— Section Title | Title |
| Launch Timeline | Diagram |
| Marketing Channels | Diagram |
| Marketing Budget and Mix | Bullets & Chart |
| Marketing Programs | Table |
| Sales Process | Bulleted List |
| Product Availability and Time Line | Diagram |
| Profit and Loss Statement | Table |
| Measures of Success | Bulleted List |
| Summary | Bulleted List |
| Next Steps | Bulleted List |

## Project Proposal

This content topic presents a structure for discussing and planning a new project. Page titles and page types are:

| Project Proposal Title Page | Title |
|---|---|
| Agenda | Bulleted List |

**Project Proposal**

| Title Page | Title |
| --- | --- |
| Introduction—Section Title | Title |
| Proposal Objectives | Bulleted List |
| Background | Bullets & Clip Art |
| Key Issues | Bulleted List |
| Proposal Overview—Section Title | Title |
| Solution | bulleted List |
| Benefits | Bullets & Chart |
| Risks | Bulleted List |
| Implementation | Bulleted List |
| Possible Alternatives | Table |
| Terms of the Proposal—Section Title | Title |
| Project Scope | Bulleted List |
| Deliverables | Bullets & Clip Art |
| Project Milestones | Diagram |
| Project Team | Organization Chart |
| Pricing/Payment Terms | Bullets & Clip Art |
| Cost/Benefit Analysis | bullets & Chart |
| Additional Considerations | Bulleted List |
| qualifications—Section Title | Title |
| Resources | Bulleted List |
| References | Bulleted List |

**Project Proposal**

| | |
|---|---|
| **Title Page** | **Title** |
| Summary | Bulleted List |
| Next Steps | Bullets & Clip Art |

## Project Status Report

This content topic enables you to prepare a regular status report for and, at the same time, analyze the progress of a project. Page titles and page types are:

| Page Title | Page Type |
|---|---|
| Project Status Report Title Page | Title |
| Agenda | Bullets & Clip Art |
| Overview—Section Title | Title |
| Project Overview | Bulleted List |
| Objectives | Diagram |
| Benefits | Bulleted List |
| Team | Organization Chart |
| Constraints | Bullets & Clip Art |
| Current Status—Section Title | Title |
| Schedule | Diagram |
| Action Items | Table |
| Current Budget Status | Bullets & Chart |
| Budget Forecast | 1 Chart |
| Going Forward—Section Title | Title |

| Page Title | Page Type |
|---|---|
| Milestones | Table |
| Risk | Bulleted List |
| Opportunities | Table |
| Next Steps | Bullets & Clip Art |
| Summary | Bullets & Clip Art |

## Quality Improvement—Juran

This content topic enables you to develop a quality improvement program for your business. Page titles and page types are:

| Page Title | Page Type |
|---|---|
| Quality Improvement Process Title Page | Title |
| Mission Statement | Bulleted List |
| Team Members | Bulleted List |
| Project Status | Diagram |
| Diagnostic Journey— Section Title | Bulleted List |
| Analysis of Symptoms | Bulleted List |
| The Vital Few | 1 Chart |
| Current Process | Diagram |
| Revisit the Mission | Bulleted List |
| Formulation of Theories | Diagram |
| Theory Test Summary | Table |
| Chart Analysis | 1 Chart |

| Page Title | Page Type |
| --- | --- |
| Histogram Analysis | 1 Chart |
| Scatter Chart Analysis | 1 Chart |
| Root Cause | Bulleted List |
| The Remedy—Section Title | Bulleted List |
| Possible Remedies | Bulleted List |
| Criteria for the Remedy | Bulleted List |
| Remedy Selection Matrix | Table |
| Remedy Design Features | Table |
| Diagram of Remedy | Diagram |
| Feedback Loop | Diagram |
| Cultural Barriers & Countermeasures | Diagram |
| Effectiveness of Remedy | 1 Chart |
| Implementation Plan | Diagram |
| Impact of the Remedy | 1 Chart |
| Other Applications of Remedy | Table |
| Potential New Projects | Bulleted List |

## Recommend a Strategy

This content topic enables you to recommend and get approval for solutions to problems and strategies for the future. Page titles and page types are:

| Page Title | Page Type |
| --- | --- |
| Recommend a Strategy Title Page | Title |

| | |
|---|---|
| Meeting Objectives | Diagram |
| History | Bulleted List |
| Sequence of Events | Diagram |
| Problem Statement | Bulleted List |
| Key Issues | Table |
| Potential Solutions | Bulleted List |
| Evaluation of Alternatives | Table |
| Recommended Strategy | Bulleted List |
| Cost Benefit Analysis | Bullets & Chart |
| Opportunity Cost | Bullets & Chart |
| Summary | Bulleted List |
| Next Steps | Bullets & Clip Art |

## Sales—Ken Wax

This content topic enables you to prepare a sales presentation that emphasizes the benefits of your products or services over your competitor's products or services. Page titles and page types are:

| Page Title | Page Type |
|---|---|
| Sales Title Page | Title |
| Before We Begin | Bulleted List |
| Our Agenda for Today | Bulleted List |
| Why the Interest in Us? | Bulleted List |
| Key Issues in Your Buying Decision | Bullets & Clip Art |
| Company-Related Issues | Basic Layout |

| Page Title | Page Type |
|---|---|
| Importance of Company Issues | Bulleted List |
| Overlooked Issues | Diagram |
| Who Has Chosen Our Product? | Diagram |
| List of Customers | 2-Column Bullets |
| What Do People Say About Us? | Diagram |
| A Few Other Opinions | Basic Layout |
| And a Few More | Basic Layout |
| You Would Be in Good Company | 2-Column Bullets |
| What Sort of ROI Can You Expect? | Bullets & Chart |
| Let's Summarize— Section Title | Title |
| Product Summary | Bulleted List |
| Your Company Summary | Bulleted List |
| Into the Future | Bulleted List |
| Use a Quote | Bulleted List |
| Benefits for You as a Customer | Bulleted List |
| Comments & Questions | Title |
| What Is the Next Step? | Bullets & Clip Art |
| Optional—Procrastinator | Bullets & Clip Art |

| Page Title | Page Type |
|---|---|
| Optional—Bargain 1 | Basic Layout |
| Optional—Bargain 2 | Bulleted List |
| Optional—Bargain 3 | Table |
| Optional—Imagination Closing | Diagram |

## Sales—Zig Ziglar

This content topic enables you to prepare a detailed sales presentation. Page titles and page types are:

| Page Title | Page Type |
|---|---|
| Sales Title Page | Title |
| Review of Understanding | Bullets & Clip Art |
| Agenda | Bulleted List |
| Thought-Provoking Question | Bullets & Clip Art |
| Key Issues | Bulleted List |
| Additional Issues | Bullets & Clip Art |
| Criteria for Your Decision | Bulleted List |
| Solution Overview | Bulleted List |
| Solution Benefits | Diagram |
| Key Aspect of Solution | Bulleted List |

| | |
|---|---|
| Pricing, Terms, and Conditions | Bulleted List |
| Cost/Benefit Analysis | Bullets & Chart |
| Implementation Considerations | Bulleted List |
| Summary | Bulleted List |
| Next Steps | Bullets & Clip Art |

## Strategic Alliance

This content topic presents many reasons for your company's strategic alliance with another company. Page titles and page types are:

| Page Title | Page Type |
|---|---|
| Strategic Alliance Title Page | Title |
| Agenda | Bulleted List |
| Alliance Goals—Section Title | Title |
| Background | Bulleted List |
| Alliance Summary | Bulleted List |
| Broad Goals for Us | Diagram |
| Broad Goals for You | Diagram |
| Specific Objectives for Us | Bullets & Clip Art |
| Specific Objectives for You | Bullets & Clip Art |
| Competitive Advantages— Section Title | Title |

| Page Title | Page Type |
| --- | --- |
| Joint Competitive Advantage | Bullets & Clip Art |
| Our Strengths | Bulleted List |
| Your Strengths | Bulleted List |
| Synergy | Bulleted List |
| Challenges for Us | Bulleted List |
| Challenges for You | Bulleted List |
| Alliance Proposal—Section Title | Title |
| Approach to the Alliance | Bulleted List |
| Timing | Diagram |
| Suggested Terms | Bulleted List |
| Managing to Success | Bulleted List |
| Next Steps | Bullets & Clip Art |

## Strategic Plan—SLF

This content topic provides a five-part strategic plan based on your company's position in the market and the strengths and weaknesses of your competitors. Page titles and page types are:

| Page Title | Page Type |
| --- | --- |
| Strategic Plan Title Page | Title |
| Five Step Agenda | Diagram |

| Page Title | Page Type |
| --- | --- |
| Business Mission | Table |
| External Environment—Section Title | Bullets & Clip Art |
| Current Environment | Diagram |
| Analysis of Driving Force | Diagram |
| Value Chain Focus: Strengths | Diagram |
| Value Chain Focus: Weaknesses | Diagram |
| Competitive Position—Section Title | Bullets & Clip Art |
| Market Analysis | Bullets & Chart |
| Analysis of Customer Purchasing | Bullets & Chart |
| Competitive Position | Table |
| Organizational Readiness | Table |
| Opportunity Assessment | Table |
| Threat Assessment | Table |
| Strategies & Action Plans—Section Title | Bullets & Clip Art |
| Qualitative Strategic Objectives | Bulleted List |
| Financial Objectives | Bulleted List |

| Page Title | Page Type |
| --- | --- |
| Growth Strategies | Diagram |
| Profit Improvement Strategies | Diagram |
| Other Strategies | Diagram |
| Business Unit Strategy Options | Table |
| Business Unit Strategic Plan | Bulleted List |
| Functional Area Strategies | Diagram |
| Action Plans by Function | Table |
| Performance Analysis— Section Title | Bullets & Clip Art |
| Revenue Performance Analysis | 2 Charts |
| Net Income Performance Analysis | 2 Charts |
| Investment Performance Analysis | 2 Charts |
| Comparison to Prior Plan | 4 Charts |
| Risks and Key Issues— Section Title | Bullets & Clip Art |
| Risks | Table |
| Key Issues | Table |

## *Training*

This content topic provides the structure for a training program for your employees or customers. Page titles and page types are:

| Page Title | Page Type |
| --- | --- |
| Training Title Page | Title |
| Introduction | Bulleted List |
| Attention-Grabber | Bullets & Clip Art |
| Reflection | Bulleted List |
| Agenda | Bulleted List |
| Overview—Section Title | Title |
| Current Skills | Bulleted List |
| Training Overview | Bulleted List |
| Terms | Table |
| Training Objectives | Diagram |
| Objectives—Section Title | Title |
| Content | Bulleted List |
| Questions & Answers | Bullets & Clip Art |
| Activity Instructions | Bullets & Clip Art |
| Activity Feedback | 2-Column Bullets |
| Objective Summary | Bulleted List |
| Session Summary—Section Title | Title |
| Training Recap | Bulleted List |

| Page Title | Page Type |
|---|---|
| Testing | Bullets & Clip Art |
| Relevance | Bullets & Clip Art |
| Helpful Hints | Table |
| Final Questions | Bulleted List |
| Next Steps | Bullets & Clip Art |
| Sources & Additional Information | Bulleted List |

► ► CHAPTER **20**

# Editing a
# Presentation

___

►► ***T****his* chapter describes various ways to edit a Freelance Graphics presentation—switching to a new SmartMaster set, changing the layout for a particular page and the typeface for all pages, copying and deleting pages, and adding tables, charts, and organization charts to presentation pages. At the end of the chapter, you'll find out how to use speaker notes and how to print all or part of a presentation. And please remember that if you have general editing questions, refer to the *Editing in SmartSuite Applications* chapter.

# ►► *Changing a Presentation*

You can change to a new SmartMaster Set or page layout at any time without affecting your presentation.

## ► *Changing to a New SmartMaster Set*

To change to a new SmartMaster set, follow these steps:

1. Choose Presentation ➤ Choose a Different SmartMaster Look. Freelance Graphics displays the Choose a Look for Your Presentation dialog box (see Figure 20.1).

2. Select a SmartMaster set from the scroll box. (Before you make your selection, scroll through the list, looking at the sample in the middle of the dialog box.)

3. Either click on OK or press Enter. Freelance Graphics changes the look and format of each page to that of the new set (see Figure 20.2).

**FIGURE 20.1** ▶

*From the Choose a Look for your Presentation dailog box, you can select a new look for your presentation.*

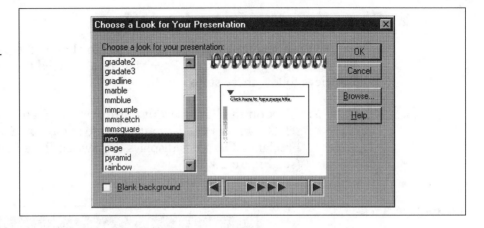

**FIGURE 20.2** ▶

*In Page Sorter view, the sample presentation with a new look*

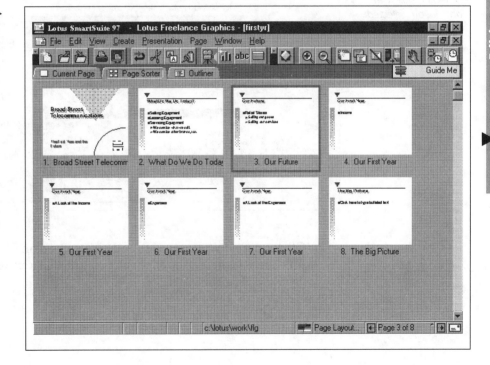

## ▶ *Changing the Page Layout*

You can change the layout of a page. To change the page layout for the current page in Current Page view or a selected page in Page Sorter view, follow these steps:

**1.** Click on the Page Layout button on the Status bar, right-click and select Switch Page Layout, or choose Page ▶ Switch Page Layout. Freelance Graphics displays the Switch Page Layout dialog box (see Figure 20.3).

**FIGURE 20.3** ▶

*The Switch Page Lay-out dialog box with a Table layout selected*

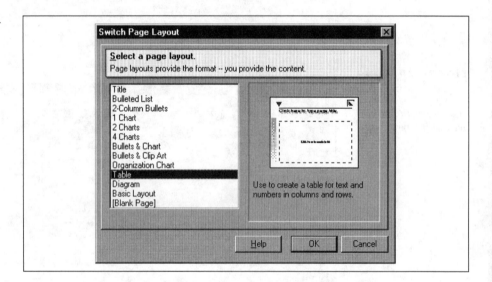

**2.** Click on a new page layout and either click on OK or press Enter. Freelance Graphics applies the new page layout to the selected page (see Figure 20.4).

**FIGURE 20.4** ▶

*A new page layout, ready for a table to be inserted*

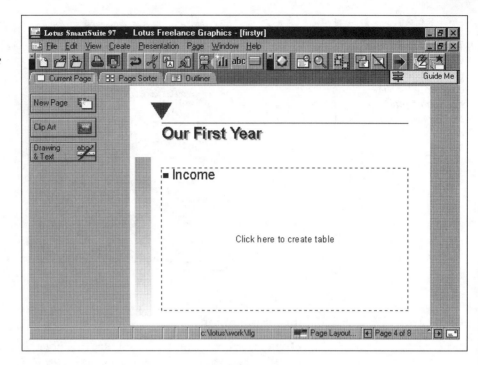

▶ ▶

Ch.
**20**

Editing a Presentation

# ▶ ▶ *Changing the Typeface on Every Page*

With one command, you can change the font for all the text, data charts, tables, and organization charts in the current presentation and for named styles. (Named styles are covered in the *Enhancing a Presentation* chapter.) Either click on the Use One Typeface for All Text SmartIcon or choose Presentation ▶ Change Typeface Globally. In the Change Typeface Globally dialog box (see Figure 20.5), select from these options:

**Choose a Typeface for All Text in Your Presentation**    Select a font for all text in your presentation from this scroll box. If you have changed from the original font and want to revert to it, select it.

**Data Charts**    Check this checkbox and select a font for all existing data charts. To change the font for future data charts, open this dialog box again and make a selection.

**FIGURE 20.5** ▶

*The Change Typeface Globally dialog box, in which you can choose a typeface for all text, data charts, tables, and organization charts*

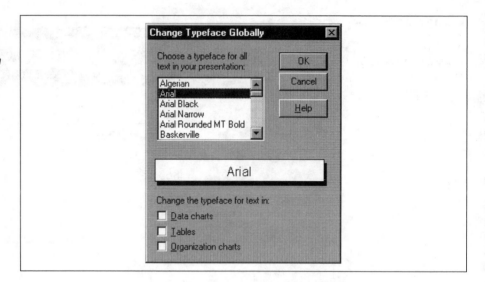

**Tables**    Check this checkbox and select a font for all tables in this presentation.

**Organization Charts**    Check this checkbox and select a font for all organization charts in this presentation.

# ►► *Duplicating a Page*

If you have worked for a long time on the formats and contents of a presentation and find that you must add a page that looks very much like the current page, click on the Duplicate Pages SmartIcon, choose Page ➤ Duplicate Page, right-click and choose Duplicate Page, or press Alt+F7. Freelance Graphics adds the duplicate page after the page on which it is based and selects the new page. You can then edit and format to make the new page unique.

# ▶▶ *Deleting a Page*

 To delete a presentation page, select it, and click on the Delete Pages SmartIcon, choose Page ➤ Delete Page, or right-click and select Delete Page. Freelance Graphics deletes the page without prompting for confirmation.

Freelance Graphics provides other ways to delete a page. In Page Sorter view, you can click on a page, and either press the Delete key or choose Edit ➤ Clear. In Outliner view, you can use the mouse pointer to drag a box around one or more pages that you want to delete (see Figure 20.6). When you release the left mouse button, Freelance Graphics extends the box from the left margin to the right margin. Then press Delete or choose Edit ➤ Clear to delete the lines within the box.

 To undo a page deletion, click on the Undo the Last Command or Action SmartIcon, choose Edit ➤ Undo Delete Page(s), or press Ctrl+Z.

**FIGURE 20.6** ▶

*Drag a box around a page to be deleted in Outliner view.*

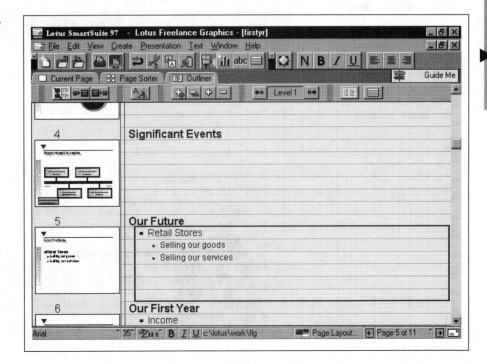

# ►► *Copying a Page from Another Presentation*

You can enhance a presentation by adding a page from another presentation. For example, you can use a page or two from a SmartMaster to add information developed by an expert in the field. Or you can add a page to use its styles, formats, and elements such as charts and tables.

To copy a page from another presentation, follow these steps:

**1.** Change to Page Sorter view by clicking on the Page Sorter tab or choosing View ► Page Sorter.

**2.** Click on the Copy Pages from Other Presentations SmartIcon or choose Page ► Copy Pages from Other Files. Freelance Graphics opens two dialog boxes: Copy Pages from Other Files and Select Presentation (see Figure 20.7).

**FIGURE 20.7** ►

*The Select Presentation dialog box with a presentation selected and its look in the sample box*

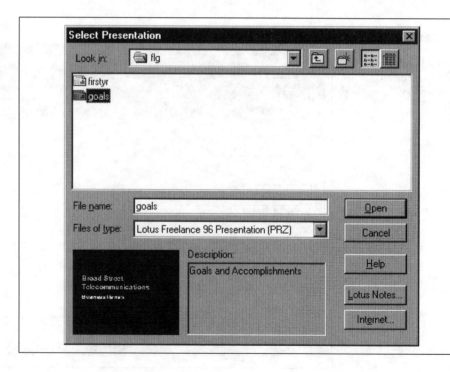

**3.** Select the presentation from which you want to copy, and click on the Open button. Freelance Graphics displays the Copy Pages from Other Files dialog box (see Figure 20.8).

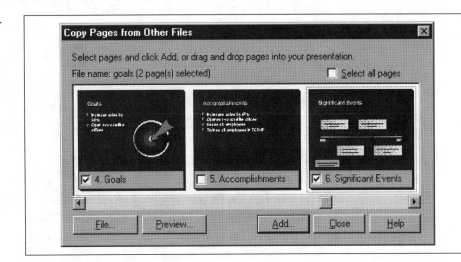

**4.** You can select pages to copy into your presentation in three ways:

- To insert all the pages in the presentation, place a checkmark in the Select All Pages checkbox, and then click on the Add button. In the Add Page(s) dialog box, select a location for the selected page(s) and click on OK.

- To select a particular page, place a checkmark in the checkbox preceding the page title, and then click on the Add button. In the Add Page(s) dialog box, select a location for the selected page(s) and click on OK.

- Drag a selected page from the Copy Pages from Other Files dialog box into your presentation.

After adding each page, Freelance Graphics automatically applies the current style to the new pages. Figure 20.9 shows the open dialog box and the newly inserted pages.

**5.** Click on Close to close the dialog box. Then edit the pages as you would any others.

**FIGURE 20.9 ►**

*Two new pages and part of the dialog box from which they came*

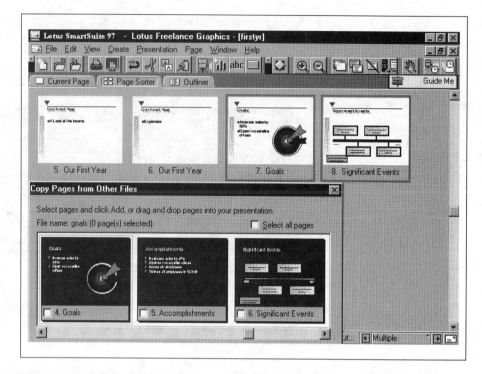

**►►TIP**

> **If you move two or more pages to a presentation, they remain as a set; you can't separate them. To allow yourself plenty of latitude, consider copying pages one at a time.**

# ►► *Adding a Table to a Presentation*

You can add a table to a presentation by creating it in Freelance Graphics or by importing it (that is, copying and pasting, embedding, or linking) from its source application.

## ► *Creating a Table*

To create a table in Freelance Graphics, follow these steps:

1. Either insert a new page with the Table page layout, or change an existing page to the Table page layout. (A quick way to add a table to any page is to select the page and choose Create ➤ Table in Current Page view.)

2. If you are working on a new page, click on Click Here to Type Page Title and type a page title in the Click Here text box.

3. Click on Click Here to Create Table in the center of the page. Freelance Graphics opens the Table Gallery dialog box (see Figure 20.10).

4. Click on one of the Select a Table Style buttons.

5. Choose the number of rows and columns from the Rows and Columns text/list boxes.

6. Either click on OK or press Enter. Freelance Graphics closes the dialog box and inserts a table on the page (see Figure 20.11).

7. Click on the table and insert text or numbers. You can move from cell to cell by clicking or by pressing Tab, Shift+Tab, the down arrow, the up arrow, the left arrow, or the right arrow; or you can click in a cell and type a value.

**Editing a Presentation**

►►

*Ch.*
**20**

**FIGURE 20.10** ►

*You use the Table Gallery dialog box to create a table and format it.*

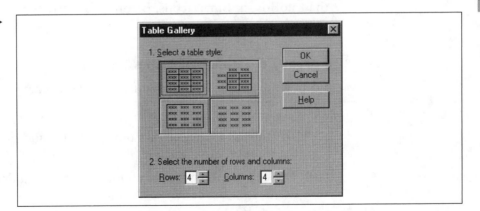

**FIGURE 20.11** ►

*A page with an
inserted table*

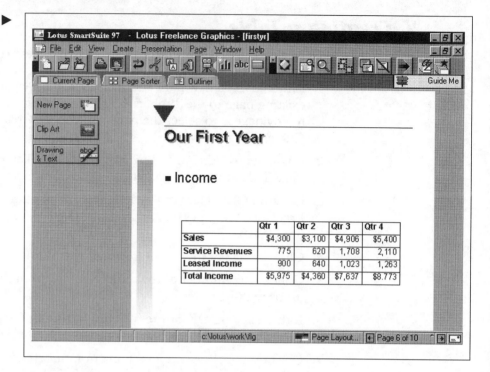

## ► *Editing a Table*

You can edit a table just as you would edit a sheet by using the mouse, the InfoBox, or SmartIcons. Before you start, click on the table to select it.

### *Editing a Table with the Mouse*

Editing the table using the mouse requires clicking on it once or twice and dragging.

- To increase the width of a table, select it and drag a border toward the right or left margin.

- To decrease the width of a table, select it and drag a column border toward the center of the table.

- To increase both the width and the height of the table and keep it in proportion, select it and drag a corner handle away from the center of the table.

- To decrease both the width and the height of the table and keep it in proportion, select it and drag a corner handle toward the center of the table.

- To move a table, select it, point to an area within its border, and drag it.

- To edit a table's contents, double-click within its border. When the table is selected, its border is thick, and an insertion pointer blinks within the cell in which you double-clicked.

## Changing Row and Column Dimensions with the InfoBox

You can change the height of selected rows or the width of selected columns using the Row/Column section of the Table Properties InfoBox (see Figure 20.12) or the Selected Cells Properties InfoBox. You cannot change the height or width of individual cells.

**FIGURE 20.12** ▶

*The Row/Column section of the Table Properties InfoBox*

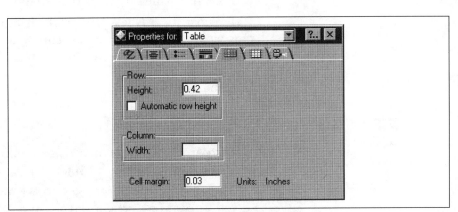

To change row and column dimensions, follow these steps:

1. Click within the table borders.

2. Choose Table ➤ Size Column/Row. Freelance Graphics opens the *Name* Properties InfoBox.

▶▶ N O T E

**If you open the InfoBox by clicking on the InfoBox SmartIcon, by choosing Table ➤ Table Properties, or by right-clicking and selecting Table Properties, you must click on the Row/Column tab.**

**3.** Select from the following options:

   **Height**     A text box in which you can type a row height. Valid values are from 0.07 to 3.00 inches.

   **Automatic Row Height**     A checkbox that when checked has Freelance Graphics set the row height. When this checkbox is checked, you cannot enter a value in the Height text box.

   **Width**     A text box in which you can type a column width. Valid values are from 0.07 to 6.00 inches.

   **Cell Margin**     A text box in which you can type the distance in the default unit of measure between the border of the selected cell(s) and the characters in the cell(s).

**4.** Close the InfoBox.

▶▶ N O T E

**You also can change row height and column width with the mouse pointer. Double-click on the table so that a wide border appears. Move the mouse pointer to a cell border until the pointer changes to a double-headed arrow. Then drag the cell border to its desired location.**

To learn about editing or enhancing text, alignment, bullets, and lines and color, see the *Editing in SmartSuite Applications* chapter.

## Changing Table Layout with the InfoBox

To change to a different table layout, follow these steps:

1. Click within the table border.

2. Click on the InfoBox SmartIcon, choose Table ➤ Table Properties, or right-click and select Table Properties. Freelance Graphics opens the  Table Properties InfoBox.

3. Click on the Layout tab. Freelance Graphics opens the Layout section of the Table Properties InfoBox (see Figure 20.13).

4. Click on the button on the right side of the Layout box to display the available table layouts.

5. Select a table layout.

6. Close the InfoBox.

**FIGURE 20.13** ▶

*The Layout section of the Table Properties InfoBox*

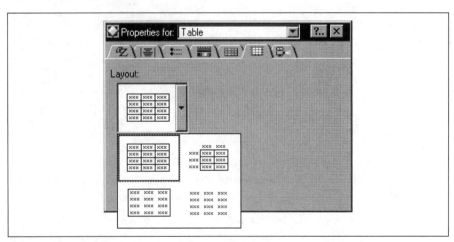

To learn about editing or enhancing text, alignment, bullets, and lines and color, see the *Editing in SmartSuite Applications* chapter.

## Inserting and Deleting Rows and Columns

You can insert and delete rows and columns using either SmartIcons or menu commands.

To insert a row, click in the row after which you want to insert the new row; then click on the Insert a Row SmartIcon, choose Table ➤ Insert ➤ Row, or right-click and select Insert Row.

 To insert a column, click in the column to the left of the location of the new column, and then click on the Insert a Column SmartIcon, choose Table ➤ Insert ➤ Column, or right-click and select Insert Column.

To insert a combination of rows and columns, follow these steps:

**1.** Choose Table ➤ Insert ➤ Row/Column. Freelance Graphics opens the Insert Column/Row dialog box (see Figure 20.14).

**FIGURE 20.14** ►

*The Insert Column/ Row dialog box showing the options that insert a new column before the selected column*

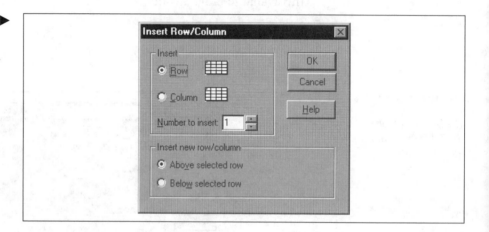

**2.** Choose the Column button to insert a column, or choose the Row button to insert a row.

**3.** Select the number of rows or columns in the Number to Insert text/list box. Valid values range from 1 to 25 columns and 1 to 43 rows.

**4.** To place the row above or the column to the left of the selected row or column, click on the Before option button.

**5.** To place the row below or the column to the right of the selected row or column, click on the After option button.

**6.** Click on OK to close the dialog box and insert the new row(s) or column(s).

To delete a row, click in the row that you want to delete; then click on the Delete Rows or Columns SmartIcon, choose Table ➤ Delete ➤ Row/Column, or right-click and select Delete Column/Row. In the Delete Column/Row dialog box, click on the Row option button, and then click on OK.

### Moving Rows and Columns

To move rows or columns, either click on the Move Row or Column SmartIcon or choose Table ➤ Move Row/Column. In the Move Row/Column dialog box (see Figure 20.15), select either the Row or Column option button to indicate whether you are moving a column or a row. Then click on an option button in the Move Row/Column group and click on OK.

*Editing a Presentation*

**FIGURE 20.15** ➤

*The Move Row/Column dialog box with the default settings*

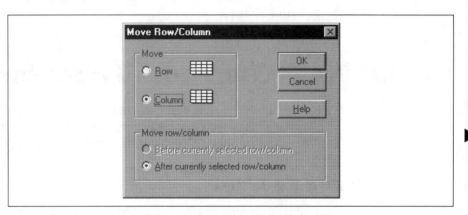

➤ ➤

Ch.
**20**

## ➤ *Importing a Table*

You can copy a table or other data into the Windows Clipboard by choosing either Edit ➤ Copy (or pressing Ctrl+C) or Edit ➤ Cut (or pressing Ctrl+X) and then choosing either Edit ➤ Paste (or pressing Ctrl+V) or Edit ➤ Paste Special to paste the table or data into the current Freelance Graphics page. You can also embed and link using OLE (see the "Linking and Embedding with OLE" section in the *What Is SmartSuite?* chapter).

To import a table (for example, a Word Pro table) into a Freelance Graphics page using cut and paste, follow these steps:

1. Create a table in another application, select it, and copy it by clicking on the Copy to the Clipboard SmartIcon, choosing Edit ➤ Copy, right-clicking and selecting Copy, or pressing Ctrl+C.

2. Make active the Freelance Graphics application window.

3. Select a page in Current Page view. (Although you can select any type of page, it's a good idea to place the table on a page with a Table page layout.)

4. Paste the table on the presentation page by clicking on the Paste the Clipboard Contents SmartIcon, choosing Edit ➤ Paste, right-clicking and selecting Paste, or pressing Ctrl+V.

5. Edit the table as you learned in the "Editing a Table" section of this chapter.

# ▶▶ Adding a Chart to a Presentation

In the same way that you can create or import a table, you can create a chart in Freelance Graphics or import it from its source application. When you import a chart, you maintain its original format.

## ▶ Creating a Chart

The centerpiece of Freelance Graphics charts is the Edit Data dialog box (see Figure 20.16) in which you can enter data and edit the chart. The options in the Edit Data dialog box are:

**Chart Preview**    A sample of the chart that changes as you add values and chart elements

**Work Area**    The cells in which you type column labels, row labels, and values

**Import Data**    A button on which you click to import data from the 1-2-3, Excel, or dBASE programs or from an ASCII numbers or text file

**Data**    A tab on which you click to add or change data to a chart. This is the default

**FIGURE 20.16** ▶

*In the Edit Data dialog box, you can fill in data and change options for a chart.*

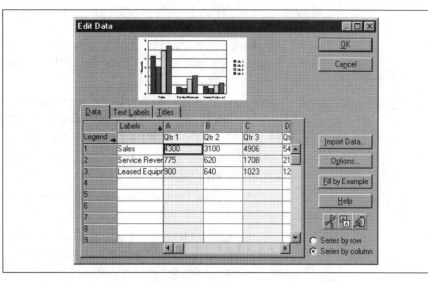

**Text labels**     A tab on which you click to edit labels in a chart

**Titles**     A tab on which you click to open the Edit Titles dialog box in which you can type three lines of chart titles; three lines of notes; and the X, Y, and 2Y axis titles

**Options**     A button on which you click to show or hide the chart preview

**Fill by Example**     A button on which you click to automatically add series of numbers with values based on selected numbers

**Cut**     A button on which you click to remove values and place them in the Clipboard

**Copy**     A button on which you click to copy values into the Clipboard

**Paste**     A button on which you click to paste values from the Clipboard into the chart

**Series in Columns**     An option button on which you click to place letter labels (for example, A, B, C, and so on) in the Legend and have numeric Labels

**Series in Rows**     An option button on which you click to place number labels (for example, 1, 2, 3, and so on) in the Legend and have letter Labels

To create a chart in Freelance Graphics, follow these steps:

1. To insert a new page in the presentation, click on the New Page button, click on the New Page SmartIcon, choose Page ➤ New Page, or press F7.

2. To change an existing page to a Chart page layout, click on the Page Layout button in the Status bar or choose Page ➤ Switch Page Layout, select a chart page type, and click on OK.

3. If you are working on a new page, click on Click Here to Type Page Title and type a page title.

4. If needed, click on the Current Page tab to switch to Current Page view.

5. Click on Click Here to Create Chart, click on the Create a Chart SmartIcon, or choose Create ➤ Chart. Freelance Graphics opens the Create Chart dialog box (see Figure 20.17).

**FIGURE 20.17**

*The Create Chart dialog box, from which you select a chart type and style*

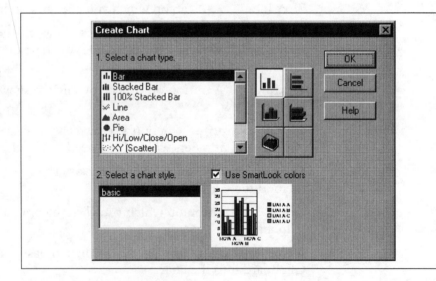

6. Click on a chart type.

7. Choose a style for the selected chart type.

8. Either click on OK or press Enter. Freelance Graphics closes the dialog box and opens the Edit Data dialog box.

**9.** Click on the chart and insert text or numbers, using the horizontal scroll bar to reveal hidden cells. You can move from cell to cell by clicking or pressing Tab, Shift+Tab, the down arrow, the up arrow, the left arrow, or the right arrow. As you fill in the chart, the sample chart changes. Figure 20.18 shows the completed Edit Data dialog box.

**FIGURE 20.18** ▶

*The completed Edit Data dialog box*

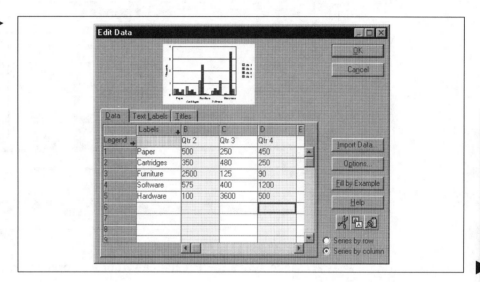

Editing a Presentation

Ch.
**20**

**10.** Click on OK. Freelance Graphics inserts the chart on the current page (see Figure 20.19).

## ▶ *Importing a Chart*

You can copy or import a chart using the same choice of Copy/Cut/Paste/Paste Special commands used to import a table. To import a chart from Word Pro (or 1-2-3 or Approach, in which you can also create charts) into a Freelance Graphics page using the Copy and Paste commands, follow these steps:

**1.** Create a chart in Word Pro or another application, select it, and copy it by clicking on the Copy to the Clipboard SmartIcon, choosing Edit ➤ Copy, right-clicking and selecting Copy, or pressing Ctrl+C.

**FIGURE 20.19** ▶

*A sample chart on the current page*

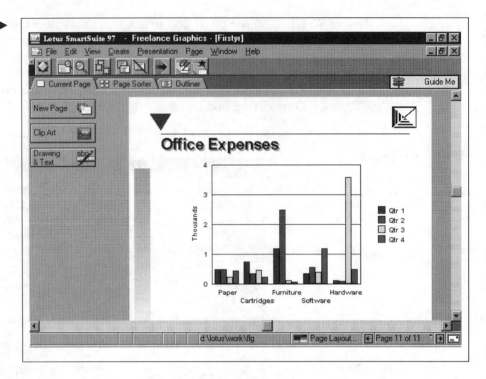

2. Make active the Freelance Graphics application window.

3. Select a page in Current Page view. (Although you can select any type of page, it's a good idea to place the chart on a page with a Chart page layout.)

4. Paste the chart on the presentation page by clicking on the Paste the Clipboard Contents SmartIcon, choosing Edit ➤ Paste, right-clicking and selecting Paste, or pressing Ctrl+V.

5. Edit the chart as you learned in the *Graphing Your Data* chapter.

# ▶▶ Adding an Organization Chart to a Presentation

You can create an organization chart page in a presentation. Creating an organization chart is very similar to creating an outline; organization charts have levels, and you use the same keys to promote or demote to different levels. Once you have added an organization chart, you can add, modify, or delete data or change or enhance its look.

## ▶ Creating an Organization Chart

To create an organization chart, follow these steps:

*1.* To insert a new page in the presentation, click on the New Page button, click on the New Page SmartIcon, choose Page ➤ New Page, or press F7.

*2.* To change an existing page to an Organization page layout, click on the Page Layout button in the Status bar or choose Page ➤ Switch Page Layout, select the Organization Chart page type, and click on OK.

*3.* If you are working on a new page, click on Click Here to Type Page Title and type a page title.

*4.* If needed, click on the Current Page tab to switch to Current Page view.

*5.* Click on Click Here to Create Organization Chart or choose Create ➤ Organization Chart. Freelance Graphics opens the Organization Chart Gallery dialog box (see Figure 20.20).

**FIGURE 20.20** ▶

*The Organization Chart Gallery dialog box*

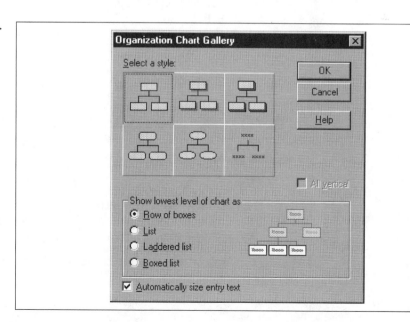

Editing a Presentation

▶ ▶

*Ch.*
**20**

**6.** Click on one of the six organization chart buttons.

**7.** Click on an option button in the Show Lowest Level of Chart As section. The illustration shows the look of the selected option button.

**8.** Either click on OK or press Enter. Freelance Graphics displays the Organization Chart Entry List dialog box (see Figure 20.21).

**FIGURE 20.21** ▶

*A filled-in Organiza-tion Chart Entry List dialog box*

**9.** Type the first entry, the top person in the organization, that person's title, and comments, pressing Enter after each line. (You need not fill in the title and comment lines.)

**10.** Fill in the next entry, a subordinate to the first entry.

11. Fill in the next entry. If the next entry is subordinate to the prior entry, press Tab. Freelance Graphics demotes that entry.

12. Continue filling in entries, pressing Enter after the end of each line in a three-line entry. Before you type the first line in the new entry, press Tab to demote it or Shift+Tab to promote it.

13. To delete an entry, press Delete.

14. When you have completed the dialog box, either click on OK or press Enter. Freelance Graphics adds the organization chart (see Figure 20.22) to the presentation.

**FIGURE 20.22** ▶

*The completed organization chart added to the presentation*

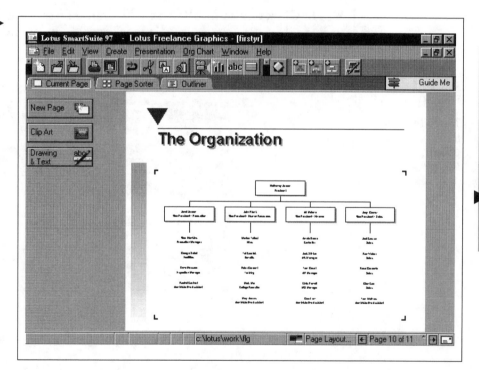

## ▶ *Editing an Organization Chart*

You can edit an organization chart in many ways: its entire frame (boxes and connecting lines), the boxes and connecting lines individually, the current box (name, title, contents, alignment, and the box and connecting lines), boxes on the same level, or subordinate boxes.

> ►►**T I P**
>
> **If you want to edit the organization chart in several ways, keep the InfoBox open and choose the next element to be edited from the Properties For drop-down list box.**

## Editing an Entire Organization Chart

To edit an entire organization chart, follow these steps:

 **1.** Click on the InfoBox SmartIcon or choose Org Chart ➤ Org Chart Properties. Freelance Graphics opens the InfoBox (see Figure 20.23).

**FIGURE 20.23** ►

*The Text section of the Organization Chart Properties InfoBox*

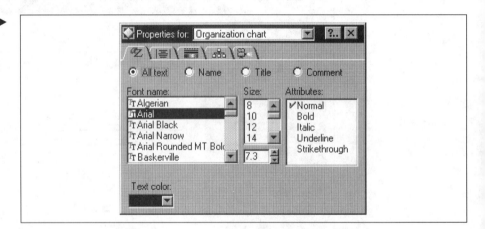

**2.** From the Properties For drop-down list box, select Organization Chart, if needed.

**3.** In the Text section, click on an option button for All Text, Name, Title, or Comment, and change the font, font size, attributes, or text color.

**4.** In the Alignment section (see Figure 20.24), click on an alignment button to change the text alignment in all the boxes.

**5.** In the Lines & Color section (see Figure 20.25), select options for the border and interior of all the boxes.

**FIGURE 20.24** ▶

*The Alignment section of the Organization Chart Properties InfoBox*

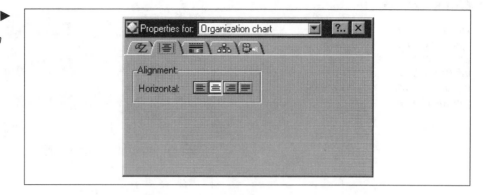

**FIGURE 20.25** ▶

*The Lines & Colors section of the Organization Chart Properties InfoBox*

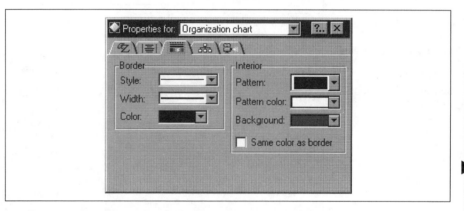

Editing a
Presentation

▶ ▶
Ch.
**20**

**6.** In the Layout section (see Figure 20.26), select a different layout or the look of the lowest level of boxes. From this section, you can edit data too.

**7.** In the Screen Show section (see Figure 20.27), select options for creating a screen show.

**8.** Close the InfoBox.

**FIGURE 20.26** ▶

*The Layout section of the Organization Chart Properties InfoBox, showing the layouts from which you can choose*

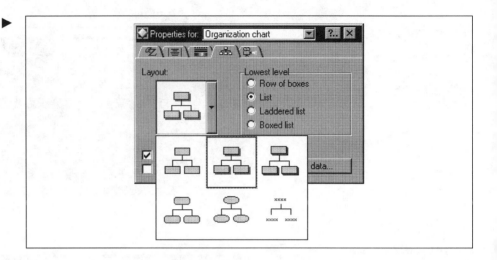

**FIGURE 20.27** ▶

*The Screen Show section of the Organization Chart Properties InfoBox*

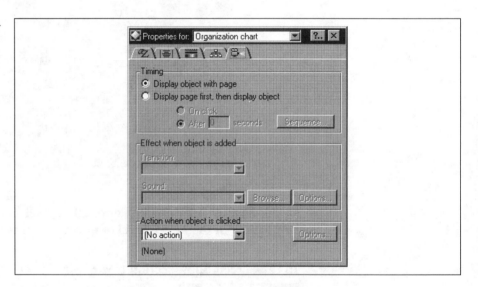

## Editing an Organization Chart Frame

To edit an organization chart *frame* (all the boxes in a chart) follow these steps:

**1.** Click on the Open InfoBox for Selected Organization Chart Frame SmartIcon or choose Org Chart ➤ Frame. Freelance Graphics displays the Lines & Color section of the Frame Properties InfoBox.

2. From the Border group, select a border style, width, or color of the borders of the boxes in the frame.

3. From the Interior group, select a pattern, pattern color, and background of the interiors of the boxes in the frame. Checking the Same Color As Border checkbox matches the border color with the interior color. (To revert to the previous interior color, open the Pattern Color drop-down palette and choose that color.)

4. Close the InfoBox.

### Editing Connecting Lines

To edit the lines connecting all the boxes in an organization chart, follow these steps:

1. Click on the Open InfoBox for Selected Org Chart Connecting Lines SmartIcon or choose Org Chart ➤ Connecting Lines. Free-lance Graphics displays the Lines & Color section of the Connecting Lines Properties InfoBox.

2. Select a line style, width, or color.

3. Close the InfoBox.

### Editing Organization Chart Boxes

To edit organization chart boxes, follow these steps:

1. Click on the Open InfoBox for Selected Organization Chart Box SmartIcon or choose Org Chart ➤ Box Properties ➤ Current Box. Freelance Graphics opens the Current Box Properties InfoBox.

2. In the Text section, click on an option button for All Text, Name, Title, or Comment, and change the font, font size, attributes, or text color.

3. In the Alignment section, click on an alignment button to change the text alignment in all the boxes.

4. In the Lines & Color section, select options for the border and interior of all the boxes.

5. Close the InfoBox.

### Editing the Current Box and Its Peers

To edit the current box and its peers (those on the same level), choose Org Chart ➤ Box Properties ➤ Current Box & Peers. Then follow the steps in the "Editing Organization Chart Boxes" section earlier in this chapter.

### Editing the Current Box and Its Subordinates

To edit the current box and its subordinates (those below this box), choose Org Chart ➤ Box Properties ➤ Current Box & Subordinates. Then follow the steps in the "Editing Organization Chart Boxes" section earlier in this chapter.

### Editing Data in an Organization Chart

To edit the data in the current organization chart, follow these steps:

1. Click on the Open InfoBox for Selected Organization Chart Box SmartIcon or choose Org Chart ➤ Edit Data. Freelance Graphics opens the Organization Chart Entry List dialog box.

2. Fill in additional entries, modify entries, or delete entries.

3. Click on OK to close the dialog box.

## ►► *Writing Speaker Notes*

When you are giving your presentation, speaker notes remind you about the topics covered on each page and help you to discuss related information.

## ► *Adding Speaker Notes to a Page*

To create speaker notes for the current page, follow these steps:

1. Select a page to make it active.

2. Either click on the Add or Edit Speaker Notes SmartIcon or choose Create ➤ Speaker Note. Freelance Graphics displays the Speaker Note—*page title* dialog box (see Figure 20.28) for the selected page.

**FIGURE 20.28** ▶

*Type your speaker notes for a particular page into the Speaker Note—page title dialog box.*

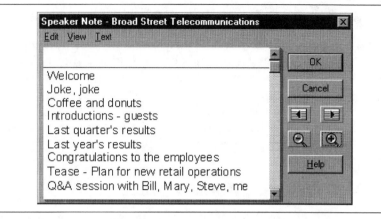

3. Type text in the large text box.

4. To move to the preceding page, click on the Prior Page button. (If you are on the first page, you will go to the last page in the current presentation.)

5. To move to the next page, click on the Next Page button. (If you are on the last page, you will go to the first page in the current presentation.)

6. To make the text appear smaller on the screen, click on the Zoom Out button.

7. To make the text appear larger on the screen, click on the Zoom In button.

8. Click on OK. In Page Sorter view, Freelance Graphics marks the page with an icon in the lower right corner of the page.

**Editing a Presentation**

▶ ▶
*Ch.*
**20**

## ► Editing Speaker Notes

Once you have added speaker notes for a page, Freelance Graphics changes the look of the Add or Edit Speaker Notes SmartIcon and changes its name to Open Speaker Note. To open the Speaker Note—*page title* dialog box to edit your notes, click on the Open Speaker Note SmartIcon or choose Page ➤ Open Speaker Note. Edit the text as you would the text in any document and click on OK when you have finished.

## ► Deleting Speaker Notes

To delete a speaker note associated with a page, follow these steps:

**1.** Select the page with the speaker notes to be deleted.

**2.** Choose Page ➤ Delete Speaker Note. Freelance Graphics opens the Delete Speaker Note dialog box (see Figure 20.29).

**3.** To delete the notes for the selected page, select the Selected Page(s) option button.

**4.** To delete all the notes for this presentation, select the All Pages option button.

**5.** Click on OK or press Enter.

**6.** Freelance Graphics prompts you to confirm the deletion.

**7.** To delete the notes, click on Continue.

**FIGURE 20.29** ►

*The Delete Speaker Note dialog box with the default setting*

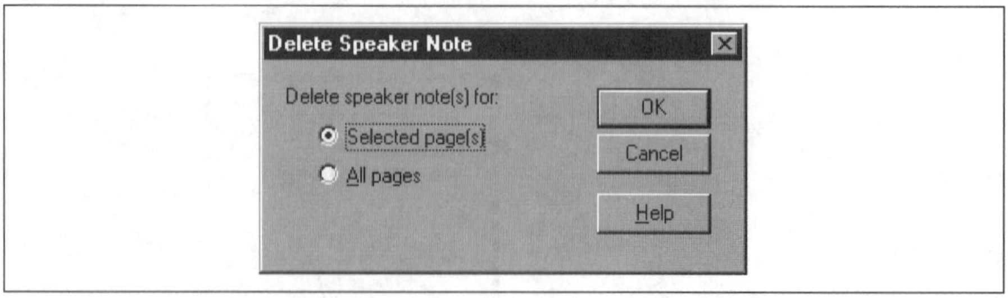

| Delete Speaker Note | ✕ |
|---|---|
| Delete speaker note(s) for: | |
| ⦿ Selected page(s) | OK |
| ○ All pages | Cancel |
| | Help |

# ▶▶ *Selecting Print Options*

You can print an entire presentation by selecting the Print command or print selected pages by choosing the Print Preview command. Each command provides its own set of options.

## ▶ *Printing a Presentation with the Print Command*

Whether you click on the Print SmartIcon, choose File ➤ Print, or press Ctrl+P, you have a choice of options for printing a Freelance Graphics presentation. This section provides a brief description of each print option shown in the Print dialog box (see Figure 20.30). After selecting options in the dialog box, either click on OK or press Enter.

**FIGURE 20.30** ▶

*In the Print dialog box, you select options to customize printing.*

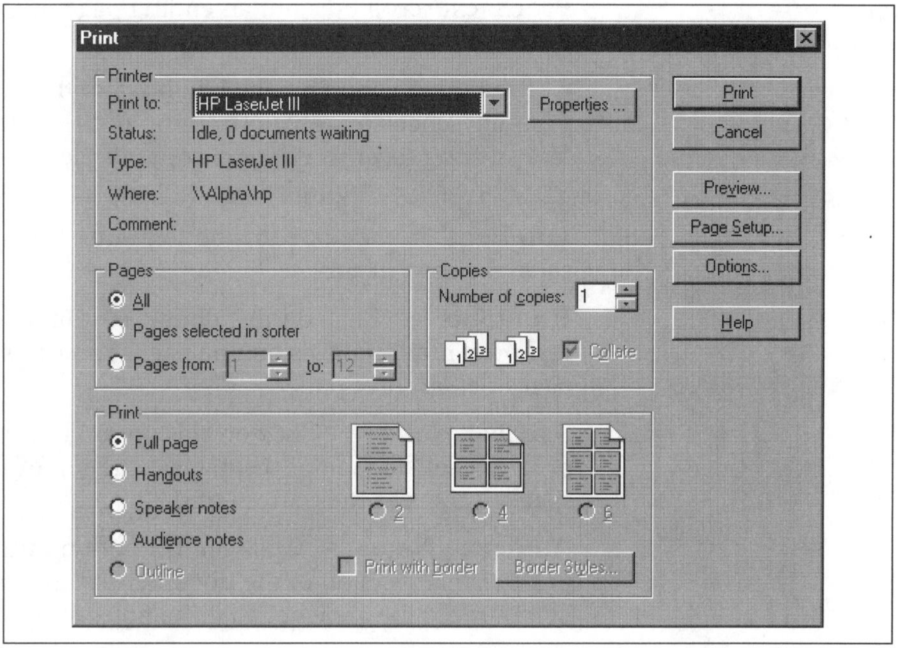

**Print To**    A drop-down list box from which you can select a printer that is attached to your computer system and installed under Windows.

**Status**    Information about the selected printer and whether it is ready for printing.

**Type**    The name of the selected printer.

**Where**    The port to which the selected printer is attached.

**Comment**    Optional additional information about the selected printer.

**Properties**    A button on which you click to view or change attributes of the selected printer

**Pages**    A group in which you select the pages to be printed: **All**, which prints all pages in the presentation; **Pages Selected in Sorter**, which prints the pages that you selected in Page Sorter view; or a range of pages with a starting page number in the **From** text/scroll box and an ending page number in the **To** text/scroll box.

**Copies**    A group in which you select the number of copies to print and check to collate (to print all the pages in one copy before starting to print the next copy) or clear (to print multiple copies of one page, multiple copies of the next page, and so on).

**Full Page**    Click on this option button if you want to print each page at full size.

**Handouts**    Click on this option button if you want to print several presentation pages on one page. You can select 2, 4, or 6 pages per sheet of paper.

**Speaker Notes**    Click on this option button if you want to print a small version of the page at the top of the paper and the speaker notes at the bottom of the page.

**Audience Notes**    Click on this option button if you want to print a small version of the document at the top of the paper, leaving room for the audience to make notes at the bottom of the page.

**Outline**    Click on this option button only in Outliner view to print only top levels of the outline. Collapsed text does not print.

**Print with Border**     When you are printing handouts, speaker notes, or audience notes, check this check box to print pages with borders.

**Border Styles**     Click on this button to open the Select Print Border Style dialog box, from which you can select several border styles if you are printing with a border.

**Print**     Click on this button to print the selected pages.

**Preview**     Click on this button to open the Print Preview dialog box in order to start previewing pages, page by page.

**Page Setup**     Click on this button to open the Page Setup dialog box, in which you can add headers and footers, change the orientation, and adjust the margins.

**Options**     Click on this button to adjust output library for printing (which can help in matching colors when printing on a color printer), print graduated fills as solid (to print graduated colors as solid colors), and/or print with blank background (without a background, you can print more quickly).

## ▶ *Printing Parts of a Presentation with the Print Preview Command*

To preview your presentation, one page at a time, click on the Preview the Print Selection SmartIcon or choose File ➤ Print Preview. Then, in the Print Preview dialog box, choose to start viewing the presentation at the first page of the presentation or the current page. The Print Preview window (see Figure 20.31) has four buttons:

**Previous**     Click on this button to go to the previous page. If you are on the first page of the presentation, you'll go to the last page.

**Next**     Click on this button to go to the next page. If you are on the last page of the presentation, you'll go to the first page.

**FIGURE 20.31** ▶

*The Print Preview window with the first page of the sample presentation on display*

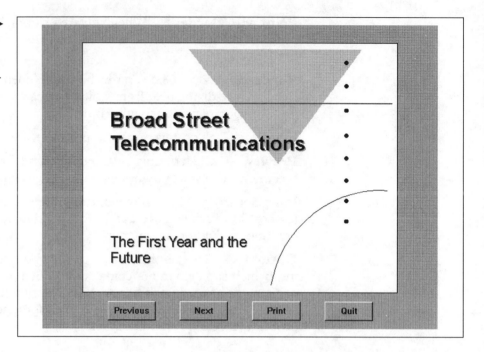

**Print**      Click on this button to open the Print dialog box so that you can print the current page. If you click on Cancel or press Esc to close the dialog box, you'll return to the view from which you selected Print Preview.

**Quit**      Click on this button to close Print Preview and return to the view from which you selected Print Preview.

► ►  ►  **CHAPTER** **21**

# Enhancing a
# Presentation

▶▶ **I**n the last chapter, you learned Freelance Graphics basics. In this chapter, you'll learn how to enhance your presentation and perhaps even turn it into an automated screen show.

## ▶▶ *Changing Click Here Text Box Formats*

You can enhance a presentation by changing text formats, much in the same way that you format Word Pro documents or 1-2-3 spreadsheets. The InfoBox for All Text Levels (see Figure 21.1) and the InfoBoxes for Level 1 Text to Level 5 Text are the central locations for reformatting Click Here text boxes, which are considered paragraphs. When you open one of these InfoBoxes, you can change text, alignment, bullets, lines and colors, screen show, and style attributes. You can find general information about all but the Screen Show section in the *Editing in SmartSuite Applications* chapter. Screen shows and the related InfoBox are covered later in this chapter.

**FIGURE 21.1** ▶

*In the All Text Levels Properties InfoBox are many options for reformatting selected paragraphs.*

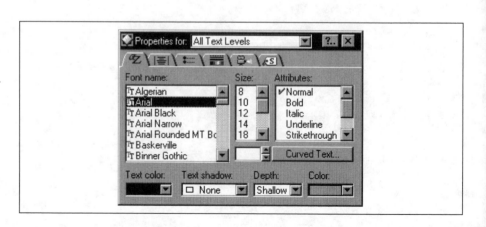

To open one of these InfoBoxes, double-click on a selection, or select text and choose Text ➤ Text Properties, choose a submenu from the Text ➤ Text Properties by Level ➤ All Levels command, or right-click and choose either the Text Properties command or Text Properties by Level and a command from the submenu. Then select options from drop-down list boxes or scroll boxes.

# ▶▶ *Illustrating a Presentation*

In Freelance Graphics, you can illustrate a presentation in a variety of ways. In the prior chapter, you learned about adding tables, charts, and organization charts and about copying finished pages from other presentations. In this section, you'll find out how to insert clip art and diagrams from a built-in library; add bitmaps with the common BMP, PCX, and TIF extensions; and import objects from other programs. For information about creating your own clip art and diagrams, see the Creating Pictures chapter. Most of the Word Pro drawing information also applies to Freelance Graphics.

## ▶ *Inserting Clip Art or a Diagram on a Page*

*Clip art* pictures are illustrations that you add to a page as-is; you cannot edit them using a conventional paint program such as Windows Paint. *Diagrams* are illustrations to which you can add text. You can access the Freelance Graphics library of clip art pictures and diagrams by going to Current Page view. You can then open the Add Clip Art or Diagram to the Page dialog box (see Figure 21.2) in one of four ways:

- Click on the Clip Art button.
- Click on the Click Here to Add Clip Art box in certain presentation pages: Title, Bullets & Clip Art, or Diagram.
- Choose Create ➤ Add Clip Art.
- Choose Create ➤ Drawing/Diagram. In the Add Diagram dialog box, click on Use a Ready-Made Diagram option button, and click on OK.

In the Add Clip Art or Diagram to the Page dialog box, choose the Clip Art or Diagram option button, select a group of pictures from the

**FIGURE 21.2** ▶

*The Add Clip Art or Diagram to the Page dialog box with its default settings*

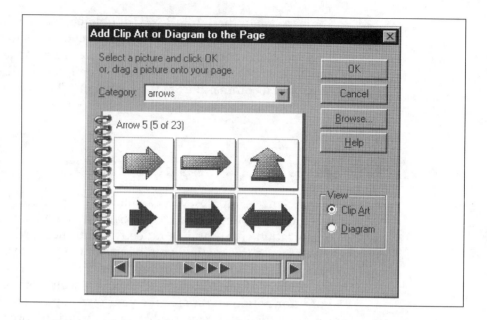

Category drop-down list box, and either look through the group by clicking on the left or right arrow at the bottom of the dialog box or scan by clicking on the Scan button. Make a selection and click on OK or press Enter to close the dialog box.

If you insert clip art or a diagram on a page that includes an area reserved for an illustration (that is, the page displays *Click Here to Add Clip Art*), the inserted picture stays within the bounds of the clip art box. If, however, you insert a picture on another type of page or outside the Click Here to Add Clip Art box, the picture is in the same location and is the same size as it was when created. For example, if you create a 2 inch by 2 inch picture using Windows Paint, Freelance Graphics inserts the same 2 inch by 2 inch picture in the presentation page.

To insert a picture on the current presentation page, follow these steps:

**1.** Starting in Current Page view, either click on the Clip Art button for any presentation page, or click on the Click Here to Add Clip Art box. Freelance Graphics opens the Add Clip Art or Diagram to the Page dialog box.

**2.** To add a clip art picture, click on the Clip Art option button.

**3.** To add a diagram, click on the Diagram option button.

**4.** Select a category from the Category drop-down list box. Free-lance Graphics displays a set of pictures.

**5.** To move through the pictures one at a time, click on the right arrow or left arrow at the bottom of the dialog box.

**6.** To scan through all the pictures in the library starting at the current group, click on the Scan button, which is at the bottom of the dialog box.

**7.** To reverse direction if you are moving toward the bottom of the library, click on the left arrow.

**8.** To reverse direction if you are moving toward the top of the library, click on the right arrow.

**9.** To stop the scan, click on the Stop Scan button.

**10.** To insert a picture onto the page, either double-click on the picture (to insert the picture and close the dialog box) or drag the picture from the dialog box to the page (to insert the picture and allow yourself to insert additional pictures).

**11.** If needed, click on OK or press Enter to close the dialog box. Figure 21.3 shows a presentation page with clip art from the Communic category; Figure 21.4 shows a diagram page in print preview.

**FIGURE 21.3** ▶

*A clip art picture just inserted on a presentation page*

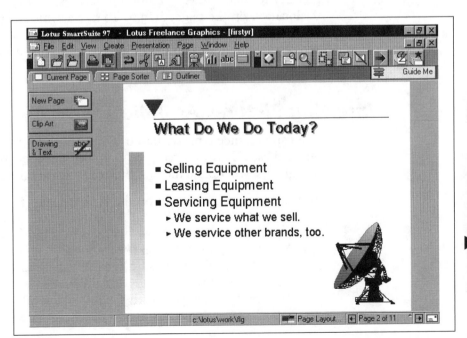

**FIGURE 21.4** ▶

*A presentation page
with a diagram*

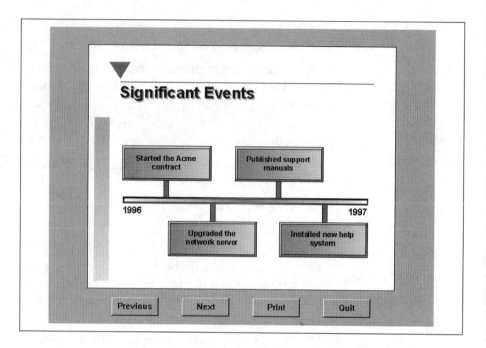

You can size and move Freelance Graphics pictures just as you would pictures in many other Windows programs. To move a symbol to a better location on the page, drag it. To size a symbol, click on a handle and move that border or corner to the desired location. To maintain the proportions of a symbol that you are sizing, move a corner handle. Figure 21.5 shows a picture being sized.

## ▶ Inserting Pictures As Bullets

You can enhance a presentation by substituting pictures for bullets in bulleted lists. Because Freelance Graphics considers presentation text paragraphs, you define the new bullet in the Paragraph Styles dialog box.

To use a picture as a bullet on the current page, follow these steps:

*1.* Starting in Current Page view, click on the Open InfoBox SmartIcon, select the text and choose Text ➤ Text Properties or Text ➤ Text Properties by Level ➤ All Levels, or right-click and choose Text Properties or Text Properties by Level ➤ All Levels. If you want to change bullets for just one level, choose the Text Properties by Level command and choose the desired level from the

**FIGURE 21.5** ▶

*A picture as it is being sized*

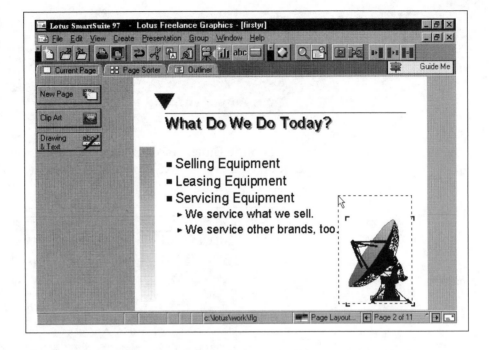

submenu. Freelance Graphics opens an InfoBox for All Text Levels or a specific level (Level 1 Text to Level 5 Text). Figure 21.6 shows the Level 1 Text Properties InfoBox.

**FIGURE 21.6** ▶

*The Text section of the Level 1 Text Properties InfoBox*

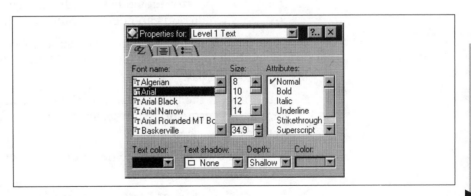

Enhancing a
Presentation

▶ ▶

*Ch.*
**21**

▶▶ **N O T E**

You can use the **All Text Levels Properties InfoBox** to change text formats in seven categories. If you choose a specific level, the InfoBox provides only three tabs: **Text, Alignment, and Bullets.**

**2.** Click on the Bullets tab. Freelance Graphics opens the bullets section of the Level 1 Text Properties InfoBox (see Figure 21.7).

**FIGURE 21.7** ▶

*The Bullets section of the Level 1 Text Properties InfoBox with an open Style drop-down palette*

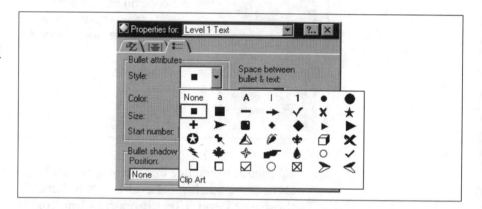

**3.** Open the Style drop-down list box. Freelance Graphics opens a box, from which you can choose a bullet or a symbol to use.

**4.** Click on Clip Art. Freelance Graphics displays the Choose Clip Art for Bullet dialog box (see Figure 21.8) with your last clip art choice on display.

**5.** Scan through the pictures and double-click on your choice. Freelance Graphics displays the selected picture in the Style drop-down list box (see Figure 21.9).

**6.** To change attributes for the new bullets, select from the options in the InfoBox.

**7.** Either click on OK or press Enter. Freelance Graphics closes the dialog box and changes the bullet symbols in front of the selection (see Figure 21.10).

**FIGURE 21.8** ▶

*The Choose Clip Art for Bullet dialog box with a clip art picture chosen*

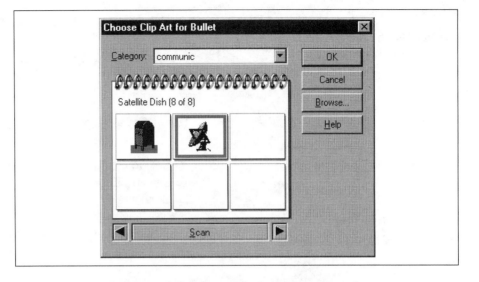

**FIGURE 21.9** ▶

*The InfoBox showing the newly added picture*

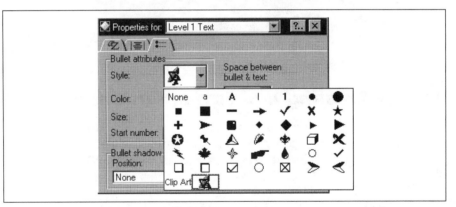

 ▶▶**T I P**

**Symbols that are composed of many lines and colors are difficult to recognize in miniature compared with one-color, two-dimensional symbols. So use multi-colored symbols sparingly.**

Enhancing a Presentation

▶▶

*Ch.*
**21**

**FIGURE 21.10** ▶

*The presentation page
with its new bullets*

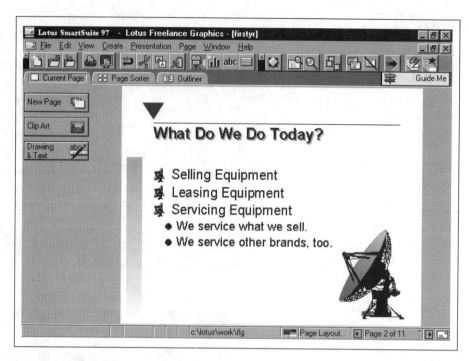

## ▶ Creating and Saving Custom Pictures

You can draw your own symbols. Although the *Creating Pictures* chapter emphasizes creating pictures using Word Pro, you can use many of the same instructions and drawing tools to create pictures in Freelance Graphics. Follow these steps to create a picture:

1. Click on the Drawing & Text button, or choose Create ▶ Drawing/Diagram, click on the Make Your Own Diagram option button, and click on OK. Freelance Graphics opens the Drawing & Text palette (see Figure 21.11).

2. Select a tool with which to draw shapes, shapes with text, and/or connectors. For information about the tools, see Table 19.2: Freelance Graphics Drawing Tool Palette. Remember that you format a picture using the InfoBox; select the picture and click on the Open InfoBox SmartIcon to open the InfoBox.

FIGURE 21.11 ▶

*The Drawing & Text palette*

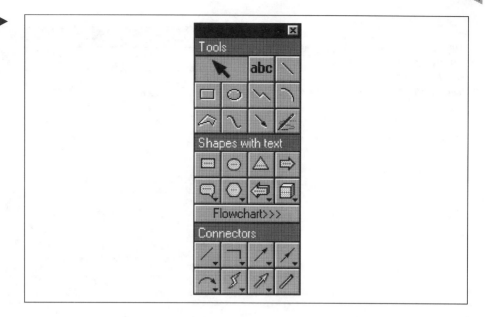

**3.** If your finished picture is made up of several objects, click on the Pointer tool and draw a box around all the objects. (Another way to select objects is to click on the first object, press and hold down Shift, and click on each additional object.) Each selected object is surrounded by its own handles; if you select many objects, the handles overlap.

**4.** Click on the Group Objects SmartIcon or choose Drawing ➤ Group. Freelance Graphics groups the objects into one object surrounded by one set of eight handles.

**5.** Choose Create ➤ Add to Library ➤ Clipart Library (or Create ➤ Add to Library ➤ Diagram Library). Freelance Graphics opens the Add to Clip Art Library dialog box (see Figure 21.12) or the

**FIGURE 21.12** ▶

*The Add to Clip Art Library dialog box, in which you specify the filename for a custom picture*

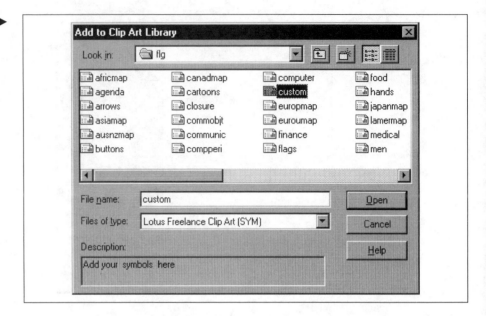

Add to Diagram Library dialog box. Name your picture and click on the Open button. Freelance Graphics closes the dialog box, adds the symbol to the specified symbol category, and returns to the presentation.

## ▶ Editing Pictures with Edit Points Mode

When a picture element is not quite right, but you don't want to re-draw the entire picture, you can edit it in points mode. Freelance Graphics marks points, which are the breaks between segments of a drawn object, with small handles.

● Arcs, arrows, and lines begin and end with points.

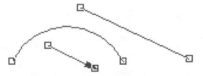

● The segments of polylines, open curves, and polygons are marked with points.

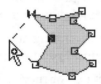

 ▶▶ **N O T E**

**Points mode is not available for rectangles, squares, ellipses, circles, or text boxes.**

 Using points mode, you can work with the smallest component of a drawn object: You can drag it to a new location, you can add or delete a point, or you can break the element at a point so that you can add more segments. To turn on points mode, click on the Turn Edit Points Mode On/Off SmartIcon, choose Edit ➤ Points Mode, or press Shift+F6. Freelance Graphics adds a small outlined cross to the mouse pointer. To turn off points mode, click on the Turn Edit Points Mode On/Off SmartIcon, choose Edit ➤ Points Mode, or press Shift+F6 again.

## *Dragging Points*

To change the shape of a drawn object, follow these steps:

*1.* Click on a point and drag it to a new location. A dashed line shows the current location of the point.

*2.* Release the left mouse button to indicate the end of dragging. Freelance Graphics fills in the changed section with the background color.

*3.* Repeats steps 1 and 2 until the drawn object is the desired size and shape.

### Adding Points to an Object

To add a point to a drawn element, follow these steps:

*1.* Click on the Add a Point SmartIcon, choose Edit ➤ Edit Points ➤ Add Point, or press Insert. Freelance Graphics adds a filled cross to the mouse pointer.

*2.* Point to the location of the new point and click. Freelance Graphics adds the new point and reverts to points mode.

*3.* To add another point, repeat steps 1 and 2.

### Deleting Points from an Object

To delete a point from a drawn element, follow these steps:

*1.* Click on the point to be deleted. Freelance Graphics marks the selected point by making the background black.

*2.* Click on the Delete a Point SmartIcon, choose Edit ➤ Edit Points ➤ Delete Points, or press Delete. Freelance Graphics deletes the point.

### Breaking an Object at a Point

To break an object into separate parts, follow these rules:

● To break an object with a beginning and an end (that is, an arc, an arrow, a line, or a polyline), you cannot select an end point.

● To break an object with a beginning and an end (that is, an arc, an arrow, a line, or a polyline), you must select one point.

● To break a polygon, select two or more noncontiguous points (that is, none of the points can be adjacent).

● To select two or more noncontiguous points, click on the first point, press and hold down the Shift key, click on the second point, click on the third point, and so on.

- To "unselect" a point, press and hold down the Shift key and click on the point.

- To undo a break, choose Edit ➤ Undo Break or press Ctrl+Z. If you have taken other actions since breaking the object, repeatedly choose Edit ➤ Undo until the Undo command changes to Undo Break.

**T I P**

**A quick way to "unselect" one or more points is to click on another object.**

To break at a point in a drawn element, follow these steps:

**1.** Select one or more points. Freelance Graphics blackens the backgrounds of the selected points.

**2.** Either click on the Break Object Apart at Selected Points Smart-Icon or choose Edit ➤ Edit Points ➤ Break at Points.

**3.** To ensure that the object has been broken, either:

- drag the segments apart while remaining in points mode, or

- turn off points mode by clicking on the Turn Edit Points Mode On/Off SmartIcon, choosing Edit ➤ Points Mode, or pressing Shift+F6. Then note the handles, which indicate the boundaries of the separate objects. Optionally, drag the segments apart.

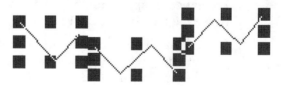

## ► *Importing a Bitmap Picture*

In almost the same way that you import tables and charts into a presentation, you can import a bitmap (BMP) picture. Simply follow these steps:

**1.** Open a presentation and, in Current Page view, display the page onto which you want to import the picture.

**2.** Choose Create ➤ Add Bitmap. Freelance Graphics displays the Add a Bitmap dialog box (see Figure 21.13).

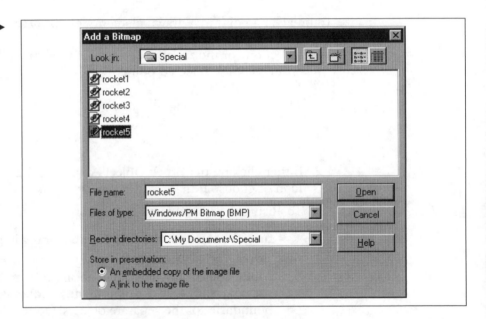

**3.** Double-click on the name of the file that you want to import. Freelance Graphics imports the picture onto the current presentation page (see Figure 21.14).

**4.** If you want to move the imported bitmap into a different area of the window, drag it. (You can also size a picture by dragging its handles.) If you drag a picture to the Click Here to Add Clip Art box, the picture takes the place and size of the box (see Figure 21.15).

**FIGURE 21.14** ▶

*A newly imported bit-map, which has not yet been dragged to its final location*

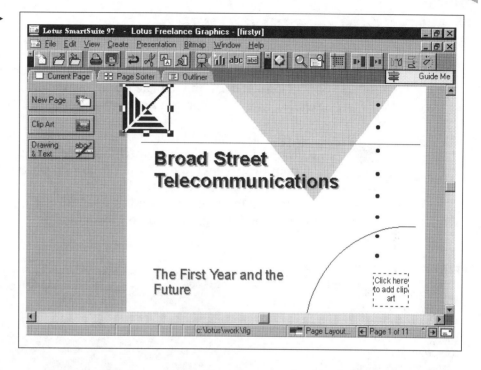

**FIGURE 21.15** ▶

*The bitmap in its final location on the presentation page*

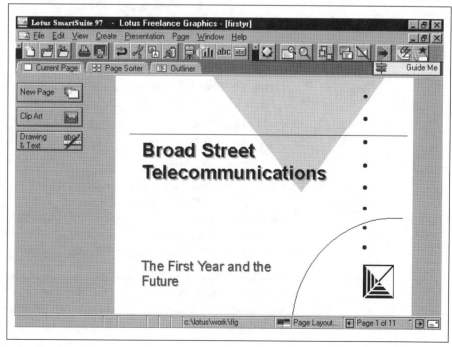

Enhancing a
Presentation

▶ ▶

Ch.
**21**

## ▶ Editing a Bitmap Picture

Although you cannot create a bitmap picture in Freelance Graphics, you can edit an imported bitmap. Using the Open InfoBox and the Bitmap SmartIcons, you can manipulate a bitmap in several ways and view it in several sizes. Simply click on a bitmap to display the Bitmap SmartIcons:

**Open InfoBox**    Click on this SmartIcon (or choose Bitmap ▶ Bitmap Properties or right-click on the bitmap and choose Bitmap Properties) to open the Bitmap Properties InfoBox (see Figure 21.16) with which you can change the look but not the size of the selected bitmap. For additional information, see the following section, "Using the Bitmap Properties InfoBox."

**FIGURE 21.16** ▶

*The section of the Bitmap Properties InfoBox in which you can change the contrast, sharpness, and brightness of an embedded bitmap*

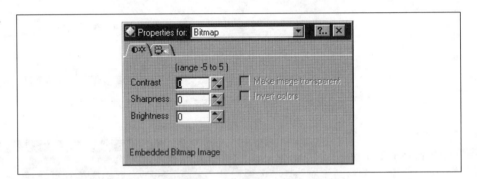

**Drag To Zoom In on an Area**    Click on this SmartIcon (or choose View ▶ Zoom In) to magnify your view of part of the page.

**Show Whole Page**    Click on this SmartIcon (or choose View ▶ Zoom to Full Page) to return to the default Current Page view of the entire page after zooming in on part of the page.

**Crop a Bitmap Image**    Click on this SmartIcon (or choose Bitmap ▶ Crop Bitmap or right-click on the bitmap and choose Crop Bitmap) to open the Crop Bitmap dialog box (see Figure 21.17). For additional information, see a following section, "Cropping and Restoring a Bitmap Image."

**Make Selected Object Larger**    Click on this SmartIcon (or choose Bitmap ▶ Object Size ▶ Enlarge 20% or right-click on the bitmap and choose Object Size ▶ Enlarge 20%) to slightly increase the size of the selected bitmap.

**FIGURE 21.17** ▶

*The Crop Bitmap dia-
log box with a bitmap
that will be cropped at
the upper right corner*

 ▶▶**N O T E**

**You can choose a menu command to change the size of
the bitmap in several ways. In addition to Enlarge 20%
and Reduce 20%, you can also choose Extra Small,
Small, Medium, Large, or Extra Large.**

 **Make Selected Object Smaller**    Click on this SmartIcon (or
choose Bitmap ➤ Object Size ➤ Reduce 20% or right-click on
the bitmap and choose Object Size ➤ Reduce 20%) to slightly decrease the size of the selected bitmap.

 **Flip Left to Right**    Click on this SmartIcon (or choose Bitmap ➤ Flip ➤ Left-Right) to flip the selected bitmap on its vertical axis (that is, the left side will be on the right and the right side
will be on the left).

 **Flip Top to Bottom**    Click on this SmartIcon (or choose Bitmap ➤ Flip ➤ Top-Bottom) to flip the selected bitmap on its horizontal axis (that is, the top will be on the bottom and the bottom
will be on the top).

 **Rotate**    Click on this SmartIcon (or choose Bitmap ➤ Rotate
or right-click and choose Rotate) to turn on rotation for the

selected bitmap. For instructions, see a following section, "Rotating a Bitmap."

## Using the Bitmap Properties InfoBox

To change the properties of the selected bitmap, follow these steps:

1. Click on the Open InfoBox SmartIcon, choose Bitmap ➤ Bitmap Properties, or right-click on the bitmap and choose Bitmap Properties. Freelance Graphics opens the Bitmap Properties InfoBox.

2. To change the *contrast*, the relationship between black and white in color and gray-scale bitmaps, select or type a value in the Contrast text/option box. Valid values are –5 (the greatest contrast) to 5 (the highest contrast). The default is 0.

3. To change the *sharpness*, the level of resolution of lines and borders in gray-scale bitmaps, select or type a value in the Sharpness text/option box. Valid values are –5 (the sharpest) to 5 (the least sharp). The default is 0.

4. To change the *brightness*, the level of luminosity for color and gray-scale bitmaps, select or type a value in the Brightness text/option box. Valid values are –5 (the bitmap is completely black) to 5 (the bitmap is completely white). The default is 0.

5. To make the bitmap transparent, click in the Make Image Transparent checkbox. This option is available only for color bitmaps.

6. To invert the colors in a monochrome bitmap, click in the Invert Colors checkbox. This option is available only for color bitmaps.

7. Click on the Close button to close the InfoBox.

## Cropping and Restoring a Bitmap Image

When you crop the selected bitmap, it is as though you are cutting off part of it with scissors. The proportions of the bitmap remain the same but part of the bitmap is gone.

To crop the selected bitmap, follow these steps:

1. Click on the Crop a Bitmap Image SmartIcon, choose Bitmap ➤ Crop Bitmap, or right-click on the bitmap and choose Crop Bitmap. The Crop Bitmap dialog box appears.

**2.** Drag handles toward the center of the bitmap until the cropped area, surrounded by the handles, is the desired size.

**3.** Click on OK. Freelance Graphics closes the dialog box and crops the bitmap.

To return the bitmap to its original size, follow these steps:

**1.** Click on the Crop a Bitmap Image SmartIcon, choose Bitmap ➤ Crop Bitmap, or right-click on the bitmap and choose Crop Bitmap. The Crop Bitmap dialog box appears.

**2.** Drag handles toward the original borders of the bitmap using the dashed box as a guide.

**3.** Click on OK. Freelance Graphics closes the dialog box and restores the bitmap.

## Rotating a Bitmap

To rotate a selected bitmap around a point in the middle of the bitmap, follow these steps:

**1.** Click on the Rotate SmartIcon, choose Bitmap ➤ Rotate, or right-click on the bitmap and choose Rotate. Freelance Graphics changes the mouse pointer.

2. To rotate the bitmap clockwise, press and hold down the left mouse button, and drag to the right side or bottom of the computer screen. The Path/Date/Time/Coordinates button on the Status bar shows how many degrees the bitmap has rotated.

3. To rotate the bitmap counterclockwise, press and hold down the left mouse button, and drag to the left side or top of the computer screen. The Path/Date/Time/Coordinates button on the Status bar shows how many degrees the bitmap has rotated.

4. When you have rotated the bitmap the desired number of degrees, release the left mouse button.

5. To rotate the bitmap again, repeat steps 1, 2, 3, and 4.

## ▶ Inserting a Logo on Every Page

To identify your company's handouts or to familiarize audiences with your logo, insert it at the same location on every page but the title page, which uses a different backdrop design. When you add a logo to every page, you are actually editing the *backdrop* (see Figure 21.18), the background design of the presentation. Note:

- You should not move the logo inside the rectangle in the middle of the backdrop.

- You should not move the logo over an area that might contain a title or page design.

- You probably should decrease the size of the logo because it is not the most important element on the page.

- You should view the entire presentation to be sure that the logo looks good on every page.

- You should print at least one page to judge whether you have to edit, move, or size the logo.

- You cannot add a logo to a page with the [Blank Page] layout.

To add a logo to every page, follow these steps:

1. In Current Page view or Page Sorter view, either click on the Place a Logo on Every Page SmartIcon or choose Presentation ➤ Add a Logo to Every Page. Freelance Graphics displays the backdrop for the presentation.

**FIGURE 21.18** ▶

*The backdrop page for the sample presentation*

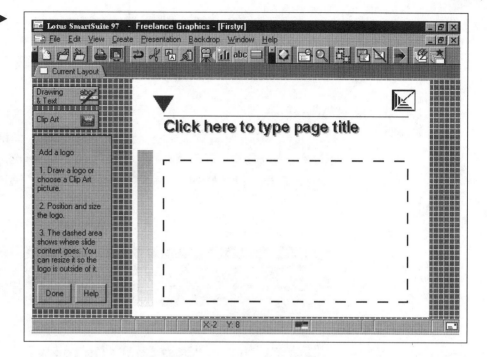

**2.** To create new art to insert on every page, click on the Drawing & Text button. Then use the tools on the Drawing & Text palette and save the picture. For additional information on creating a picture in Freelance Graphics, see a preceding section, "Creating and Saving Custom Pictures."

**3.** To add a bitmap to each page, choose Create ➤ Add Bitmap. From the Add a Bitmap dialog box, double-click on the desired filename. For additional information on adding a bitmap, see a preceding section, "Importing a Bitmap Picture."

**4.** To add a clip art picture to each page, choose Create ➤ Add Clip Art. From the Add Clip Art or Diagram to the Page dialog box, double-click or drag the desired picture onto the backdrop. For additional information on adding a bitmap, see a preceding section, "Inserting Clip Art or a Diagram on a Page." To learn more about editing a backdrop, see the "Changing the Look of the Backdrop" section near the end of this chapter.

**5.** Once you have inserted the picture, drag it to its final location.

**Enhancing a Presentation**

▶▶

*Ch.*
**21**

6. Size the logo. Figure 21.19 shows a sample page with a logo in the upper right corner.

7. To return to the presentation, choose Presentation ➤ Return to Presentation Pages or press Shift+F9.

▶▶**N O T E**

**To add the logo to the title page of a presentation, choose Presentation ➤ Edit Page Layouts, follow the preceding steps 2, 3, or 4, and then do steps 5 and 6.**

**FIGURE 21.19** ▶

*A sample page with a logo included*

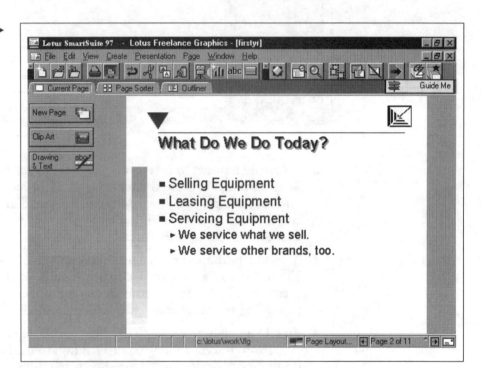

## ▶▶ *Creating a Screen Show*

In previous sections of this chapter, you learned how to insert objects such as clip art onto a single page. In this section, you'll find out how to convert all the pages in a presentation into a screen show using additional special effects: movies and sound files, transitions between pages, and bullets that are added progressively to a page.

## ▶ About the Screen Show Section of the InfoBox

The Screen Show section of the InfoBox (see Figure 21.20) is the centerpiece of a screen show and is available in one format or another for particular effects (that is, sound, movies, and so on). You use the options in this InfoBox to time the display of text on a page, arrange pages in sequence, skip a page, add bullets one at a time to a page, specify a transition effect, add a sound, and define an action when you click on a text block or other object. The options in the Screen Show section of the InfoBox are:

**Display Text/Object with Page**     An option button that you select to simultaneously display a presentation page with its text or objects. If you select this option button, the only available page effect is an action when you click on the current text block. This is the default.

**Display Page First, Then Display Text/Object**     An option button that you select to display a blank presentation page and then add its text. If you select this option button, a variety of page effects options are available.

**On Click**     An option button on which you click to have an object appear when you click the left mouse button. If you have selected the Display Text with Page option button, this option is not available.

**After *n* Seconds**     An option button that when selected enables you to display text or an object at a specific time after the previous object appeared on the page. If you have selected the Display Text with Page option button, this option is not available.

**Sequence**     A button on which you click to open the Screen Show Sequence Overview dialog box in which you can specify the order in which the objects with associated effects appear on the current page. If you have selected the Display Text/Object with Page option button, this option is not available.

**Display Bullets**    A drop-down list box from which you can choose the way in which bullets appear on the current page: All at Once (the default) or One at a Time. If you have selected the Display Text with Page option button, all the bullets on the page appear simultaneously. If you have selected a page without bullets, this option does not appear in this section of the InfoBox.

**Dim Previous Bullets**    A checkbox with which you can specify whether previously displayed bullets are dimmed once the next bullet appears. A checked checkbox dims previous bullets. If you have selected the Display Text with Page option button or if Display Bullets is set to All at Once, this option is not available. If you have selected a page without bullets, this option does not appear in this section of the InfoBox.

**Transition**    A drop-down list box from which you choose a visual effect that occurs between the prior page and the current page. If you have selected the Display Text with Page option button, this option is not available.

**Sound**    A text box in which you insert the name of a sound file that will accompany the current object or text. If you have selected the Display Text with Page option button, this option is not available.

**Browse**    A button on which you can click to browse for sound files to attach to the current object or text.

**Options (Effect When Text Block Is Added group)**
A button on which you click to open the Options for the current wave (WAV) file dialog box to select attributes for the sound. If you have not selected a sound, this button is not available.

**Action When Text Block Is Clicked**    A drop-down list box with which you associate an action with a click on the selected text block. Options from which you can choose are No Action (the default), Jump, Run Application, Play Sound, Play Movie, and Run Show.

**Options (Action When Text Block Is Clicked group)**
A button on which you click to specify attributes of the selected action. This button is not available if there is no action or if you have chosen Jump, Run Application, or Run Show from the Action When Text Block Is Clicked drop-down list box.

**FIGURE 21.20** ▶

*The Screen Show section of the All Text Levels Properties InfoBox with all the default settings*

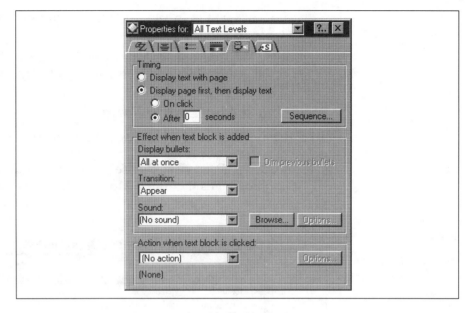

## ▶ Adding a Movie to a Screen Show

A movie can be a brief diversion, introduce or end an important topic, or signal the end of one page and the start of the next.

- You can automatically play a movie at a particular time after its page appears, or you can play a movie by clicking.

- You can play a movie continuously or specify the number of times that it should play.

- You can run the movie at one of three speeds.

- You can either embed a movie in a presentation or link to the movie file.

Freelance Graphics supports three types of movies:

- Gold Disk Animation Works Movies, which have an AWM extension and which are supported by the Windows Media Control Interface (MCI).

- All movie types supported by the Windows Media Control Interface (MCI). To see the list of devices supported by your computer, open the Control Panel, double-click on the Multimedia icon, click on the Advanced tab, and click on the plus sign preceding Media Control Devices.

● Gold Disk Add Impact Movies, which have an AIM extension. Freelance Graphics includes a library of AIM movies.

### Inserting a Movie on a Page

To add a movie to the current page, follow these steps:

**1.** In Current Page view, choose Create ➤ Add Movie. Freelance Graphics opens the Add a Movie dialog box (see Figure 21.21).

**FIGURE 21.21** ▶

*The Add a Movie dialog box with a movie selected*

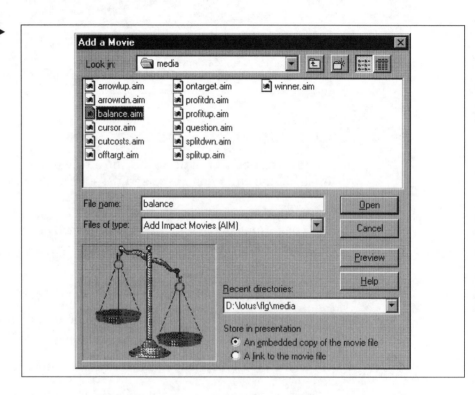

**2.** Select a filename from the list in the middle of the dialog box. Freelance Graphics displays an illustration in the sample box and inserts the name of the file in the File Name text box.

**3.** To play the movie before committing to it, click on the Preview button.

**4.** To embed the movie in the presentation (that is, copy the file), click on the An Embedded Copy of the Movie File option button.

**5.** To link to the movie (that is, establish a connection to the file in its original location), click on A Link to the Movie File.

**6.** Click on Open. Freelance Graphics closes the dialog box and inserts the movie in its default position on the page. If the movie runs across the screen, Freelance Graphics adds a horizontal scroll bar to the bottom of the work area (see Figure 21.22). If the movie takes place in a small area, a small rectangle and button (see Figure 21.23) or a small heading appear on the page.

**FIGURE 21.22** ▶

*A page with an embedded movie, which will run across the screen*

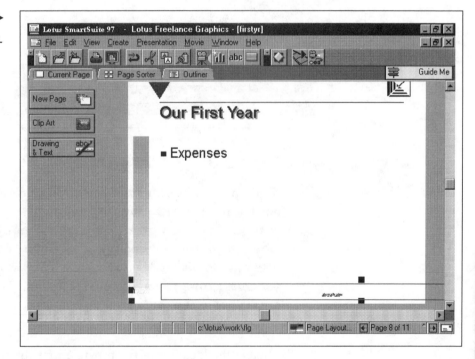

**FIGURE 21.23** ▶

*A page with an embedded movie and the default movie icon*

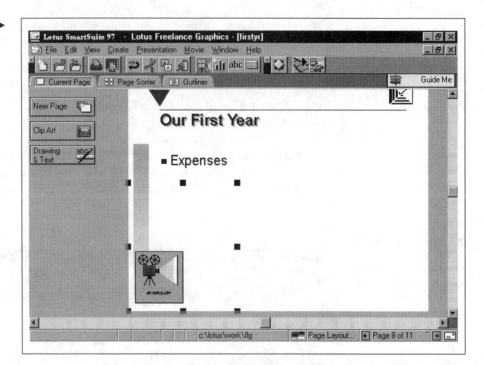

> **TIP**
>
> **If you plan to use this presentation as a TeamShow, embed the presentation file and all files associated with it. If you do not, all the files will not be available when the person to whom you send the presentation attempts to play it. If you create a TeamShow, Freelance Graphics prompts you to convert linked files to embedded ones.**

**7.** To change the location of the movie, move the mouse pointer to the movie icon or the heading within the box, press and hold down the left mouse button, and drag.

**8.** To resize the background box for the movie, drag one or more handles. Note that when you decrease the size of the box, you may make it too small for the movie to fit.

## Playing a Movie Outside a Screen Show

You might want to play a movie to time it or to check changes to its attributes. To play a movie without running a screen show, follow these steps:

*1.* Click on the movie icon. Freelance Graphics adds handles to the area in which the movie is located.

*2.* Either click on the Play a Movie SmartIcon or choose Movie ➤ Play. Freelance Graphics inserts a box with a black background and plays the movie on it.

## Editing a Movie

To edit movies, use the Movie Properties InfoBox (see Figure 21.24). Options in this InfoBox are:

**Display Movie As Icon on Page**     An option button that you select to display a movie icon on the current presentation page. If you select this option button (the default), you cannot play the movie using special effects such as clicking on a button (other than the Play a Movie SmartIcon) or setting it to start at a certain time after the page is revealed.

**Display Page First, Then Play Movie**     An option button that you select to display a blank presentation page and then play the movie. If you select this option button, movie starting and page sequence effects are available.

**FIGURE 21.24** ▶

*The Screen Show section of the Movie Properties InfoBox*

Enhancing a Presentation

*Ch.*
**21**

**On Click**    An option button on which you click to have an object appear on which you can click to play the movie. If you have selected the Display Movie As Icon on Page option button, this option is not available.

**After *n* Seconds**    An option button that when selected enables you to time, in seconds, how long between the appearance of the page and the start of the movie. If you have selected the Display Movie As Icon on Page option button, this option is not available.

**Sequence**    A button on which you click to open the Screen Show Sequence Overview dialog box in which you can specify the order in which the objects with associated effects appear on the current page. If you have selected the Display Movie As Icon on Page option button, this option is not available.

**Options**    A button on which you click to open the Options for the *MOVIE*.AIM dialog box (where *MOVIE* represents the current movie) to select attributes for playing the movie.

## Attaching a Movie to an Object

You can attach a movie to an object or to text on a page. During a screen show, you can then click on the object to play the movie. To attach a movie to an object, follow these steps:

1.  Select an object or a text block.

2.  Click on the Open InfoBox SmartIcon; choose a Properties command from the Text, Group, Table, Chart, Bitmap, or Org Chart menu; or right-click on the object and choose a Properties command. Freelance Graphics opens the InfoBox.

3.  If needed, click on the Screen Show tab.

4.  From the Action When Object Is Clicked drop-down list box, select Play Movie (see Figure 21.25), and click on the Options button. The Play Movie dialog box appears.

5.  Select a filename.

6.  To embed the file in the presentation, click on An Embedded Copy of the Movie File.

7.  To link the file to the presentation, click on A Link to the Movie File.

**FIGURE 21.25** ▶

*The Screen Show section of the Group Properties InfoBox with Play Movie selected*

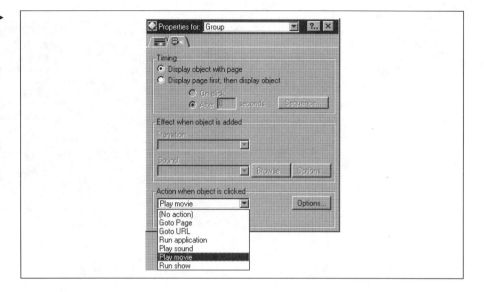

**8.** Click on Open.

**9.** In the InfoBox, click on the Options button. The Options for *MOVIE*.AIM dialog box (see Figure 21.26) appears.

**10.** Select from these options:

**Play Continuously**  Select this option button to play the movie continuously. To stop the movie, press the Esc key.

**Play *n* Time(s)**  Select this option button and type a number in the text box to play the movie a certain number of times.

**Speed**  From this drop-down list box, select the speed at which you want the movie to run: Slow, Medium, or Fast.

**Location**  From this drop-down list box, Select the location of the movie.

**An Embedded Copy of the Movie File**  Click on this option button to embed the movie. This button is available only if you have linked to the movie file when opening it.

**A Link to the Movie File**  Click on this option button to link to the movie file. This button is available only if you have linked to the movie file when opening it.

Enhancing a
Presentation

▶ ▶

*Ch.*
**21**

**FIGURE 21.26** ►

*The Options for BALOON1.AIM dialog box with its default settings*

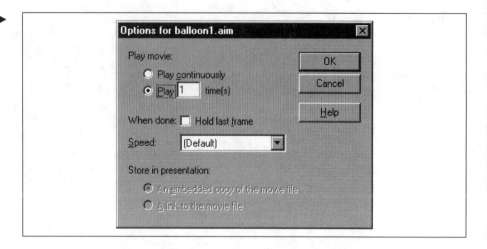

**Options for balloon1.aim**

Play movie:
○ Play continuously
◉ Play 1 time(s)

When done: ☐ Hold last frame

Speed: [(Default)]

Store in presentation:
◉ An embedded copy of the movie file
○ A link to the movie file

OK
Cancel
Help

**11.** Click on OK to close the dialog box.

## ► *Adding Bullets Progressively*

In a page with a bulleted list, you can add one bulleted item at a time and, thus, talk about each item as it appears on the page.

►► **N O T E**

> **This feature applies only to top-level bullets; bulleted items under a top-level item appear on a page at the same time their "parent" bullet appears.**

To add bulleted items one by one to a page, follow these steps:

**1.** In Current Page view, select a page with a bulleted list containing two or more bulleted items.

**2.** Choose Page ➤ Bullet Build. Freelance Graphics adds appropriate pages and opens the Screen Show section of the All Text Levels Properties InfoBox with bullet options selected: One at a Time is selected from the Display Bullets drop-down list box, and the Dim Previous Bullets checkbox is checked (see Figure 21.27).

**3.** Click on the Close button to close the InfoBox. The next time you run the presentation, the bullet options will be in place.

**FIGURE 21.27** ▶

*The Screen Show section of the All Text Levels Properties InfoBox with bullet options selected*

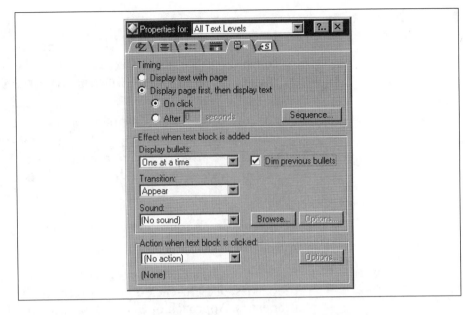

▶▶**NOTE**

**To delete these bullet options, open the InfoBox, click on the Screen Show tab, and select All at Once from the Display Bullets drop-down list box. Then close the InfoBox.**

## ▶ *Specifying Transitions between Pages*

When you put on a screen show, it's exciting to use a special effect to enhance the transition from one page to another. Using the Screen Show section of the InfoBox, you can specify a transition effect used to display the current page.

> **▶▶TIP**
>
> **Some of these effects flash by if you have a fast computer. When you first start using Freelance Graphics, experiment and find the effects that work best for you and the computer on which you plan to run the screen show. Many times, trying effects one at a time with the first page of a screen show allows you to see the effect more clearly; starting the screen show seems to slow the transition down a bit.**

To specify an opening transition for the current page in Current Page view, follow these steps:

1. Click on the Open InfoBox SmartIcon, choose Page ➤ Page Properties, or right-click on the current page and choose Page Properties. Approach opens the Page section of the Page Properties InfoBox.

2. Click on the Screen Show tab. Freelance Graphics switches to the Screen Show section of the Page Properties InfoBox (see Figure 21.28).

3. Select a transition effect from the Transition scroll box.

4. After choosing other options, click on the Close button. Freelance Graphics adds the transition to the chosen page and closes the dialog box.

**FIGURE 21.28** ▶

*The Screen Show section of the Page Properties InfoBox*

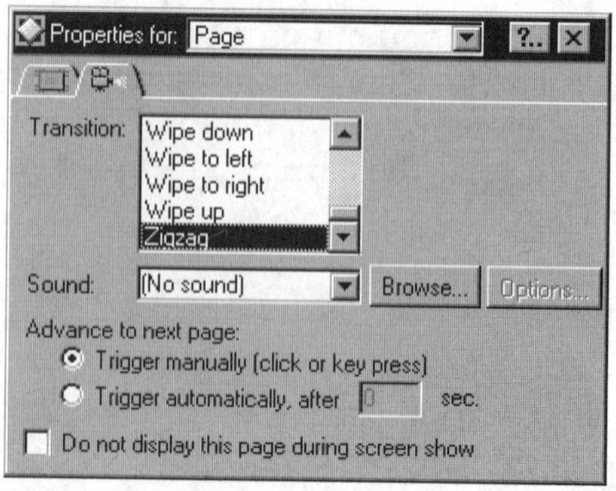

## ▶ *Adding Sound to a Screen Show*

You can use sound to introduce an important topic, to accompany a movie, or to signal the start of a new page. You can add sound to any page or to any object in a presentation.

- You can automatically play a sound file at a particular time after its page appears or by clicking.

- You can play a sound file either during or after the transition from one page to the next.

- If you play a sound file after a page transition, you can play it continuously or a set number of times.

- You can choose to finish playing a sound file before the next automatic event occurs.

- You can either embed a sound file in a presentation or link to the sound file.

Freelance Graphics supports two types of sound files:

- Wave files, which have a WAV extension. Freelance Graphics includes a library of wave files. Look for Windows 95-based wave files in the WINDOWS.MEDIAPLT and WINDOWS.MEDIA folders.

- MIDI clips, which have an MID extension. If your installed copy of Windows 95 includes MIDI clips, you will find them in the WINDOWS.MEDIAPLT and WINDOWS.MEDIA folders.

### Inserting a Sound File on a Page

To add sound to the current page, follow these steps:

 **1.** While working in any view, click on the section of the page with which you want to associate the sound, click on the Open InfoBox SmartIcon; choose Text ➤ Text Properties, Page ➤ Page Properties, or another Properties command; or right-click on the page and choose a Properties command. Freelance Graphics opens the InfoBox.

▶▶ **N O T E**

**To add a sound file in Outliner view, click on the picture or icon in the left margin after you open an InfoBox and click on the Screen Show tab.**

**2.** Click on the Screen Show tab.

**3.** Click on the Display Page First, Then Display Text or Object option button. Freelance Graphics makes active the Sound text box and the Browse and Option buttons.

**4.** Click on the Browse button. Freelance Graphics opens the Attaching Sounds to: *object* dialog box (see Figure 21.29).

**5.** Select a filename from the list of files in the middle of the dialog box. Freelance Graphics inserts the name of the file in the File Name text box.

**6.** To play the sound before committing to it, click on the Play button.

**7.** To embed the sound in the presentation (that is, copy the file), click on the An Embedded Copy of the Sound File option button.

**FIGURE 21.29** ▶

*The Attaching Sounds to:* object *dialog box*

| Attaching sounds to: Group | | | ✕ |
|---|---|---|---|

Look in: 📁 media

| applause | jazzy | rain |
|---|---|---|
| carskid | **lionroar** | shiphorn |
| cheering | phone | ticking |
| chime_a | pluck_a | trumpet |
| chime_b | pluck_b | whistle |
| intro | pluck_c | |

File name: lionroar              Open

Files of type: Wave Files (WAV)      Cancel

Recent directories: C:\lotus\flg\media

Store in presentation:                Play
  ⦿ An embedded copy of the sound file      Help
  ○ A link to the sound file

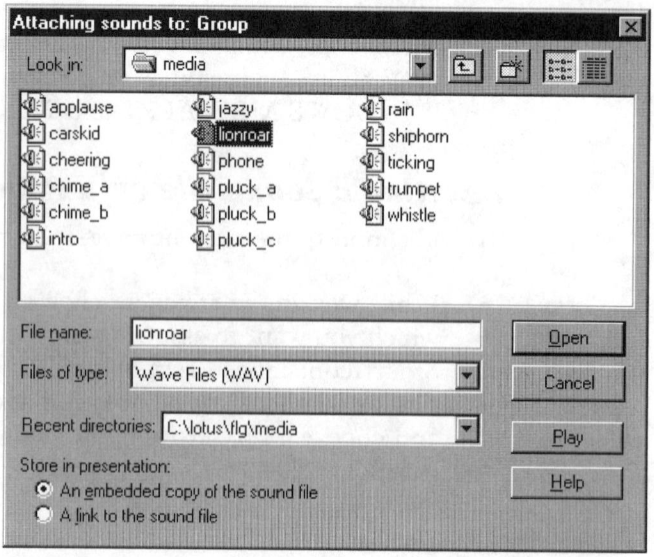

**8.** To link to the sound (that is, establish a connection to the file in its original location), click on A Link to the Sound File.

**9.** Click on Open. Freelance Graphics closes the dialog box and returns to the InfoBox.

▶▶ **T I P**

> **If you plan to use this presentation as a TeamShow, embed the presentation file and all files associated with it. If you do not, all the files will not be available when the person to whom you send the presentation attempts to play it. If you create a TeamShow, Freelance Graphics prompts you to convert linked files to embedded ones.**

## Changing Sound Attributes in a Screen Show

To change attributes such as the time at which a sound file starts playing, whether it plays continuously or a particular number of times, its sequence with other page events, and to change the way it is stored, use the Options for *SOUNDFILE*.EXT dialog box (see Figure 21.30). Options in this dialog box are:

**During Transition**　　An option button that you select to start playing the sound file as the current page appears.

**After Transition**　　An option button that you select to start playing the sound file after the page appears.

**Play Continuously**　　Select this option button to play the sound file continuously. To stop the sound file, press the Esc key.

**Play *n* Time(s)**　　Select this option button and type a number in the text box to play the sound file a certain number of times.

**Sequencing**　　Check this checkbox to finish playing the sound before the next page effect starts.

**An Embedded Copy of the Sound File**　　Click on this option button to embed the sound file. This button is available only if you have linked to the sound file when opening it.

**A Link to the Sound File** Click on this option button to link to the sound file. This button is available only if you have linked to the sound file when opening it.

**FIGURE 21.30** ▶

*The Options for the SOUNDFILE.EXT dialog box with the After Transition option button selected*

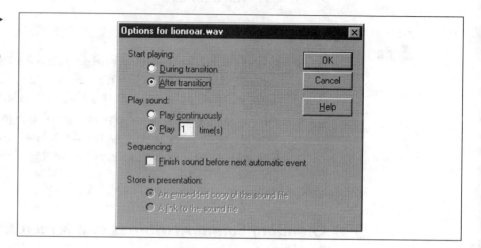

## ▶ *Specifying the Sequence of Objects on a Page*

You can control the sequence in which objects appear and events happen on a page. For example, if you associate a sound with a title, be sure that the title (and its sound) appear and play before a bulleted list and its sound, and finish up with a sound file and a movie that play when you click on a button. To specify the order of objects as they appear on a page, click on the Sequence Objects in a Screen Show SmartIcon, choose Presentation ▶ Sequence Objects on Page, or in the Screen Show section of the Movie Properties, Group Properties, or All Text Levels Properties InfoBox, click on the Sequence button. In the Screen Show Sequence Overview dialog box (see Figure 21.31), you can rename objects, move the objects so that they play in a different order, and view their attributes and the objects with which they are associated.

**FIGURE 21.31** ▶

*The Screen Show Sequence Overview dialog box with renamed objects*

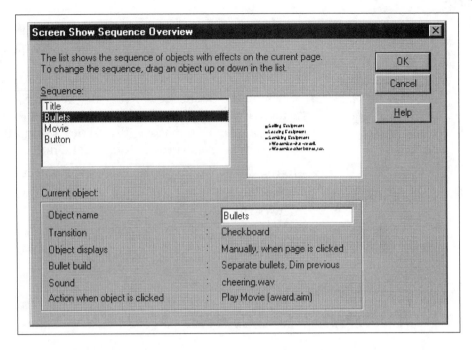

## Renaming Sequence Objects

As Freelance Graphics adds an effect to a page, it gives it a name, Object n, where n represents the order in which you added it to the page. When a page has several effects that must appear in a particular order, renaming each effect can help you to keep better track—especially if you use a name that reminds you of how the effect fits into the overall page. To rename a sequence object in the Screen Show Sequence Overview dialog box, follow these steps:

*1.* Click on the Sequence Objects in a Screen Show SmartIcon, choose Presentation ➤ Sequence Objects on Page, or in the Screen Show section of the Movie Properties, Group Properties, or All Text Levels Properties InfoBox, click on the Sequence button.

*2.* In the Sequence text box, click on the object to be renamed.

*3.* In the Object Name text box, overtype the current name.

*4.* Repeat steps 2 and 3 for other names.

*5.* To close the dialog box, click on OK.

### Changing the Sequence of Objects on a Page

To control the sequence in which objects appear in a screen show, follow these steps:

1. Click on the Sequence Objects in a Screen Show SmartIcon, choose Presentation ➤ Sequence Objects on Page, or in the Screen Show section of the Movie Properties, Group Properties, or All Text Levels Properties InfoBox, click on the Sequence button.

2. In the Sequence text box, click on the object to be moved.

3. When the mouse pointer changes to a hand, drag the object to its new position on the list.

4. Repeat steps 2 and 3 to move other objects.

5. To close the dialog box, click on OK.

# ▶▶ Running a Screen Show

You can show your presentation on your computer monitor manually or automatically. If you run a screen show manually, you control when the next page appears; you don't have to worry about synchronizing your comments and the screen show. If you run the show automatically, you can set the speed at which pages change. You can also set the screen show to run continuously, which works very well at conferences and expositions.

During a screen show, you can branch to a specific presentation page, start an application, draw on the screen using the mouse pointer, or temporarily stop the show.

To start a screen show on the first page of the current presentation, click on the Run Screen Show from Beginning SmartIcon, press Alt+F10, or choose Presentation ➤ Run Screen Show ➤ From Beginning. To start a screen show at the current page, press Alt+F11 or choose Presentation ➤ Run Screen Show ➤ From Current Page. Freelance Graphics starts the screen show using the default screen show settings or the effects that you have specified. You can also create a screen show to run on a computer that may not have Freelance Graphics installed.

To control the screen show, you can click a mouse button or press a key.

| To take this action: | Press: | Click: |
| --- | --- | --- |
| Display the next page | Enter or PgDn | The left mouse button |
| Display the previous page | PgUp | The right mouse button |
| Pause the screen show | Spacebar | N/A |
| Resume a paused screen show | Spacebar | N/A |
| Display the Screen Show Pages dialog box (see Figure 12.32) to jump to another page in the screen show or to quit the show | Esc | N/A |
| Display the List Pages dialog box to stop the screen show | Esc | N/A |

**FIGURE 21.32** ▶

*The Screen Show Pages dialog box*

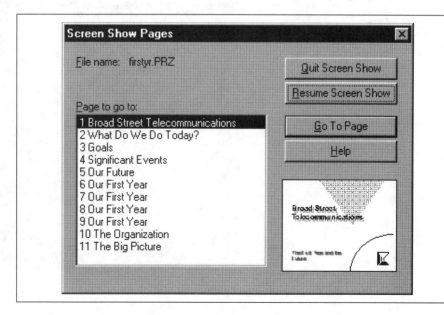

►►N O T E

**If you don't like the look of the screen show dimensions on your desktop, try optimizing it. To do so, choose File ➤ Print and from the Print To drop-down list box, select Screen Show. Then click on the Close button. This can adjust the dimensions of the pages in the show to your desktop dimensions. However, remember to select a printer from the Print To drop-down list box the next time you want to print presentation pages on a printer.**

# ►► *Editing a Screen Show*

When you want to define and change attributes for the entire screen show, use the Set Up Screen Show dialog box (see Figures 21.33, 21.34, and 21.35). To open this dialog box, choose Presentation ➤ Set Up Screen Show.

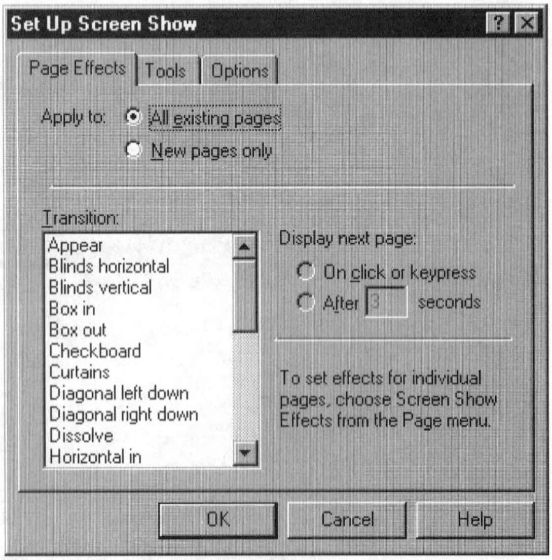

**FIGURE 21.33** ►

*The Page Effects section of the Set Up Screen Show dialog box*

| Set Up Screen Show | ? X |
| --- | --- |

Page Effects | Tools | Options

Apply to:  ◉ All existing pages
           ○ New pages only

Transition:
Appear
Blinds horizontal
Blinds vertical
Box in
Box out
Checkboard
Curtains
Diagonal left down
Diagonal right down
Dissolve
Horizontal in

Display next page:
○ On click or keypress
○ After 3 seconds

To set effects for individual pages, choose Screen Show Effects from the Page menu.

OK | Cancel | Help

**FIGURE 21.34** ▶

*The Tools section of the Set Up Screen Show dialog box*

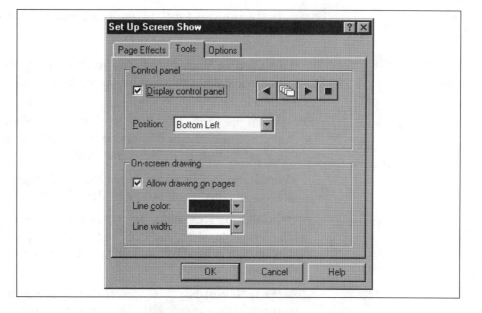

**FIGURE 21.35** ▶

*The Options section of the Set Up Screen Show dialog box*

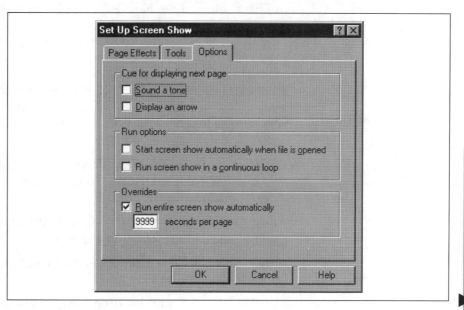

These are the options for the Page Effects section of the Set Up Screen Show dialog box:

**All Existing Pages**    Click on this option button to apply all the changes you make in this dialog box to all the pages currently in the presentation.

**New Pages Only**    Click on this option button to apply all the changes you make in this dialog box to all pages that you add to the presentation from this time forward.

**Transition**    To add a transition to all pages, select a transition effect from this scroll box. The default transition is Appear.

**On Click or Keypress**    Click on this option button to display the next page when you click the mouse or press a key. This option button is available only if you have selected the New Pages Only option button.

**After *n* Seconds**    Click on this option button to display the next page after *n* seconds. This option button is available only if you have selected the New Pages Only option button.

These are the options for the Tools section of the Set Up Screen Show dialog box:

**Display Control Panel**    Check this checkbox to display a control panel with which you can control the show. For more information, see the following section, "Controlling a Running Screen Show."

**Position**    From this drop-down list box, which is available only if you check the Display Control Panel checkbox, select one of four positions for the control panel.

**Allow Drawing on Pages**    Check this checkbox to enable drawing lines on presentation pages.

**Line Color**    From this drop-down color palette, select a color for lines that you draw on pages.

**Line Width**    From this drop-down list box, select the width of lines that you draw on pages.

These are the options for the Options section of the Set Up Screen Show dialog box:

**Sound a Tone**    Check this checkbox to have Freelance Graphics sound a tone as a cue for displaying the next page.

**Display an Arrow**    Check this checkbox to have Freelance Graphics show an arrow graphic as a cue for displaying the next page.

**Start Screen Show Automatically When File Is Opened**
Check this checkbox to have the screen show start automatically when you open the presentation file. The show ends after all screens have been displayed; Freelance Graphics ends if you are currently using it only to run the screen show.

 ▶▶ **T I P**

> To stop a show from automatically running every time you open it, press Esc once the show starts and click on Quit Screen Show. Then open the Set Up Screen Show dialog box, and clear the Start Screen Show Automatically When File Is Opened checkbox.

**Run Screen Show in a Continuous Loop**    Check this checkbox to run the screen show continuously.

**Run Entire Screen Show Automatically**    Check this checkbox to temporarily run this screen show automatically instead of its usual condition—the manual advance from page to page.

***n* Seconds per Page**    In this text box, type a numeric value representing the length of time, in seconds, that each page will be on display. Valid values range from 1 to 9999.

## ▶ *Controlling a Running Screen Show*

You can control the order of pages displayed during a screen show by using the Screen Show control panel, which allows you to control the page sequence manually.

Enhancing a
Presentation

▶▶

*Ch.*
**21**

The Screen Show control panel, which you can display on your desktop as a screen show runs, consists of four buttons with which you can go to a specific page or stop the screen show.

To display the control panel, follow these steps:

1. Choose Presentation ➤ Set Up Screen Show. Freelance Graphics opens the Set Up Screen Show dialog box.

2. Click on the Tools tab to display the Tools section of the Set Up Screen Show dialog box.

3. Click on the Display Control Panel checkbox.

4. From the Position drop-down list box, select the position of the control panel: Top Right, Bottom Right, Bottom Left, or Top Left. Try to select a location in which there are no objects on any page in the presentation.

5. Click on OK. Freelance Graphics closes the dialog box.

When you start the screen show, the Screen Show control panel appears in the location that you specified.

## ►► Creating Your Own SmartMaster Set

If you want to design your own unique SmartMaster set, work with a completely "blank slate." To start, create a new presentation. From the New Presentation dialog box (see Figure 21.36), select [No Content Topic] so that you can choose your own combination of page layouts, and select Blank so that you can design your own page background.

Of course, you can save some time (and perhaps make your life easier) by selecting a content topic and building a background behind that or by selecting a look and adding your own content to predefined page layouts.

The following sections show how to edit the page backdrop and how to edit page layouts.

**FIGURE 21.36** ▶

*The New Presentation
dialog box, from which
you can customize a
blank presentation*

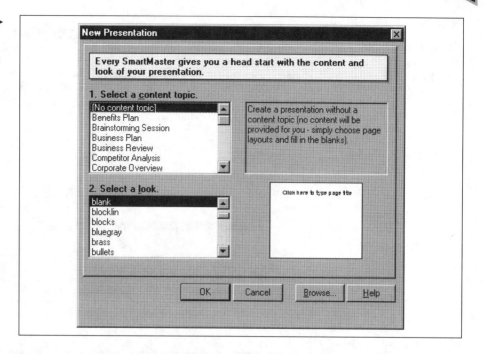

## ▶ *Creating a Blank Presentation*

To create a blank presentation, follow these steps:

*1.* Click on the Create a New File SmartIcon or choose File ➤ New
Presentation. Freelance Graphics opens the New Presentation dialog box.

*2.* Select [No Content Topic] from the Select a Content Topic scroll
list, select Blank from the Select a Look scroll list, and click on
OK. Freelance Graphics displays the New Page dialog box.

*3.* To start with a completely blank page, select [Blank Page](see Figure 21.37).

*4.* Click on OK. Freelance Graphics displays a blank page (see Figure 21.38) for an untitled presentation.

**FIGURE 21.37** ▶

*The New Page dialog box with [Blank Page] selected*

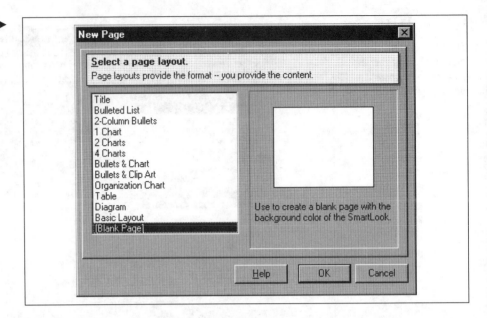

**FIGURE 21.38** ▶

*A blank page in a new untitled presentation*

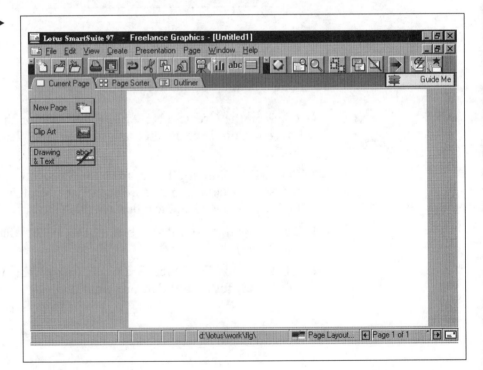

## ▶ *Editing a Page Backdrop*

Editing a blank backdrop enables you to design the background for all presentation pages (except the title page). Using the Presentation ➤ Edit Backdrop command, you can add a background pattern, pattern color, or background color or add a graphic on all presentation pages but the title page. To learn about inserting a graphic, such as a logo, on the backdrop, see the "Inserting a Logo on Every Page" section earlier in this chapter. To find out how to edit a title page, see the following section, "Editing Page Layout."

To edit a presentation backdrop, choose Presentation ➤ Edit Backdrop. Freelance Graphics displays a page with a default page title Click Here box against a "gridded" background (see Figure 21.39).

**FIGURE 21.39** ▶

*A page ready to be edited*

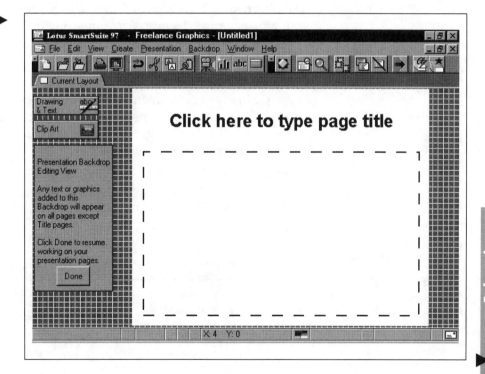

Enhancing a Presentation

▶▶

*Ch.*
**21**

### Editing a Click Here Text Block

To edit the Click Here text block, click on the text block and either click on the Open InfoBox SmartIcon or choose "Click Here" ➤ "Click Here" Properties. The "Click Here" Properties InfoBox is composed of seven sections.

The options in the Text section of the "Click Here..." Block InfoBox (see Figure 21.40) are:

**Font Name**    From this scroll box, select one of the fonts installed on your computer and under Windows.

**Size**    From this scroll box, select a point size for the selected text. You also can type or select a point size from the option box/text box at the bottom of the scroll box.

**Attributes**    In this scroll box, click on effects with which you can enhance the selection. Attributes include Normal, Bold, Italic, Underline, Strikethrough, Superscript, and Subscript. Table 3.5 lists the equivalent SmartSuite shortcut keys and key combinations.

**Text Color**    Click on any part of this drop-down box to display a palette of colors from which you can choose for the selected text—either for display onscreen or for printing on a color printer installed on your computer system.

**Text Shadow**    Click on this drop-down list box to display a list of shadows that you can apply to text. Options include None (the default), Below Right, Below Left, Above Right, and Above Left.

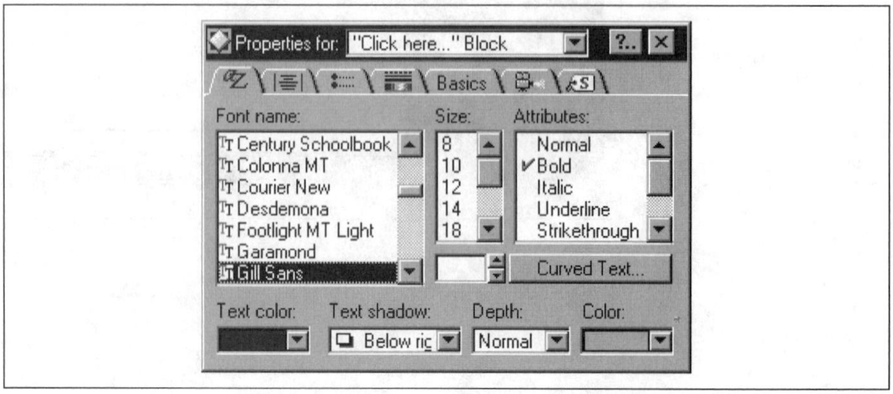

**FIGURE 21.40** ▶

*The Text section of the "Click Here... " Block Properties InfoBox*

**Depth**     Click on this drop-down list box to display a list of shadow depths: Shallow (the default), Normal, or Deep.

**Color**     Click on this drop-down list box to open a palette from which you can choose a shadow color.

The options in the Alignment section of the "Click Here... " Block Properties InfoBox (see Figure 21.41) are:

**Alignment**     Click on a Horizontal button to align text between the left and right margins of its bounding box, marked by the handles around the selected block of text. Click on a Vertical button to align text between the top and bottom margins of the bounding box.

**Space Between**     From the Lines and Paragraphs drop-down list boxes, select the space between lines and paragraphs.

**Indent**     In the 1st Line, Left, and Right text boxes, type the values (ranging from 0.00 to 22.03) by which lines in the text block are indented from the first line at the left margin, the remaining lines at the left margin, and the right margin.

**Wrap Text**     Check this checkbox to apply word wrap to the text block. The default is a checked checkbox.

**FIGURE 21.41** ▶

*The Alignment section of the "Click Here... " Block Properties InfoBox*

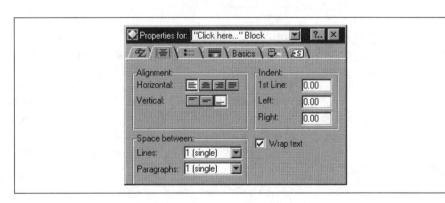

The options in the Bullets section of the "Click Here... " Block Properties InfoBox (see Figure 21.42) are:

**Bullet Attributes**     In this group are options for bullets' appearance: Style, a drop-down list box from which you choose the bullet

Ch.
**21**

Enhancing a
Presentation

character or number type; Color, a drop-down palette from which you choose the bullet color; Size, a text/option box from which you select the bullet size; and Start Number, a text box in which you type the starting number for a numbered list.

**Bullet Shadow**     In this group are options for bullets' shadow: Position, a drop-down list from which you choose the location of a shadow behind the bullet; Depth, a drop-down list from which you choose the size of the shadow; and Color, a drop-down palette from which you choose the shadow color.

**Space between Bullet & Text**     A drop-down list from which you choose the distance between the bullet and its associated text.

**FIGURE 21.42** ►

*The Bullets section of the "Click Here... " Block Properties InfoBox*

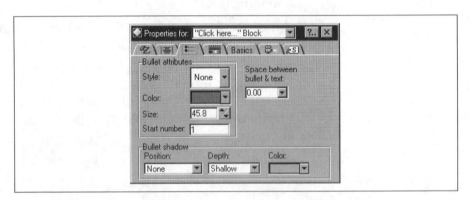

 The options in the Lines and Color section of the "Click Here..." Block Properties InfoBox (see Figure 21.43) are:

**Border**     From the Style drop-down list box, select the line style of the border around the block. The default is None, or no border; a value of None means that the Width and Color selections do not have an effect. From the Width drop-down list box, select the border line width. From the Color drop-down palette, select the border line color.

**Shadow**     From this drop-down list box select the shadow behind the block.

**Interior**     From the Pattern drop-down palette, select the pattern of the interior of the block. The default is black (a solid pattern). If you choose None, there is no pattern. From the Pattern Color drop-down palette, select the foreground color of the pattern. From the Background drop-down palette, select the background color of the pattern. Check the Same Color As Border checkbox to match the Pattern Color with the Color in the Border group.

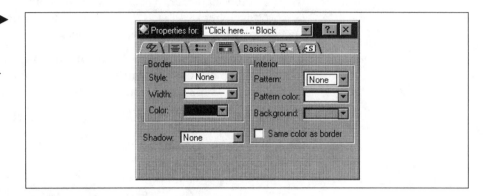

**Basics** The options in the Basics section of the "Click Here..." Block Properties InfoBox (see Figure 21.44) are:

**Type of Block**   From this drop-down list box, choose the type of block for the selection: Text (the default), Clip Art, Chart, Org Chart, Table, Diagram, or Button.

**WARNING**

**If you have applied colors to the block or its border, selecting a different type of block may change the colors. If you intend to select a different type of block, do that first and then apply colors.**

**ID Number**   In this text box, type a number from 1 to 100 to change the ID and, therefore, the position of the selected Click Here block. For more information about mapping Click Here blocks, refer to the Details section of "Changing the ID of 'Click Here...' Blocks" help topic under "Click Here... Blocks."

**Use Click Here Block Guide**   Check this checkbox to control the placement and size of multiple Click Here blocks on a page. A cleared checkbox, the default, allows you to resize Click

Here blocks manually. For more information, refer to the "Overview" help topic under "Click Here... Blocks."

**Set Click Here Block Guide Order**    To change the placement of the Click Here block within the Click Here Block Guide (if you have checked Use Click Here Block Guide), check this checkbox. The default is a cleared checkbox.

**Use Standard Prompt**    From this drop-down list box, select the prompt to appear within the Click Here block. The default is Click Here to Type Page Title.

**Attach Script**    Click on this button to create or edit a script. This button is available only if you are editing a content topic.

**FIGURE 21.44** ►

*The Basics section of the "Click Here... " Block Properties InfoBox*

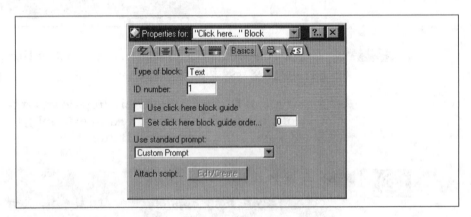

 The options in the Screen Show section of the "Click Here..." Block Properties InfoBox (see Figure 21.45) are described in the "Creating a Screen Show" section, which appears earlier in this chapter.

 The options in the Styles section of the "Click Here..." Block Properties InfoBox (see Figure 21.46) are:

**Text Style for Current Text Block**    Select a name of a text style for the current text block from this scroll box. The default style is Page Title.

**Reset to Style**    Click on this button to reset the text style for the current text block to the default style.

**FIGURE 21.45** ▶

*The Screen Show section of the "Click Here..." Block Properties InfoBox*

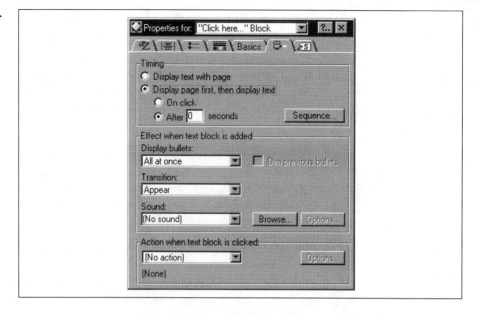

**FIGURE 21.46** ▶

*The Styles section of the "Click Here... " Block Properties InfoBox*

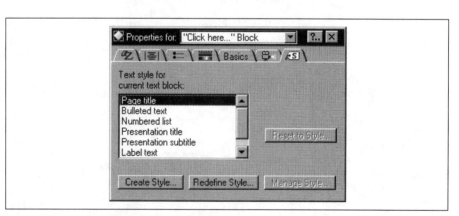

**Create Style**    Click on this button to open the Create Style dialog box in which you can name and describe a text style based on the current options in the "Click Here..." Block Properties InfoBox. Clicking on OK saves the named style.

**Redefine Style**    Click on this button to open the Redefine Style dialog box in which you can redefine a previously named text style using the current options in the "Click Here..." Block Properties InfoBox. This button is not available if you choose the (None) text style from the Text Style for Current Text Block scroll box.

**Manage Style**   In the Styles sections of other InfoBoxes, you can click on this button to open the Manage Styles dialog box in which you can rename, delete, or copy a style from another file. This button is not available in this InfoBox.

## Changing the Look of the Backdrop

To edit the backdrop, click on the blank page and either click on the Open InfoBox SmartIcon or choose Backdrop ➤ Page Properties. The Backdrop Properties InfoBox is composed of one section: Lines and Color.

The options in the Backdrop Properties InfoBox (see Figure 21.47) are:

**Pattern**   From this drop-down palette, select the pattern of the backdrop. The default is black (a solid pattern). If you choose None, there is no pattern.

**Pattern Color**   From this drop-down palette, select the foreground color of the pattern—the color of the backdrop if you have chosen black (a solid pattern). The default is white.

**Background**   From this drop-down palette, select the background color of the pattern. The default is white.

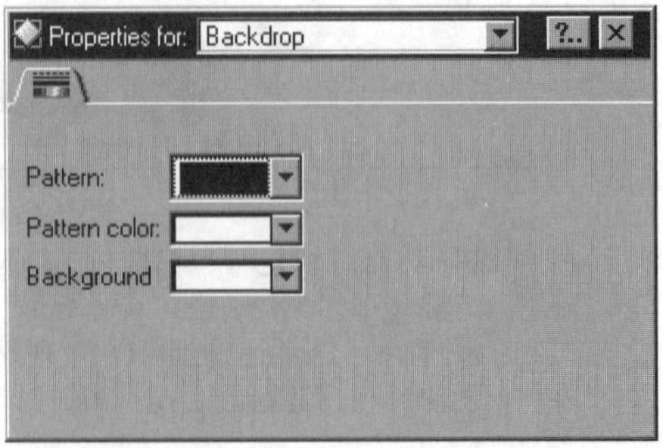

**FIGURE 21.47** ►

*The Backdrop Properties InfoBox with its default settings*

To return to the presentation, click on the Close button, choose Presentation ➤ Return to Presentation Pages, or press Shift+F9.

## ▶ *Editing Page Layout*

If you are creating a custom presentation, you don't have to stop at customizing text blocks or changing the color or pattern of the backdrop. In this section, you'll learn how to change the layout of default pages. The centerpiece of page layout editing is the Edit Page Layout dialog box (see Figure 21.48). Here, you can change both layout and backdrop attributes of selected pages. To open the Edit Page Layout dialog box, choose Presentation ➤ Edit Page Layouts.

To edit the backdrop, click on Presentation Backdrop and click on the Edit button. Then follow the instructions in the previous section, "Editing a Page Backdrop."

**FIGURE 21.48** ▶

*The Edit Page Layout dialog box from which you can change the backdrop or layout of the selected page*

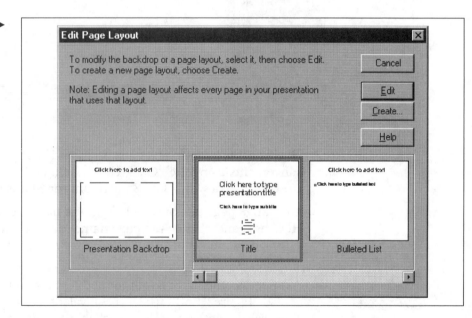

### *Editing a Presentation Page*

To edit a page, follow these steps:

**1.** Click on the page in the scroll box at the bottom of the Edit Page Layout dialog box, and then click on Edit. Use the scroll box to move through all the presentation pages. The dialog box closes and the selected page appears (see Figure 21.49).

**FIGURE 21.49** ►

*A title page ready to be edited*

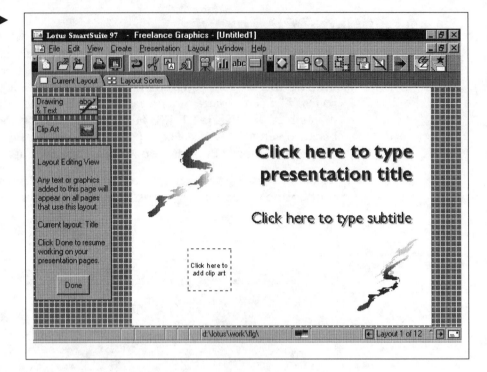

2. To edit a Click Here box, click on it, and change formats and enhancements using the "Click Here..." Block Properties InfoBox or a text properties InfoBox, SmartIcons, or Status bar buttons.

3. To change page attributes, click on the page, outside any Click Here box, and change the page name, description, lines and colors, or screen show using the Page Properties InfoBox or SmartIcons.

4. To select another page layout to modify, click on the Layout Sorter tab (see Figure 21.50), which is equivalent to the Page Sorter tab. Then select another page and click on the Current Layout tab, which is equivalent to the Current Page tab, and change the page using the preceding steps.

5. When you have completed your work, return to the presentation by clicking on the Done button, choosing Presentation ➤ Return to Presentation Pages, or pressing Shift+F9.

**FIGURE 21.50** ▶

*The Layout Sorter section*

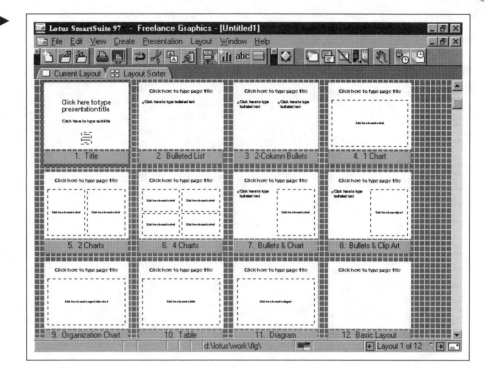

# PART SIX

► ► ► CHAPTER **22**

# Scheduling with Organizer

►► **I**n this chapter and the next, you'll learn about Organizer, a personal information manager (PIM) that you can use in business or in your personal life. Remember that you can learn the basics of opening and saving files by reviewing the *Getting Acquainted with Smart-Suite* chapter, and you can review editing concepts in the *Editing in SmartSuite Applications* chapter.

This chapter covers Organizer basics, using the Calendar section to demonstrate. At the same time you're learning about Organizer, you'll see how the Calendar works.

## ►► *Introducing Organizer*

Organizer is an all-purpose personal information manager that looks like an on-screen version of an organizer notebook.

With Organizer, you can do the following:

- Track and control many of your activities, including keeping a daily diary, scheduling appointments, setting alarms so that you can keep your appointments and remember your anniversaries, recording incoming and outgoing telephone calls, and even starting an application at a particular time.

- Accumulate text, graphics, and diagrams in a notebook.

- Keep an up-to-date to-do list, and expand on to-do items in the notebook.

- Maintain an address book—with both business and personal information—that is arranged in alphabetic or category order. You can import names and addresses from Approach or other database programs. You can also dial telephone numbers from your address book if you have a modem up and running.

- Keep an anniversary list that is arranged in alphabetic, category, or even zodiac order.

- Record both incoming and outgoing telephone calls with their duration; view call entries by date, name, company, status, or category.

- Maintain and view a yearly planner, which illustrates your projects and schedule day by day.

- Add new sections or customize sections to suit your own information management purposes.

- Keep multiple Organizer files so that you can separate your business and personal obligations.

- Print your Organizer information on pages that are compatible with almost any label or personal organizer binder.

# ▶▶ *Viewing the Organizer Window*

The opening Organizer application window (see Figure 22.1) contains a title bar, a menu bar, and SmartIcons, just as described in the *Getting Acquainted with SmartSuite* chapter. Organizer also has its own unique work area and set of tools.

## ▶ *Organizer SmartIcons*

To learn how SmartIcons work, see the *Getting Acquainted with SmartSuite* chapter.

## ▶ *The Work Area*

On the left side of the work area is a tool palette, described in Table 22.1.

The work area displays your electronic personal organizer, with the following sections:

**Calendar**    Use the Calendar section to track your appointments and meetings, set alarms, and keep a diary, if you wish. Figure 22.2 shows the opening pages of the Calendar section.

**FIGURE 22.1** ▶

*The opening Organizer window shows today's Calendar.*

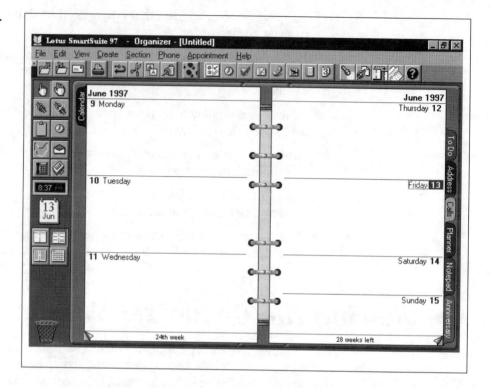

▶ **TABLE 22.1:** *Organizer Work Area Tools*

| Tool | Menu Command and Shortcut Key | Description |
|---|---|---|
| | N/A; N/A | Selects an entry for editing or for drag and drop |
| | N/A; N/A | Picks up an entry and drops in on another page |
| | N/A; N/A | Creates a link |
| | N/A; N/A | Breaks a link |
| | Edit ▶ Cut or Edit ▶ Paste; Ctrl+X or Shift+Del to cut; Ctrl+V or Shift+Ins to paste | Copies an entry into the Clipboard; pastes the contents of the Clipboard |

▶ **TABLE 22.1:** *Organizer Work Area Tools (continued)*

| Tool | Menu Command and Shortcut Key | Description |
|------|-------------------------------|-------------|
| | Create ➤ Appointment; Ins | Adds a new entry to the Calendar |
| | Create ➤ Task; Ins | Adds a new entry to the To Do list |
| | Create ➤ Address; Ins | Adds a new entry to the Address book |
| | Create ➤ Call: Ins | Adds a new entry to the Calls section |
| | Create ➤ Event; Ins | Adds a new entry to the Planner |
| | Create ➤ Page; Ins | Adds a new entry to the Notepad |
| | Create ➤ Anniversary; Ins | Adds a new entry to the Anniversary list |
| | File ➤ Meeting Notices | Shows your meeting notices if you are a member of a workgroup |
| | File ➤ TeamMail | Sends or receives mail if you are a member of a workgroup |
| | Phone ➤ Dial; Ctrl+D | Dials a telephone call |
| | File ➤ Print; Ctrl+P | Prints information from a section |
| 8:49 PM | N/A; N/A | Displays your current computer system time |
| 13 Jun | N/A; N/A | Displays your current computer system day and month |
| | Edit ➤ Clear; Del | Deletes dragged entries accompanied by an animated flame |

**FIGURE 22.2** ▶

*The opening pages of the Calendar section*

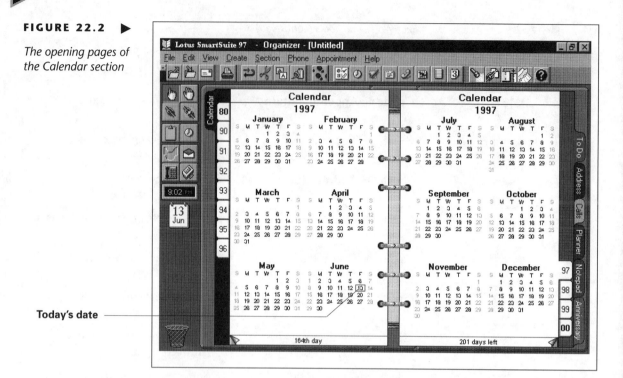

Today's date

**To Do**    Use the To Do section to write down your plans and let Organizer arrange them by date and priority. Figure 22.3 shows a page in a typical To Do section.

**Address**    Use the Address section to keep names and both business and home addresses and telephone numbers (which can be used in a Word Pro mail merge). In addition, you can dial telephone numbers and keep a log of your calls. Figure 22.4 shows two pages of the Address section.

**Calls**    Use the Calls section to record both incoming and outgoing telephone calls, time calls, redial calls, and schedule future calls. Figure 22.5 shows two entries in the Calls section.

**Planner**    Use the Planner section to show graphically your schedule of meetings, projects, vacations, and other events. Figure 22.6 shows an unfolded Planner.

**FIGURE 22.3** ▶

*A page in the To Do section, filled in with tasks*

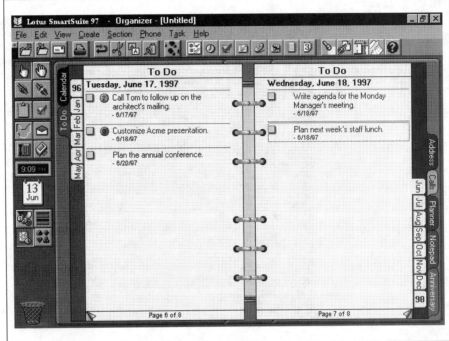

**FIGURE 22.4** ▶

*Two pages of the Address section*

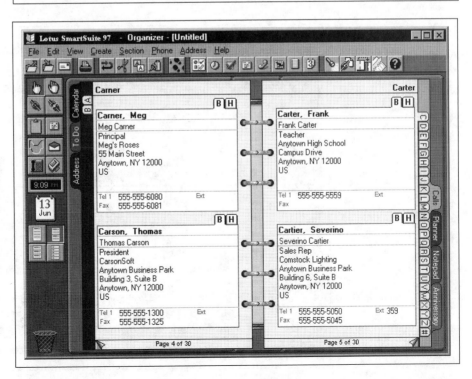

**FIGURE 22.5** ►

*Two entries in the Calls section*

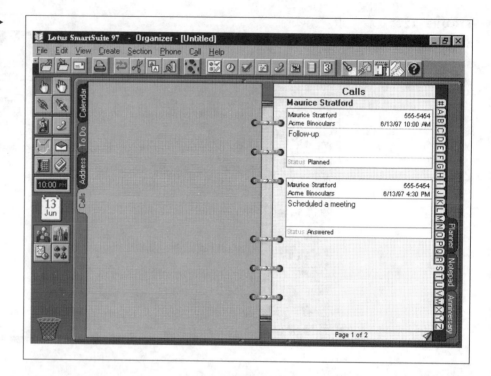

**FIGURE 22.6** ►

*An unfolded Planner, with several events marked*

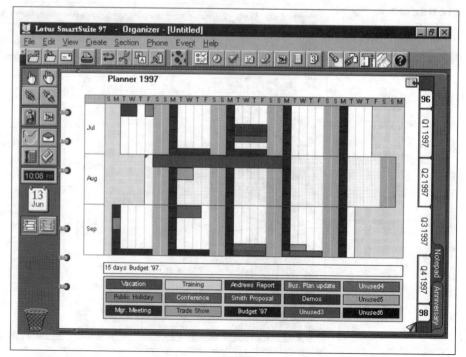

**Notepad**    Use the Notepad section to write notes and memos. You can also import text, spreadsheet data, charts, organization charts, and graphics and export information to other applications running under Windows. Figure 22.7 shows an entry in the Notepad section.

**FIGURE 22.7** ▶

*An entry in the Notepad section*

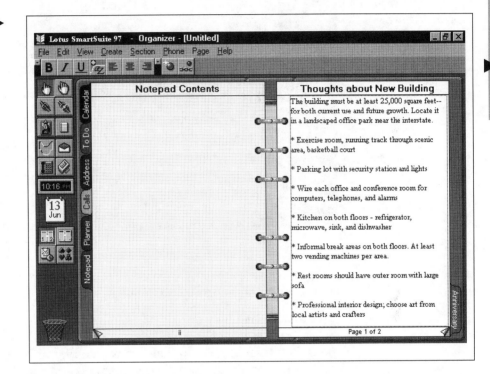

**Anniversary**    Use the Anniversary section to register anniversaries and birthdays for this year and future years. Figure 22.8 shows an entire year in the Anniversary section.

# ▶ ▶ *Opening an Organizer File*

Starting Organizer for the first time or opening a new file in Organizer means that you have new, empty Calendar, To Do, Address, Calls, Planner, Notepad, and Anniversary sections with which to work. You can

**FIGURE 22.8** ►

*The entire year in the Anniversary section*

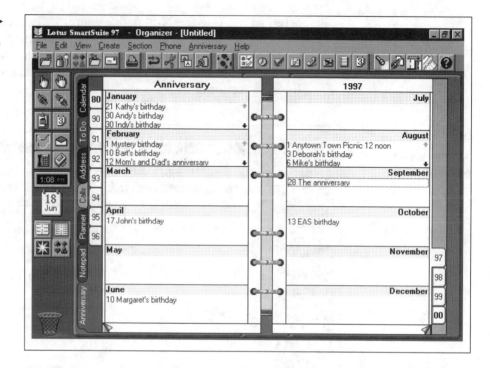

use multiple Organizer files to separate your business, personal, and volunteer activities, or you can keep everything in one file.

You can automatically open a particular file when you start Organizer. Choose File ➤ User Setup ➤ Organizer Preferences. When Organizer opens the Organizer Setup dialog box (see Figure 22.9), type the path and filename in the Automatically Open text box, and click on OK. To learn more about the Organizer Setup dialog box, refer to the *Customizing Your SmartSuite Environment* appendix.

To identify a particular Organizer file, type appropriate information in the text box on the right side of the very first page in the organizer:

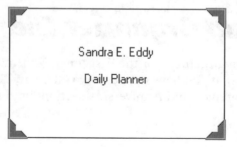

**FIGURE 22.9** ▶

*In the Organizer Preferences dialog box, you can specify a file that opens automatically when you start Organizer.*

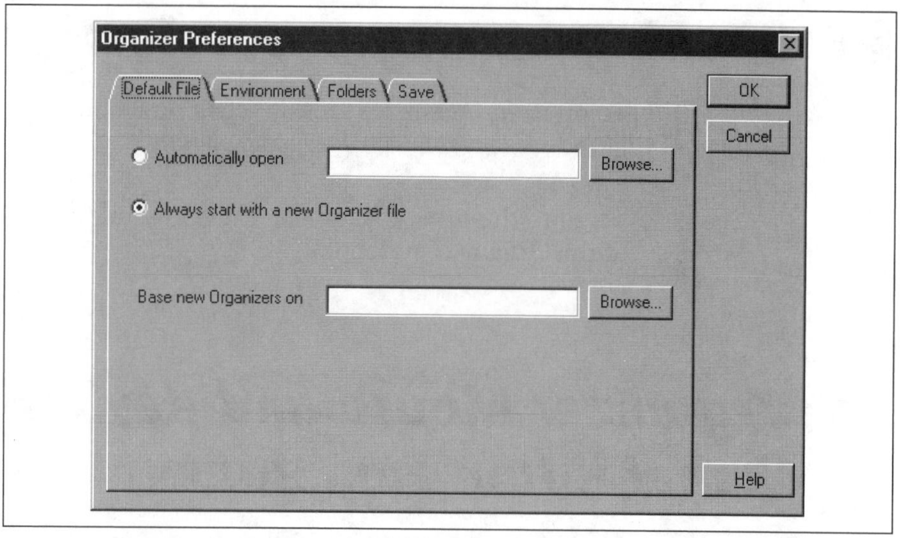

▶▶**NOTE**

**When you open an ORG or OR2 file from a previous version of Organizer, Organizer automatically converts it to the OR3 format. Either choose File ➤ Open, press Ctrl+O, or click on the Open SmartIcon at the left side of the SmartIcon bar. In the Open dialog box, open the List Files of Type drop-down list box, select Organizer 1.*x* (\*.ORG) or Organizer 2.*x* (\*.OR2), and double-click on the ORG or OR2 file. When Organizer asks if you want to convert the file, click on OK. Organizer converts the file, showing you its progress, and then asks if you would like to always open the file when Organizer starts up. Answer either Yes or No. (You can designate only one file to open automatically.) Organizer then opens the file.**

# ►► Opening an Organizer Section

To open an Organizer section, click on its tab.

To go to the first or last page of the Organizer, click on a nontab area of the Organizer notebook.

# ►► Organizer Mouse and Keyboard Combination Functions

In Organizer, you use the following special mouse/keyboard functions to navigate, select, or embed the time and/or date:

| Action | Purpose |
|---|---|
| Ctrl+Click on a tab | Return to the last page you viewed or edited |
| Click on a tab | Go to the first page of a section |
| Shift+Click on a tab | Go to the last page of a section |
| Click on the edge of the "front cover" of the notebook | Go to the front of the notebook |
| Click on the edge of the "back cover" of the notebook | Go to the back of the notebook |
| Ctrl+Click on an entry | Add the clicked-on entry to the selection |
| Shift+Click on an entry | Add all entries from the end of the previous selection to the clicked-on entry |
| Shift+Click on the time to the left of the notebook | Embed the time (e.g., 10:06 PM) in text that you are editing in a Create *Entry* dialog box |

| Action | Purpose |
|---|---|
| Shift+Click on the date to the left of the notebook | Embed the date (e.g., 2/2/97) in text that you are editing in a Create *Entry* dialog box |
| Ctrl+Shift+Click on the date to the left of the notebook | Embed the date and time in text that you are editing in a Create *Entry* dialog box |

## ▶▶ *Working in the Calendar Section*

To open the Calendar section, click on its tab or choose Section ➤ Turn To ➤ Calendar. Then go to a particular date:

- Go to a date in this year's annual calendar, displayed across both opening pages, by double-clicking on it. Notice that today's date is surrounded by a red border (if you have a color monitor).

- Go to a date in another year by clicking on a year tab (clicking on 80 displays all the years in the 1980s, clicking on 90 displays every year in the 1990s, and clicking on 00 displays calendars for the first 10 years in the 21st century and 10, which leads to the next ten years, and so on) on the edge of the page. Then double-click on the date in the annual calendar.

- Go to a date on the previous or next page by clicking on the page turner, the curled page at the bottom of the left or right sides of the Calendar.

 ▶▶ **T I P**

> **To open the Calendar and go to today's date, click on the Date icon on the left side of the Organizer window.**

### ▶ *Displaying a Calendar Format*

You can display an Organizer Calendar in four views:

 Click on the View Day per Page button (the default) to display two pages each having one day with half-hour time increments. This is especially useful if you keep a detailed diary.

Click on the View Work Week button to display the work week and two small Saturday and Sunday sections on two facing pages.

 Click on the View Week per Page button to display two weeks having seven identical-sized sections on two facing pages.

 Click on the View Month button to display five or six weeks, including all the days in the current month, on two facing pages.

  **TIP**

**The buttons are not displayed when you are viewing the annual calendars at the beginning of the section. To display the buttons, turn to any Calendar page.**

## ▶ Scheduling Your Activities

You schedule activities in two basic ways: one for today or another day that is displayed on the current Calendar page or pages, and one for days that are not currently displayed.

### Scheduling an Activity on the Current Calendar Page

The quickest and most straightforward way to schedule an activity for a day displayed on the current Calendar page is to follow these steps:

1. Open the Calendar or choose Section ➤ Turn To ➤ Calendar.

2. Double-click on the date on which the appointment will occur. Organizer displays the page on which the date appears. If you are displaying the Calendar pages in the Day per Page format, Organizer displays the times in half-hour increments; so you can skip to step 4.

3. Click on the Calendar page. Organizer displays the times for that day in increments that depend on the type of calendar display (that is, Work Week, Week per Page, or Month). You can move up

(or down) to earlier (or later) times by clicking on the small upward (or downward) pointing arrow at the top (or bottom) right of the page.

**4.** Double-click on the desired time. Organizer opens the Create Appointment dialog box (see Figure 22.10).

**FIGURE 22.10** ▶

*A filled-in Create Appointment dialog box*

**5.** Type appointment information in the Description text box.

**6.** To set the appointment time and length, either:

- Click on the downward-pointing arrow at the right side of the Time drop-down list box and drag the starting and ending times on the time tracker. For more information about the time tracker, see the section called "Setting the Time and Length of an Appointment."

- Type a value or click on the + or – buttons in the Duration text/option box.

**7.** To indicate that this appointment is tentatively scheduled at the specified date and time, check the Pencil In checkbox.

8. To make this appointment confidential, check the Confidential checkbox.

9. Click on OK. Organizer closes the dialog box and inserts the appointment on the appropriate calendar page.

## Scheduling an Activity on Any Date

To schedule an activity for any day, whether or not it's displayed on the current Calendar page, follow these steps:

1. Click on the Calendar tab or choose Section ➤ Turn To ➤ Calendar.

2. Click on the Click to Create an Appointment SmartIcon, click on the Click to Create an Entry button, choose Create ➤ Appointment, or press Insert. Organizer opens the Create Appointment dialog box.

3. Either type a date, or click on the downward-pointing arrow to the right side of the Date drop-down text/list box and select from the calendar that appears:

```
◀      May 1997      ▶
Su Mo Tu We Th Fr Sa
27 28 29 30  1  2  3
 4  5  6  7  8  9 10
11 12 13 14 15 16 17
18 19 20 21 22 23 24
25 26 27 28 29 30 31
```

4. Type appointment information in the Description text box.

5. To find the first available free time, repeatedly click on the Find Time button. (To enable Organizer to search for time on weekends, you must change your Calendar preferences; choose View ➤ Calendar Preferences, check Include Weekends in Find Time Search in the Calendar Preferences dialog box, and click on OK.)

6. Fill in or select other options in the dialog box (see steps 6, 7, and 8 in the preceding section).

7. Click on OK. Organizer closes the dialog box and inserts the appointment on the appropriate calendar page.

## ► *Editing an Appointment*

To edit an appointment, select it and choose Edit ➤ Edit Appointment, or press Ctrl+E. In the Edit Appointment dialog box, which looks just like the Create Appointment dialog box, select or change options using the previous steps as a guide.

You can bypass the Edit Appointment dialog box and go to the appropriate dialog box by selecting an appointment and choosing one of the following:

- To categorize an appointment, choose Appointment ➤ Categorize or press F5. Then fill in the Categorize dialog box.

- To set or change an alarm, choose Appointment ➤ Alarm or press F6. Then fill in the Alarm dialog box.

- To specify a repeating appointment, choose Appointment ➤ Repeat or press F7. Then fill in the Repeat dialog box.

- To associate a cost code with the appointment, choose Appointment ➤ Cost or press F8. Then fill in the Cost dialog box.

- To make an appointment confidential in a password-protected file, choose Appointment ➤ Confidential or press F4.

## ► *Deleting an Appointment*

To delete an appointment, drag it to the Wastebasket, select it and press Delete, or choose Edit ➤ Clear.

## ► *Setting the Time and Length of an Appointment*

You can use the time tracker (see Figure 22.11) to set the starting time, the duration, and, implicitly, the ending time for an appointment. Open the time tracker by double-clicking on an appointment or by clicking on the downward pointing arrow for the Time drop-down list box in the Create Appointment dialog box or the Edit Appointment dialog box.

**FIGURE 22.11** ▶

*The time tracker showing a lunchtime appointment*

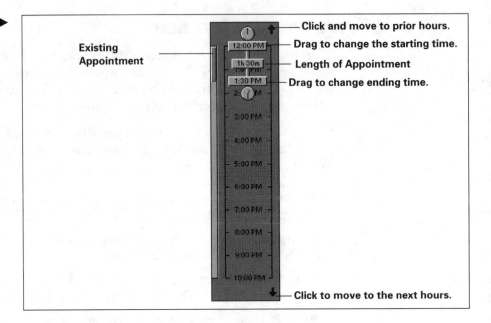

When you fill in an appointment window, the starting time tracker time matches the time displayed in the window. The default time tracker is set to one-hour appointments. You can adjust the length of an appointment in three ways:

- You can drag the top time to change the starting time and/or duration.

- You can drag the bottom time to change the ending time and/or duration.

- You can drag the time tracker by the duration time in order to change the beginning and ending appointment times but keep the same length. When you drag the time tracker, the times change in five-minute increments and remain within the current work day.

You can press keys or use the mouse as you drag the time tracker to force certain behavior:

- Hold down the Shift key as you drag the time tracker, and it moves in 30-minute increments.

- Move the mouse pointer to the upward-pointing arrow at the upper right corner of the time tracker, click, and hold down the left mouse button to scroll to times before 8:00 AM.

- Move the mouse pointer to the downward-pointing arrow at the lower right corner of the time tracker, click, and hold down the left mouse button to scroll to times after 6:00 PM.

When the Create Appointment dialog box is open and you have already scheduled appointments for the selected day, blue, green, and possibly red bars are on the left side of the time tracker. The blue bars represent time blocks for previously scheduled appointments, and the green bar represents the appointment that you are currently scheduling. If you see a red bar, you are scheduling a conflicting appointment.

▶▶ **N O T E**

> **To copy an appointment to another day that is currently displayed (remember that you can display five or six weeks at a time), press and hold down Ctrl, and drag and drop the appointment. You can drag the appointment to the Clipboard tool, display the date to which you want to move the appointment, and drag the appointment from the Clipboard to the Calendar page.**

## ▶ *Scheduling Conflicting Appointments*

Let's say that you use Organizer to schedule a long block of time to catch up on paperwork. You might also want to schedule a quick telephone call during that time. Organizer allows you to schedule a conflicting appointment but makes sure that you reply to a prompt and marks the appointments with a vertical red line on the Calendar page.

When you schedule a conflicting appointment, Organizer displays the Conflicting Appointment dialog box (see Figure 22.12). To confirm the appointment, click on OK. To change the time of the appointment, either click on the Find Time button to have Organizer find your next free time or select or type a new time, and then click on OK. If you are creating this appointment from another page of the Calendar and you can't currently see the date of the conflicting appointment, click on the Turn To button to display the date and its other entries.

**FIGURE 22.12** ▶

*The Conflicting Appointment dialog box*

## ▶ *Setting an Alarm for an Appointment*

You can set an alarm as a reminder that it's almost time for an event—in the Calendar, To Do, Calls, Planner, and Anniversary sections. To set an alarm for an appointment, follow these steps:

**1.** Click on the Calendar tab or choose Section ➤ Turn To ➤ Calendar.

**2.** Click on the Click to Create an Appointment SmartIcon, click on the Click to Create an Entry button, choose Create ➤ Appointment, or press Insert. Organizer opens the Create Appointment dialog box. (If you want to set an alarm for an existing appointment, select the appointment and click on the Assign an Alarm to the Current Entry SmartIcon, choose Edit ➤ Edit Appointment, or press Ctrl+E. Go to step 4.)

**3.** Define the appointment: Date, Time, Duration, and Description.

**4.** Click on the Alarm button. Organizer opens the Alarm dialog box (see Figure 22.13) with the date and time of the appointment displayed.

**5.** Specify the number of minutes (from 0 to 23 hours and 59 minutes) before an appointment that you want the alarm to sound. The default is 5.

**6.** To play an alarm tune, open the Tune drop-down list box and select the tune. If you want to display an alarm message box without an alarm sounding, select (None). To test the tune, click on the Play button.

**FIGURE 22.13** ▶

*In the Alarm dialog box, you can set the amount of time before an appointment that the alarm sounds.*

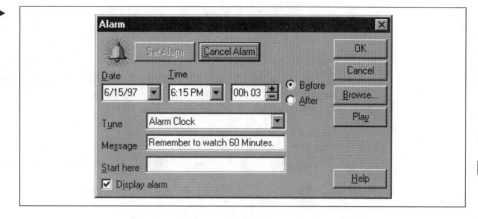

7. To display a message in the alarm box, type it in the Message text box.

8. Click on OK. Organizer closes the dialog box and returns to the Calendar.

Organizer must be running for an alarm to sound or an alarm message to display. When the alarm goes off, Organizer plays a tune if you have selected one—whether Organizer is maximized, restored, or minimized. Whether or not you have selected a tune, Organizer displays another Alarm dialog box (see Figure 22.14) when the alarm goes off.

You can turn off or delay an Organizer alarm. To turn off the alarm, click on OK. To have the alarm go off again at a specified time, set a time in the Snooze For list box (the default is five minutes), and click on the Snooze button.

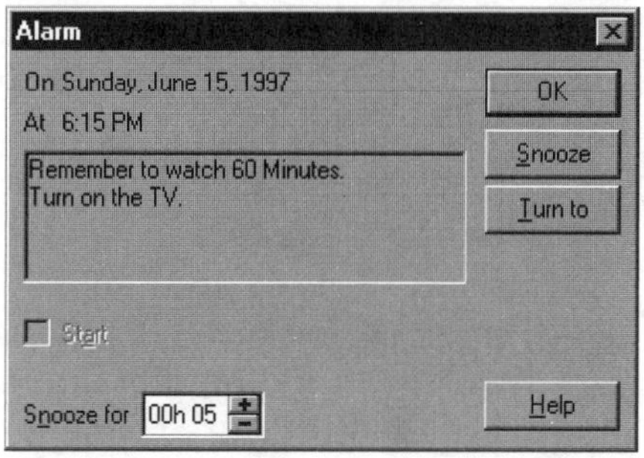

**FIGURE 22.14** ▶

*The Alarm dialog box that appears when the alarm goes off*

Organizer can display icons representing options for appointments: that you have made it confidential, set an alarm for it, made it a repeating appointment, penciled it in, or assigned a category to it. To select appointment icons for display, choose View ➤ Calendar Preferences, check the appropriate checkbox, and click on OK. Table 22.2 illustrates the appointment icons.

▶ **TABLE 22.2:** *Appointment Icons*

| Icon | Indicates |
| --- | --- |
| 🔒 | A confidential appointment |
| 🔔 | An appointment with an alarm |
| 🔁 | A repeating appointment |
| ✏️ | A penciled-in appointment |
| ▦ | A categorized appointment |

## ▶ *Running an Application from within the Calendar*

You can run an application from within Organizer (that is, the Calendar, To Do, Calls, Planner, and Anniversary sections) at a set time. To run an application from Calendar, follow these steps:

*1.* Click on the Calendar tab or choose Section ➤ Turn To ➤ Calendar.

*2.* Click on the Click to Create an Appointment SmartIcon, click on the Click to Create an Entry button, choose Create ➤ Appointment, or press Insert. Organizer opens the Create Appointment dialog box. (If you want to run an application from an existing appointment, select the appointment and either choose Edit ➤ Edit Appointment or press Ctrl+E. Go to step 4.)

**3.** Define the appointment: Date, Time, Duration, and Description.

**4.** Click on the Alarm button. Organizer opens the Alarm dialog box.

**5.** If needed, adjust the date and time on which you want to start the application.

**6.** In the Start Here text box, type the exact path and executable file-name of the application to be started and go to step 9.

**7.** If you aren't sure about the path and name of the executable file to be started, click on the Browse button. Organizer displays the Launch Application Browse dialog box (see Figure 22.15).

**FIGURE 22.15** ▶

*The Launch Application Browse dialog box with a folder and file selected*

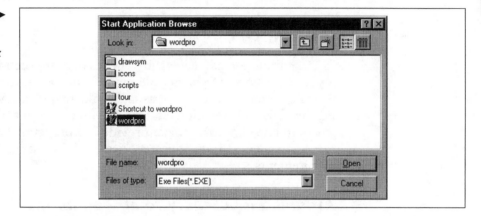

**8.** Select the name of the file that you want to execute. You may have to search through folders and subfolders until you find it.

**9.** Click on Open. Organizer returns to the Alarm dialog box and fills in the Launch text box.

**10.** Click on OK. Organizer closes the dialog box and returns to the Calendar.

Figure 22.16 shows the Alarm dialog box with the Start Here text box filled in.

**FIGURE 22.16** ▶

*The Alarm dialog box
containing the path
and name of the appli-
cation to be launched*

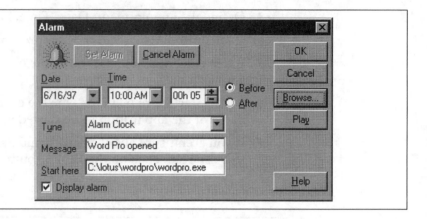

# ▶ *Using Categories*

In Organizer, you can categorize entries in every section. For example, if you use a single Organizer file for all your needs, you can separate your life into categories such as Calls, Clients, Ideas, Meetings, Personal, Travel, Vacation, and so on; you can even assign several categories to one entry. Organizer provides 13 predefined categories; you can add, rename, or delete categories until the list matches your own requirements.

## *Assigning a Category to an Appointment*

To assign a category to an appointment, follow these steps:

*1.* Click on the Calendar tab or choose Section ▶ Turn To ▶ Calendar.

*2.* Click on the Click to Create an Appointment SmartIcon, click on the Click to Create an Entry button, choose Create ▶ Appointment, or press Insert. Organizer opens the Create Appointment dialog box. (If you want to run an application from an existing appointment, select the appointment and either choose Edit ▶ Edit Appointment or press Ctrl+E. Go to step 4.)

*3.* Define the appointment: Date, Time, Duration, and Description, and so on.

*4.* Open the Categories drop-down list box.

**5.** Click on a selection. Continue clicking until you have assigned all the desired categories. Organizer highlights selected categories.

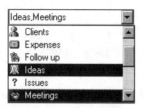

**6.** To remove a category, click on it again. Organizer removes the highlight.

**7.** When you have completed the dialog box, click on OK. Organizer closes the dialog box, returns to the Calendar page, and displays the category names under the bottom line of the appointment.

## Adding a Category

To add a category to the predefined list, follow these steps:

**1.** Click on the Click to Create and Edit Categories SmartIcon or choose Create ➤ Categories. Organizer opens the Categories dialog box (see Figure 22.17).

**FIGURE 22.17** ▶

*The Categories dialog box with a symbol about to be selected*

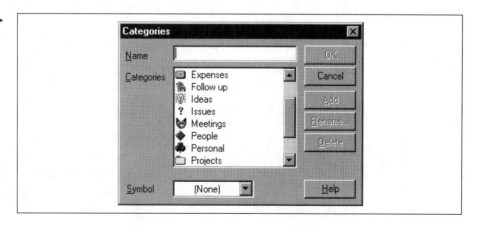

**2.** Type a category name in the Name text box.

**3.** Select a symbol from the Symbol drop-down list box.

4. If you want to add more categories, click on Add. Organizer adds the entry to the category list.

5. Repeat steps 2, 3, and 4 until you have finished.

6. Click on OK. Organizer closes the dialog box and adds the entry to the category list.

## Renaming a Category

To rename a category, follow these steps:

1. Click on the Click to Create and Edit Categories SmartIcon or choose Create ➤ Categories. Organizer opens the Categories dialog box.

2. Click on a category in the Categories scroll list.

3. Click on Rename. Organizer displays the Rename Category dialog box.

4. In the New Name text box, type the new category name, and click on OK.

5. Optionally, select a new or the same symbol.

6. Click on OK again. Organizer closes the dialog box.

 ▶▶N O T E

You can use these same steps to change the symbol for a category.

### Deleting a Category

To delete a category, follow these steps:

1. Click on the Click to Create and Edit Categories SmartIcon or choose Create ➤ Categories. Organizer opens the Categories dialog box.

2. Click on a category in the Categories scroll list.

3. Click on Delete. Organizer asks you to confirm the deletion.

4. Click on Yes. Organizer returns to the Categories dialog box.

5. Click on OK. Organizer closes the dialog box.

## ▶ Specifying a Cost Code for an Appointment

You can specify a customer code and a cost code for an appointment (and for entries in the To Do, Calls, Planner, and Anniversary sections). When you specify these codes, you can track the expenses associated with a particular customer and related activities. You can then export the information in ASCII Text (*.TXT) or ANSI Text (*.TXT) format to another SmartSuite or Windows application, such as a 1-2-3 spreadsheet or a Word Pro document.

To specify a cost code for a Calendar entry, follow these steps:

1. Click on the Calendar tab or choose Section ➤ Turn To ➤ Calendar.

2. Click on the Click to Create an Appointment SmartIcon, click on the Click to Create an Entry button, choose Create ➤ Appointment, or press Insert. Organizer opens the Create Appointment dialog box. (If you want to specify a cost code for an existing appointment, select the appointment and either click on the Attach a Cost Code SmartIcon, choose Edit ➤ Edit Appointment, or press Ctrl+E. Go to step 4.)

3. Define the appointment: Date, Time, Duration, and Description.

4. Click on the Cost button. Organizer displays the Cost dialog box (see Figure 22.18).

**FIGURE 22.18** ►

*In the Cost dialog box, you can specify a customer code and a cost code.*

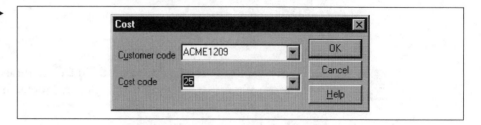

5. Fill in the Customer Code text/drop-down list box with the customer name or code and fill in the Cost Code text/drop-down list box with the price per hour or code. (If you have already defined a code, you can select it from the list.)

6. Click on OK. Organizer closes the dialog box.

7. Click on OK again. Organizer closes the Create Appointment dialog box.

►►**TIP**

**If cost codes don't appear with an entry, you can choose View ➤ Calendar Preferences, check the Cost Code checkbox, and click on OK.**

## ► Securing Organizer Files and Appointments

You can use a password to restrict the viewing and editing of an appointment. Before making an appointment confidential, protect your Organizer file with a password.

### Setting a Password for an Organizer File

You can assign a password to an Organizer file to protect it from others.

When someone attempts to open a secured file, he or she is denied access until the defined password is typed. Organizer passwords are case-sensitive; so if you type all uppercase letters for a password defined using lowercase letters, Organizer does not allow access to the file.

You can assign passwords to grant three levels of access: Owner, Assistant, and Reader.

- An *Owner* has complete editing rights to your file, can view confidential entries, and can assign passwords.

- An *Assistant* can view and edit all but entries that the Owner has marked as confidential.

- A *Reader* can view all but confidential entries.

To define a password, follow these steps:

**1.** Click on the Click to Protect a File with Access Rights and a Password SmartIcon, choose File ➤ User Setup ➤ Passwords, or press Ctrl+U. Organizer displays the Passwords dialog box (see Figure 22.19).

**FIGURE 22.19** ▶

*The Passwords dialog box with passwords in three text boxes*

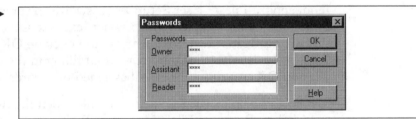

**2.** Type a password in the Owner text box. Organizer automatically inserts the same password in the Assistant and Reader text boxes.

**3.** Optionally, type a different password in the Assistant text box. Organizer automatically inserts the same password in the Reader text box.

**4.** Optionally, type a different password in the Reader text box.

**5.** Click on OK. Organizer opens the Verify Passwords dialog box (see Figure 22.20).

**FIGURE 22.20** ▶

*The Verify Passwords dialog box as it looks with only an Owner password to verify*

▶▶ **W A R N I N G**

**It is extremely important for you to write down the password and put it in a secure place. If you forget your password, you no longer have access to the protected file.**

**6.** Retype one, two, or three passwords in one, two, or three text boxes.

**7.** Click on OK.

To delete the passwords for a secured file, open the file, and click on the Click to Protect a File with Access Rights and a Password Smart-Icon, choose File ➤ User Setup ➤ Passwords, or press Ctrl+U. In the Passwords dialog box, leave the Owner text box and optionally the Assistant and Reader text boxes empty, and click on OK. In the Verify Password box, also click on OK without filling in the text boxes. Then click on OK two more times. All assigned passwords are removed.

To change the passwords in a secured file, open the file, and click on the Click to Protect a File with Access Rights and a Password Smart-Icon, choose User Setup ➤ Passwords, or press Ctrl+U. In the Password dialog box, type one or more new passwords, and click on OK. Type the same passwords in the Verify Password box, and click on OK.

## ▶ Creating Repeating Appointments

When you have a regular appointment or meeting, you can create a repeating appointment. For example, you can schedule a meeting on every Monday or on the 1st and 15th forever or for a limited period. You also can create repeating entries in the Calls, To Do, Anniversary, and Planner sections.

The Repeat dialog box (see Figure 22.21) controls repeating appointments. As you select options for a repeating appointment, keep looking at the contents of the Your Select box; you'll be able to tell if you're on the right track.

**FIGURE 22.21** ▶

*The Repeat dialog box, which controls repeating appointments*

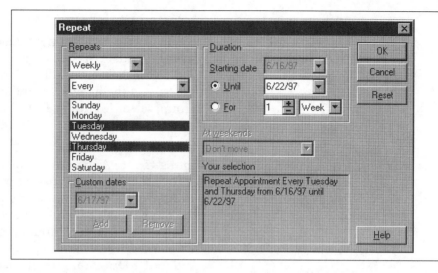

These are examples of several repeating appointments and the Repeat dialog box options used to schedule them:

| **Appointment** | **Selected Options** |
|---|---|
| Every Monday at 9:00 AM for the next year | In the Create Appointment dialog box, specify the date of the first appointment, and select the time and the duration. In the Repeat dialog box, from the Repeats group, select Weekly, Every, and Monday; and in the Duration group, select 1 and Year. |

 ▶ ▶ N O T E

> To select multiple days (for example, Tuesday and Thursday), click on the first day, press and hold down the Ctrl key, and click on the next day. While you hold down the Ctrl key, you can continue to select days. Release the Ctrl key when you have completed your selection. To select a range of days (for example, Monday to Friday), click on the first day, press and hold down the Shift key, and click on the last day in the range. Then release the Shift key.

| Appointment | Selected Options |
|---|---|
| The 1st and 15th of every month for the next year | In the Create Appointment dialog box, specify the date of the first appointment, and select the time and the duration. In the Repeat dialog box, from the Repeats group, select Monthly (Dates) and 1st, hold down Ctrl, and select 15th; and in the Duration group, select 1 and Year. |
| Every Monday, Wednesday, and Friday for three months | In the Create Appointment dialog box, specify the date of the first appointment, and select the time and the duration. In the Repeat dialog box, from the Repeats group, select Weekly, Monday, hold down Ctrl, and select Wednesday and Friday; and in the Duration group, select 3 and Months. |
| Every other Thursday until June 26, 1997 | In the Create Appointment dialog box, specify the date of the first appointment, and select the time and the duration. In the Repeat dialog box, from the Repeats group, select Weekly, Every Other, and Thursday; and in the Duration group, click on Until and type 6/26/97. |
| December 4 and 5; January 11 and 30 | In the Create Appointment dialog box, specify December 4, and select the time and the duration. In the Repeat dialog box, from the Repeats group, select Custom, click on the downward-pointing arrow in the Custom Dates group, click on December 5, click on Add, click on the downward-pointing arrow in the Custom Dates group, click on the right-pointing arrow on the calendar, click on January 11, click on Add, click on the downward-pointing arrow in the Custom Dates group, click on 30, and click on Add. |

To create a repeating appointment, follow these steps:

1. Click on the Calendar tab or choose Section ➤ Turn To ➤ Calendar.

2. Click on the Click to Create an Appointment SmartIcon, click on the Click to Create an Entry button, choose Create ➤ Appointment, or press Insert. Organizer opens the Create Appointment dialog box. (If you want to specify a repeating appointment for an existing appointment, select the appointment and either click on the Attach a Cost Code SmartIcon, choose Edit ➤ Edit Appointment, or press Ctrl+E. Go to step 4.)

3. Define the appointment: Date, Time, Duration, and Description.

4. Click on the Repeat button. Organizer displays the Repeat dialog box.

5. Fill in or select options in the Repeat dialog box using the previous examples as your guide.

6. When you have finished selecting options, click on OK. Organizer returns to the Create Appointment dialog box.

7. Click on OK again. Organizer returns to the Calendar page.

## ▶ *Moving an Appointment to Another Day*

To move an appointment to a day that you can see on the open Calendar pages, drag it to its new day.

To move an appointment to a day that you cannot see, follow these steps:

1. Click on the Click to Move an Entry tool at the top right of the toolbox.

2. Click on the appointment to be moved. Organizer changes the mouse pointer to an entry icon.

3. Go to the page that holds the day to which you want to move the appointment.

4. Click on the new day. Organizer drops the appointment onto the new day and deactivates the tool.

▶▶ **N O T E**

**To copy an appointment to a new location, press Ctrl when you drop the appointment. Organizer keeps the original appointment in its starting date and a copy in the new date.**

If you are networked with other computers, you can go beyond tracking your own meetings and appointments; you can schedule meetings, invite attendees, and reserve resources. For further information, see the Organizer *User Manual,* and the Organizer help facility.

# 23

# Managing Data
# with Organizer

▶▶ **I**n the previous chapter, you found out how to manage your time using Organizer, and you learned many Calendar basics. In this chapter, you'll find out how to manage data. In the To Do, Address, Notepad, Planner, Anniversary, and Call sections, you can track your ideas, plan for the days ahead, and store important names, addresses, birthdays, and anniversaries. You can also store telephone numbers and track completed, attempted, and incoming telephone calls.

As you read and work through these pages, be aware that the features covered in the previous chapter work in most of the Organizer sections described here. For example, you can set alarms, launch applications, categorize, and create repeating entries in all but the Address section. For detailed information about using these features, please refer to the *Scheduling with Organizer* chapter.

# ▶▶ *Working in the To Do Section*

You can use an Organizer To Do list to put all your tasks in one place and list them according to priority, status, starting date, and category. The following sections will help you create and maintain your own To Do list.

## ▶ *Displaying a To Do Format*

To go to the To Do section, click on the To Do tab or choose Section ➤ Turn To ➤ To Do. You can display a To Do list in one of four views:

 Click on the View by Priority button (the default) or choose View ➤ 1 By Priority to display tasks by priority (1, 2, 3, and None).

Click on the View by Status button or choose View ➤ 2 By Status to display tasks by status (Overdue, Current, Future, and Completed).

 Click on the View by Start Date button or choose View ➤ 3 By Start Date to display tasks by starting date (one tab per month).

 Click on the View by Category button or choose View ➤ 4 By Category to display tasks by category (all the currently defined categories and un-categorized tasks arranged under alphabetic tabs).

## ▶ *Adding a Task to the To Do List*

To add a task to your To Do list, follow these steps:

**1.** Click on the To Do tab or choose Section ➤ Turn To ➤ To Do.

**2.** Click on the Click to Create an Entry button or the Click to Create a Task SmartIcon, click on a page, press Insert, or choose Create ➤ Task Organizer opens the Create Task dialog box (see Figure 23.1).

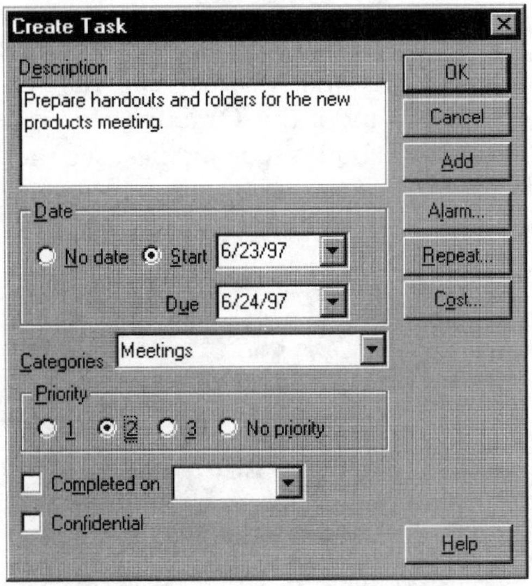

**FIGURE 23.1** ▶

*The filled-in Create Task dialog box*

Create Task dialog box showing:

- **Description**: Prepare handouts and folders for the new products meeting.
- **Date**: ○ No date ● Start 6/23/97 Due 6/24/97
- **Categories**: Meetings
- **Priority**: ○ 1 ● 2 ○ 3 ○ No priority
- ☐ Completed on
- ☐ Confidential
- Buttons: OK, Cancel, Add, Alarm..., Repeat..., Cost..., Help

3. Type a description of the task in the Description text box. The text box holds thousands of characters, but it's best to type just a few lines at the most.

4. Type or select a starting date (today's date is the default):

| 6/23/97 ▼ |
| ◄ June 1997 ► |
| Su Mo Tu We Th Fr Sa |
| 1 2 3 4 5 6 7 |
| 8 9 10 11 12 13 14 |
| 15 16 17 18 **19** 20 21 |
| 22 23 24 25 26 27 28 |
| 29 30 1 2 3 4 5 |

5. Type or select an ending date (today is the default) from the drop-down calendar.

6. To categorize this task, select from the Categories drop-down list box.

7. Set a Priority. The default is No Priority, the top priority is 1, and the lowest is 3.

8. Check the Confidential checkbox if you want this task to be confidential (that is, read-only or not viewable by certain individuals) and if this Organizer file is password-protected. For information about securing files, see the *Scheduling with Organizer* chapter.

9. Click on OK. Organizer adds the task to the To Do list.

►► **N O T E**

**You can set alarms for tasks, associate cost codes with entries, and define repeating entries in the To do section. See the *Scheduling with Organizer* chapter for more information.**

Organizer To Do list tasks are color-coded:

- **Red text** indicates a task entry that is overdue (beyond its due date and not checked as complete).

- **Green text** indicates a current task, which falls on today's date.

- **Blue text** indicates a task that you will start and complete at a future date.

- **Black text** with a green check in the box preceding the entry is a task that you have checked as complete.

Figure 23.2 shows tasks in various stages of completion and with different priorities.

**FIGURE 23.2** ▶

*Tasks in various stages of completion*

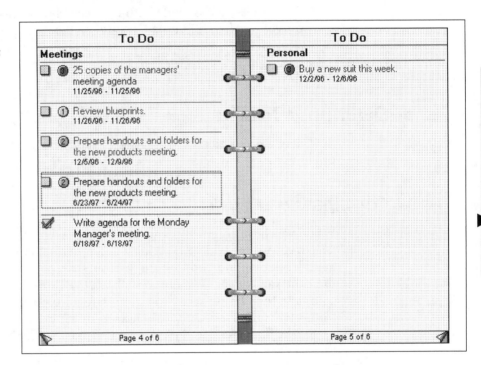

Managing Data with Organizer

Ch.
**23**

## ▶ *Editing a Task*

To edit a task, double-click on it (to edit its text on the page), select it and choose Edit ➤ Edit Task, or press Ctrl+E. In the Edit Task dialog box, which looks just like the Create Task dialog box, select or change options using the previous steps as a guide.

You can bypass the Edit Task dialog box and go to the appropriate dialog box by selecting a task and choosing one of the following:

- To categorize a task, choose Task ➤ Categorize or press F5. Then fill in the Categorize dialog box.

- To set or change an alarm, choose Task ➤ Alarm or press F6. Then fill in the Alarm dialog box.

- To specify a repeating task, choose Task ➤ Repeat or press F7. Then fill in the Repeat dialog box.

- To associate a cost code with the task, choose Task ➤ Cost or press F8. Then fill in the Cost dialog box.

- To make a task confidential in a password-protected file, choose Task ➤ Confidential or press F4.

## ▶ Deleting a Task

To delete a task, drag it to the Wastebasket, select it and press Delete, or choose Edit ➤ Clear.

## ▶ Completing a Task

When you have completed a task, you can delete it if you don't need to keep a record, or you can mark it as complete. To mark a task as completed, select it and choose Edit ➤ Edit Task, or press Ctrl+E. When the Edit Task dialog box appears, check the Completed On checkbox to complete the task on today's system date, or type or select the date from the Completed On text box/drop-down calendar. Organizer closes the dialog box and places a checkmark in the box preceding the entry.

## ▶ Displaying To Do Tasks in the Calendar

To display To Do tasks for a particular Calendar date or range of dates or in the Planner section, follow these steps:

*1.* Click on the Click to Show an Entry in Multiple Sections Smart-Icon or choose Section ➤ Show Through. Organizer opens the Show Through dialog box (see Figure 23.3).

**FIGURE 23.3** ▶

*The Show Through dialog box, in which you can select section entries to be displayed in the Calendar or Planner*

2. Open the Show Into drop-down list box and select either Calendar or Planner.

3. In the From list, click on To Do, the section to be displayed.

4. Click on OK. Organizer closes the dialog box and displays tasks on appropriate dates in the Calendar or Planner.

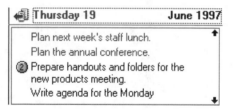

 ▶▶ **N O T E**

**To end the display of tasks in the Calendar or Planner, open the Show Through dialog box, and click on the section in the From list to remove the highlight. Click on OK to close the dialog box.**

# ▸▸ *Working in the Address Section*

In the Address section, you can produce a list of names and addresses, search for View or addresses on a list, dial a telephone number (if you have a modem), and import and export information to other Windows applications. Figure 23.4 shows the dialog box that you fill in when adding new business and home name and address information to the Address section.

**FIGURE 23.4** ▸

*The Create Address dialog box, which you fill in with new Address information for both business and home*

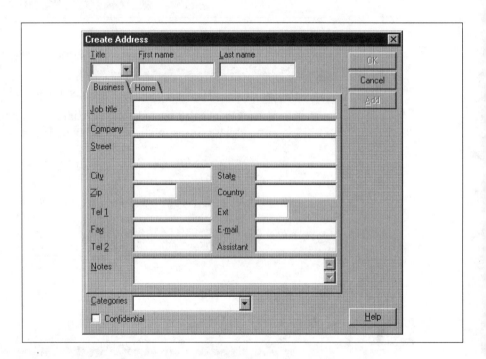

## ▸ *Displaying an Address Format*

You can display an Address book in four views:

 Click on the View All button or choose View ➤ 1 All to display one complete set of business or home data on a page.

 Click on the View Address button (the default) or choose View ➤ 2 Address to display two sets of business or home name, company, address, and telephone data on a page.

Click on the View Contact button or choose View ➤ 3 Contact to display three sets of business or home name, company, telephone, and e-mail data on a page.

 Click on the View Phone button or choose View ➤ 4 Phone to display 18 sets of business or home names and primary telephone data on a page.

## ▶ Entering Names, Addresses, and Other Information

Enter names and addresses into the fields by tabbing from field to field or by clicking on a field and either typing or selecting information from a drop-down list box. (You also can add information to a drop-down list.)

The Create Address dialog box contains two sections: Business and Home, marked by tabs. The information in three fields at the top of the dialog box and the categories by which you identify an individual appear in both sections of the dialog box. Other fields—for address, telephone, fax, and e-mail—appear on both Business and Home sections of the dialog box, although in a different layout.

These are the fields in the business and home sections of the Create Address dialog box:

**Title**    Mr., Ms., Miss, Mrs., Dr., and Prof. If a title isn't on this drop-down list/text box, you can type it. (Once you add this information, it appears in both sections of the dialog box.)

**First Name, Last Name**    The individual's name. (This information also appears under both business and home tabs.)

**Job Title**    The individual's position in the company.

**Company**    The company with which the individual is associated.

**Street**    Several lines for a street address, post office box, apartment, and so on. (You can enter separate addresses for business and home.)

**City**    The city in which the individual's business (Business tab) and/or home (Home tab) are located.

**State**    The state in which the individual's business (Business tab) and/or home (Home tab) are located. Either spell the entire name or use the two-letter postal abbreviation.

Managing Data with Organizer

Ch. **23**

▶▶ **N O T E**

**After you type a company name and press Enter, Organizer searches through the address book for a record with the same text in the Company field. If a duplicate is found, the Similar Address Found dialog box appears. Check its contents, click on OK, and Organizer adds address and telephone information to the new record.**

**Zip**    The business (Business tab) and/or home (Home tab) zip code.

**Country**    The country in which the business is located.

**Tel 1**    The primary telephone number (for example, 1-555-555-5555 or 555-5555) for this individual. For more information about connecting a modem and automatically dialing the telephone, see "Working in the Calls Section," later in this chapter.

**Ext**    Telephone extension. You can enter one number for business and one for home.

**Fax**    The fax number. You can enter one number for business and one for home.

**E-mail**    An e-mail address for this individual. You can enter one address for business and one for home.

**Tel 2**    Another telephone number for the individual or company. You can enter one number for business and one for home.

**Assistant**    The name of the individual's assistant or a person whom you can call instead of the individual.

**Categories**    The category or categories that best fit this individual. (This information also appears under both Business and Home tabs.)

**Notes**    Any user-defined information about this individual (for example, likes, dislikes, hobbies, the last order, names of family members, and so on. You can enter one note for business and another for home. Notes can help you personalize telephone calls to business contacts.

**Confidential**     Check this checkbox to hide this record from those who don't have the appropriate password. For information about securing files, see the *Scheduling with Organizer* chapter.

**Spouse**     The name of the individual's spouse.

**Children**     The name of the individual's children.

To insert a record, follow these steps:

1. Click on the Address tab or choose Section ➤ Turn To ➤ Address.

2. Click on the Click to Create an Entry button, the Click to Create an Address Record SmartIcon, press Insert, choose Create ➤ Address, or double-click on the blank part of a page.

3. Complete the dialog box, and click on OK. Organizer adds the information to the Address book and displays the page (see Figure 23.5) on which the information is stored.

**FIGURE 23.5** ▶

*Two facing pages of filled-in name and address information*

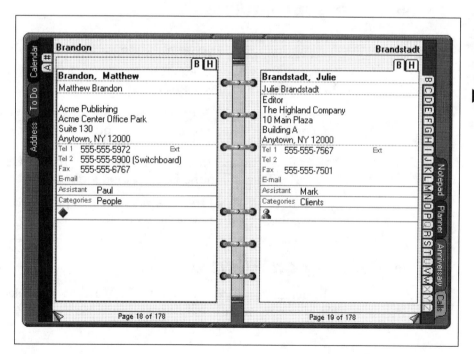

▶▶**TIP**

**You can choose whether to display business information, home information, or a combination. Choose View ➤ Address Preferences to open the Address Preferences dialog box. From the Foreground Tab drop-down list box, click on Business, to display business information (the default), Home, to display home information, or Select, to determine whether to display business or home information for a particular record. Click on OK to close the dialog box. Another way to switch between Business and Home is to choose Address ➤ Business (or press Ctrl+B) or Address ➤ Home (or press Ctrl+H).**

## ▶ Editing an Address

To edit an address, double-click on it, select it and choose Edit ➤ Edit Address, or press Ctrl+E. In the Edit Address dialog box, which looks just like the Create Address dialog box, select or change options using the previous steps as a guide.

You can bypass the Edit Address dialog box and go to the appropriate dialog box by selecting an address and choosing one of the following:

- To categorize an address, choose Address ➤ Categorize or press F5. Then fill in the Categorize dialog box.

- To make an address confidential in a password-protected file, choose Address ➤ Confidential or press F4.

## ▶ Deleting an Address

To delete an address, drag it to the Wastebasket, select it and press Delete, or choose Edit ➤ Clear.

## ▶ *Copying an Entry to a New Entry*

You can copy the current address entry to a new entry so that you can save steps in adding a new but related record, such as another individual working in the same department. You can have Organizer copy specific fields: the Full Address, Short Address, All, Name, Phone, Fax, Fax Header, Notes, Home, or Business. To copy the active address entry to a new entry, follow these steps:

1. Choose Edit ➤ Copy Special. Organizer opens the Copy Special dialog box, as shown in Figure 23.6.

2. From the Fields drop-down list box, select the fields to be added. The Fields text box shows the fields to be added using the current selection. After making a selection, view the field or fields to be copied in the sample box.

3. Click on OK. Organizer copies the information to the Clipboard. Notice that the Clipboard tool contains a small Address icon, indicating that it contains address information.

4. Either drag the icon from the Clipboard tool or choose Edit ➤ Paste. Organizer copies the information from the selected fields to a new record, where you can edit it to make it unique.

**Managing Data with Organizer**

▶ ▶

*Ch.*
**23**

**FIGURE 23.6** ▶

*The Copy Special dialog box with a record displayed*

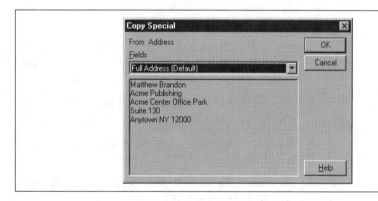

## ▶ Finding Information in Organizer

You can easily find information in Organizer—not only in the current section but also throughout Organizer. To search for information in Organizer, follow these steps:

**1.** Click on the Click to Find Text SmartIcon, choose Edit ➤ Find, or press Ctrl+F. Organizer displays the Find dialog box (see Figure 23.7).

**FIGURE 23.7** ▶

*The Find dialog box with the results of a search for Michael*

**2.** In the Find text box, type a *search string*, the text for which you are searching. You can type a partial word or use the wildcard ★ to search for a combination of characters.

**3.** To search for an exact match of upper- and lowercase characters, check the Case Sensitive checkbox.

**4.** To search for an entire word, not a partial word, check the Whole Word checkbox.

**5.** To search through one section, open the Section drop-down list box and click on a selection. To search through every section, click on the All Sections option button.

**6.** To clear the list after this search, click on Clear List (the default); to add the results of the next search to this one, click on Append to List.

7. To find the next occurrence of the search string, click on Find Next.

8. To find all occurrences of the search string, click on Find All.

9. To turn to the selected entry on the Occurrences scroll list, click on Turn To.

10. To close the dialog box, click on Close.

## ▶ *Filtering Information*

Another way to search within an Organizer file is by filtering your information. An Organizer *filter* uses criteria that you specify to gather a subset of information for one or more sections. For example, you can find all the addresses in a particular city or state in order to call only those individuals. Or you can find all Calendar entries for a certain cost code.

After creating a filter, you can save it or add it to a menu so that you can use it again at any time.

To create a filter, follow these steps:

1. Click on the Click to Create and Edit Filters SmartIcon or choose Create ▶ Filters. Organizer opens the Filters dialog box, as shown in Figure 23.8.

2. Click on New. Organizer displays the New Filter dialog box (see Figure 23.9).

3. Type the filter name in the Name text box.

4. From the Section drop-down list box, click in an empty box, and select the section for which you are creating the filter.

5. Click in the next box in the row under the Field column, open the Field drop-down list box, and select the field in which the filtering takes place.

6. Click in the next box in the row under the Test drop-down list box, open the Test drop-down list box, and select a condition with which Organizer tests the field.

Managing Data
with Organizer

Ch.
**23**

**FIGURE 23.8** ▶

*The Filters dialog box with one filter already created*

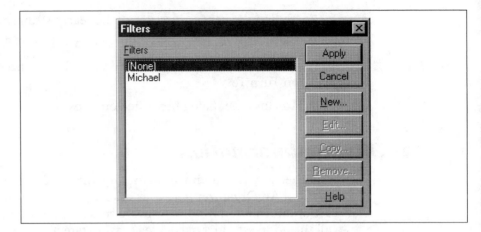

**FIGURE 23.9** ▶

*The New Filter dialog box with fields defined for a new filter*

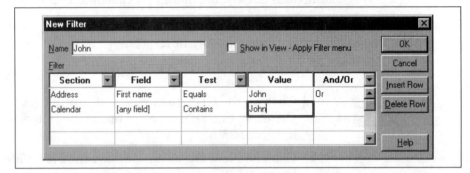

**7.** Click in the next box in the row under the Value text box and type the value for which the filter is searching. (If you want Organizer to display a prompt box in which you type a value, precede the typed value with a question mark.)

**8.** Click in the next box in the row under the And/Or drop-down list box, and select AND or OR if you want to add another row of conditions. Once you have clicked in the first cell in a new row, you don't need to click in succeeding boxes to make sure that values are entered in that row; Organizer is programmed to insert values appropriately.

**9.** To add other conditions to this filter, repeat steps 4 through 8.

**10.** To add a menu item to the View Apply Filter menu, check the Show in View - Apply Filter Menu checkbox.

**11.** When you have completed building the filter, click on OK. If your filter is valid, Organizer closes the dialog box and saves the filter. Otherwise, Organizer displays a message. After editing the filter, click on OK. Repeat this step until the filter is valid.

**12.** Click on Apply. Organizer runs the filter against the section or sections for which you created it. At the conclusion of a search, the affected sections contain only records and entries that match the filter. For example, all the Calendar pages except for those that match are blank, and in Notepad, all pages except for those that match are missing.

 To clear a filter, click on the Click to Create and Edit Filters SmartIcon or choose Create ➤ Filters. In the Filters dialog box, select (None) and click on Apply.

 To edit a filter, click on the Click to Create and Edit Filters SmartIcon or choose Create ➤ Filters. In the Filters dialog box, select the filter you want to edit and click on Edit. In the Edit Filter dialog box (see Figure 23.10), change the options and values, and click on OK.

 You can copy a filter and then edit it under its new name. Thus, you don't have to create a slightly different filter from scratch. To copy a filter, click on the Click to Create and Edit Filters SmartIcon or choose Create ➤ Filters. In the Filters dialog box, select the filter you want to copy and click on Copy. In the Copy Filter dialog box, overtype the name, edit the filter, and then click on OK.

 To delete a filter, click on the Click to Create and Edit Filters SmartIcon or choose Create ➤ Filters. In the Filters dialog box, select the filter and click on Remove. To confirm the deletion, click on Yes. Click on Close.

# ▶▶ *Working in the Notepad Section*

In the Organizer Notepad, you can keep detailed notes about ideas, projects, and so on. In fact, it's possible to have an Organizer notebook with only Notepad sections.

**Managing Data with Organizer**

▶▶

*Ch.*
**23**

**FIGURE 23.10** ▶

*The New Filter dialog box with a four-line filter*

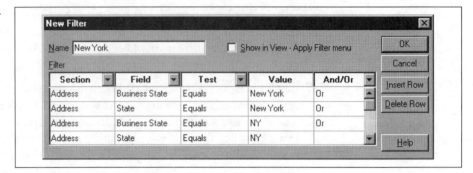

## ▶ Displaying a Notepad Format

You can arrange the pages in the Notepad section in four ways:

 Click on the View by Page Number button or choose View ➤ 1 By Page Number (the default) to arrange the pages by the current order in which you have placed the pages.

 Click on the View by Title button or choose View ➤ 2 By Title to arrange the pages alphabetically by page title.

 Click on the View by Date button or choose View ➤ 3 By Date to arrange the pages by creation date—from the oldest page to the newest.

 Click on the View by Category button or choose View ➤ 4 By Category to arrange pages by category.

## ▶ Adding an Entry to the Notepad

To add an entry to the Notepad section, follow these steps:

1. Click on the Notepad tab or choose Section ➤ Turn To ➤ Notepad.

 2. Click on the Click to Create an Entry button, double-click on the first, second, or last page of the section, press Insert, or choose Create ➤ Page. Organizer opens the Create Page dialog box (see Figure 23.11).

**FIGURE 23.11** ▶

*In the Create Page dialog box, you control all aspects of a new Notepad page.*

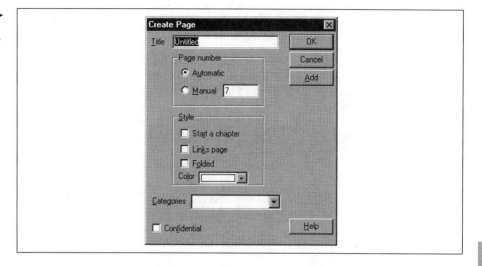

3. Type a title in the Title text box.

4. To automatically number the pages in the Notepad, click on Automatic. To manually number this page, click on Manual and type a value in the text box.

5. Choose page styles:

   **Start a Chapter**   Creates a new chapter for this Notepad page.

   **Links Page**   Links this page to another page or entry in the file.

   **Folded**   Creates a wide, foldable page, which includes a button with which you can unfold or fold the page.

   **Color**   Click on the downward-pointing arrow to open a palette from which you can choose a background color for the page.

6. To categorize this page, select from the Categories drop-down list box.

7. Check the Confidential checkbox to make this page confidential if this Organizer file is password-protected.

▶ ▶

*Ch.*
**23**

**8.** To add the page but keep the dialog box so that you can add another page, click on Add.

**9.** To add the page and close the dialog box, click on OK. Organizer adds the page or pages to the Notepad section and inserts an entry in the table of contents.

## ▶ Using the Notepad Section SmartIcons

When you open the Notepad section of an Organizer file, two short SmartIcons bars replace the default bar. You can use some of the SmartIcons to edit selected text; the rightmost SmartIcons enable you to insert an object and manage object links. Table 23.1 illustrates and describes each SmartIcon.

▶ **TABLE 23.1:** *Organizer Notepad SmartIcons*

| SmartIcon | Dialog Box options | Shortcut Key | Description |
|---|---|---|---|
| **B** | Click on the Font SmartIcon to open the Font dialog box; click on Bold to apply boldface; click on Regular to remove formatting. | Ctrl+B | Applies or removes boldface from selected text |
| *I* | Click on the Font SmartIcon to open the Font dialog box; click on Italic to apply italics; click on Regular to remove formatting. | Ctrl+I | Applies or removes italics from selected text |
| U | Click on the Font SmartIcon to open the Font dialog box; check the Underline checkbox to underline selected text; clear the Underline checkbox to remove the underline. | Ctrl+U | Underlines or removes the underline from selected text |
| | N/A | N/A | Opens the Font dialog box |
| | Choose Page ➤ Align to open the Align dialog box. | Ctrl+L | Aligns the selected paragraph with the left margin |

▶ **TABLE 23.1:** *Organizer Notepad SmartIcons (continued)*

| SmartIcon | Dialog Box options | Shortcut Key | Description |
|---|---|---|---|
| | Choose Page ➤ Align to open the Align dialog box. | N/A | Centers the selected paragraph between the left and right margins |
| | Choose Page ➤ Align to open the Align dialog box. | Ctrl+R | Aligns the selected paragraph with the right margin |
| | Create ➤ Object | N/A | Inserts an object in the current page |
| | Edit ➤ OLE Links | N/A | Updates and manages the links to the selected object |

## ▶ *Editing a Page*

To edit a page, go to the page and double-click on it, select it and choose Edit ➤ Edit Page, or press Ctrl+E. When the Edit Page dialog box opens, edit the text or select options, and click on OK. To add, change, enhance, or delete the text on the page, click on the page and work as you would in a word processor. To leave edit mode, press F2.

You can bypass the Edit Page dialog box and go to the appropriate dialog box by selecting a page and choosing one of the following:

- To categorize a page, choose Page ➤ Categorize or press F5. Then fill in the Categorize dialog box.

- To assign page attributes, choose Page ➤ Page. Then fill in the Page dialog box.

- To change alignment of text on the page, choose Page ➤ Align. Then fill in the Align dialog box.

- To import a graphic or a text file, choose Page ➤ File. Then fill in the File dialog box.

- To make a task confidential in a password-protected file, choose Page ➤ Confidential or press F4.

## ▶ Deleting a Page

To delete a page, drag it to the Wastebasket. You can also select it and press Delete or choose Edit ➤ Clear.

# ▶▶ Working in the Planner Section

The Planner presents a graphical view of a year's events. You can look at color-coded entries and see the time—up to four adjacent or eight overlapping blocks per day—that you have reserved for events.

## ▶ Displaying a Planner Format

You can look at the Planner in two ways:

Click on the Quarter per Page button or choose View ➤ 1 Quarter per Page to display the Planner over four pages—one for each quarter of the year.

Click on the Year per Page button or choose View ➤ 2 Year per Page (the default) to display the Planner for one year on one page.

## ▶ Adding an Event

In Planner, you can add an event in two ways: You can click on the legend at the bottom of the page and then click on a date in the grid, or you can fill in a dialog box.

The easy way to add an event in the Planner is to click on its block in the legend and click near the top of one of the blocks in the morning or afternoon on the desired date. (If you click toward the bottom of a block, you may inadvertently insert an overlapping event.) You also can click on the block in the legend and drag across the dates on which you want to place the event. (If you drag across a weekend, the event is placed there as well.) You can drag across a block but not down and across other blocks on the same day or range of days; once you've added an event to a single block, you can't incorporate additional blocks. You can also drag an entire event to another block of time— perhaps to the afternoon from the morning or to the next week.

You can insert as many as four events in a morning and four more in the afternoon—if you overlap the entries. To insert an overlapping event, click on the bottom of an existing event. Remember that you can drag an event into place. The best way to master inserting multiple events on a day or a block of days is to practice, practice, practice.

To add an event to the Planner section using a dialog box, follow these steps:

**1.** Click on the Planner tab or choose Section ➤ Turn To ➤ Planner.

**2.** Click on the Click to Create an Entry button, click on the Click to Create an Event SmartIcon, press Insert, double-click on a date, or choose Create ➤ Event. Organizer opens the Create Event dialog box (see Figure 23.12).

**FIGURE 23.12** ▶

*The Create Event dialog box*

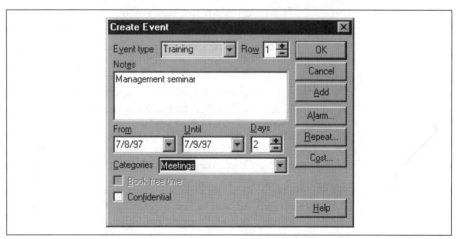

**3.** Choose an event type from the Event Type drop-down list box.

**4.** Select one of the four rows from the Row list box.

**5.** Type anything related to the event in the Notes text box.

**6.** Type or select a starting date from the From drop-down list box. If you click on the downward-pointing arrow, a calendar from which you can choose appears:

```
        ◄      June 1997      ►
        Su Mo Tu We Th Fr  Sa
         1  2  3  4  5  6   7
         8  9 10 11 12 13  14
        15 16 17 18 19 [20] 21
        22 23 24 25 26 27  28
        29 30  1  2  3  4   5
```

**7.** Type or select an ending date from the Until drop-down list box. If you click on the downward-pointing arrow, a calendar from which you can choose appears. You also can select the duration of an event by typing or selecting a value from the Days list box.

**8.** To categorize the event, select from the Categories drop-down list box.

**9.** Check the Book Free Time checkbox to insert this event into the Calendar, which helps you to avoid scheduling conflicts. The default is a cleared checkbox.

**10.** Check the Confidential checkbox to make this event confidential if this Organizer file is password-protected. The default is a cleared checkbox.

**11.** To set an alarm for the event, click on Alarm, fill in the Alarm dialog box, and click on OK.

**12.** To define this as a repeating event, click on Repeat, fill in the Repeat dialog box, and click on OK.

**13.** To associate a cost code with this event, click on Cost, fill in the Cost dialog box, and click on OK.

**14.** To insert this event without closing this dialog box (so that you can add other events), click on Add.

**15.** To insert this event and close the dialog box, click on OK.

## ▶ *Editing an Event*

To change the attributes for an event, go to the event and double-click on it, select it and choose Edit ➤ Edit Event, or press Ctrl+E. When the Edit Event dialog box opens, select options or type in the text boxes, and click on OK.

You can bypass the Edit Event dialog box and go to the appropriate dialog box by selecting an event and choosing one of the following:

- To categorize an event, choose Event ➤ Categorize or press F5. Then fill in the Categorize dialog box.

- To set or change an alarm, choose Event ➤ Alarm or press F6. Then fill in the Alarm dialog box.

- To specify a repeating event, choose Event ➤ Repeat or press F7. Then fill in the Repeat dialog box.

- To associate a cost code with the event, choose Event ➤ Cost or press F8. Then fill in the Cost dialog box.

- To make an event confidential in a password-protected file, choose Event ➤ Confidential or press F4.

## ▶ *Deleting an Event*

To delete an event, drag it to the Wastebasket. If the Delete Repeating Event dialog box (see Figure 23.13) appears, select an option, and click on OK.

The options in the Delete Repeating Event dialog box are:

**Just This One**     Deletes the event from this date. If you added two events at separate times, however, Planner treats each as separate.

**All**     Deletes the entire block of events that you added.

**All Previous**     Deletes this event and all previous events in this range.

**All Future**     Deletes this event and all the next events in this range.

**All Until**     Deletes this event and all the next events in this range until the date that you type in the text box or select from the calendar that pops up.

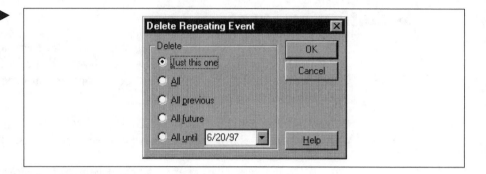

## ► *Naming an Event*

To change or define the name of an event or (Unused) in the legend at the bottom of the Planner, either double-click on the name or choose View ► Planner Preferences, and click on the Key button. In the Planner Key dialog box (see Figure 23.14), double-click on a title, overtype the event name, and then click on OK twice.

# ►► *Working in the Anniversary Section*

You can use the Anniversary section to track important birthdays and anniversaries. Remember that you can choose to display Anniversary entries in the Calendar section, and you can set alarms so that you'll never send a belated birthday card again.

## ▶ *Displaying an Anniversary Format*

You can display anniversary entries in four ways:

 Click on the View by Month button or choose View ➤ 1 By Month (the default) to display entries three months to a page.

 Click on the View by Year button or choose View ➤ 2 By Year to display all the entries for an entire year on two facing pages.

 Click on the View by Zodiac button or choose View ➤ 3 By Zodiac to display entries by their zodiac signs.

 Click on the View by Category button or choose View ➤ 4 By Category to arrange pages by category in the order in which they were added.

## ▶ *Adding an Entry to the Anniversary List*

To add an entry to your Anniversary list, follow these steps:

 **1.** Click on the Anniversary tab or choose Section ➤ Turn To ➤ Anniversary.

**2.** Click on the Click to Create an Entry button, click on the Click to Create an Anniversary SmartIcon, double-click on a blank part of a page in the section, press Insert, or choose Create ➤ Anniversary. Organizer opens the Create Anniversary dialog box (see Figure 23.15).

**Managing Data with Organizer**

▶▶

Ch.
**23**

**FIGURE 23.15** ▶

*The Create Anniversary dialog box*

| Create Anniversary | ✕ |
|---|---|
| Description | OK |
| Mike's birthday | Cancel |
| | Add |
| Date 8/6/97 ▼ | Alarm... |
| Categories Personal ▼ | Repeat... |
| ☑ Occurs on same date every year | Cost... |
| ☐ Confidential | |
| | Help |

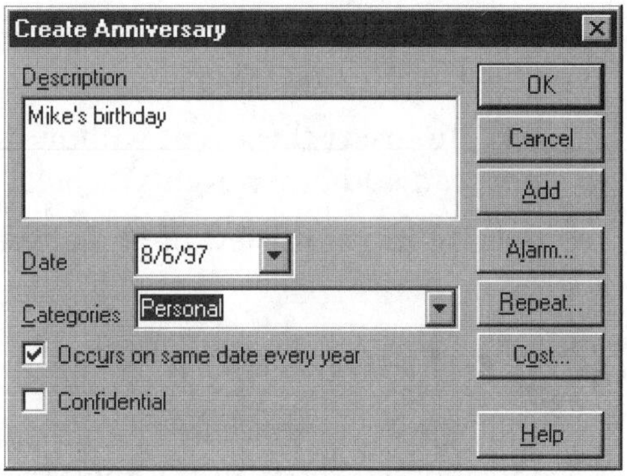

3. Type a description of the event in the Description text box.

4. Type or select a date from the Date drop-down list box. If you click on the downward-pointing arrow, a calendar from which you can choose appears:

```
    ◀      August 1997      ▶
   Su Mo Tu We Th  Fr  Sa
   27  28  29  30  31   1   2
    3   4   5  [6]  7   8   9
   10  11  12  13  14  15  16
   17  18  19  20  21  22  23
   24  25  26  27  28  29  30
   31   1   2   3   4   5   6
```

5. To categorize the event, select from the Categories drop-down list box.

6. Check the Occurs on Same Date Every Year checkbox to mark a birthday or anniversary date. If you are tracking holidays, which can occur on different dates each year, clear this checkbox. The default is a checked checkbox.

7. Check the Confidential checkbox to make this entry confidential if this Organizer file is password-protected. The default is a cleared checkbox.

8. To set an alarm for this event, click on Alarm, fill in the Alarm dialog box, and click on OK.

9. To define this as a repeating event, click on Repeat, fill in the Repeat dialog box, and click on OK.

10. To associate a cost code with this event, click on Cost, fill in the Cost dialog box, and click on OK.

11. To insert this event without closing this dialog box (so that you can add other events), click on Add.

12. To insert this event and close the dialog box, click on OK.

## ▶ Editing an Anniversary

To change the attributes for an anniversary, double-click on it, select it and choose Edit ▶ Edit Anniversary, or press Ctrl+E. When the Edit Anniversary dialog box opens, edit the text, select options, and click on OK.

You can bypass the Edit Anniversary dialog box and go to the appropriate dialog box by selecting an anniversary and choosing one of the following:

- To categorize an anniversary, choose Anniversary ➤ Categorize or press F5. Then fill in the Categorize dialog box.

- To set or change an alarm, choose Anniversary ➤ Alarm or press F6. Then fill in the Alarm dialog box.

- To specify a repeating event, choose Anniversary ➤ Repeat or press F7. Then fill in the Repeat dialog box.

- To associate a cost code with the anniversary, choose Anniversary ➤ Cost or press F8. Then fill in the Cost dialog box.

- To make the anniversary occur every year, choose Anniversary ➤ Occurs Every Year. If a checkmark precedes the command, the anniversary occurs every year.

- To make an anniversary confidential in a password-protected file, choose Anniversary ➤ Confidential or press F4.

### ▶ *Deleting an Anniversary*

To delete an anniversary, drag it to the Wastebasket, or select it and press Delete or choose Edit ➤ Clear.

# ▶▶ *Working in the Calls Section*

Making and receiving telephone calls may be the most important aspect of your working day; so it's a good idea to be very careful about keeping a record of your calls—both incoming and outgoing, attempted and completed. Using the Calls section, you can also time calls, redial calls, and schedule future calls.

Open the Calls section by clicking on its tab or choosing Section ➤ Turn To ➤ Calls.

## ▶ *Displaying a Calls Section Format*

You can display the Calls section in four views:

 Click on the View by Name button or choose View ➤ 1 By Name to display entries alphabetically by last name. This is the default.

 Click on the View by Company button or choose View ➤ 2 By Company to display entries alphabetically by company name.

 Click on the View by Date button or choose View ➤ 3 By Date to display entries arranged by date—from oldest to newest.

 Click on the View by Category button or choose View ➤ 4 By Category to display entries arranged by category.

## ▶ *Getting Ready to Dial*

Organizer enables automatic dialing if a telephone is properly connected to your modem, which in turn must be connected correctly to your computer. Before trying to dial your telephone, check that Organizer recognizes the communications (COM) port to which the modem is attached. Because these settings may not match your Windows 95 dialing properties, it is very important to do this. To check your modem settings, follow these steps:

*1.* Choose File ➤ User Setup ➤ Telephone Dialing. Organizer opens the Telephone Dialing dialog box, as shown in Figure 23.16.

**FIGURE 23.16** ▶

*The Dialer Preferences dialog box with some typical options selected or changed*

| Telephone Dialing | |
|---|---|
| **Dial using** | |
| Device: Practical Peripherals PM144MT ▼   Configure... | OK |
| | Cancel |
| Address: Address 0 ▼ | |
| **Phone number lookup** | |
| Search for names & companies in 📷 Address ▼ | Help |

2. From the Port drop-down list box, select the communications port to which your modem is connected. If you have a serial mouse, it's probably connected to COM1 (the default). If you aren't sure of the communications port for your modem, try COM2 first.

3. If your telephone is touchtone, click on Tone (the default); otherwise, click on Pulse.

4. Select or type other options. When you are in doubt, use the Organizer defaults.

5. After you have completed the dialog box, click on OK.

If you have problems getting a dial tone or in hanging up, refer to "Troubleshooting Modem Settings" under the "Modems" topic in the help facility. In addition, if the TECHNOTE.OR2 file is in the \ORG2\ORGFILES directory, open it, and look at the chapter, "Autodialer & Modem." Another source of help is your modem's user documentation.

## ▶ *Autodialing a Telephone Number*

To dial a telephone number, follow these steps:

1. Click on the Telephone icon, click on the Dial a Number Smart-Icon, drag an entry from any Organizer section to the Telephone icon, choose Phone ➤ Dial, or press Ctrl+D. Organizer displays the Dial dialog box (see Figure 23.17). If you dragged an entry from the Address book to the Telephone icon, the Number is already filled in.

▶ ▶
Ch.
**23**

**Managing Data with Organizer**

**FIGURE 23.17** ▶

*Organizer's Dial dialog box, from which you can dial a telephone number*

| Dial | ☒ |
|---|---|

| | First name | Last name | Dial... |
|---|---|---|---|
| Contact | Maurice | Stratford ▼ | Cancel |
| Company | Acme Binoculars ▼ | | |
| Phone at | The phone number entered below ▼ | | |

Phone number
☐ Use Country and Area codes

| Area code | Phone number | Ext |
|---|---|---|
| | 555-5454 | |

Country code
United States of America (1) ▼

Dialing from  Default Location ▼   Dialing properties...

Dial using  Compaq Presario 144 ▼   Configure...   Help

2.  If the First Name, Last Name, and Company text boxes are empty, you can fill them in; however, it's not required. If the individual you are calling is in your address book, you can open the drop-down list boxes and select the last name and company.

3.  If the Number text box is empty, type a telephone number (for example, 1-555-555-5555 (long distance) or 555-5555 (local). If the individual you are calling is in your address book, you can open the drop-down list boxes and select the telephone number. You can edit the number, if needed.

4.  To dial the number, click on Dial. The Dialing dialog box (see Figure 23.18) displays the number and allows you to automatically enter information in the phone log, hang up, or redial.

**FIGURE 23.18** ►

*The Dialing dialog box*

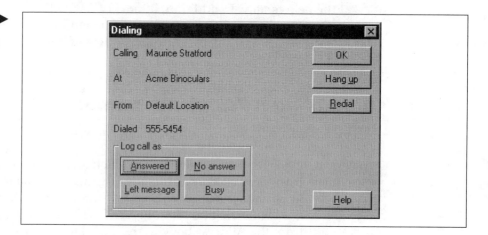

## ► Quick-Dialing a Telephone Number

Organizer can dial the number of an entry in any section. Just click on the entry, and click on the Click to Dial the Number of the Current Entry SmartIcon, choose Phone ➤ Quick Dial, or press Ctrl+Q. Organizer dials the telephone number without displaying the Dial dialog box. You also can quick-dial the last number that you dialed.

## ► *Creating a Future Telephone Call*

Before you make a telephone call, you can document it in detail. Just fill in and select options from the Create Call dialog box. To plan and optionally make and record a call, follow these steps:

1. Click on the Call tab or choose Section ➤ Turn To ➤ Call.

2. Click on the Click to Create an Entry button, click on the Click to Create a Calls Entry SmartIcon, double-click on a blank part of a page in the section, press Insert, or choose Create ➤ Call. Organizer opens the Contact section of the Create Call dialog box (see Figure 23.19).

**FIGURE 23.19** ►

*The Contact section of the Create Call dialog box*

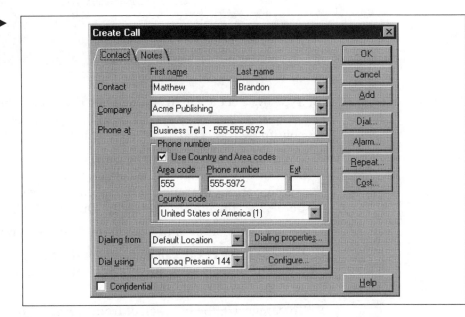

3. Type or select a name, company name, and telephone number from the First Name, Last Name, Company, and Phone At text/drop-down list boxes, respectively. Note that the address information in the drop-down list boxes come from the Address section.

4. Click on the Notes tab. Organizer opens the Notes section of the Create Call dialog box (see Figure 23.20).

Managing Data with Organizer

Ch.
**23**

**FIGURE 23.20** ▸

*The Notes section of the
Create Call dialog box*

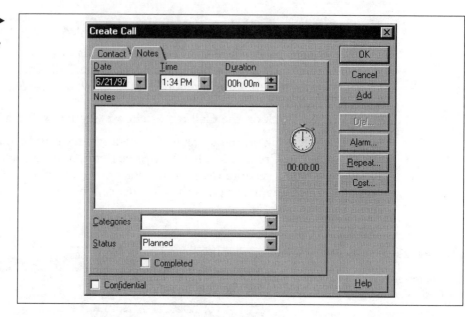

**5.** Type or select a date from the Date drop-down list box. Today's
computer system date is the default. If you click on the downward-
pointing arrow, a calendar from which you can choose appears.

**6.** Type or select a time from the Time drop-down list box. The current
computer system time is the default. If you click on the downward-
pointing arrow, the time tracker appears. You can select a duration
from either the time tracker or the Duration list box.

**7.** Type a description of the call in the Notes text box.

**8.** If needed, select the call status from the Status drop-down list
box. The default is Planned. If you select Follow up, Organizer inserts a follow-up call to this call.

**9.** To categorize the call, select from the Categories drop-down
list box.

**10.** Check the Confidential checkbox (in either section of the dialog
box) to make this entry confidential if this Organizer file is password-
protected. The default is a cleared checkbox.

**11.** Check the Completed checkbox if you have completed the call.
The default is a cleared checkbox.

**12.** To set an alarm for the call, click on Alarm (in either section of
the dialog box), fill in the Alarm dialog box, and click on OK.

13. To define this as a repeating call, click on Repeat (in either section of the dialog box), fill in the Repeat dialog box, and click on OK.

14. To associate a cost code with this call, click on Cost (in either section of the dialog box), fill in the Cost dialog box, and click on OK.

15. To stop the Stopwatch, click on or near it; to reset the Stopwatch, click again.

16. To add this call to the Calls section without closing this dialog box (so that you can add other calls), click on Add (in either section of the dialog box).

17. To add this call to the Calls section and close the dialog box, click on OK.

## ► *Tracking an Incoming Call*

When a call comes in, you can time it and record information about it. To track an incoming call, follow these steps:

1. After you pick up the receiver, choose Phone ➤ Incoming Call. Organizer opens the Create Call dialog box and starts the Stopwatch to start timing the call.

2. At the conclusion of the call, hang up the receiver, and click on the Stopwatch.

3. Fill in the text boxes and select options as you would when creating a call.

4. Click on OK. Organizer closes the dialog box and inserts the record of the call in the Calls section.

## ► *Defining a Follow-up Call*

To define a follow-up call, select the call that you want to follow up, and choose Call ➤ Follow Up. Fill in the Create Follow Up Call dialog box. If you set an alarm, you'll get a reminder to make the follow-up call.

As you are making a telephone call, you can define it as a follow-up call by selecting the Follow Up status from the Status drop-down list box.

## ▶ *Editing a Call*

To change the attributes for a call, double-click on it, select it and choose Edit ➤ Edit Call, or press Ctrl+E. When the Edit Call dialog box opens, edit the text, select options, and click on OK.

You can bypass the Edit Call dialog box and go to the appropriate dialog box by selecting a call and choosing one of the following:

- To categorize a call, choose Call ➤ Categorize or press F5. Then fill in the Categorize dialog box.

- To set or change an alarm, choose Call ➤ Alarm or press F6. Then fill in the Alarm dialog box.

- To specify a repeating event, choose Call ➤ Repeat or press F7. Then fill in the Repeat dialog box.

- To associate a cost code with the call, choose Call ➤ Cost or press F8. Then fill in the Cost dialog box.

- To make a call confidential in a password-protected file, choose Call ➤ Confidential or press F4.

- To complete a call, choose Call ➤ Completed.

## ▶ *Deleting a Call*

To delete a call, drag it to the Wastebasket, select it and press Delete, or choose Edit ➤ Clear.

# ▶▶ *Selecting Print Options*

Printing in Organizer is almost the same as printing in any other Smart-Suite application. The main differences are the number of available paper layouts and the options in the Print dialog box.

▶▶**N O T E**

> You can add a new page layout or edit an existing layout. Choose Edit ➤ Layouts or press Ctrl+Y and make your changes in the Layouts dialog box. For further information, see "Customizing Layout Styles" or "Selecting Layout Options" in the help facility or click on the Help button in the dialog box to get related help.

Whether you decide to print by choosing File ➤ Print, pressing Ctrl+P, clicking on the Print SmartIcon, or dragging an entry to the Click to Print Information button, you have a choice of options that are tailored for printing a particular Organizer section. These pages provide a brief description of each print option shown in the Print dialog box (see Figure 23.21). After selecting options in the dialog box, click on OK.

The options in the Print dialog box are:

**Section**    Selects the section to be printed (that is, Calendar, To Do, Address, and so on).

**Layout**    Selects the layout format. Each section has its own default layout. To view a sample of the layout before printing, click on the Layouts button.

**Paper**    Selects page dimensions or a particular planner size. To view a sample of the paper and to see the actual dimensions, click on the Layouts button and then click on the Paper button.

**Single Sided**    Prints on a single side of each sheet. This is the default.

**Double Sided**    Prints on both sides of each sheet. When printing double-sided, Organizer prompts you to turn the paper to the second side and insert it in the printer.

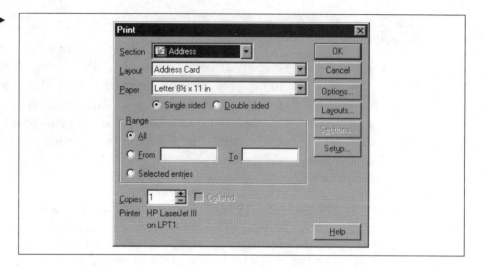

**Range**     You have three options:

> **All**     Prints all the information from the selected section.
>
> **From**     Prints a range starting with a value such as the
> page number, starting name, or date in the first text/list box
> and ending with the ending value in the To text/list box.
>
> **Selected Entries**     Prints entries that you selected be-
> fore you chose File ➤ Print.

**Copies**     Selects or types the number of copies that you want
to print.

**Collated**     Prints all the pages of a section, starting with the
first page and ending with the last page before starting to print the
next copy.

For more information about printing in Organizer, see the Organizer
documentation or look up "Printing" in the help facility.

# APPENDICES

# A

# Installing Lotus SmartSuite

▶▶ **T**his appendix provides information about installing a Smart-Suite application. Before installing SmartSuite, you should have already installed Windows 95 or a more recent version, if available, and installed printers and other peripheral devices. To ensure that you can reinstall a SmartSuite application if something happens to your original installation disks, and if you are installing from floppy disks, you should also make copies of the disks and store them away from your computer.

You can install all the SmartSuite programs or individual SmartSuite programs using the following procedures.

# ▶▶ *Minimum Hardware and Software Requirements*

These are the minimum requirements for installing a SmartSuite application:

- An IBM PC or 100% compatible personal computer with an 80486 microprocessor or greater.

- Microsoft Windows 95 or a more recent version.

- At least 16 megabytes of RAM (*random access memory*), your computer's main memory and temporary storage area. This ensures that you can run at least one SmartSuite application. The more RAM you have, the better a SmartSuite application runs and the more applications you can run simultaneously.

- A floppy disk drive, 3.5-inch high-density, or a CD-ROM drive for installation.

- An IBM 8514, SVGA (super VGA), or VGA monitor.

- A mouse or other pointing device.

- At least 57 megabytes of hard disk drive space for a minimum installation of all SmartSuite applications. The amount of space required depends on the files that you choose to install. For a complete installation, which includes all SmartSuite features, tours, SmartMaster templates, the Help system for all SmartSuite applications, and sample files, reserve at least 140 megabytes.

# ▶▶ *Installing SmartSuite Programs*

Installing SmartSuite is easy. The installation program displays a series of dialog boxes that help you decide which options and programs to choose. In the early stages of installation, be prepared to choose the type of installation:

**Default Install** The recommended choice; the installation program installs the SmartSuite application and selects the most appropriate options for you. Note that not all options are installed using the Default Install.

**Customized Install** For experienced users; the installation program allows you to select the SmartSuite application files that you want to install. Use Customized Install if you want to install every file associated with a particular program or with the entire SmartSuite.

**Install for Laptops** The installation program installs the minimum number of application files.

 ▶▶ **N O T E**

If you want to reinstall a SmartSuite application at a later time and choose another installation type, simply run the installation program again.

Installation

▶▶

*App.*

**A**

## ► *Installing SmartSuite Applications Using the Default Install*

To install a SmartSuite application using Default Install, follow these steps:

1. With Windows 95 running, insert the first installation disk or CD into the appropriate drive.

2. Click on the Start button, click on Run, and type **d:\install** in the Open text box, where *d* represents the identifier of the disk drive or CD-ROM drive. Click on OK. The installation program displays preliminary screens and opens the Welcome to the Lotus SmartSuite Installation Program dialog box.

 ►► **N O T E**

> **If the installation window automatically appears on your desktop, click on Install on the left side of the window.**

3. Type your name and company name in the appropriate text boxes if the text boxes are empty and click on Next.

4. Confirm that the names you entered are correct. The Specify Lotus SmartSuite Directory dialog box appears.

5. Click on Yes. The Specify Lotus SmartSuite Directory dialog box appears.

6. Click on Next to accept the current folders. The Select Lotus SmartSuite Applications dialog box appears with all applications— SmartCenter, 1-2-3, Word Pro, Freelance Graphics, Approach, Organizer, ScreenCam, and Suite DocOnline—selected for installation.

 ►► **N O T E**

> **If you are installing SmartSuite on a computer on which there is already a copy, the install program displays a message that warns you that the old version's files will be overwritten unless you choose another folder in which to install the new version.**

▶▶**T I P**

**In the Select Lotus SmartSuite Applications dialog box, you can select specific applications to be installed. So if you need to reinstall an application or add a previously uninstalled application, check or clear checkboxes until only the applications you want to install are checked.**

**7.** Click on Next. The installation program displays the Install Options dialog box.

**8.** Click on Next to select the Default Features—Automatic Install. If you have any questions about the types of installation you can select, click on the Help button. The installation program evaluates your computer and may display dialog boxes that prompt you to change settings. The Select Program Folder dialog box opens.

▶▶**N O T E**

**If the installation program detects a previous version of a SmartSuite application, it displays a message prompting you to save the previous version's SmartMasters.**

**9.** Select the folder in which you want application shortcuts to be placed. Click on Next. The installation program asks whether you want to start copying files to your hard drive.

**10.** Click on Yes. The installation begins.

**11.** If you are installing from floppy disks, the installation program prompts you to insert the next one and either click on OK or press Enter. If you are installing from a CD-ROM, you will not be prompted. The installation program shows you how the installation is progressing and informs you when it is complete.

**12.** Click on Done to return to Windows. If the Lotus SmartSuite Registration dialog box appears, complete the remaining steps in this procedure.

Installation

▶▶

*App.*

**13.** Fill in all the text boxes in the dialog box. Click on Next. Another Lotus SmartSuite Registration dialog box opens.

**14.** Answer the questions in the dialog box. Click on Next. Another Lotus SmartSuite Registration dialog box opens.

**15.** Answer the questions in the dialog box. Click on Next. The registration program checks your modem, dials, and sends the Smart-Suite registration information.

**16.** Click on Done. You are returned to your Windows desktop.

## ▶ Installing a SmartSuite Application Using the Custom Install

After installing selected SmartSuite applications or to install an application for the first time, you can select Custom Install, which enables you to add features not installed in the Default Install.

 ▶▶ **T I P**

> **The Default Install does not automatically install all the features that are covered in the user documentation and the Help system. Word Pro's Grammar Checker is an example; the only way to install it is to use Custom Install.**

To install a SmartSuite application using the Custom Install, follow these steps:

**1.** With Windows 95 running, insert the first installation disk or the CD into the appropriate disk drive.

**2.** Click on the Start button, click on Run, and type ***d:\install*** in the Open text box, where *d* represents the identifier of the disk drive or the CD-ROM drive. Click on OK. The installation program displays preliminary screens and opens the Welcome to the Lotus SmartSuite Installation Program dialog box.

**N O T E**

> If the installation window automatically appears on your desktop, click on Install on the left side of the window.

**3.** Type your name and company name in the appropriate text boxes if the text boxes are empty, and click on Next.

**4.** Confirm that the names you entered are correct. The Specify Lotus SmartSuite Directory dialog box appears.

**5.** Click on Yes. The Specify Lotus SmartSuite Directory dialog box appears.

**6.** Click on Next to accept the current folders. (If the installation program has detected a previous version of a SmartSuite application, it displays a message telling you that the previous version's files will be overwritten unless you select a different folder.) The Select Lotus SmartSuite Applications dialog box appears with all applications—SmartCenter, 1-2-3, Word Pro, Freelance Graphics, Approach, Organizer, ScreenCam, and Suite DocOnline— selected for installation.

**N O T E**

> In the Select Lotus SmartSuite Applications dialog box, you can select specific applications to be installed. So if you need to reinstall an application or add a previously uninstalled application, check or clear checkboxes until only the applications you want to install are checked.

**7.** Click on Next. The installation program displays the Install Options dialog box.

**8.** Select Customize Features—Manual Install, and click on Next. The Select SmartSuite Applications to Customize dialog box opens.

**9.** Select a SmartSuite Application to customize and click on the Customize button. The Customize Features dialog box opens.

App.
**A**

Installation

**10.** Click on the tabs at the top of the dialog box to review the features of the application. If the checkbox preceding a feature is checked, it is already installed; if the checkbox is cleared, the feature is not installed.

**11.** To view sections of the dialog box with tabs not on display, click on the right-pointing or left-pointing arrow at the top right of the dialog box.

**12.** Check the checkboxes for the features to be installed, and then click on OK.

**13.** Click on Next.

**14.** Answer Yes or No to go through a series of dialog boxes. The Select Program Folder dialog box opens.

 ▶▶ **N O T E**

> **If the installation program detects a previous version of a SmartSuite application, it asks you if you want to save the previous version's SmartMasters in a backup folder.**

**15.** Select the folder in which you want application shortcuts to be placed. Click on Next. The installation program asks whether you want to start copying files to your hard drive.

**16.** Click on Yes. The installation begins.

**17.** If you are installing from floppy disks, the installation program prompts you to insert the next one and either click on OK or press Enter. If you are installing from a CD-ROM, you will not be prompted. The installation program shows you how the installation is progressing and informs you when it is complete.

**18.** Click on Done to return to Windows. If the Lotus SmartSuite Registration dialog box appears, complete the remaining steps in this procedure.

**19.** Fill in all the text boxes in the dialog box. Click on Next. Another Lotus SmartSuite Registration dialog box opens.

**20.** Answer the questions in the dialog box. Click on Next. Another Lotus SmartSuite Registration dialog box opens.

**21.** Answer the questions in the dialog box. Click on Next. The registration program checks your modem, dials, and sends the SmartSuite registration information.

**22.** Click on Done. You are returned to your Windows desktop.

 **T I P**

> **If you are installing from CD-ROM, you'll want to know that SmartSuite online documentation in the Adobe Acrobat PDF format is located in the \ACROREAD folder. Because many of these files are very large, it is best to leave them on the CD-ROM rather than copying them onto your hard drive. To open a file and read it using the Acrobat reader, insert the CD-ROM disk in the CD-ROM drive, open Windows Explorer, open the \ACROREAD folder on the CD-ROM drive, and double-click on the icon representing the file that you want to open.**

# ▶▶ *Removing a SmartSuite Application from Your Computer*

If you ever want to delete a SmartSuite application from your computer, Windows 95 handles the deletion by deleting files and references to files.

To delete a SmartSuite application, follow these steps:

**1.** Open the Control Panel by using one of these methods:

- Click on the Start button, point to Settings, and click on Control Panel.
- Double-click on the My Computer icon on your Desktop and double-click on the Control Panel icon.

Installation

▶▶

*App.*

**A**

2. Double-click on the Add/Remove Programs icon. Windows opens the Install/Uninstall section of the Add/Remove Programs Properties dialog box.

3. Click on the program to be removed and click on the Add/Remove button. Windows asks you to confirm the file deletion.

4. To delete the program, click on Yes.

# Customizing Your SmartSuite Environment

**T**his appendix provides information about customizing your working environment in the SmartCenter and in each of the SmartSuite applications. The first part is an overview of ways in which you can change your environment, application by application. The second part deals with customizing SmartIcons.

# ▶▶ *Changing Your SmartCenter Environment*

You can change the properties of the SmartCenter using the Smart-Center Properties command on the Control menu, and you can change the properties of a particular drawer using the shortcut menu associated with that drawer. You can modify the look and position of the SmartCenter and specify sounds and drawer speed. For individual drawers, you can change the label on the drawer front and the drawer handle.

## ▶ *Changing SmartCenter Properties*

To change SmartCenter Properties, click on the Lotus button on the left side of the SmartCenter and choose SmartCenter Properties. The SmartCenter Properties dialog box contains three sections: Basics, Effects, and Appearance.

The Basics section contains these options:

> **Reserve Minimum Space for SmartCenter**  Check this checkbox to make more space available for the work area in the current application. The default is a cleared checkbox.

**Display Popup Help**    Check this checkbox (the default) to display pop-up help information about the drawer over which you have moved the mouse pointer.

**SmartCenter Position**    Click on the Top of Screen option button (the default) to place the SmartCenter at the top of the desktop; click on the Bottom of Screen option button to place the SmartCenter at the bottom of the desktop.

The Effects section contains these options:

**Event**    From this drop-down list box, select an event (such as an opening or a closing drawer) with which you want to associate a sound.

**Sound**    From this drop-down list box, select a sound to associate with the selected event.

**Browse**    Click on this button to open the Browse for Open Drawer Sound dialog box, with which you can find other sounds (WAV) to associate with an event.

**Drawer Speed**    Slide from Slow to Fast to control the speed with which drawers open.

The Appearance section contains options for the appearance of the drawer fronts. To match a texture to your computer system, look at the brief resolution description to the right of the sample texture. Then click on a texture to select it.

## ▶ *Changing Drawer Properties*

To change properties for a particular drawer, right-click on it and select Drawer Properties. The Drawer Properties dialog box provides these options:

**Drawer Label**    In this text box, type the name that you want to appear on the front of the drawer.

**Drawer Handle**    From this drop-down list box, select the smaller graphic that you want to appear on the right side of the drawer front.

# ▶▶ *Changing Your 1-2-3 Environment*

In 1-2-3, you can determine the way in which you start 1-2-3 and create a workbook, sort values in a workbook, drag and drop values from one cell or range to another, and automate certain actions, and you can select the default fonts and point sizes, the locations in which you store particular files, and so on. You can customize 1-2-3 using the 1-2-3 Preferences dialog box.

## ▶ *Changing 1-2-3 Preferences*

Choose File ➤ User Setup ➤ 1-2-3 Preferences to open the User Setup dialog box, in which you can specify user defaults in five sections: General, New Workbook Defaults, File Locations, Recalculation, and Classic Keys.

The General section contains these options:

**Show Welcome Dialog**    Check this checkbox (the default) to start 1-2-3 without a prompting dialog box.

**Maximize 1-2-3 Window**    Check this checkbox (the default) to start 1-2-3 in a maximized window.

**Sort Numbers before Words**    Check this checkbox (the default) to place numbers before words when sorting.

**Sort Blank Cells to Bottom**    Check this checkbox (the default) to place blank cells after numbers or words when sorting.

**Country Sort Order**    From this drop-down list box, select a sorting order determined by country. The default sort order is Generic Sorting.

**Number of Recent Files to Show**    Type or select a value from 0 to 10 to set the number of recent files to be displayed at the bottom of the File menu. The default is 5. To open one of the files on the File menu, simply click on the filename or type the underlined number preceding the filename.

**Show New Workbook Dialog**    Check this checkbox (the default) to display the New Workbook dialog box when you choose File ➤ New Workbook. If you clear this checkbox, 1-2-3 opens a new empty workbook instead.

**Undo**    Check this checkbox (the default) to activate the Edit ➤ Undo command.

**Beep on Error**    Check this checkbox (the default) so that a beep sounds when an error occurs or when 1-2-3 encounters a {Beep} command in a macro. To hear a beep, you must have installed a sound card, and sounds must be enabled in Windows 95.

**Use "Total" to Sum Automatically**    Check this checkbox (the default) to have 1-2-3 automatically total columns when you type **Total** or **Totals** at the bottom of columns or when you type **Total** or **Totals** at the right side of rows.

**Update Links When Opening Workbooks**    Check this checkbox to automatically update links between files when you open a 1-2-3 file associated with links. The default is a cleared checkbox.

**Drag and Drop Cells**    Check this checkbox (the default) to be able to drag-and-drop cells with your mouse.

**Confirm Overwrite for Drag and Drop**    Check this checkbox (the default) to have 1-2-3 warn you if drag-and-drop will overwrite data.

**Run File Opened Scripts, Autoexecute Macros**    Check this checkbox (the default) to automatically run macros associated with a file when you open the file.

**Show Warning When Saving As a Wk ★ File**    Check this checkbox (the default) to display a message when you select a Wk★ file type for saving.

**Interpret Entry of Years 00-49 as 21st Century**    Check this checkbox (the default) to precede two-digit years between 00-49 as 2000 to 2049.

**Set Dates to Always Display 4-Digit Years**    Check this checkbox to always display years ina four-digit format. The default is a cleared checkbox.

The New Workbook Defaults section contains these options:

**Font Name**    Select a font name for new and existing files (when you open them) from the scroll box. The default is Arial.

**Size**    Select a point size for new and existing files (when you open them) from the scroll box. The default is 12.

**Text Color** Open this drop-down list box to display a color palette from which you can select a new default text color for new and existing files (when you open them). The starting default color is black.

**Background Color** Open this drop-down list box to reveal a color palette from which you can select a new default cell background color for new and existing files (when you open them). The starting default color is white.

**Use Windows Default Colors for Text and Background** Returns the defaults to the original settings (for example, black text on a white background).

**Column Width** Type or select a column width value from 1 to 240 characters. The default is 9.

**Row Height** Click on an option button to select a row height or to automatically fit the size of the default font (the default). If you select a row height, the values range from 1 to 255, and the default value is 14, if you select this option.

The File Locations section shows the default locations of workbook files, SmartMaster templates, automatically opened files, and add-ins. To change a location, simply overtype the current path with the new path. You can click on the Browse button to choose folders and subfolders that make up a path.

The Recalculation section contains these options:

**Automatic** Click on this option (the default) to recalculate formulas automatically when you change values in the current worksheet.

**Manual** Click on this option to recalculate formulas manually when you press F9.

**Natural** Click on this option button (the default) to recalculate formulas in the current worksheet by their dependence on other formulas. 1-2-3 recalculates formulas not dependent on other formulas first and recalculates dependent formulas later.

**By Column** Click on this option button to recalculate the formulas in the current worksheet in order by column. 1-2-3 starts its recalculation in the top left corner and then moves down each column from left to right.

**By Row**    Click on this option button to recalculate the formulas in the current worksheet in order by row. 1-2-3 starts its recalculation in the top left corner and then moves down each column from top to bottom.

**Number of Iterations**    Select or type the number of times 1-2-3 repeats its recalculations if you have selected By Column or By Row or if you have selected Natural and 1-2-3 identifies a *circular reference* (a cell value that depends on itself for calculation, which can cause invalid results).

The Classic Keys section contains these options:

**TAB Moves Right One Screen, ENTER Confirms**    Click on this option button to control the results of pressing the Tab and Enter keys while working in a workbook. Pressing Tab moves the cursor to the next screen to the right; pressing Enter confirms the value entered in the current cell.

**TAB Moves Right One Cell, ENTER Confirms and Moves Down**    Click on this option button (the default) to control the results of pressing the Tab and Enter keys while working in a workbook. Pressing Tab moves the cursor to the next cell to the right; pressing Enter both confirms the value entered in the current cell and moves to the next cell down.

**Display 1-2-3 Classic Menu by Pressing**    From this drop-down list box, select the character that when pressed opens the Classic menu at the top of the desktop. If you have used 1-2-3 since its DOS days, you may be more comfortable using the Classic menu from time to time. To close the menu, press Esc.

# ▶▶ *Changing Your Word Pro Environment*

In Word Pro, you can specify the way in which you select default formats and user setup options and view documents.

## ▶ Changing User Preferences

Choose File ➤ User Setup ➤ Word Pro Preferences or click on the Word Pro Preferences SmartIcon to open the Word Pro Preferences dialog box, in which you can specify a variety of user preferences in four sections: General, Locations, Default Files, and Personal.

The General section contains these options:

**Automatically Time Save Every *n* Minutes**   Check this checkbox (the default) and either type or select a value (10 minutes is the default) in the text/list box to have Word Pro automatically save your documents. As you work on a document, Word Pro keeps track of the number of minutes since the last save. When the count reaches the minutes specified and you pause in your work, Word Pro saves the document.

**Auto Back Up Documents (.BAK)**   Check this checkbox to create a backup file, with a BAK extension, whenever you save a document. The default is a cleared checkbox.

**Disable**   From this drop-down list box, check the features that you would like to disable. Items preceded with a checkmark are disabled.

**Keyboard**   From this drop-down list box, check the keyboard changes affected by the language that you are using. The default is No Changes.

**Load Word Pro Maximized**   Check this checkbox (the default) to start Word Pro in a maximized window.

**Load Files Maximized**   Check this checkbox (the default) to load files in maximized windows.

**Load in Clean Screen View**   Check this checkbox to start Word Pro using the Clean Screen options that you selected in the View Preferences dialog box. The default is a cleared checkbox.

**Show File New Dialog Box**   Check this checkbox to display the File New dialog box when you choose File ➤ New. If you clear this checkbox, Word Pro opens a new empty document instead.

**Undo Levels**   Open this drop-down list box to specify the number of actions that Word Pro will go back to undo. The default is 20 levels. To undo an action, Word Pro must save the prior settings in a storage area (buffer). So, for every undo level, Word Pro must set aside a buffer. For this reason, when you select more levels, Word Pro's processing speed slows.

**Recent Files**     Type or select a value from 0 to 5 to set the number of recent files to be displayed at the bottom of the File menu. The default is 4. To open one of the files on the File menu, simply click on the filename or type the underlined number preceding the filename.

**Measure In**     From this drop-down list box, select the unit of measure to be used as the default. You can select Inches, Centimeters, Picas, or Points.

**Markup Options**     Click on this button to open the Markup Options for *user name* dialog box, with which you can specify the look of newly inserted text, deletions, and comments.

The Locations section shows the default locations of documents, SmartMaster templates, SmartIcons, backup files, user dictionaries, glossaries, and scripts. To change a location, simply overtype the current path with the new path. You can click on the Browse button to choose folders and subfolders that make up a path. Other options in this section are:

**Use Working Directory**     Check this checkbox to use the folder in which you are currently working to save files and as the starting point for opening other files. A cleared checkbox (the default) uses the folders and subfolders indicated in the text boxes in this section.

**Use Working Type**     Check this checkbox to use the file type with which you are currently working when saving and opening files. A cleared checkbox (the default) uses the Lotus Word Pro (LWP) file type.

**Retain Name of Imported Files**     Check this checkbox (the default) to keep the complete name and extension of files that you import from other applications.

The Default Files section shows the default names of the plain Smart-Master document, the user dictionaries, the glossary file, and the file type. To change a path and/or name, simply overtype the current path and name with the new path and name. You can click on the Browse button to choose folders and subfolders that make up a path.

The Personal section, with which Word Pro can fill in Click Here boxes in documents, contains these options:

**User Name**    Type the name of the individual who uses this copy of Word Pro. This name is the one that is "stamped" in Word Pro (for example, in Notes and in some Word Pro templates). The default is the name entered at installation.

**Initials**    Type the initials (a maximum of six characters) to be inserted on notes and comments. The default is the first letter of every part (for example, first name, middle initial, and last name) of the name entered at installation.

**Title**    Type the title of the individual who uses this copy of Word Pro.

**Company**    Type the company name of the individual who uses this copy of Word Pro. The default is the name entered at installation.

**Address** *n*    Type one, two, or three address lines.

**Post Code**    Type the postal code or zip code.

**Phone**    Type the voice telephone number.

**Fax**    Type the fax telephone number.

**E-Mail**    Type the e-mail address of the individual who uses this copy of Word Pro.

**Other Personal Data**    Type a maximum of four lines of personal information.

## ▶ *Changing View Preferences*

Choose View ➤ Set View Preferences or click on the View Preferences SmartIcon to open the View Preferences dialog box, in which you can specify document-viewing options in four sections: Show, Zoom, Outline, and Clean Screen.

The Show section contains these options:

**Show Marks**    From this drop-down list box, check entries to display marks (All, Tabs, Returns, Rulers, Page Breaks, Section Breaks, Column Breaks, Bookmarks, OLE/DDE Marks, New Page Styles, Comment Marks, and Anchors) in documents.

**Show Ruler**    Check this checkbox to display a horizontal ruler in the application window. The default is a cleared checkbox, that is, a hidden ruler.

**Show Vertical Ruler**    Check this checkbox to display a vertical ruler in the application window. The default is a cleared checkbox.

**Show Margin Guides**    Check this checkbox (the default) to display vertical lines that mark the margins of the document.

**Show Margins in Color**    Check this checkbox to display the margins in a color or with a pattern. The default is a cleared checkbox.

**Show Parallel Column Grid Lines**    Check this checkbox to display vertical lines that mark the borders of columns. The default is a cleared checkbox.

**Show Table Row/Column Headings**    Check this checkbox to show row and column headings (such as spreadsheet labels) in a table when you are editing it. The default is a cleared checkbox.

**Show Table Guides**    Check this checkbox (the default) to show the gridlines marking the borders of cells in a table.

**Show Page Gauge**    Check this checkbox (the default) to show a page location indicator in the right margin when you drag the scroll box in the vertical scroll bar.

**Show Graphics**    Check this checkbox (the default) to display pictures in frames. If you clear this checkbox, Word Pro displays a frame but not the picture within.

**Show Divider Tabs**    Check this checkbox to display division divider tabs. The default is a cleared checkbox.

**Show Click Here Blocks**    Check this checkbox (the default) to display Click Here Blocks in which you can insert information or graphics in a document.

**Show Misspelled Words**    Check this checkbox to highlight words not found in the dictionary. The default is a cleared checkbox.

**Make Default**    Check this checkbox (the default) to make the current options the default.

The Zoom section contains these options:

**Show Draft**    Check this checkbox to view your document in draft view, which shows some text formatting but does not include page breaks, headers, footers, and some graphics. The default is a cleared checkbox.

**Zoom Level**    Click on this option button (the default) and select a zoom level from the drop-down list box. The default zoom level is 100%.

**Custom Level**    Select a value to set the custom view to a value from 10% to 400%. The default is 91%. Then when you choose View ➤ Zoom To ➤ Custom Level, Word Pro zooms the document to the specified value.

**View to Show Multiple Pages**    Click on this option button and select from 2 (the default) to 20 pages displayed on the desktop at one time.

The Outline section contains these options:

**Show Outline**    Check this checkbox to display documents in outline view.

**Show Outline Buttons**    Check this checkbox (the default) to display buttons representing the division or outline level of each paragraph in the document.

**Show Level Indents**    Check this checkbox (the default) to indent each paragraph by its outline level.

**Show Outline Button for Headings Only**    Check this checkbox to display outline buttons for paragraphs with heading styles only. The default is a cleared checkbox.

**Show Only Headings When Collapsed to Level**    Check this checkbox to display headings only when the document is fully collapsed. The default is a cleared checkbox.

**Wrap within Window**    Check this checkbox (the default) to wrap the document text so that it is all visible within the work area.

**Quick Outline Setup Using Paragraph Styles**    Click on this button to open the Set Outline Style Sequences dialog box, with which you can specify outline sequences.

The Clean Screen section contains options with which you can display (a checked checkbox) or hide (a cleared checkbox) screen elements when you choose View ➤ Show/Hide ➤ Clean Screen. You can show or hide these elements: the title bar, menu bar, SmartIcons bars, status bar, horizontal and vertical scroll bars, and the return icon on which you click to end the Clean Screen display and return to the standard Word Pro desktop.

# ▶ ▶ *Changing Your Approach Environment*

In Approach, you can define preferences by choosing File ➤ User Setup ➤ Approach Preferences. This opens the Approach Preferences dialog box, which contains seven sections: Display, Order, Password, Dialer, Database, Index, and General.

The Display section contains these options:

**SmartIcons**    Check this checkbox (the default) to display the SmartIcons bar on the Approach window.

**Status Bar**    Check this checkbox (the default) to display the Status bar at the bottom of the Approach window.

**Action Bar**    Check this checkbox (the default) to display the action bar under the SmartIcons bar.

**View Tabs**    Check this checkbox (the default) to display the view tabs right below the SmartIcons bar on the Approach window.

**Title Bar Help**    Check this checkbox (the default) to display in the title bar a short description of the selected menu or command.

**Welcome Dialog**    Check this checkbox (the default) to display a Welcome dialog box when you first start Approach.

**Report Summaries**    Check this checkbox (the default) to display summaries when viewing a report in the Design or Print Preview environment. Note that you must have also chosen View ► Show Data.

**Data**    Check this checkbox (the default) to show your data in the Design environment.

**Rulers**    Check this checkbox to display the rulers in the Design environment. The default is a cleared checkbox.

**Add Field Dialog**    Check this checkbox to display the Add Field dialog box in the Design Environment. The default is a cleared checkbox.

**Tools Palette**    Check this checkbox (the default) to display the drawing tools palette in the Design Environment.

**Custom Controls**    Click on this button to open the Custom Controls dialog box in which you can select controls to add to the tools palette.

**Show Grid**    Check this checkbox (the default) to show the grid in the Design environment.

**Units**    Open this drop-down list box to select the unit of measure: inches (the default) or centimeters.

**Snap to Grid**    Check this checkbox to have graphic elements snap to the grid when you move or create them. The default is a cleared checkbox.

**Width**    Click on this drop-down list box to choose the width of the grid (in inches): $\frac{1}{16}$, $\frac{1}{12}$ (the default), $\frac{1}{8}$, $\frac{1}{4}$, or $\frac{1}{2}$. If you choose a small width measurement, you'll be able to fine-tune the positions of elements on forms.

**Default Style**    Click on this button to open the Define Style dialog box in which you can specify default font, lines and color, label, picture, and background options.

**Save Default**    Click on this button to save these settings as the new defaults. Approach saves the settings to the APPROACH.INI initialization file. Clicking on OK without clicking on Save Default uses the defaults only in the current file.

The Order section contains these options:

**Maintain Default Sort For**     Open this drop-down list box and select the database affected by changes in order.

**Fields**     Select a sort field from this scroll box.

**Add**     Click on this button to add the selected sort field to the Fields to Sort on box.

**Remove**     Click on this button to remove the selected field from the Fields to Sort on box.

**Clear All**     Click on this button to clear all the fields from the Fields to Sort on box.

**Sort Order**     From this drop-down list box, select the default sort order: Ascending (from A to Z) or Descending (from Z to A). Ascending is the default.

**Fields to Sort On**     A box containing selected sort fields.

The Password section contains these options:

**Database**     Open this drop-down list box and select a database, if needed.

**Read/Write Password**     To define a read/write password for this database, check the checkbox and type a password in the text box. Retype the password in the Confirm Password dialog box; then click on OK.

**Read-Only Password**     To define a read-only password for this database, check the checkbox and type a password in the text box. Retype the password in the Confirm Password dialog box; then click on OK.

**TeamSecurity**     Click on this button to open the TeamSecurity dialog box in which you can assign access rights for the selected database.

The Dialer section contains these options:

**Modem Port**     Open this drop-down list box and select the communications port to which your modem is connected.

**Baud Rate**    Open this drop-down list box and select your modem's baud rate.

**Dial Prefix**    In this text box, type the code for your dial prefix, or accept the default code.

**Dial Suffix**    In this text box, type the code for your dial suffix, or accept the default code.

**Hangup**    In this text box, type the code to "hang up" the modem, or accept the default code.

**Initialize**    In this text box, type the code to initialize the modem, or accept the default code.

**Access Code**    In this text box, type the access code to dial out, or accept the default code.

**Do Not Dial**    In this text box, type the code that you want to use to stop dialing.

**Tone**    Click on this option button (the default) if your telephone is the touch-tone type.

**Pulse**    Click on this option button if your telephone is the pulse type.

The Database section contains these options:

**Database**    Open this drop-down list box and select the database to which you will apply changes to the defaults. The current database is already selected.

**Make All Fields in Database Read-Only**    Check this checkbox to make all the fields in the selected database read-only. This prevents others from editing your work. The default is a cleared checkbox.

**DOS or OS/2 (PC-8)**    Check this option to use characters from the PC-8 character set.

**Windows (ANSI)**    Check this option (the default) to use characters from the ANSI character set furnished with Windows.

**Compress**    Click on this button to compress the selected database.

The Index section contains these options:

**Database**    Open this drop-down list box and select the database to which you will apply changes to the defaults. The current database is already selected.

**Add Index**    Click on this button to add the selected index to the current database in order to maintain it for either dBASE or FoxPro. This button does not always appear in this dialog box.

**Close Index**    Click on this button to close the selected index and no longer maintain it for either dBASE or FoxPro.

The General section contains these options:

**Calculated Fields in the Join Dialog**    Check this checkbox to display calculated fields in the Join dialog box when you are joining databases. The default is a cleared checkbox.

**Add Field Dialog after Creating New Fields**    Check this checkbox (the default) to display the Add Field dialog box after you add a new field to a database.

**Cancel Macro Dialog When Running Macros**    Check this checkbox to display the Cancel Macro dialog box while you are running a macro. The default is a cleared checkbox.

**Use Enter Key to Move between Fields**    Check this checkbox to be able to use the Enter key in the same way that you use the Tab key to move from field to field. The default is a cleared checkbox.

**Expand Drop-Down Lists Automatically**    Check this checkbox to have Approach open drop-down lists when you tab into fields with drop-down list boxes. The default is a cleared checkbox.

**Download Data before Print Preview**    Check this checkbox to have Approach download a copy of the current database to your hard drive whenever you go to the Print Preview environment. The default is a cleared checkbox.

**Lock Records Using Optimistic Record Locking**    Check this checkbox (the default) to allow simultaneous editing by individuals on a networked version of Approach. When two users work on the same record, Approach allows the first user to save and then alerts the second user that someone has just changed the record and asks whether he or she wants to overwrite those changes.

**Default Directories**     Click on this button to specify a default working directory and a default SmartMaster directory.

# ▶▶ *Changing Your Freelance Graphics Environment*

In Freelance Graphics, you can determine the look of the application window and how your presentation pages appear when you first start Freelance Graphics. You can also specify save, undo, drawing tools, and other options. In addition, you can specify the unit of measure, select grid options, and select certain formats.

## ▶ *Changing User Setup*

Choose File ▶ User Setup ▶ Freelance Preferences to open the Freelance Graphics Preferences dialog box, which provides these options:

**Skip the Standard Startup Dialogs and Bring Up a Blank Page with No Look (Blank Background)**     Check this checkbox to start Freelance Graphics without displaying the opening dialog boxes. The default is a cleared checkbox.

**Startup View**     Click on an option button in this group to open Freelance Graphics in a particular view: Current Page (Full Page), Page Sorter, or Outliner. Current Page is the default.

**Replicate**     Click on an option button in this group to indicate the position of a replicated object; click on Place Copy on Original to place the replicated object exactly on top of the original object, or click on Offset Copy from Original (the default) to place the replicated object so that you can see both the replicated and original objects.

**Drawing Tools**     In this group, click on the Keep Tool Active option button to keep active the drawing tool that you selected, or click on the Revert to Pointer option button (the default) to activate the pointer tool.

**Color Chooser**   In this group, click on the Standard Chooser option button (the default) to select a two-section color palette and library, or click on the Designer's Chooser option button to select a three-section color selection, color palette, and library.

**Save**   Click on an option button in this group to indicate the way that you want to save files. Click on Replace (the default) to replace the prior version of this file when you save. Click on Backup to save the current version and save the prior version as a backup file. Click on Confirm to have Freelance Graphics prompt you to replace or back up the file or to cancel the save process.

**Auto Timed Save**   Check this checkbox and either type or select a value to have Freelance Graphics automatically save the current file every 1 to 99 minutes, with a default of 10 minutes. The default is a cleared checkbox.

**Recent Files**   Check this checkbox, (the default), and either type or select a value from 1 to 5 (the default) to set the number of recent files to be displayed at the bottom of the File menu. To open one of the files on the File menu, click on the filename or type the underlined number preceding the filename.

**Disable Black & White Palettes**   Check this checkbox to use the Microsoft Windows black and white options for printing on a black and white printer or other printing device. The default is a cleared checkbox, or the Freelance Graphics color options are used.

**Keep Text Overrides When Changing a Look**   Check this checkbox to keep the changes that you have made to the text in a presentation when you change to another SmartMaster. The default is a cleared checkbox.

**Scanning Speed**   Type the number of seconds with which you can view objects when you have clicked on the Scan button. Valid values range from 0.1 to 100 seconds; the default is 1 second.

**File Locations**   Click on this button to open the File Locations dialog box in which you can change the default location of presentations, SmartMaster files, and backup files.

**Undo**   Click on the Enable (the default) or Disable option button to turn on or off Edit ➤ Undo.

# ▶ Changing the Unit of Measure and Specifying Grid Options

Choose View ➤ Set Units & Grids to open the Set Units & Grids dialog box, in which you can change your unit of measure and specify grid options. The options in this dialog box are:

**Units**    Click on an option button in this group to select the default unit of measure: Inches [System] (the default), Centimeters, Inches, Millimeters, Picas, or Points.

**Display Grid**    Check this checkbox to display the grid, which allows you to align objects on presentation pages. The default is a cleared checkbox.

**Snap to Grid**    Check this checkbox (or press Shift+F7) to place objects on the grid lines as you add them to the page. Objects already on the page do not snap to the grid after you select this option; you must move them. The default is a cleared checkbox.

**Horizontal Space**    Type a value for the measurement between horizontal dots on the grid. The default value is 0.2 inches or the equivalent for your default unit of measure.

**Vertical Space**    Type a value for the measurement between vertical dots on the grid. The default value is 0.2 inches or the equivalent for your default unit of measure.

# ▶ Changing View Preferences

Choose View ➤ Set View Preferences to open the Set View Preferences dialog box, from which you can choose the following options:

**Show Page Borders**    In this group, click on one of three option buttons: selecting Recommended Drawing Area displays a border indicating the margins; Printable Area displays a border indicating the area that your current printer driver can print; and None (the default) does not display any border.

**Coordinates**    Check this checkbox, the default, to display X and Y coordinates in the edit line, between the menu bar and SmartIcons.

**Drawing Ruler** Check this checkbox to display horizontal and vertical rulers using the default unit of measure. The default is a cleared checkbox.

**Text Block Ruler** Check this checkbox to display a ruler within an open text block box. The default is a cleared checkbox.

**Cursor Size** Choose Big Crosshair or Small Crosshair (the default) for drawing on a presentation page. Press Shift+F4 to switch between big and small crosshairs.

# ▶▶ *Changing Your Organizer Environment*

In Organizer, you can change the look of the notebook—the size of section tabs, the color of the notebook cover and inside tab pages—and you can select display preferences.

## ▶ *Changing Organizer Preferences*

Choose File ➤ User Setup ➤ Organizer Preferences to open the Organizer Preferences dialog box, which provides four sections: Default File, Environment, Folders, and Save.

The Default File section contains these options:

**Automatically Open** Click on this option button and select an Organizer file to automatically open when you start Organizer. Click on the Browse button to find the file, if needed.

**Always Start with a New Organizer File** Click on this option button (the default) to open a new Organizer file when you start Organizer. Click on the Browse button to find the file, if needed.

**Base New Organizers On** In this text box, type the name of the existing Organizer file on which you want to base new files.

The Environment section contains these options:

**Clock & Today's Date**    Check this checkbox (the default) to display the time and date in the application window.

**Animated Page Turn**    Check this checkbox (the default) to animate the page turn.

**Display Missed Alarms**    Check this checkbox (the default) to have Organizer display any alarms that have been triggered since you last exited Organizer.

**Mouse Pointer**    In this group, click on the Plain option button to display monochrome mouse pointers, click on the Color option button (the default) to display colorful mouse pointers, or click on Animated to display some animated mouse pointers.

**Favorite Alarm Tune**    From this drop-down list box, select from many alarm tunes.

**Sound**    From this scroll box, select a sound to associate with a particular event.

**Play**    Click on this button to play the selected sound.

**Stop**    Click on this button to stop playing the selected sound.

**Sounds**    Click on this button to open the Sounds dialog box so that you can modify Windows sounds.

**Mute Organizer Sounds**    Check this checkbox to turn off sounds in Organizer. The default is a cleared checkbox.

**Week Starts On**    From this drop-down list box, select the day (Sunday or Monday) on which your Organizer week will start. This affects the display of the annual calendar.

The Folders section shows the default locations of the Organizer files, paper layouts, custom SmartIcons, and backup files. To change a path and/or name, simply overtype the current path and name with the new path and name. You can click on the Browse button to choose folders and subfolders that make up a path.

The Save section contains these options:

**After Each Change**    Click on this option button to save after every editing change you make.

**Every *n* Minutes**    Click on this option button to automatically save the file every *n* minutes.

**Ask for Confirmation First**    If you check the checkbox, Organizer prompts you before an automatic save.

**Only When Told**    Click on this option button to save only when you want.

**Create Backup When Opened**    Check this checkbox to have Organizer save the previously saved version of the file as a backup whenever you save this version of the file. Organizer does not allow you to check this checkbox if you select After Each Change as your save option. The default is a cleared checkbox.

**Make Backup Now**    Click on this button to back up the Organizer file.

▶▶ **N O T E**

> The options in the Save section of the Organizer Preferences dialog box are not available until you have saved the current file.

## ▶ *Changing Section Preferences*

You can change preferences for each section by opening the View menu and choosing the bottom command from the menu (Calendar Preferences, To Do Preferences, Address Preferences, Calls Preferences, Planner Preferences, Notepad Preferences, or Anniversary Preferences). In the resulting dialog box, select options that make Organizer easier to use.

### *Calendar Preferences*

The Calendar Preferences dialog box contains these options:

**View**    Click on an option button in this group to select the way in which you view this section when you start Organizer. Your choices are Day per Page, Work Week, Week per Page, or Month.

**Options**    In this group, select options or check or clear checkboxes to select the look of a page. You can choose a starting and ending hour, time slots (from 5 to 60 minutes), and the default duration (from 5 to 60 minutes) for an activity, and you can show icons representing activities, conflicting appointments, and the time tracker. You can include weekends in a search and can turn to an entry that you just created or edited.

**Show**    In this group, select checkboxes and fill in a text box to select the look of an entry. You can display the end time, duration, categories, and cost code for an entry. You can display all or some lines of a description.

## To Do Preferences

The To Do Preferences dialog box contains these options:

**View**    Click on an option button in this group to select the way in which you view this section when you start Organizer. Your choices are Priority, Status, Start Date, Category, or Due Date or Completion Date.

**Options**    In this group, select options or check or clear checkboxes to select the look of a page. You can choose a starting heading or priority code, and you can show page tabs, icons representing the type of activity, and completed tasks. You can delete a task when it's completed, and you can turn to an entry that you just created or edited.

**Show**    In this group, select checkboxes and fill in a text box to select the look of an entry. You can display the start date, due date, completed date, categories, and cost code for an entry. You can display all or some lines of a description.

**Status Color**    In this group, select from drop-down palettes to change the color of a task by status: Overdue, Current, Future, and Completed.

## Address Preferences

The Address Preferences dialog box contains these options:

**View**    Click on an option button in this group to select the way in which you view this section when you start Organizer. Your choices are All, Address, Contact, and Phone.

**Options**    In this group, select options or check or clear checkboxes to select the look of a page. You can choose whether the Business, Home, or the Selected information is displayed, and you can select the location of the next heading on a page. You can show or hide address tabs, an index line, and an icon indicating that an address is locked. You can choose to turn to an entry that you just created or edited.

**Default Envelope/Label Format**    From this drop-down list box, select the number representing the format of an envelope. Choose Format 1 to print an envelope to be mailed within the United States, Canada, or Australia. To identify other formats, refer to the "Changing Preferences in Address" topic in the help facility.

**Sort By**    In this group, select an option button, and optionally a field, to select the way in which the address book is sorted.

**Fields**    Click on this button to open the Field Labels dialog box to edit field names.

## Calls Preferences

The Calls Preferences dialog box contains these options:

**View**    Click on an option button in this group to select the way in which you view this section when you start Organizer. Your choices are Person, Company, Date, and Category, or Status, Number, or Incomplete.

**Options**    In this group, select options or check or clear checkboxes to select the look of a page. You can choose the way in which you display the next heading, whether to show page tabs, and show completed calls. You can show icons representing activities, and you can turn to an entry that you just created or edited.

**Show**    In this group, select checkboxes and fill in a text/list box to select the look of an entry. You can display the name, company, status, categories, number, date and time, and cost code for an entry. You can display all or some lines of a description.

## Planner Preferences

The Planner Preferences dialog box contains these options:

**View**    Click on an option button in this group to select the way in which you view this section when you start Organizer. Your choices are Quarter or Year.

**Options**    In this group, select options or check or clear checkboxes to select the look of a page. You can choose a starting and ending hour, show or hide the key, automatically unfold the planner, and turn to an entry that you just created or edited.

**Key**    Click on this button to open the Planner Key dialog box in which you can change the name of an existing key or type a new key name.

## Notepad Preferences

The Notepad Preferences dialog box contains these options:

**View**    Click on an option button in this group to select the way in which you view this section when you start Organizer. Your choices are Page Number, Title, Date, and Category.

**Options**    In this group, select options or check or clear checkboxes to select the look of a page. You can choose how to start a chapter, how to display the table of contents, and how to number pages. You can show icons representing activities, and you can turn to an entry that you just created or edited.

**Show**    In this group, select checkboxes and fill in a text box to select the look of an entry. You can display the Title and Categories.

### Anniversary Preferences

The Anniversary Preferences dialog box contains these options:

**View**    Click on an option button in this group to select the way in which you view this section when you start Organizer. Your choices are Month, Year, Zodiac, and Category.

**Options**    In this group, select options or check or clear checkboxes to select the look of a page. You can choose the way in which you start headings and whether to show page tabs. You can show icons representing activities, select a page color, and turn to an entry that you just created or edited.

**Show**    In this group, select checkboxes and fill in a text box to select the look of an entry. You can display the date, categories, and cost code for an entry. You can display all or some lines of a description.

## ► Changing the Contents and Look of Your Organizer

Choose Section ➤ Customize to open the Customize dialog box, in which you can define new sections, rename and delete existing sections, include sections from other Organizer files, change the look of the Organizer binder, and select a font. The Customize dialog box contains three sections: Sections, Book, and Fonts.

The Sections section contains these options:

**Tabs**    Click on a tab name to perform an action on it.

- To move it above the previous tab on the list, click on Up. Up is inactive if the first section is selected.
- To move it below the next tab on the list, click on Down. Down is inactive if the last section is selected.
- To change its color, open the Color drop-down list box and make a selection.

**Add**    Click on this button to open the Add New Section dialog box to add and name a new section. For example, you can add a second Calendar section and use it as a diary.

**Rename**     Click on this button to open the Rename Section dialog box in which you can type a new name. This option is not available for renaming the front page or back page of the organizer.

**Remove**     Click on this button to remove the selected section. When the message box appears, click on Yes to remove the section, or click on No to return to the Customize dialog box without deleting. This option is not available for renaming the front page or back page of the organizer.

**Include**     Click on this button to open the Include Section dialog box so that you can include a section from another Organizer file.

**Picture**     Click on this button to open the Picture - *section* dialog box so that you can insert a picture in the selected section.

**Color**     Choose a tab color for the selected section from this drop-down palatte.

The Book section contains these options:

**Color**     Open this drop-down list box to select a color for the cover of the organizer.

**Texture**     Open this drop-down list box to select a texture for the cover of the organizer.

**Size to Name**     Check this checkbox (the default) to adjust the size of a tab to the size of its name.

**Overlap by *n*%**     Check this checkbox (the default) and type a value from 0 to 100 in the text box. The default is 15%.

**Width**     From this drop-down list box, select the width of the tabs: Narrow, Medium (the default), or Wide.

**Open To**     From this drop-down list box, select the section or page to turn to when you start Organizer. Today (today's date in the Calendar) is the default.

The Fonts section contains these options:

**Default**     Click on this option button (the default) to select an 8-point display font. To see the effects of your selection, look at the sample.

**Medium**     Click on this option button to select a 10-point display font. To see the effects of your selection, look at the sample.

**Large**     Click on this option button to select a 12-point display font. To see the effects of your selection, look at the sample.

**Scale with Window Size**     Check this checkbox to keep the text in height-width proportion. The default is a cleared checkbox.

# ▶▶ *Customizing SmartIcons*                                    ▶ ▶

In every SmartSuite application, you can change the displayed Smart-Icons. You can add or remove SmartIcons, change their location on the application window, and change their size. In fact, you can even create your own SmartIcons. For more information about the topics covered in this section, refer to your SmartSuite documentation or select "SmartIcons" from the Help facility's Index window.

To display a dialog box in which you can customize SmartIcons, either choose File ➤ User Setup ➤ SmartIcons Setup, or click on a small downward-pointing arrow in the SmartIcons bar and choose SmartIcons Setup.

## ▶ *Changing SmartIcon Sets*

Add a SmartIcon to an existing set by selecting the set from the Bar Name drop-down list box. Then drag an icon from the Available Icons scroll box to the SmartIcons bar at the top of the dialog box.

▶▶**T I P**

> **You can space icons by dragging a Spacer between them. The spacer is the first Icon in the Available Icons scroll box. This action allows you to separate unrelated buttons.**

To remove a SmartIcon from the set, drag it off the set. (You don't need to drag it back to its original position in the Available Icons scroll box.) To move a SmartIcon to another location on its bar, simply drag it to its new position on the bar.

To save a SmartIcons set, click on the Save Set button. In the Save Set of SmartIcons dialog box, name the set and its filename, and click on OK.

To delete a SmartIcons set, click on the Delete Set button. In the Delete Sets dialog box, select the set to be deleted, click on OK, and respond to the Warning message box.

## ▶ Changing the Size of SmartIcons

Open the Icon Size drop-down list box to select the icon size. Selecting Large provides the advantage of a display that is easier to see, but there is room for fewer SmartIcons on a bar. Selecting Regular, the default, enables the display of 20 or more SmartIcons. The number of SmartIcons actually displayed in the application window depends on the size of the window itself. (There is no Small option.)

## ▶ Moving a SmartIcons Bar

To move a SmartIcons bar, follow these steps:

1. Move the mouse pointer under a downward-pointing arrow on the SmartIcons bar. The mouse pointer cursor changes to a hand.

2. Drag the bar to its new location:

   • If you drag the bar to the bottom, the left side, or the right side of the desktop, it is long and narrow.

   • If you drag the bar within the work area, it floats, and you can adjust its borders by dragging.

## ▶ Hiding and Revealing a SmartIcons Bar

The SmartIcons bar is actually made up of one, two, or more bars, which you can hide or display individually. To display the entire SmartIcons bar (if it is hidden), choose View ➤ Show SmartIcons (except in Organizer). To hide the entire SmartIcons bar (if it is displayed), choose View ➤ Hide SmartIcons. You can also hide the SmartIcons bar by clicking on any downward-pointing arrow on the SmartIcons bar and choosing Hide All SmartIcons.

Many SmartIcons bars contain one, two, or three downward-pointing arrows. Each arrow indicates the beginning of a context SmartIcons bar related to a certain activity. To hide or display a particular Smart-Icons bar, click on the downward-pointing arrow to the left of the first SmartIcon on the bar. From the shortcut menu, choose Hide This Bar of SmartIcons.

At the bottom of the SmartIcons shortcut menu are names of particular SmartIcons bars that are associated with the current bar. A checkmark preceding a name indicates that the bar is on display. To display a hidden bar, click on its name on the shortcut menu. To hide a displayed bar, click on its name.

Customizing
SmartSuite

App.
B

▶ ▶ **APPENDIX**

# C

# SmartSuite
# and the Internet

———

**A**ll SmartSuite applications include Internet features. From all applications you can access Lotus corporate and support sites on the World Wide Web and can download files using FTP (File Transfer Protocol). Using features built into some applications, you can save files to the Internet, publish pages to the World Wide Web, and open a file on the Internet. This appendix is a quick reference to SmartSuite Internet features. For additional information on using the SmartSuite Internet features, start at the "Internet" topic in each application's help facility.

To fully use the SmartSuite Internet features, you must have a way to dial in—either via a direct connection or via an Internet service provider. For example, in Windows 95, you can define a Dial-Up Networking connection to your provider. SmartSuite applications will then dial in to your provider and the Internet using your connection information. You should also have installed an Internet browser to be able to access the Lotus home page, support home page, and support FTP site.

The topics covered in this appendix are:

- Specifying Internet FTP Options
- Specifying HTML Import and Export Options
- Opening a File from the Internet
- Saving a File to the Internet
- Publishing a File on the Internet
- Providing Host Information
- Getting Internet Support from Lotus
- Creating a Web Page using Word Pro

# ▶▶ *Specifying Internet FTP Options*

 You can automatically connect to an FTP site by specifying options in the Internet Options dialog box. Click on the Internet Options Smart-Icon. Then, choose File ➤ Internet ➤ FTP Connection Setup. The options in the FTP Connection Setup dialog box are:

**Auto Connect Open from Internet**  Check this checkbox to automatically log on to a server when you choose File ➤ Internet ➤ Open from Internet. The default is a cleared checkbox.

**Auto Connect Save to Internet**  Check this checkbox to automatically log on to a server when you choose File ➤ Internet ➤ Save to Internet. The default is a cleared checkbox.

**FTP Server to Connect To**  From this drop-down list box (which appears twice in this dialog box), select the FTP server to which you want to connect.

**Capture Record of Open from Internet**  Check this checkbox to keep a log of the files that you open from the Internet. The default is a cleared checkbox.

**Hosts**  Click on this button to open the FTP Hosts dialog box in which you can specify connection information for a host server. For more information about this dialog box, see the "Providing Host Information" section on a following page.

# ▶▶ *Specifying HTML Import and Export Options*

To specify import and export options for HTML files in Word Pro, choose File ➤ Internet ➤ HTML Import/Export Options. Word Pro opens the HTML Import/Export Options dialog box. The options in this dialog box are:

**Always Display This Dialog Box before Importing**  Check this checkbox (the default) to open the HTML Import/Export Options dialog box so that you can change import options.

SmartSuite and the Internet

▶▶
App.
C

**Import As Source Code**    Check this checkbox to import a source code version of the HTML document. The default is a cleared checkbox.

**Show Unknown Tags in Comment Notes**    Check this checkbox (the default) to show tags that do not conform to the selected HTML standard as comments.

**Download Graphics from the Internet**    Check this checkbox (the default) to automatically download graphics associated with the HTML document when importing the document.

**Embed Graphics in Document**    Check this checkbox (the default) to store the graphics files with the HTML document with which they are associated.

**Character Encoding**    From this drop-down list box, select the special character set that your system supports.

**Always Display This Dialog Box before Exporting**    Check this checkbox (the default) to open the HTML Import/Export Options dialog box so that you can change export options.

**Copy Linked Graphics When Saving Locally**    Check this checkbox (the default) to copy graphic files when saving on your computer or network.

**Path of Graphics When Saving to Internet**    In this group, click on an option button to specify the path for graphic files associated with the HTML document to be exported. Click on Same As Document to use the same path as the document; click on Specify a Single Path for All Graphics to specify that all graphics remain in the same folder; or click on Specify a Path for Each Graphic to specify a particular path for each graphic.

# ▶▶ Opening a File from the Internet

You can use the same command to open files from the Internet in 1-2-3, Word Pro, Approach, and Freelance Graphics. Click on the Open a File from the Internet SmartIcon or choose File ➤ Internet ➤ Open from

Internet to open the Open from Internet dialog box. The dialog box options vary depending on the server type. If you select an FTP server, the options are:

**Server Type**    Click on the FTP or WWW option button to indicate the server with which you want to open one or more files.

**FTP Servers**    From this drop-down list box, select the address of the FTP server.

**List by Description**    Check this checkbox (the default) to display a description of the server rather than the name.

**Hosts**    Click on this button to open the FTP Hosts dialog box in which you can specify connection information for a host server. For more information about this dialog box, see the "Providing Host Information" section on a following page.

**Connect**    Click on this button to connect to the Internet.

**Look In**    From this drop-down list box, select the folder or directory in which the file to be opened is located.

**Up One Level**    Click on this button to go to the drive or folder immediately above the current drive or folder.

**New Folder**    Click on this button to create a new folder in the current drive.

**File Name**    In this text box, type the name of the file to be opened.

**List Files of Type**    From this drop-down list box, select the type of file to be opened.

If you select a WWW server, the options are:

**Server Type**    Click on the FTP or WWW option button to indicate the server with which you want to open one or more files.

**File Name**    In this text box/drop-down list box, type or select the name of the file that you want to open.

**Use Proxy**    Check this checkbox to access the Internet through a firewall defined as a proxy server. This option applies to those with networked computers. The default is a cleared checkbox.

**Proxy**    From this drop-down list box, select the address of the proxy server. This option is available only if you check the Use Proxy checkbox.

**Edit Proxies**    Click on this button to open the Edit Proxies dialog box with which you can add or edit the proxy address and the port and specify the default proxy. This option is available only if you check the Use Proxy checkbox.

# ▶▶ *Saving a File to the Internet*

 You can save a file to the Internet in 1-2-3, Word Pro, Approach, and Freelance Graphics. Click on the Save a File to the Internet SmartIcon or choose File ➤ Internet ➤ Save to Internet to open the Save to Internet dialog box.

## ▶ *Saving a File to the Internet in 1-2-3, Word Pro, and Freelance Graphics*

In 1-2-3, Word Pro, and Freelance Graphics, select options in the Save To Internet dialog box. The options in this dialog box are:

**FTP Servers**    From this drop-down list box, select the address of the FTP server.

**List by Description**    Check this checkbox (the default) to display a description of the server rather than the name.

**Hosts**    Click on this button to open the FTP Hosts dialog box in which you can specify connection information for a host server. For more information about this dialog box, see the "Providing Host Information" section on a following page.

**Connect**    Click on this button to connect to the Internet.

**Save In**    From this drop-down list box, select the folder or directory in which the file to be saved is located.

 **Up One Level**    Click on this button to go to the drive or folder immediately above the current drive or folder.

 **New Folder**    Click on this button to create a new folder in the current drive.

**File Name**    In this text box, type the name of the file to be saved.

**Save As Type**    From this drop-down list box, select the type of file to be saved.

**Save HTML Graphics As Files on Server**    Check this checkbox (the default) to also save the graphics associated with this file. This option is available only in Word Pro.

**Save**    Click on this button to save the selected file.

### ▶ Saving a File to the Internet in Approach

In Approach, select options in the Save To Internet dialog box. The options in this dialog box are:

**Current View Only**    Click on this option button to save this view of the current database.

**All of the Views**    Click on this option button to save all views of the current database.

**Include Data From**    From this drop-down list box, choose whether to save the file with all its joined databases (the default) or blank databases, the Found Set of records, or the current record.

## ▶▶ Publishing a File on the Internet

With 1-2-3, Word Pro, Approach, and Freelance Graphics, you can publish files on the World Wide Web. The procedures for publishing in some applications are somewhat different than publishing in others.

### ▶ Publishing a File using 1-2-3

Choose File ➤ Internet ➤ Publish a Range to the Internet to open the first of several dialog boxes. In the first dialog box, select a range and click on Next. In the next, select a table format and click on Next. Then, create a page on which the table will be inserted and click on Next. Finally, preview the page and/or publish it on the Web.

## ► *Publishing a File on the Internet Using Word Pro and Approach*

 Click on the Save to Internet As HTML SmartIcon or choose File ➤ Internet ➤ Publish As Web Page(s). Unless you have checked the Do Not Show Me This Message Again checkbox, Word Pro displays the Publish As Web Page dialog box, which provides an overview of publishing a document as a Web page. You can either read the contents of the dialog box or click on the Help button to access the Word Pro Internet help topics. Click on OK to open the Save to Internet dialog box, which provides these options:

**FTP Servers**     From this drop-down list box, select the address of the FTP server.

**List by Description**     Check this checkbox (the default) to display a description of the server rather than the name.

**Hosts**     Click on this button to open the FTP Hosts dialog box in which you can specify connection information for a host server. For more information about this dialog box, see the "Providing Host Information" section on a following page.

**Save In**     From this drop-down list box, select the address to which you'll publish the file.

 **Up One Level**     Click on this button to go to the drive or folder immediately above the current drive or folder.

 **New Folder**     Click on this button to create a new folder in the current drive.

**File Name**     In this text box, type the name of the file to be saved.

**Save As Type**     From this drop-down list box, select the type of file to be saved.

**Save HTML Graphics As Files on Server**     Check this checkbox (the default) to also save the graphics associated with this file.

**Save**     Click on this button to save the selected file.

## ▶ *Publishing a File on the Internet Using Freelance Graphics*

 Click on the Publish As Web Pages SmartIcon or choose File ➤ Internet ➤ Publish to Web. Unless you have checked the Do Not Show Me This Message Again checkbox, Freelance Graphics opens the Publish to Web Page(s) Instructions dialog box, which provides an overview of publishing a presentation as a Web page. Read the contents of the dialog box and click on OK to open the Publish As Web Page(s) Options dialog box. The options in this dialog box are:

**Movie and Sound Files**    Click on this checkbox to publish movies and sound files along with the presentation. The default is a cleared checkbox.

**A Link to a Copy of the Presentation**    Click on this checkbox to run the presentation on the Web, in Freelance Graphics, or using the Mobile Screen Show Player. The default is a cleared checkbox.

**A Button Linked to the Lotus Home Page**    Click on this checkbox (the default) to add a button that links the presentation to the Lotus home page.

**A Table of Contents with Links to Each Page**    Click on this checkbox (the default) to embed a table of contents with links to each page in the presentation.

**Speaker Notes Appended Below Each Page**    Click on this checkbox (the default) to insert your speaker notes at the bottom of the page to which they are related.

**An E-Mail Address at the Bottom of Each Page**    Click on this checkbox to insert an e-mail address link at the bottom of each page. The default is a cleared checkbox.

**Name**    In this text box, type the name of the individual associated with the e-mail address. This option is available only if you have checked the An E-Mail Address at the Bottom of Each Page checkbox.

**Address**    In this text box, type the e-mail address of the person whose name will appear on the page. This option is available only if you have checked the An E-Mail Address at the Bottom of Each Page checkbox.

SmartSuite and the Internet

▶ ▶

*App.*

**C**

**Resolution**   From this drop-down list box, select the resolution of the presentation's GIF files.

**HTML 2.0**   Check this checkbox to use HTML version 2.0 as your standard for the HTML tags created for the presentation. The default is a cleared checkbox.

**Type of Server**   Click on the CERN or NCSA option button to further choose the HTML version 2.0 standard.

**Netscape Enhanced HTML 2.0**   Check this checkbox (the default) to use Netscape Enhanced HTML version 2.0 as your standard for the HTML tags created for the presentation.

# ►► *Providing Host Information*

You must provide connection information before you can open or save a file using FTP. Click on the Internet Options SmartIcon or choose File ► Internet ► FTP Connection Setup. Then click on the Hosts button to open the FTP Hosts dialog box, which provides these options:

**Host Description**   In this text box/drop-down list box, either type or select a description of the host to which you will connect.

**Host Address**   In this text box, type the URL of the host to which you will connect.

**User ID**   In this text box, type the user ID that you use to access the site. If you have checked the Anonymous FTP checkbox, a SmartSuite application gives you a user ID of anonymous.

**Password**   In this text box, type the password that you use to access the site. If you have checked the Anonymous FTP checkbox, your password is your e-mail address.

**Save Password**   Check this checkbox (the default) to save the password so that you don't have to reenter it each time you access this host.

**Initial Directory at Remote Host**   In this text box, type the directory that you first visit when you access this site.

**Anonymous FTP**   Check this checkbox (the default) to access this FTP site using anonymous FTP (that is, you don't need to provide a special user ID or a special password; your e-mail address is the password).

**Passive (PASV)**   Check this checkbox to access the Internet through a firewall supporting passive transfers. This option applies to those with networked computers. The default is a cleared checkbox.

**Use Proxy**   Check this checkbox to access the Internet through a firewall defined as a proxy server. This option applies to those with networked computers. The default is a cleared checkbox.

**Proxy**   From this drop-down list box, select the address of the proxy server. This option is available only if you check the Use Proxy checkbox.

**Edit Proxies**   Click on this button to open the Edit Proxies dialog box with which you can add or edit the proxy address and port and specify the default proxy. This option is available only if you check the Use Proxy checkbox.

**New**   Click on this button to define a new host.

**Save**   Click on this button to save the host information.

**Delete**   Click on this button to delete information on the selected host.

# ▶▶ *Getting Internet Support from Lotus*

All the SmartSuite Help menus provide three commands with which you can go to Lotus Internet sites without explicitly opening your browser and dialing your provider.

- Click on the Go to Lotus Home Page SmartIcon or choose Help ➤ Lotus Internet Support ➤ Lotus Home Page to go to the Lotus home page (`http://www.lotus.com/`) on the World Wide Web.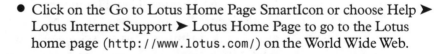

- Click on the Go to Lotus Customer Support Home Page Smart-Icon or choose Help ➤ Lotus Internet Support ➤ Lotus Customer Support to go to the Lotus customer support page (`http://www.support.lotus.com/`) on the World Wide Web.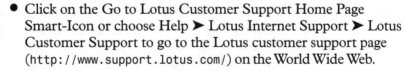

- Click on the Go to Lotus Customer Support FTP Site SmartIcon or choose Help ➤ Lotus Internet Support ➤ Lotus FTP Site to go to the Lotus customer FTP support page (`ftp://ftp.support.lotus.com/`).

# ▶▶ *Creating a Web Page using Word Pro*

You can use Word Pro to create pages for the World Wide Web. Before you get started, it's a good idea to choose File ➤ Internet ➤ Show Web Authoring Tools, which opens a set of buttons with which you can edit and publish the page.

The Web Authoring Tools are:

**Arrows**    Click on an arrow to display the prior or next file.

**Create Link**    After selecting text in the document, click on this button to insert a link using the A tag.

**Edit Link**    After selecting a link in the document, click on this button to change the link URL or the type of link.

**Preview in Browser**    Click on this button to open your default browser and view the document.

**Publish to Internet**    Click on this button to open the Publish As Web Page dialog box from which you can post the page on the Internet. You can also open this dialog box by choosing File ➤ Internet ➤ Publish As Web Page(s).

**Open Web Page**    In this text box, type the Web or FTP address of a file to be opened.

Create a Web page as you would another Word Pro document. Click on the Create a New Document SmartIcon (to create a blank document) or choose File ➤ New Document (either to create a blank document or use a SmartMaster). Although you can start with a blank document, the best way to create a Web page is by using a SmartMaster. Then, the document will have a set of built-in styles, each related to an HTML tag. (To use a style, select text, click on the Style button in the status bar, and choose a style.) Word Pro provides SmartMasters, including background graphics, for corporate and personal pages and for corporate intranets. Once a SmartMaster is onscreen, click on the Click Here blocks and overtype or insert graphics. For more information about Word Pro and the Internet, see the topic "Working with Word Pro and the Internet" in the Word Pro help facility.

# Quick Reference
# to Workgroups

►► ***U**sing* SmartSuite team features, you can exchange messages and files with people whose computers are networked with or attached to yours or, in some cases, to whom you can send a file using e-mail or a floppy disk. Team features include TeamMail, TeamReview, TeamConsolidate, TeamShow, and TeamSecurity. This appendix is a quick reference to and overview of selected SmartSuite Team commands and dialog boxes. For more information about Team features and workgroup computing, see the help facilities for each of the SmartSuite applications.

 ►►**TIP**

**Good starting places in the help systems are the Overview: TeamMail, Overview: TeamReview, Overview: TeamConsolidate, Overview: TeamShow, and Overview: TeamSecurity topics.**

# ►► *TeamMail*

Using TeamMail—available in 1-2-3, Word Pro, Approach, Freelance Graphics, and Organizer—you can send messages, files, and selected data to individuals defined to your e-mail system. To access the Team-Mail feature, click on the Send E-Mail (or New Message or Send Data by Electronic Mail) SmartIcon, choose File ➤ TeamMail in 1-2-3, Word Pro, Freelance Graphics, or Organizer, or choose File ➤

TeamMail ➤ Send New Message in Approach. The options in Team-Mail (or TeamMail for Lotus Freelance in Freelance Graphics) dialog boxes are:

**Approach File With**     Check this checkbox, and from the drop-down list box, select the databases that you want to attach: All data-bases (the default) associated with this database or blank databases. Click on an option button: Current View Only or All of the Views (the default). The default is a cleared checkbox. (Approach)

**Attach Mobile Screen Show Player, Too**     Check this check-box to attach the Mobile Screen Show Player to this message. This checkbox is not available when you have selected the Message Only option button. (Freelance Graphics)

**Current Document, As an Attachment**     Click on this option button to attach the current document to this message. (Word Pro)

**Current Presentation, As an Attachment**     Click on this option button to attach the current presentation to this message. (Freelance Graphics)

**Don't Include Address Entries in Message Body**     Check this checkbox to exclude address entries from the message. (Organizer)

**Message Only**     Click on this option button to send the mes-sage with no attachments. (1-2-3, Word Pro, Freelance Graphics, and Organizer)

**Message with Current Selection's Text As Message Body** Click on this option button to use the current text selection as the message. (Word Pro, Organizer)

**Paste in Picture of the Selection**     Check this checkbox (the default) to paste a picture of the selected range in the message. This checkbox is available only if you have clicked on the Message Only option button. (1-2-3)

**Message with Selected Entries As Message Body**     Click on this option button to use the selected entries as the message. (Organizer)

**People I Select from the Mail Directory**    Click on this option button to distribute the message to selected people from the mail directory selected from the Address Book. (Organizer)

**People from the Selected Addresses**    Click on this option button to distribute the message to selected people from the Address Book. (Organizer)

**Send a Snapshot of the Current View**    Check this checkbox to send a Windows Metafile "picture" of the current view with the message. (Approach)

**Specified Pages, As an Attachment**    Click on this option button to attach selected pages to the message. (Freelance Graphics)

**Workbook with Message**    Click on this option button to attach the current workbook to the message. (1-2-3)

# ▶▶ *TeamReview*

Using TeamReview—a feature in 1-2-3, Word Pro, and Freelance Graphics—members of your team can add comments to a saved file after examining it and send it back to you. Reviewers can add freehand drawings and typed notes to the information but cannot edit or delete the file itself.

## ▶ *TeamReview in Word Pro*

To access the TeamReview feature in Word Pro, either click on the TeamReview SmartIcon, or choose File ▶ TeamReview. Word Pro opens the TeamReview Assistant dialog box, which contains three sections.

The options in the Step 1: Who section of the Word Pro TeamReview Assistant dialog box are:

**Add the People (Editors) Who You Want to Review This Document**    From this list box, select the individuals that you want to review this document.

**Add**    Click on this button to add a reviewer to the reviewer list.

**Remove**    Click on this button to remove a reviewer from the reviewer list.

**Verify Editors By**    From this drop-down list box, select the name by which Word Pro will verify the reviewer: Word Pro User Name, OS Login, or E-mail Login.

**Allow Alternate Verification**    Check this checkbox to enable a custom verification method. This checkbox is active only if you choose OS Login or E-mail Login from the Verify Editors By drop-down list box.

**Back**    Click on this button to move to the previous section of the dialog box. If you are in the first section, this button is dimmed.

**Next**    Click on this button to move to the next section of the dialog box. If you are in the last section, this button is dimmed.

**Done**    Click on this button to indicate that you have completed selecting options and want to distribute the document.

 ▶▶ **N O T E**

> **The Back, Next, Done, Cancel, and Help buttons appear in all three sections of this dialog box.**

The options in the Step 2: What section of the Word Pro TeamReview Assistant dialog box are:

**Set Options for All People to Review and Comment**
Click on this option button to specify the same options for all reviewers. This is the default.

**Set Specific Options for All People Sharing the Document**
Click on this option button to specify certain options for all reviewers of the current document.

**Edits Are**    From this drop-down list box, select whether editing is allowed, or select the version(s) in which editing can take place. You can allow editing in the current version, in a newer version, or in both, or you can not allow editing. This option is available only if you select the Set Specific Options for All People Sharing the Document option button.

**Limited To**   From this drop-down list box, select editing limits: (no limits), all edits marked up, no version creation or review, no editing of named styles, no copying or saving as a new file, and no printing. The default is (no limits). You can select more than one of these options.

**Greeting Will Suggest**   From this drop-down list box, select whether the accompanying greeting informs the editor of the editing limits: (nothing), editing in new version, markup of edits, and review and comment tools. The default is (nothing). You can select more than one of these options.

**Set Specific Options for Specific People**   Click on this option button to set editing limits for certain people.

**Options**   Click on this button to open the TeamSecurity dialog box with which you can specify access rights, editing rights, and other protection. For more information, see the "TeamSecurity" section on a following page.

**Display Greeting with This Text**   Check this checkbox to display a greeting when the reviewer opens the distributed document. If you start filling in the box under this checkbox, Word Pro checks the checkbox. The default is a cleared checkbox.

**Request Editor's Remark on Close**   Check this checkbox to prompt the reviewer for a typed comment when closing the document.

The options in the Step 3: How section of the Word Pro TeamReview Assistant dialog box are:

**Distribute Document By**   From this drop-down list box, select the means of distribution: to a file that you can copy to a disk, to a file on the Internet, or to Notes; or save and send or route using e-mail.

**TeamReview in 1-2-3**   To access the TeamReview Assistant dialog box, choose File ➤ TeamReview. In the dialog box, select a range to be sent and click on OK.

## ▶ *TeamReview in Freelance Graphics*

 To access the TeamReview feature in Freelance Graphics, either click on the TeamReview SmartIcon, or choose File ➤ TeamReview ➤ Distribute for Review. Freelance Graphics opens the TeamReview Instructions dialog box. Click on OK to display the Distribute for TeamReview dialog box.

The options in this dialog box are:

**Distribute Presentation By** From this drop-down list box, select the means of distribution: posting in a Notes database or in a public directory, routing via-email, or saving to floppy disk (the default).

**Path and File Name/Notes Database** In this text box, type the path, including the filename, or the name of the Notes database to which you want to distribute the presentation. This text box is not available if you have chosen routing through e-mail or saving to a floppy disk.

**Notify Reviewers by E-Mail** Check this checkbox to send reviewers notification that you have sent the presentation via e-mail or to a Notes database.

**Reviewer Privileges** Click on an option button to have the reviewers comment or comment and edit the distributed database. Editing requires a user password.

**Browse** Click on this button to find the name of a Notes database to which you want to distribute this file. This button is available only if you will be distributing this file to a Notes database.

# ▶▶ *TeamConsolidate*

With TeamConsolidate, you can split parts of a 1-2-3 workbook or Word Pro document, save them as individual versions or documents, distribute them to members of your team, and get the pieces back again to merge them into a single file. To access the TeamConsolidate feature in Word Pro, for example, either click on the TeamConsolidate SmartIcon, or choose File ➤ TeamConsolidate. The options in the TeamConsolidate dialog box are:

**Select the Files to Compare to Your Current File** Identify the files that you want Word Pro to compare against the current document. You can select from files on your computer, files on the network to which your computer is attached, and files on the Internet.

**Add Files** Click on this button to open the Browse dialog box from which you can select files to compare.

**Remove** Click on this button to remove selected files from the list.

**Internet** Click on this button to display the Open from Internet dialog box from which you can select an Internet file to compare.

**Protect Current Version of This Document?** Click on the Yes option button to consolidate and insert markups into a new version of the file, thereby protecting the current version; click on the No button to consolidate comparisons and insert markups into the current version of the file, thereby overwriting it.

**What Do You Want to Do with the Consolidated Document?** Click on the Leave the Consolidated Document in This File option button to leave the consolidated copy and markups in the current version of the file; click on the Put the Consolidated Document into a Copy of This File button to insert the consolidated copy and markups in a new unnamed and unsaved file.

# ▶▶ *TeamSecurity*

 With TeamSecurity, you can password-protect the current Word Pro document or Approach (APR) file to restrict the files to the original author and selected reviewers and to specify levels of access. To access the TeamMail feature, either click on the TeamSecurity SmartIcon, or choose File ➤ TeamSecurity.

## ▶ *The Word Pro TeamSecurity Dialog Box*

In Word Pro, the TeamSecurity dialog box is composed of three sections: Access, Editing Rights, and Other Protection. The options in the Access section of the TeamSecurity dialog box are:

**Who Can Open (Access) This File** In this group, you can indicate one or more individuals who can open the current file:

**Anyone (Unprotected)** Click on this option button to allow anyone with access to your computer to open the current file. This is the default.

**Anyone with This Password**     Click on this option button to allow anyone with a valid password to open the current file.

**Change**     Click on this button to open the Enter New File Password dialog box in which you can type a password. The Change button is available only if you click on the Anyone with This Password option button.

**Current Editors Only**     Click on this option button to allow only reviewers assigned to this document to open it.

**Original Author Only**     Click on this option button to allow only the original author to open the current document.

**Who Can Open This Dialog, and Change Access, Editing Rights, and Other Protection Options**     In this group, you can indicate one or more individuals who can open the TeamSecurity dialog box and change access rights, editing rights, and other security options:

**Anyone (Unprotected)**     Click on this option button to allow anyone with access to your computer to change security options. This is the default.

**Anyone with This Password**     Click on this option button to allow anyone with a valid password to change security options.

**Change**     Click on this button to open the Enter New File Password dialog box in which you can type a password. The Change button is available only if you click on the Anyone with This Password option button.

**Only**     Click on this option button to make active the drop-down list box from which you can select one individual who can open this dialog box and specify access, editing, and protection rights. The default is the registered user of this version of Word Pro.

**Verify Editors Using**     From this drop-down list box, select the means of verification: the Word Pro user name (the default), the OS login, or the E-mail login.

**Allow Alternate Verification**     Check this checkbox to enable a custom verification method. This checkbox is active only if you choose OS Login or E-mail Login from the Verify Editors by drop-down list box.

The options in the Editing Rights section of the TeamSecurity dialog box are:

**Editor's Name/How They Can Edit This Document**     This scroll box lists the names of the reviewers of this document and current editing rights.

**New Editor**     Click on this button to open the New Editor dialog box with which you can type the name of a new editor for the current document.

**Delete Editor**     Click on this button to delete the selected editor after confirming the deletion.

**Markup**     Click on this button to open the Markup Options for *editorname* dialog box with which you can specify markup options, including text and background color, highlighter/comment color, and markup characteristics for insertions and deletions.

**Edits Are**     From this drop-down list box, select the version(s) in which edits are allowed. You can allow editing in the current version, in a newer version, or both, or you can not allow editing. This option is available only if you select the Set Specific Options for All People Sharing the Document option button.

**Limited to**     From this drop-down list box, select editing limits: (no limits), no version creation or review, no editing of named styles, no copying or saving as a new file, and no printing. The default is (no limits).

**Greeting Will Suggest**     From this drop-down list box, select whether the accompanying greeting informs the editor of the editing limits: (nothing), editing in new version, markup of edits, and review and comment tools. The default is (nothing).

The options in the Other Protection section of the TeamSecurity dialog box are:

**Display All Division Tabs in Document**     Check this checkbox to display all division tabs to anyone accessing the document. The default is a cleared checkbox.

**Protection Settings for Division**     From this drop-down list box, select a division to which you want to apply protection.

**Hide Entire Division**     Check this checkbox to hide the selected division to prevent it from being edited. The default is a cleared checkbox.

**Honor Protection on Frames and Table Cells**     Check this checkbox (the default) to prevent reviewers from changing protected frames and table cells.

**Allow Editing of Protected Text**     Check this checkbox (the default) to allow reviewers to change protected text.

**Show Hidden Text**     Check this checkbox (the default) to display text that has been hidden.

**Disable Version Review**     Check this checkbox to restrict reviewers to viewing the current version of the document only. The default is a cleared checkbox.

**Disable Notes/FX of TeamSecurity Fields**     Check this checkbox to prevent Word Pro from exchanging data in TeamSecurity fields with Notes. The default is a cleared checkbox.

**Require Running of Startup Scripts**     Check this checkbox to run startup scripts associated with the current document when a reviewer opens the document. The default is a cleared checkbox.

**Edit Click Here Block Prompts On-Screen**     Check this checkbox to allow a reviewer to change Click Here Blocks. The default is a cleared checkbox.

## ▶ *The Approach TeamSecurity Dialog Box*

In Approach, the TeamSecurity dialog box consists of one section. The options in the Approach TeamSecurity dialog box are:

**User Privilege Level**     Select one or more user privilege levels and then click on a button to add, delete, change, or copy the security options for that level. You can select from Manager, Designer, Editor, and/or Reader levels.

▶▶ **N O T E**

**To select two or more contiguous levels, click on the first level, press and hold down the Shift key, and click on the last level. Then release the Shift key. To select two or more noncontiguous levels, press and hold down the Ctrl key, and click on each level. Then release the Ctrl key.**

**Edit**    Click on this button to open the Edit TeamSecurity dialog box to edit the settings for the selection in the box. For information about this dialog box, see the following section, "The Approach Edit TeamSecurity Dialog Box."

**New**    Click on this button to open the Edit TeamSecurity dialog box to create new security settings.

**Copy**    Click on this button to open the Edit TeamSecurity dialog box to copy the settings for the selection in the box.

**Delete**    Click on this button to delete the selected category after confirming the deletion.

## ▶ The Approach Edit TeamSecurity Dialog Box

Choose File ➤ TeamSecurity and click on the Edit or New button to open the Edit TeamSecurity dialog box, which contains these options:

**Group or User Name**    From this drop-down list box, select the group or user name whose security options you want to change. You can select Manager, Designer, Editor, or Reader.

**Approach File Password**    In this text box, type the password for the current file.

**Database Password**    Click on this button to open the Password section of the Approach Preferences dialog box to specify passwords for the current database.

**Database**    Click on this tab (the default) to allow the selected category editing rights (a checked checkbox) or not (a cleared checkbox) of the current database or to require passwords to access it.

**View**     Click on this tab to allow the selected category to gain access to (a checked checkbox) or to not see (a cleared checkbox) views in the current database.

**Advanced**     Click on this tab to open a section in which you can allow the selected category to have designer privileges, change passwords, or both.

# Index

Note to the Reader:  First level entries are in **bold**. Page numbers in **bold** indicate the principal discussion of a topic or the definition of a term. Page numbers in *italic* indicate illustrations.

## Numbers and Symbols

**1-2-3.** *See* Lotus 1-2-3
**1-2-3 Preferences dialog box, 205–207, 1004–1007**
Classic Keys section, 107
File Locations section, 1006
General section, 1004–1005
New Workbook Defaults section, 1005–1006
Recalculation section, 205–207, *206, 207*, 1006–1007
**.123 extension,** 75
**\* (asterisk)**
in Approach, 619
in Lotus 1-2-3, 162–163, 165
**@ (at sign).** *See* @functions
**^ (caret) in Lotus 1-2-3,** 162–163, 165
**= (equal to) in Lotus 1-2-3,** 163–164, 165
**> (greater than) in Lotus 1-2-3,** 163–164, 165
**>= (greater than or equal to) in Lotus 1-2-3,** 163–164, 165
**< (less than) in Lotus 1-2-3,** 163–164, 165
**<= (less than or equal to) in Lotus 1-2-3,** 163–164, 165
**~ (minus sign) in Lotus 1-2-3,** 162–163, 165
**<> (not equal to) in Lotus 1-2-3,** 163–164, 165
**( ) (parentheses) in Lotus 1-2-3,** 165
**+ (plus sign) in Lotus 1-2-3,** 162–163, 165
**? (question mark) in Approach,** 619–620
**/ (slash) in Lotus 1-2-3,** 162–163, 165
**~ (tilde) in Approach,** 620

## A

**ABS keyword in Lotus 1-2-3 macros,** 325
**absolute cell references in Lotus 1-2-3,** 167–168
**accessing.** *See* opening
**accessing**
FTP sites, 1035, 1042–1043
the Internet, 13, 1034
Lotus support sites on the Internet, 1043

**Action bar in Approach,** 544–545, *545*, 617–618
**adding.** *See also* entering; inserting; installing
in Approach
records to databases, 590–591
repeating panels to forms, 647–640, *649, 650*
report title pages, 664–665
summaries to reports with PowerClick SmartIcons, 674, 675–676, *677*
summaries to reports with Summary dialog box, 673–675, *675*
in Freelance Graphics
bullets progressively in screen shows, 882–883, *883*
points to objects, 862
speaker notes to current page, 840–841, *841*
notes and text boxes to Lotus 1-2-3 charts, 260–261, *261*
to SmartCenter drawers
application icons, 25–26
drawers, 23–24, *24, 25,* 26
folders, 26–27
names and addresses to Addresses drawer, 36–37, *36*
in Word Pro
borders, patterns, or colors to tables, 509–511, *509*
frames to documents, 441–442
SmartCorrect entries, 361–362, *361,* 371–373, *372*
SmartIcons to SmartIcons toolbar, 368, 380, 384
**addition,** in Lotus 1-2-3, 162–163, 165
**Address power fields in Word Pro,** 518
**Address section in Organizer,** 918, 956–961, 1025
copying entries, 961, *961*
creating address entries, **957–960,** *959*
deleting addresses, 960
display formats, 956–957
displaying home and/or business information, 960
editing addresses, 960
preferences, **1025**
**Addresses drawer in SmartCenter bar,** 17, **33–39.** *See also* drawers
adding names and addresses, 36–37, *36*

# M

# S

# W

# X

# Z

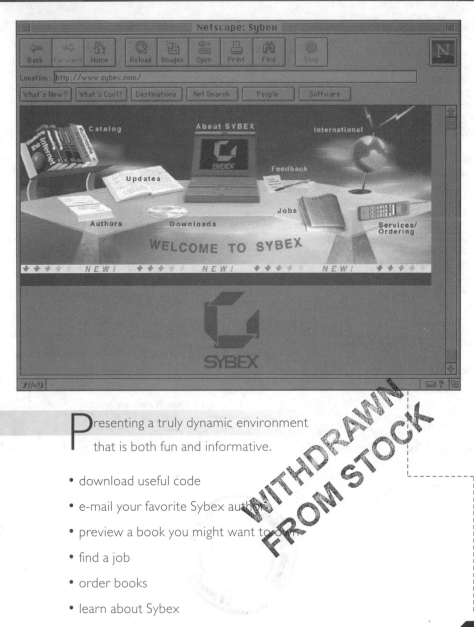